Ordnance Survey

STREET ATLAS
Durham

Contents

III	Key to map symbols
IV-V	Key to map pages
VI	Administrative and post code boundaries
1	Street maps
238	Explanation of street index reference system
238	Key to town, village and rural locality abbreviations in index
240	Index of hospitals, railway stations, schools, shopping centres, street names and universities

PHILIP'S

First colour edition published 1996 by

Ordnance Survey
Romsey Road
Maybush
Southampton SO16 4GU

and

George Philip Ltd.
an imprint of Reed Books
Michelin House, 81 Fulham Road, London SW3 6RB
and Auckland, Melbourne, Singapore and Toronto

ISBN 0-540-06365-7 (Philip's, hardback)
ISBN 0-540-06366-5 (Philip's, wire-o)

ISBN 0-319-00849-5 (Ordnance Survey, hardback)
ISBN 0-319-00850-9 (Ordnance Survey, wire-o)

To the best of the Publishers' knowledge, the
information in this atlas was correct at the time of
going to press. No responsibility can be accepted
for any errors or their consequences.

The representation in this atlas of a road, track or
path is no evidence of the existence of a right of way.

Printed and bound in Spain by Cayfosa

Key to map symbols

Symbol	Description
	Motorway
	Primary Routes (Dual carriageway and single)
	A Roads (Dual carriageway and single)
	B Roads (Dual carriageway and single)
	C Roads (Dual carriageway and single)
	Minor Roads
	Roads under construction
	County boundaries
	All Railways
	Track or private road
	Gate or obstruction to traffic (restrictions may not apply at all times or to all vehicles)
	All paths, bridleways, BOAT's, RUPP's, dismantled railways, etc.

The representation in this atlas of a road, track or path is no evidence of the existence of a right of way

174 Adjoining page indicator

Acad	Academy	Mon	Monument
Cemy	Cemetery	Mus	Museum
C Ctr	Civic Centre	Obsy	Observatory
CH	Club House	Pal	Royal Palace
Coll	College	PH	Public House
Ex H	Exhibition Hall	Л0ɛr	Reservoir
Ind Est	Industrial Estate	Ret Pk	Retail Park
Inst	Institute	Sch	School
Ct	Law Court	Sh Ctr	Shopping Centre
L Ctr	Leisure Centre	Sta	Station
LC	Level Crossing	TH	Town Hall/House
Liby	Library	Trad Est	Trading Estate
Mkt	Market	Univ	University
Meml	Memorial	YH	Youth Hostel

Symbol	Description
	British Rail station
	Private railway station
	Bus, coach station
	Ambulance station
	Coastguard station
	Fire station
	Police station
	Casualty entrance to hospital
	Churches, Place of worship
H	Hospital
i	Information Centre
P	Parking
	Post Office
	Public Convenience
	Important buildings, schools, colleges, universities and hospitals
River Soar	Water Name
	Stream
	River or canal (minor and major)
	Water Fill
	Tidal Water
	Woods
	Houses

0	¼	½	¾	1 mile

0	250m	500m	750m	1 Kilometre

The scale of the maps is 5.52 cm to 1 km (3½ inches to 1 mile)

The small numbers around the edges of the maps identify the 1 kilometre National Grid lines

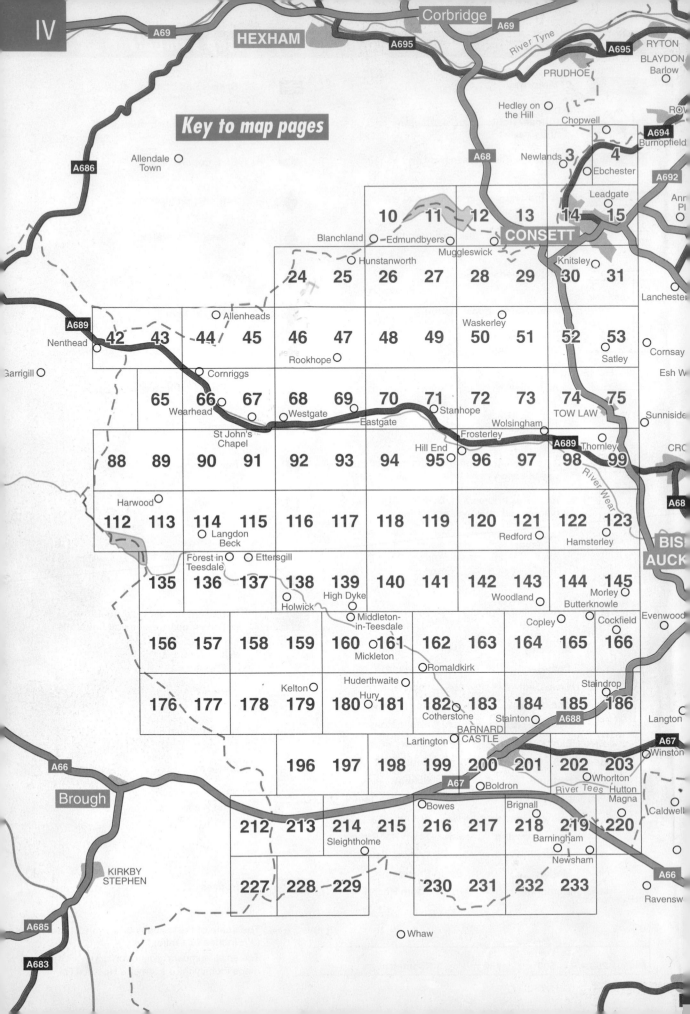

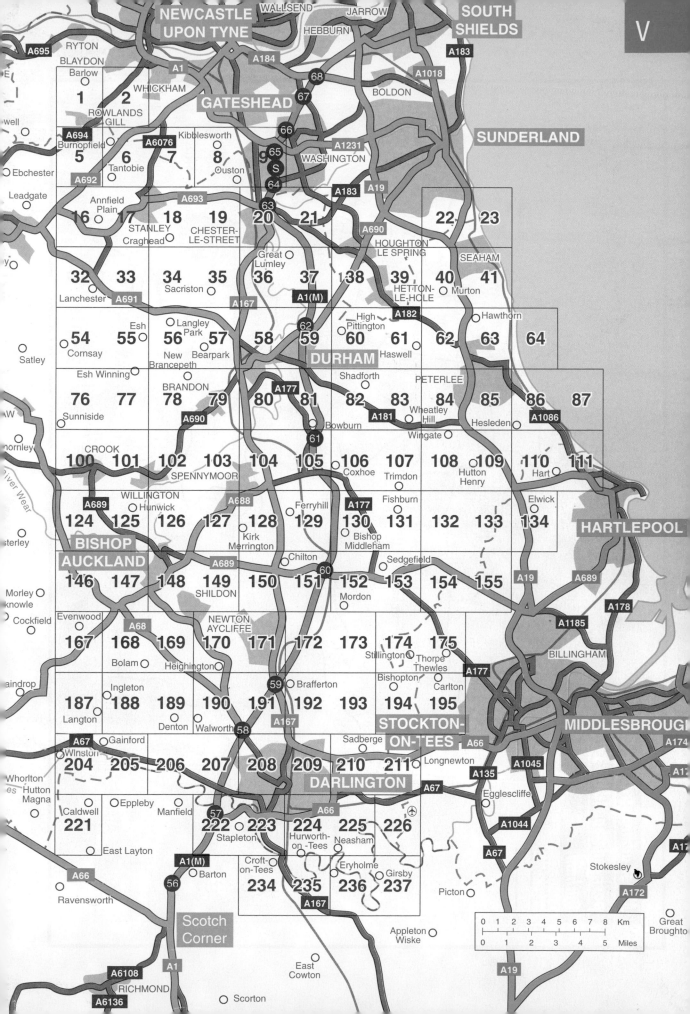

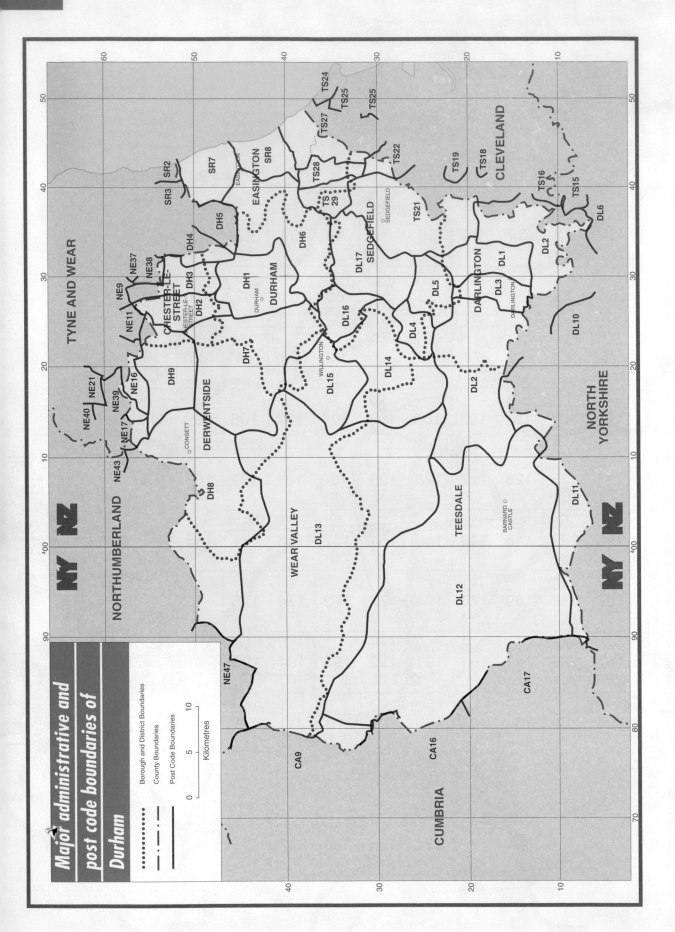

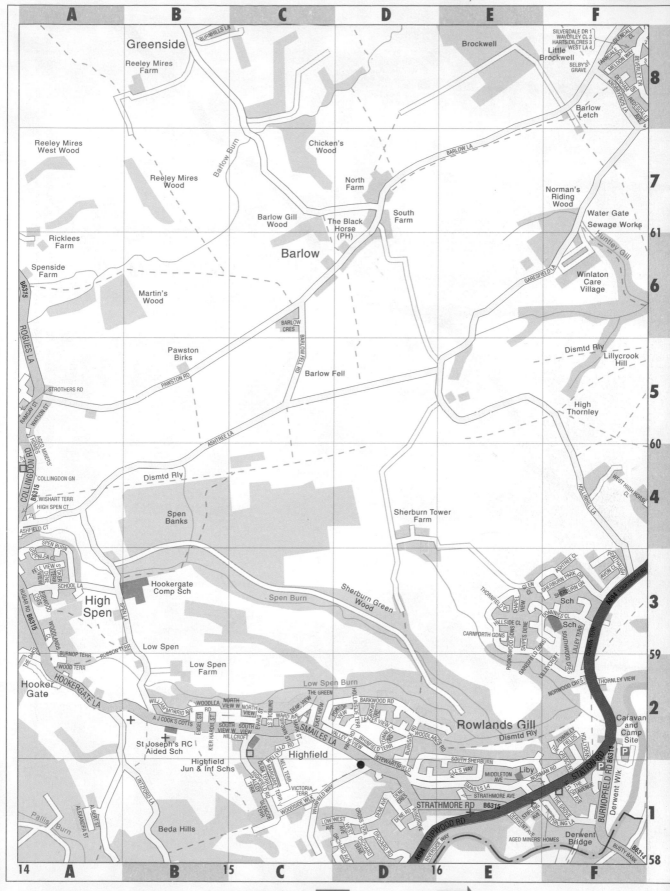

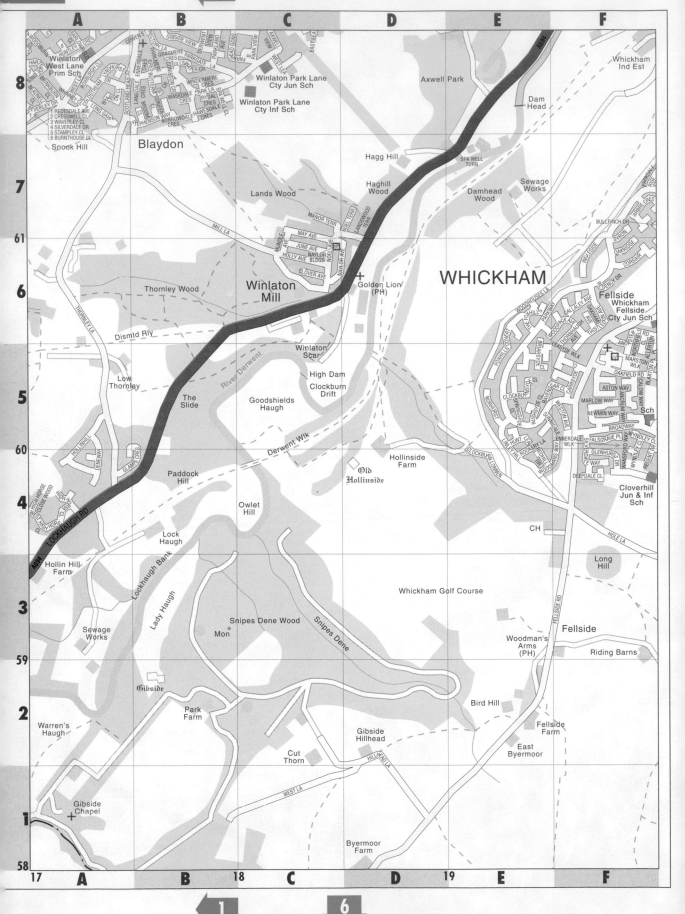

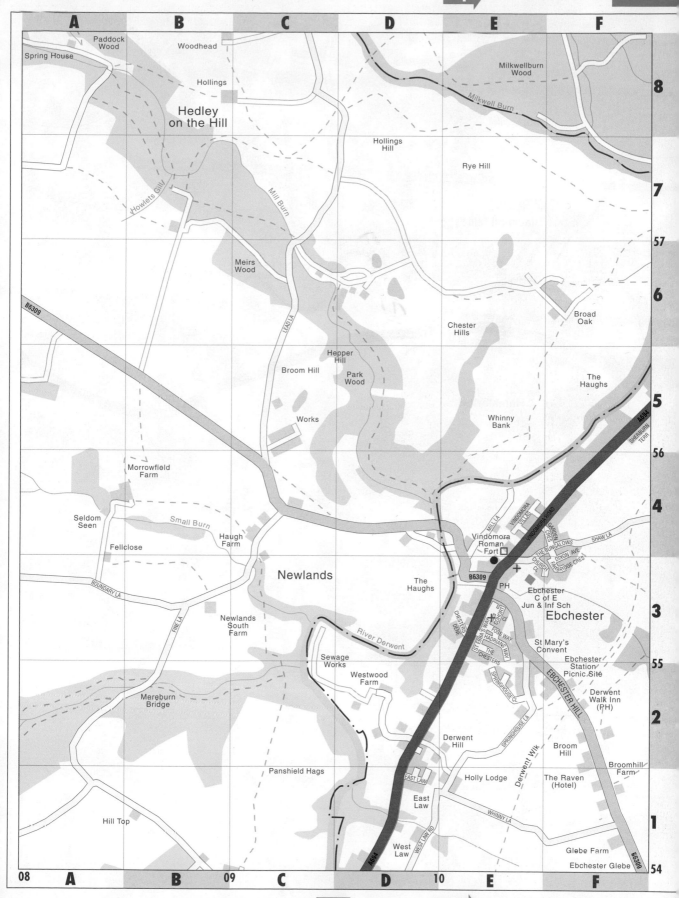

A   B   C   D   E   F

8
7
57
6
5
56
4
3
55
2
1
54

Paddock Wood
Spring House
Woodhead
Hollings
Hedley on the Hill
Milkwellburn Wood
Milkwell Burn
Hollings Hill
Rye Hill
Howlets Gill
Mill Burn
Meirs Wood
Broad Oak
Chester Hills
Lead La
Hepper Hill
Broom Hill
Park Wood
The Haughs
Works
Whinny Bank
B6309
Morrowfield Farm
Seldom Seen
Small Burn
Haugh Farm
Fellclose
Vindomora Roman Fort
Mill La
Vindomora Hills
The Bungalows
Vindomora Road
Garden Cres
Shaw La
Dixon Ave
Tarbridge Cres
Newry Cl
B6309
PH
Ebchester C of E Jun & Inf Sch
Ebchester
Newlands
The Haughs
Chesters Dene
Foss Way
St Ebba's Wk
Hadrian's Way
The Chesters
St Mary's Convent
Ebchester Station Picnic Site
Boundary La
Newlands South Farm
River Derwent
Fine La
Sewage Works
Westwood Farm
Springhouse Cl
Ebchester Hill
Derwent Walk Inn (PH)
Mereburn Bridge
Springhouse La
Derwent Hill
Derwent Wlk
Broom Hill
Broomhill Farm
The Raven (Hotel)
Panshield Hags
Holly Lodge
Hill Top
East Law
East Law
West Law Rd
West Law
Whinny La
Glebe Farm
Ebchester Glebe
A694
B6309

3

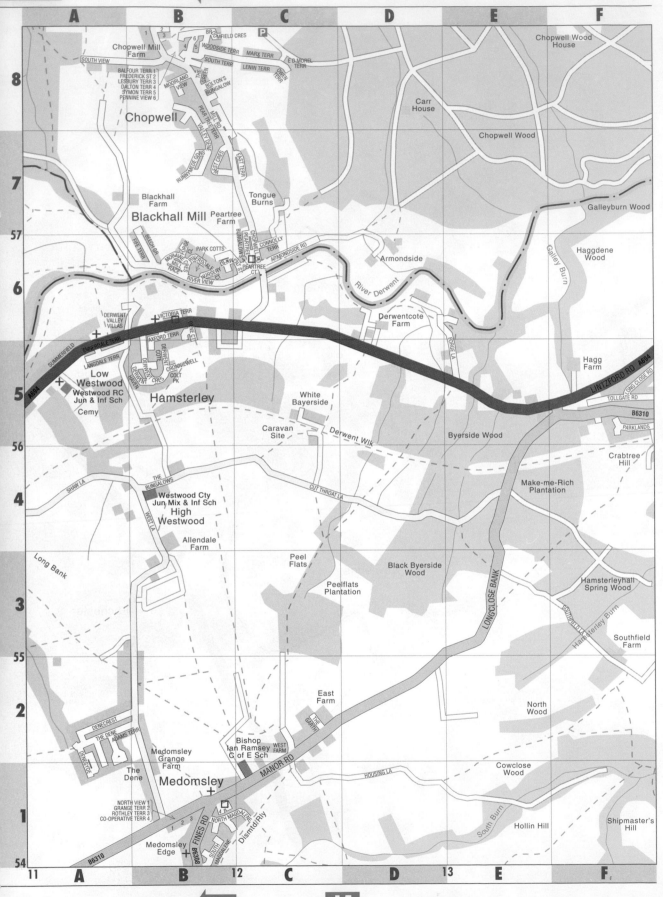

8

Chopwell Mill Farm

SOUTH VIEW

BALFOUR TERR 1
FREDERICK ST 2
LESBURY TERR 3
DALTON TERR 4
SYMON TERR 5
PENNINE VIEW 6

Chopwell

MOORLAND VIEW

BOLTON'S BUNGALOW

THE GREEN

WOODSIDE TERR

MARX TERR

SOUTH TERR

LENIN TERR

E D MOREL TERR

Chopwell Wood House

Carr House

Chopwell Wood

7

Blackhall Farm

Tongue Burns

VALLEY DENE

PEAR TREE TERR

WEST CRES

EAST TERR

Galleyburn Wood

57

Blackhall Mill

Peartree Farm

BESOR LA

FIRE TERR

MORAVIAN TERR

MILL RACE

PARK COTTS

GATESDALE

BUNGALOWS

CHOPWELL ST

RIVER VIEW

BLAW ST

NURSERY CT

PEARTREE CT

A ARMONDSIDE RD

CONNOLLY TERR

Armondside

River Derwent

Haggdene Wood

GALLEY BURN

6

DERWENT VALLEY VILLAS

VICTORIA TERR

AXFORD TERR

DERWENT CT

Derwentcote Farm

FORGE LA

Hagg Farm

LINTZFORD RD

LONG CLOSE RD

A694

SUMMERFIELD

EMERDALE TERR

LANGDALE TERR

DERWENT COTE

CRONNIEWELL

COLT PK

TOLLGATE RD

A694

Low Westwood

Westwood RC Jun & Inf Sch

Cemy

Hamsterley

DERWENT HAVEN

DERWENT CRES

White Bayerside

Byerside Wood

B6310

PARKLANDS

5

Caravan Site

Derwent Wlk

Crabtree Hill

56

SHAW LA

THE BUNGALOWS

CUT THROAT LA

Make-me-Rich Plantation

4

WEST LA

Westwood Cty Jun Mix & Inf Sch

High Westwood

Peel Flats

Black Byerside Wood

LONG CLOSE BANK

Hamsterleyhall Spring Wood

Allendale Farm

Peelflats Plantation

SOUTHFIELD

HAMSTERLEY BURN

3

Long Bank

Southfield Farm

55

East Farm

North Wood

2

DENECREST

THE DENE

ADAMS TERR

DENESIDE

THE GARTH

Bishop Ian Ramsey C of E Sch

WEST FARM

Cowclose Wood

Medomsley Grange Farm

MANOR RD

HOUSING LA

The Dene

Medomsley

NORTH VIEW 1
GRANGE TERR 2
ROTHLEY TERR 3
CO-OPERATIVE TERR 4

FINES RD

NORTH MAGDALENE

Dismtd Rly

South Burn

Hollin Hill

Shipmaster's Hill

1

Medomsley Edge

SOUTH MAGDALENE

B6310

54

3   15

1
6

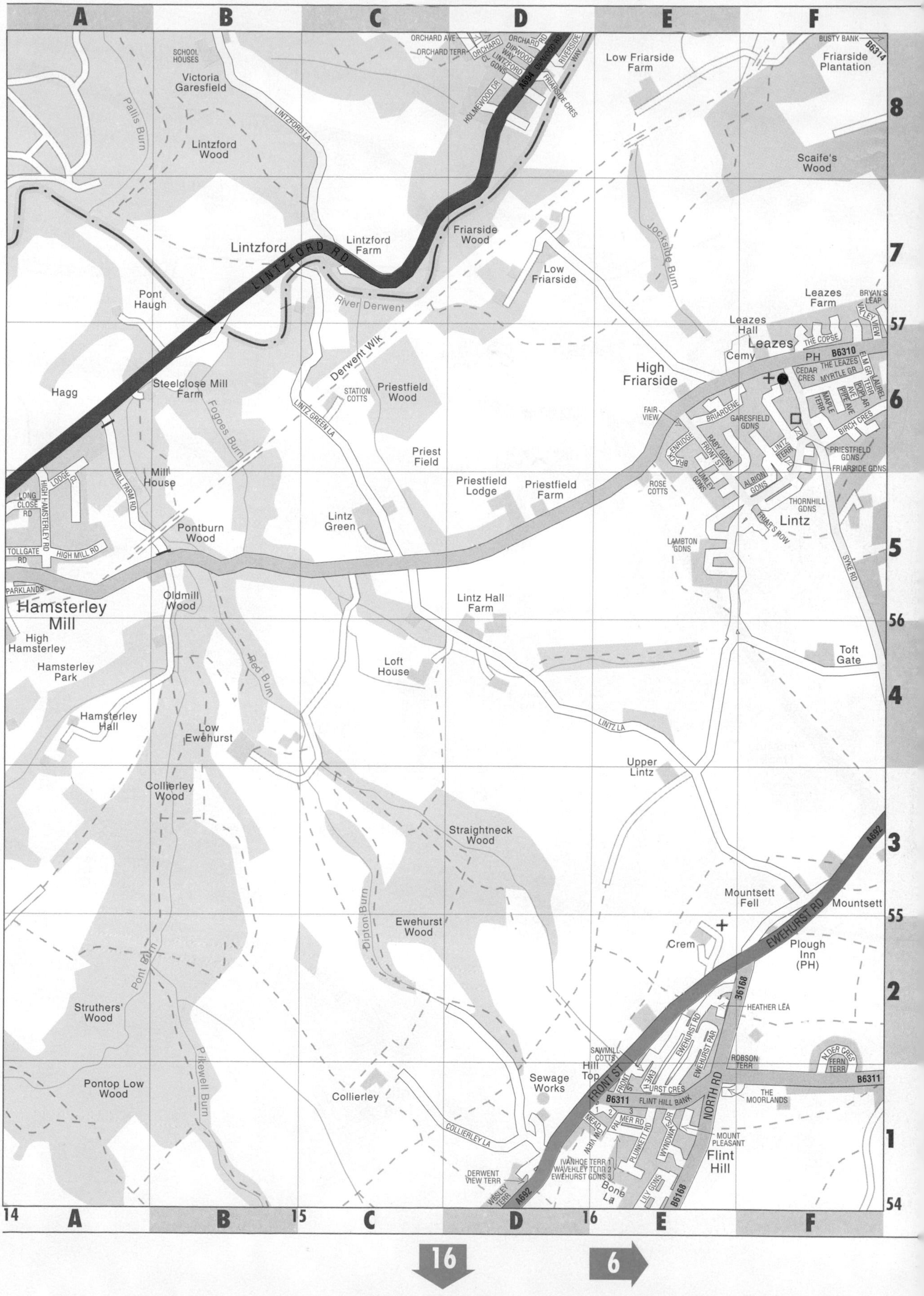
A
B
C
D
E
F
8
7
6
5
4
3
2
1
57
56
55
54
14
15
16
SCHOOL HOUSES
Victoria Garesfield
Pallis Burn
Lintzford Wood
LINTZFORD LA
ORCHARD AVE
ORCHARD TERR
ORCHARD CL
DIPWOOD WAY
LINTZFORD GDNS
HOLMEWOOD DR
A694
DERWENT RD
RIVERSIDE WAY
FRIARSIDE CRES
Low Friarside Farm
BUSTY BANK
B6314
Friarside Plantation
Scaife's Wood
Lintzford
LINTZFORD RD
Lintzford Farm
Friarside Wood
Jockside Burn
Low Friarside
River Derwent
Pont Haugh
Leazes Farm
BRYAN'S LEAP
VALLEY VIEW
Leazes Hall
Leazes
THE COPSE
Cemy
PH
B6310
CEDAR CRES
THE LEAZES
ELM GR
TERR
MYRTLE GR
LAUREL
POPLAR
MAPLE TERR
PINE AVE
BIRCH CRES
Derwent Wlk
High Friarside
Hagg
Steelclose Mill Farm
STATION COTTS
Priestfield Wood
Fogoes Burn
LINTZ GREEN LA
FAIR VIEW
BRIARDENE
GARESFIELD GDNS
RABY GDNS
FRONT ST
ENRIDGE
LINTZ TERR
PRIESTFIELD GDNS
FRIARSIDE GDNS
Priest Field
LUMLEY GDNS
ALBION GDNS
LODGE CL
HIGH HAMSTERLEY RD
MILL FARM RD
Mill House
LONG CLOSE RD
Priestfield Lodge
Priestfield Farm
ROSE COTTS
THORNHILL GDNS
Lintz
Lintz Green
FRIAR'S ROW
Pontburn Wood
TOLLGATE RD
HIGH MILL RD
LAMBTON GDNS
SYKE RD
PARKLANDS
Hamsterley Mill
Oldmill Wood
Lintz Hall Farm
High Hamsterley
Hamsterley Park
Red Burn
Loft House
Toft Gate
Hamsterley Hall
Low Ewehurst
LINTZ LA
Upper Lintz
Collierley Wood
Straightneck Wood
A692
Dipton Burn
Mountsett Fell
Mountsett
Ewehurst Wood
Crem
EWEHURST RD
Plough Inn (PH)
Pont Burn
B6168
Struthers' Wood
HEATHER LEA
SAWMILL COTTS
Hill Top
FRONT ST
EWEHURST RD
EWEHURST PAR
ROBSON TERR
ALDER CRES
FERN TERR
B6311
Pontop Low Wood
Pikewell Burn
Sewage Works
URST CRES
THE MOORLANDS
NORTH RD
B6311
FLINT HILL BANK
MEADOW
MER RD
Collierley
COLLIERLEY LA
PLUNKETT RD
WYNDWAYS DR
MOUNT PLEASANT
IVANHOE TERR 1
WAVERLEY TERR 2
EWEHURST GDNS 3
Flint Hill
DERWENT VIEW TERR
WESLEY TERR
Bone La
LILY GDNS

16
6

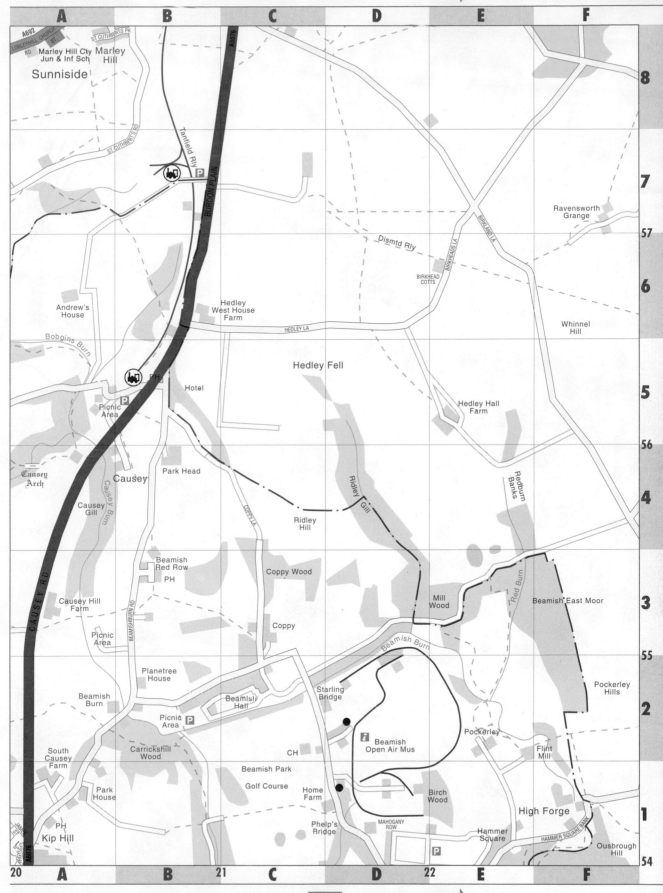

A B C D E F

8
7
57
6
5
56
4
3
55
2
1
54

20 A B 21 C D 22 E F

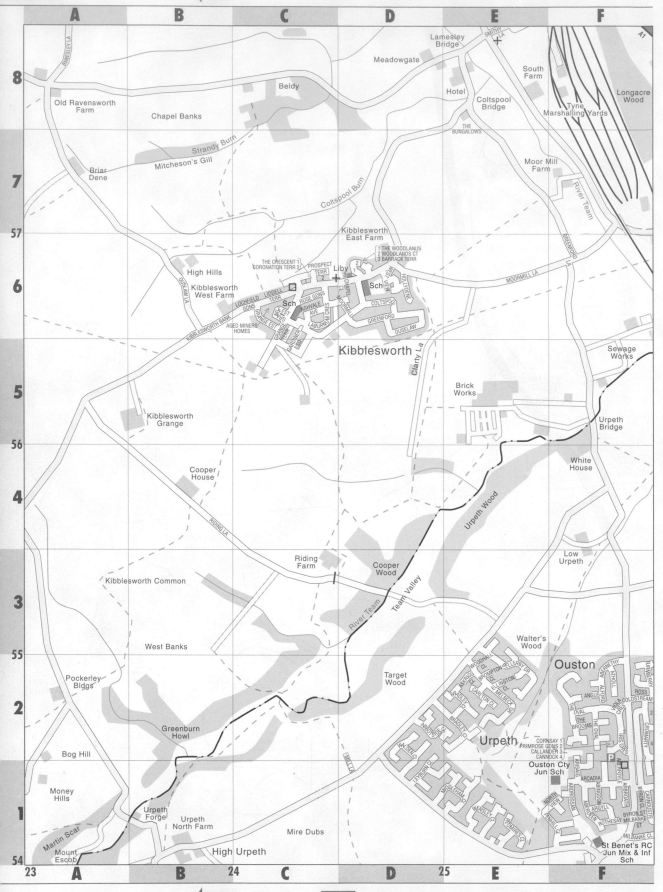

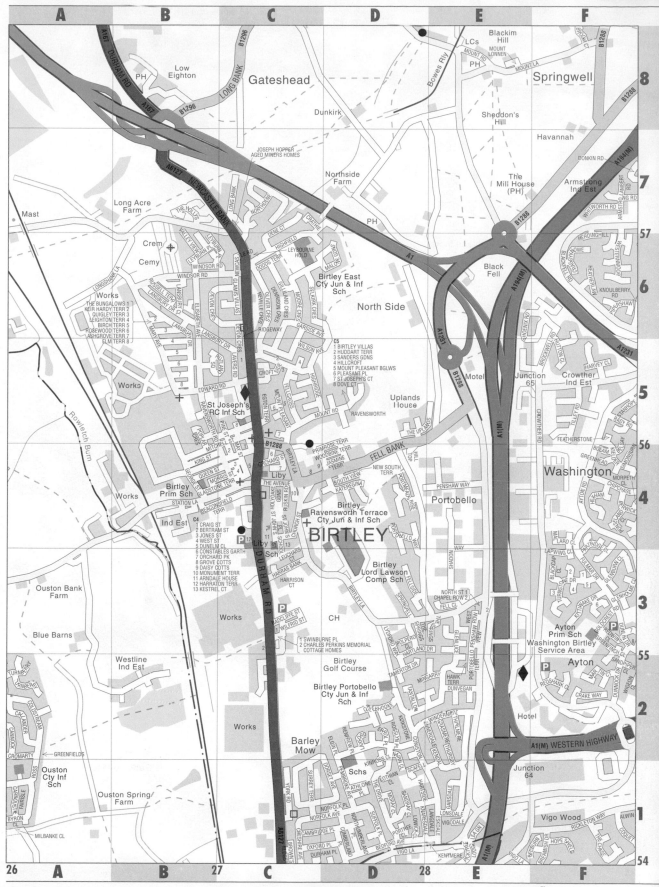

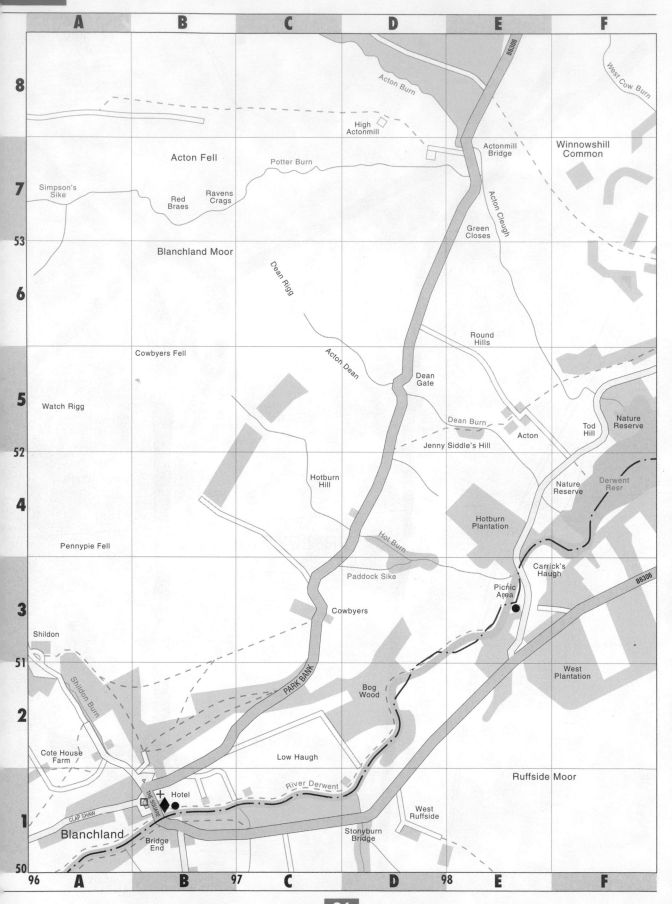

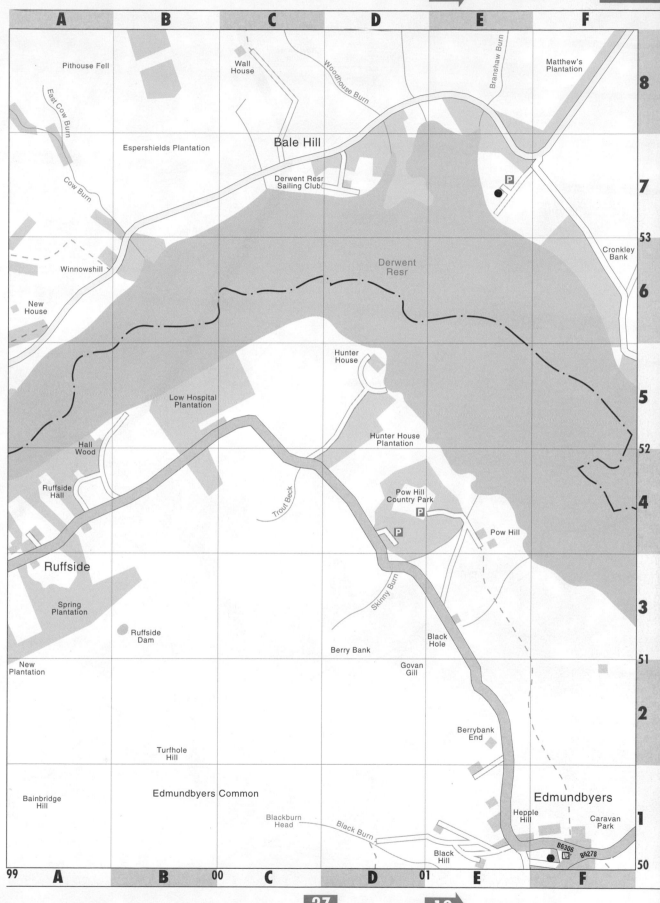

A   B   C   D   E   F

8

Pithouse Fell

East Cow Burn

Wall House

Matthew's Plantation

Branshaw Burn

Espershields Plantation

Bale Hill

Woodhouse Burn

Cow Burn

P

7

Derwent Resr Sailing Club

53

Cronkley Bank

Winnowshill

Derwent Resr

6

New House

Hunter House

5

Low Hospital Plantation

Hunter House Plantation

52

Hall Wood

Ruffside Hall

Trout Beck

Pow Hill Country Park

4

P

Pow Hill

Ruffside

Skinny Burn

P

Spring Plantation

3

Ruffside Dam

Black Hole

Berry Bank

51

New Plantation

Govan Gill

2

Berrybank End

Turfhole Hill

Edmundbyers Common

Edmundbyers

1

Bainbridge Hill

Hepple Hill

Caravan Park

Blackburn Head

Black Burn

Black Hill

B6306

B6278

50

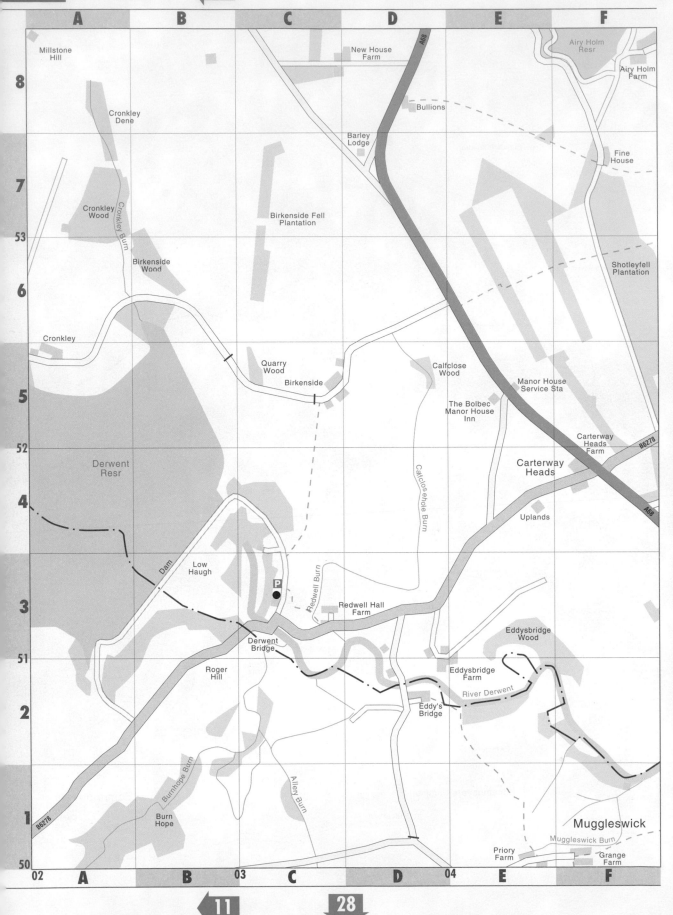

A B C D E F

8
7
53
6
52
5
4
3
51
2
1
50

02 A B 03 C D 04 E F

Millstone Hill
Cronkley Dene
Cronkley Wood
Cronkley Burn
Birkenside Wood
Cronkley
Derwent Resr
Dam
Low Haugh
Roger Hill
Burnhope Burn
Burn Hope
Allery Burn
Quarry Wood
Birkenside
Birkenside Fell Plantation
New House Farm
Barley Lodge
Bullions
Airy Holm Resr
Airy Holm Farm
Fine House
Shotleyfell Plantation
Calfclose Wood
The Bolbec Manor House Inn
Manor House Service Sta
Carterway Heads Farm
Carterway Heads
Catclosehole Burn
Redwell Burn
Redwell Hall Farm
Uplands
Eddysbridge Wood
Eddysbridge Farm
River Derwent
Eddy's Bridge
Derwent Bridge
Muggleswick
Muggleswick Burn
Priory Farm
Grange Farm
B6278
A68

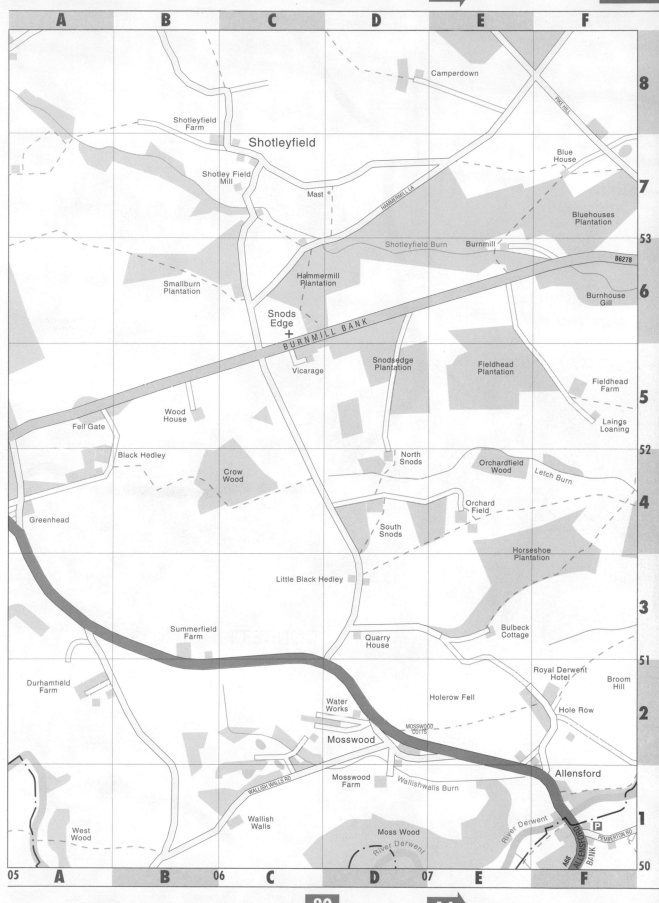

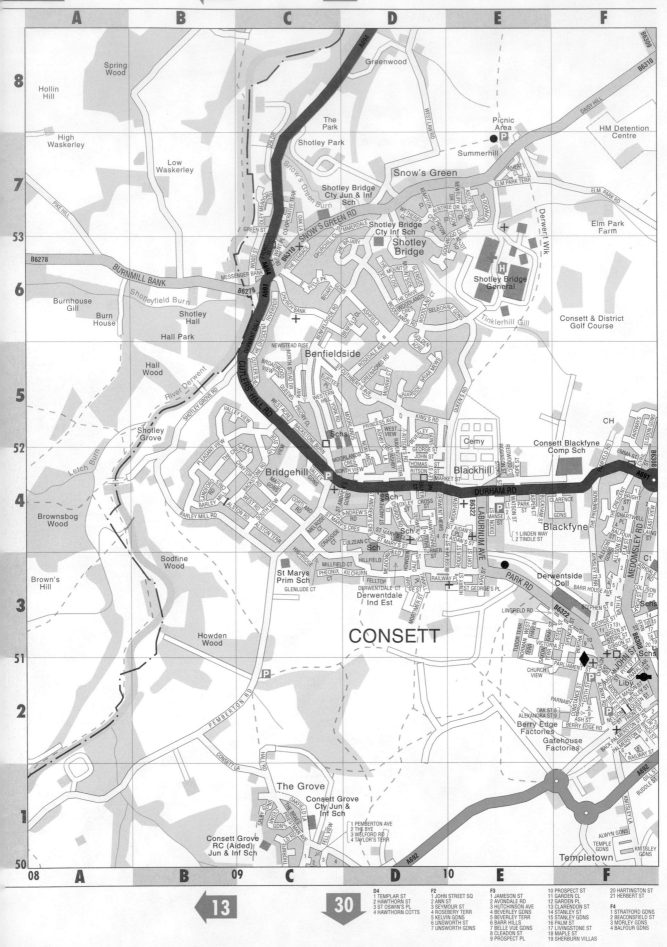

A B C D E F

8

7

53

6

5

52

4

3

51

2

1

50

Hollin Hill
High Waskerley
Spring Wood
Low Waskerley
Greenwood
The Park
Shotley Park
Picnic Area
Summerhill
Snow's Green
HM Detention Centre
Elm Park Farm
Elm Park Rd
Daisy Hill
B6310
B6309

Shotley Bridge Cty Jun & Inf Sch
Shotley Bridge Cty Inf Sch
Shotley Bridge
Shotley Bridge General
H
Consett & District Golf Course

B6278
BURNMILL BANK
Shotleyfield Burn
B6278
Messenger Bank
Burnhouse Gill
Burn House
Shotley Hall
Hall Park
Shotley Grove Rd
River Derwent
Letch Burn
Shotley Grove
Hall Wood
Brownsbog Wood
Brown's Hill
Benfieldside
Newstead Rise
Tinklerhill Gill
CUTLERS HALL RD

Bridgehill
St Marys Prim Sch
Derwentdale Ind Est
Sodfine Wood
Howden Wood
Pemberton Rd
Consett La
Hall Rd

CONSETT
Blackhill
Cemy
Consett Blackfyne Comp Sch
CH
Blackfyne
DURHAM RD
A691
B6308
LABURNUM AVE
PARK RD
Derwentside Coll
MEDOMSLEY RD
B6322
B6306
Schs
JOHN ST
Liby
CHURCH VIEW
Berry Edge Factories
Gatehouse Factories
A692
Templetown
Temple Gdns
Knitsley Gdns
Alwyn Gdns
B692
Buddle St

The Grove
Consett Grove Cty Jun & Inf Sch
Consett Grove RC (Aided) Jun & Inf Sch
1 Pemberton Ave
2 The Bye
3 Welford Rd
4 Taylor's Terr

D4
1 TEMPLAR ST
2 HAWTHORN ST
3 ST OSWIN'S PL
4 HAWTHORN COTTS

F2
1 JOHN STREET SQ
2 ANN ST
3 SEYMOUR ST
4 ROSEBERY TERR
5 KELVIN GDNS
6 UNSWORTH ST
7 UNSWORTH GDNS

F3
1 JAMESON ST
2 AVONDALE RD
3 HUTCHINSON AVE
4 BEVERLEY GDNS
5 BEVERLEY TERR
6 BARR HILLS
7 BELLE VUE GDNS
8 CLEADON ST
9 PROSPECT PL

10 PROSPECT ST
11 GARDEN CL
12 GARDEN PL
13 CLARENDON ST
14 STANLEY ST
15 STANLEY GDNS
16 PALM ST
17 LIVINGSTONE ST
18 MAPLE ST
19 SHERBURN VILLAS

20 HARTINGTON ST
21 HERBERT ST

F4
1 STRATFORD GDNS
2 BEACONSFIELD ST
3 MORLEY ST
4 BALFOUR GDNS

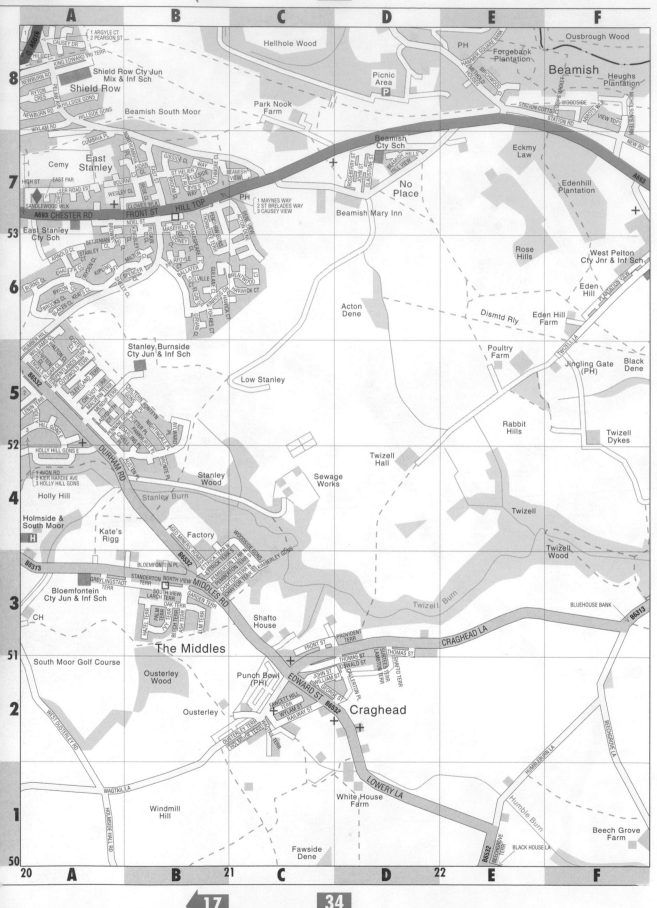

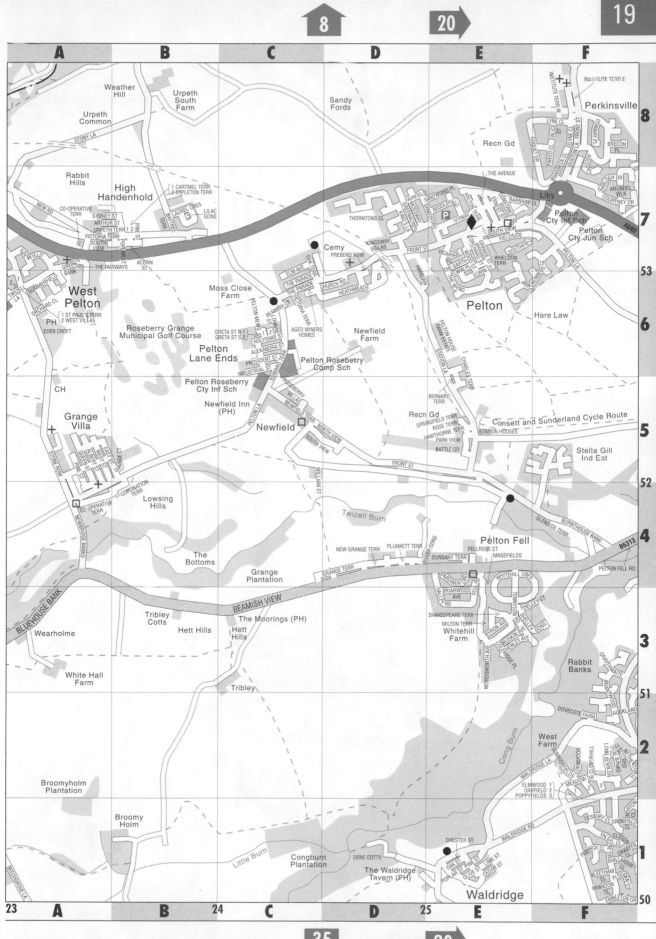

A   B   C   D   E   F

8

Ouston Villa Farm

Drum Ind Est

DRUM RD
FIRST AVE
SECOND AVE

Park View Comp Sch

BEDFORD AVE
VIGO LA
BARLEY MOW

A6127
DURHAM RD

KINGSWAY
GREENHILL
NORTH RD
WEAR LODGE
LOMBARD DR

NORTH LODGE

SINCLAIR DR
NAPIER CL
HAMPTON CT
AVE
MERLIN DR

PICKTREE LODGE
MORNINGSIDE
EASTLANDS
WOODLANDS
GRAYLANDS
LAMBTONS
ASH MEADOWS
PICKTREE LA

A1(M)

H The Washington

VILLAGE CTR
WINSTER
WELLHOPE
BREAMISH DR
VIGO LA
HARTHOPE
GRASSLEES
ROCKHOPE

Rickleton Prim Sch

BONEMILL LA

Rickleton

7

A693

DRUM RD
Dismtd Rly
LOW FLATTS RD

GREENHURST AVE
DEAN PK

NORTH DR
LINFORT
PICKTREE FARM COTTS

Picktree

Rickleton Wood

53

6

Plough Inn (PH)

High Flatts Farm

High Flatts

Works

South Pelaw

A693
A6127
A163
B6290
BLIND LA

Pelaw House

Cherry Banks

Junction 63

A167
A183

The Raceground

The Bottoms

Lambton Park

5

LILAC GR
CHERRY TREE RD
SYCAMORE AVE
WILLOWVALE
HOLLYCREST
ROSEWOOD GDNS
BEECHWOODS
FIRTREES
CONYERS AVE
PELAW AVE
PELAW PL
PELTON LA
CONYERS
CONYERS GDNS
CONYERS RD
PARK VIEW
PELAW CRES
PELAW RD
LAUREL CL

Schs

Highfield Day H

HIGHFIELD RISE
ARCADIA AVE
MAYFIELD GDNS
SPRINGFIELD GDNS
CASTLE NEW

BROADWAY
TUDOR RD
HADRIAN AVE
ATKINSON RD
APPLEDORE GDNS

PARK RD N

B6290
CAMPERDOWN AVE
RICKLETON AVE
CHERRY
SHIELDS RD

Sewage Works

CHESTER RD
Chester New Bridge

Lambton Bridge

Ayrie's Bank

BLACK DR
NEWBRIDGE BANK

52

Stella Gill
ELMWAY
HAZEL AVE
ASHLEIGH
GLEN TERR
MAPLEWOOD
CHERRY TREE RD
PARK RD
THE CLOSE
HILDA TERR
SOUTH ST
GLENMORE
GLEN BARR
GLENHOLM GDNS
PELAW BANK
PROSPECT RD
HILLSIDE
CASTLE NEW

Ct C Ctr
The Orchard
PICKTREE COTTS
PICKTREE LA
HOGARTH

B6313

River Wear

The Haughs

A183

4

CHESTER-LE-STREET

B6313
WHITEHILL LA

Whitehill Hall

Cragside
Lingholme

PELTON FELL RD

GLEN TERR

Schs

NORTH BURNS
SOUTH BURNS
Canada
TWELFTH AVE
ELEVENTH AVE
TENTH AVE
SIXTH AVE
FIFTH AVE
THE GREEN
SEVENTH AVE
EIGHTH AVE
NINTH AVE
THE AVENUE
MURRAY PL
MURRAY RD

P

ASHLEY TERR
CO-OPERATIVE ST
STUART ST

P

GREENBANK ST
POPLAR TERR
CONE TERR

ROMAN AVE
LINDSFARNE AVE

PARK RD N
PARK RD N

B6290

The Hags

Ford Cottage
Hag Bridge

The Haughs

A1(M)

Garden House

3

WYNYARD
DELAVAL
THE CRESCENT
FOURTH AVE
THIRD AVE
THE GARDENS
Sch
BULLION LA
GAINFORD
KIMBLESWORTH
SANDERS MEMORIAL HOMES

Chester-le-Street Sta

Chester-le-Street Sch

BEDE AVE
COOKSON TERR
STATION RD
ELM ST
AVONDALE TERR
POPULAR
FRONT ST
WESLEY
HIGH CHARE
MIDDLE CHARE
ST CUTHBERT'S WLK

P P P

Cestria & Park View Schs

P

Liby

PARK ROAD CENTRAL

Lumley Park

Lumley Castle

CH

51

AUCKLAND
BRANGWYN
GIBBSIDE
MATFEN CT
CARTMEL CT
Chester-le-Street Hermitage Comp Sch

RIDLEY AVE
SECOND AVE
GRAY AVE
VINOLIA
KIMBLE
Newker & West Lane Schs
OAKDALE TERR
BOULMER CL
VIVIAN
EDWARD TERR
NICHOLAS ST
CLIFTON RD
CLIFFORD TERR
ANFIELD

MAINS PARK RD
FARDEN PK AVE
ST CUTHBERT AVE
HAWTHORN TERR
HOLMLANDS
Sch
Wear

ROPERY LA

B1284

Lumley New Bridge

LUMLEY NEW RD

Lumley Castle

Golf Course

Broad Wood

2

WALDRIDGE LA
AUCKLAND
FENTON CL
NORTON CL
WALDRIDGE RD
PENNINE VIEW
CHILTERN AVE
MALVERN AVE
CLEVELAND AVE
CHEVIOT RD
KAFFIR
RANMOOR
BENRIDGE PK
General H
WESTWOOD
THOMAS ST
ERNEST TERR

RELTON TERR
VANE TERR
WELDON TERR
STANLEY TERR
GEORGE ST
Cemy

LUMLEY TERR
LAMBTON TERR
BROADWOOD VIEW
RANSOME GDNS

MILBURN CL

Sports Ctr

Durham Cty Cricket Gnd

Weardale Way

1

ALNWICK
INGRAM
REDESDALE RD
RREDALE RD
ROTHBURY
BARDON DR
PORTLAND RD
CLIFTON CL
CHATTON
WESTRAY
LOMOND
BASSENTHWAITE AVE
ULLSWATER AVE
DUNVEGAN AVE
WINDERMERE AVE
ENNERDALE PL
HAWES AVE
THIRLMERE AVE
RYDAL RD
ORCHARD TERR
ARD GDNS
DENE VILLAS
JOLLIFFEST
CRICHTON AVE

Chester-le-Street Red Rose Cty Jun & Inf Sch

Lumley Riding

50

EMBLETON DR
CHILLINGHAM DR
The Hermitage

A167

26 A   **27** B   C   D **28** E   F

C2
1 REAY CT
2 GIBBS CT
3 PENTLAND CT
4 LAWSON CT
5 RIDDELL CT

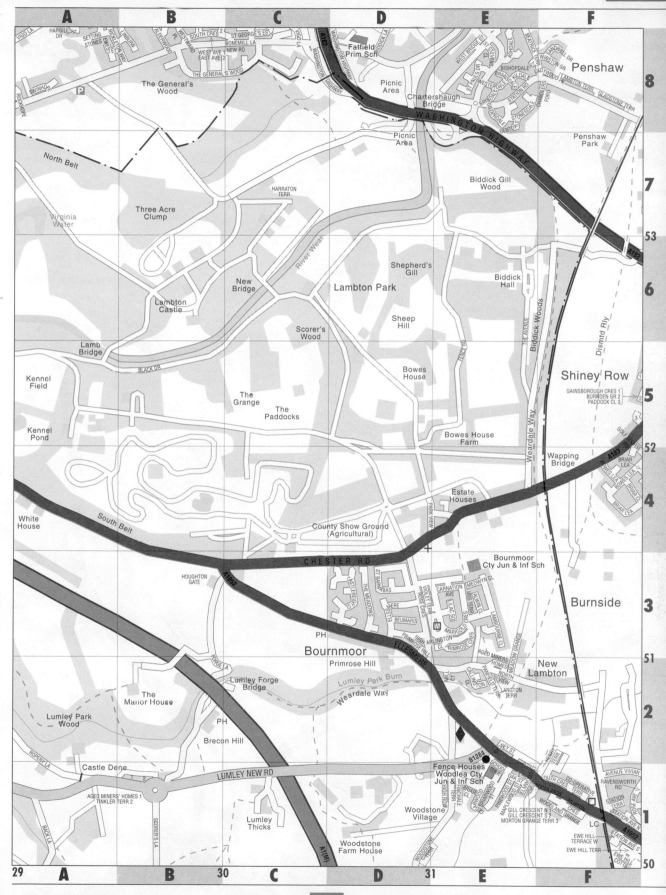

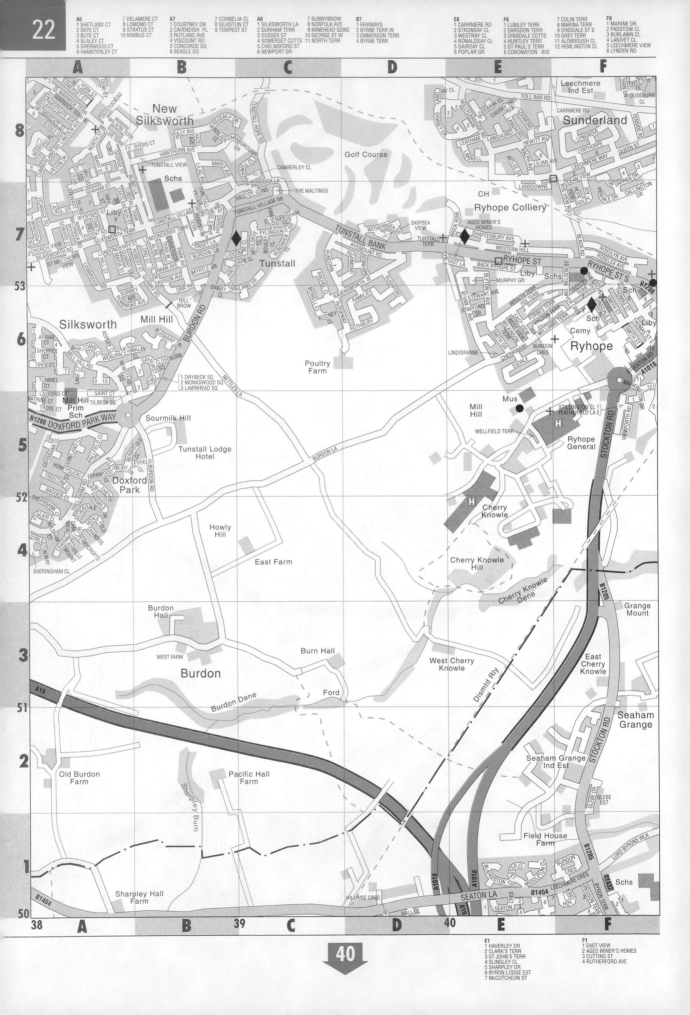

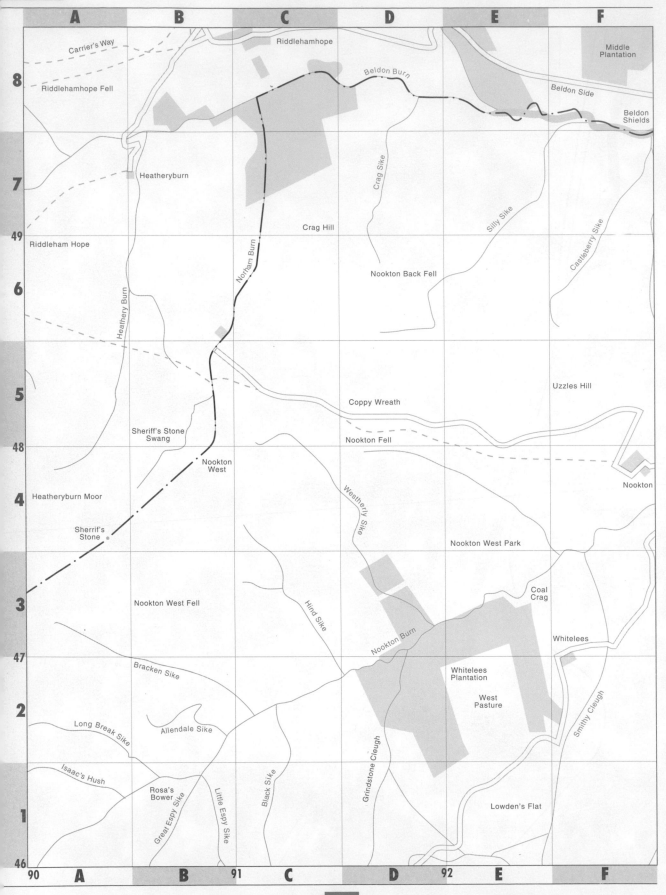

A   B   C   D   E   F

8

Carrier's Way

Riddlehamhope Fell

Riddlehamhope

Beldon Burn

Middle Plantation

Beldon Side

Beldon Shields

7

Heatheryburn

Crag Sike

49

Riddleham Hope

Crag Hill

Silly Sike

Castleberry Sike

Nookton Back Fell

6

Heathery Burn

Norham Burn

5

Uzzles Hill

Coppy Wreath

Sheriff's Stone Swang

Nookton Fell

48

Nookton West

Nookton

4

Heatheryburn Moor

Westherly Sike

Nookton West Park

Sherrif's Stone

Coal Crag

3

Nookton West Fell

Hind Sike

Nookton Burn

Whitelees

47

Bracken Sike

Whitelees Plantation

Smithy Cleugh

2

Long Break Sike

Allendale Sike

West Pasture

Isaac's Hush

Grindstone Cleugh

Black Sike

1

Rosa's Bower

Great Espy Sike

Little Espy Sike

Lowden's Flat

46

90   A   B   91   C   D   92   E   F

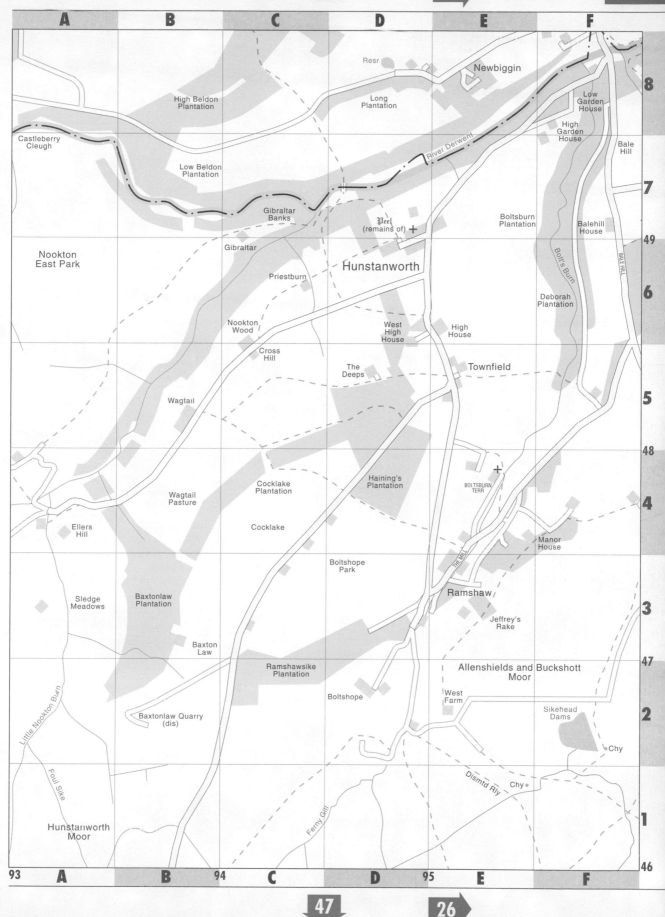

A B C D E F

8
7
49
6
5
48
4
3
47
2
46
1

Newbiggin
Resr
Long Plantation
High Beldon Plantation
Castleberry Cleugh
Low Beldon Plantation
Gibraltar Banks
River Derwent
Low Garden House
High Garden House
Bale Hill
Boltsburn Plantation
Balehill House
Gibraltar
Peel (remains of)
Hunstanworth
Priestburn
Bolt's Burn
Bale Hill
Nookton East Park
Deborah Plantation
Nookton Wood
West High House
High House
Townfield
Cross Hill
The Deeps
Wagtail
Boltsburn Terr
Haining's Plantation
Cocklake Plantation
Wagtail Pasture
Ellers Hill
Cocklake
Manor House
Boltshope Park
Jeffrey's Rake
Sledge Meadows
Baxtonlaw Plantation
Ramshaw
Baxton Law
Allenshields and Buckshott Moor
Ramshawsike Plantation
West Farm
Sikehead Dams
Baxtonlaw Quarry (dis)
Boltshope
Chy
Little Nookton Burn
Dismtd Rly
Chy
Foul Sike
Ferny Gill
Hunstanworth Moor

25
10

A   B   C   D   E   F

River Derwent

Rope Barn

8

Buckshott Farm

Stony Burn

Allenshields

Near Haw Burn

Horden Sike

Bock Sike

West Sike

Stonyburn Head

7

Allenshields

Buckshott Park

49

Balehill Plantation

Pedamsoak

6

Pedamsoak Sike

Pedam's Oak

Buckshott Fell

Taylor's Shaft (dis)

Chop Hardy

5

Abbey Weathers

48

Edmondbyers Common

4

Belmount

Sunnyside

Burnhope Burn

Beaulie Sike

Sandyford

Burn Hope

3

47

Near Sandyford

Eudon Burn

The Middles

Haygarth's Flat

2

Far Sandyford

Canal Hill

1

Black Hill

Burnhope Dam

46

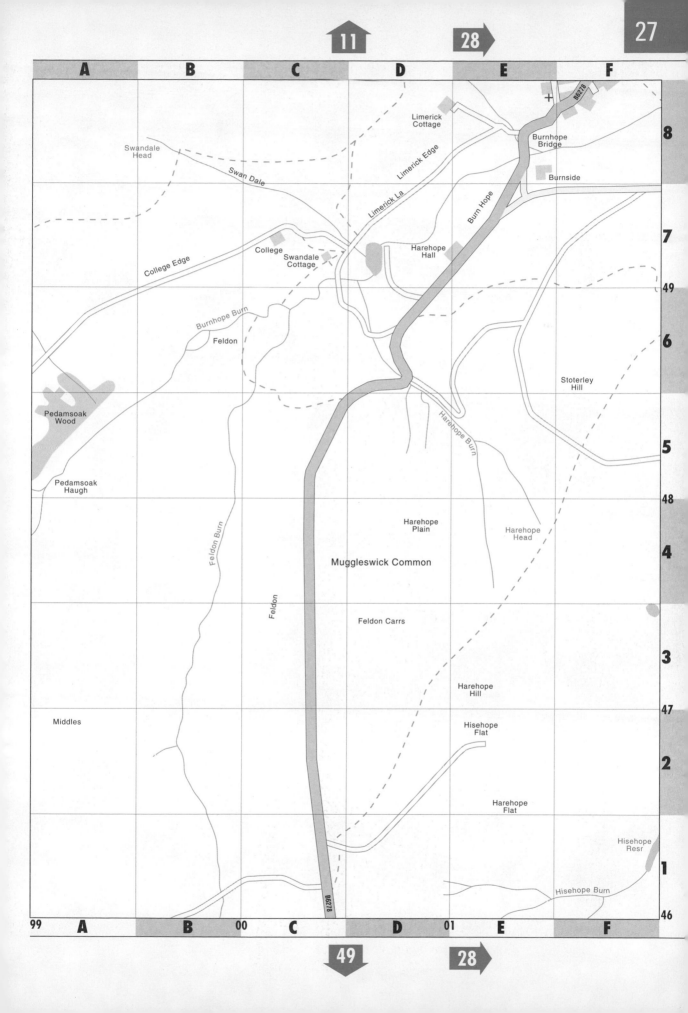

A   B   C   D   E   F

8

Swandale
Head

Limerick
Cottage

Burnhope
Bridge

B6278

Swan Dale

Limerick Edge

Burnside

7

Limerick La.

Burn Hope

49

College Edge

College

Swandale
Cottage

Harehope
Hall

Burnhope Burn

6

Feldon

Stoterley
Hill

Pedamsoak
Wood

Harehope Burn

5

48

Pedamsoak
Haugh

Feldon Burn

Harehope
Plain

Harehope
Head

4

Muggleswick Common

Feldon

Feldon Carrs

3

Harehope
Hill

47

Middles

Hisehope
Flat

2

Harehope
Flat

Hisehope
Resr

1

B6278

Hisehope Burn

46

99   A   B   00   C   D   01   E   F

27
12

A B C D E F

8

East Cot House

Allery Burn

Lane Head

Calf Hall

Bashaw Bank

Fox Yards

West Cot House

Key West

7

Muggleswick Park

Hall

Stony Hill

Three Curricks

Hasling Dene

Shield Farm

49

Black Cleugh Crags

Cuddy's Stables

Srawberry Hill

Dyke House

6

Lamb Shield Farm

Black Cleugh

Juniper Hill

Struthers Sike

Calfclose Hill

Lambshield Moss

Coalgate Burn

Coal Gate

Hisehope Bridge

GOLDHILL LA

Railgap Burn

Lair Banks

5

Black Burn

48

Birkhot

Lambshield Sikes

Hise Pasture

Whinny Hill

Carp Shield

4

Muggleswick Common

Cushat Leazes

Round Hill

Cross Rig

Catchwater

Hisehope Burn

Seavy Sike

Goldhill Edge

3

Black Hill

47

Blackpool Hill

Backstone Burn

Hise Hope

2

PH

The Pike

Heather View

Hisehope Resr

Smiddy Shaw House

Smiddy Shaw Resr

1

P

Hisehope House

46

02 A B 03 C D 04 E F

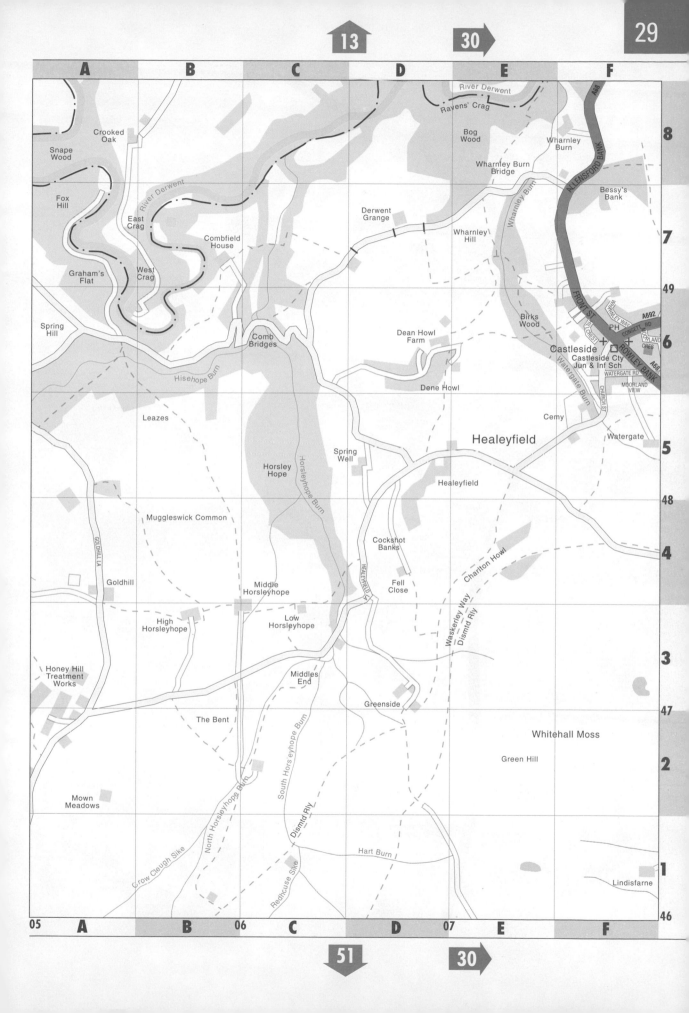

Snape Wood
Crooked Oak
Fox Hill
East Crag
Graham's Flat
West Crag
Spring Hill
Combfield House
Comb Bridges
River Derwent
Hisehope Burn
Leazes
Horsley Hope
Horsleyhope Burn
Spring Well
Mugglewick Common
Goldhill
Honey Hill Treatment Works
GOLDHILL LA
Middle Horsleyhope
High Horsleyhope
Low Horsleyhope
The Bent
Mown Meadows
North Horsleyhope Burn
South Horsleyhope Burn
Crow Cleugh Sike
Redhouse Sike
Dismtd Rly
Middles End
Greenside
Hart Burn

River Derwent
Ravens' Crag
Bog Wood
Wharnley Burn
Wharnley Burn Bridge
Derwent Grange
Wharnley Hill
Dean Howl Farm
Dene Howl
Healeyfield
Healeyfield
Cockshot Banks
Fell Close
Charlton Howl
HEALEYFIELD LA
Wasterley Way
Dismtd Rly
Whitehall Moss
Green Hill
Lindisfarne

Wharnley Burn
ALLENSFORD BANK
A68
Bessy's Bank
Birks Wood
49
Castleside
Castleside Cty Jun & Inf Sch
FRONT ST
PH
WHARNLEY WAY
HILL CREST
CONSETT RD
A692
LELAND CRES
ROWLEY BANK
A68
Watergate RD
CHURCH ST
MOORLAND VIEW
Watergate Burn
Cemy
Watergate
6
5
48
4
3
47
2
1
46

8
7
49
6
5
48
4
3
47
2
1
46

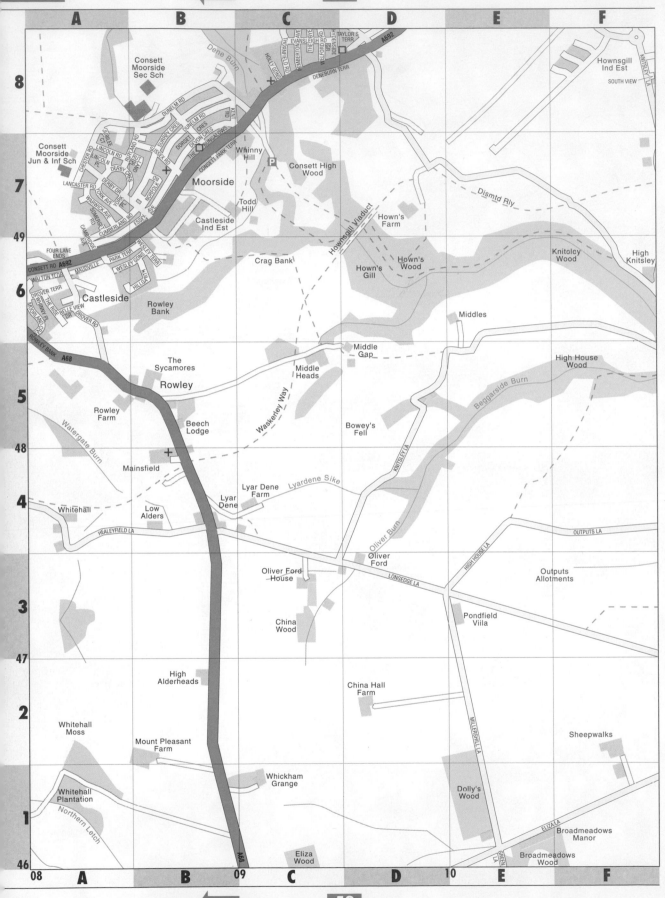

A | B | C | D | E | F

8

Consett
Moorside
Sec Sch

Dene Burn

Evansleigh

Taylor's
Terr

RAINFIELD RD
PEMBERTON AVE
THE DRIVE
HYDE PK
GROVE M
HOLLY ENDS
A692

DENEBURN TERR

SOUTH VIEW

Hownsgill
Ind Est

KNITSLEY LA

Consett
Moorside
Jun & Inf Sch

DUNELM RD
VUBLER
CHESTER RD
LINCOLN PL
RUTLAND RD
BUTLAND RD
DERBY DR
NORFOLK RD
DUNELM RD
DORSET
DEVON CRES
DUNINGA GVS
KENT RD
SURREY CRES
CRES
SUSSEX RD
DERBY DR
THE
CONSETT PARK TERR
Whinny
Hill
P
Consett High
Wood

Hown's
Farm

Dismtd Rly

7

LANCASTER RD
YORK AVE
WARWICK AVE
SOMERSET
ESSEX
AVE
CUMBERLAND RD
CAMBRIDGE
AVE

Moorside

Castleside
Ind Est

Todd
Hill

Crag Bank

Hown's
Gill

Hown's
Wood

Knitsley
Wood

High
Knitsley

49

Four Lane
Ends
CONSETT RD A692
MAUDVILLE
PARK TERR
WESLEY GDNS TERR
WESLEY TERR
HILLGA

Hownsgill Viaduct

6

WALTON TERR
DROVER TERR
THE RISE
WHINNY
MOORLAND RD
BELLE VIEW
DR
DROVER RD

Castleside

Rowley
Bank

Middles

A68

The
Sycamores

Middle
Gap

High House
Wood

5

Rowley

Rowley
Farm

Beech
Lodge

Middle
Heads

Waskerley Way

Bowey's
Fell

Beggarside Burn

KNITSLEY LA

48

Watergate Burn

Mainsfield

Lyar Dene
Farm

Lyardene Sike

4

Whitehall

Low
Alders

Lyar
Dene

Oliver Burn

HEALEYFIELD LA

OUTPUTS LA

Oliver
Ford

HIGH HOUSE LA

3

Oliver Ford
House

LONGEDGE LA

Outputs
Allotments

China
Wood

Pondfield
Villa

47

2

High
Alderheads

China Hall
Farm

MILLERSHILL LA

Sheepwalks

Whitehall
Moss

Mount Pleasant
Farm

Whickham
Grange

Dolly's
Wood

ELIZA LA

1

Whitehall
Plantation

Northern Letch

GREEN

Broadmeadows
Manor

Broadmeadows
Wood

46

A68

Eliza
Wood

08 | A | B | 09 | C | D | 10 | E | F

A B C D E F

8
7
49
6
5
48
4
47
2
1
46

Works PERCY GDNS

Delves Lane Cty
Jun Mix & Inf Schs

← KNITSLEY LA

+ Delves

Caribbees
Plantation

Stockerley
Ridge

High
Woodside

WOODSIDE BANK

Low Castle
Dene

High Castle
Dene Farm

Castle
Hill

Stockerley Burn

Black
Wood

BRIAR DALE

GREENWAY
CT

MEADOW VIEW

PIXLEY DELL

Delves
Lane
Ind Est

WOODLANDS VIEW

SUNNINGDALE

Little
Greencroft

Stockerley
Bridge

STOCKERLEY LA

Dismtd Rly

HOWNSGILL DR

Knitsley

Low
Farm

Back
Gill

Backgill Burn

VALLEY
VIEW

BUTSFIELD LA

East Knitsley
Grange

West Knitsley
Grange

Hurbuck
Cotts

Hurbuck

Beggarside Burn

Knitsley Burn

Knitsley
Bridge

Knitsley
Mill

Sewage
Works

Sunnyside
Farm

Dam
Wood

Smallhope Burn

48

Dyke
Nook

OUTPUTS LA

HUMBERHILL LA

New House
Farm

Woodlands Park

Barley
Hill

NEWBIGGIN LA

Dunleyford
House

ELIZA LA

Woodlands
Hall

David's
Town

Woodlands
Park Farm

Windy Hill

Humber
House

LONGEDGE LA

KNITSLEY LA

Red
House

Redhouses
Bridge

Rippon Burn

Sawmill
Wood

HUMBERHILL LA

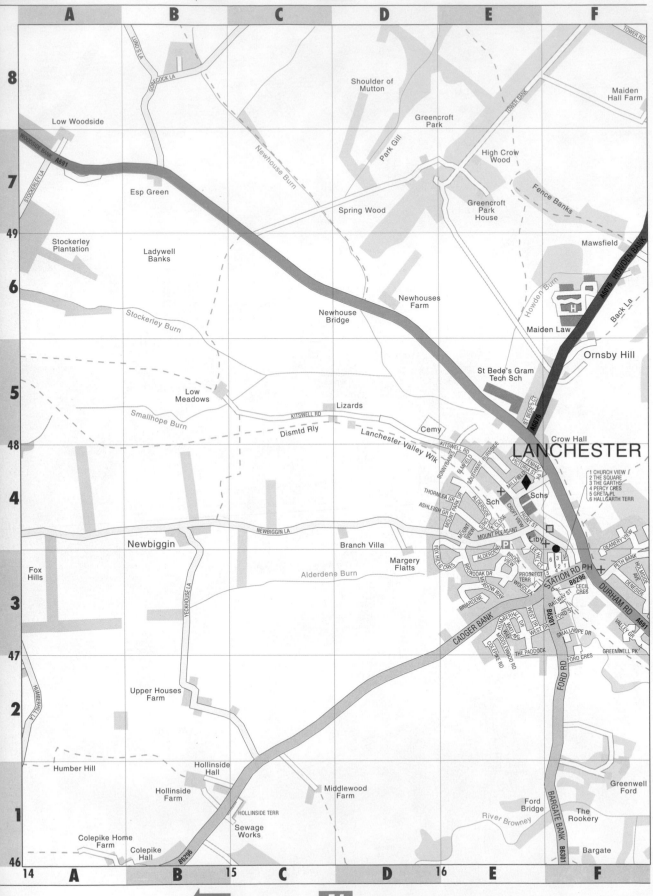

LANCHESTER

1 CHURCH VIEW
2 THE SQUARE
3 THE GARTHS
4 PERCY CRES
5 GRETA PL
6 HALLGARTH TERR

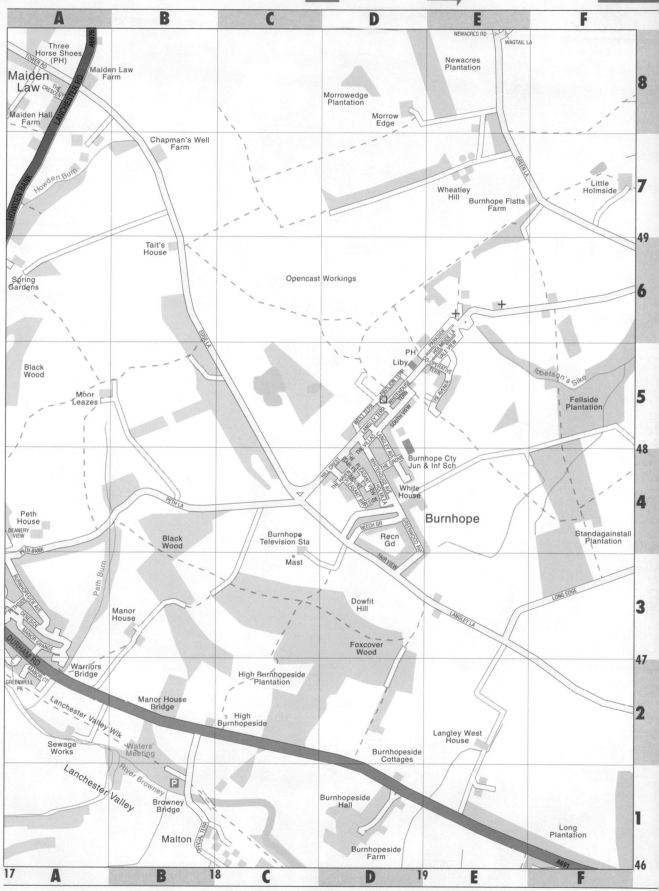

A B C D E F

8
7
49
6
5
48
4
47
3
2
1
46

Maiden Law
Three Horse Shoes (PH)
TOWER RD
Maiden Law Farm
THE CRESCENT
LANCHESTER RD
A6076
Maiden Hall Farm
HOWDEN BANK
Howden Burn

Chapman's Well Farm

NEWACRES RD
WAGTAIL LA
Newacres Plantation

Morrowedge Plantation
Morrow Edge

GREEN LA
Little Holmside

Tait's House

Wheatley Hill
Burnhope Flatts Farm

Spring Gardens
Opencast Workings

EDGE LA

Black Wood

Moor Leazes

PAYSIDE
HOLMSIDE LA
VALE VIEW
CO-OPERATIVE TERR
THE AVENUE
PH
Liby
PAVILION TERR
RIDDEHOUSE TERR
WEST TERR
LANGLEY TERR
SOUTH VIEW
Ibbetson's Sike
Fellside Plantation

THE VILLAS
LANGLEY AVENUE
THE GROVE
HILL CREST
THE PLEASANT
THE GABLES INT
THE HAVEN
THE PLEASANT TERR
WHITEHOUSE AVE
HOLMLEA
PLEASANT BROWSIDE
Burnhope Cty Jun & Inf Sch

PETH LA
White House

Burnhope

Peth House
DEANERY VIEW
PETH BANK

Black Wood

Burnhope Television Sta
Mast

BEECH GR
Recn Gd
GREENWOOD AVE
FAIR VIEW

Standagainstall Plantation

LANGLEY LA
LONG EDGE

BURNHOPESIDE AVE
PETHSIDE AVE
DENESIDE
MANOR GRANGE
DURHALL RD
MANOR CT
GREENWELL PK

Manor House

Dowfit Hill

Foxcover Wood

Warriors Bridge

Path Burn

Manor House Bridge

High Burnhopeside Plantation

High Burnhopeside

Burnhopeside Cottages

Langley West House

Lanchester Valley Wlk
Sewage Works
Waters' Meeting
River Browney

P
Browney Bridge
OFFICIAL TERR

Lanchester Valley

Malton

Burnhopeside Hall

Burnhopeside Farm

Long Plantation
A691

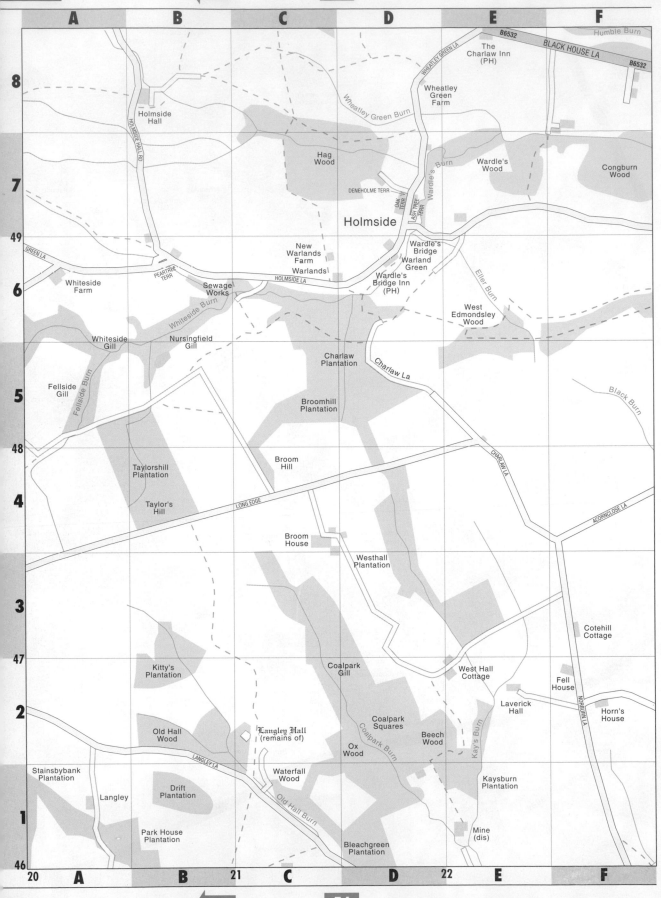

A   B   C   D   E   F

8

Holmside Hall
HOLMSIDE HALL RD

Wheatley Green Burn
WHEATLEY GREEN LA
The Charlaw Inn (PH)
B6532
BLACK HOUSE LA
Humble Burn
B6532

Hag Wood
Wardle's Burn
Wheatley Green Farm
Wardle's Wood
Congburn Wood

7

DENEHOLME TERR
OAK TERR
ASH TREE TERR

Holmside

49

GREEN LA
New Warlands Farm
Warlands
PEARTREE TERR
HOLMSIDE LA
Wardle's Bridge
Warland Green
Wardle's Bridge Inn (PH)
Eller Burn

6

Whiteside Farm
Sewage Works
Whiteside Burn
West Edmondsley Wood

Whiteside Gill
Nursingfield Gill
Charlaw Plantation
Charlaw La

Fellside Gill
Fellside Burn
Broomhill Plantation
Black Burn

5

48

Taylorshill Plantation
Broom Hill
CHARLAW LA

4

Taylor's Hill
LONG EDGE
ACORNCLOSE LA

Broom House
Westhall Plantation

3

Cotehill Cottage

47

Kitty's Plantation
Coalpark Gill
West Hall Cottage
Fell House
NORBURN LA
Horn's House

2

Old Hall Wood
Langley Hall (remains of)
Coalpark Squares
Coalpark Burn
Ox Wood
Beech Wood
Kay's Burn
Laverick Hall

Stainsbybank Plantation
Langley
LANGLEY LA
Drift Plantation
Waterfall Wood
Old Hall Burn
Kaysburn Plantation

1

Park House Plantation
Bleachgreen Plantation
Mine (dis)

46

20   A   B   21   C   D   22   E   F

A **B** **C** **D** **E** **F**

Little Burn
Sewage Works
Cong Burn
BLACK HOUSE LA
BEECHGROVE LA
Congburn Bridge
Dismtd Rly
Mine (dis)
Waldridge Fell
P
P
P
WALDRIDGE RD
Waldridge Hall Farm
Beech Wood
HAUXLEY OR
8

Deneacres
Edmondsley Cty Jun & Inf Sch
BRAESIDE
JUBILEE CL
Wanister Hill
Wanister Bog
South Burn
WALDRIDGE LA
7

APPLEDORE GDNS 1
WATSON'S BLDGS 2
STOBART ST 3
FRONT ST 4
FLEECE TERR 5
TYZACK ST
FLEECE COTTS
PH
Nettlesworth Hill
BEANLEY LA
49

East Farm
Edmondsley
Sacriston Wood
WOODSIDE VIEW
BRUCE ST
HAMILTON TERR
STORE COTTS
Daisy Hill
Scrogs
Felledge Farm
6

MELBOURNE TERR
EDMONDSLEY LA
HEUGH EDGE
WESTHILL ST
DALESIDE
Nettlesworth West House
Howlmire Gill
Black Burn
West Hill
5

MOUNT PLEASANT 1
EAST ST 2
Charlaw
SOUTH VIEW
ASHFIELD DR
CROSS LA
DENESIDE
Sewage Works
Nettlesworth
CONYERS
BROADMIRES TERR
THE GREEN
Sch Liby
BOYNTONS
GAIR CT
AGED MINERS' HOMES
UGLY LA
48

ACORNCLOSE LA
CHARLAW CL
ACORN CL
FULFORTH WAY
TIMBER CL
RYDAL CL
CONSTON DR
LINGEY CL
St Bedes RC Jun & Inf Sch
CHURCH PARK
DAVISON TERR
Sacriston
BROOKSIDE
MINORSIDE
WITTON AVE
GRESON ST
OAKWOOD
1 ROSEWOOD CL
2 NEWTOWN VILLAS
3 CROSSLEA
4 MEADOW VIEW
5 GRAHAM CT
6 LOW GRAHAM ST
AGED MINER'S HOMES
PARK VIEW
THE CRESCENT
HILLMEADS
GLENMEADS
TANMEADS
OAK CRES
CEDAR AVE
B6312
4

LABURNUM CT 1
WEST VIEW 2
CHURCH ST
ELM CL
Plawsworth Cty Inf Sch
Cemy
SPRINGSIDE
WOODLAND TERR
Barras Hill
HAWTHORN CL
SYCAMORE RD
BRIAR CL
Tan Hills
Kimblesworth
3

ERRINGTON BGLWS 3
KIRKWOOD 4
FRONT ST
Recn Gd
VICTORIA ST
ELLIOTT ST
JOHN ST
WATER ST
PLAWSWORTH RD
LINKWAY
ROSE CRES
FERN RD
CENE CRES
LAVENDER GDNS
UPHILL DR
Barrashill Wood
EAST PAR
ELM CRES
SOUTH VIEW
47

Fulforth Wood
WESTWARD VIEW
CHARLAW TERR
WITTON RD
VALLEY VIEW
SOMERSBY
ST THOMAS'
MAFEKING
FRENCH CL
Liby
P
CROSSWAY'S
WESTON ST
5
CROSSFIELD
LILAC AVE
VIOLA CRES
HOLLY CRES
PENSHAW VIEW
Findon Hill
RED LANDS
FELLSIDE VIEW
CATHEDRAL VIEW
2

Now Hill
WOODSIDE
DURHAM RD
Sacriston Jun & Inf Schs
HIGH GRAHAM ST 7
DOROTHY TERR 8
FYNDOUNE 9
CRAIGLAND VILLAS 10
DUNELM
10
FINDON HILL
HOLMLANDS VILLAS
EASTWOOD
BROWBANK
WHITBURN
Fulworth
New Close
THE CRESCENT
ROSE LEA
Fyndoune Community Coll
Wellsprings Farm
Kimblesworth Grange
1

MORBURN PK
BRIAR LEA
HILLSIDE
SACRISTON LA
HOLLY LEA
GREEN LEA
OAK LEA
FYNDOUNE WAY
FINDON AVE
SCOTS LEA
BROOKSIDE
CHESTER GDNS
B6312
Red House Farm
B6312
Nor Burn
46

A **B** **C** **D** **E** **F**

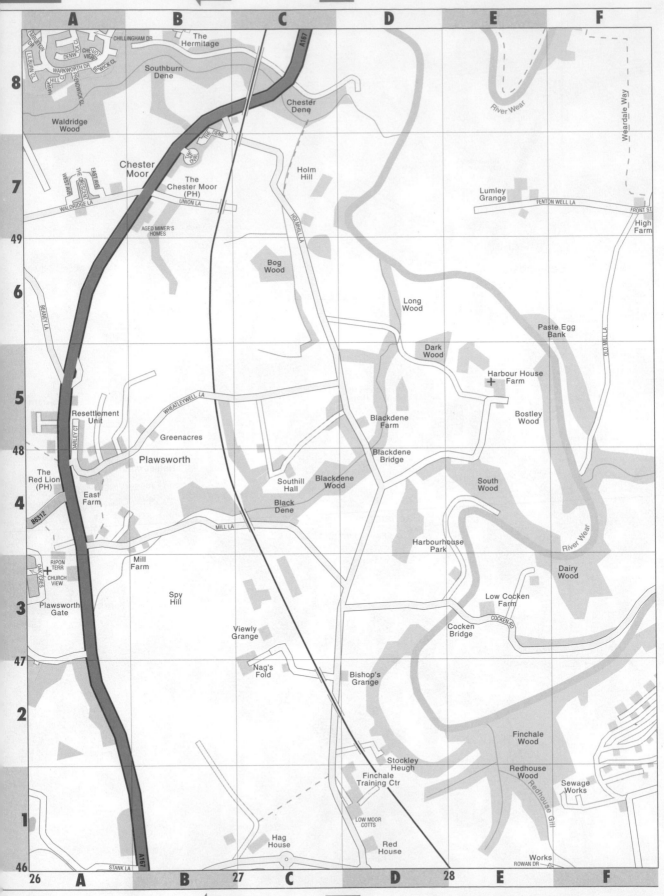

A B C D E F

8

7

49

6

5

48

4

3

47

2

1

46

Chillingham Dr
The Hermitage
Southburn Dene
Chester Dene
Waldridge Wood
Chester Moor
The Chester Moor (PH)
Holm Hill
Aged Miner's Homes
Bog Wood
Lumley Grange
FENTON WELL LA
FRONT ST
High Farm
River Wear
Weardale Way
Long Wood
Paste Egg Bank
Dark Wood
Harbour House Farm
Resettlement Unit
WHEATLEYWELL LA
Greenacres
Plawsworth
Blackdene Farm
Bostley Wood
The Red Lion (PH)
East Farm
Blackdene Bridge
Southill Hall
Blackdene Wood
South Wood
Black Dene
MILL LA
Harbourhouse Park
River Wear
Mill Farm
RIPON TERR
CHURCH VIEW
OAK CRES
Spy Hill
Dairy Wood
Low Cocken Farm
COCKEN RD
Cocken Bridge
Plawsworth Gate
Viewly Grange
Nag's Fold
Bishop's Grange
Finchale Wood
Stockley Heugh
Finchale Training Ctr
Redhouse Wood
Sewage Works
Redhouse Gill
Hag House
Low Moor Cotts
Red House
Works
ROWAN DR
STANK LA
A167
B6312
BEANEY LA
DARLEY CT
WEST AVE
WALDRIDGE LA
UNION LA
HOLMILL LA
OLD MILL LA

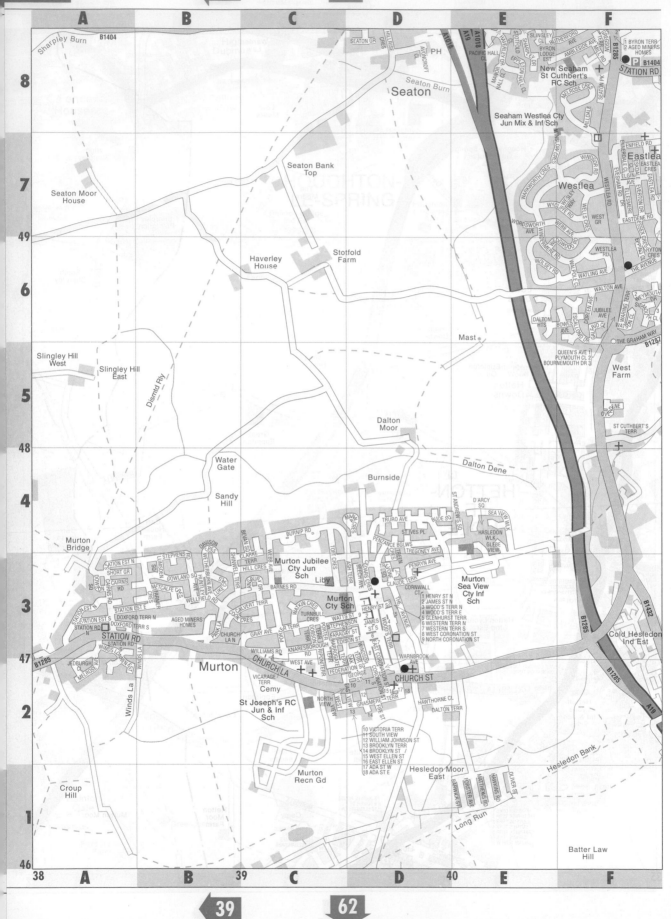

A   B   C   D   E   F

8

7

49

6

5

48

4

47

2

1

46

Sharpley Burn   B1404

Seaton GR

Seaton Burn

Seaton

Seaton Bank Top

Seaton Moor House

Haverley House

Stotfold Farm

Slingley Hill West

Slingley Hill East

Dismtd Rly

Mast

Dalton Moor

Dalton Dene

Water Gate

Burnside

Sandy Hill

Murton Bridge

Murton Jubilee Cty Jun Sch

Liby

Murton Cty Sch

Murton Sea View Cty Inf Sch

Station Rd

Aged Miners Homes

Murton

Church La

Williams Rd

West Ave

Vicarage Terr

Cemy

St Joseph's RC Jun & Inf Sch

Church St

Hawthorne Cl

Dalton Terr

North View

Murton Recn Gd

10 Victoria Terr
11 South View
12 William Johnson St
13 Brooklyn Terr
14 Brooklyn St
15 West Ellen St
16 East Ellen St
17 Ada St W
18 Ada St E

Hesledon Moor East

Hesledon Bank

Croup Hill

Long Run

Batter Law Hill

New Seaham St Cuthbert's RC Sch

1 Byron Terr
2 Aged Miners Homes

Station Rd

B1404

Seaham Westlea Cty Jun Mix & Inf Sch

Eastlea

Westlea

West Farm

St Cuthbert's Terr

Queen's Ave 1
Plymouth Cl 2
Bournemouth Dr 3

The Graham Way

Cold Hesledon Ind Est

B1285

A19

1 Henry St N
2 James St N
3 Wood's Terr N
4 Wood's Terr E
5 Glenhurst Terr
6 Western Terr N
7 Western Terr S
8 West Coronation St
9 North Coronation St

B1285

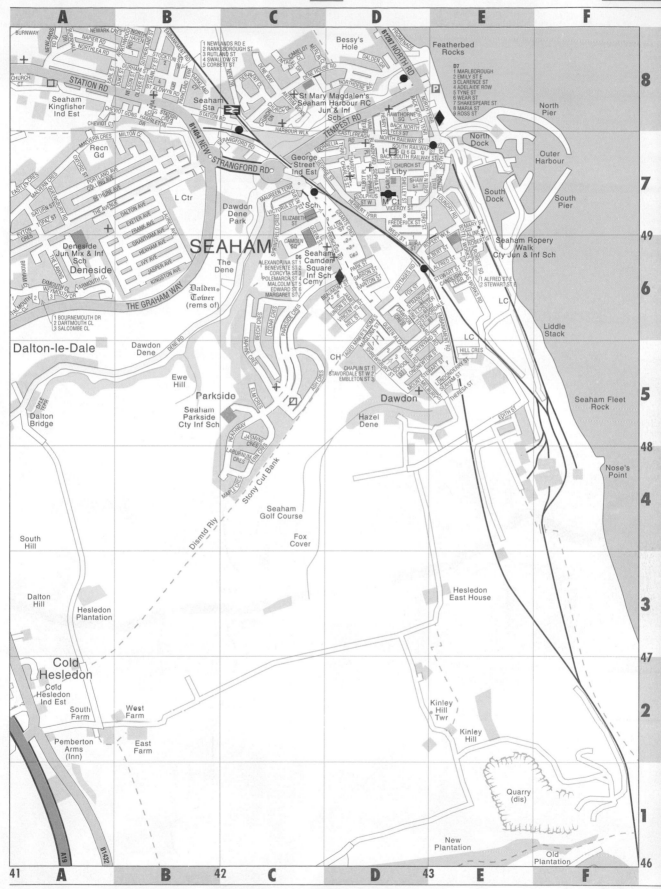

SEAHAM

Dalton-le-Dale

Dalden
Tower
(rems of)

THE GRAHAM WAY

Parkside

Seaham
Parkside
Cty Inf Sch

Dawdon

Dawdon Dene

Ewe Hill

Hazel Dene

Seaham
Golf Course

Fox Cover

South Hill

Dalton Hill

Hesledon Plantation

Cold Hesledon

Cold Hesledon Ind Est

South Farm

West Farm

East Farm

Pemberton Arms (Inn)

Dalton Bridge

Dalton-le-Dale

Dismtd Rly

Stony Cut Bank

Hesledon East House

Kinley Hill Twr

Kinley Hill

Quarry (dis)

New Plantation

Old Plantation

Nose's Point

Seaham Fleet Rock

Liddle Stack

Seaham Ropery Walk Cty Jun & Inf Sch

North Pier

Outer Harbour

South Pier

North Dock

South Dock

Featherbed Rocks

Bessy's Hole

North Railway St

Seaham Kingfisher Ind Est

Seaham Sta

STATION RD

NEW STRANGFORD RD

George Street Ind Est

Dawdon Dene Park

Deneside

Deneside Jun Mix & Inf Sch

The Dene

L Ctr

Recn Gd

Seaham Camden Square Inf Sch

St Mary Magdalen's Seaham Harbour RC Jun & Inf Sch

B1287 NORTH RD

B1404

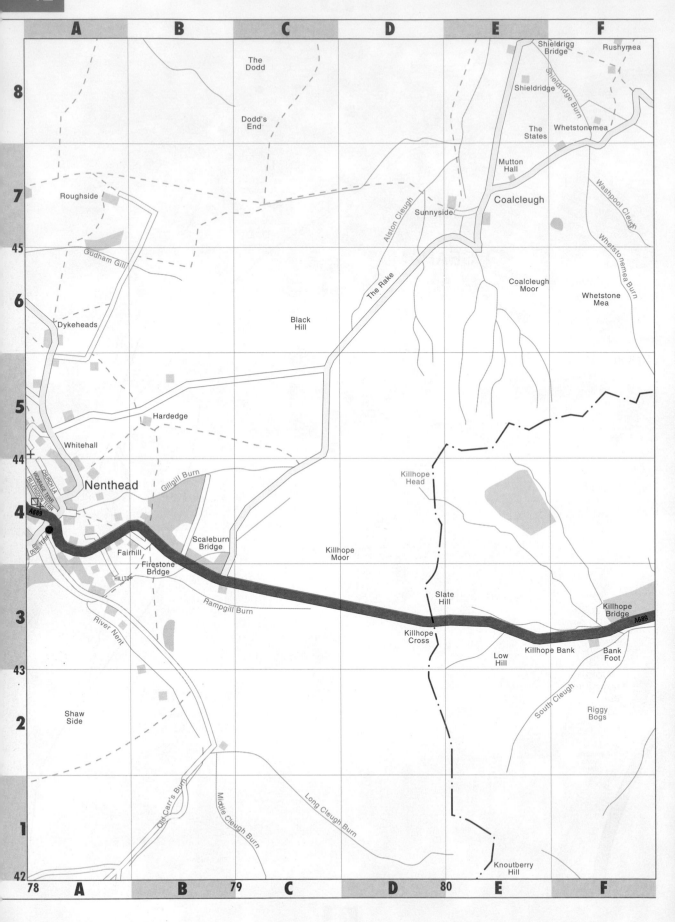

A B C D E F

8
The Dodd
Dodd's End

7 Roughside
45 Gudham Gill
Shieldrigg Bridge
Rushymea
Shieldridge
Shieldridge Burn
The States
Whetstonemea
Mutton Hall
Coalcleugh
Alston Cleugh
Sunnyside

6 Dykeheads
The Rake
Black Hill
Coalcleugh Moor
Whetstone Mea
Washpool Cleugh
Whetstonemea Burn

5 Hardedge
Whitehall
44 Nenthead
Gillgill Burn
Killhope Head

4 A689
Fairhill
Scaleburn Bridge
Firestone Bridge
HILLTOP
Killhope Moor
Slate Hill
Killhope Bridge
A689

3 River Nent
Rampgill Burn
Killhope Cross
Killhope Bank
Bank Foot
Low Hill
43
Shaw Side
South Cleugh
Riggy Bogs

2
Old Carr's Burn
Middle Cleugh Burn
Long Cleugh Burn

1
Knoutberry Hill
42

Shivery Hill

Middlehope Head

Deep Cleugh

White Mere

Todd's Sike

Doctor's Hush

Groove Sike

Roundhill Sike

Hetty Well

Varty's Sike

8

Bridge Cleugh

Long Mere

Round Hill

7

Coalcleugh Moor

Middlehope Moor

45

Green Hills

Killhope Law

Allendale Common

Coulson's Sike

Bowey Mere

Carriers' Way

Blackcleugh Burn

6

Weardale Way

Groat Hill

5

Hard Hills

Killhopelaw Sike

44

Killhope Moor

High Linn

Bentyhill End

4

Cleugh Head

Betty's Cleugh

Carriers' Hill

Hard Sike

Hill Top

White Hall

Cleugh House

Band Edge

Snodberry Cleugh

Killhope

Far House

Holy Well

3

Green Swang

Kidd's Dam

Clevison Currick

43

Killhope Burn

Park Level Mill

Killhope Wheel (Mus)

Snodberry

Puddingthorn Moor

Broad Meres

Gold Hill

2

Appleby Currick

Weardale Forest

Green Hill

Weardale Way

Cowhorse Hill

Cowhorse Hush

Wellhope Moor

Slit Foot

1

Quarry Hill

Collior Hill

New Level Hill

A689

42

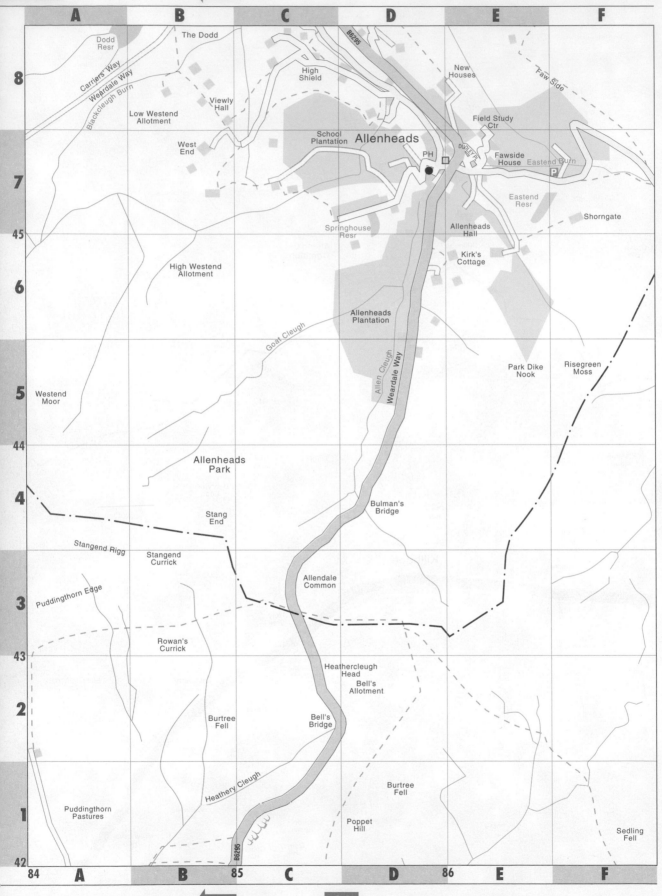

Dodd Resr

The Dodd

Carriers' Way

Weardale Way

Blackcleugh Burn

Low Westend Allotment

Viewly Hall

West End

High Shield

School Plantation

Allenheads

B6295

New Houses

Faw Side

Field Study Ctr

PH

Dudley PI

Fawside House

Eastend Burn

P

Shorngate

45

Springhouse Resr

Allenheads Hall

Eastend Resr

High Westend Allotment

Kirk's Cottage

6

Allenheads Plantation

Park Dike Nook

Risegreen Moss

Goat Cleugh

Allen Cleugh

Weardale Way

5

Westend Moor

44

Allenheads Park

4

Stang End

Bulman's Bridge

Stangend Rigg

Stangend Currick

Puddingthorn Edge

Allendale Common

3

Rowan's Currick

43

Heathercleugh Head

Bell's Allotment

2

Burtree Fell

Bell's Bridge

Burtree Fell

Heathery Cleugh

Poppet Hill

1

Puddingthorn Pastures

Sedling Fell

B6295

42

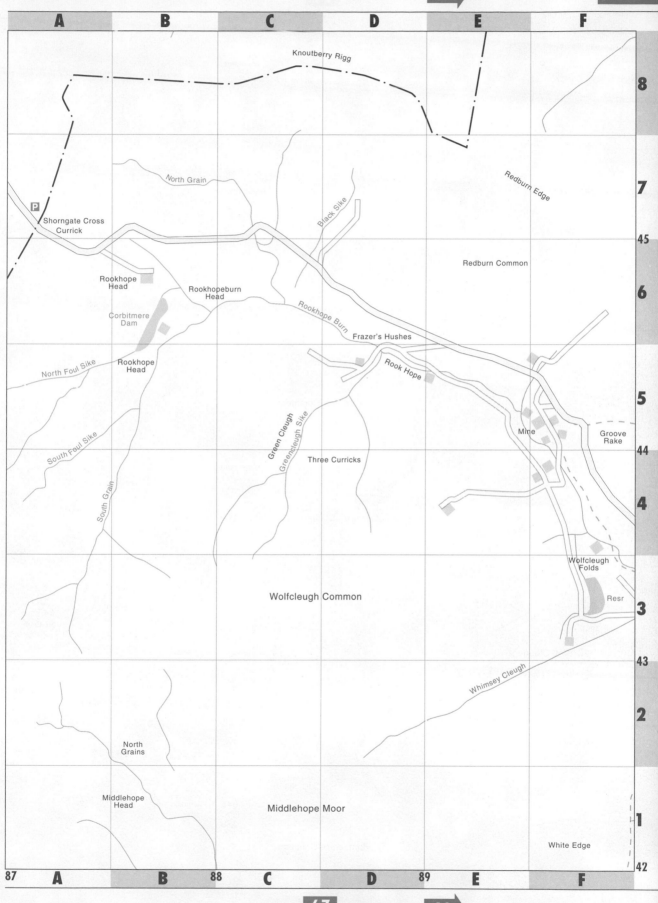

A B C D E F

8

Knoutberry Rigg

Redburn Edge

7

North Grain

P

Shorngate Cross
Currick

Black Sike

45

Redburn Common

6

Rookhope
Head

Rookhopeburn
Head

Rookhope Burn

Corbitmere
Dam

Frazer's Hushes

North Foul Sike

Rookhope
Head

Rook Hope

5

Mine

Groove
Rake

44

South Foul Sike

Green Cleugh

Greencleugh Sike

Three Curricks

4

South Grain

Wolfcleugh
Folds

Wolfcleugh Common

Resr

3

43

Whimsey Cleugh

2

North
Grains

Middlehope
Head

Middlehope Moor

1

White Edge

42

87 A B 88 C D 89 E F

A B C D E F

8

North Grain

South Grain

Bokenbank Sike

Grindstone Cleugh

Shooting
Cabin

Hackford's
Hush

7

Hackford's
Dam

Black Hags

45

6

Dry Rigg

5

Redburn Common

44

Groove
Rake

Rookhope Chimney
(course of)

Snow
Wreaths

Hawk Sike

Red Burn

4

Hawk
Hill

Thorny
Slit

Bield
Hill

Redburn

Rispey Sike

Bank
Foot

3

Mine
(dis)

Rushy
Hole

Redburn
Mine

Wolf Cleugh

43

Lintzgarth

Wolf Cleugh
Common

Rispey
Mill

2

Rookhope Burn

Lintzgarth
House

Wolf
Cleugh

Scar Sike

Shafts
(dis)

Lintzgarth
Bield

Lintzgarth
Plantation

1

Lintzgarth Common

42

90 A B 91 C D 92 E F

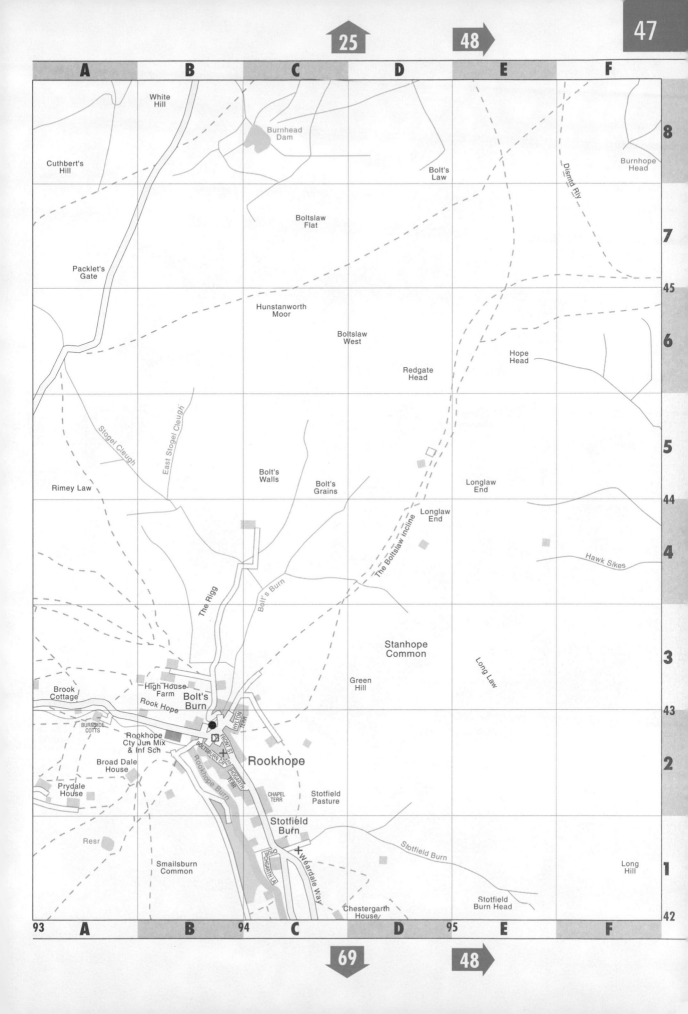

A B C D E F

8

Sladeyford Sike

Pike Sike

Horseshoe Plain

Dead Friars Bank

Tongue

Eudonburn Head

7

Dead Friars

45

Horseshoe West End

Mast

Horseshoe Hill

6

Dismtd Rly

Meadows Edge

Bell's Hill

5

East Nipton Burn

44

Hawk Sikes

4

Steward Shield Meadow

West Whiteley Burn

Smiddy Burn

Stanhope Burn

Shooting Box

3

Whiteley Rigg

43

Delph Holes

Stanhope Common

North Thatch Burn

2

South Thatch Sike

Gibb Carrs

1

Cot Hill

Quarry Hills

Gibb Hill

Brownley Hill

42

96 A B 97 C D 98 E F

A   **B**   **C**   **D**   **E**   **F**

8

Little
Pike

Hawkburn
Head

P

Waskerley Way

7

Meeting
Stack

+

Resr

Frosterley Cut

Chy

45

Skaylock
Hill

6

Waskerley Beck

5

Waskerley
Resr

Treatment
Works

Teel Gill

44

Walsingham
Park Moor

4

3

Waskerley Park

Ewe Law Sike

43

2

Washpool Gill

Shooting
Box

Slateyford
Plantation

1

Weather Law

Catchwater
Plantation

42

02   **A**   **B**   03   **C**   **D**   04   **E**   **F**

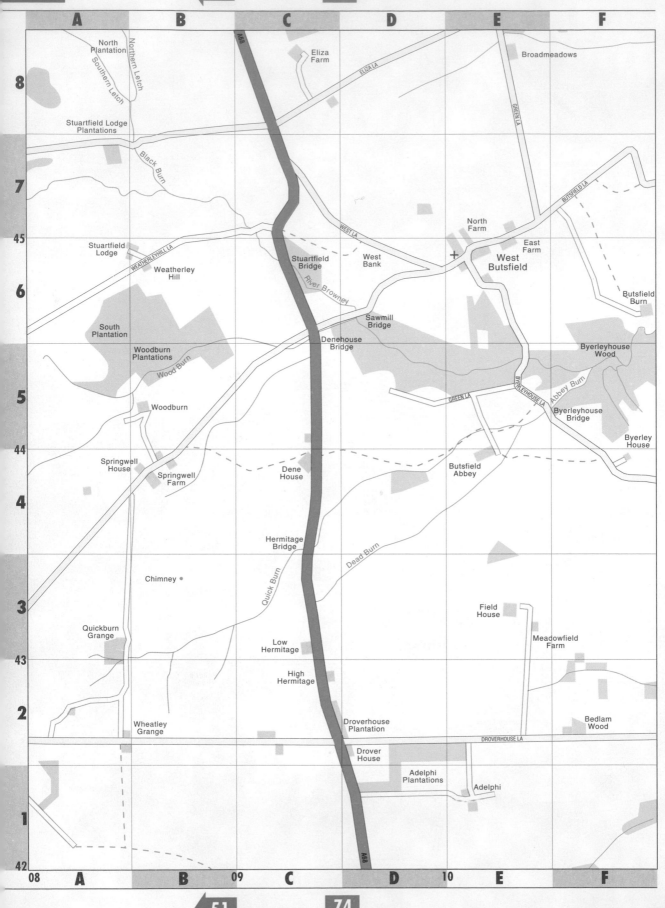

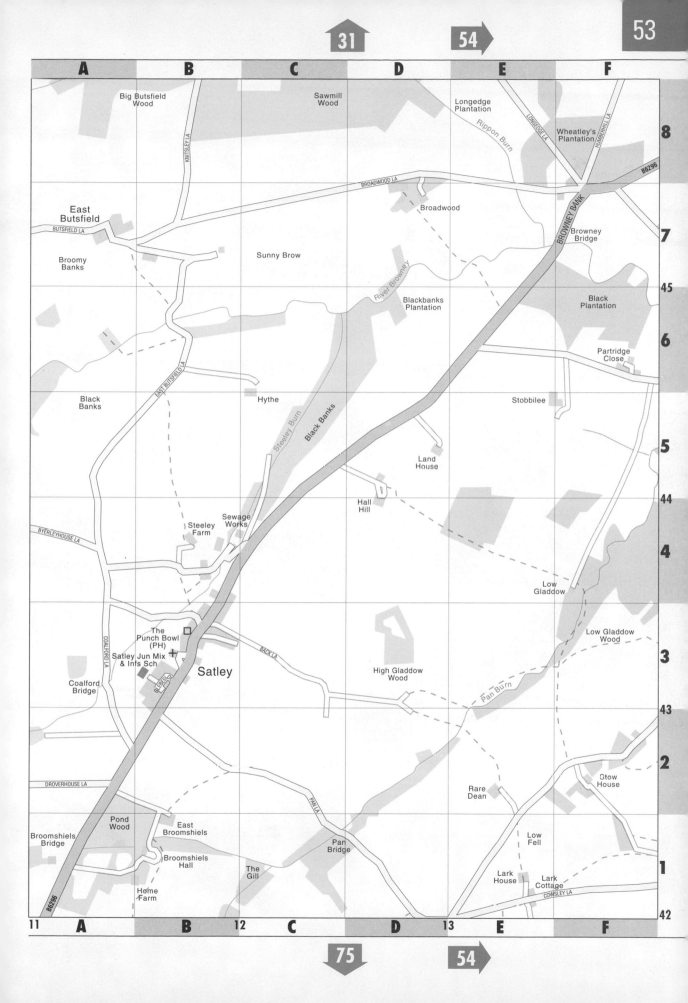

A B C D E F

Big Butsfield Wood

Sawmill Wood

Longedge Plantation

Rippon Burn

Wheatley's Plantation

8

B6296

Broadwood La

Broadwood

Browney Bank

Browney Bridge

7

East Butsfield

Butsfield La

Broomy Banks

Sunny Brow

River Browney

Blackbanks Plantation

Black Plantation

45

East Butsfield La

6

Partridge Close

Black Banks

Hythe

Steeley Burn

Black Banks

Stobbilee

Land House

5

Byerleyhouse La

Sewage Works

Steeley Farm

Hall Hill

44

4

Low Gladdow

Low Gladdow Wood

Coalford La

The Punch Bowl (PH)

Satley Jun Mix & Infs Sch

Satley

Back La

High Gladdow Wood

Pan Burn

3

Coalford Bridge

43

2

Droverhouse La

Pan La

Rare Dean

Stow House

Pond Wood

East Broomshiels

Broomshiels Bridge

Broomshiels Hall

The Gill

Pan Bridge

Low Fell

Lark House

Lark Cottage

1

Home Farm

Cowsley La

B6296

42

11 A B 12 C D 13 E F

53
32

A   B   C   D   E   F

8

B6296

Black House Farm

Throstle Nest

Greenwell Farm

B6301

HOLEHOUSE LA

B6296

Hole House

Colepike Mill

Lead Hill

BARGATE BANK

7

Triangle Plantation

Bleach Green

River Browney

45

Square House

HAMSTEELS LA

Partridgeclose Mill Bridge

Ragpathside Plantation

Squarehouse Cotts

6

Ragpath Side

RAGPATH LA

Lowmill Bridge

CORNSAY LA

5

Lowmill Wood

Click-Em-Inn Farm

44

Clickemin Hill

B6301

4

East Ravensbush Wood

Cornsay House

Grange Farm

Cornsay

North Ravensbush Wood

Black Horse Inn (PH)

POST OFFICE ROW

3

South Farm

Low Row

43

Greenacres

Lane Foot

Hedleyhope Burn

2

Bell's House

The Firtree (PH)

Lodge House Farm

COWSLEY LA

HEDLEYHILL LA

IVESLEY LA

B6301

1

Cowsley

B6301

42

14   A   B   15   C   D   16   E   F

A   B   C   D   E   F

Hollybush

Love's
Wood

Langley
Mill

Langley
House

A691

8

Lanchester Valley Wlk   River Browney

Lanchester Valley

Biggen
Farm

Biggen House
Farm

Blackburn

7

45

Hamsteels
Hall

Malton
House

HAMSTEELS BANK

Cemy

HAMSTEELS LA

Biggin
Terrace

Blackburn Beck

6

Hamsteels Beck

LOW MOOR RD

Weather
Hill

Greenland
Drift

ESH BANK

North
Farm

5

Greenland

GREENLAND RD

Esh CE
Sch

PH

44

WILK'S
HILL

AGED MINER'S
HOMES

CHURCH VIEW

FOLD

FRONT ST

GREEN CT

HILL CRES

HALL RD

Esh Laude
RC Sch

Esh

STEADMAN'S LA

MARLEY'S
COTTS

FRONT ST

PH

Greenland Bank

Eshe
Laude

4

B6301

Quebec

LAUDE BANK

Esh
Hall

COMMERCIAL ST

Cornsay
Colliery

Clifford's House
Farm

CLIFFORD'S BANK

Hag
Wood

3

PH

B6302

Hedleyhope Burn

Heugh

43

SOUTH TERR

HEDLEYHILL LA

B6301

Rowley

Castle
Steads

Newhouse

2

Rowley Burn

Rowley
Gillots

Hamsteels Cty
Jun & Inf
Sch

ROSE CT
VALLEY GARTH
CLIFFORDS
GATE
BRIAR DENE
VALLEY DR
INVERNESS GR
WESTERN AVE
FIR CRES
ASH CRES
WILLOW RD
ROWLEY CRES
ROWLEY LINK

BURNSIDE

SWALLOW
CL

FALCON WAY

WOODLANDS RD

FIR TERRACES

WOODLAND RD
FLATS

NEWHOUSE AVE

FAIR VIEW

B6302

B6302

1 NEWHOUSE RD
2 WOOD VIEW
3 DURHAM RD

SOUTH TERR

COPPICE HILL

B6302

1

42

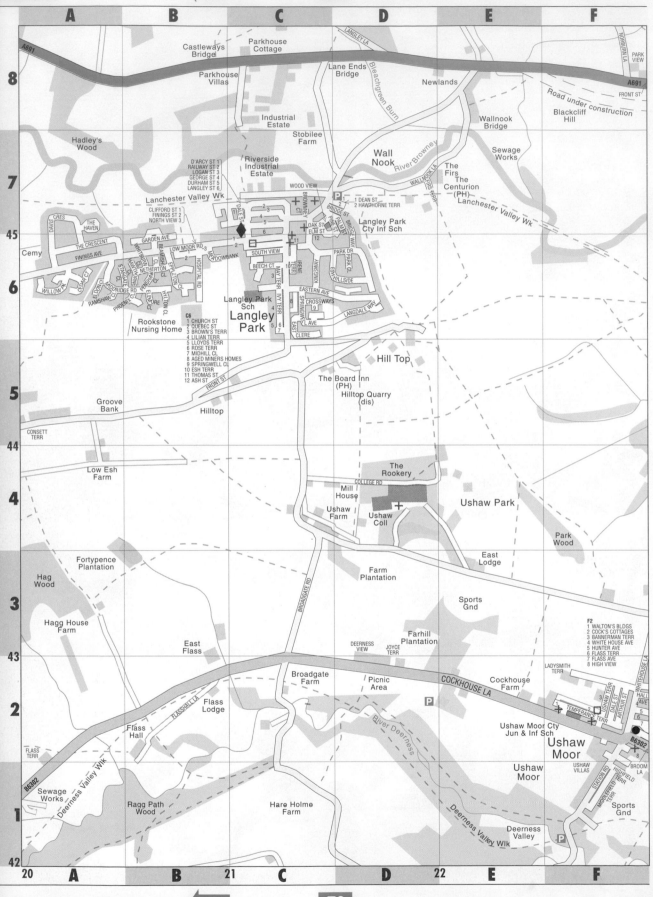

A B C D E F

8

A691

Castleways Bridge
Parkhouse Cottage
Parkhouse Villas

Langley La
Lane Ends Bridge
Newlands

Bleachgreen Burn

Wall Nook

A691
Norburn La
Park View
Front St
Road under construction
Blackcliff Hill

7

Hadley's Wood

Industrial Estate

Stobilee Farm

River Browney

Wallnook Bridge

Sewage Works

D'ARCY ST 1
RAILWAY ST 2
LOGAN ST 3
GEORGE ST 4
DURHAM ST 5
LANGLEY ST 6

Riverside Industrial Estate

WOOD VIEW

Lanchester Valley Wk

Wallnook La

The Firs
The Centurion (PH)
Lanchester Valley Wk

CLIFFORD ST 1
FININGS ST 2
NORTH VIEW 3

45

DAVIS CRES
THE HAVEN

The Crescent
Finings Ave
Cemy

GARDEN AVE
Low Moor Rd

MEADOWBANK
SOUTH VIEW

1 DEAN ST
2 HAWTHORNE TERR

OAK ST
ELM ST

Langley Park Cty Inf Sch

Park Dr
Park Cl

6

WILLOW PK

RAMSHAW'S
STARGATE RD
PHOENIX CL
HAWTHORNE
NETHERTON

HYLTON CL

HOSPITAL RD

BEECH CT

MAY TERR
IVY TERR
IRENE TERR
SPRINGWELL
EAST

EASTERN AVE
CROSSWAYS
AWESOME

EHILLSIDE

ELAVE
CLERE

LANGDALE WAY

Langley Park Sch
Langley Park

C6
1 CHURCH ST
2 QUEBEC ST
3 BROWN'S TERR
4 LILIAN TERR
5 LLOYDS TERR
6 ROSE TERR
7 MIDHILL CL
8 AGED MINERS HOMES
9 SPRINGWELL CL
10 ESH TERR
11 THOMAS ST
12 ASH ST

Rookstone Nursing Home

Hill Top

5

Groove Bank

Hilltop

FRONT ST

The Board Inn (PH)
Hilltop Quarry (dis)

CONSETT TERR

44

Low Esh Farm

The Rookery

4

East Flass

Mill House

Ushaw Farm

COLLEGE RD

Ushaw Coll

Ushaw Park

East Lodge

Park Wood

Fortypence Plantation

Hag Wood

Farm Plantation

Sports Gnd

3

Hagg House Farm

East Flass

BROADGATE RD

DEERNESS VIEW

JOYCE TERR

Farhill Plantation

F2
1 WALTON'S BLDGS
2 COCK'S COTTAGES
3 BANNERMAN TERR
4 WHITE HOUSE AVE
5 HUNTER AVE
6 FLASS TERR
7 FLASS AVE
8 HIGH VIEW

43

Broadgate Farm

Picnic Area

COCKHOUSE LA

Cockhouse Farm

LADYSMITH TERR

WHITEHOUSE LA

2

FLASSHALL LA

Flass Lodge

Flass Hall

River Deerness

TEMPERANCE TERR
USHAW TERR
DALE ST
ARTHUR ST
HALL AVE

Ushaw Moor Cty Jun & Inf Sch

Ushaw Moor

Ushaw Villas

STATION RD
HIGHFIELD TERR
MORFIELD TERR

BROOM LA
B6302

FLASS TERR

B6302

Sewage Works

Deerness Valley Wlk

Ragg Path Wood

Hare Holme Farm

Deerness Valley Wlk

Deerness Valley

Sports Gnd

1

42

20 A B 21 C D 22 E F

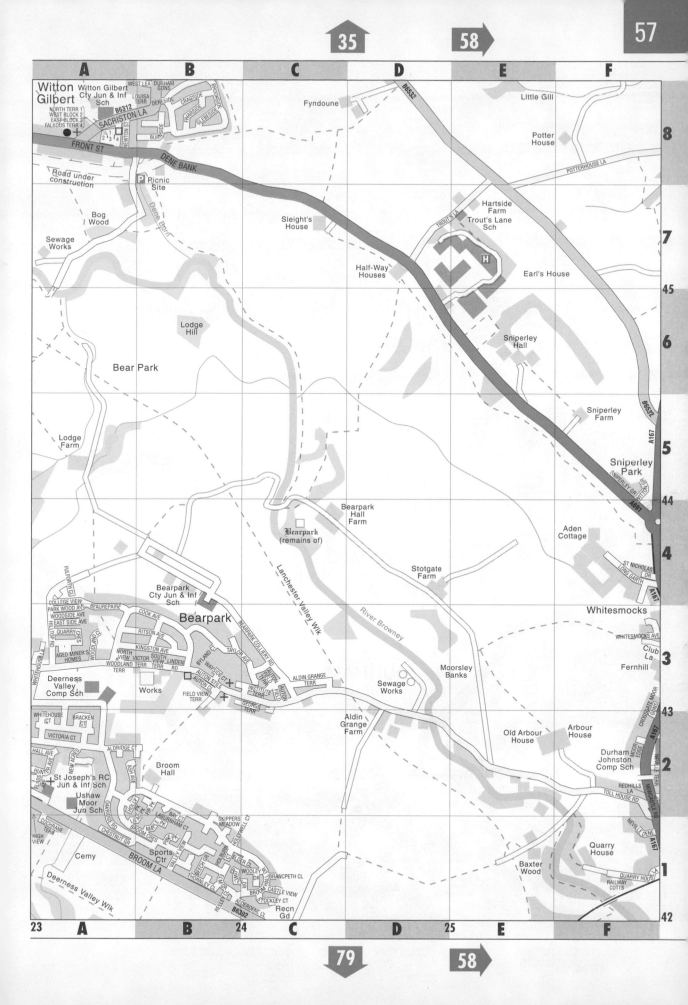

Witton Gilbert

Witton Gilbert Cty Jun & Inf Sch
WEST LEA
DURHAM GDNS
LOUISA TERR
DENESIDE
CRAGSIDE
FIRMARSIDE
GLEBESIDE
BROOMSIDE
BURYSIDE
NORTH TERR 1
WEST BLOCK 2
EAST BLOCK 3
FALKOUS TERR 4
B6312
SACRISTON LA
NEWTON ST
FRONT ST
DENE BANK

Fyndoune
Little Gill
Potter House
B6532
POTTERHOUSE LA

Road under construction
P Picnic Site

Bog Wood
Dene Burn
Sewage Works

Sleight's House
Half-Way Houses
Hartside Farm
Trout's Lane Sch
TROUT'S LA
H
Earl's House
Sniperley Hall

Lodge Hill
Bear Park
Sniperley Farm
B6532
A167

Lodge Farm
Sniperley Park
SNIPERLEY GR

Bearpark Hall Farm
Bearpark (remains of)
Stotgate Farm
Aden Cottage
A691
A167
St Nicholas DR
LONG GARTH

Bearpark Cty Jun & Inf Sch
Lanchester Valley Wlk
River Browney
Whitesmocks
WHITESMOCKS AVE

COLLEGE VIEW
PARK WOOD
WOODSIDE AVE
EAST SIDE AVE
HILLTOP RD
FULFORTH CL
BEAUREPAIRE
WOODLAND
QUARRY CRES
COOK AVE
RITSON AVE
KINGSTON AVE
NORTH VIEW VICTOR TERR
SOUTH VIEW
LINDEN RD
WOODLAND TERR
Bearpark
BYLAND CT
TAYLOR AVE
BEARPARK COLLIERY RD
AUTON STILE
AUTON FIELD
ANTON TERR
ALDIN GRANGE TERR
Moorsley Banks
Club La
Fernhill
CROSSGATE MOOR GDNS
A167
MOOR EDGE

Aged Miner's Homes
WHITEHOUSE LA
Deerness Valley Comp Sch
Works
INSTITUTE TERR
FIELD VIEW TERR
GEORGE TERR
Sewage Works
Old Arbour House
Arbour House
Durham Johnston Comp Sch

WHITEHOUSE CT
BRACKEN CT
VICTORIA CT
HALL AVE
NEW ACRES
HUNTER AVE
FLASS AVE
ALDRIDGE CT
ASH AVE
Broom Hall
Aldin Grange Farm
REDHILLS LA
TOLL HOUSE RD
NEWCASTLE RD
NEVILLE TERR
A167

St Joseph's RC Jun & Inf Sch
Ushaw Moor Jun Sch
HIGH VIEW
COCHRANE TERR
Cemy
OAKRIDGE RD
CHESTNUT RD
BROOM CRES
LABURNHAM CT
Sports Ctr
SKIPPERS MEADOW
HOLLYWELL CT
NEVILLE DENE
Quarry House
Baxter Wood
QUARRY HOUSE LA

BROOM LA
Deerness Valley Wlk
THORNLEY CL
BEECH CL
HOLBURN
WOOLEY DR
ELDER CL
BRANCPETH CL
CASTLE VIEW
POCKLEY CT
ALDERDENE CL
Recn Gd
B6302
Railway Cotts

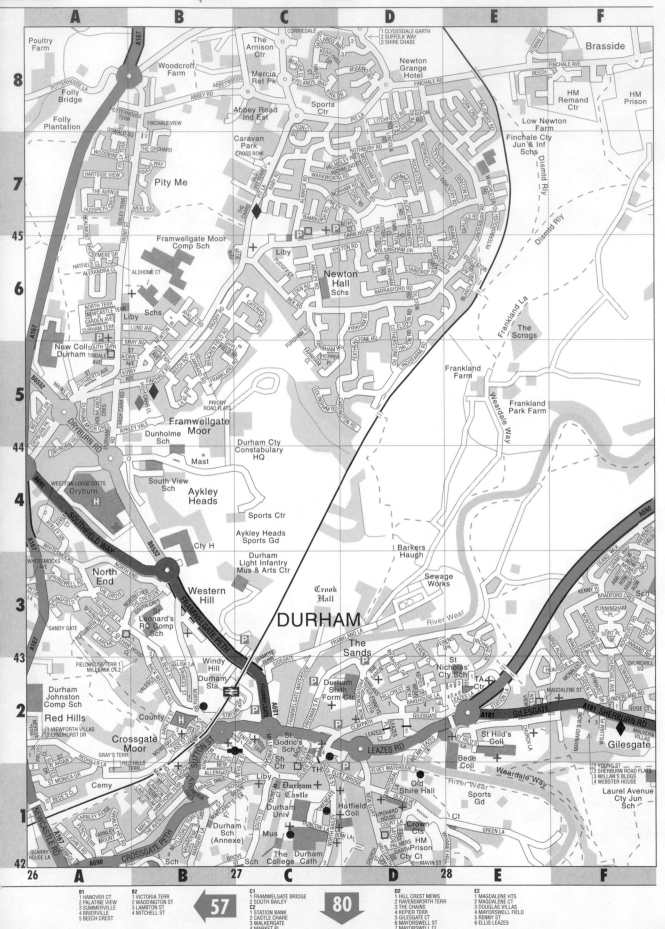

B1
1 HANOVER CT
2 PALATINE VIEW
3 SUMMERVILLE
4 BRIERVILLE
5 BEECH CREST

B2
1 VICTORIA TERR
2 WADDINGTON ST
3 LAMBTON ST
4 MITCHELL ST

C1
1 FRAMWELGATE BRIDGE
2 SOUTH BAILEY
C2
1 STATION BANK
2 CASTLE CHARE
3 WALKERGATE
4 MARKET PL

D2
1 HILL CREST MEWS
2 RAVENSWORTH TERR
3 THE CHAINS
4 KEPIER TERR
5 GILESGATE CT
6 MAYORSWELL ST
7 MAYORSWELL CL

E2
1 MAGDALENE HTS
2 MAGDALENE CT
3 DOUGLAS VILLAS
4 MAYORSWELL FIELD
5 RENNY ST
6 ELLIS LEAZES

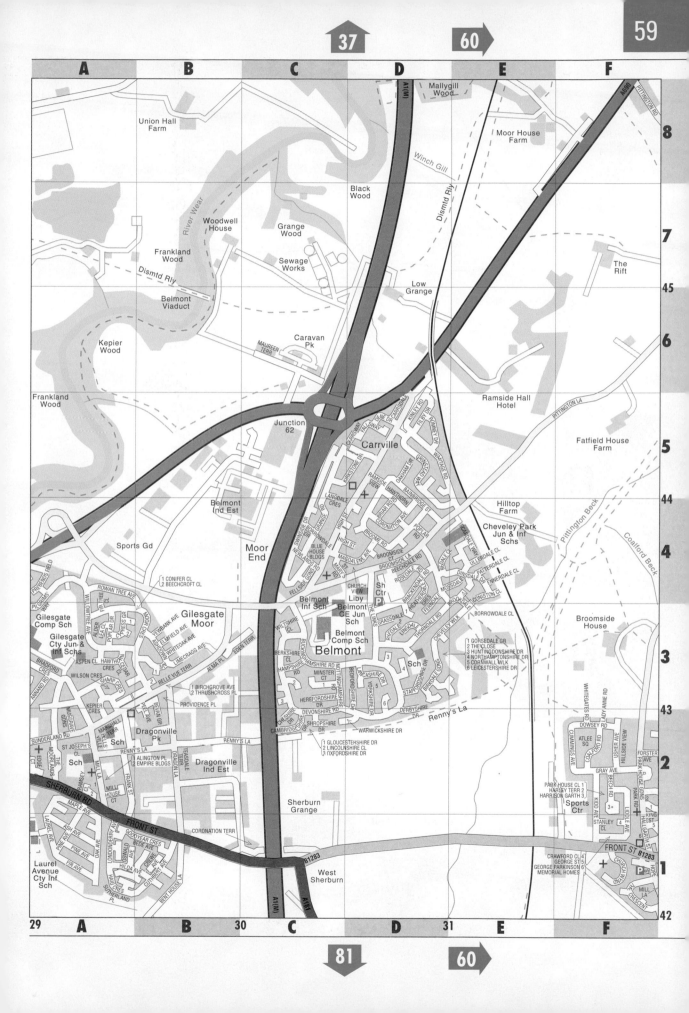

A B C D E F

8 Pitfield House
Homer Hill Farm

High Moorsley

VALLEY VIEW

High Moorsley Farm

MOORSLEY RD

7

PITTINGTON RD

Cobbler's Hill

Quarryhouse Wood

45

Pittington Hill

Hillside Farm

ELEMORE LA

PITTINGTON LA

STATION RD

PH

FRONT ST   HIGH ST

CORONATION CRES

6 Low Pittington

1 WELLINGTON ST
2 HILLSIDE GROVE
3 GRAHAM TERR
4 HALLGARTH VIEW

LADY'S PIECE LA

ELEMORE ST

ST JOHN'S RD   ST LAWRENCE RD

ST LAWRENCE

NORMAN TERR   NEWBY LA

Willow Garth

GLEN'S FLATS

PRIORS GRANGE

5 Pittington Cty Jun & Inf Sch

HALLGARTH LA

High Pittington

The Moor

Horseshoe Wood

SOUTH END

44

Coldwell Burn

MANOR VIEW

CHURCH VALE

COALFORD LA

Sewage Works

White's Wood

4 Hallgarth Farm

Hallgarth Manor (Hotel)

MOOR COTTAGES

Littletown

Dog Kennel Bank

Hallgarth

CROSS ST

PLANTATION AVE

Duke of York (PH)

Hastings House

3 Pittington Bridge

Coalford Beck

Littletown Farm

Littletown House

LITTLETOWN LA

43 Stand Bridge

2

FORSTER AVE

Sherburn Cty Jun & Inf Sch

COOKSHOLD LA

Cook's Hold Farm

Saw Mill

Black Banks

PARK HOUSE GDNS

MITFORD CR

GEORGE ST

NELSON TERR

MELDON AVE

WHALTON CL

Sherburn

Sherburn Hill

YELL CRES

NORTH VIEW

SOUTH VIEW

EAST VIEW

JUBILEE CRES

1

B1283

PEART CL

CHAPEL CT

NEW ST

SOUTH ST

FRONT ST

KINNOCK CL

HALLGARTH VILLAS

BROADVIEW VILLAS

ALSTON WLK

LOCAL AVE

WEST VIEW

WESLEY TERR

BANNERMAN TERR

AGED MINERS HOMES

Sherburn Hill Cty Mix Inf Sch

THE CROFT

PINDERS WAY

JUBILEE CRES

High House Farm

FRONT ST

PH

B1283

1 CO-OPERATIVE VILLAS
2 BRIGHTON TERR
3 DURHAM LA

42

MILL LA

32 A B **33** C D **34** E F

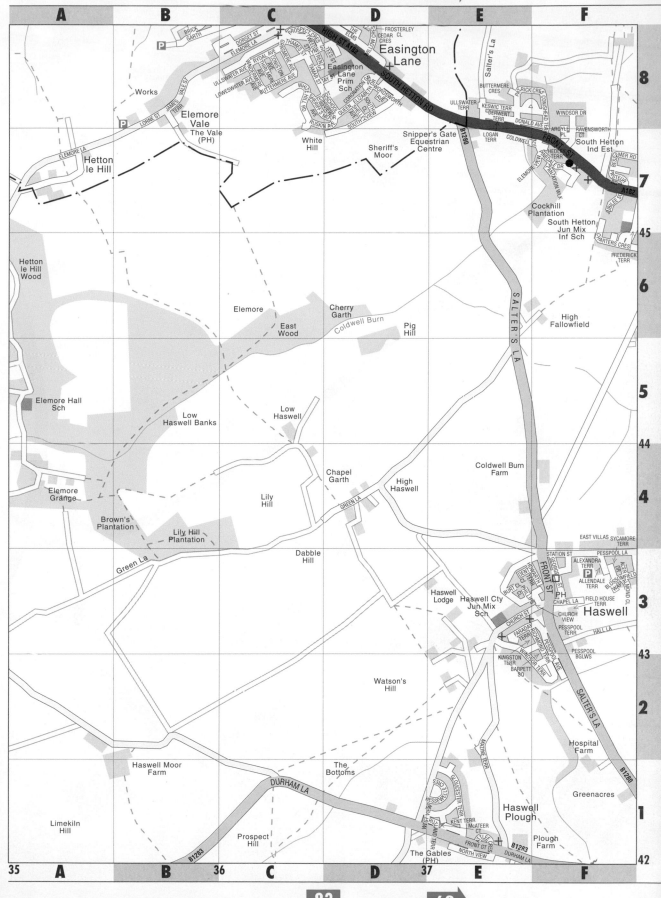

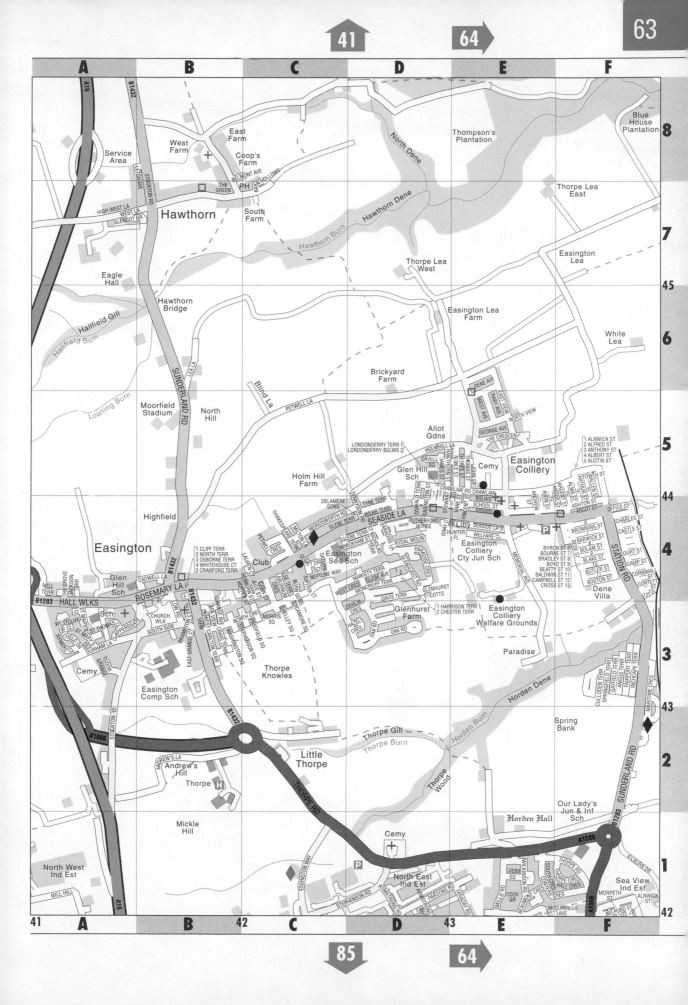

A B C D E F

8

Blue House Plantation

Thompson's Plantation

North Dene

Thorpe Lea East

West Farm

East Farm

Coop's Farm

BELMONT AVE

BOG HOLLOWS

PH

THE GREEN

Hawthorn

South Farm

Hawthorn Dene

Hawthorn Burn

7

Thorpe Lea West

Easington Lea

45

Eagle Hall

Hawthorn Bridge

Hallfield Gill

Hallfield Burn

SUNDERLAND RD

LEY LA

Easington Lea Farm

White Lea

6

Loaning Burn

Moorfield Stadium

North Hill

Blind La

PETWELL LA

Brickyard Farm

DENE AVE

WEST AVE

RABY AVE

EAST VIEW

NORTH VIEW

GEORGE AVE

THE CRESCENT

Allot Gdns

Cemy

Easington Colliery

1 ALNWICK ST
2 ALFRED ST
3 ANTHONY ST
4 ALBERT ST
5 AUSTIN ST

5

LONDONDERRY TERR 1
LONDONDERRY BGLWS 2

Holm Hill Farm

Glen Hill Sch

HOLMHILL LA

CAVELL SQ

JAMES ST

JOHN ST

THOMAS ST

HARRY ST

MARY ST

HARTHORN ST

STEWART ST

GRAY ST

CRAWLAW RD

CRAWLAW BGLWS

SCHOOL ST

TOWER ST

ALLEN ST

ARGENT ST

ANGUS ST

ANDREW ST

ALMA ST

ARTHUR ST

ASHTON ST

ASCOT ST

OFFICE ST

CHARLES ST

CASTLE ST

44

DELAMERE GDNS

WORDSWORTH RD

TENNYSON RD

TYNE TERR

WEAR TERR

GLEBE TERR

OSWALD TERR

SEASIDE LA

Liby

SEASIDE LA S

RUTHERFORD HOUSE

HUNTER PL

WELFARE CL

P

BROWNING ST

BARWICK ST

BOLAM ST

BLAKE ST

BUTLER ST

CORNWALL

CORTEY

STATION RD

COURT ST

CAMP ST

4

Highfield

SHAKESPEARE TERR

PETWELL CRES

1 CLIFF TERR
2 NORTH TERR
3 OSBORNE TERR
4 WHITEHOUSE CT
5 CRANFORD TERR

MILTON LA

Club

CROFT DR

JUPITER ST

SATURN ST

NICHOLAS ST

WICKHAM TERR

PARADISE LA

RYDAL MOUNT

PARADISE CRES

MANISTY TERR

GLEBE AVE

MONCRIEFF TERR

Easington Sec Sch

GLENHURST RD

Easington Colliery Cty Jun Sch

MEMORIAL AVE

GLENHURST COTTS

BYRON ST 6
BOURNE ST 7
BRADLEY ST 8
BOYD ST 9
BEATTY ST 10
BALDWIN ST 11
CAMPBELL ST 12
CROSS ST 13

Dene Villa

Easington

Glen Hill Sch

CADWELL LA

ROSEMARY LA

B1432

LAUREN CT

ALDER CT

LABURNUM

HOPPER ST

ADE ST

BURN GDNS

SYCAMORE SQ

NEPTUNE WAY

WEST CRES

DAVIS TERR

DEHLIA CRES

HAZEL CRES

OAK RD

OAK RD

Glenhurst Farm

1 HARRISON TERR
2 CHESTER TERR

Easington Colliery Welfare Grounds

MILL TERR

THE GROVE

JACKSON TERR

B1283 HALL WLKS

Sch

ST MARY'S

ST THOMAS

CAPPERGATE

CHURCH WLK

SOUTH SIDE

GRANGE AVE

CRAIG TERR

WEST CARLTON TERR

WASHINGTON SQ

NORTH CRES

MORRIS SQ

SHELLEY SQ

Thorpe Knowles

Paradise

Horden Dene

CULLODEN TERR

SPRINGFIELD TERR

GAYFIELD TERR

ANGUS TERR

FAIRPORT TERR

MONCAPE TERR

MARITIME CRES

3

43

WESTCLIFF

ST ANNS

FIELD DR

ST JOHN'S

DURHAM LA

RYMERS

TUDOR GRANGE

EAST GRANGE CT

SPA VIEW

BRAMBLING CT

LOW RD

STEPHENSON SQ

HORDEN BURN

Spring Bank

Cemy

Easington Comp Sch

A1086

A19

STOCKTON RD

B1432

ANDREW'S LA

Andrew's Hill

Thorpe

H

Little Thorpe

Thorpe Gill

Thorpe Burn

Thorpe Wood

Horden Hall

Our Lady's Jun & Inf Sch

B1283

A1086

SUNDERLAND RD

KILBURN DR

2

1

Mickle Hill

Cemy

North East Ind Est

WEBB SQ

WILKINSON RD

THORPE CRES

HALL CRES

SOUTH CRES

SEA VIEW

Sea View Ind Est

MORPETH ST

ALNWICK ST

North West Ind Est

MILL HILL

ESSINGTON WAY

P

STEPHENSON RD

ARMSTRONG

PARSONS RD

FARADAY ST

SMAILE RD

COOK GR

BETHAM

CRES

McGUINNESS LANE

BELFORD ST

A1086

42

A B C D E F

8

7

45

6

5

44

4

3

43

2

1

42

44 A 45 C 46 D E F

Blue House
Plantation
Hive Point

Beacon
Point
Beacon
Hill
*Shippersea
Bay*
Shippersea
Point

Shot
Rock

Loom

Busiers
Holes
Bed
Slide
Fox Holes
Fox Holes
Dene
Horden Burn
Horden
Dene

Horden
Point

Warren House Gill

Ash Gill

Sea View
Ind Est

A B C D E F

8
Low Puddingthorn
Heathery Cleugh
B6295
High Greenfield
Burtree Fell
Sedling Burn
A689
Lanehead
SCHOOL HILL
Middle Burnt Hills
Cornriggs
Rough Hill
Weardale Way
Cogley
Burtree Pastures
Coptcleugh

7
Heathery Bridge
Heatherycleugh
Weardale Way
CORNRIGGS
Holyhead
CROSS LA
Sedling Mine (dis)

41
Low Allers
B6295
Copthill
COPTHILL

6
High Allers
Hill Farm
Hill Farm
Cowshill
High Grain
Burtreeford Bridge
BURTREE FORD
LONGHORN ENDS
Queensbury

Moss Moor
Northgrain
Burtree Ford
Killhope Burn

5
Green Pit
Halliwell House

40
Bents Head
NORTHGRAIN
West Fall Farm
Newfield

4
Cleugh House
Black Cleugh Ford
Blackcleugh
Mount Haley
Wearhead Mix Jun & Inf Sch
BENTS LA
WEST FALL
Wearhead
Westfall Bridge
Bail Hill
Elmford Cleugh
Whitestones Farm

Burnhope Moor
Stripe Head
Stonedrass
Wearhead Bridge
FRONT ST
Weardale Way
River Wear
Elmford Bridge
Low Whitestones

3
Duntertwell Sike
Pryhill
Burnhope Burn
VEDRA
Lane Side
Waterside Farm
CARRWAY BANK
West Blackdene
BLACKDENE

Burnhope Scars
Rigg Foot
Middle Rigg
Low Rigg
Irestone
LANEHILL
BRIAR HILL

39
Wham
High Rigg
IRESTONE LA
Ling Riggs

2
Burnhope Resr
The Rigg
White Hills
CAUSEWAY RD
LANEHILL
FRONT ST
A689
STONY PATH
Ireshopeburn

1
High House
West Grain
East Grain
Whin Sike
Battle Spots
GRASSHILL CSWY
Slack House
Greenwell
Ireshope Burn
Earnwell Sike
Doghill

38
Ireshope Plains

84 A 85 C D 86 E F

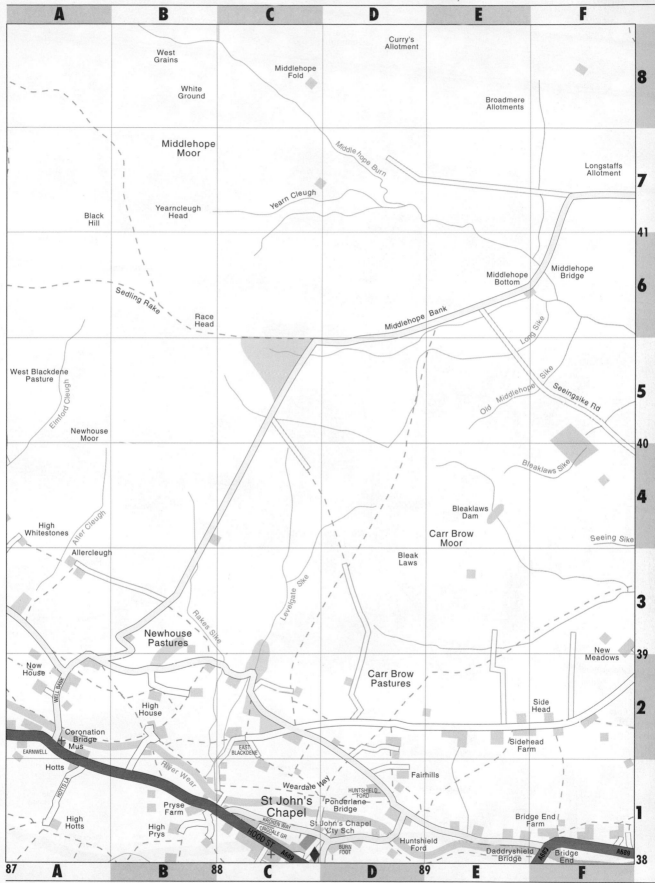

A   B   C   D   E   F

West
Grains

White
Ground

Middlehope
Fold

Curry's
Allotment

Broadmere
Allotments

Longstaffs
Allotment

8

Middlehope
Moor

Middle hope Burn

Yearn Cleugh

Yearncleugh
Head

Black
Hill

7

41

Middlehope
Bottom

Middlehope
Bridge

6

Sedling Rake

Race
Head

Middlehope Bank

Long Sike

Seeingsike Rd

Old Middlehope Sike

West Blackdene
Pasture

Elmford Cleugh

Newhouse
Moor

Bleaklaws Sike

5

40

4

High
Whitestones

Aller Cleugh

Allercleugh

Carr Brow
Moor

Bleaklaws
Dam

Seeing Sike

Bleak
Laws

Rakes Sike

Levelgate Sike

Newhouse
Pastures

New
Meadows

3

39

Now
House

WELL BANK

High
House

Carr Brow
Pastures

Side
Head

2

Coronation
Bridge
Mus

EARNWELL

Hotts

HOTTS LA

River Wear

EAST
BLACKDENE

Sidehead
Farm

High
Hotts

Pryse
Farm

High
Prys

St John's
Chapel

Weardale Way

BROKEN WAY

LONGDALE GR

HOOD ST

A689

Ponderlane
Bridge

BURN
FOOT

St John's Chapel
Cty Sch

HUNTSHIELD
FORD

Fairhills

Huntshield
Ford

Daddryshield
Bridge

Bridge End
Farm

A689

Bridge
End

A689

1

38

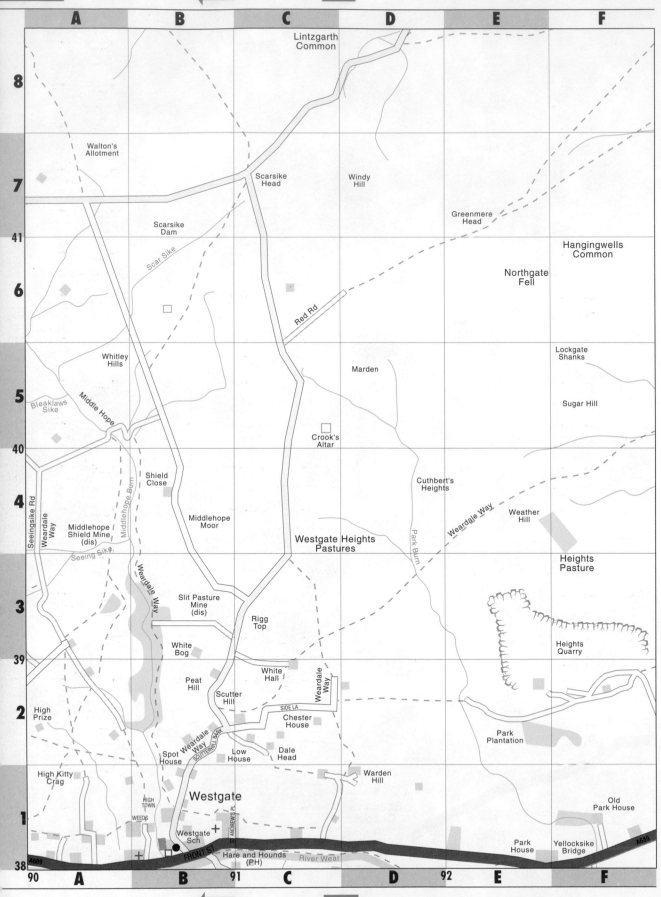

A B C D E F

8

7

41

6

Lintzgarth
Common

Walton's
Allotment

Scarsike
Head

Windy
Hill

Greenmere
Head

Scarsike
Dam

Hangingwells
Common

Scar Sike

Northgate
Fell

Red Rd

Whitley
Hills

Marden

Lockgate
Shanks

Bleaklaws
Sike

Middle Hope

Sugar Hill

5

40

4

3

39

2

1

38

Crook's
Altar

Shield
Close

Cuthbert's
Heights

Weardale Way

Weather
Hill

Heights
Pasture

Seeingsike Rd

Weardale Way

Middlehope
Shield Mine
(dis)

Middlehope Burn

Middlehope
Moor

Westgate Heights
Pastures

Park Burn

Seeing Sike

Weardale Way

Slit Pasture
Mine
(dis)

Rigg
Top

Heights Quarry

White
Bog

Peat
Hill

White
Hall

Weardale Way

High
Prize

Scutter
Hill

SIDE LA

Chester
House

Park
Plantation

Spot
House

Weardale Way

SCUTTERHILL BANK

Low
House

Dale
Head

High Kitty
Crag

Warden
Hill

Old
Park House

HIGH
TOWN

Westgate

WEEDS

Westgate Sch

ST ANDREW'S PL

Park
House

Yellocksike
Bridge

A689

FRONT ST

Hare and Hounds
(PH)

River Wear

A689

90 A B 91 C D 92 E F

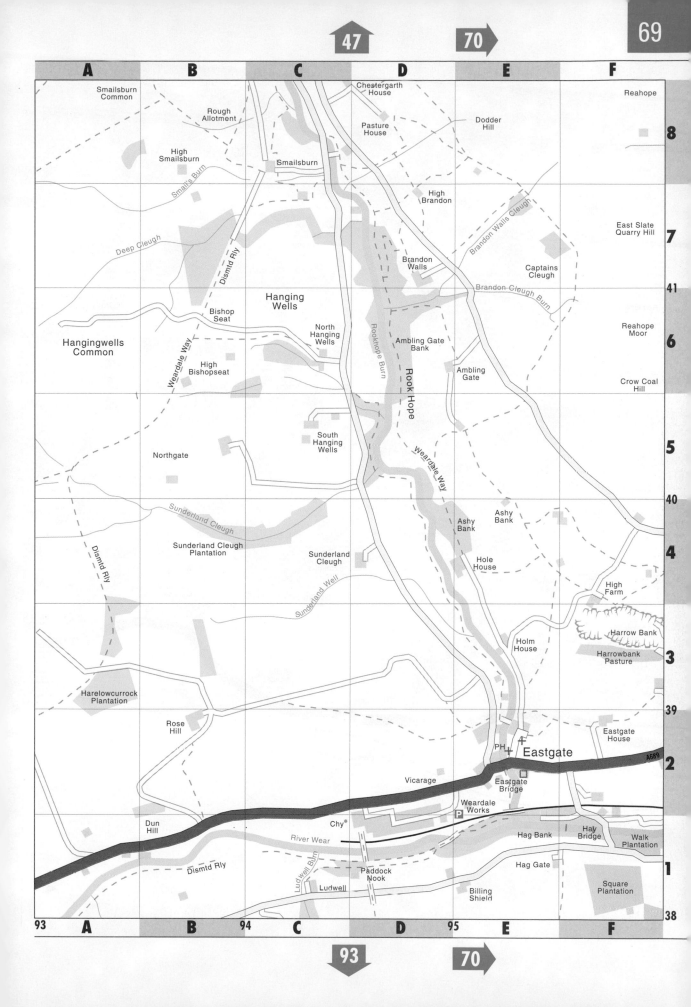

A B C D E F

Smailsburn Common

Rough Allotment

Chestergarth House

Pasture House

Dodder Hill

Reahope

8

High Smailsburn

Smailsburn

Small's Burn

High Brandon

East Slate Quarry Hill

7

Deep Cleugh

Dismtd Rly

Bishop Seat

Hanging Wells

Brandon Walls

Brandon Walls Cleugh

Captains Cleugh

Brandon Cleugh Burn

41

Hangingwells Common

Weardale Way

High Bishopseat

North Hanging Wells

Rookhope Burn

Ambling Gate Bank

Rook Hope

Ambling Gate

Reahope Moor

6

Crow Coal Hill

Northgate

South Hanging Wells

Weardale Way

5

Sunderland Cleugh

Ashy Bank

40

Dismtd Rly

Sunderland Cleugh Plantation

Sunderland Cleugh

Sunderland Well

Ashy Bank

Hole House

High Farm

4

Harrow Bank

Holm House

Harrowbank Pasture

3

Harelowcurrock Plantation

39

Rose Hill

Eastgate House

PH Eastgate

A689

2

Vicarage

Eastgate Bridge

Dun Hill

Chy

Weardale Works

P

Hag Bank

Hay Bridge

Walk Plantation

River Wear

Dismtd Rly

Ludwell Burn

Paddock Nook

Hag Gate

1

Ludwell

Billing Shield

Square Plantation

38

93 A B 94 C D 95 E F

69
48

A   B   C   D   E   F

8

Shank Sike

Hope House

High House

Park Plantation

Longwell Sike

7

Deep Sike

Reahope Burn

Park Shops

Clint's Plantation

Shield Hurst

41

Isaac Sike

Reahope Moor

Stoneby Sike

Fiddle Plantation

Noah's Ark

West Pasture

6

Stanhope Burn

Pease Mires

Stanhope Common

Mount Pleasant

Spring Plantation

Keeper's Lodge

Widley Field

Hungry Hill

5

Black Hill

Belle Vue

40

Bewdley Plain

Bewdley

Green Head Cottage

Allerton Burn

Allerton Wood

4

Spain's Field

West Bewdley

Green Head

Stanhope Hall

Greenfoot Caravan Site

Kell's Bank

Thrush Nest

Guy's Close

Stanhope Bridge

Horn Hall

B6278

A689

3

Brock Bank

Sweet Wells

Golden Lands

B6278

East Softley Plantation

Hare Law

39

A689

Howl John

Weardale Way

West Softley Plantation

B6278

2

White House Farm

Horsley Burn Wood

River Wear

Snow Field

Horsley Burn Farm

Aller Gill House

Crutch Bank

Walk Plantation

Aller Gill Cottage

1

Horsley Hall

Horsley Burn

B6278

Hag Top

38

96   A   B   97   C   D   98   E   F

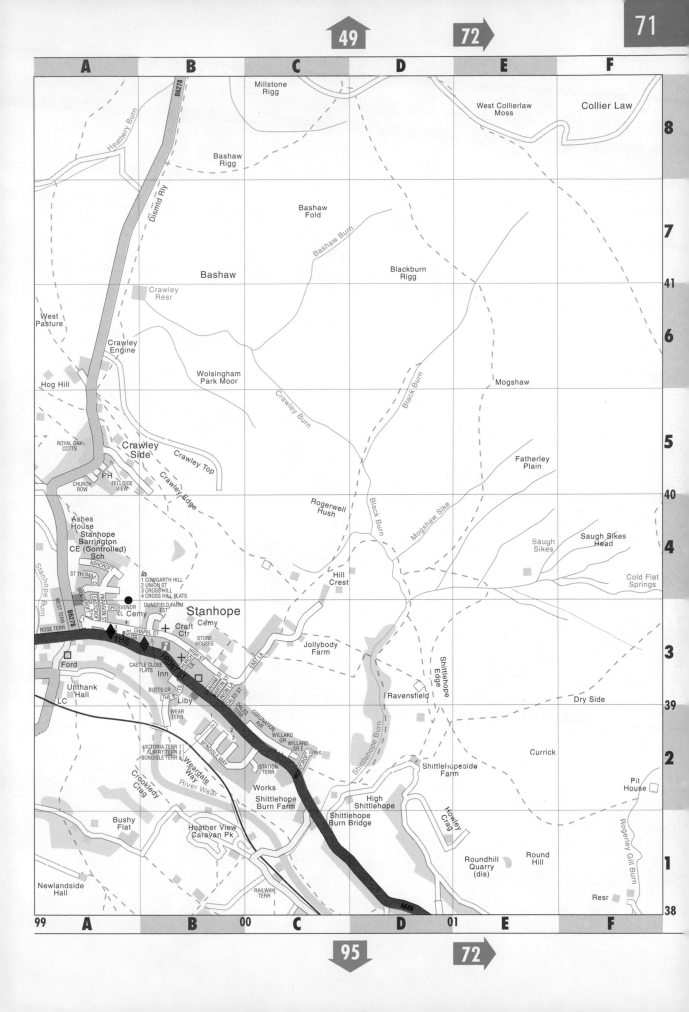

A | B | C | D | E | F

Millstone
Rigg

West Collierlaw
Moss

Collier Law

8

B6278

Bashaw
Rigg

Dismtd Rly

Bashaw
Fold

7

Bashaw Burn

41

Bashaw

Blackburn
Rigg

Crawley
Resr

West
Pasture

6

Crawley
Engine

Mogshaw

Wolsingham
Park Moor

Hog Hill

Crawley Burn

Black Burn

ROYAL OAK
COTTS

Fatherley
Plain

5

Crawley
Side

Crawley Top

40

CHURCH
ROW

PH

FELLSIDE
VIEW

Crawley Edge

Rogerwell
Hush

Mogshaw Sike

Saugh Sikes

Saugh Sikes
Head

Ashes
House

Stanhope
Barrington
CE (Controlled)
Sch

Black Burn

Cold Flat
Springs

4

ASHCROFT

St THOMAS CL

ASHCROFT

A3

Hill
Crest

1 COWGARTH HILL
2 UNION ST
3 CROSS HILL
4 CROSS HILL FLATS

Stanhope Burn

WEST TERR

B6278

PARAGON ST

EASTCROFT

WESTCROFT

GROSVENOR
CL

DUNSFIELD FARM
EST

Cemy

Stanhope

Cemy

ROSE TERR

CHAPEL ST

Craft
Ctr

STONE
HOUSES

Jollybody
Farm

3

THE NK

FRONT ST

HIGH ST

CHURCH LA

EAST LA

Shittlehope Edge

Ford

CASTLE CLOSE
FLATS

GRAHAM ST

MARTIN ST

UNION ST

DALES ST

Ravensfield

Dry Side

Inn

Unthank
Hall

BUTTS CR

THE BUTTS

Liby

DALES TERR

CORONATION
AVE

39

LC

WEAR
TERR

BONDISLE WAY

WILLARD
GR

WILLARD
GR E

Shittlehope Burn

Currick

VICTORIA TERR 1
ALBERT TERR 2
BONDISLE WAY

STATION
TERR

WESTGROVE GDNS

Shittlehopeside
Farm

2

Crookledy
Crag

Weardale
Way

River Wear

Works

Shittlehope
Burn Farm

High
Shittlehope

Howley
Crag

Pit
House

Bushy
Flat

Heather View
Caravan Pk

Shittlehope
Burn Bridge

Roundhill
Quarry
(dis)

Round
Hill

Rogerley Gill Burn

1

Newlandside
Hall

RAILWAY
TERR

A689

Resr

38

A B C D E F

8

East Collierlaw
Moss

Weather
Law

Tunstall Burn

Tunstall Burn
Head

7

Swinburne's
Currick

Cock
Lake

41

Shooting
Box

Wolsingham Park Moor

6

5

Thornhope
Sikes

Millsbull Sike

Carr
Stones

40

Red
Brae

4

Thornhope
Moor

Park Wall Edge

Fatherley
Hill

3

Thornhope
House

Thornhope Beck

39

2

Ladley
Wood

Thornhope Nook

Rogerley High
Plantation

Mast

1

Ladley

38

INTAKE LA

Intake
Plantation

Intake
Farm

02 A 03 B C 04 D E F

A   B   C   D   E   F

8

Stoney Allotment

Far Ling

Slaty Ford

Tunstall House Farm

Quarry Wood

Backhouse Wood

Kirkley House

Glen Wood

Rough Allotment Plantation

Tunstall Resr

Backstone Bank Wood

Ninety Acre Allotment

7

Tank Wood

Ninety Acre Plantation

41

Foresters Lodge Cottage

Backstone Bank

Spring Plantation

6

Prisoners Wood

Tunstall Cottages

Victory Wood

5

High Jofless

Jofless Cottage

40

Low Jofless

Students Wood

4

Justice Plantation

Park Wall

Long Plantation

Bishop Oak

Waskerley Beck

3

Park Wall Plantation

Gale Cottage

39

Thistlewood Farm

High Fawnlees

Middle Fawnlees

Baal Hill Wood

2

THISTLEWOOD LA

Low Fawnlees

Ladley Wood

High Doctor Pasture

Thistlewood House

Trod Beck

Thornhope Beck

Fawnlees Hall

Baal Hill House

Hollywood Hall

1

Sunny Bank Plantation

The Lodge

86296

A   B   C   D   E   F

8

Wharndean
Wood

Springwell
Cottage
Farm

A68

B6296

7

Dismtd Rly

41

Greenfield
Cottage

Sand Edge

6

Low
Houselop

High House
Farm

Wolsingham
North Moor

High Stoop

High
Houselop

5

Middle
Houselop

The Brown
Horse
(PH)

Ward's End
Cottages

40

A68

Houselop Beck

Armond Carr
Works

4

Redmires

Viewly
Hill

3

Dodd
Hill

Richmond
Farm

39

Castle
Hills

Armond
Carr

Sandy
Carr

Houselop
Bridge

Houselope
Grange

2

Redgate
Grange

Houselopbridge
House

B6297

Mount
Pleasant

Grey's
Well

1

Redgate
Farm

REDGATE BANK

Redgate
Head

B6297

THISTLEWOOD LA

B6296

Redgate
Hall

New
Row

LOW REDGATE BANK

38

08   A   B   09   C   D   10   E   F

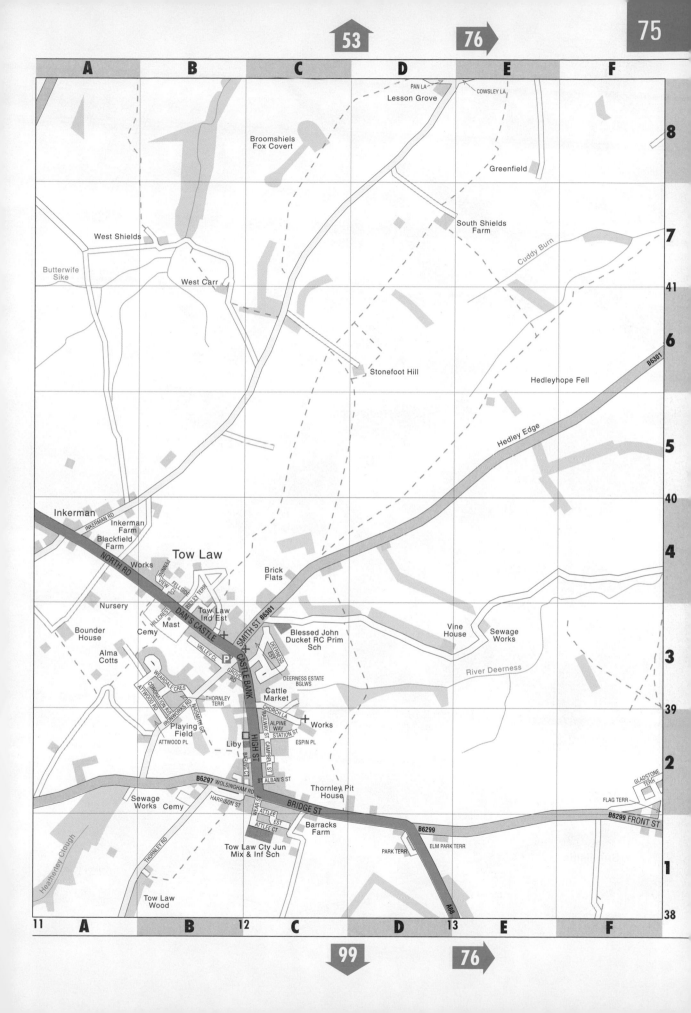

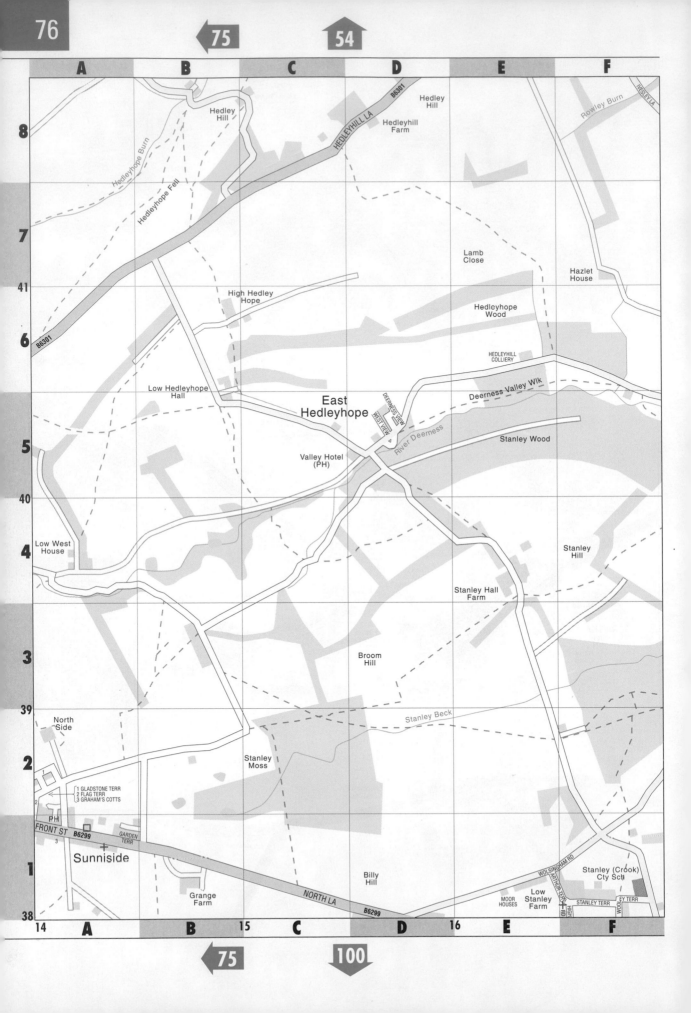

A B C D E F

Ivesley Wood

Old Ivesley Farm

WOODLANDS RD
DENE PK
OSPREY CL
ARBOURCOURT AVE
HILL VIEW
WOOD VIEW
B6302
BRANDON RD
CORONATION HOMES
COPPICE HILL
SOUTH TERR Sch
RAVEN CL
CYPRESS PK
BIRCH PL
HOLBURN RD
NEWHOUSE RD
WEST VIEW
DURHAM RD
BURNELL RD
ACTON RD
PINE VIEW VILLAS
MERLIN CT
RIDDING RD
EDWARD ST
ALBERT ST
GEORGE ST
CRAWFORD RD
The Bungalows
THE OAKS
THE LARCHES
REDWOOD
PINETREE
RIDDING RD
THE WYNDS
MARKET PL
P
STATION VIEW
STATION RD
Holburn Bridge

Esh Winning

Liby

ROWAN CL

COLLEGE VIEW

WOODLAND PL
WOODLAND TERR

Holburn Wood

Park Wood

Cemy

Esh Winning Cty Jun & Inf Sch

WEST VIEW

Holburn Beck

New Ivesley

IVESLEY LA

Deerness Valley Wlk

Water House Bank

41

Long Hill Wood

Waterhouses

Deerness Valley

IVESLEY COTTS

PH

HEDLEYHILL TERR

OLD WOLSINGHAM RD

River Deerness

PUTTON'S BANK

STATION ST
RUSSELL ST

Rabbit Hill

6

Standalone

Little Brier Wood

Crow Gill

Standalone Wood

Waterhouses Wood

Stanley Beck

40

West Wood

WATER HOUSE RD

BRANDON LA

West Brandon Farm

4

Wooley Hill

SANDY LONNEN

Baal Hill

WEST BRANDON RD

3

WOLSINGHAM RD

High Wooley

Weather Hill Wood

Caliph's Wood

39

Weather Hill House

2

Birks Wood

Stockley Beck

Stockley Gill

Stockley Gill Plantation

1

8

7

5

A B C D E F

8

Biggin
Farm

Park
Lodge

Redburn
Wood

River Deerness

Deerness
Valley

Eshwood
Hall

Esh
Wood

Red Burn

WOODBINE TERR
PROSPECT PL

BEWLEY TERR 1
BENVILLE TERR 2
HAWTHORN TERR 3

THE
BUNGALOWS

BRAUNESPATH
EST

FAIRFALLS
TERR

ROCK TERR
EDWARD TERR
PROSPECT TERR
CO-OPERATIVE TERR

WALTONS TERR

New
Brancepeth

TUSCAN CL

New Brancepeth
Cty Jun & Inf Sch

DODIC RD

ROWLEY CL

PRINGLE PL

7

Hill
House

41

PRINGLE
CL

PRINGLE
GR

Pringle
House

6

Long Hill
Wood

Stob
House

5

North
Wood

PIT LA

Cemy

BRANDON LA

40

Pithouse East
Plantation

4

East Brandon
Wood

Pithouse
Plantation

CHERRY PK 1
LABURNAM PK 2

3

Rabbit Hill
Plantation

Bowser's
Gill

Morley
Farm

MORLEY LA

MAPLE

BRANCEPETH TERR

SCRIPTON GILL RD

FOREST

Scripton
Gill

FOREST VIEW

ASHBROOK CL

39

Caliph's Gill

Littlewhite
Farm

BEECHCROFT AVE 3
CAMBERLEY DR 4

2

South
Brandon Farm

Brawn's
Den

WOLSINGHAM RD

Quarry
Hill

Quarryhill
Cottages

Brandon-Bishop Auckland Walk

A590

Tunstall Burn

1

Stockley Beck

Goodwell
Farm

Stockley Gill
Wood

P

GOODWELL LEA

THE OLD FORGE

THE GLEBE

1 WILLIAM RUSSELL HOMES
2 FOXES ROW

A590

DURHAM
RD

38

20 A B 21 C D 22 E F

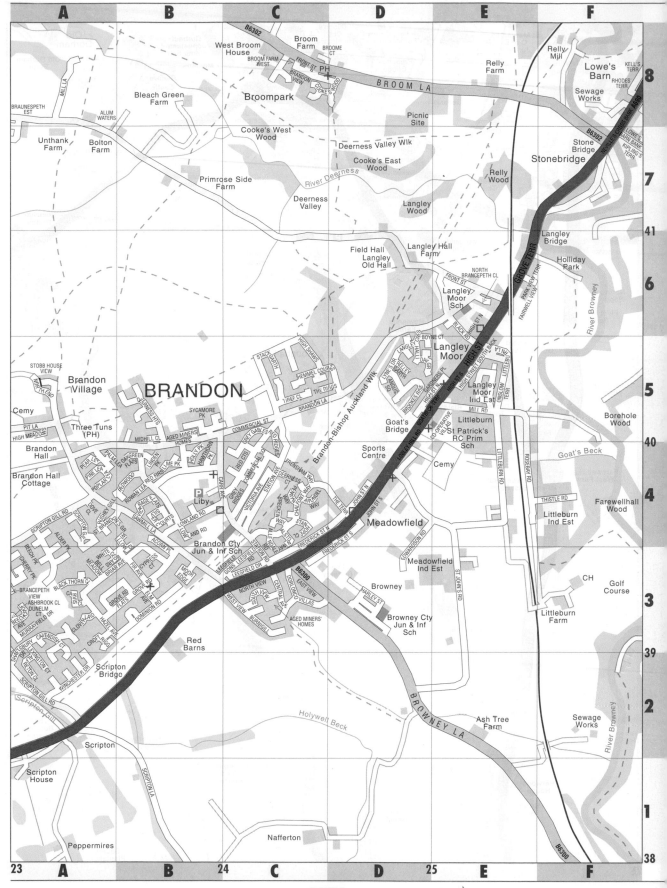

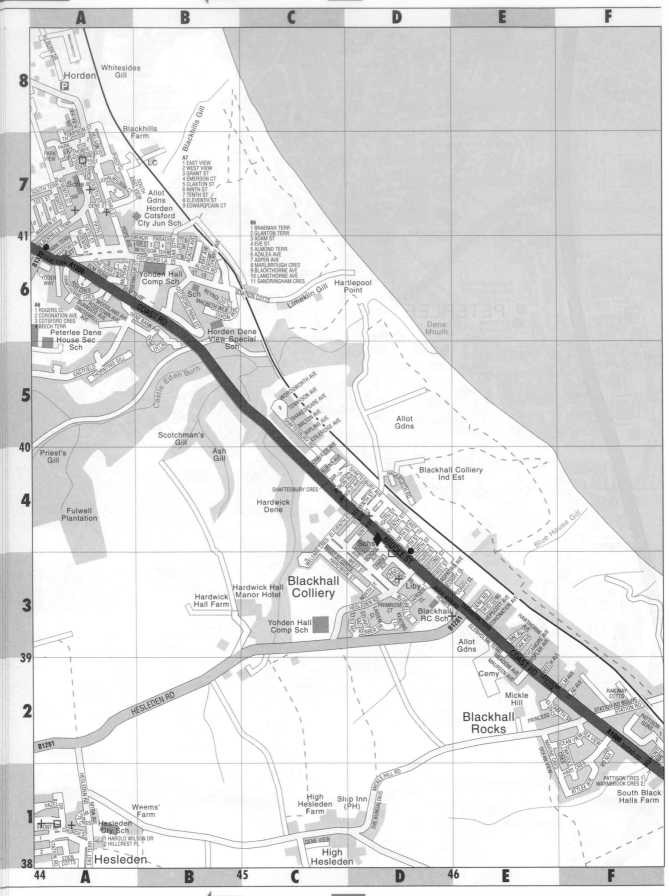

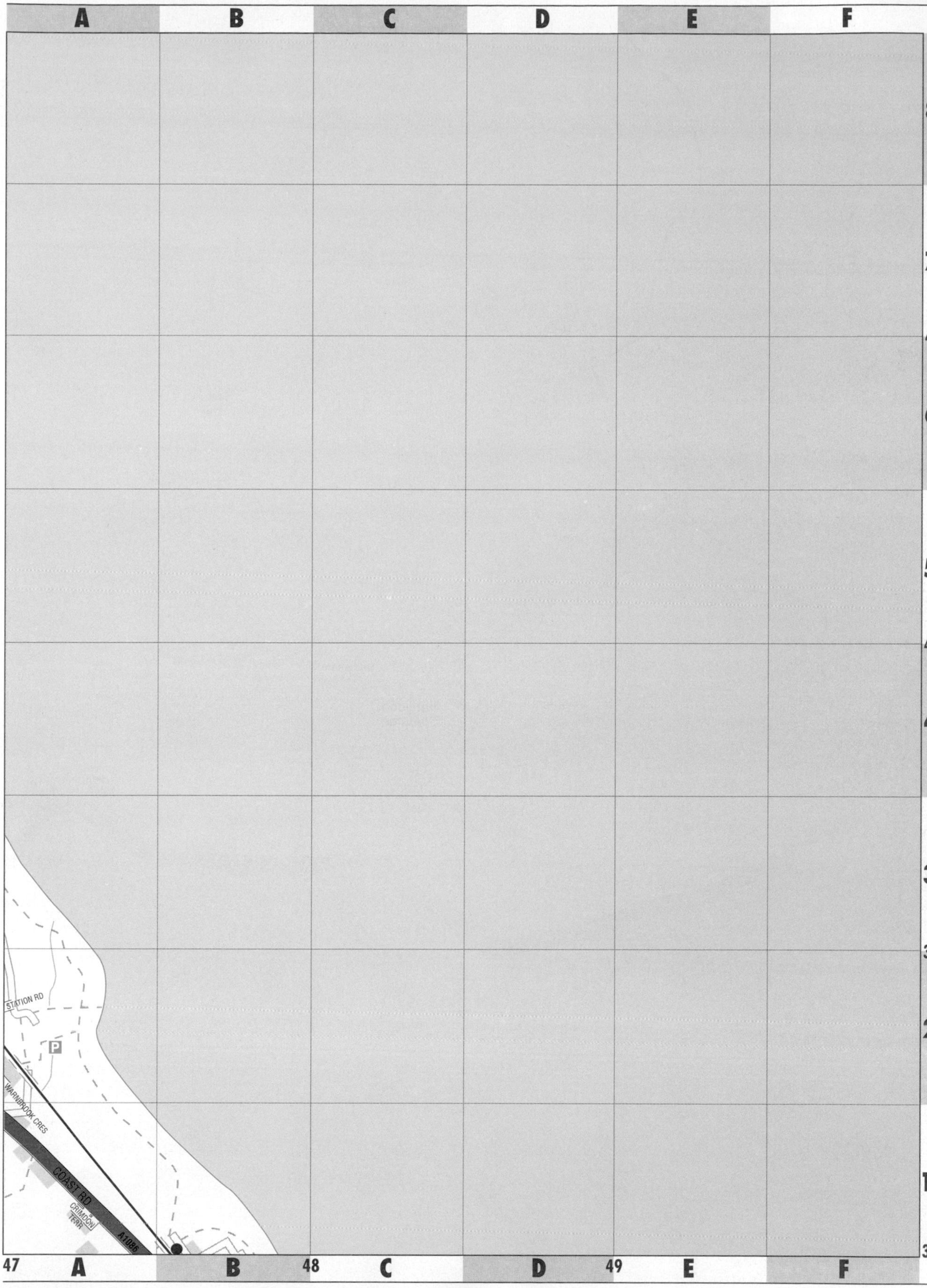

	A	B	C	D	E	F

8

7

41

6

5

40

4

3

39

2

1

38

STATION RD

P

WARNBROOK CRES

COAST RD

CRIMDON TERR

A1086

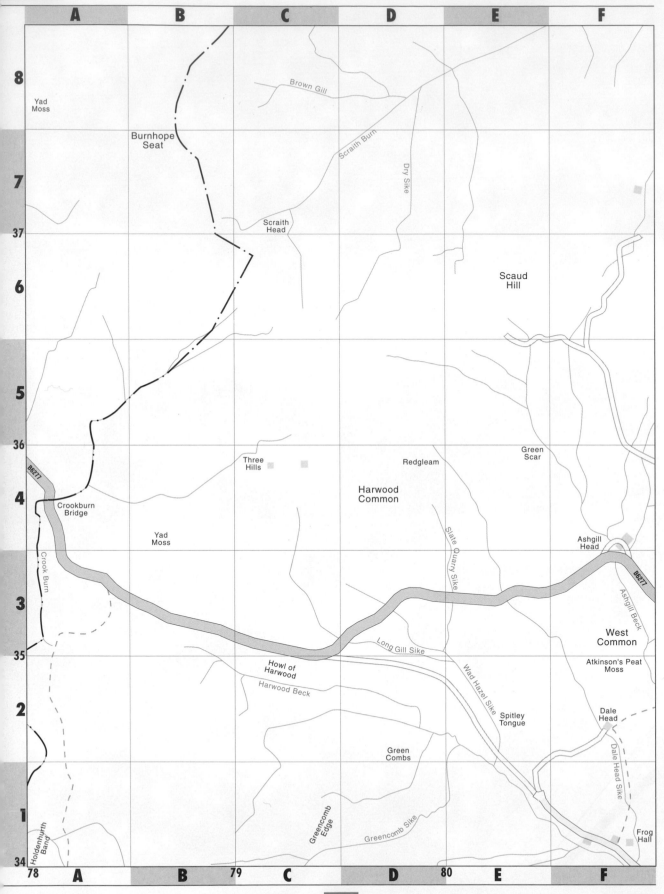

A B C D E F

8 Yad Moss
Brown Gill
Burnhope Seat
Scraith Burn
Dry Sike
7
37 Scraith Head
Scaud Hill
6
5
36 Green Scar
Three Hills
Redgleam
Harwood Common
4 Crookburn Bridge
Yad Moss
Slate Quarry Sike
Ashgill Head
Crook Burn
3 West Common
35 Long Gill Sike
Howl of Harwood
Atkinson's Peat Moss
Harwood Beck
Wad Hazel Sike
2 Spitley Tongue
Dale Head
Green Combs
Dale Head Sike
1 Greencomb Edge
Greencomb Sike
34 Holdenhurth Band
Frog Hall

78 A B 79 C D 80 E F

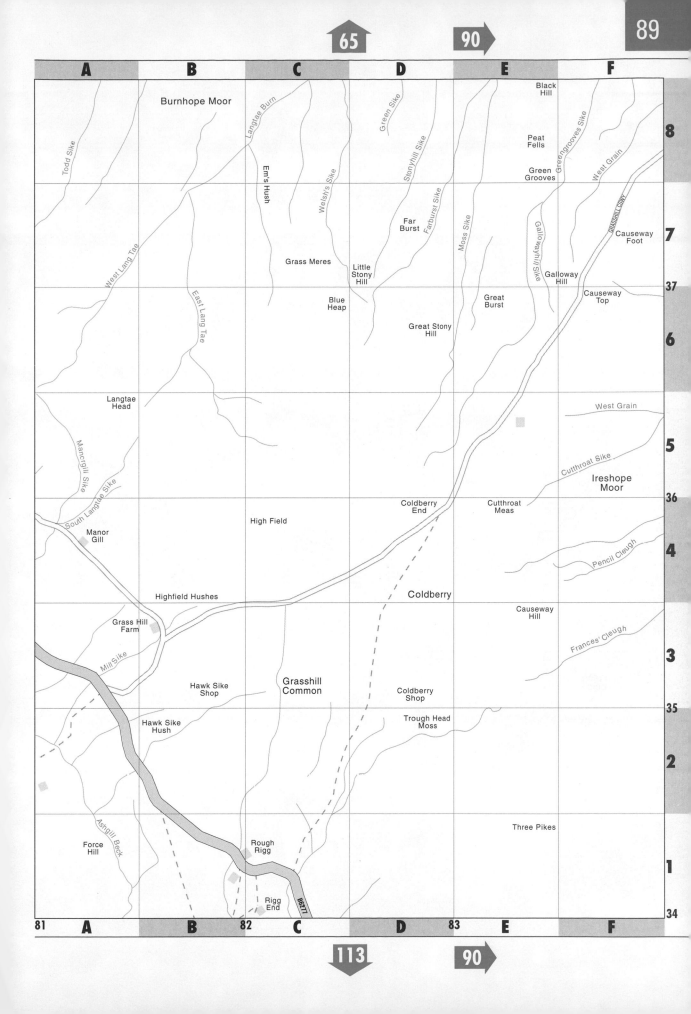

89
66

A **B** **C** **D** **E** **F**

Hawkwell
Head

8

GRASSHILL SWT

The
Hags

Greenwell
Crags

Reatcleugh Sike

Ireshope
Plains

Ires
Hope

Black
Rigg

7

Wham
Pasture

Rowantree
Plantation

Ireshope Burn

Groove Heads Sike

Gravel Edge

37

Broad Sike

The
Burst

6

West Grain

Clints
Crags

Ireshope
Moor

5

Grooves Cleugh

Deep Cleugh

Cormick's Currock
Rigg

Harthope
Moor

Jenny Meggy's Sike

Nein
Head

Peat
Rigg

36

Bulls
Head

Noon
Hill

Birk Sike

4

Long Sike

3

Langdon
Common

Harthope
Head

35

Langdon
Head

Langdon
Head
Shop

2

West Beck

Three
Comb

1

Langdon Beck

Westbeck
Hush

34

84 **A** **B** 85 **C** **D** 86 **E** **F**

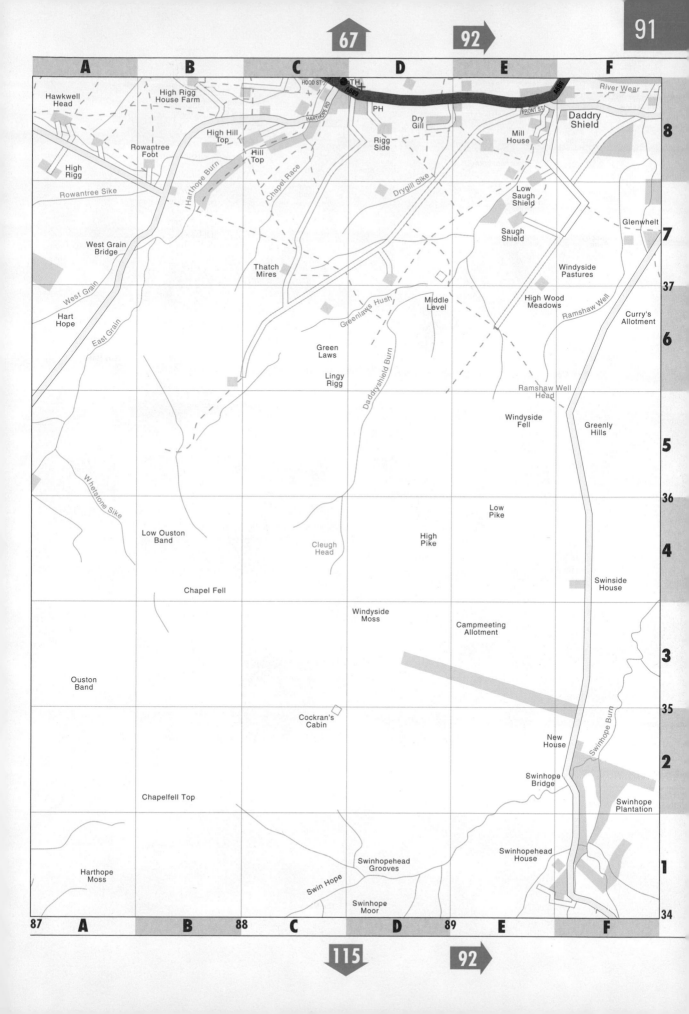

Hawkwell Head

High Rigg House Farm

High Hill Top

Hill Top

Rowantree Foot

High Rigg

Rowantree Sike

Harthope Burn

Chapel Race

HARTHOPE RD

HOOD ST

A689

TH

PH

Rigg Side

Dry Gill

Drygill Sike

Mill House

Daddry Shield

River Wear

FRONT ST

A689

Low Saugh Shield

Glenwhelt

Saugh Shield

Windyside Pastures

West Grain Bridge

Thatch Mires

High Wood Meadows

Curry's Allotment

Ramshaw Well

West Grain

Hart Hope

East Grain

Greenlaws Hush

Middle Level

Green Laws

Lingy Rigg

Daddryshield Burn

Ramshaw Well Head

Windyside Fell

Greenly Hills

Whetstone Sike

Low Ouston Band

Cleugh Head

High Pike

Low Pike

Swinside House

Chapel Fell

Windyside Moss

Campmeeting Allotment

Ouston Band

Swinhope Burn

Cockran's Cabin

New House

Chapelfell Top

Swinhope Bridge

Swinhope Plantation

Swinhopehead House

Harthope Moss

Swinhopehead Grooves

Swin Hope

Swinhope Moor

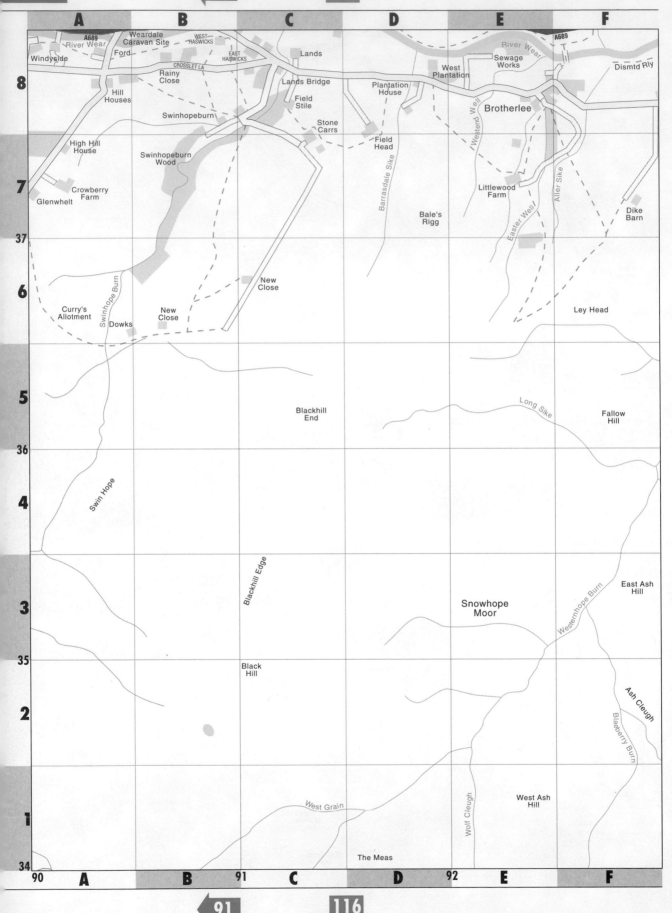

A B C D E F

Windyside
River Wear
A689
Ford
Weardale
Caravan Site
WEST
HASWICKS
EAST
HASWICKS
Lands
River Wear
A689
West
Plantation
Sewage
Works
Dismtd Rly

8

Hill
Houses
Rainy
Close
CROSSLET LA
Lands Bridge
Field
Stile
Plantation
House
Brotherlee

Swinhopeburn
Stone
Carrs
Field
Head
Westend Well

High Hill
House
Swinhopeburn
Wood
Barrasdale Sike
Littlewood
Farm
Aller Sike
Dike
Barn

7

Crowberry
Farm
Bale's
Rigg
Easter Well

Glenwhelt

37

Swinhope Burn
New
Close
Ley Head

6

Curry's
Allotment
Dowks
New
Close

5

Blackhill
End
Long Sike
Fallow
Hill

36

Swin Hope

4

Blackhill Edge
Westernhope Burn
East Ash
Hill

3

Snowhope
Moor

35

Black
Hill
Ash Cleugh

2

Blaeberry Burn

West Grain
Wolf Cleugh
West Ash
Hill

1

The Meas

34

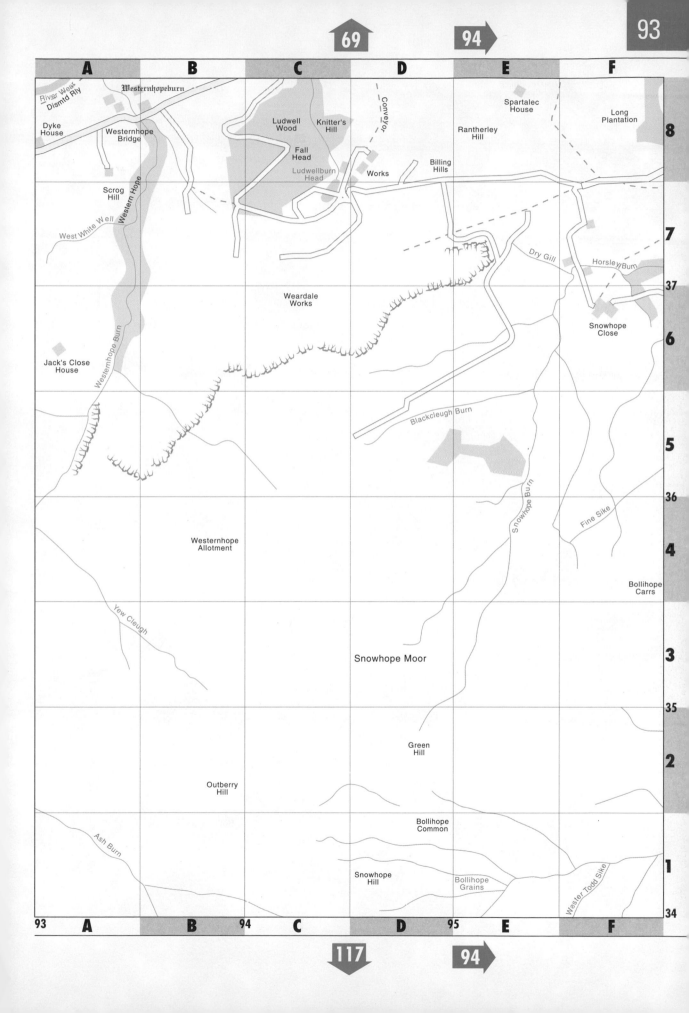

River Wear
Dismtd Rly
Westernhopeburn
Dyke House
Westernhope Bridge
Ludwell Wood
Knitter's Hill
Conveyor
Spartalec House
Rantherley Hill
Long Plantation
Scrog Hill
Fall Head
Ludwellburn Head
Works
Billing Hills
Western Hope
West White Well
Weardale Works
Dry Gill
Horsley Burn
Snowhope Close
Westernhope Burn
Jack's Close House
Blackcleugh Burn
Snowhope Burn
Fine Sike
Bollihope Carrs
Westernhope Allotment
Yew Cleugh
Snowhope Moor
Green Hill
Outberry Hill
Bollihope Common
Ash Burn
Snowhope Hill
Bollihope Grains
Wester Todd Sike

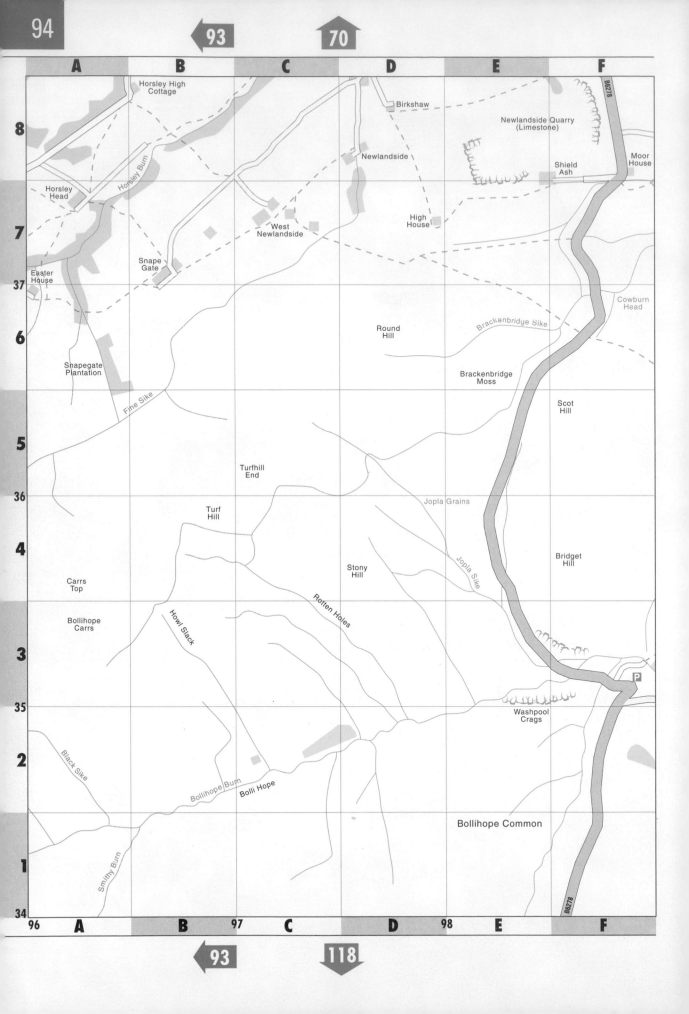

A **B** **C** **D** **E** **F**

8

Horsley High Cottage

Birkshaw

Newlandside Quarry (Limestone)

Moor House

Newlandside

Horsley Burn

Shield Ash

7

West Newlandside

High House

Horsley Head

Easter House

Snape Gate

37

Cowburn Head

Round Hill

Brackenbridge Sike

6

Snapegate Plantation

Brackenbridge Moss

Fine Sike

Scot Hill

5

Turfhill End

36

Turf Hill

Jopla Grains

4

Carrs Top

Stony Hill

Jopla Sike

Bridget Hill

Bollihope Carrs

Howl Slack

Rotten Holes

3

Washpool Crags

35

Black Sike

2

Bollihope Burn

Bolli Hope

Bollihope Common

1

Smithy Burn

B6278

34

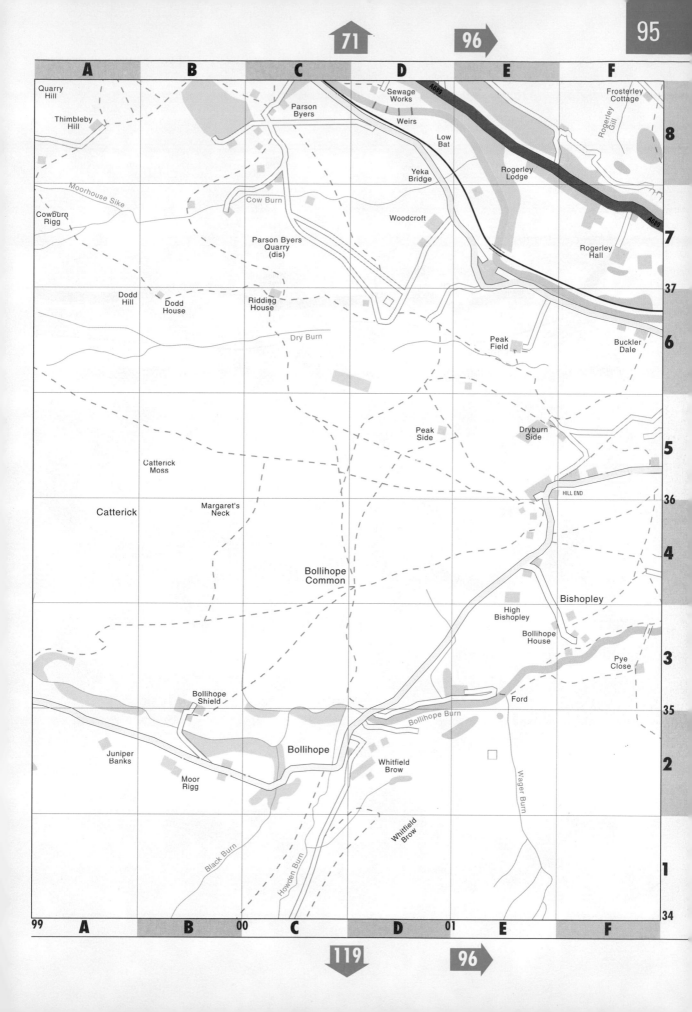

A B C D E F

Quarry Hill

Thimbleby Hill

Moorhouse Sike

Cowburn Rigg

Parson Byers

Cow Burn

Parson Byers Quarry (dis)

Dodd Hill

Dodd House

Ridding House

Dry Burn

Sewage Works

Weirs

Low Bat

Yeka Bridge

Woodcroft

Peak Field

Peak Side

Catterick Moss

Catterick

Margaret's Neck

Bollihope Common

Bollihope Shield

Juniper Banks

Moor Rigg

Bollihope

Whitfield Brow

Black Burn

Howden Burn

Whitfield Brow

Bollihope Burn

Ford

Wager Burn

High Bishopley

Bollihope House

Pye Close

Bishopley

HILL END

Dryburn Side

Buckler Dale

Frosterley Cottage

Rogerley Gill

Rogerley Lodge

Rogerley Hall

A689

8
7
37
6
5
36
4
3
35
2
1
34

95
72

A B C D E F

8

7

Wiserley
Hill

High
Barn

Willow Green Burn

Newlands
Hall

A689

WESTFIELD

Willow Green Gill

West
Newlands

37

KIRK
RISE

STOCKLEY
CRES

STOCKLEY GR

PH

Willow
Green

A689

Frosterley
Bridge

FRONT ST

CROMER LEA

Green Bank

P

MELLBUT
BANK

HOLMEFIELD

WEAR VIEW

CROFT
TERR

GLEBE VIEW

WESTERN
HILL

THE
BATTS

LC

Sewage
Works

6

Frosterley

River Wear

Broadwood

Landieu

The Ellands
Caravan Pk

LC

Bridge End

Frosterley
South Cty
Sch

East
Bridge End

Works

BELLE
VUE

5

Miln House
Farm

Wise Eel
Bridge

West
Biggins

East
Biggins

36

Low Bishopley

Bollihope Burn

WHITE
KIRKLEY

North
Rigg

4

Harehope Burn

Harehope Gill

East Biggins
Cottage

Harehope

Harvey
Hill

3

Fine
House

35

Fine Gill

Folly
Plantation

2

Fine Burn

Weardale Way

Allotment
Plantations

1

Allotment
House

34

02 A B 03 C D 04 E F

95
120

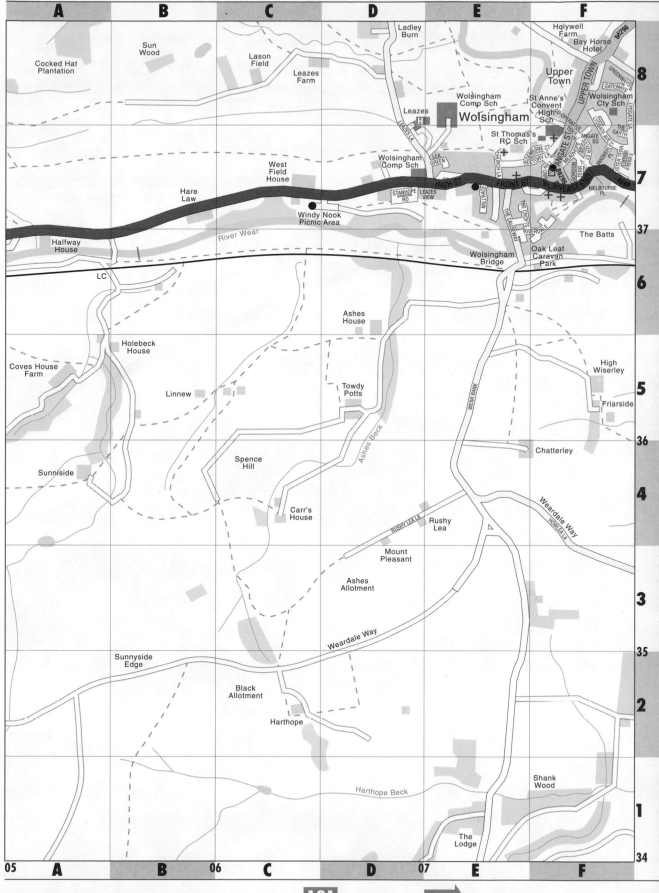

Cocked Hat Plantation

Sun Wood

Lason Field

Leazes Farm

Ladley Burn

Holywell Farm

Bay Horse Hotel

Upper Town

Wolsingham Comp Sch

Leazes

St Anne's Convent High Sch

Wolsingham Cty Sch

Wolsingham

St Thomas's RC Sch

West Field House

Hare Law

Wolsingham Comp Sch

Lea Green

HIGH ST

LEAZES LA

STANHOPE RD

LEAZES VIEW

Windy Nook Picnic Area

FRONT ST

THE CROFTS

MILLRACE

THE CAUSEWAY

RIVERDALE

The Batts

Halfway House

River Wear

Wolsingham Bridge

Oak Leaf Caravan Park

LC

Holebeck House

Ashes House

Coves House Farm

Linnew

High Wiserley

Friarside

Spence Hill

Towdy Potts

Ashes Beck

WEAR BANK

Chatterley

Sunniside

Carr's House

RUSHY LEA LA

Rushy Lea

Weardale Way

HOWLEA LA

Mount Pleasant

Ashes Allotment

Weardale Way

Sunnyside Edge

Black Allotment

Harthope

Harthope Beck

Shank Wood

The Lodge

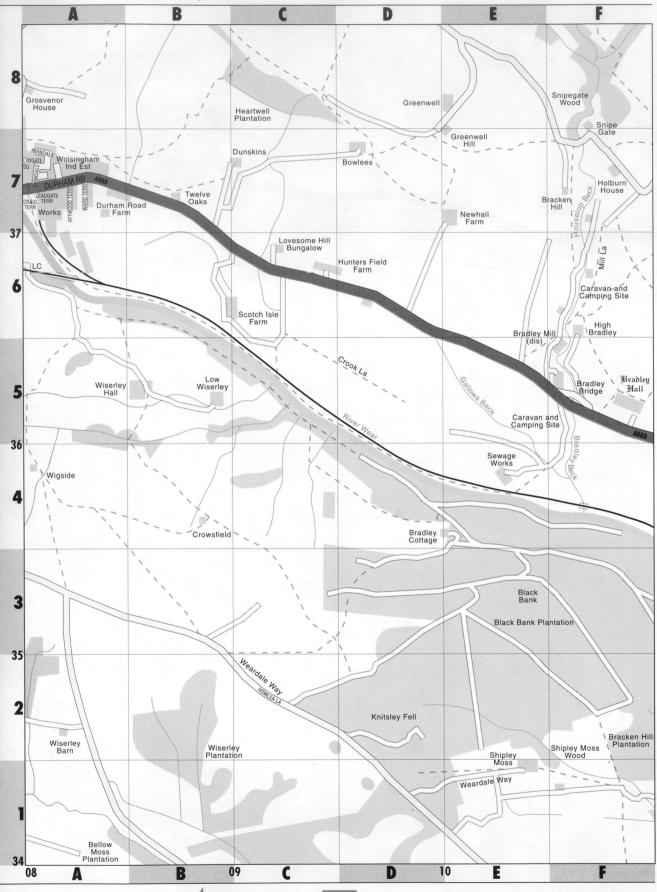

A   B   C   D   E   F

8

Grosvenor House

Heartwell Plantation

Greenwell

Snipegate Wood

Snipe Gate

Dunskins

Bowlees

Greenwell Hill

FERNDALE
LYDGATE SQ
LYNDALE
Wolsingham Ind Est

7   DURHAM RD   A689

Twelve Oaks

Newhall Farm

Bracken Hill

Holburn House

CRAIG TERR
LEADGATE TERR
ATTWOOD TERR
WARD TERR

Durham Road Farm

Works

37

LC

Lovesome Hill Bungalow

Hunters Field Farm

Bradley Mill (dis)

Caravan and Camping Site

High Bradley

6

Scotch Isle Farm

Crook La

Gallows Beck

Bradley Hall

5

Wiserley Hall

Low Wiserley

River Wear

Caravan and Camping Site

Bradley Bridge

A689

36

Wigside

Sewage Works

Bradley Beck

Houselop Beck

Mill La

4

Crowsfield

Bradley Cottage

Black Bank

Black Bank Plantation

35

Weardale Way

HOWLEA LA

Knitsley Fell

2

Wiserley Barn

Wiserley Plantation

Shipley Moss Wood

Bracken Hill Plantation

Shipley Moss

Weardale Way

1

34   Bellow Moss Plantation

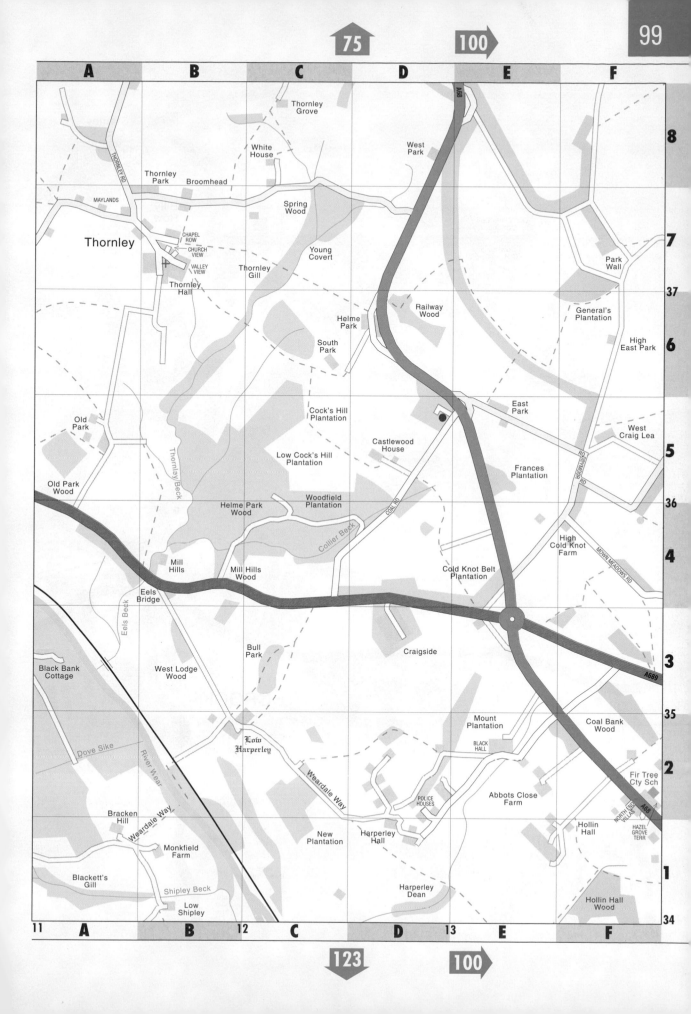

99
76

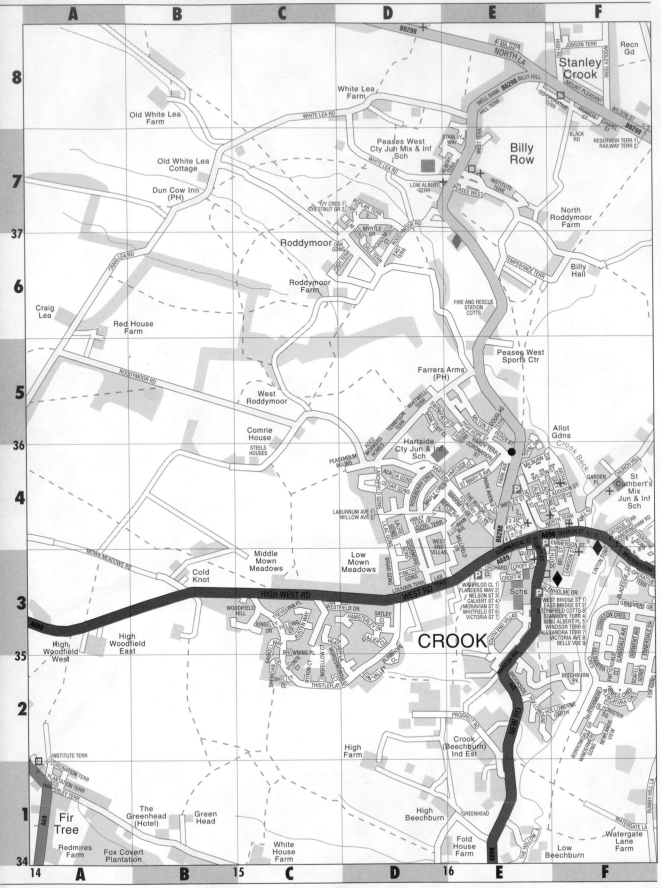

A map of Crook, showing areas including Stanley Crook, Billy Row, Roddymoor, Fir Tree, High Beechburn, and Low Beechburn.

Key place names and labels visible on the map:

Grid references: A, B, C, D, E, F (columns); 1, 34, 35, 2, 3, 36, 4, 37, 5, 6, 7, 8 (rows); 14, 15, 16 (bottom)

Old White Lea Farm, Old White Lea Cottage, Dun Cow Inn (PH), White Lea Farm, White Lea Rd, B6299, North La, Stanley Crook, Recn Gd, Jobson Terr, Wooley Terr, Wilson St, High Rd, Alma Terr, Mount Pleasant, Well Bank, Hill Terr, West Terr, B6298 Billy Hill, Co-Operative Terr, Francis St, Chapel St, Black Rd, Reservoir Terr 1, Railway Terr 2, Peases West Cty Jun Mix & Inf Sch, Stanley Way, Albert Terr, Low Albert Terr, Peases West, Institute Terr, Billy Row, North Roddymoor Farm, Temperance Terr, Billy Hall, Ivy Cres 1, Chestnut Gr 2, Poplar Terr, Myrtle Gr, Elm Gdns, Oak Gdns, High Terr, Dale Terr, Roddymoor Rd, East Terr, Roddymoor, Roddymoor Farm, Fire and Rescue Station Cotts, Prebs Lea Rd, Craig Lea, Red House Farm, Roddymoor Rd, West Roddymoor, Comrie House, Peases West Sports Ctr, Crook Beck, Allot Gdns, Farrers Arms (PH), Steels Houses, Peaseholm Bglws, Abled Workers Homes, Whitwell Terr, Swingfield Terr, Park Foot Ct, Tennyson Terr, High Hope St, Milton St, Douglas St, Percy St, Royal Gr, Milburn St, Church Hill, St Cuthbert's Mix Jun & Inf Sch, Hartside Cty Jun & Inf Sch, Hartside Ct, Hardy Terr, Coronation St, Wilson St, Gladstone St, Arthur St, Garden Pl, Acacia Gdns, Cedar Gdns, Larchfield Gdns, Roseberry Cres, Maple Cres, St Mary's Ave, Park Ave, Park Avenue Cl, Foundry Fields, Wesley St, Addison St, Albert St, North Terr, George Terr, Sandringham Rd, Osborne St, Laburnum Ave 1, Willow Ave 2, Holly Terr, Hazel Terr, Groom Ct, Beech La, Lishman St, Millfield, West End Villas, B6298, Kellett St, Commercial St, Church St, Mown Meadows Rd, Middle Mown Meadows, Cold Knot, Low Mown Meadows, Laurel Gdns, Lilac Gdns, Sycamore Gdns, Pinetree Gdns, Briar Gdns, Louvain Terr, West Rd, Lax Terr, A690, Orchard Cl, Queen St, South St, Dawson St, Emmerson Rd, Lintom Terr, Co-Operative Terr, West Street Bottom, Woodifield Hill, Trevelyan Pl, Westfield Dr, Hamsterley Dr, Satley Cl, Croft St, Croft Cl, Waterloo Cl 1, Flanders Way 2, Nelson St 3, Calvert St 4, Moravian St 5, Whitfield St 6, Victoria St 7, Schs, Glenholme Dr, West Bridge St 1, East Bridge St 2, Greenfield Cotts 3, Stanhope Terr 4, King Albert Pl 5, Windsor Terr 6, Alexandra Terr 7, Victoria Ave 8, Belle Vue 9, Grasmere Gr, Bladeside, Coniston Cres, Derwent Ave, Ennerdale Dr, High Woodfield West, High Woodfield East, Kingsley Dr, Fielding Way, Austen Way, Collier Gr, Heatherlea, Windsor Terr, Browning Pl, Longfellow Ct, Fern Valley, Bunhope Cl, South End Villas, Jobson Ave, Broomside, Hollowdene, Beechburn Pk, Patterdale Cl, Scafell Gdns, Langdale Ave, Lowther Cres, Holmes Cres, Homister Sq, Newlands View, Borrowdale Gr, Buttermere Gdns, Wastwater Ave, Blencathra Cres, Esk Gdns, Windermere Gdns, Newlands Gdns, Gaskell Way, Sheridan Cl, Shelley Cl, Byron Ct, Thistleflat Rd, Prospect Rd, CROOK, High Farm, Crook (Beechburn) Ind Est, New Rd, High Beechburn, Greenhead, Institute Terr, Coronation Terr, Plantation Terr, Harperley Terr, A68, Fir Tree, Redmires Farm, Fox Covert Plantation, The Greenhead (Hotel), Green Head, White House Farm, High Beechburn, Greenhead, The Hollow, Fold House Farm, Low Beechburn, Watergate La, Rumby La, Watergate Lane Farm, A689

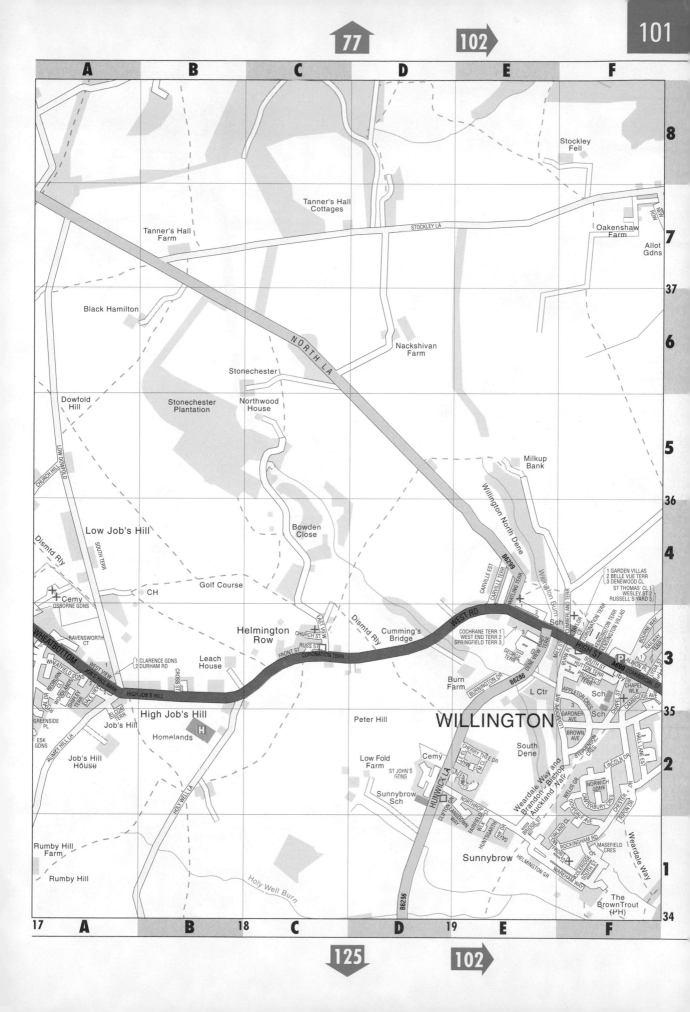

A B C D E F

8
7
37
6
5
36
4
3
35
2
1
34

Stockley Fell

Tanner's Hall Cottages

STOCKLEY LA

Oakenshaw Farm

NEW ROW

Allot Gdns

Tanner's Hall Farm

Black Hamilton

NORTH LA

Nackshivan Farm

Dowfold Hill

Stonechester

Northwood House

Stonechester Plantation

Milkup Bank

CHURCH HILL

LOW DOWFOLD

Low Job's Hill

SOUTH TERR

Bowden Close

Willington North Dene

Willington Burn

B6299

Dismtd Rly

CH

Golf Course

CARVILLE TERR
CARVILLE EST

WATLING TERR

1 GARDEN VILLAS
2 BELLE VUE TERR
3 DENEWOOD CL
ST THOMAS' CL 1
WESLEY ST 2
RUSSELL'S YARD 3

Cemy
OSBORNE GDNS

Helmington Row

EAST VIEW

CHURCH ST

RUSS ST

FRONT ST

CORONATION TERR

Dismtd Rly

Cumming's Bridge

WEST RD

COCHRANE TERR 1
WEST END TERR 2
SPRINGFIELD TERR 3

Willington Terr

DENE VIEW TERR

HIGH ST

KENSINGTON TERR
KENSINGTON VILLAS

CORONATION TERR

UMBERLAND TERR

BOURNE WAY

Railway

Sch

RAVENSWORTH CT

WEST VIEW

JOB'S HILL BANK

WHEATBOTTOM

WHEATFIELD GDNS

1 CLARENCE GDNS
2 DURHAM RD

Leach House

GEORGE TERR

Burn Farm

BURNINGTON DR

B6286

L Ctr

ALBION PL

A690

P
Lbry

COMMERCIAL ST

MILL LANE

HUTTON TERR

PROSPECT TERR

APPLETON CRES

Chapel WLK

Sch

CAMBRIDGE AVE

HALL LANE EST

High Job's Hill

H

Homelands

Peter Hill

WILLINGTON

South Dene

GARDNER AVE

BROWN AVE

STEPHENSON CRES

NORWICH GDNS

LINCOLN DR

CHESTER DR

RIPON DR

DOVEDALE AVE

GREENSIDE PL

ESK GDNS

Job's Hill House

CROSS ST

HOLY WELL LA

ELCOAT TERR

Low Fold Farm

Cemy

ST JOHN'S GDNS

HUNWICK LA

Sunnybrow Sch

CHERRY TREE DR

ELM CL

GREEN VS

NORTHROP CL

CLIFTON GDN

LANSDOWN WAY

FAIRFIELD WLK

HUNTS GARTH

BRIDGES ST

Weardale Way and Brandon - Bishop Auckland Way

WELLS GR

CANTERBURY CRES

ORLAND CL

ROCKINGHAM RD

PROM

SOUTHS ST

WOLSINGHAM WAY

ORCHARD CT

WAREHAM WAY

HELMINGTON GR

MASEFIELD CRES

Weardale Way

Rumby Hill Farm

Rumby Hill

Holy Well Burn

Sunnybrow

B6286

The Brown Trout (PH)

17 A B 18 C D 19 E F 34

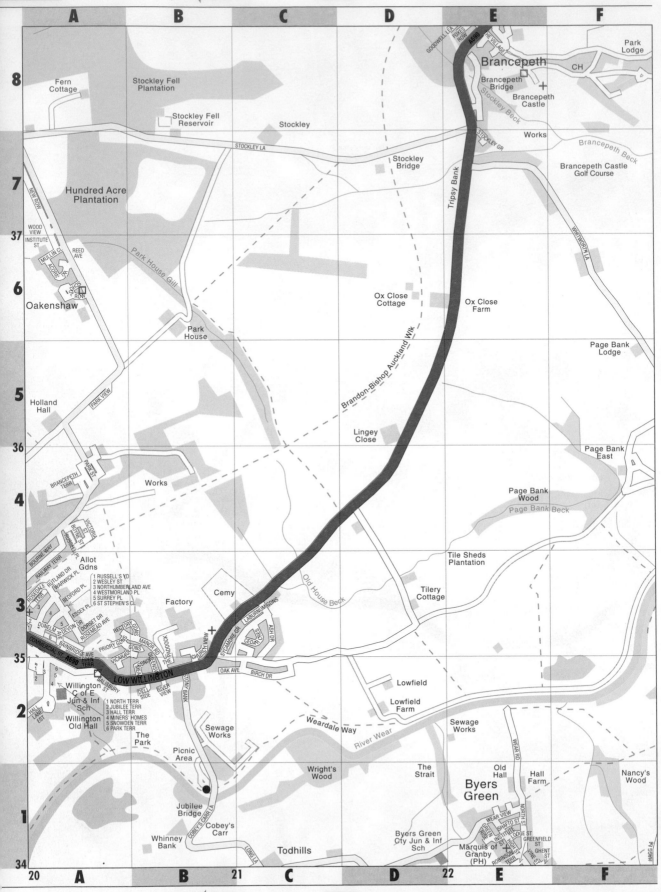

A   B   C   D   E   F

BROWNEY LA
B6300

Nafferton Gill
High Burnigill
Burnigill

8

Tudhoe Lodge

Holywell Beck
Holywell

SCRIPTON LA

Holywell Hall

7

NICK NACK Beck

37

East Park

East Park Cottage

Weardale Way

Coldstream Farm

6

River Wear

Brancepeth Beck

Spring Wood

5

Black House

36

Tudhoe Village

WHITWORTH LA

Page Bank

NEW ROW

THE GREEN

CHAIR LA

MILL LA

4

Park Hill Lodge

Stanner's Farm

Page Bank Bridge

Charhill Wood

Dark Gill Wood

Woodhouse Farm

Sewage Works

Valley Burn

Hall Farm

Lower Burtons

Trotter Wood

EBBERSTON CT
NEWBURGH CT
EASBY CT
CARTMEL CL
GLASTONBURY CL
CANTERBURY CT
GERVAULX CT
RIEVAULX CT
ELLESMERE 2
DUNELM CT
WINCHESTER CT
WANSBECK CL
TROUTBECK CL

3

35

STANNER'S LA

Brick Kiln Wood

Church Wood

Whitworth Park

Whitworth Hall

Middle Burtons

MOSSMERE
BUTTERMERE
KENTMERE
WINDERMERE
ROSSMERE
KELDMERE
TANMERE
KINMORE
COLDMERE
GLENMORE
GRASMERE
BIRCHMERE
CARR LA
PARKDALE
FARNDALE
BARNSDALE

SCARGILL DR
MIDDLEHAM DR

Cow Plantation

Tudhoe Grange

WOOD VUE

2

HARE LA

WHITWORTH RD

Burton Beck

Burton Beck Farm

ROSEDALE
WESTERDALE
PARKSIDE
GLASSIDE
CARR ST
WESTFIELDS

Ox Close Cty Jun & Inf Sch

OX CLOSE CRES

TYNE CRES
TEES CRES
VINE RD
DURHAM RD
WOOD VUE
DENESIDE

1

New Town

Upper Burtons

North Park Lodge Farm

Oxford Rd

VILLAGE ST
TA Ctr
13

King St Cty Jun & Inf Sch
10 11

HIGH GRANGE
KING WILLIAM ST
HOLBURN

34

F1
1 BURN TERR
2 BROOK ST
3 THOMPSON ST
4 O HANLAN ST
5 ARMOURY ST
6 KING WILLIAM ST
7 KING JAMES ST
8 CHEAPSIDE
9 ST ANDREW'S LA
10 KING WILLIAM CT
11 KING WILLIAM GRANGE
12 JACKSON ST
13 PARK PAR

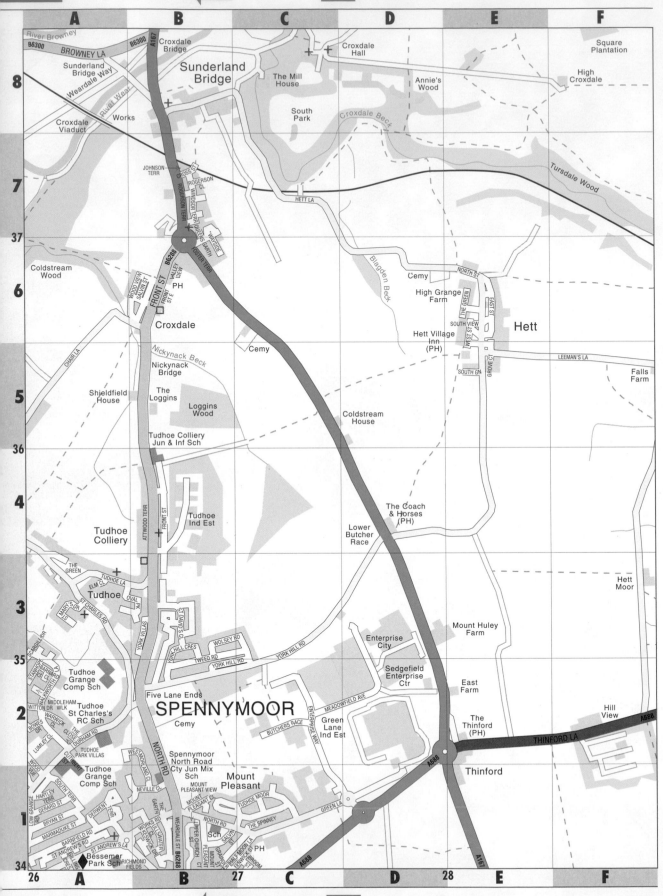

A   B   C   D   E   F

B6300   BROWNEY LA
River Browney
Sunderland Bridge Way
Weardale Way
Croxdale Viaduct
Works
River Wear
B6300   A167
Croxdale Bridge
Sunderland Bridge
The Mill House
South Park
Croxdale Hall
Annie's Wood
Croxdale Beck
Square Plantation
High Croxdale
Tursdale Wood

8
7
37
6
5
36
4
3
35
2
1
34

JOHNSON TERR
CROSS ST
ROGERSON CL
WINDSOR TERR
QUEEN'S GARTH
ROGERSON TERR
FOSTER TERR
HETT LA
Blagden Beck
Cemy
North St
High Grange Farm
The Green
South View
Hett Village Inn (PH)
South Gn
Hett
Leeman's La
Falls Farm
East St
West St
Grove Ct

B6288
FRONT ST
WOOD VIEW
SALVIN ST
FRONT ST E
MILL HALEY
PH
Croxdale
Coldstream Wood
CHAR LA
Nickynack Beck
Nickynack Bridge
Shieldfield House
The Loggins
Loggins Wood
Tudhoe Colliery Jun & Inf Sch
Cemy
Coldstream House

ATTWOOD TERR
FRONT ST
Tudhoe Colliery
Tudhoe Ind Est
The Coach & Horses (PH)
Lower Butcher Race

THE GREEN
TUDHOE LA
ELM CL
OVAL
YORK VILLAS
Tudhoe
ST CHARLES RD
ST DAVID'S CL
YORK HILL CRES
WOLSEY RD
TWEED RD
YORK HILL RD
YORK HILL RD
Hett Moor
Mount Huley Farm

MARY'S CR
SCARGILL DR
STANHOPE
BARNARD
WALKWORTH CL
Tudhoe Grange Comp Sch
Five Lane Ends
SPENNYMOOR
Cemy
Enterprise City
Sedgefield Enterprise Ctr
East Farm
Hill View
A688

MIDDLEHAM WLK
WITTON DR
WARWICK CL
DURHAM ST
The CLOSE
Tudhoe St Charles's RC Sch
BUTCHERS RACE
MEADOWFIELD AVE
Green Lane Ind Est
ENTERPRISE WAY
Mount Pleasant
The Thinford (PH)
Thinford
THINFORD LA

LUMLEY CL
BOWES GR
WESTMORLAND CL
Tudhoe Park Villas
Tudhoe Grange Comp Sch
NEVILLE CL
NORTH RD
Spennymoor North Road Cty Jun Mix Sch
MOUNT PLEASANT VIEW
MOUNT PLEASANT CL
TUDHOE MOOR
THE SPINNEY
NORTH RD
GREEN LA
A688
A688
A167

LOW GRANGE VIEW
HARTLEY TERR
GERARD ST
BRYAN ST
MARMADUKE ST
BARNFIELD RD
St ANDREW'S RD
St ANDREW'S LA
Bessemer Park Sch
RICHMOND FIELDS
WORKS RD
THE GARTH
WEARDALE ST
B6288
GRANGE
UPPER CHURCH ST
FINAL MOOR LA
KESWICK DR
BROOM
SALVIN ST
PH
Sch

26   A   B   27   C   D   28   E   F

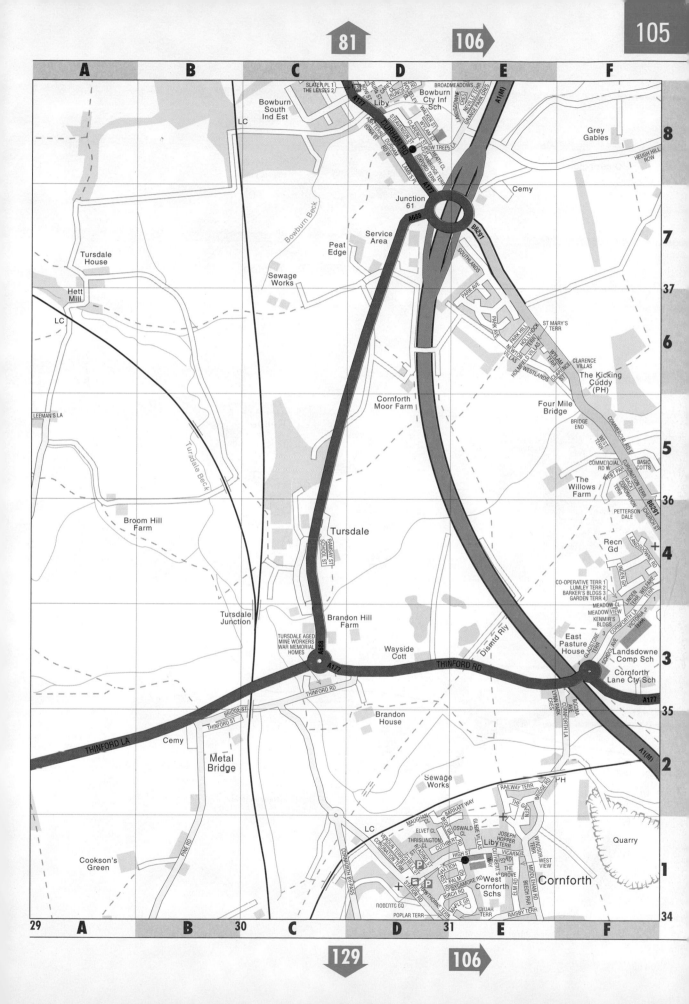

A B C D E F

8

7

37

6

5

36

4

3

35

2

1

34

32 A B 33 C D 34 E F

Old Quarrington
Quarrington Farm
HEUGH HALL ROW
Quarrington Quarry
Quarrington Quarry

Quarry Plantation

Quarry Plantation

Mast
Beacon Hill
Cassop Hill
Cassop
Cty Jun & Inf Sch
B6291
FRONT ST
BELLE AVE
CHURCH ST
Quarrington Hill
Ind Est
AGED MINERS'
HOMES
FRONT ST S
The Half Moon
(PH)
St Helen's
Cres
STEETLEY TERR.
NELL CRES
CAROLE
DUNES
HAZEL
AVE
MALCOLM
AVE
DAVID TERR
HAWTHORN
CRES
Quarrington
Hill

ANN AVE
MARY CRES
SCHOOL AVE
MORLEY CRES
Cemy
Church Kelloe
Kelloe Beck
Kelloe Cty Sch
Jun Mix & Inf
Kelloe
FRONT ST
EAST HETTON AGED
WORKMEN'S HOMES
BURNETT CRES

Coxhoe Bank
Plantation
Joint Stocks
Quarry
PARKWAY
AVE
TATE AVE
WOODLAND
AVE
WOODLAND CRES
WOODLAND CRES
SHARON AVE
FRONT ST

BEECHFIELD RISE
BROWNING WAY
PICTERSON DALE
BROWNLESS TE
CHURCH FRONT ST E
B6291
CORNFORTH LA
APPLEGARTH
HEDLEIGH CT
PELHAM
CT
THE CEDARS
THE FEDARS
OAKWOOD
MULBERRY
THE TERR
PADDOCK
FISHBURN WAY
THE GRANGE
GRANGE CRES
GREEN CRES
THE GROVE
STATION RD
BELGRAVE AVE
BELGRAVE CT
FRONT ST
The Avenue
Avenue Farm
A4
1 CHURCH ST
2 LANDSDOWNE RD
3 SANDERSON ST
4 COOPERATIVE TERR
5 BLACKGATE W
6 BLACKGATE E
Coxhoe
Coxhoe Wood
East House
Farm
Farm
Cottages
Sewage
Works
Dismtd Rly
Bradyll
Street

Raisby
Quarries

Coxhoe Pottery
Black Horse (PH)
A177
STATION RD
Coxhoe Bridge
Coxhoe Beck
Coxhoe Beck
Dismtd Rly

West House
Farm
Garmondsway

A1(M)
A177
Simonside
Garmondsway
Middle Farm
Garmondsway
East Farm

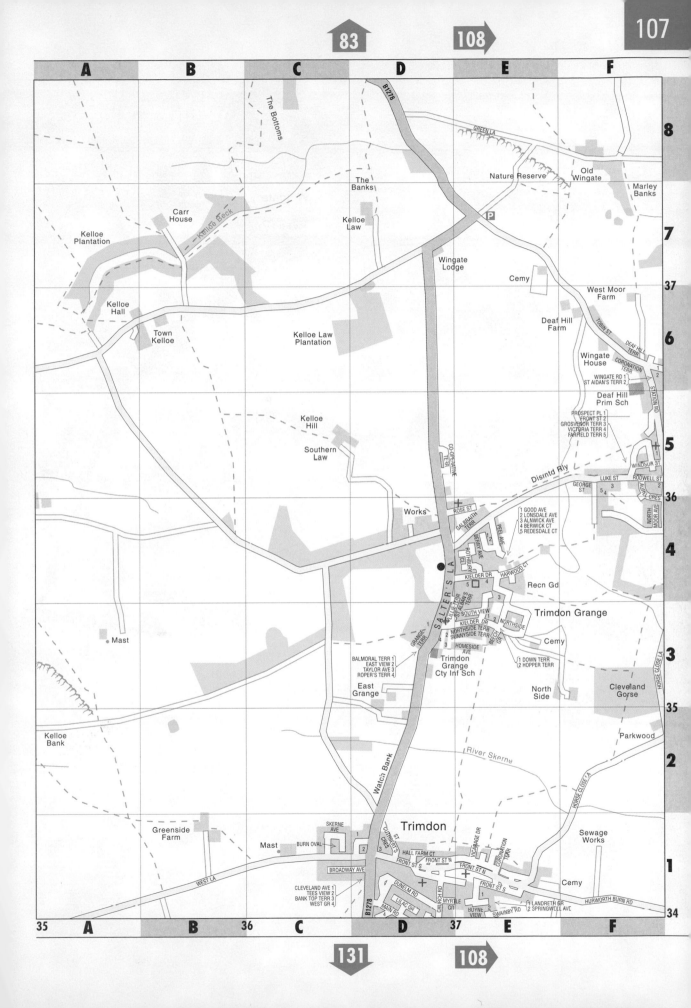

A B C D E F

8

Nature Reserve

The Bottoms

Old Wingate

Marley Banks

The Banks

Kelloe Law

Carr House

Kelloe Plantation

7

37

Wingate Lodge

Cemy

West Moor Farm

Kelloe Hall

Deaf Hill Farm

6

Town Kelloe

Kelloe Law Plantation

Wingate House

WINGATE RD 1
ST AIDAN'S TERR 2

Deaf Hill Prim Sch

PROSPECT PL 1
FRONT ST 2
GROSVENOR TERR 3
VICTORIA TERR 4
FARFIELD TERR 5

Kelloe Hill

5

WINDSUR 3

Southern Law

Disntd Rly

LUKE ST

RODWELL ST

GEORGE ST

AUREL CRES

36

NORTH MOOR AVE

Works

ROSE ST

1 GOOD AVE
2 LONSDALE AVE
3 ALNWICK AVE
4 BERWICK CT
5 REDESDALE CT

4

GALBRAITH TERR

PEEL AVE

BERRY AVE

ROTHBURY

HARWOOD CT

KIELDER DR

Recn Gd

ST ALBAN'S TERR

SOUTH VIEW

Trimdon Grange

KIELDER DR

NORTHSIDE

Cemy

NORTHSIDE TERR
SUNNYSIDE TERR

BECK GR

GRANGE TERR

HOMESIDE AVE

1 DOWN TERR
2 HOPPER TERR

3

BALMORAL TERR 1
EAST VIEW 2
TAYLOR AVE 3
ROPER'S TERR 4

Trimdon Grange Cty Inf Sch

North Side

Cleveland Gorse

East Grange

HORSE CLOSE LA

35

Mast

Kelloe Bank

Parkwood

River Skerne

2

Watch Bank

HORSE CLOSE LA

Greenside Farm

SKERNE AVE

Trimdon

Sewage Works

Mast

BURN OVAL

ST CUTHBERT'S CRES

VICARAGE DR

CORONATION TERR

Cemy

BROADWAY AVE

WEST LA

HALL FARM CT

FRONT ST N

FRONT ST N

FRONT ST S

HURWORTH BURN RD

CLEVELAND AVE 1
TEES VIEW 2
BANK TOP TERR 3
WEST GR 4

DUNELM RD

CHURCH RD

MYRTLE GRN

FRONT ST S

1 LANDRETH GR
2 SPRINGWELL AVE

B1278

MAIN RD

LILAC GH

HUYNE VIEW

SWAINBY RD

1

34

A B C D E F

8

Wingate Grange Farm

Pickering Hill

CUMMINGS SQ 1
FORSTER SQ 2
WILLIAMSON SQ 3

SNAITH TERR
NATTRESS TERR

VICARAGE EST

1 HOWDEN GDNS
2 ARMSTRONG AVE

CARADOC RD

KING'S RD
CORONATION RD
DUN CRES
PARTRIDGE TERR
NEW CROSS ROW
QUEEN'S RD
FOREST GATE
WOODLAND VIEW
BRUCE CRES
SALTER'S LA
NORTH ROW
NORTH RD
DAWSON RD
GRAY SQ
GULLY RD

B1280

Wingate

Wellfield Comp Sch

Wingate Cty Jun Sch

MOOR LA

Beech House

7

Wingate Grange Ind Est

Cemy

Wingate Cty Inf Sch

37

Low Grange Farm

FRONT ST

Tilery Farm

6

Wingate Grange

PICKERING'S
CHAPEL ST
JOHNSTON ST
MARKET CRES
ROWLANDS TERR
LAKE VIEW
LAKE BANK TERR
STATION RD
CHURCH ST
STATION LA
FRONT ST

TOWNEND CT

Wingate RC Sch

St Aidan's Terr

Deaf Hill

BEECH GR
WATSON CRES
WOOD VIEW
ASH GR
MAY CRES
RUSSELL CRES
SYCAMORE CRES
LILAC CRES
WINGATE RD
NATTRESS TERR
LABURNUM AVE
SPRINGDALE
LABURNUM SQ
PURVIS TERR
MALVERN CRES
MARGARET TERR
HOLME LEA TERR
CINNAMON DR

Welfare Park

Station Town

DORMAND CT
BRACKENDALE CT
FERNDALE CL
BEACHDALE
NELWOOD EST
MILBANK TERR

Rodridge Cottage Farm

CRAVEN'S BLDGS

5

Dismtd Rly

West Woodburn

BURN VALLEY GDNS 1
BRIDGE TERR 2
ELLERBOURNE TERR 3
HEATON TERR 4

36

COMMERCIAL ST
ST PAUL'S RD
LAWSON'S ST
LANGDALE OVAL
LOW HOGG ST
PARK RD
HORSE CLOSE LA

Trimdon Colliery

Dyke House Farm

Low Dyke St

Langdale

Beaumont Nursery

Bridgefield Farm

4

Langley Beck

Hurworth Bryan

Woodlands Close

B1280

3

Dismtd Rly

35

Park House

2

Hurworth Burn

White Hurworth Farm

Haswell to Hart Countryside Wlk

Hurworth Burn Resr

1

River Skerne

34

HURWORTH BURN RD

38 A B 39 C D 40 E F

A B C D E F

8
7
37
6
5
36
4
3
35
2
1
34

Thacmyers

Heads Hope

Heads Hope Dene

Mill Hill

Hallow Hill

Castle Eden Inn (PH)

Castle Eden

Eden Vale

Bleachery Dene

The Bleachery

DENE VIEW

HEATH VIEW

Fairfield Farm

MANOR HOUSE EST

Rodridge Hall

Hutton Henry

MANOR HOUSE EST

Hutton Henry C of E Sch (Jun & Inf)

Allot Gdns

Plough Inn (PH)

The Common

MANOR HOUSE EST

Hutton House

Bowman's Plantation

Hulam

BELLOWS BURN LA

Cemy

EIGHT HOUSES

THE OAKS

FRONT ST

HUTTON CRES

SOUTH VIEW

ELLERBOURNE TERR

LEECHMIRE TERR

ASHBOURNE CT

Rodridge Farm

West Common

Village Farm

Leechmire

Gravel Hill

Clay Pool Beck

Sheraton Hill

Blankeley Hill

Fleet Shot

Sedgewick Hill

SHERATON BANK

A19

South Wingate

Red Barns

Sheraton Hall Farm

Hart Bushes Hall

Ben Knowle Belt

Catlow Hall Farm

Fardenhill Plantation

Rixown

B1280

Catley Hill

Dismd Rly

Black Hurworth Farm

Wood Close Farm

Farden Hill

Roper's Wood

109
86

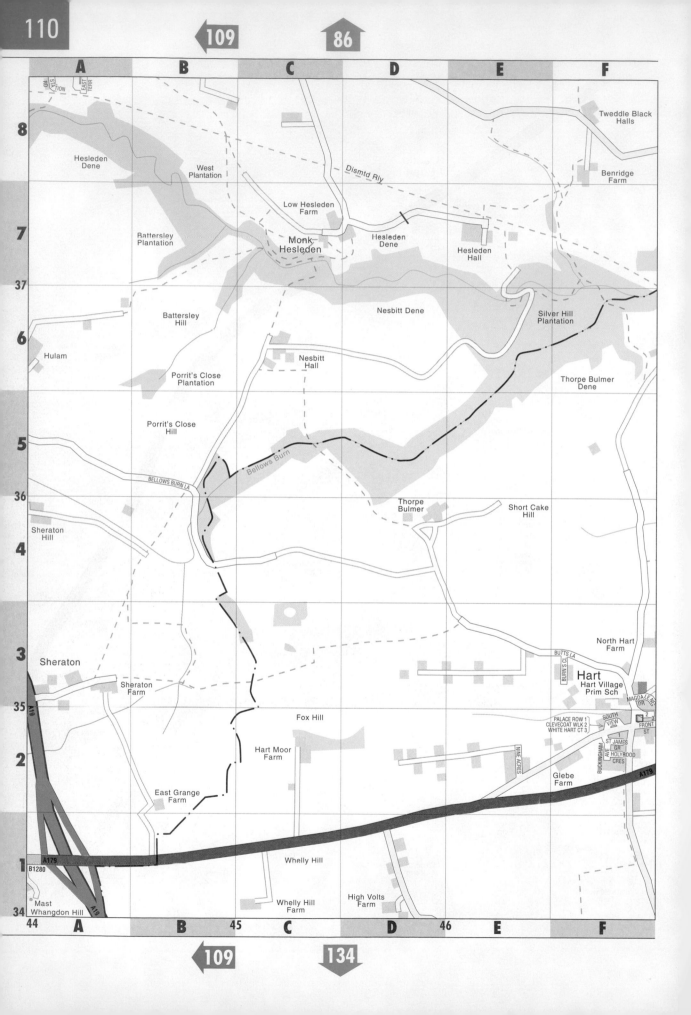

A · B · C · D · E · F

8

Tweddle Black Halls

Hesleden Dene

West Plantation

Benridge Farm

Dismtd Rly

7

Low Hesleden Farm

Battersley Plantation

Monk Hesleden

Hesleden Dene

Hesleden Hall

37

Battersley Hill

Nesbitt Dene

Silver Hill Plantation

6

Hulam

Porrit's Close Plantation

Nesbitt Hall

Thorpe Bulmer Dene

Porrit's Close Hill

Bellows Burn

5

Thorpe Bulmer

Short Cake Hill

36

BELLOWS BURN LA

Sheraton Hill

4

North Hart Farm

3

Sheraton

BUTTS LA

BURN'S CL

Hart

Hart Village Prim Sch

Sheraton Farm

MAGDALE

35

A19

PALACE ROW 1
CLEVECOAT WLK 2
WHITE HART CT 3

SOUTH VIEW

2
3
FRONT ST

Fox Hill

ST JAMES GR

HOLYROOD CRES

2

Hart Moor Farm

BUCKINGHAM AVE

NINE ACRES

Glebe Farm

A179

East Grange Farm

1

A179

Whelly Hill

B1280

34

Mast Whangdon Hill

A19

Whelly Hill Farm

High Volts Farm

44 · A · B · 45 · C · D · 46 · E · F

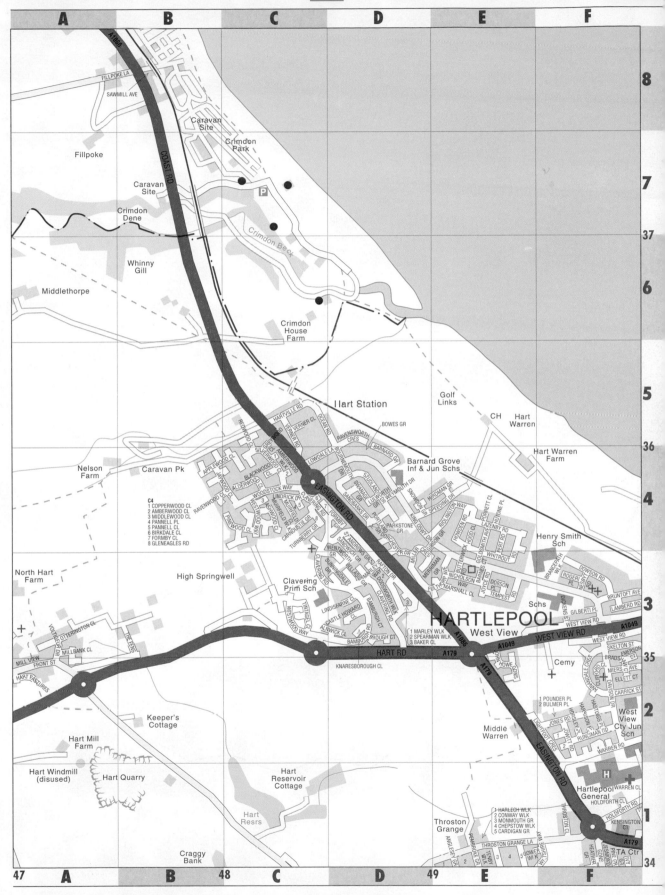

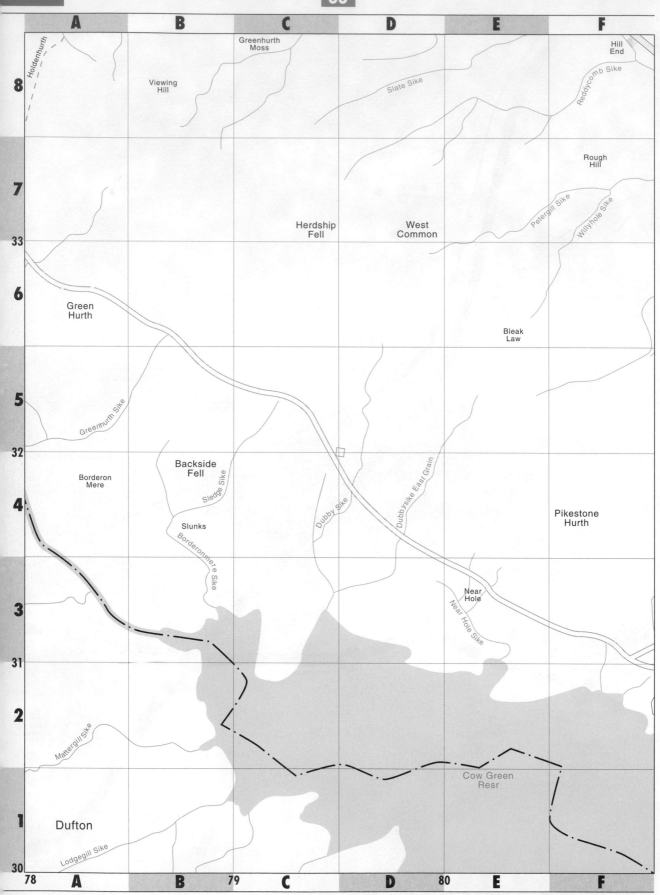

A　B　C　D　E　F

Holdenhurth

Greenhurth
Moss

Viewing
Hill

Hill
End

Slate Sike

Reddycomb Sike

8

Rough
Hill

7

Herdship
Fell

West
Common

Petergill Sike

Willyhole Sike

33

6

Green
Hurth

Bleak
Law

5

Greenhurth Sike

32

Borderon
Mere

Backside
Fell

Sledge Sike

Dubby Sike

Dubbysike East Grain

Pikestone
Hurth

4

Slunks

Borderonmere Sike

3

Near
Hole

Near Hole Sike

31

2

Mattergill Sike

Cow Green
Resr

1

Dufton

Lodgegill Sike

30

78　A　　B　79　C　　D　80　E　　F

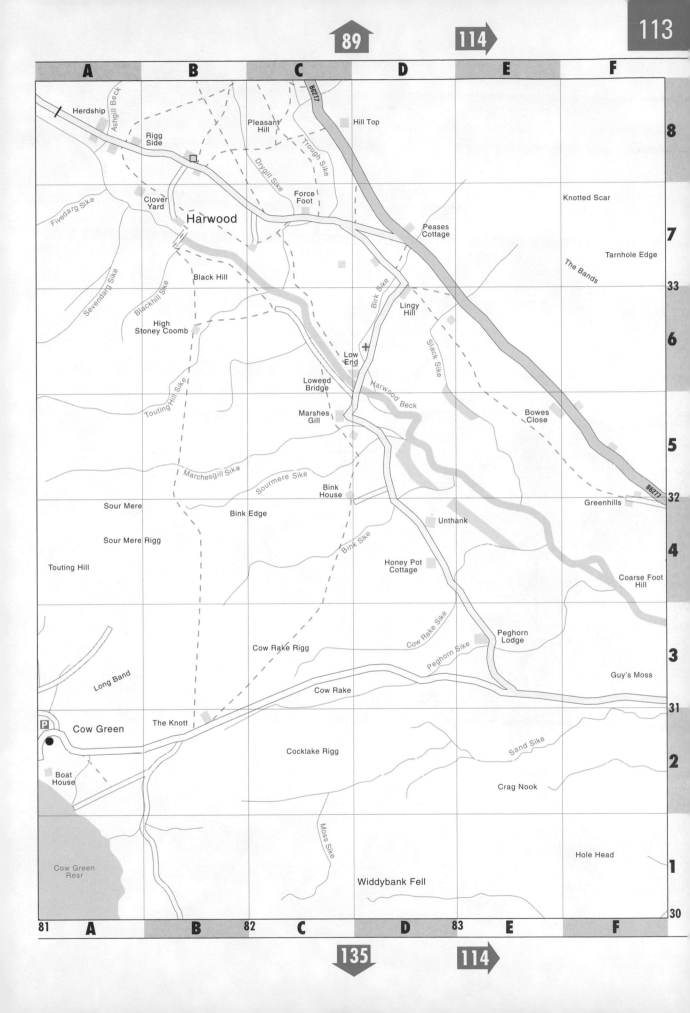

A   B   C   D   E   F

Herdship
Ashgill Beck
Rigg Side
Pleasant Hill
Hill Top
B6277
Trough Sike
Drygill Sike
Fivedarg Sike
Clover Yard
Force Foot
Harwood
Knotted Scar
Peases Cottage
The Bands
Tarnhole Edge
Black Hill
Sevendarg Sike
Blackhill Sike
Birk Sike
Lingy Hill
High Stoney Coomb
Low End
Slack Sike
Touting Hill Sike
Lowend Bridge
Harwood Beck
Bowes Close
Marshes Gill
B6277
Marchesgill Sike
Sourmere Sike
Bink House
Greenhills
Sour Mere
Bink Edge
Unthank
Sour Mere Rigg
Bink Sike
Coarse Foot Hill
Touting Hill
Honey Pot Cottage
Cow Rake Sike
Peghorn Lodge
Cow Rake Rigg
Peghorn Sike
Long Band
Cow Rake
Guy's Moss
Cow Green
The Knott
Sand Sike
Cocklake Rigg
Boat House
Crag Nook
Cow Green Resr
Moss Sike
Hole Head
Widdybank Fell

8
7
33
6
5
32
4
3
31
2
1
30

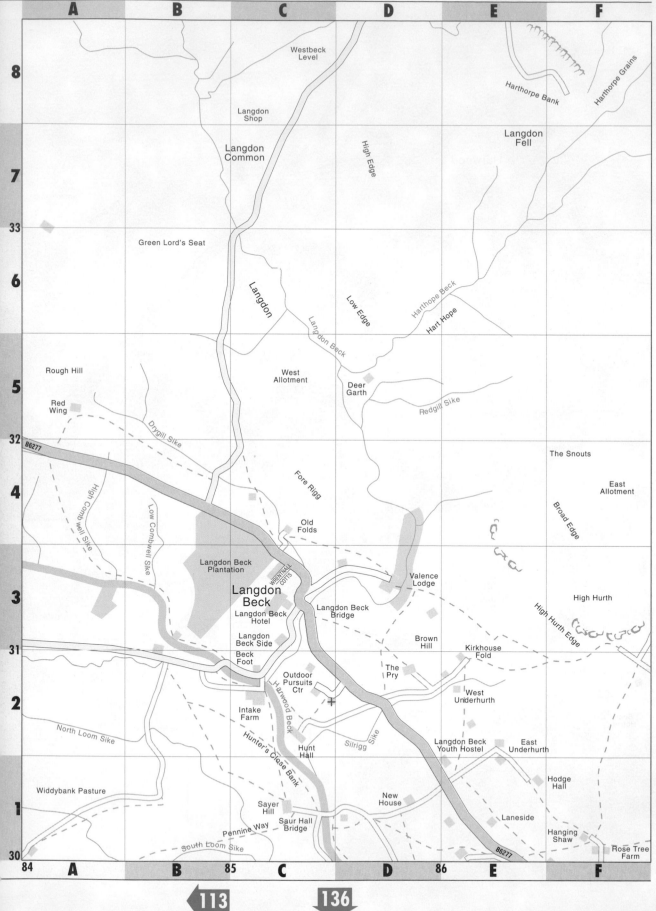

A B C D E F

Claypit Burn

Elph Cleugh

Swinhope Burn Head

Black Scar

Fendrith Hill

Swinhope Head

P

Short Bowers

Dora's Seat

Church Bowers

Long Mere

Longmere Sike

Hare Law Sike

Blacklaw Moss

Ettersgill Common

White Mere

Little Thatchpot Sike

Thatch Pot

Black Law

Wester Head

High Flood Beck

Thatchpot Sike

Wester Beck

Thatchpot Rigg

New Strake Shop

Beck Head Dales

Fouts Pot Pit

West Binks Edge

Green Hills

East Binks Edge

High Beck Head

Holmfield Sike

Chester Sike

Ettersgill Beck

Whinfield Sike

Wool Pits Hill

Archer Rigg Sike

Scar End

High House

Winsley Sike

Egg Pot

Bank Top

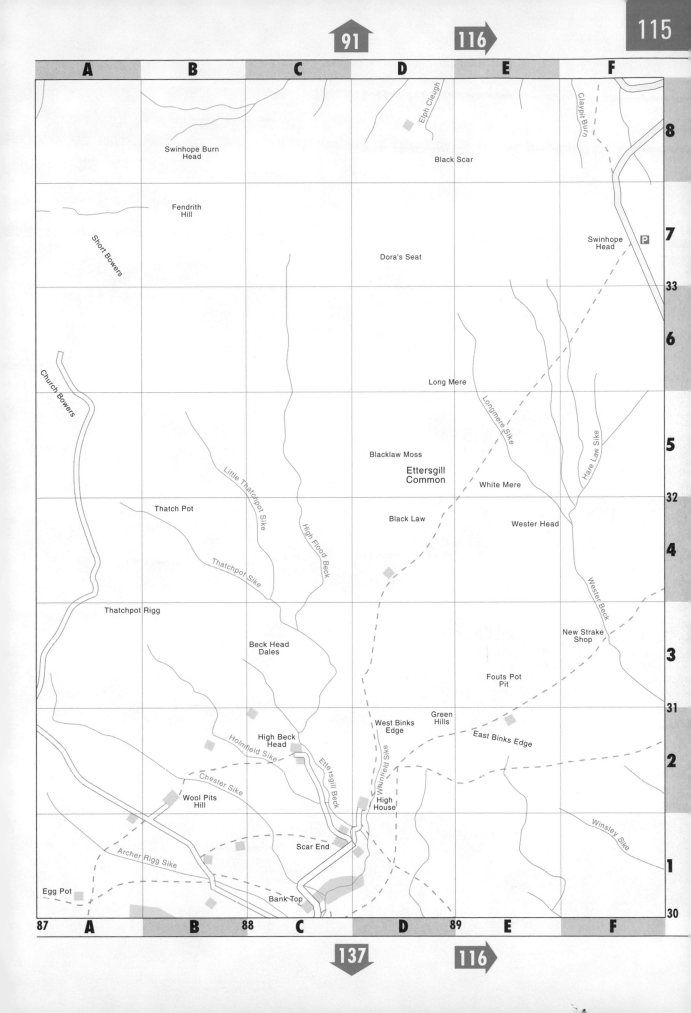

115
92

	A	B	C	D	E	F

8

West Grain

Green Sike

Wolf Cleugh

Westernhope Moor

Hawk Crag

Wolfcleugh Head

7

Blaeberry Burn

33

Blaeberry Grains

Blaeberry Cleugh

6

Black Hill

Broperygill Sike

5

Three Folds Sike

32

Pike Law

Flushie Mere

Broadley Hill

Rowantreegill Sike

4

Newbiggin Common

James's Hill

Carr Crags

3

Green Fell

Ford

Flushiemere House

31

Flushiemere Beck

2

Wester Beck

Bales Allotment

Bleagill Sike

Weather Beds

Goreemoss Sike

Bales Hush

Bleagill Allotment

1

Watson's Bridge

Blea Gill

Winsley Sike

Lingy Rigg

30

90	A	B	91	C	D	92	E	F

115
138

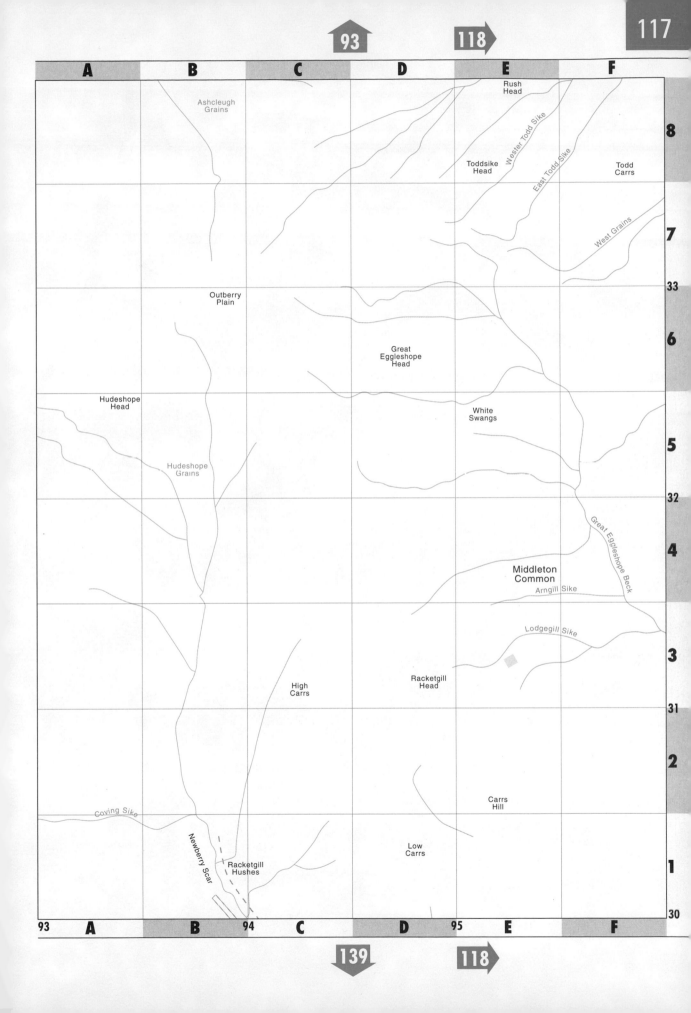

A **B** **C** **D** **E** **F**

Ashcleugh
Grains

Rush
Head

Wester Todd Sike

East Todd Sike

Toddsike
Head

Todd
Carrs

8

West Grains

7

33

Outberry
Plain

Great
Eggleshope
Head

6

Hudeshope
Head

White
Swangs

5

Hudeshope
Grains

32

Great Eggleshope Beck

Middleton
Common

4

Arngill Sike

Lodgegill Sike

3

Racketgill
Head

High
Carrs

31

2

Carrs
Hill

Coving Sike

Newberry Scar

Low
Carrs

Racketgill
Hushes

1

30

A   B   C   D   E   F

Smithy Burn

Low Black Hill

B6278

8   Bracken Hills

Harnisha Flat

Harnisha Burn

Harnisha Gill

Harnisha Carrs

High Black Hill

7   East Grains

Harnisha Head

33

6

B6278

5

Raven Seat

Three Laws

Harnisha Hill

32

Little Egleshope
Grains

4

Candlesieve Sike

3   Great Eggles
Hope

Great Eggleshope Beck

31

Round
Hill

2   Shooting
House

Littlegill Sike

White Hill

1   Dusty Gill

Manorgill
Hushes

30

96   A   B   97   C   D   98   E   F

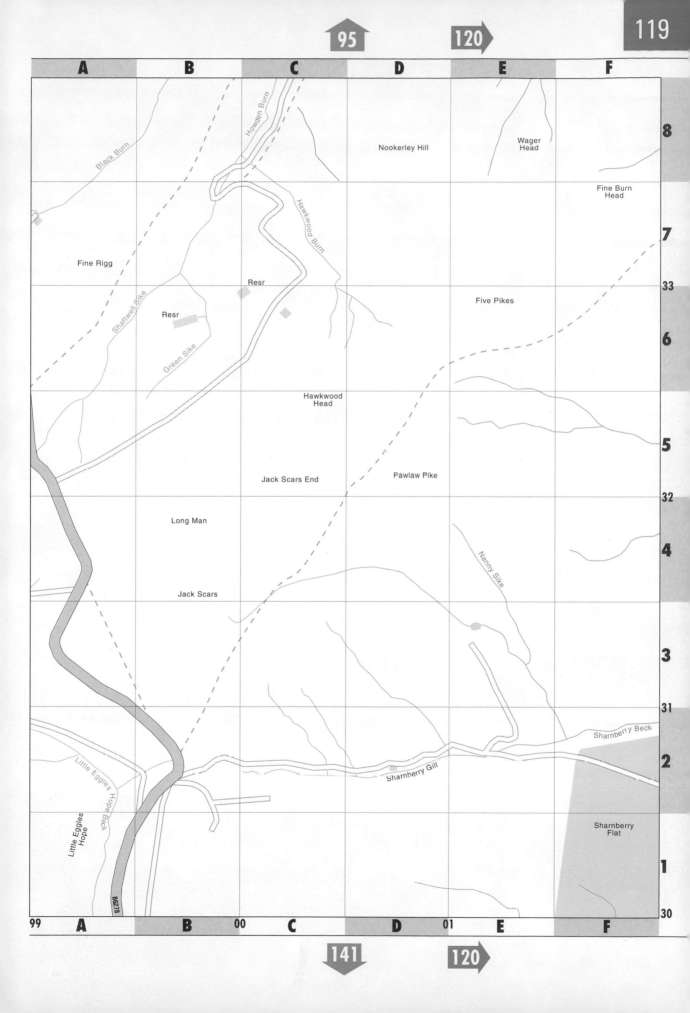

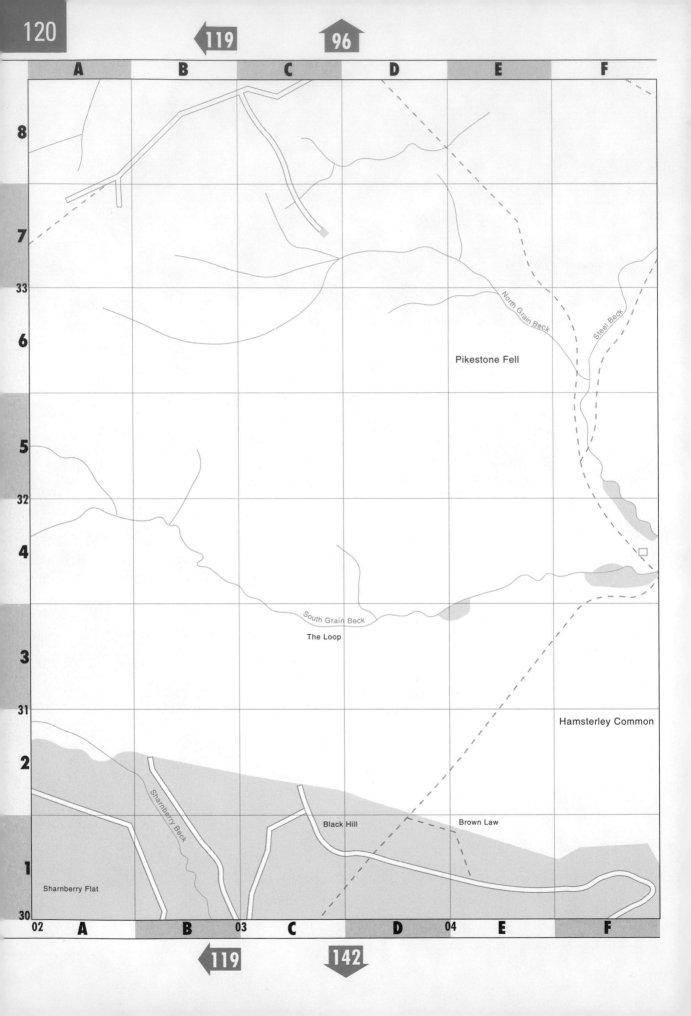

A B C D E F

8

7

33

6

Pikestone Fell

North Grain Beck

Steel Beck

5

32

4

South Grain Beck

The Loop

3

31

Hamsterley Common

2

Sharnberry Beck

Black Hill

Brown Law

1

Sharnberry Flat

30

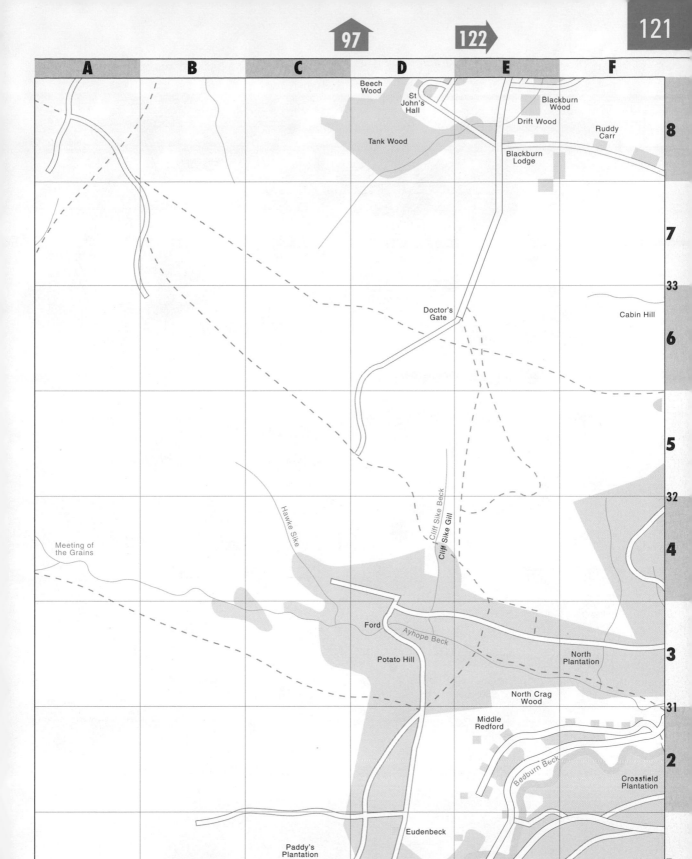

A   B   C   D   E   F

8

7

33

6

5

32

4

3

31

2

1

30

Beech Wood
St John's Hall
Blackburn Wood
Drift Wood
Tank Wood
Ruddy Carr
Blackburn Lodge

Doctor's Gate
Cabin Hill

Hawke Sike
Cliff Sike Beck
Cliff Sike Gill

Meeting of the Grains

Ford
Ayhope Beck
North Plantation

Potato Hill
North Crag Wood

Middle Redford

Bedburn Beck
Crossfield Plantation

Eudenbeck

Paddy's Plantation

Nest Plantation

Frog Wood

A B C D E F

8

East
Belt

Knitsley
Cottage

Dryderdale
Plantation

Knitsley
Plantation

West Shipley
Farm

High
Shipley
Wood

7

Shull
Lodge

Dryderdale
Farm

Shull

Dryderdale Beck

Dryderdale
Hall

Harthope Beck

HOWLEA LA

33

Shull
Bank

Shull Bank
Wood

The
Castles

6

West Moor
Plantation

SHULL LANK

North
Wood

Harthope
Wood

Low
Burnlea
Row

Stanhope La

5

White
Lodge

Hoppyland
Hall

East Knotty
Hill Wood

Harthope Mill
(dis)

West Knotty
Hill

32

West Hoppyland
Allotments

West
Hoppyland
Farm

Benchy
Bank

Caravan
Pk

Black
Lodge

Newhall
Farm

New
Hall
Wood

4

Mill
Plantation

Bedburn
Old Hall

Bedburn

Redford
Allotments

REDFORD LA

Bedburn
Hall

Red Hill Top
Plantation

Hatcase

Mill Race

Bedburn Beck

3

Toll

Visitor
Ctr
ℹ

White
Hill
Top

Red
Hill
Top

Low Redford
Wood

Coronation
Farm

Low
Redford
Bridge

Windy Bank
Wood

Eden
Hall

Quarry
House

31

Low
Redford

Black Hill Top
Plantation

2

Windy
Bank

Black Hill Top
Farm

High
House
Farm

Numbers
Farm

WINDY BANK RD

Rackwood
Hill

East
Rackwood
Hill

1

West
Rackwood
Hill

30

08 A B 09 C D 10 E F

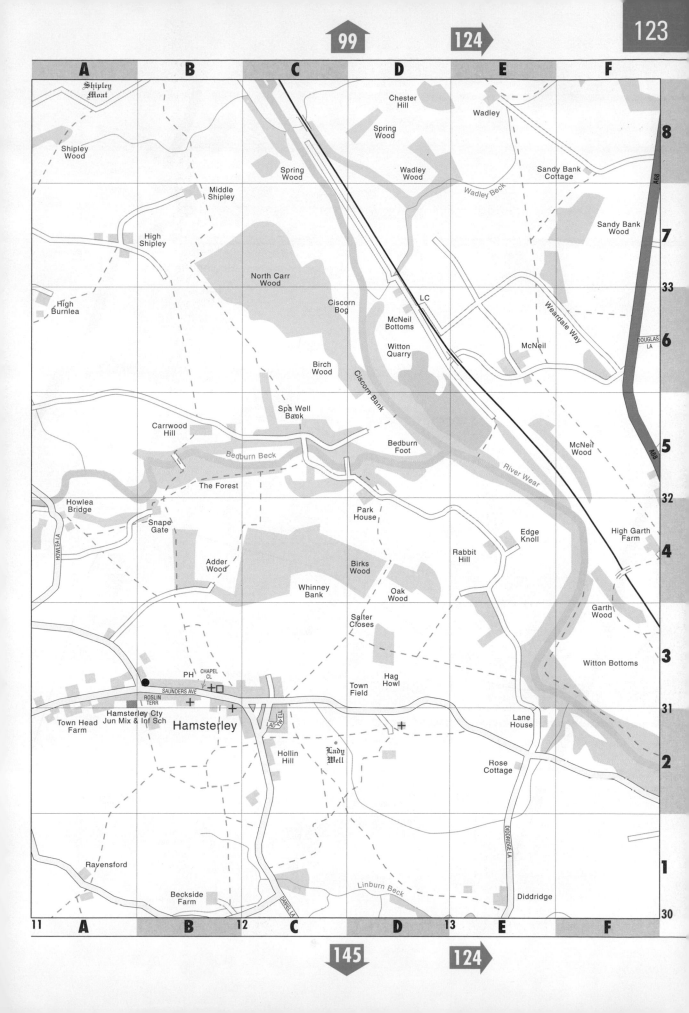

A **B** **C** **D** **E** **F**

Shipley Moat

Shipley Wood

8

Chester Hill

Wadley

Spring Wood

Spring Wood

Wadley Wood

Wadley Beck

Sandy Bank Cottage

Middle Shipley

Sandy Bank Wood

7

High Shipley

33

North Carr Wood

High Burnlea

Ciscorn Bog

LC

6

McNeil Bottoms

McNeil

Birch Wood

Witton Quarry

Weardale Way

DOUGLAS LA

Ciscorn Bank

Spa Well Bank

Carrwood Hill

Bedburn Beck

Bedburn Foot

5

River Wear

McNeil Wood

32

The Forest

Howlea Bridge

Park House

Edge Knoll

High Garth Farm

HOWLEA LA

Snape Gate

4

Adder Wood

Birks Wood

Rabbit Hill

Garth Wood

Whinney Bank

Oak Wood

Witton Bottoms

3

Salter Closes

Town Field

Hag Howl

Lane House

31

PH CHAPEL CL

SAUNDERS AVE

ROSLIN TERR

Hamsterley Cty Jun Mix & Inf Sch

Hamsterley

LADY WELL

Town Head Farm

Hollin Hill

Lady Well

Rose Cottage

2

DIDDRIDGE LA

Ravensford

1

Beckside Farm

DARNELL LA

Linburn Beck

Diddridge

30

11 **A** **B** **12** **C** **D** **13** **E** **F**

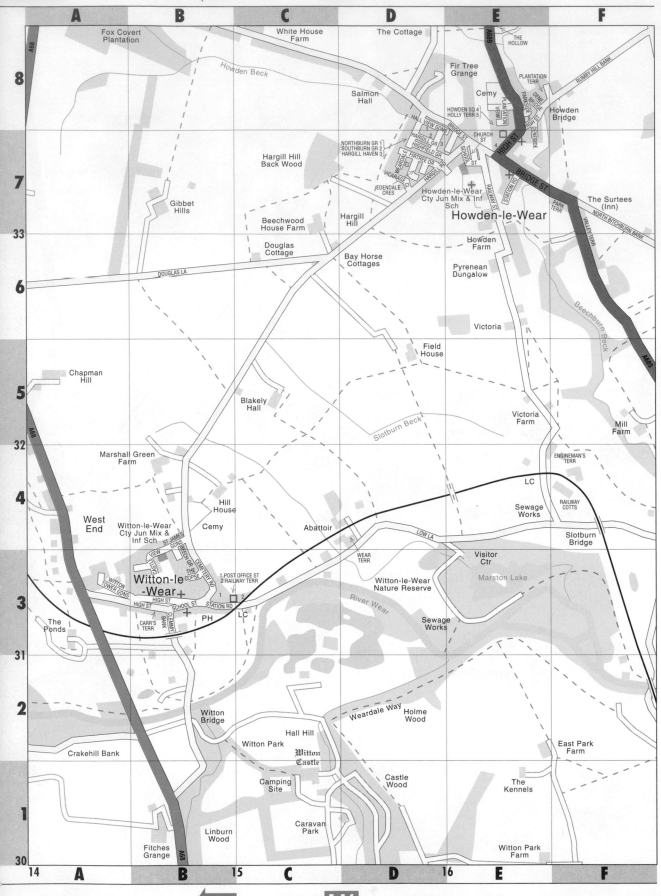

A **B** **C** **D** **E** **F**

Fox Covert Plantation

White House Farm

The Cottage

THE HOLLOW

A689

8

Howden Beck

Salmon Hall

Fir Tree Grange

Cemy

PLANTATION TERR

RUMBY HILL BANK

Howden Bridge

HALL VIEW GDNS

HOWDEN SQ 4 HOLLY TERR 5

BRIDGE ST

CHURCH ST

HIGH ST

PARKSIDE

DENE BRIDGE

DENESIDE

Hargill Hill Back Wood

NORTHBURN GR 1 SOUTHBURN GR 2 HARGILL HAVEN 3

HIGHFIELD GR

HARGILL GR 3

SCHOOL ST

BRIDGE ST

7

WEARDALE CTS

FIRTREE DR

VICARAGE

HARGILL RD

RAILWAY ST

STATION RD

PARK TERR

The Surtees (Inn)

33

EDENDALE CRES

Hargill Hill

Howden-le-Wear Cty Jun Mix & Inf Sch

Howden-le-Wear

VALLEY TERR

NORTH BITCHBURN BANK

Beechwood House Farm

Douglas Cottage

Bay Horse Cottages

Howden Farm

6

DOUGLAS LA

Pyrenean Bungalow

Beechburn Beck

Victoria

Field House

A689

5

Chapman Hill

Blakely Hall

Slotburn Beck

Victoria Farm

Mill Farm

32

A68

Marshall Green Farm

ENGINEMAN'S TERR

LC

4

Hill House

Abattoir

LOW LA

Sewage Works

RAILWAY COTTS

West End

Witton-le-Wear Cty Jun Mix & Inf Sch

Cemy

WEAR TERR

Visitor Ctr

Slotburn Bridge

ST JAMES GDNS

CASTLE VIEW

BEECH GR

THE COPSE

CEMETERY RD

1 POST OFFICE ST 2 RAILWAY TERR

Witton-le-Wear Nature Reserve

Marston Lake

WITTON TOWER GDNS

Witton-le-Wear

HIGH ST

STATION RD

LC

River Wear

Sewage Works

3

CARR'S TERR

HIGH ST

CLEMMY BANK

SCHOOL ST

PH

The Ponds

31

Witton Bridge

Weardale Way

Holme Wood

2

Hall Hill

Witton Park

Witton Castle

East Park Farm

Crakehill Bank

Castle Wood

The Kennels

Camping Site

1

Linburn Wood

Caravan Park

Witton Park Farm

30

Fitches Grange

A68

14 **A** **B** **15** **C** **D** **16** **E** **F**

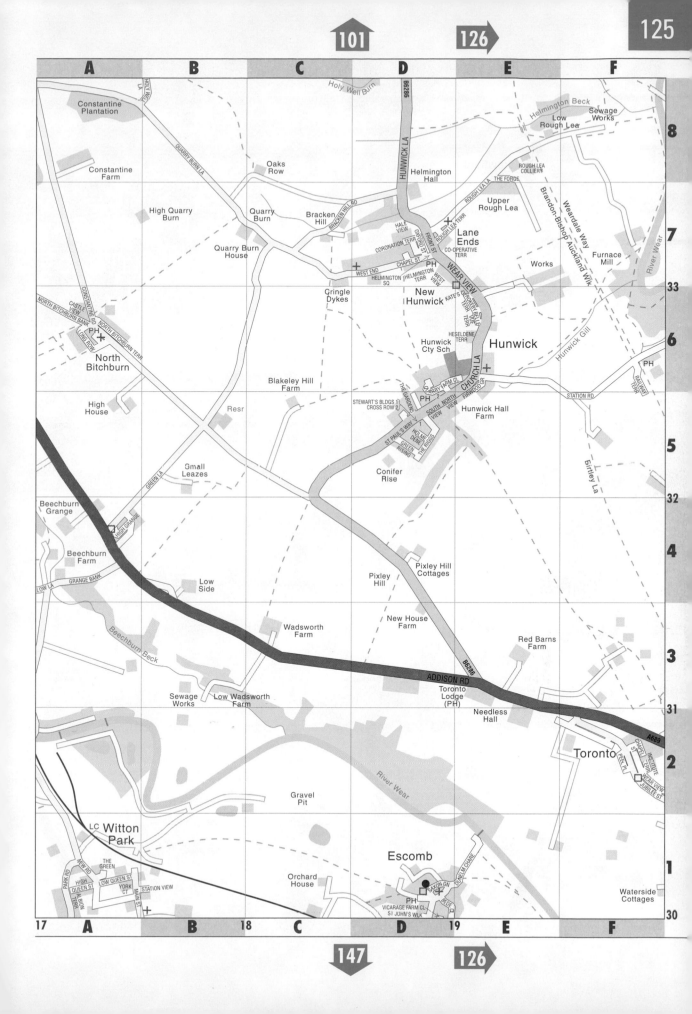

101
126
147
126

A   B   C   D   E   F

Holy Well Burn

B6286

HUNWICK LA

Helmington Beck

Constantine
Plantation

Low
Rough Lea

Sewage
Works

8

Constantine
Farm

Oaks
Row

Helmington
Hall

ROUGH LEA RD

THE FORGE

Rough Lea
Colliery

River Wear

High Quarry
Burn

Quarry
Burn

Bracken
Hill

HALF
VIEW

Upper
Rough Lea

7

Quarry Burn
House

Quarry Burn

OXFORD ST

FRONT ST

CORONATION TERR

ROUGH LEA TERR

Lane
Ends

Brandon-Bishop Auckland Wlk

Weardale Way

Furnace
Mill

33

West End

WEST END

CHAPEL ST

HELMINGTON
SQ

HELMINGTON
TERR

HELMINGTON
TERR

WEST
VIEW

PH

KATE'S

CROCKERY BELT

New
Hunwick

WEAR VIEW

Works

Gringle
Dykes

CROCKERY BELT

VIEW

TERR

6

Constantine Rd

CASTLE
VIEW

North Bitchburn Bank

North Bitchburn Terr

LONG ROW

PH

Hunwick
Cty Sch

Hunwick Cty Sch

HESELDENE
TERR

Hunwick

Hunwick Gill

PH

RAILWAY
TERR

North
Bitchburn

Blakeley Hill
Farm

CHURCH LA

STATION RD

High
House

Resr

THE GARDENS

STEWART'S BLDGS 1
CROSS ROW 2

QUARRY FARM 01

PH

SOUTH
VIEW

NORTH
VIEW

FIRWOOD GR

Hunwick Hall
Farm

5

Green La

Small
Leazes

ST PAUL'S WAY

HOLME
DENE

THE RIDGES

HOLME
DENE

GREEN
RISING

Conifer
Rise

Birtley La

32

Beechburn
Grange

HIGH GRANGE

Pixley Hill
Cottages

4

Beechburn
Farm

GRANGE BANK

LOW LA

Low
Side

Pixley
Hill

New House
Farm

Red Barns
Farm

3

Beechburn Beck

Wadsworth
Farm

ADDISON RD

B6286

Toronto
Lodge
(PH)

31

Sewage
Works

Low Wadsworth
Farm

Needless
Hall

A689

Toronto

INSTITUTE

CHAPEL TERR

PEEL PL

PEAR VIEW

JUBILEE ST

2

Gravel
Pit

River Wear

Escomb

DUNELM CHARE

Witton
Park

LC

PARK RD

NEW RD

THE
GREEN

HIGH
QUEEN
ST

ALBION
TERR

YORK
CT

LOW QUEEN ST

STATION VIEW

MAIN ST

Orchard
House

SAXON GN

BEDE

SAXON ST

PH

VICARAGE FARM CL
ST JOHN'S WLK

Waterside
Cottages

1

30

17   A   B   18   C   D   19   E   F

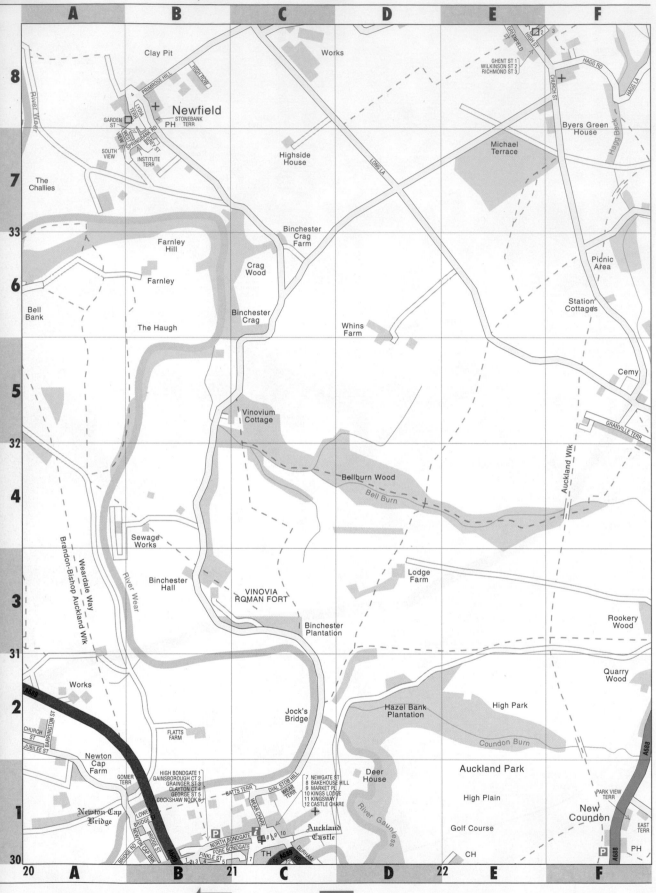

103 128

A B C D E F

Hagg Farm
HAGG LA

Bishop's Close Cottages

Auckland Wlk

High Whitworth Farm

Whitworth House Sch

Spennymoor Comp Sch

Bishop's Close

Bishop's Close

PARK PAR
PARK NORTH ST
LIBY L Ctr
SILVER ST
HIGH ST
CHURCH ST
BAMBURGH PARK
CLARENCE HOUSE
Wesleyan Rd

Old Park Terr

PAGE GR
WESTMOOR CT
WHITWORTH CL
DUNCOMBE CL
WEST TERR
HAWTHORN

TODD ST 1
VYNER ST 2
ROBERT ST 3
PRINCESS ST 4
WHITWORTH TERR 5
EDEN ST 6

ST PAUL'S RISE
OAK TERR
FLORA AVE
BELLE VUE ST
CLYDE TERR
LOTHIAN ST
OSBORNE VILLA
VICTORIA GDNS
CHESTNUT AVE
EDEN RD
ASH TERR
BEECH AVE
CHARLES
PRINCESS
CARR RD
JACKSON ST
DICKENS ST
CAMBRIDGE ST
DRAKE ST
STRATTON ST
SOUTH ST
RAFT ST
WEIR ST
CRAGSIDE
HOLINMEE
TIMOTHY TERR
THISTLE CL
EDDERTON CL
A688

Old Park Hall Farm

Spennymoor West Cty Inf Sch

Spennymoor Comp Lower Sch Est

Windsor Ave

33

Park Plantation

Middlestone Moor

AGED MINERS HOMES
ALBION ST
HEATHER GR
NORTH DR
MOORSIDE
BRIAR GR
THORN
FERN GR
ROCK RD
HEATH RD
CENTRAL DR
GRAYSON RD
HAWTHORN
LYNE RD
HIGHCROFT

Cemy

Moor Farm Est

6

Old Park Lodge Farm

Binchester Moor

OMORNE TERR
DURHAM RD
WHITWORTH MEADOWS
WATSON ST
WEST ST
GIBBON ST
CASTLEGARTH
WILTON RD
DURHAM ST
Middlestone Moor Sch
SOUTH VIEW
SOUTH CT

White Wings Farm

NORTH CLOSE RD

North Close Farm

5

REEL ST
GLADSTONE ST
GRANVILLE TERR

Binchester

Low House Farm

32

Low House

B6288

4

Low House Farm

Hall Heads

WEST VIEW
B6287
MERRINGTON HEIGHTS
East Farm
HOPKINSON PL
RICHARDSON PL
PH
THE CROFT

3

Park Head Farm

Westerton

Works

Mast

Middlestone

HIGH RD
LOW RD
EDEN VIEW
The Ship (PH)

EDEN TERR

31

QUARRY HOUSES

South Bank

2

Etty Hill

Leasingthorne Farm

Coundon Burn

Township Field

Leeholme

STAINEMORE TERR
WESTERTON RD
YORK
HARTLEY AVE
FARM AVE
ADD
NOTTINGHAM ST
POTTS ST
FRICKINGHAM ST
KENT ST
SANDRINGHAM TERR
HEREFORD ST
CAMBRIDGE ST
LEEHOLME RD
WINDSOR TERR
MICKLE GR

1 LINCOLN ST
2 PEMBROKE ST
3 BUCKINGHAM TERR

WEST PK
FREDERICK ST
CURLISH TERR
LINGWELL DENE
WELLINGTON DENE
WESTERTON VIEW

B6287
LEEHOLME RD
3 2 1

1

149 128

8 7 33 6 5 32 4 3 31 2 1 30

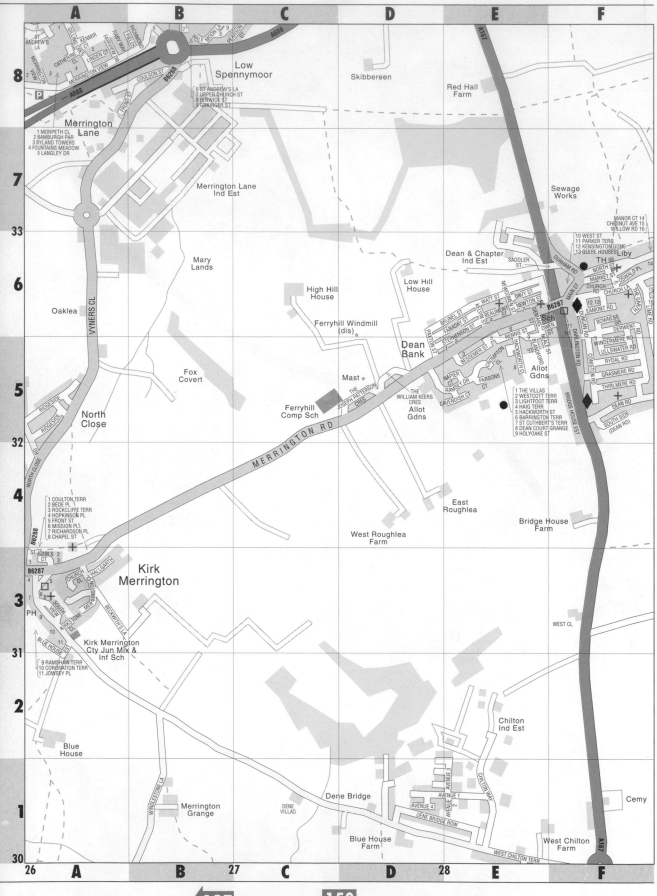

Low
Spennymoor

Merrington
Lane

1 MORPETH CL
2 BAMBURGH PAR
3 BYLAND TOWERS
4 FOUNTAINS MEADOW
5 LANGLEY DR

6 ST ANDREW'S LA
7 UPPER CHURCH ST
8 FENWICK ST
9 GRAINGER ST

Skibbereen

Red Hall
Farm

Merrington Lane
Ind Est

Sewage
Works

Mary
Lands

Oaklea

High Hill
House

Low Hill
House

Dean & Chapter
Ind Est

MANOR CT 14
CHESNUT AVE 15
WILLOW RD 16

10 WEST ST
11 PARKER TERR
12 KENSINGTON GDNS
13 GLEBE HOUSES

TH
Liby

Ferryhill Windmill
(dis)

Dean
Bank

Fox
Covert

Mast

North
Close

Ferryhill
Comp Sch

Allot
Gdns

1 THE VILLAS
2 WESTCOTT TERR
3 LIGHTFOOT TERR
4 HAIG TERR
5 HACKWORTH ST
6 BARRINGTON TERR
7 ST CUTHBERT'S TERR
8 DEAN COURT GRANGE
9 HOLYOAKE ST

THE WILLIAM KEERS
CRES

Allot
Gdns

Bridge House
Farm

East
Roughlea

1 COULTON TERR
2 BEDE PL
3 ROCKCLIFFE TERR
4 HOPKINSON PL
5 FRONT ST
6 MISSION PL
7 RICHARDSON PL
8 CHAPEL ST

West Roughlea
Farm

Kirk
Merrington

ST JOHN'S
CT

PH

Kirk Merrington
Cty Jun Mix &
Inf Sch

WEST CL

Chilton
Ind Est

9 RAMSHAW TERR
10 CORONATION TERR
11 JOWSEY PL

Blue
House

Merrington
Grange

DENE
VILLAS

Dene Bridge

AVENUE 1
AVENUE 3
AVENUE 4
AVENUE 2
DENE BRIDGE ROW

Cemy

Blue House
Farm

West Chilton
Farm

WEST CHILTON TERR

A B C D E F

8
33
7
6
5
32
4
3
31
2
1
30

East Howle
Dismtd Rly

Coxhoe
Junction

A6
1 SOUTH VIEW
2 STRATFORD GDNS
3 MANOR VIEW
4 DUNELM TERR
5 HIGHLAND TERR
6 HIGHCLIFFE TERR
7 GREENFIELDS
8 EAST VIEW
9 MILFORD TERR
10 GREGORY TERR
11 WEST VIEW

Cleves Cross
Cty Jun & Inf
Sch

The Carrs

Stone Quarry

Chy
Thrislington Works

Thrislington Plantation

Ferryhill
Broom Cottages
Cty Jun & Inf Sch

The Broom

Ferryhill Rosebank Sch

Cleves Cross Grange

L Ctr

Cleves Ave

Cemy

Ruffers Plantation

Rough Furze Quarry (dis)

Sewage Works

A5
1 BEDE TERR
2 RUTHERFORD TERR
3 ROSS TERR
4 CONVERS TERR
5 BROOM COTTS

Allot Gdns

B5
1 CLEVE COTTS
2 DUNCOMBE TERR
3 GREY TERR
4 PEACE HAVEN
5 ROWLANDSON TERR
6 OSBORNE TERR
7 MAGDALENE TERR
8 LOVAINE TERR
9 GLADSTONE TERR

GLADSTONE VILLAS

Rudd Hill
RUDDS HILL

HIGH ST
MILLS BLDGS

WALKER TERR
DENNISON TERR
ELDON TERR

BACK ELDON TERR
CLIVE ST
WOLSELEY ST
TRAFALGAR ST
NELSON ST
HAIG ST

Lough House

Ferryhill Station

Lough House Bank

MORRISON TERR
MAINSFORTH RD

Recn Gd

CROFT GDNS

CHAPEL ROW

ARTHUR TERR

ENCOMBE TERR

Nable Hill

South Farm

Mainsforth

Little Chilton

FEVERSHAM TERR

Ferryhill Station Jun & Inf Sch

CARLTON TERR
CHURCH ST
WENSLEY TERR
MAINSFORTH FRONT ROW

Chilton Lane

FIRWOOD TERR

GEORGE ST
COMMERCIAL ST

SUTEES TERR

WILLIAM ST

COCHRANE TERR

The Carrs

Wheel Hill

LAUREL RD
SAXON RD
LILAC RD

Chilton East House

GIPSY LA

Sewage Works

Great Chilton Farm

Chilton Hall

Park Hill

Thrundle

Dismtd Rly

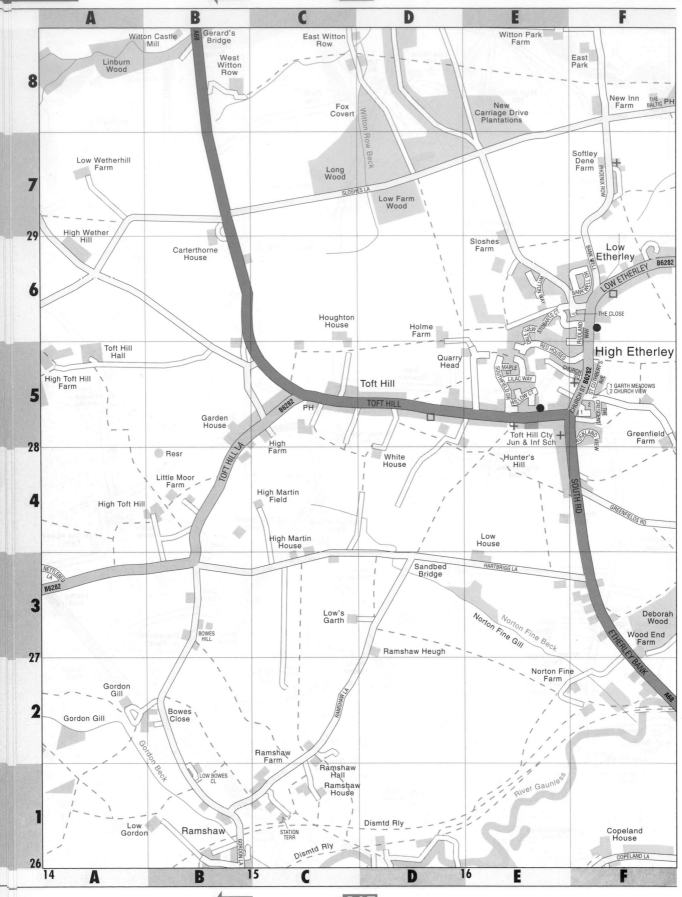

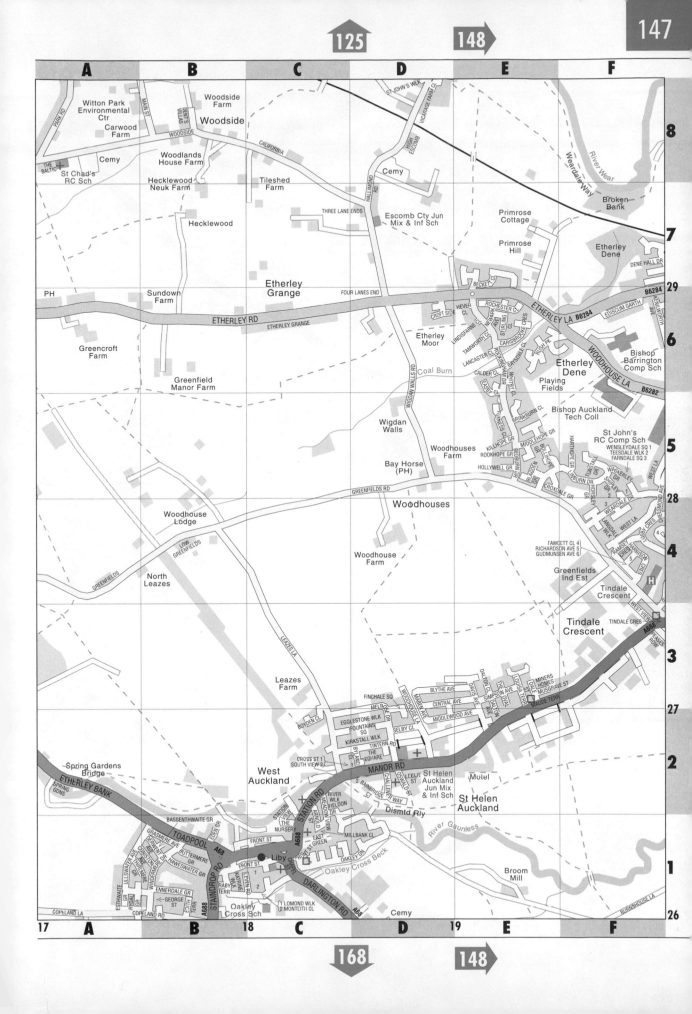

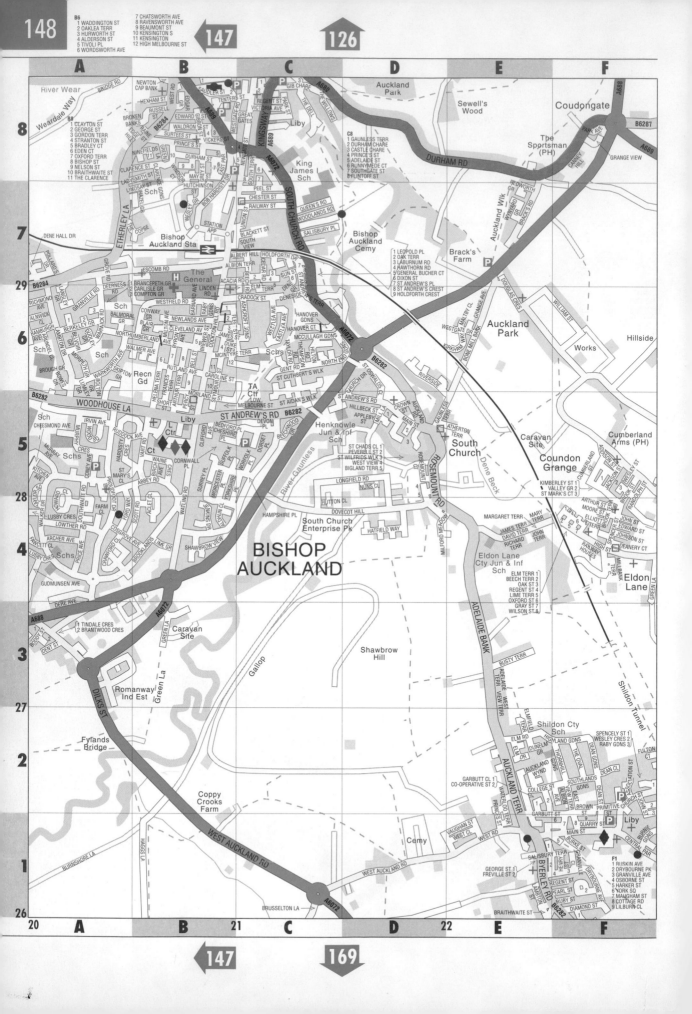

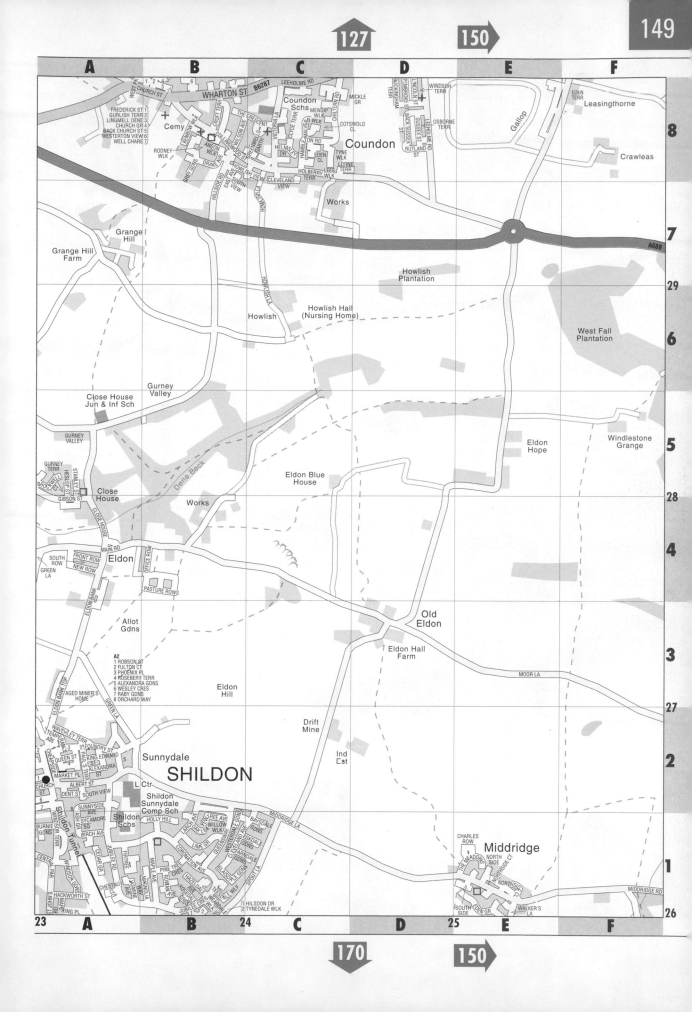

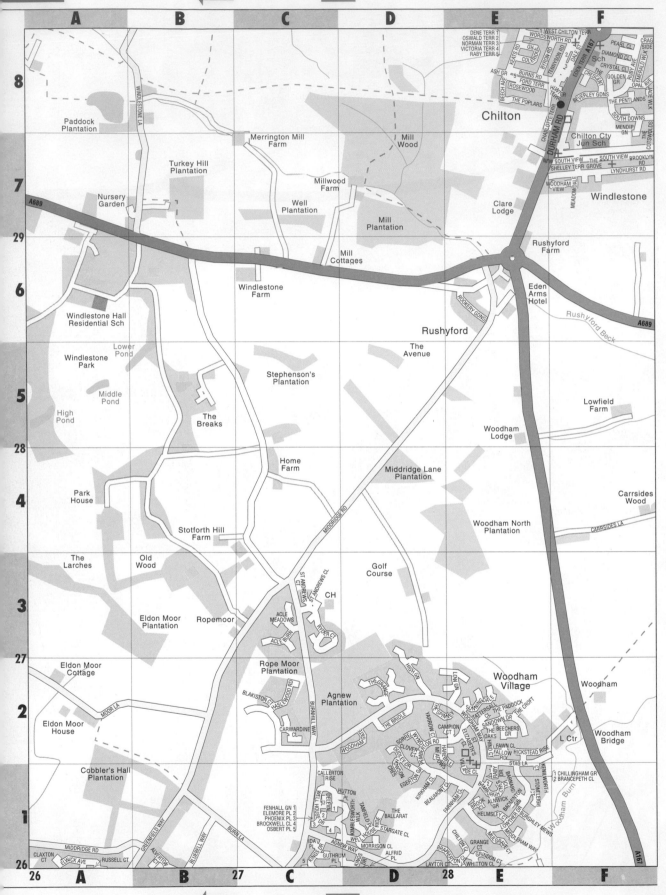

129
152

A **B** **C** **D** **E** **F**

Thrundle

1 CRAGSIDE
2 EMERALD WLK
ALDWIN CL
SKIRLAW
SHANKLY CL
FCL
KIRKHAM
CL
VILLIERS CL
ALINGTON
CL

Chilton
Grange

Dismtd Rly
Lark
Hill

8

OPAL AVE
JADE WLK
CORONATION RD

3 GRAMPIAN WAY
4 PENNINE WAY
5 MALVERN

Kay's
Hill

GIPSY LA

SOUTH DOWNS

ALBERT ST
ARTHUR ST
PROSPECT TERR

HAMBLETON WAY

Nunstainton
East

7

6 THE COTSWOLDS
7 SOUTH VIEW
8 LYNDHURST RD
9 BROOKLYN RD

Standalone

A1(M)

29

Depot

Sewage
Works

Nunstainton
Grange
Cottages

Junction 60

6

Borehole
Plantation

Nunstainton
Grange

Nunstainton
Carrs

A689

Low
Farm

5

Pityme
Wood

High
Farm

Bradbury

28

RUSHYFORD BECK

Nunstainton Grange
Carrs

River Skerne

Bradbury
Plantation

CARRSIDES LA

Carrsides

Carrsides
Carrs

4

Bradbury
Carrs

3

27

Little
Isle

Great
Isle

WOODHAM BURN

The Isle

Swan Carr
Farm

2

Low
Copelaw

1

A1(M)

26

29 **A** **B** **30** **C** **D** **31** **E** **F**

172
152

← 151
130

A B C D E F

8

A1(M)

Dismtd Rly

The Carrs

Green Knowles

Low Hardwick

Brick Kiln Plantation

7

River Skerne

Tile Shed Plantation

Hardwick Hall Hotel

A177

Hardwick Hall Country Park

29

Black Plantataion

Serpentine Lake

6

Nunstainton Carrs

Brakes Farm

Hardwick Park

West View

SANDY BANK

A177

Bath Plantation

West Lodge

East Lodge

STATION RD

QUEENS DR

A689

5

A689

Tilery

Sands Hall

Firtree Hill

Sands Farm

Sedgefield Racecourse

28

Firtree Hill Cottage

Firtree Hill Plantation

Stables

Caravan Site

4

West Winds

Mordon Moor

3

Mordon North Farm

Mordon Wood

27

Peter's La

2

Harpington Hill

Hopper House

Village Farm

HARPINGTON VIEW

AYCLIFFE LA

Manor House

Mordon

Mordon Carrs

South Moor Farm

1

Mordon Cottage Farm

Brookfield House

26

Black Wood

Embleton

Hill House

Embleton Farm

Low Swainston

Close Wood

Red Gap Moor

Middle Swainston

Close Farm

Red Gap Cottage

Close Wood

Red Gap

Black Moor Plantation

Newton Hanzard Plantations

Close Beck

Middle Swainton Plantation

THUNDERBUCK DR

NEWTON HANZARD LONG DR

Newton Hanzard Beck

Low Newton Hanzard

High Newton Hanzard

Swart Hole Plantation

Woodside

BLACK SQUARES DR

BRIERLEY DR

NURSERY DR

HARTLEPOOL RD

Forester's Lodge

Salter House Wood

SALTER HOUSES

North Lodges

Wynyard Park C of E Sch

Seaham New Plantation

THE WYND

THE GRANARY

Wynyard Village

CASTLEREAGH

THE RACECOURSE

Fanny's Glen

SALTER HOUSE DR

THE COPPICE

Whinny Moor Cottage

COAL LA

A689

Black Corner Plantation

WELLINGTON DR

Kennel Hill Plantation

The Paddocks

Wynyard Park

Horse Shoe Plantation

BRIERLEY DR

Brierley Beck

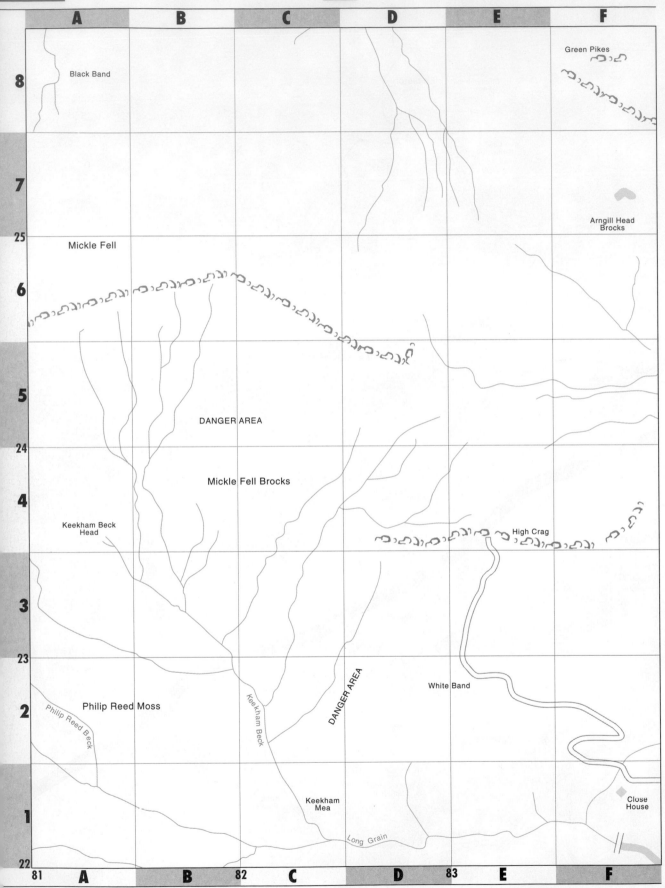

| | A | B | C | D | E | F |

Black Band

Green Pikes

8

7

Arngill Head
Brocks

25

Mickle Fell

6

5

DANGER AREA

24

Mickle Fell Brocks

4

Keekham Beck
Head

High Crag

3

23

White Band

Philip Reed Moss

2

DANGER AREA

Philip Reed Beck

Keekham Beck

Close
House

Keekham
Mea

1

Long Grain

22

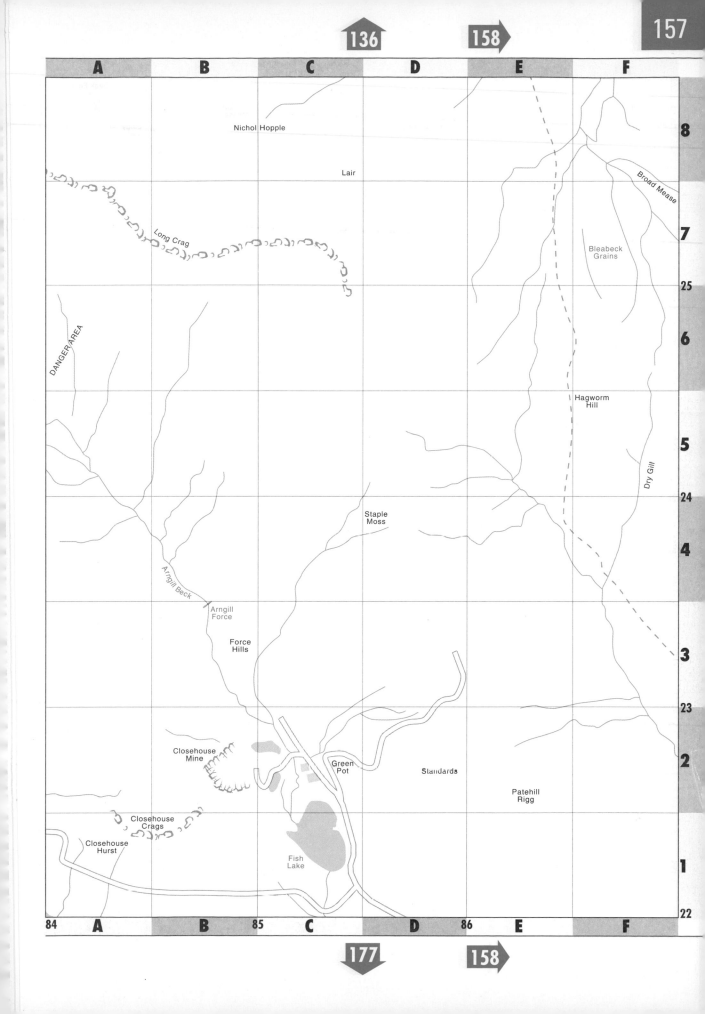

A B C D E F

8

Nichol Hopple

Lair

Broad Mease

7

Long Crag

Bleabeck
Grains

25

DANGER AREA

6

Hagworm
Hill

Dry Gill

5

24

Staple
Moss

4

Arngill Beck

Arngill
Force

23

Force
Hills

Closehouse
Mine

Green
Pot

Standards

2

Patehill
Rigg

Closehouse
Crags

Closehouse
Hurst

Fish
Lake

1

22

84 A B 85 C D 86 E F

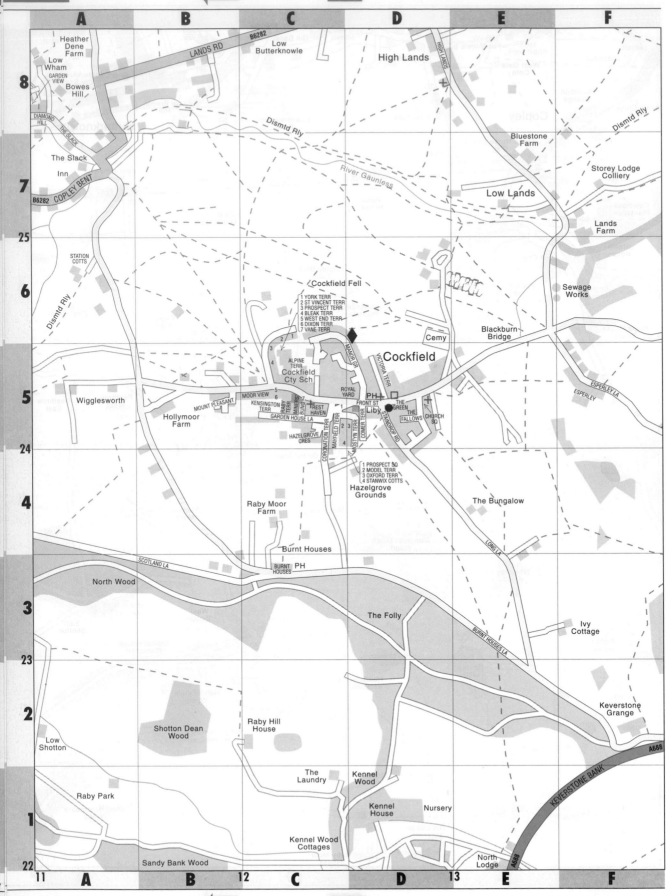

A B C D E F

8

Heather Dene Farm
Low Wham
GARDEN VIEW
Bowes Hill
DIAMOND HILL
THE SLACK

LANDS RD
B6282
Low Butterknowle

High Lands

HIGH LANDS

Dismtd Rly

Bluestone Farm

Dismtd Rly

7

The Slack Inn
B6282
COPLEY BENT

River Gaunless

Low Lands

Storey Lodge Colliery

Lands Farm

25

STATION COTTS

Dismtd Rly

6

Cockfield Fell

1 YORK TERR
2 ST VINCENT TERR
3 PROSPECT TERR
4 BLEAK TERR
5 WEST END TERR
6 DIXON TERR
7 VANE TERR

Cemy

Blackburn Bridge

Sewage Works

5

Wigglesworth

Hollymoor Farm

MOUNT PLEASANT
MOOR VIEW
KENSINGTON TERR
RABY TERR
MINERS BUNGS
GARDEN HOUSE LA
REST HAVEN

ALPINE TERR
Cockfield Cty Sch

MANOR GR

ROYAL YARD

FRONT ST
PH
Liby
THE GREEN
THE FALLOWS
CHURCH SQ

Cockfield

VICTORIA TERR

CORNER TERR

ESPERLEY LA

ESPERLEY

24

HAZELGROVE CRES

CORONATION TERR
MAYFIELD TERR
MOSTYN TERR

STANDROP RD

1 PROSPECT SQ
2 MODEL TERR
3 OXFORD TERR
4 STANWIX COTTS

The Bungalow

4

Raby Moor Farm

Hazelgrove Grounds

LONG LA

Burnt Houses

SCOTLAND LA

BURNT HOUSES
PH

3

North Wood

The Folly

BURNT HOUSES LA

Ivy Cottage

23

2

Shotton Dean Wood

Raby Hill House

Keverstone Grange

Low Shotton

A688

1

Raby Park

The Laundry

Kennel Wood

Kennel House

Nursery

KEVERSTONE BANK

Kennel Wood Cottages

North Lodge

A688

22

Sandy Bank Wood

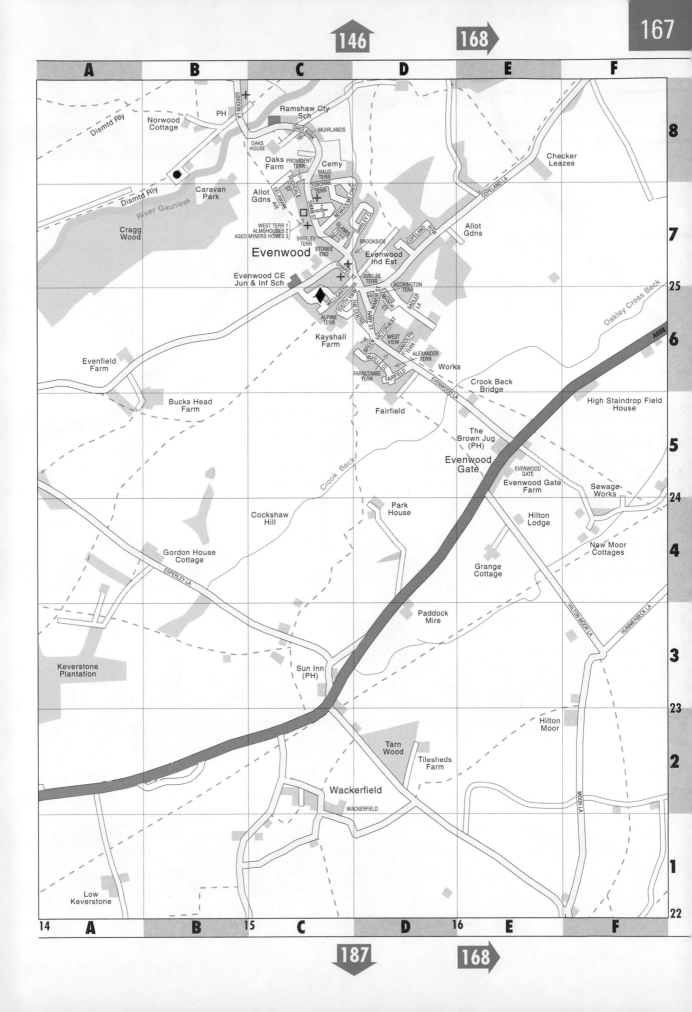

Dismtd Rly
Norwood Cottage
PH
GORDON LA
Ramshaw Cty Sch
MUIRLANDS
OAKS HOUSE
Caravan Park
Dismtd Rly
River Gaunless
Oaks Farm
OAKS BANK
PROVIDENT TERR
Cemy
MAUD TERR
Checker Leazes
Cragg Wood
Allot Gdns
DEANDALE AVE
ROONDALE ST
OSBORNE TERR
NEWHOLME CRES
SWAN ST
SHIRLEY CL
COPELAND LA
WEST TERR 1
ALMSHOUSES 2
AGED MINERS HOMES 3
SHIRLEY TERR
GLAMIS
BROOKSIDE
COPELAND ROW
Allot Gdns
Evenwood
STONES END
Evenwood Ind Est
25
Evenwood CE Jun & Inf Sch
CHAPEL ST
WELLGARTH
JUBILEE TERR
MANOR CT
MANOR ST
ACCRINGTON TERR
SADLER LA
Oakley Cross Beck
SOUTH VIEW
THE CENTRE
HABY ST
ALPINE TERR
A688
Kayshall Farm
VICTORIA ST
WEST VIEW
RANDOLPH TERR
ALEXANDER TERR
6
THE GREEN
NEVILLE CL
FARNCOMBE TERR
FAIRFIELD
Works
Evenfield Farm
Crook Beck Bridge
High Staindrop Field House
Bucks Head Farm
Fairfield
The Brown Jug (PH)
Crook Beck
Evenwood Gate
EVENWOOD LA
5
Evenwood Gate Farm
Sewage Works
24
Cockshaw Hill
Park House
Hilton Lodge
New Moor Cottages
Gordon House Cottage
ESPERLEY LA
Grange Cottage
4
Paddock Mire
HILTON MOOR LA
HUMMERBECK LA
Keverstone Plantation
Sun Inn (PH)
3
23
Hilton Moor
Tarn Wood
Tilesheds Farm
2
Wackerfield
MOOR LA
WACKERFIELD
Low Keverstone
1
22

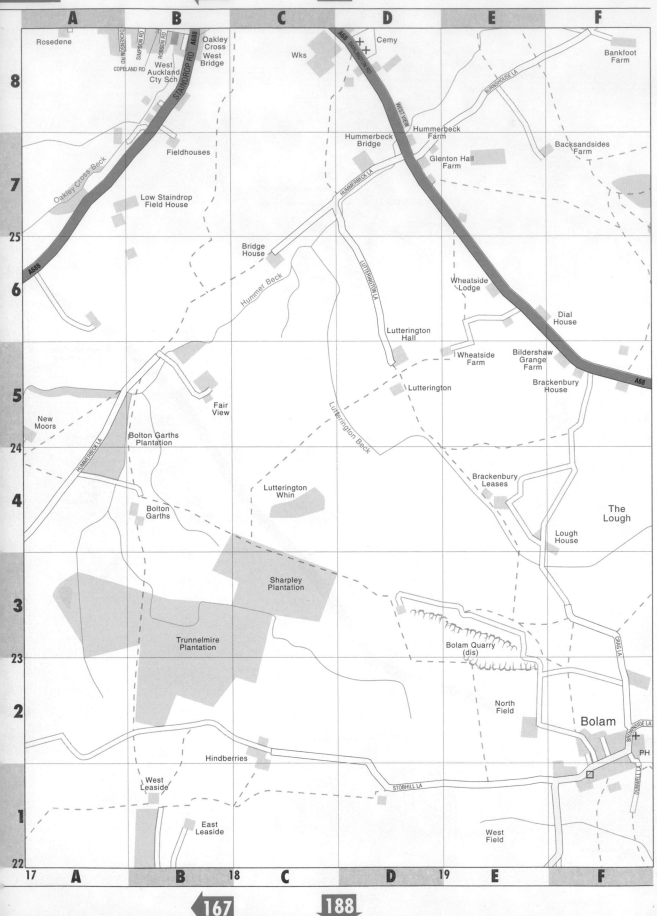

A B C D E F

8

Rosedene

Oakley Cross West Bridge

West Auckland Cty Sch

DICKENSON RD
SIMPSON RD
ROBSON RD
COPELAND RD
STAINDROP RD
A688

Wks

Cemy

A68 DARLINGTON RD

Bankfoot Farm

BURNSHOUSE LA

WEST VIEW

Fieldhouses

Hummerbeck Bridge

Hummerbeck Farm

Backsandsides Farm

7

Oakley Cross Beck

Low Staindrop Field House

HUMMERBECK LA

Glenton Hall Farm

25

A688

Bridge House

Hummer Beck

LUTTERINGTON LA

6

Wheatside Lodge

Dial House

Lutterington Hall

Wheatside Farm

Bildershaw Grange Farm

A68

5

New Moors

Fair View

Lutterington

Brackenbury House

Bolton Garths Plantation

Lutterington Beck

24

HUMMERBECK LA

4

Bolton Garths

Lutterington Whin

Brackenbury Leases

Lough House

The Lough

3

Sharpley Plantation

Bolam Quarry (dis)

23

Trunnelmire Plantation

CRAG LA

2

North Field

Bolam

BROWNSIDE LA

PH

Hindberries

STOBHILL LA

DUNWELL LA

West Leaside

1

East Leaside

West Field

22

17 A 18 B C 18 D 19 E F

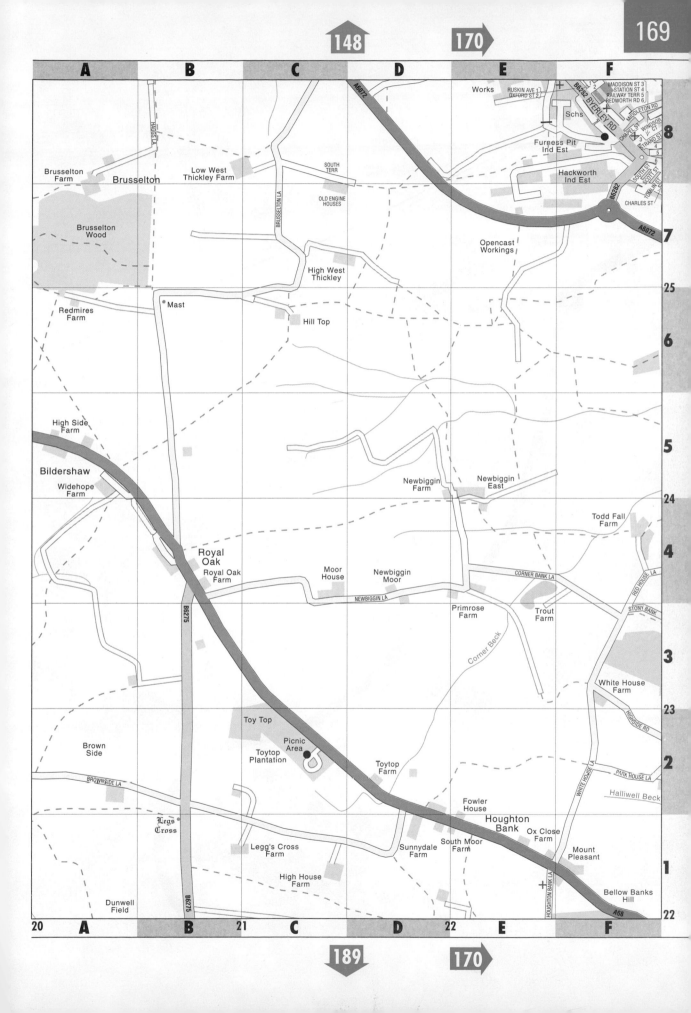

A B C D E F

Works

MADDISON ST 3
STATION ST 4
RAILWAY TERR 5
REDWORTH RD 6
RUSKIN AVE 1
OXFORD ST 2

B6282
BYERLEY RD
MIDDLETON RD

Schs

CHAPEL ST
WINDSOR

8

Furness Pit
Ind Est
STRAND ST

Brusselton
Farm

Brusselton

Low West
Thickley Farm

SOUTH
TERR

Hackworth
Ind Est

SOUTH ST
SCOTT ST
CONLIN ST

CHARLES ST

B6282

Brusselton
Wood

BRUSSELTON LA

OLD ENGINE
HOUSES

A6072

7

Opencast
Workings

A6072

Redmires
Farm

Mast

High West
Thickley

Hill Top

25

6

High Side
Farm

5

Bildershaw

Newbiggin
Farm

Newbiggin
East

Todd Fall
Farm

24

Widehope
Farm

Royal
Oak

Royal Oak
Farm

Moor
House

Newbiggin
Moor

CORNER BANK LA

RED HOUSE LA

STONY BANK

4

NEWBIGGIN LA

Primrose
Farm

Trout
Farm

B6275

Corner Beck

White House
Farm

HIGHSIDE RD

3

23

Brown
Side

Toy Top

Picnic
Area

Toytop
Plantation

Toytop
Farm

WHITE HOUSE LA

PARK HOUSE LA

Halliwell Beck

2

BROWNSIDE LA

Fowler
House

Houghton
Bank

Ox Close
Farm

Legs
Cross

Legg's Cross
Farm

Sunnydale
Farm

South Moor
Farm

Mount
Pleasant

1

High House
Farm

HOUGHTON BANK LA

Bellow Banks
Hill

B6275

Dunwell
Field

A68

22

20 A 21 B C 22 D E F

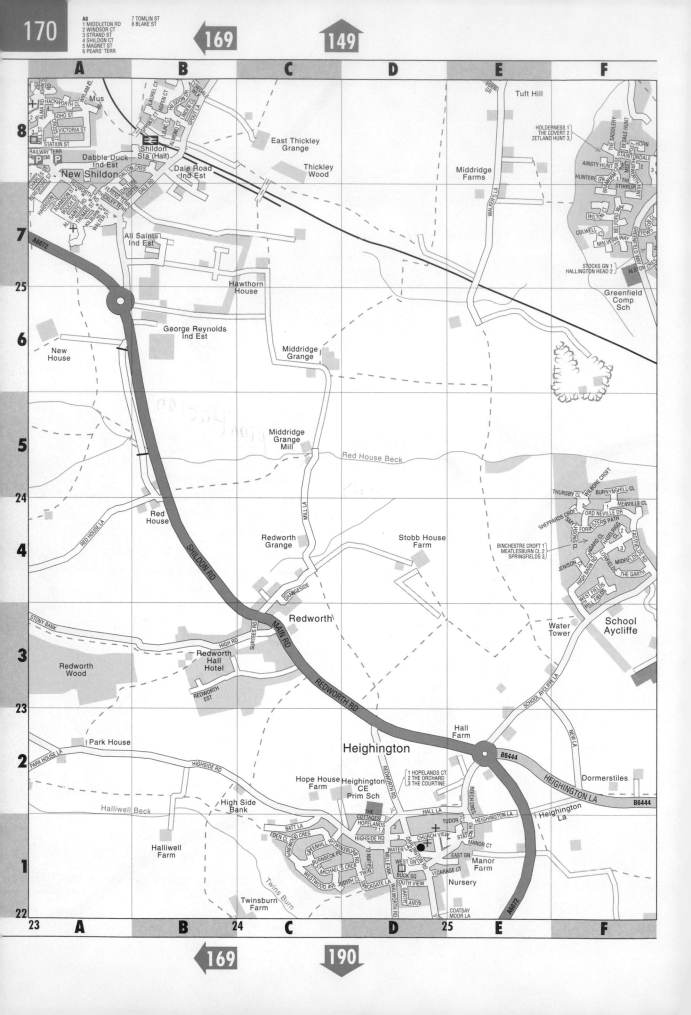

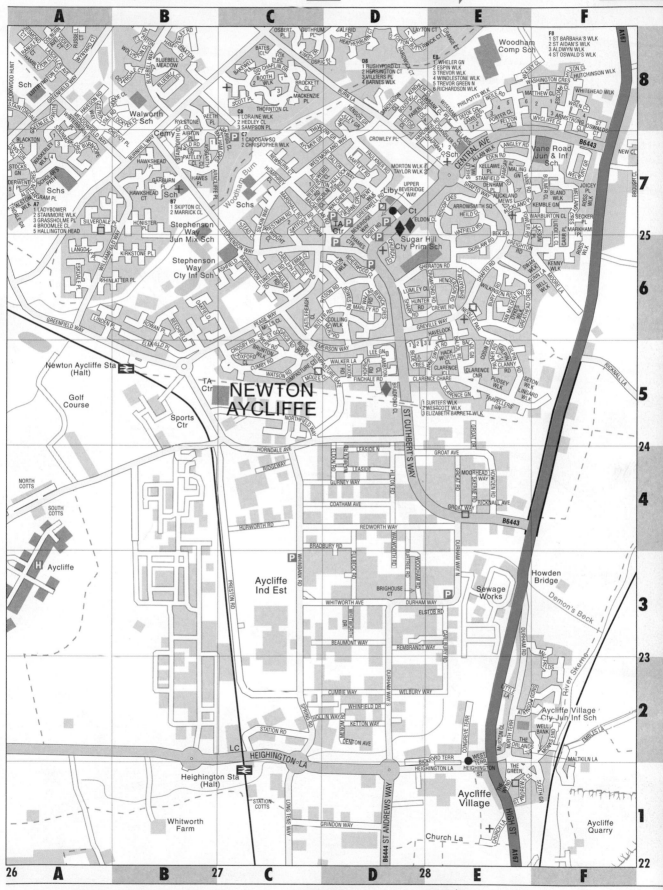

171
151

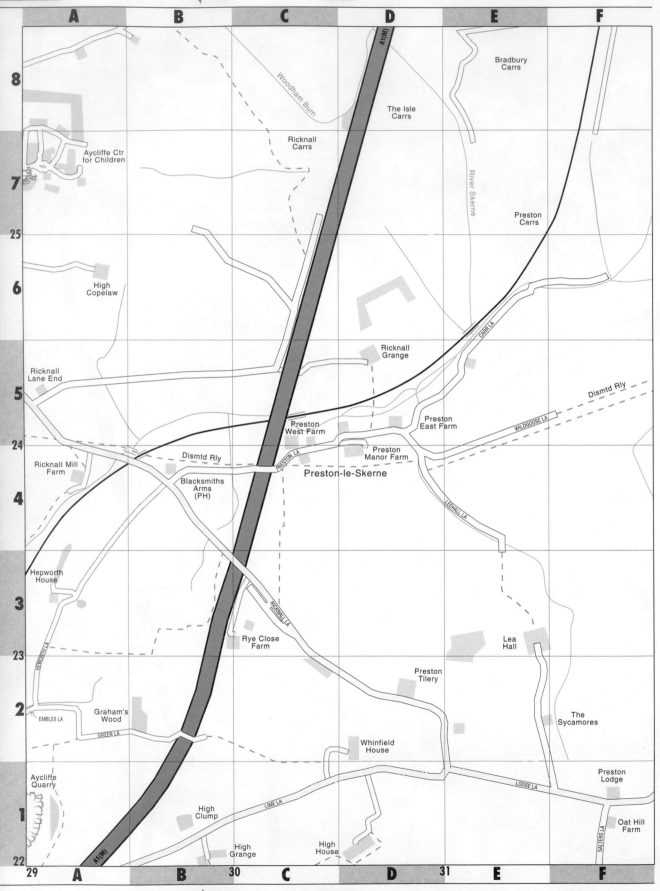

A B C D E F

8

7

25

6

5

24

4

23

3

2

1

22

29 A B 30 C D 31 E F

Bradbury
Carrs

The Isle
Carrs

Woodham Burn

Ricknall
Carrs

River Skerne

Preston
Carrs

Aycliffe Ctr
for Children

BROUGH CT

High
Copelaw

CARR LA

Ricknall
Grange

Dismtd Rly

Ricknall
Lane End

WILDGOOSE LA

Preston
West Farm

Preston
East Farm

Ricknall Mill
Farm

Dismtd Rly

Preston LA

Preston
Manor Farm

Preston-le-Skerne

Blacksmiths
Arms
(PH)

LEEHALL LA

HEWORTH LA

Hepworth
House

RICKNALL LA

Lea
Hall

Rye Close
Farm

Preston
Tilery

23

EMBLES LA

Graham's
Wood

The
Sycamores

GREEN LA

Whinfield
House

LODGE LA

Preston
Lodge

Aycliffe
Quarry

High
Clump

LIME LA

SALTERS LA

Oat Hill
Farm

High
Grange

High
House

A1(M)

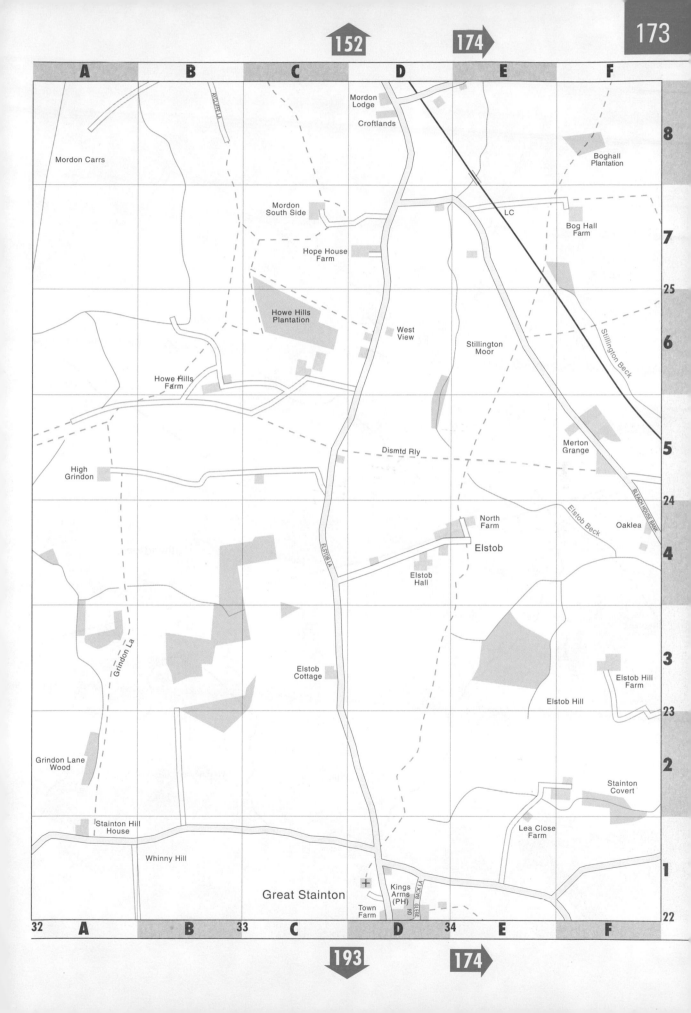

173
153

A B C D E F

8

Foxton
Wood

Shotton Beck

7

Shotton

FOXTON LA

Gilly
Hill

25

Crowdy
Hall

North
Farm

Shotton
Moor

Foxton
Farm

6

Foxton

South
Farm

Rafter Dene

Foxton Beck

5

Whitton
Three Gates

24

Lamb's
Hill

Stillington

William Cassidi
(C of E)
Prim Sch

4

Works

LOWSON ST

MORRISON ST

STILLINGTON
IND EST

Moordale
Bottom

IRONMASTERS WAY

Stillington Beck

P.H.

MESSINES LA

WE CARE GR

BELL
SQ

THE
CROFTS

REDMARSHALL

SOUTH ST

WEST HSE

WILTON
ST

MANOR DR

MANOR
WLK

BLEACH HOUSE BANK

KIRK
ST

APP CRES

3

SOUTH AVE

Bleach House
Bridge

MOUNT
PLEASANT

MOUNT PLEASANT RD

Mount Pleasant
GR

MOUNT
PLEASANT
CL

23

Round
Hill

MOUNT
PLEASANT
WLK

Town
Farm

2

Stillington
Bridge

Old
Stillington

West House
Farm

Mill
Bridge

West
Farm

Bishopton
Mill

Stillington
Foot Bridge

Bishopton Beck

COBBY CASTLE LA

1

MILL LA

22

35 A B 36 C D 37 E F

A   B   C   D   E   F

Old Homer Carr
Plantation

Newlands

Golden
Elders

Woodside

8

Flat Wood

Grindon
Grange

Railway
Cottages

7

Grindon

25

Castle Eden Walkway Country Park

Whitton Moor
Farm

Thorpe
Leazes

Woodside
Farm

Thorpe
Wood

6

DURHAM RD

Station House
Visitor Ctr

Fulthorpe
Garage

5
P

24
BLAKESTON LA

Hell Hole

Hellhole La

Blakeston
Bridge

4

Hall Bank

St James Cl
NORTH

Thorpe Beck

SCHOOL CL
MIDDLE BANK
BANK TERR
WYNARD CT

Thorpe
Thewles

New
Bridge

3

Mill Terr

PH
MANOR COTTS
VICARS CL

New Grange
Farm

HAMILTON CT

A177

23

Townend
Farm

Letch Beck

Evergreen

Whitton

Whitton
House
Farm

Dismtd Rly

2

MILL LA

Carlton
Grange

MILLBANK
TERR

Greystone

HOLMS LA

Sewage
Works

Whitton Beck

Thorntree
Farm

1

THORPE RD
LILAC CL

22

38   A   B   39   C   D   40   E   F

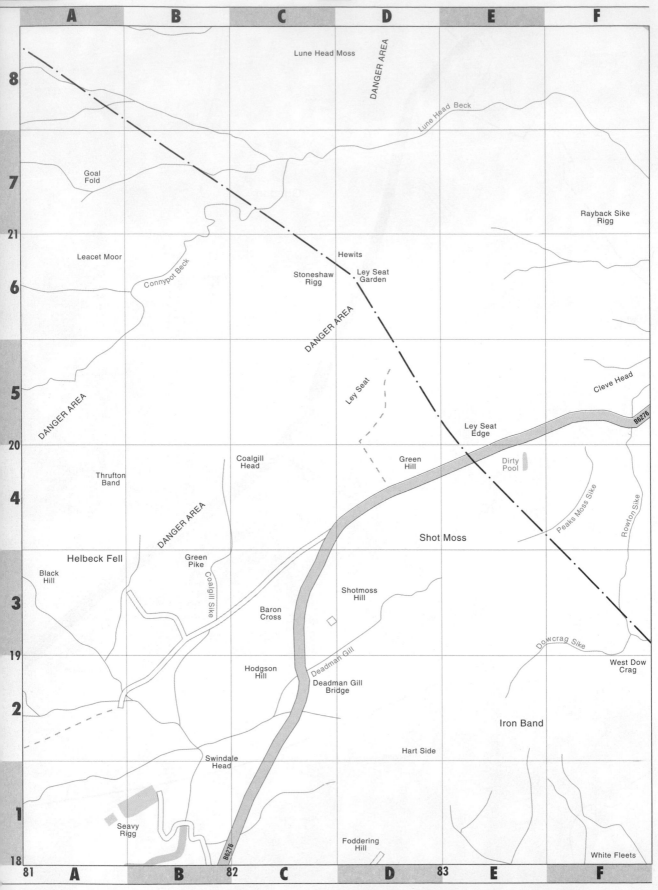

A　　　B　　　C　　　D　　　E　　　F

8

7

21

6

5

20

4

3

19

2

1

18

Lune Head Moss

DANGER AREA

Lune Head Beck

Goal Fold

Rayback Sike Rigg

Leacet Moor

Connypot Beck

Hewits

Stoneshaw Rigg

Ley Seat Garden

DANGER AREA

Ley Seat

Cleve Head

B6276

Ley Seat Edge

Dirty Pool

Green Hill

Coalgill Head

Thrufton Band

DANGER AREA

Peaks Moss Sike

Rowton Sike

DANGER AREA

Shot Moss

Helbeck Fell

Green Pike

Coalgill Sike

Black Hill

Shotmoss Hill

Baron Cross

Dowcrag Sike

Hodgson Hill

Deadman Gill

West Dow Crag

Deadman Gill Bridge

Iron Band

Hart Side

Swindale Head

B6276

Seavy Rigg

Foddering Hill

White Fleets

81　　A　　　B　　82　　C　　　D　　83　　E　　　F

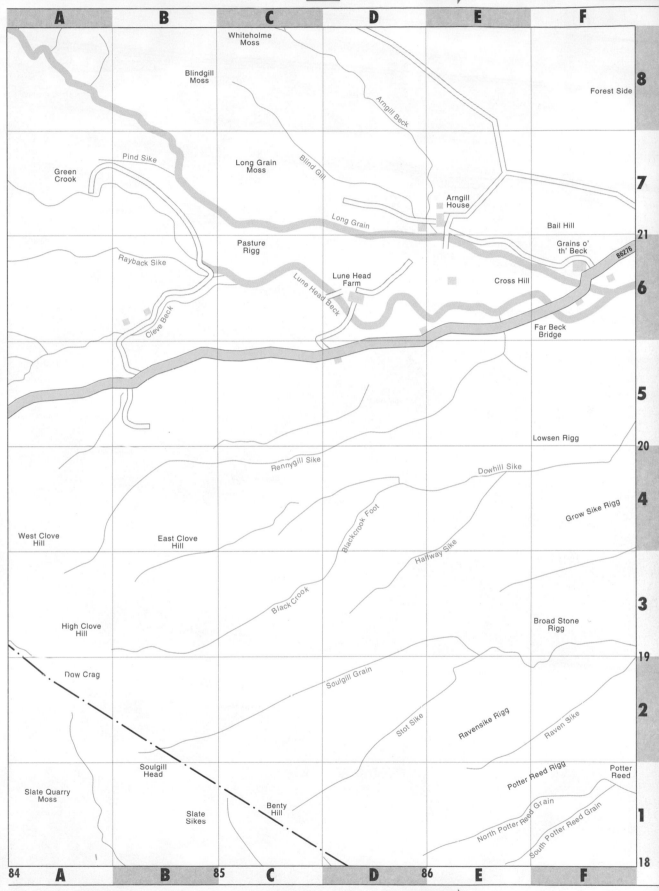

A   B   C   D   E   F

Whiteholme
Moss

Blindgill
Moss

Forest Side

8

Arngill Beck

Pind Sike

Long Grain
Moss

Blind Gill

7

Green
Crook

Arngill
House

Bail Hill

Long Grain

21

Pasture
Rigg

Grains o'
th' Beck

Rayback Sike

Lune Head
Farm

Cross Hill

B6276

6

Cleve Beck

Lune Head Beck

Far Beck
Bridge

5

Lowsen Rigg

20

Rennygill Sike

Dowhill Sike

4

Blackcrook Foot

Grow Sike Rigg

West Clove
Hill

East Clove
Hill

Halfway Sike

Broad Stone
Rigg

3

High Clove
Hill

Black Crook

19

Dow Crag

Soulgill Grain

2

Stot Sike

Ravensike Rigg

Raven Sike

Soulgill
Head

Potter Reed Rigg

Potter
Reed

Slate Quarry
Moss

Slate
Sikes

Benty
Hill

North Potter Reed Grain

South Potter Reed Grain

1

18

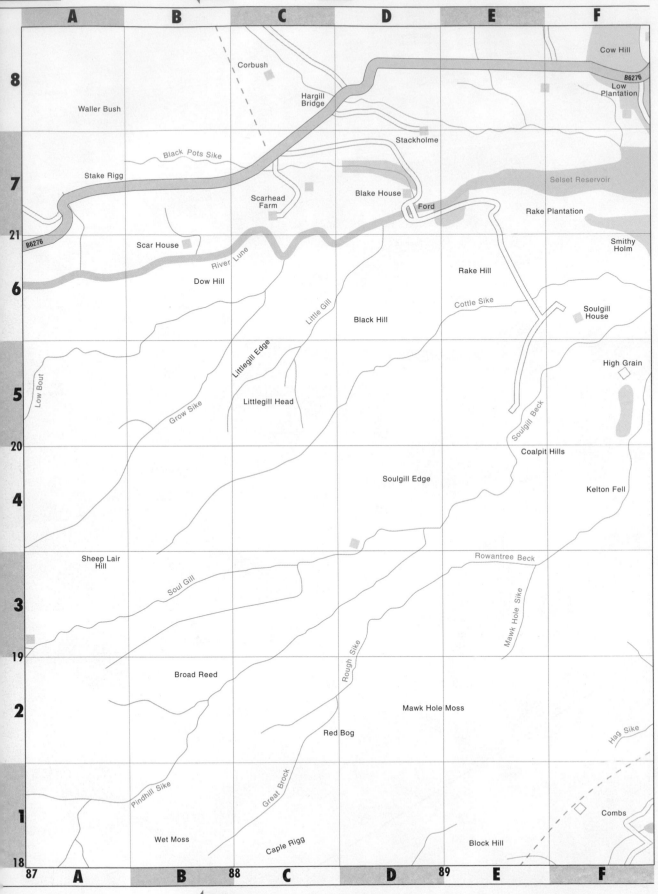

A B C D E F

8

Cow Hill

Corbush

Waller Bush

Hargill Bridge

B6276

Low Plantation

Stackholme

Black Pots Sike

Selset Reservoir

7

Stake Rigg

Scarhead Farm

Blake House

Ford

Rake Plantation

21

B6276

Scar House

River Lune

Smithy Holm

Dow Hill

Rake Hill

6

Cottle Sike

Soulgill House

Little Gill

Black Hill

Low Bout

Littlegill Edge

High Grain

5

Grow Sike

Littlegill Head

Soulgill Beck

20

Coalpit Hills

Soulgill Edge

4

Kelton Fell

Rowantree Beck

Sheep Lair Hill

Soul Gill

Mawk Hole Sike

3

Rough Sike

19

Broad Reed

2

Mawk Hole Moss

Hag Sike

Red Bog

Pindhill Sike

Great Brock

1

Combs

Wet Moss

Block Hill

Caple Rigg

18

87 A B 88 C D 89 E F

A B C D E F

B6276

Cop Top

Sleights
Pasture

Brown Rigg

GRASSHOLME LA

Grassholme
Farm

8

Wemmergill Hall
Farm

Low
Selset

Grassholme

P

Grassholme
Resr

Selset Resr

Selset
Weir

KELTON LA

Lunedale
How

7

Sun Plantation

Whey Sike

21

Knowle
House

Hunter
House

Beck
Head

6

Green Gill

Kelton

Lane
Head

Pennine Way

Bella
House

Three
Chimneys

Kelton
Bottom

5

Locks

Mickleton Moor

20

Well Rigg

Black Hill

Kelton Hill

4

White Hill

Foul Sike Gill

Hard Rigg

Black Hill

Cock Lake

East Carni Gill

West Hunder

Hunder Sike

3

Hunderthwaite Moor

19

Mea Sike

P

West
Carnigill

East
Carnigill

Foul Sike
Farm

Primrose Hill

Sleetburn
Farm

Club
House

P

2

Balderhead Resr

Wether
Hill

1

Broad Shaw

Blea Gill

Overflow
Basin

18

90 A B 91 C D 92 E F

179
160

A   **B**   **C**   **D**   **E**   **F**

8

Grassholme Resr

Easter Beck

Swarthy Top

Wester Beck

Millstone Grits

Harker Springs

Harker Hill

GRASSHOLME LA

7

KELTON LA

Botany

BOTANY RD

Brownberry

21

6

Brownberry Moss

Howgill Head

Howgill Grange

Kelton Moss

How Gill

5

Great Moss

Blake Hill

Howgill Bridge

Hury

20

Bull Hill

Bullhill Sike

Rokehole Sike

4

Roke Hole

Hill Gill Farm

Brier Dykes

Acre Sike

Hillgill Plantation

3

Hazelgarth Rigg

Totter Bank

Hillgill Bridge

East New Houses

Hury Resr

East Hunder

West New Houses

Low New Houses

19

Needless Bridge

Blind Beck

Birk Hat Hills

Blackton House

Willoughby Hall

2

Blind Beck

Pennine Way

High Birk Hat

Blackton Resr

Pitcher House

Birk Hat

1

Blackton Bridge

River Balder

Mere Beck

East Friar House

Bleak Rigg

18

179
197

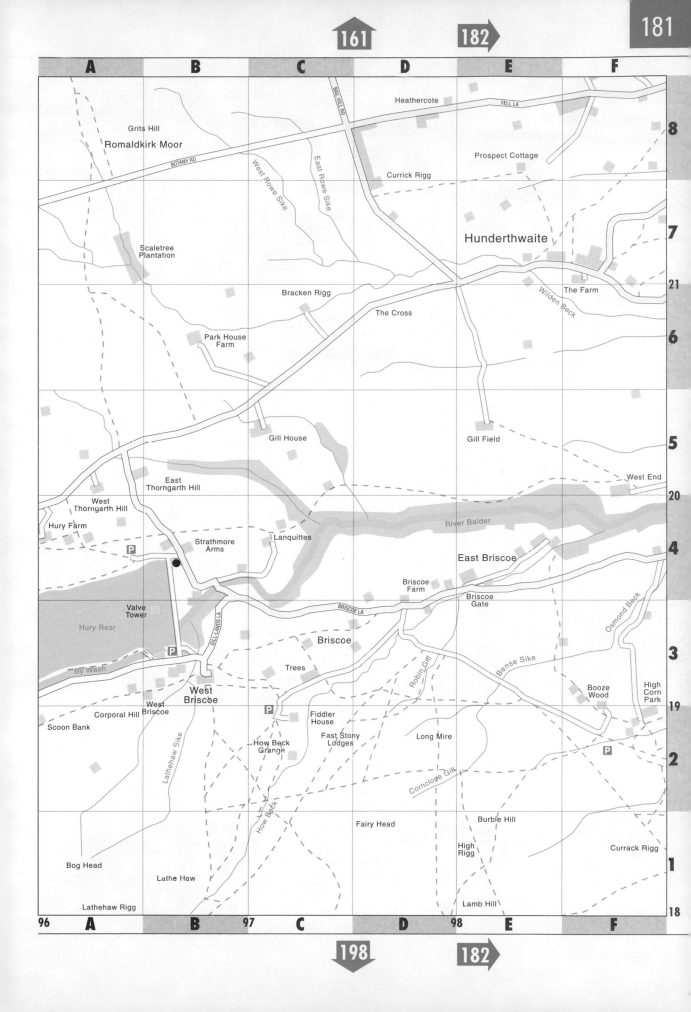

161
182

A   B   C   D   E   F

Heathercote

FELL LA

Grits Hill

8

Romaldkirk Moor

BOTANY RD

Prospect Cottage

West Rowe Sike

East Rowe Sike

BALL HILL RD

Currick Rigg

Hunderthwaite

7

Scaletree
Plantation

21

Wilden Beck

The Farm

Bracken Rigg

6

The Cross

Park House
Farm

Gill House

Gill Field

5

East
Thorngarth Hill

West End

20

West
Thorngarth Hill

River Balder

Hury Farm

Strathmore
Arms

Lanquittes

East Briscoe

4

Valve
Tower

Briscoe
Farm

Briscoe
Gate

Osmond Beck

Hury Resr

BRISCOE LA

Briscoe

Bense Sike

Booze
Wood

High
Corn
Park

3

By Wash

Trees

Robin Gill

GILL LANDS LA

West
Briscoe

West
Briscoe

Corporal Hill

Fiddler
House

Long Mire

19

Scoon Bank

How Beck
Grange

East Stony
Lodges

Cornclose Gill

2

Lathehaw Sike

How Beck

Fairy Head

Burble Hill

Currack Rigg

Bog Head

High
Rigg

1

Lathe Haw

Lamb Hill

Lathehaw Rigg

18

198
182

181
162

A **B** **C** **D** **E** **F**

FELL LA
B6277
B6278

8

HOLLIN CRES

Great Wood

Raygill Beck

High Shipley

Low Garth

Wildon Grange

7

Phillis Wood

Teesdale Way

21

Hard Ings

Dismtd Rly

HARDINGS

Gueswick Hills

Shipley Wood

Quarryhouse Farm

Woden Croft

River Tees

6

Buck Hill

Wilden Beck

Wilden Wood

Teesdale Way

Wilden Bridge

5

River Balder

Doe Park

SPOUT BANK

Thwaite Hall

Low Shipley

Balder Bridge

20

West Park

Balder Grange

Hallgarth Hill

Osmond Bridge

SHIPLEY TERR

4

CROFT VIEW

PH

NICHOLSON TERR

DEMESNE LA

North Corn Park

SUNNYVIEW COTTS

Cotherstone Cty Jun & Inf Sch

Corn Park

Scalehow Rigg

Cotherstone

MIRE LA

3

Bonny Hill

East Corn Park

MARWOOD VIEW

HUGH CT

Cemy

GREENFIELDS

MARWOOD TERR

Lancelands

THE CLOSE

Lance Beck

Cuckoo

Crookbeck House

Dismtd Rly

STATION TERR

19

Crook Beck

Lance Bridge

Durble Beck

2

Common Sike

Casset How

Mense House

Butter Stone

Works

1

Works

Waskey Wood

Spring Wood

B6277

18

Naby

NABY LA

99   **A**   **B**   00   **C**   **D**   01   **E**   **F**

181
199

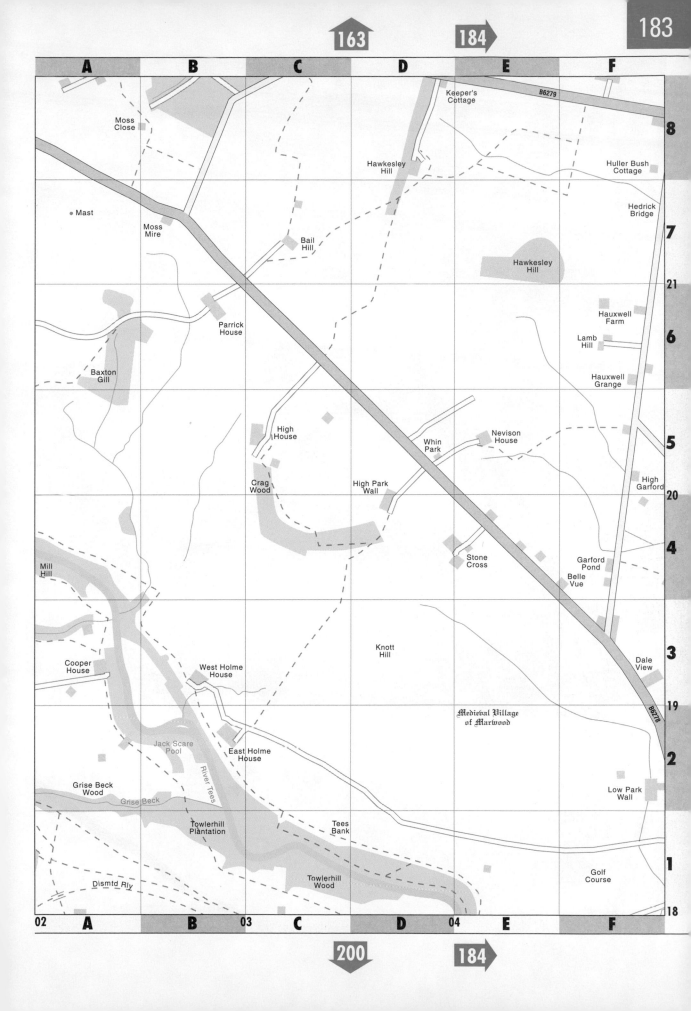

Moss
Close

Keeper's
Cottage

B6279

Huller Bush
Cottage

8

Hawkesley
Hill

Hedrick
Bridge

Mast

Moss
Mire

Bail
Hill

7

Hawkesley
Hill

21

Hauxwell
Farm

Parrick
House

Lamb
Hill

6

Baxton
Gill

Hauxwell
Grange

High
House

Whin
Park

Nevison
House

5

Crag
Wood

High Park
Wall

High
Garford

20

Stone
Cross

Garford
Pond

4

Mill
Hill

Belle
Vue

Cooper
House

Knott
Hill

Dale
View

3

B6278

West Holme
House

19

Medieval Village
of Marwood

Jack Scare
Pool

East Holme
House

2

Grise Beck
Wood

Grise Beck

River Tees

Towlerhill
Plantation

Low Park
Wall

Tees
Bank

Golf
Course

1

Towlerhill
Wood

Dismtd Rly

18

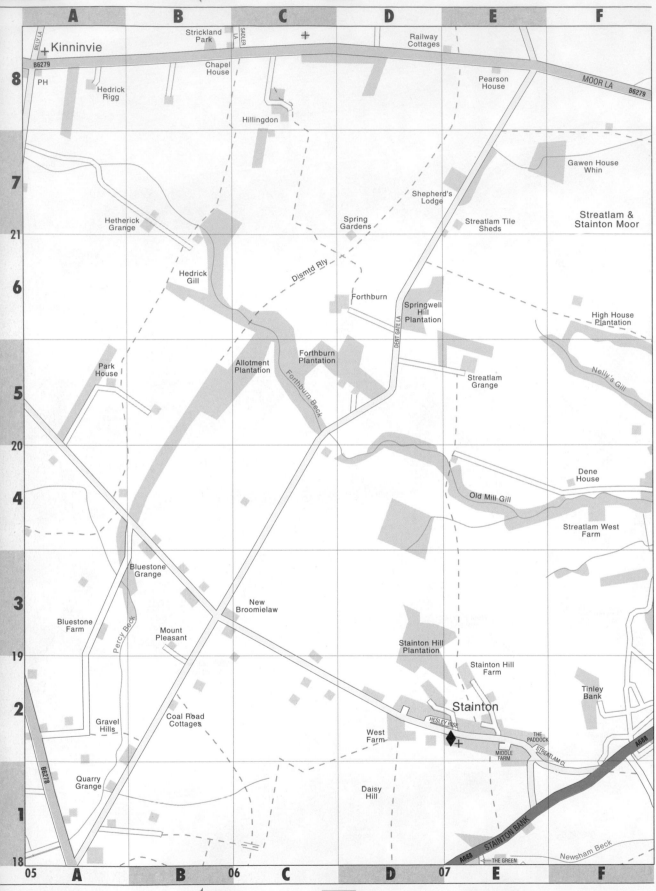

Kinninvie

Strickland Park

Railway Cottages

B6279

PH

Hedrick Rigg

Chapel House

Hillingdon

Pearson House

MOOR LA

B6279

8

Gawen House Whin

Hetherick Grange

7

Shepherd's Lodge

Spring Gardens

Streatlam Tile Sheds

Streatlam & Stainton Moor

21

Dismtd Rly

Hedrick Gill

6

Forthburn

Springwell Hill Plantation

High House Plantation

Nelly's Gill

Allotment Plantation

Forthburn Plantation

Forthburn Beck

DENT GATE LA

Streatlam Grange

Park House

5

20

Old Mill Gill

Dene House

4

Streatlam West Farm

Bluestone Grange

Percy Beck

3

New Broomielaw

Stainton Hill Plantation

19

Bluestone Farm

Mount Pleasant

Stainton Hill Farm

Tinley Bank

2

Gravel Hills

Coal Road Cottages

Stainton

HESLEY RISE

West Farm

THE PADDOCK

STREATLAM CL

A688

B6278

Quarry Grange

MIDDLE FARM

Daisy Hill

STAINTON BANK

1

A688

THE GREEN

Newsham Beck

18

165
186
202
186

A **B** **C** **D** **E** **F**

Raby Home Farm

8

Langley Beck

West Bulrush Wood

Raby Moor House

West Farm

Ladyclose Wood

7

Gawen House

Bolton Hill

M O O R   L A

21

Bolton Hill Plantation

West Lodge

6

Friars' Cote House

Staindrop Moor

Moor Beck

Blakeley

B6279

Friars' Cote Gill

Scaife House

High House

Ford

5

East Fog Close

SNOTTERTON LA

Stud Farm

North Drive Clump

20

Streatlam Grove

Snotterton Hall

4

Ford

Woodend Farm

Sudburn Beck

Forthburn Beck

Streatlam Park

Dunn House Farm

3

Sewage Works

Great Wood

Dun House Wood

A688

Streatlam Home Farm

19

Oak Lea

CLEATLAM BACK LA

East Lodge

Ralston House

2

Lodge Plantation

Picnic Area

Depot

South View

High Barford

Barford Camp

1

Broomielaw

Newsham Beck

18

08 **A** **B** 09 **C** **D** 10 **E** **F**

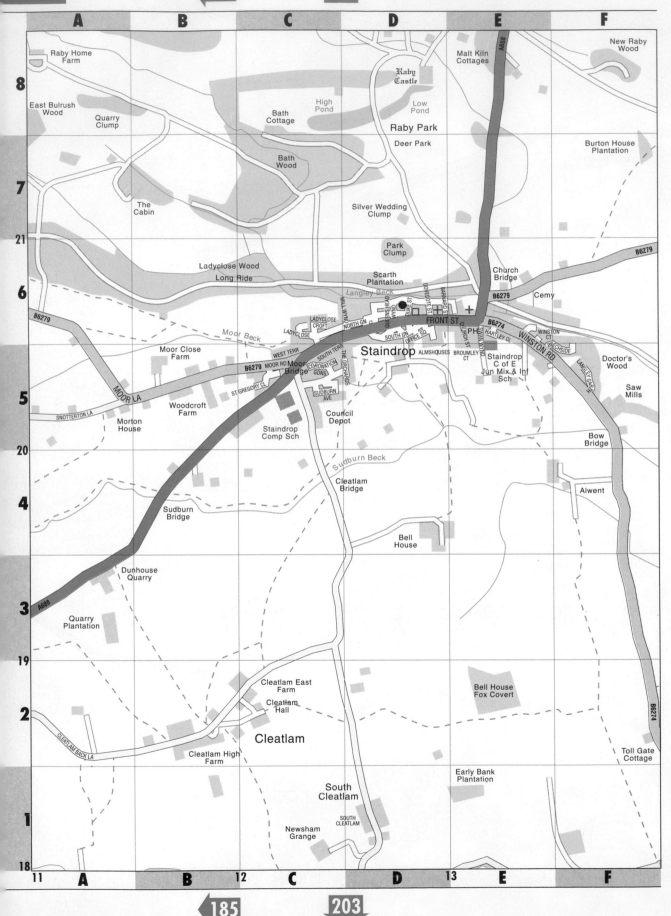

A B C D E F

8

Raby Home Farm

East Bulrush Wood

Quarry Clump

Bath Cottage

High Pond

Raby Castle

Low Pond

Malt Kiln Cottages

New Raby Wood

A688

7

The Cabin

Bath Wood

Raby Park

Deer Park

Burton House Plantation

21

Silver Wedding Clump

6

Ladyclose Wood

Long Ride

Park Clump

Scarth Plantation

Langley Beck

Church Bridge

B6279

Cemy

B6279

Moor Beck

MILL WYND

QUEENS HEAD WYND

DUKE ST

BARNARD ST

DOVECOTE ST

CHURCH ST

SWAN WYND

FRONT ST

B6274

WINSTON CT

BEECHSIDE

WINSTON RD

Moor Close Farm

Ladyclose Croft

Ladyclose

NORTH GN

SOUTH GN

OFFICE SQ

Staindrop

Almshouses

PH

Staindrop C of E Jun Mix & Inf Sch

BROUMLEY CT

HARTLEY CL

LANGLEY BECK

Doctor's Wood

WEST TERR

SOUTH TERR

CORONATION GDNS

THE ORCHARDS

B6279 Moor RD Moor Bridge

MOOR LA

St GREGORY CL

SUDBURN AVE

Saw Mills

5

SNOTTERTON LA

Woodcroft Farm

Morton House

Staindrop Comp Sch

Council Depot

Bow Bridge

20

Sudburn Beck

Cleatlam Bridge

Alwent

4

Sudburn Bridge

Bell House

Dunhouse Quarry

A688

3

Quarry Plantation

19

Cleatlam East Farm

Cleatlam Hall

Bell House Fox Covert

B6274

2

CLEATLAM BACK LA

Cleatlam

Cleatlam High Farm

South Cleatlam

Early Bank Plantation

Toll Gate Cottage

1

Newsham Grange

SOUTH CLEATLAM

18

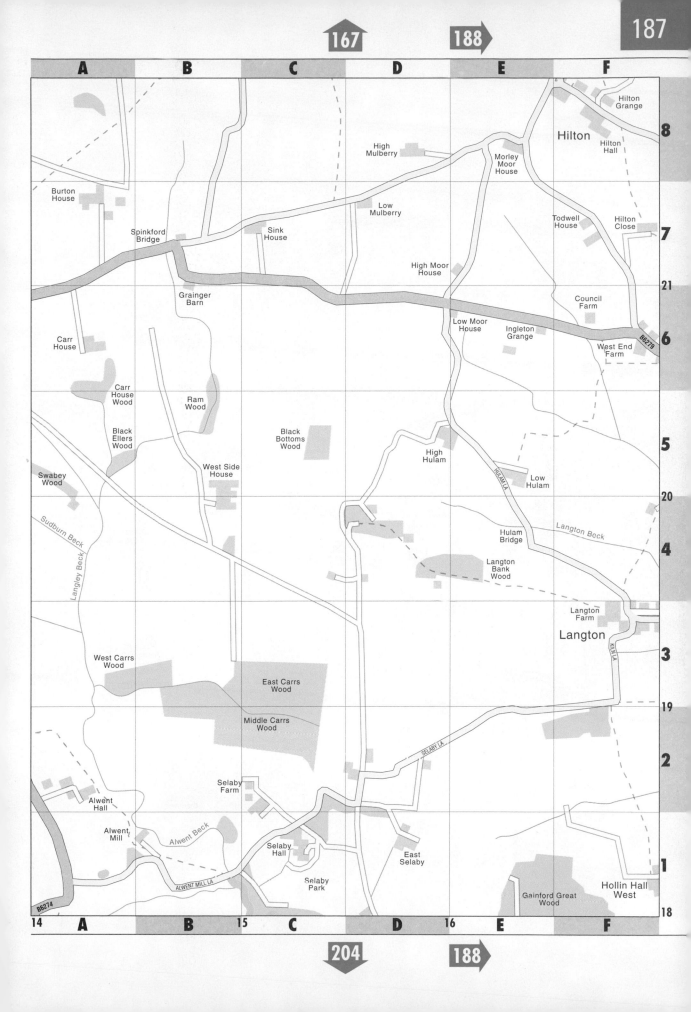

167
188

A   B   C   D   E   F

8

Hilton

Hilton
Grange

Burton
House

High
Mulberry

Morley
Moor
House

Hilton
Hall

Low
Mulberry

Todwell
House

Hilton
Close

7

Spinkford
Bridge

Sink
House

High Moor
House

21

Grainger
Barn

Low Moor
House

Ingleton
Grange

Council
Farm

Carr
House

West End
Farm

B6279

6

Carr
House
Wood

Ram
Wood

Black
Bottoms
Wood

High
Hulam

Low
Hulam

HULAM LA

5

Black
Ellers
Wood

West Side
House

20

Swabey
Wood

Hulam
Bridge

Langton Beck

Langton
Bank
Wood

4

Sudburn Beck

Langley Beck

West Carrs
Wood

Langton
Farm

Langton

KILN LA

3

East Carrs
Wood

19

Middle Carrs
Wood

Selaby
Farm

SELABY LA

2

Alwent
Hall

Alwent
Mill

Alwent Beck

Selaby
Hall

East
Selaby

1

B6274

ALWENT MILL LA

Selaby
Park

Gainford Great
Wood

Hollin Hall
West

18

14   A   15   B   C   15   D   16   E   F

204
188

187
168

A B C D E F

8

Hilton
Plantation

Quarry
House

Morton
Heads

Morton
Tinmouth

7

Hilton
Whin

West
Farm

East
Farm

21

6

Black Horse
(PH)

MANOR
COTTS

SCHOOL
HOUSES

B6279

MANOR RD

SPRINGWELL

HILLSIDE

CHURCH VIEW

THE GARTH

CHURCH
ROW

RANSON CT

FRONT ST

GAINFORD RD

Ingleton C of E
Controlled
Sch

Ingleton

Killerby Beck

KILN LA

5

The
Mill

New House
Farm

Killerby Hall
Farm

NORTH LA

Woodside

20

Middleton
House

Morley
Hill

Killerby
Garths

Killerby

4

Langton

LANGTON

Langton Beck

CAKESMIRE LA

Killerby
Bridge

B6279

3

BACK LA

THE GREEN

19

Headlam

2

Ford Dike
Bridge

Ford Dike

FORD DIKE LA

RIGG HEAD

Headlam
Hall

Headlam Beck

Dyance
Plantation

1

Hollin Hall
East

COCK LA

Hillhouse
Hill

Dyance
Bridge

Dyance Beck

Dyance Bottom

18

17 A 18 B C D 19 E F

189
170

A B C D E F

8 Elm Grange
Westholme
Page Farm
Deneville
Broom Dykes North
Dene Bridge Farm
Dene Bridge

7 Cock Inn Farm
Burrell Moor
CROSS LANES
The Dog (PH)

21 Walworth Moor Farm
Coatsay Moor
New House Farm
Dene Beck

6 Grimshaw Cottage

Greystones

5 Cowfold Farm
COWFOLD LA
Walworth Gate
Ivy Cottage
WEST AUCKLAND RD
A6072

20 Throstle Nest
Cowfold Plantation

4 New Moor Farm
Throstle Nest Plantation
Swan House Farm
WEST AUCKLAND RD

Silver Hill
BACK LA
Silverhill Plantation
Humbleton Farm

3 North Farm

19 The Rookery
Coldsides

2 Walworth
Walworth Grange
Peel Acres
Weezey Hill

1 Walworth Park
Cuckoo House
NEWTON LA

18

23 A B 24 C D 25 E F

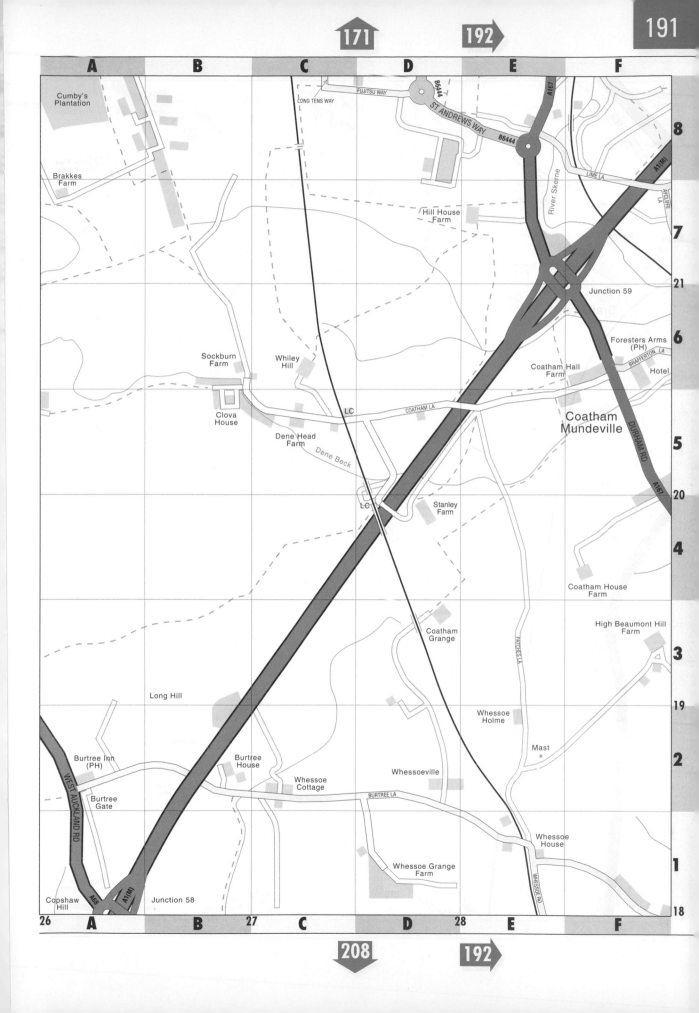

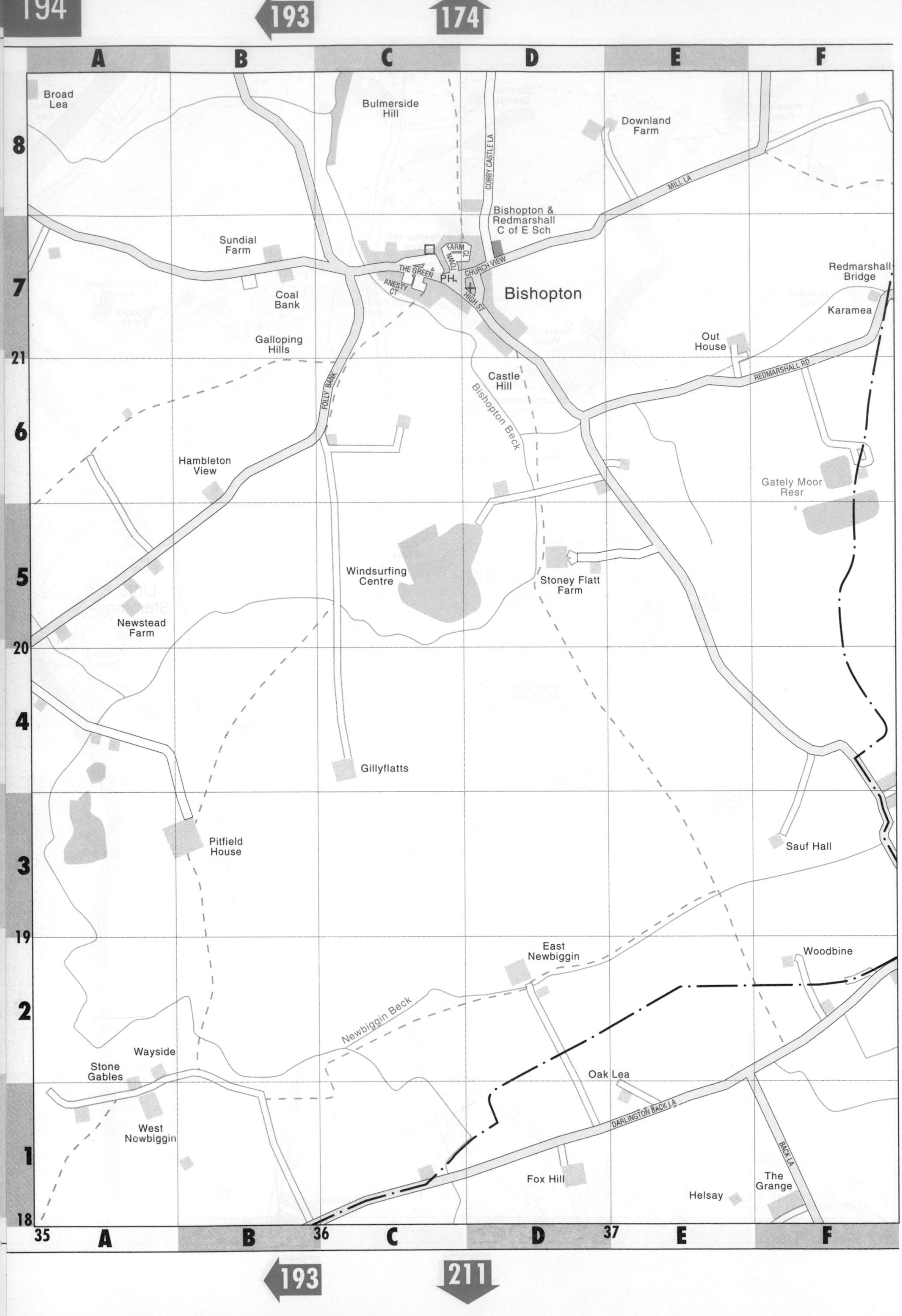
193
174
A
B
C
D
E
F
Broad Lea
Bulmerside Hill
Downland Farm
COBBY CASTLE LA
MILL LA
Bishopton & Redmarshall C of E Sch
Sundial Farm
FARM CT
TOWN
THE GREEN
PH
CHURCH VIEW
ANESTY CT
HIGH ST
Bishopton
Coal Bank
Redmarshall Bridge
Karamea
Galloping Hills
Out House
REDMARSHALL RD
Castle Hill
FOLLY BANK
Bishopton Beck
Hambleton View
Gately Moor Resr
Windsurfing Centre
Stoney Flatt Farm
Newstead Farm
Gillyflatts
Pitfield House
Sauf Hall
East Newbiggin
Woodbine
Newbiggin Beck
Wayside
Stone Gables
Oak Lea
DARLINGTON BACK LA
West Newbiggin
BACK LA
Fox Hill
The Grange
Helsay
8
7
21
6
5
20
4
3
19
2
1
18
35
36
37
193
211

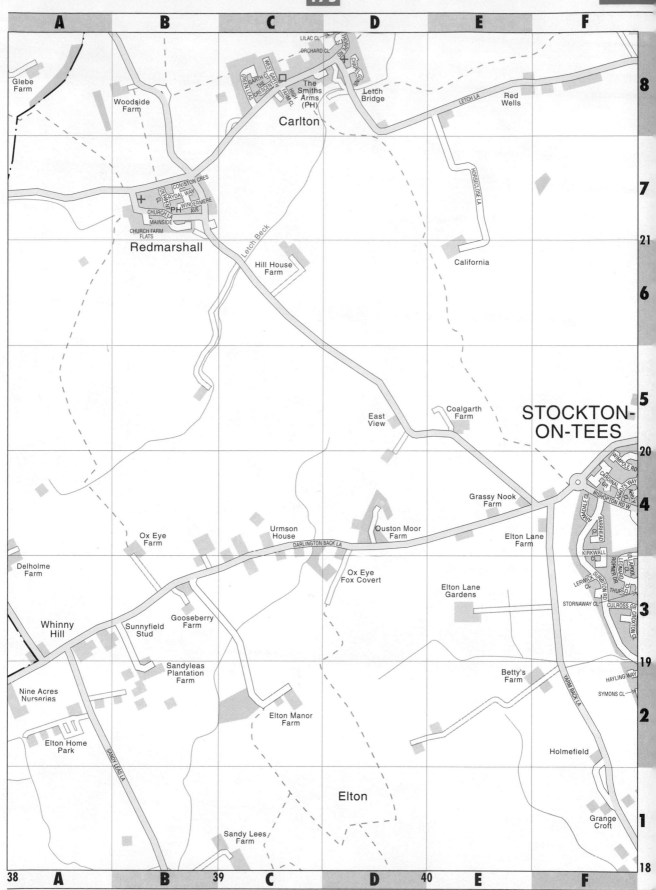

Glebe Farm

Woodside Farm

Carlton

LILAC CL
ORCHARD CL
THE GREEN LEAS
WEST GARTH
THE CRESCENT
GARTH
HIGH FARM CL
The Smiths Arms (PH)
Letch Bridge
CHAPEL GDNS
THORPE LA BK

LETCH LA
Red Wells

HORSECLOSE LA

CONISTON CRES
RYDAL WAY
DERWENT CL
PH
WINDERMERE AVE
CHURCH LA
MAINSIDE
CHURCH FARM FLATS
Redmarshall

Letch Beck

Hill House Farm

California

East View

Coalgarth Farm

STOCKTON-ON-TEES

WIMPOLE RD
CARDINAL GR
ABBEY GR
ST IVES WAY
BISHOPTON RD W
ARMDALE CL
BARRHEAD
ULLAPOOL
LEONARD
ROPNER DR
THURSO
KIRKWALL CL
LERWICK CL
SURBITON RD
STORNAWAY CL
CULROSS GR
CROXTON CL

Grassy Nook Farm

Elton Lane Farm

Ox Eye Farm

Urmson House

DARLINGTON BACK LA

Ouston Moor Farm

Delholme Farm

Ox Eye Fox Covert

Elton Lane Gardens

Whinny Hill

Sunnyfield Stud

Gooseberry Farm

Sandyleas Plantation Farm

Betty's Farm

HAYLING WAY
SYMONS CL

Nine Acres Nurseries

YARM BACK LA

Holmefield

Elton Home Park

SANDY LEAS LA

Elton Manor Farm

Elton

Grange Croft

Sandy Lees Farm

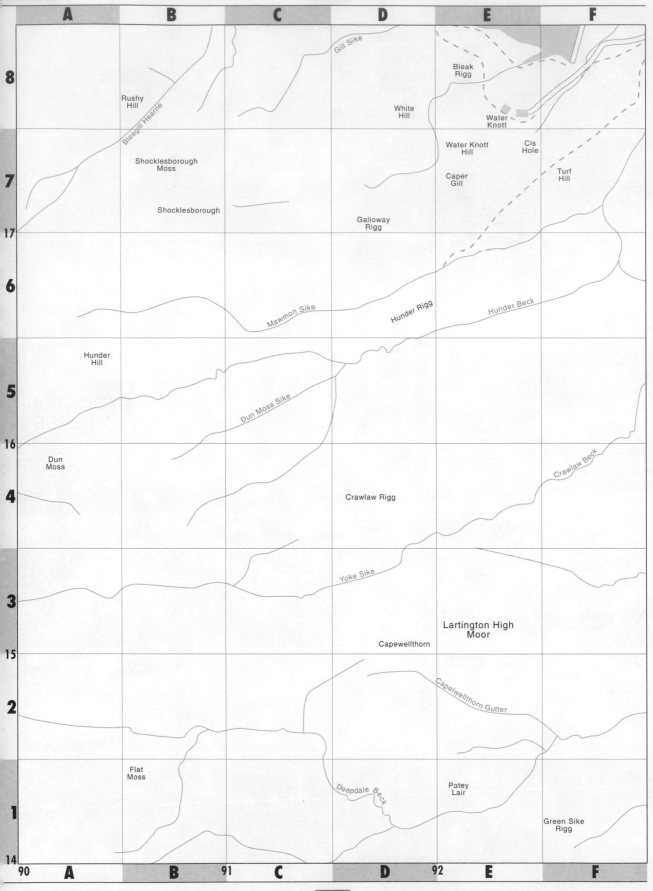

A   B   C   D   E   F

8

Rushy
Hill

Gill Sike

Bleak
Rigg

White
Hill

Water
Knott

Bleagill Hearne

Shocklesborough
Moss

Water Knott
Hill

Cis
Hole

7

Shocklesborough

Caper
Gill

Turf
Hill

17

Galloway
Rigg

6

Mawmon Sike

Hunder Rigg

Hunder Beck

Hunder
Hill

5

Dun Moss Sike

16

Dun
Moss

Crawlaw Beck

4

Crawlaw Rigg

3

Yoke Sike

Lartington High
Moor

Capewellthorn

15

Capelwellthorn Gutter

2

Flat
Moss

Deepdale Beck

Patey
Lair

1

Green Sike
Rigg

14

90   A   B   91   C   D   92   E   F

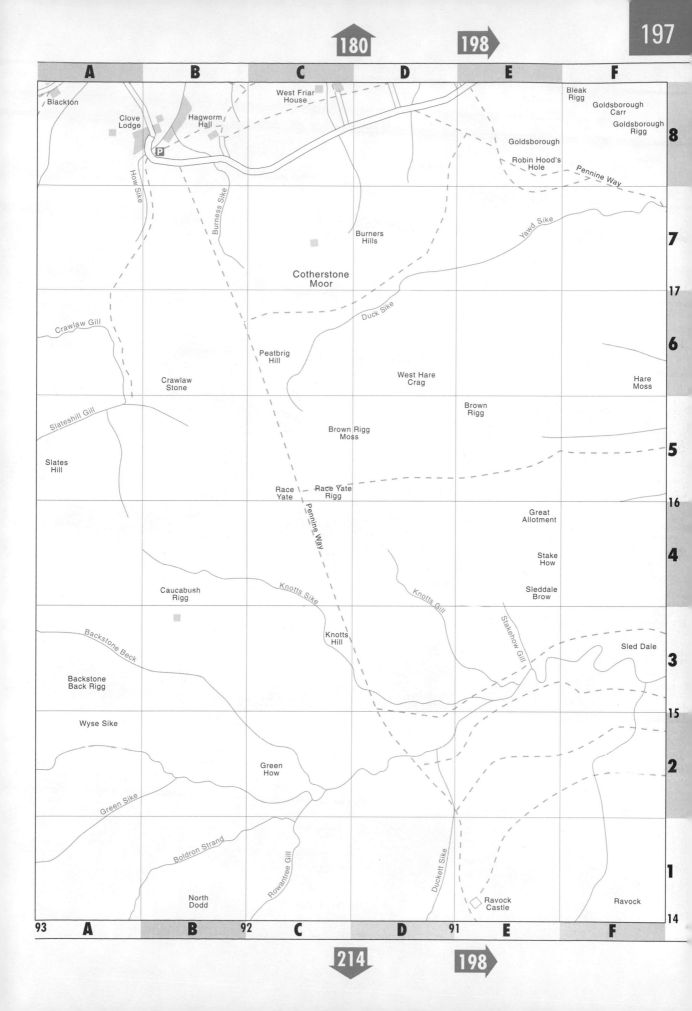

A B C D E F

8

7

17

6

5

16

4

15

3

2

1

14

Blackton
Clove Lodge
Hagworm Hall
West Friar House
How Sike
Burness Sike
Burners Hills
Cotherstone Moor
Bleak Rigg
Goldsborough Carr
Goldsborough Rigg
Goldsborough
Robin Hood's Hole
Pennine Way
Yawd Sike
Crawlaw Gill
Duck Sike
Peatbrig Hill
West Hare Crag
Hare Moss
Crawlaw Stone
Brown Rigg
Slateshill Gill
Brown Rigg Moss
Slates Hill
Race Yate
Race Yate Rigg
Great Allotment
Pennine Way
Stake How
Sleddale Brow
Caucabush Rigg
Knotts Sike
Knotts Gill
Stakehow Gill
Sled Dale
Backstone Beck
Knotts Hill
Backstone Back Rigg
Wyse Sike
Green How
Green Sike
Boldron Strand
Rowantree Gill
Duckett Sike
Ravock Castle
Ravock
North Dodd

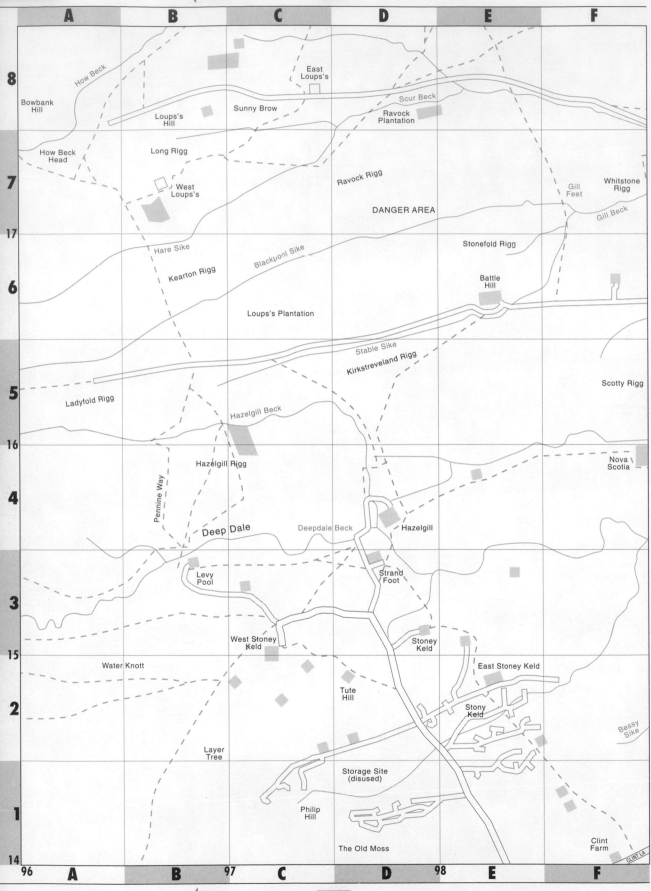

A B C D E F

8

Bowbank
Hill

How Beck

Loups's
Hill

East
Loups's

Sunny Brow

Scur Beck

Ravock
Plantation

How Beck
Head

Long Rigg

West
Loups's

Ravock Rigg

DANGER AREA

Gill
Feet

Whitstone
Rigg

Gill Beck

7

17

Hare Sike

Kearton Rigg

Blackpool Sike

Stonefold Rigg

Battle
Hill

6

Loups's Plantation

Stable Sike

Kirkstreveland Rigg

Ladyfold Rigg

Scotty Rigg

5

Hazelgill Beck

Hazelgill Rigg

Pennine Way

Nova
Scotia

16

4

Deep Dale

Deepdale Beck

Hazelgill

Levy
Pool

Strand
Foot

West Stoney
Keld

Stoney
Keld

East Stoney Keld

3

15

Water Knott

Tute
Hill

Stony
Keld

Bessy
Sike

2

Layer
Tree

Storage Site
(disused)

Philip
Hill

Clint
Farm

CLINT LA

1

14

The Old Moss

96 A B 97 C D 98 E F

A   B   C   D   E   F

Scur Beck

North Gill Wood

NABY LA

Scur Beck

B6277

Scurbeck Bridge

Lartington

8

The Green

B6277

North Gill Bridge

North Gill

LARTINGTON LA

North Gill

Lartington Green

LARTINGTON GREEN LA

7

Battle Hill Range

Dismtd Rly

Washfold Bridge

Gill Beck

Whin Covert

17

West Pasture

6

The Rigg

CAT CASTLE COTTS

Crag Pond

Cat Castle

Scotty Rigg

Crag Hill

Low Crag

5

Crag Hill

Dismtd Rly

16

Nova Scotia

Low Thornberry

Raven's Nest

High Crag

Deepdale Beck

North Field

4

Nabb Bridge

Weather Hill

Nabb Farm

Crag Bridge

North Thornberry

Thornberry

3

Fountain Head

THORNBERRY LA

15

Bessy Sike

South Thornberry

Cow Close

A67

2

Cow Close

Milestone House

Brookside

Dismtd Rly

Hulands Farm

1

CLINT LA

Myre Keld Farm

Black Lodge

A67

14

199
183

A   B   C   D   E   F

8

Grotto Wood
Pecknell
Towler Hill

Lartington Hall

Lartington Hall Park

Scur Beck

Dismtd Rly

Pecknell Wood

Percy Beck Bridge

Wool House

Percy Beck

B6277

Montgomery RD
WOODSIDE

7

LARTINGTON LA

Teesdale Way

Flatts Wood

River Tees

WOODSIDE

WELLINGTON RD

17

Low Fish Pond

Ray Gill

Dockon Flatt Wood

DENE RD   CECIL RD

RABY AVE   VANE RD

VERE RD

6

Raygill

B6277

FLAXFIELD

Picnic Site

PLATTS RD   GALGATE

A67

HORSE MARKET

Barnard Castle Bridge

Osmond Flatt

Deepdale Beck

Deepdale Wood

HM Young Offender Institution

DEERBOLT BANK

ULLATHORNE RISE

B6277

THE SILLS

THE BANK

5

BOWES RD

STARTFORTH PARK

DARK LA   STANMORE CL

LOW STARTFORTH RD

BOLDRON LA

TEESDALE

GILL LA

THORNGATE WYND   THORNGATE

16

Smart Gill

Gill Beck

GRAY LA 1
BRIDGE INN YD 2

Startforth Morrit Memorial CE Sch

Startforth

THE LENDINGS

4

Westwood

Startforth Hall

Startforth Hall Farm

CHURCH BANK

North Field

Dismtd Rly

Smart Gill

Startforth Grange

Wise Hill

ABBEY LA

Thorsgill Farm

3

Blades Field

Pearson Moor

Thorsgill Bridge

15

Boldron Moor

Thorsgill Beck

Boldron Whins

2

A67

B6277

Cottage Farm

Boldron

Manyfold Beck

1

George and Dragon (PH)

Princess Charlotte Wood

14

North Side

WEST LA

West Roods

West Hall

B6277

02   A   B   03   C   D   04   E   F

A   B   C   D   E   F

8

Harmire Bridge
Manor House
CH
Harmire Enterprise Pk
Redwell Inn
Works
B6278
Black Beck
Black Beck Bridge
A688
THE CRESCENT
THE AVENUE
THE OVAL
THE GREEN
Stainton Grove
Dismtd Rly
Dismtd Rly
Stell Plantation

7

RAILWAY TERR
HARMIRE RD
STRATHMORE RD
WOODLANDS RD
HARMIRE
WOODSIDE
MONTALBO RD
HAWTHORN DR
FAIRFIELD RD
WELLINGTON RD
MAYWOOD DR
Sch
CLEVELAND RD
Sports Ctr
Teesdale Comp Sch
PROSPECT PL
A688
DICKENS RD
NORTHFIELD
HIGH RIGGS
TOWN PASTURE LA
West Town Pasture
East Town Pasture

17

FIFE RD
STRATHMORE CT
MAYFIELD
CAMBRIDGE TERR
CORONATION ST
BEDE RD
VERE RD
MARSHALL ST
GALGATE
GROVE PK
BEACONSFIELD CT
Bede
H
Richardson
H
CHURCHILL RD
HILTON RD
DAL RD
GRETA RD
Barnard Castle Jun & Inf C of E Controlled Schs
Marden Farm
DARLINGTON RD

6

Liby
P
1 LOW MILL
2 GEORGE ST
3 WARE CT
4 PEARSON TERR
KING ST
ALBERT CL
VICTORIA RD
RICHARDSON
SHERWOOD CL
ZETLAND RD
GREEN LA
BARNARD CASTLE
A67
MOUNT EFF RD

5

HALL ST
QUEEN ST
WOOD ST
BIRCH RD
WILSON ST
DUNELM CT
St Mary's Sch
WATSON CT
CROOK LA
KAY YAT
BARTLEMERE
P
Bowes Mus
Barnard Castle Sch
Horse Market
MARKET PL
ST MARYS CL
PARSONS LONNING
NEWGATE
MOUNT EFF LA
Mount Eff

16

THE BANK
UPRIORY BANK
BRIDGE INN YD
GRAY LA
Demesnes
ABBEY TERR
Demesnes Mill Farm
Lowfield Garden
Sally Gill Plantation

4

THE LENDINGS
Lendings
East Lendings Caravan Pk
ABBEY LA
WESTWICK RD
Westwick

3

Thorsgill Wood
Teesdale Way
Bow Bridge
Mains House
Westfield

15

Egglestone Abbey (remains of)
River Tees
Abbey Bridge
Tees Bank
Tees Bank Plantation

2

Holly Lane Plantation
Tees Bank
P
Castle Farm
Waterloo Plantation
Colton Plantation

1

Dowson's Gill
Manyfold Beck Wood
Manyfold Beck
Rokeby Grange
MORTHAM LA

14

A   B   C   D   E   F

8

Low Barford

Humbleton Hill

Stell Plantation

Wether Hill

7

Westwick Moor

Humbleton

17

6

A67

Black Bull Farm

DARLINGTON RD

Dial House

A67

Hoy House

Arlaw Banks

Whorlton High Grange

5

Hill House Farm

Sledwich Wood

16

West Shaws

4

Whorlton Beck

Middle Wood

3

Burnholme Farm

SLEDWICH COTTS

Red House

Grange Farm

GRANGE COTTS

Sledwich Hall

Whorlton Grange

GRANGE TERR

East Shaws

15

Whorlton

THE STEADINGS

Bridge Inn (PH)

2

Whorlton Banks

Whorlton Bridge

River Tees

West Thorpe

Whorlton Lido

MORTHAM LA

Dairy Bridge

Mortham

Teesdale Way

1

Mortham Tower

Thorpe

Rokeby Park

THORPE HALL

14

08   A   B   09   C   D   10   E   F

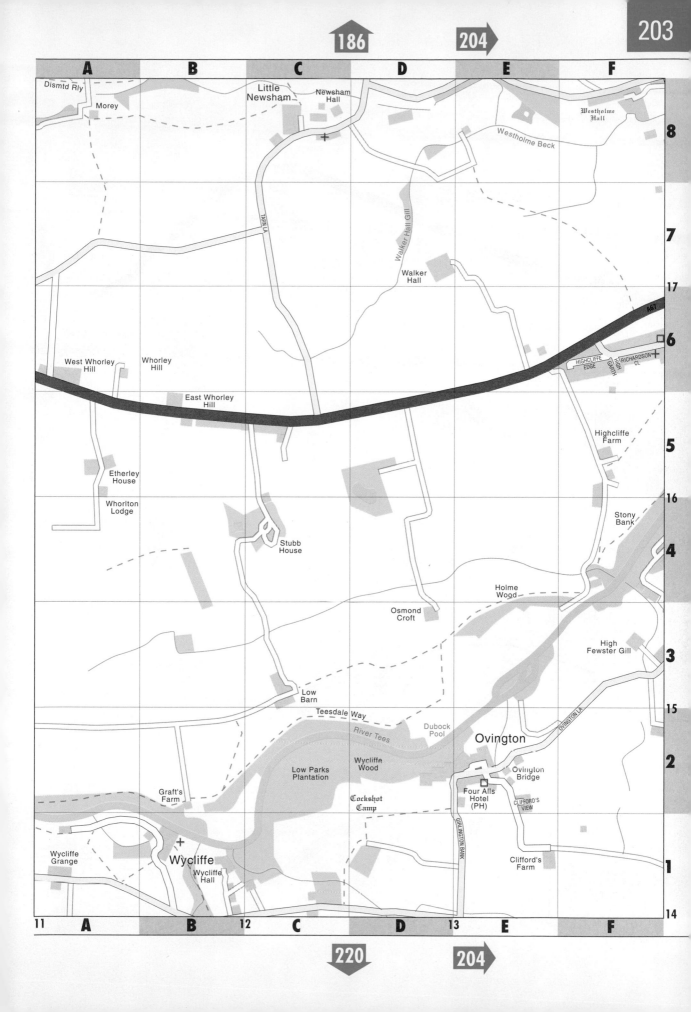

Dismtd Rly

Morey

Little
Newsham

Newsham
Hall

Westholme
Hall

Westholme Beck

TARN LA

Walker
Hall

Walker Hall Gill

A61

HIGHCLIFFE
EDGE

HIGH
GARTH

RICHARDSON
CL.

West Whorley
Hill

Whorley
Hill

East Whorley
Hill

Highcliffe
Farm

Etherley
House

Stony
Bank

Whorlton
Lodge

Stubb
House

Holme
Wood

High
Fewster Gill

Osmond
Croft

Low
Barn

Teesdale Way

OVINGTON LA

River Tees

Dubock
Pool

Ovington

Graft's
Farm

Low Parks
Plantation

Wycliffe
Wood

Ovington
Bridge

CLIFFORD'S
VIEW

Four Alls
Hotel
(PH)

GIRLINGTON BANK

Cockshot
Camp

Wycliffe
Grange

Wycliffe

Wycliffe
Hall

Clifford's
Farm

A | B | C | D | E | F

8

Westholme Beck
Westholme Bridge
Gainford Great Wood

Alwent Beck
Selaby Basses
Dismtd Rly
Winfield
Primrose Hill Farm

7

B6274
Station Farm
West Tees Bridge
River Tees

Balmer Hill

Vicarage Farm

17

A67
SPA RD
B6274
PH
CHURCH MEWS
Church Farm
Hedgeholme Wood
PIGGY LA
HIGH ROW
LOW RD

6

Gainford Controlled Prim Sch
Sewage Works
Winston
Hedgeholme
Barforth Hall
Cemy

Hedgeholme Bank

5

Winston Bridge
Winston Gate
Hill Top
St Lawrence's Chapel

BOAT LA

16

Winston Bridge Caravan Pk
Barforth Whins

4

OVINGTON LA
BERRY BANK
Moor Row
Chapel Gill

Greener Hill

3

Barforth Grange

15

Pudding Hill
PUDDING HILL RD

2

Ovington Grange

1

Greystone West
Greystone
Main Moor Hill
Cote Hill
B6274
Sough Hill

14

14 | A | B | 15 | C | D | 16 | E | F

A | B | C | D | E | F

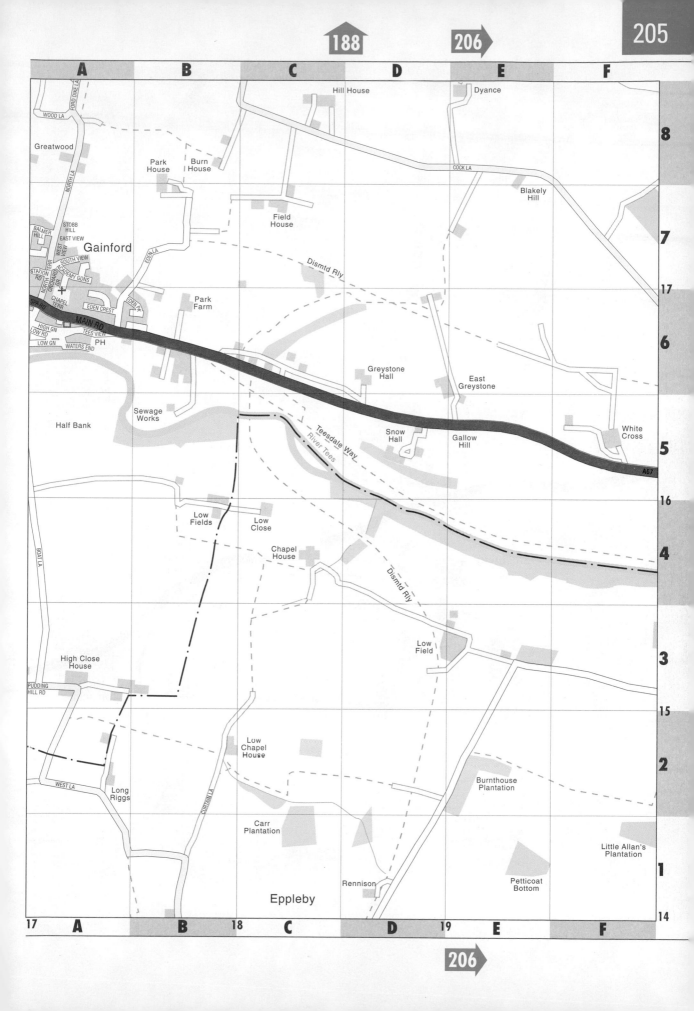

Hill House
Dyance

8

WOOD LA
FORD DIKE LA

Greatwood

Park
House
Burn
House

NORTH LA

COCK LA

Blakely
Hill

Field
House

7

BALMER
HILL
STOBB
HILL
EAST VIEW
WEST
VIEW
SOUTH VIEW

Gainford

EDEN LA

Dismtd Rly

17

STATION
RD
NORTH TERR
ORCHARD
GR
ACADEMY GDNS
CHAPEL
TERR

Park
Farm

EDEN CREST
EDEN PK

SPA RD
MAIN RD
HIGH GN
LOW RD
LOW GN
TEES VIEW
PH
WATERS END

6

Greystone
Hall

East
Greystone

Half Bank

Sewage
Works

Snow
Hall

Gallow
Hill

White
Cross

Teesdale Way
River Tees

A67

5

BOAT LA

16

Low
Fields

Low
Close

Chapel
House

Dismtd Rly

4

Low
Field

High Close
House

3

PUDDING
HILL RD

15

Low
Chapel
House

Burnthouse
Plantation

2

WEST LA

Long
Riggs

CURTAIN LA

Carr
Plantation

Little Allan's
Plantation

Petticoat
Bottom

1

Rennison

Eppleby

14

17 | A | B | 18 | C | D | 19 | E | F

205
189

A B C D E F

Dyance Beck

8

Beck Whin

Fulbeck Bridge

B6279

Hopewell

The Cottages

High Carlbury Farm

7

Fanny Barks

Ullnaby Hall

B6279

17

Piercebridge Grange

Hobson Hill

6

Piercebridge Beck

COCK LA

ULNABY LA

Dismtd Rly

5

Works

Cabin House

Carlbury Cottage

Carlbury Crossing Cottage

A67

16

The Wheatsheaf (PH)

B6275

Station House

Carlbury

B6275

ROMAN VIEW

B6275

Low Carlbury

Carlbury Mill

4

Piercebridge Farm

THE GREEN

Tofts

Piercebridge +

Teesdale Way

High Coniscliffe Jun Sch

WEST CL

The Mill House

BRIDGE END

River Tees

The Spotted Dog (PH)

MILL LA

ULNABY BECK

The George (Hotel)

Kathleen Wood

ST EDWIN'S CL

THE GREEN

A67

West Wood

Cliffe Hall

Betty Watson's Hill

3

Home Farm

Cliffe

Quarry

High Coniscliffe +

15

Holme House

2

Allan's Grange

Cliffe Bank

Gatehouse Plantation

Crabby Plantation

Glebe Farm

1

Great Allan's Plantation

Cliffe Bank Cottages

B6275

Manfield Gill

14

20 A B 21 C D 22 E F

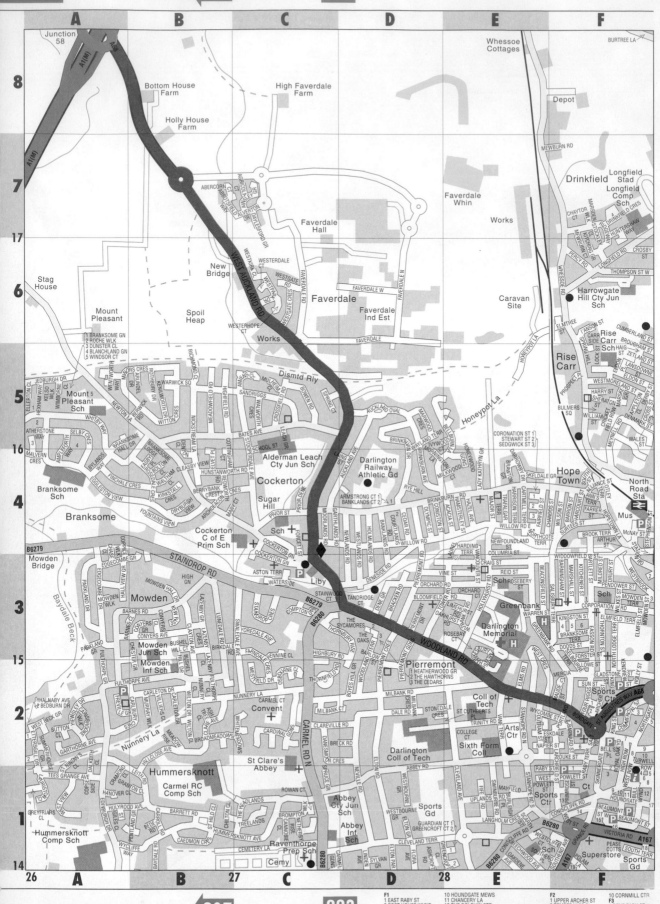

F1
1 EAST RABY ST
2 POST HOUSE WYND
3 BUCKTON'S YD
4 EAST ROW
5 CHURCH ROW
6 BAKEHOUSE HILL
7 HORSE MARKET
8 MARKET PL
9 BLACKWELLGATE

10 HOUNDGATE MEWS
11 CHANCERY LA
12 THE DOLPHIN CTR
13 LARCHFIELD HOUSE
14 NORTHUMBERLAND ST
15 WELLINGTON COURT MEWS
16 SOUTH ARDEN ST
17 FEETHAMS
18 FEETHAMS S
19 OAKLEA CT

F2
1 UPPER ARCHER ST
2 TEMPERANCE PL
3 UNION ST
4 QUEEN ST
5 CROWN ST
6 WINSTON ST
7 PROSPECT PL
8 PREBEND ROW
9 PRIESTGATE

10 CORNMILL CTR
F3
1 DENE PARK CT
2 MELVILLE ST
3 WESTBROOK ST
4 CHELMSFORD ST
5 OAKLANDS TERR
6 DERWENT ST

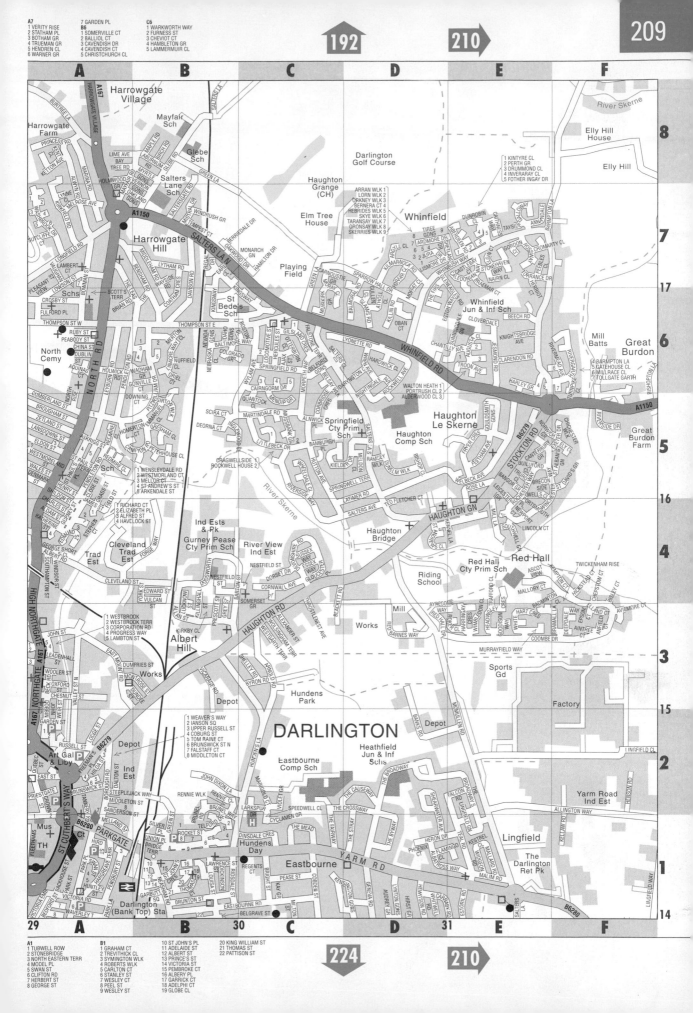

209 193

A   B   C   D   E   F

8

Burdon
Hall

Burdon
Gardens

7

BISHOPTON LA

Carcut Beck

17

CHAPEL ROW 1
EAST VIEW 2
STAINTON VIEW 3
HILLSIDE TERR 4
LAUREL TERR 5
CHURCH VIEW 6
DARLINGTON RD 7

Well House
Farm

Works

Sadberge
C of E Sch

Hill
Cottage

HILL HOUSE LA

NORTON BACK LA

NORTON CRES

NORTON RD

DALE RD
ABBEY RD

6

Village
Hall

EAST CL
THE ORCHARD
WEST VIEW
BEACON CHURCH LA
GRANGE PK
MIDDLETON RD

Buck Inn
(PH)

Sadberge

STOCKTON RD

A66

Beacon
Hill

BEACON HILL

Sadberge Resr
(dis)

Lea
Close

A1150

Little
Burdon

Bumper
Hill

5

BUESS LA

Toft
Hill

16

4

Sadberge
Hall

Sadberge Hall
Farm

Street House
Farm

3

Dismtd Rly

The
Kennels

15

South
Burdon

The
Anchorage

2

LINGFIELD CL

LINGFIELD WAY

DUDLEY RD

Ashtree
Cottage

Highfield
Farm

ALLINGTON
WAY

Morton Palms
Farm

Allot
Gdns

SADBERGE RD

The
Fighting Cocks
(PH)

1

MORTON RD

Yarm Road
Ind Est

A66

Palm
Bridge

Works

HAXBY
STATION RD

HARPERS
TERR

WILD GR

Acolan
House

A67

PALM TREE
VILLAS
STATION
TERR

HEATHFIELD
PK

PALM TREE PK

A67

14

32   A   B   33   C   D   34   E   F

194

A B C D E F

8
Larberry Pastures

NORTON BACK LA

Salter Carr Farm
DARLINGTON BACK LA

BACK LA

7
Bewley Hill

Longnewton Resr

17

Newton Grange Farm

6
Farfields Farm

Rectory Farm

Longnewton

Eddlethorpe Farm

Hang Thorn Farm

A66

Ivanhoe

THE WILLOW CHASE
THE CLOSE
THE YEW WLK
WOODLANDS
WAY
PARKSIDE
THE CLOSE
DARLINGTON RD
FARFIELDS CL.

Newton South Grange

5
Vane Arms (PH)

West End Farm

16

Spring House Farm

Hardstones Farm

Londonderry Cottage

Middle Town Farm

4

Mill Hill Farm

White House Farm

3

Lyndale
MILL LA

West Moor

15

West Gate Fox Covert

Burnwood Beck

2

High Goosepool Farm

Long Plantation

Westgate Farm

West Hartburn Farm

Sewage Works

1

A61

14

35 A B 36 C D 37 E F

96

E Pastu

Bar Pas

Sle

A   B   C   D   E   F

North Side

Bowes Hutchinsons CE Aided Prim Sch

Myre Keld Farm

High Broats

THE STREET

Low Broats

A66

Unicorn Hotel (PH)

CASTLE TERR

THE STREET

Bowes Cross Farm

LOW RD

Stone Bridge

THE WYND

THE ANNUMS

Bowes

West Low Fields

Low Field Farm

Gilmonby Bridge

Gilmonby

River Greta

Low Field

East Lowfields Farm

Gilmonby Farm

Greta Farm

Mid Low Field

LONG CLOSE LA

Chert Gill Plantation

A66

Ch

Howlugill

Square Plantation

Craddock's Plantation

Whorlands

Plover Hall

White Close Hill

Pry Rigg

How Low Gill

Crake Gill Sike

West Ling

Quarry Hill

High Green Fell

Green Fell Plantation

The Rigg

Hong Kong Plantation

Farewell

The Combs

Low Green Fell

Scargill Low Moor

Pinlow Hill

Eller Beck

Long Side

Millstone Hill

Eller Beck Rigg

Seavy Sike

Spanham West Hill

Spanham Scar

Spanham

93   99   A   B   00   C   D   01   E   F

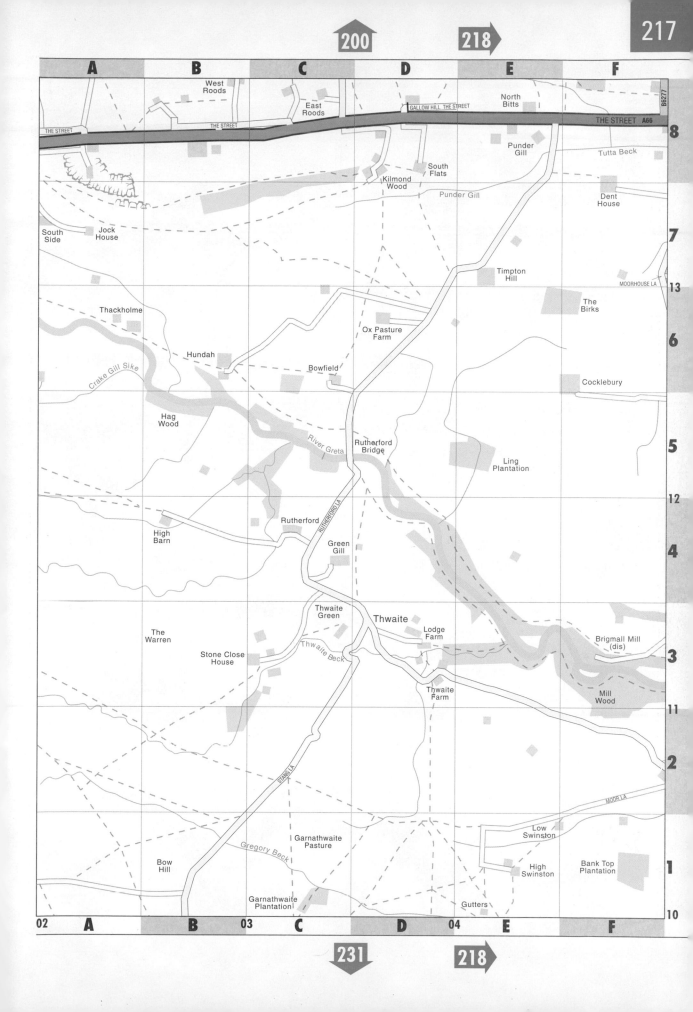

200
218

A B C D E F

West
Roods

East
Roods

GALLOW HILL THE STREET

North
Bitts

THE STREET

THE STREET

THE STREET A66

B6277

8

Punder
Gill

Tutta Beck

South
Flats

Kilmond
Wood

Punder Gill

Dent
House

South
Side

Jock
House

7

Timpton
Hill

MOORHOUSE LA

13

Thackholme

The
Birks

Ox Pasture
Farm

6

Hundah

Bowfield

Cocklebury

Crake Gill Sike

Hag
Wood

River Greta

Rutherford
Bridge

Ling
Plantation

5

12

High
Barn

Rutherford

RUTHERFORD LA

Green
Gill

4

Thwaite
Green

Thwaite

Lodge
Farm

Brigmall Mill
(dis)

The
Warren

Stone Close
House

Thwaite Beck

Thwaite
Farm

Mill
Wood

3

11

STANG LA

Low
Swinston

MOOR LA

2

Bow
Hill

Gregory Beck

Garnathwaite
Pasture

High
Swinston

Bank Top
Plantation

1

Garnathwaite
Plantation

Gutters

10

02 A B 03 C D 04 E F

231
218

217
201

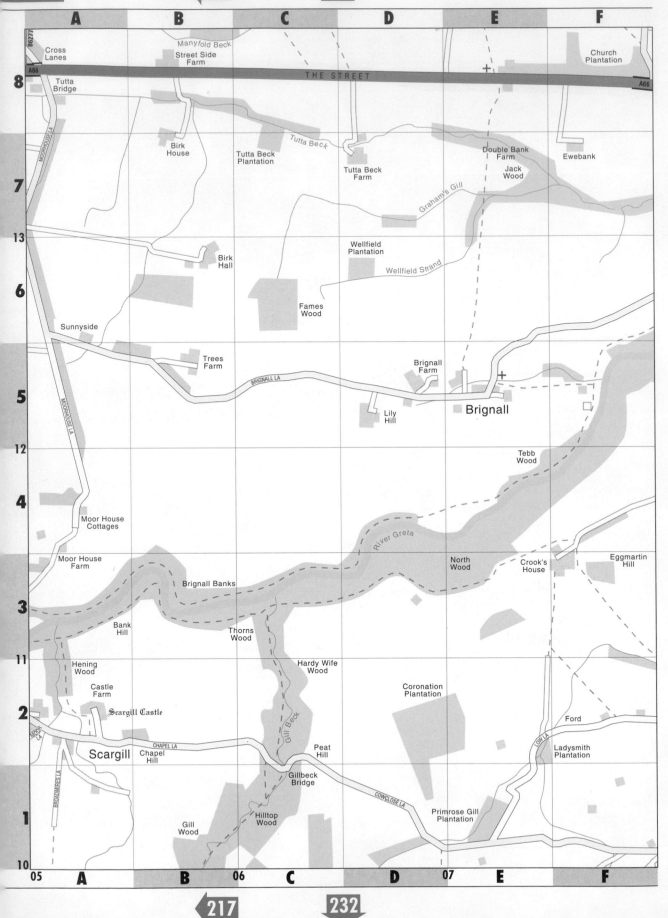

A B C D E F

Cross Lanes
Street Side Farm
Manyfold Beck
Church Plantation
THE STREET
A66
A66

8

Tutta Bridge
Birk House
Tutta Beck
Tutta Beck Plantation
Tutta Beck Farm
Double Bank Farm
Jack Wood
Ewebank
Graham's Gill

7

13

Birk Hall
Wellfield Plantation
Wellfield Strand

6

Fames Wood

Sunnyside
Trees Farm
BRIGNALL LA
Brignall Farm
Brignall

5

Lily Hill

12

Tebb Wood

4

Moor House Cottages

River Greta

Moor House Farm
Brignall Banks
North Wood
Crook's House
Eggmartin Hill

3

Bank Hill
Thorns Wood

11

Hening Wood
Hardy Wife Wood

Castle Farm
Coronation Plantation

2

Scargill Castle
Gill Beck
Ford
Low La
Ladysmith Plantation

Scargill
CHAPEL LA
Chapel Hill
Peat Hill

Gillbeck Bridge
COWCLOSE LA
MOOR LA
BROADMIRES LA

1

Gill Wood
Hilltop Wood
Primrose Gill Plantation

10

05 A B 06 C D 07 E F

MOORHOUSE LA
B6277

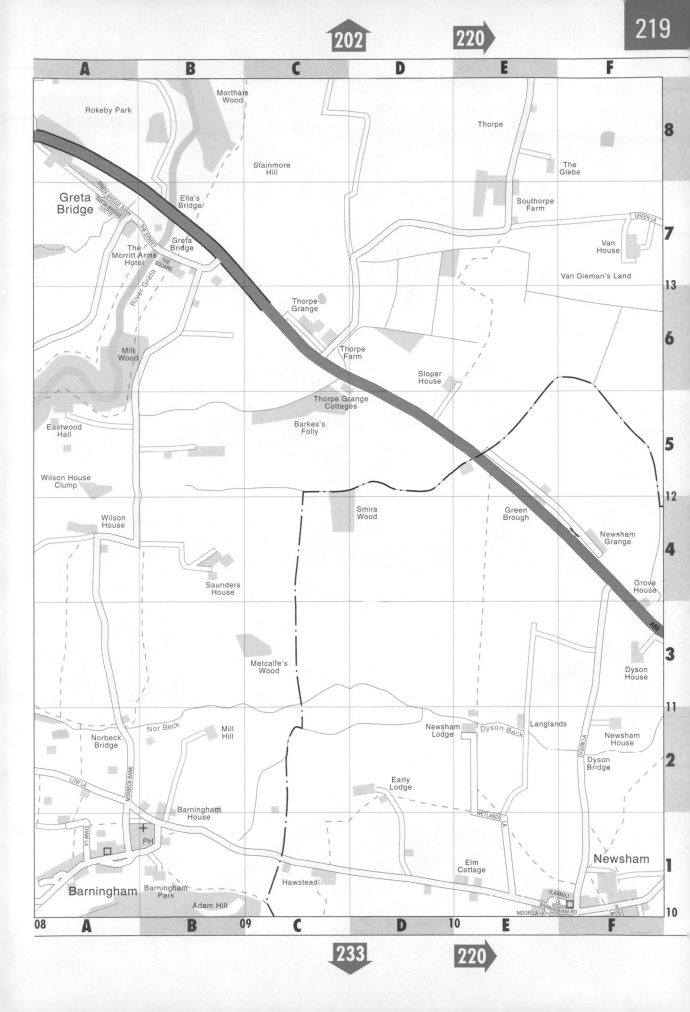

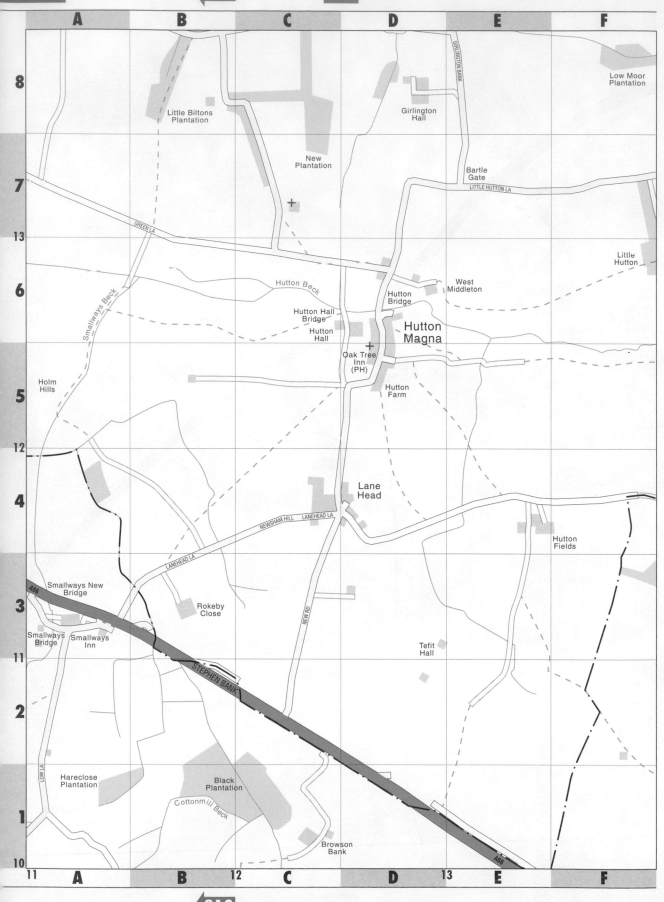

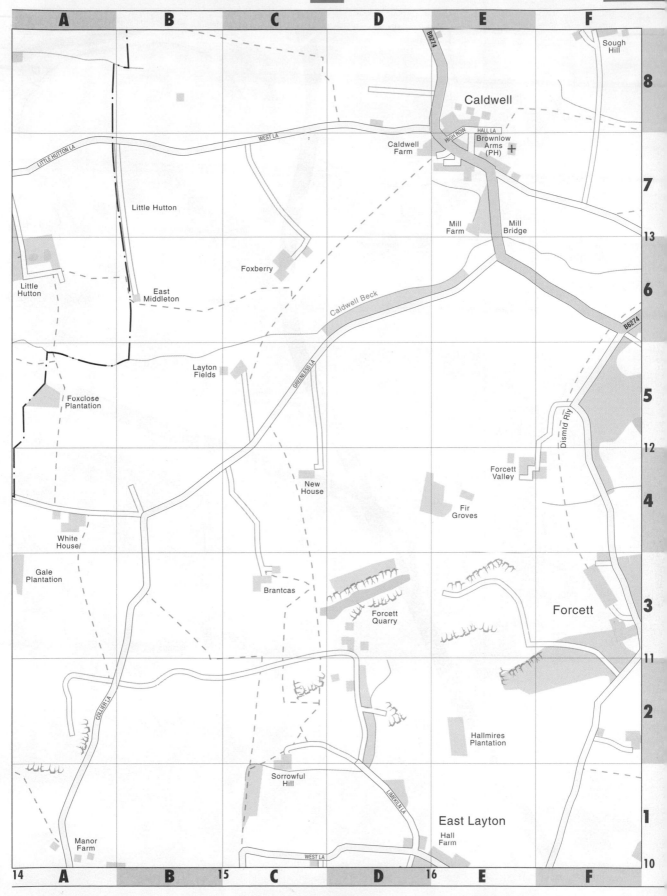

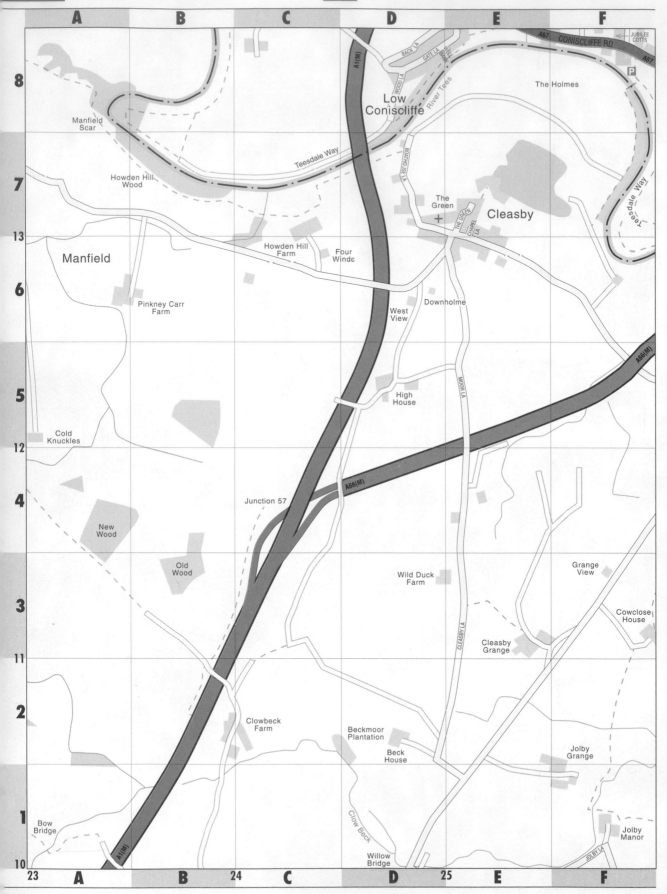

A | **B** | **C** | **D** | **E** | **F**

8

Manfield Scar

Howden Hill Wood

7

13

Manfield

Four Winds

Howden Hill Farm

Pinkney Carr Farm

6

West View

Downholme

Low Coniscliffe

The Green

Cleasby

The Holmes

BACK LA

GATE LA

BOWBANK

A67 CONISCLIFFE RD

A67

JUBILEE COTTS

Teesdale Way

River Tees

BOATHOUSE LA

THE GREEN

CHAPEL LA

Teesdale Way

5

High House

MOOR LA

A66(M)

Cold Knuckles

12

Junction 57

4

New Wood

Old Wood

A66(M)

Wild Duck Farm

Grange View

Cowclose House

3

Cleasby Grange

11

CLEASBY LA

Clowbeck Farm

2

Beckmoor Plantation

Beck House

Jolby Grange

Bow Bridge

Clow Beck

Jolby Manor

1

Willow Bridge

A1(M)

JOLBY LA

10

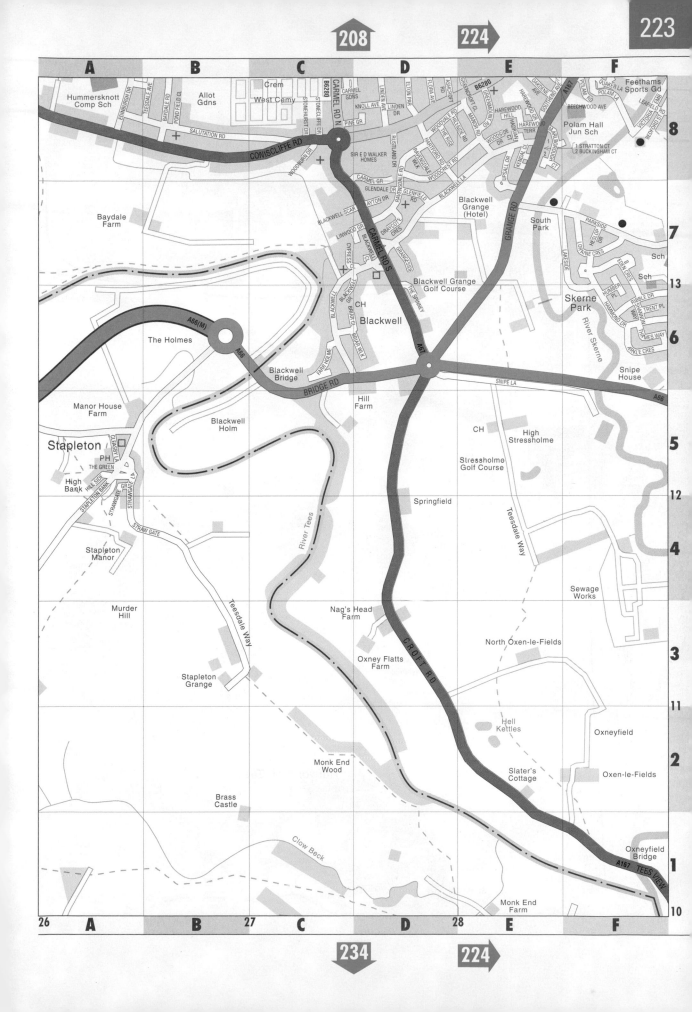

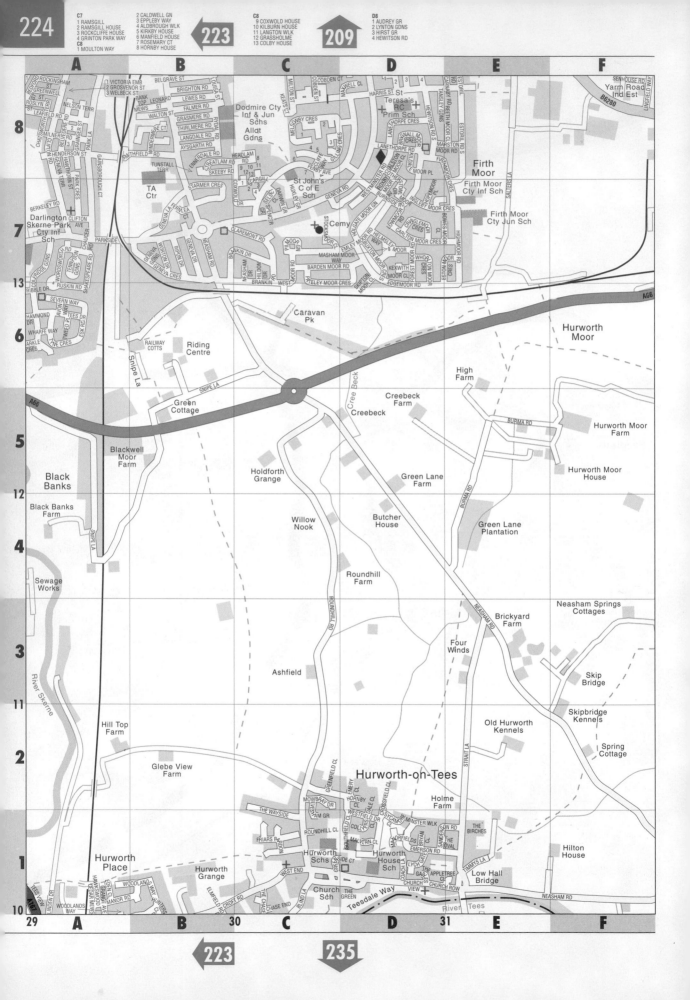

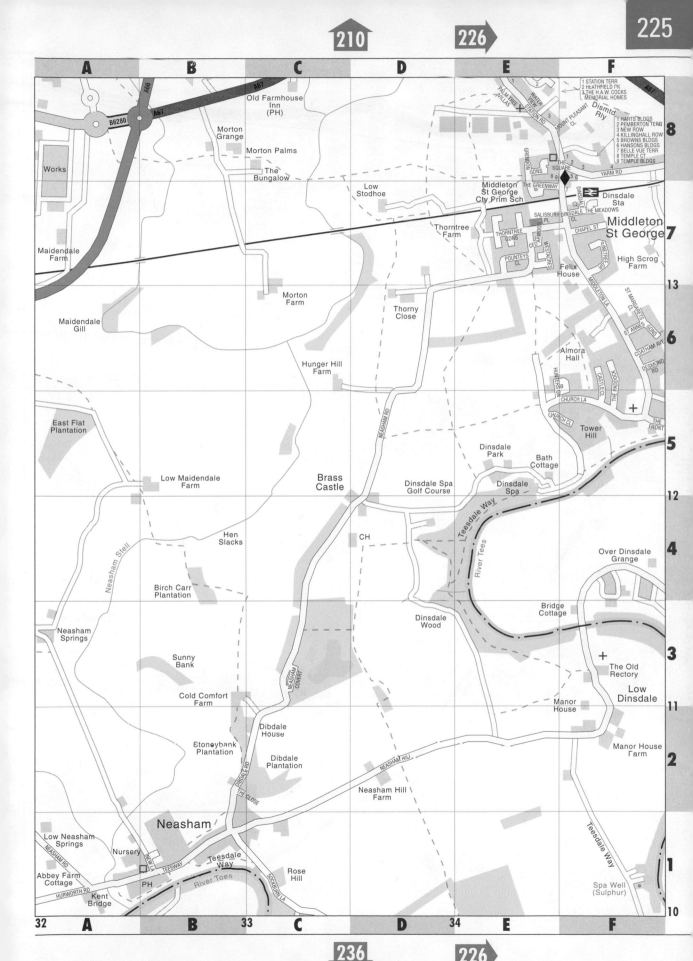

A B C D E F

8

Works

B6280

A67

Old Farmhouse
Inn
(PH)

Morton
Grange

Morton Palms

The
Bungalow

Low
Stodhoe

Middleton
St George
Cty Prim Sch

1 STATION TERR
2 HEATHFIELD PK
3 THE H.A.W. COCKS
  MEMORIAL HOMES

Dismtd
Rly

1 HARTS BLDGS
2 PEMBERTON TERR
3 NEW ROW
4 KILLINGHALL ROW
5 BROWNS BLDGS
6 HANSONS BLDGS
7 BELLE VUE TERR
8 TEMPLE CT
9 TEMPLE BLDGS

PALM TREE VILLAS

MOUNT PLEASANT

WATER STATION RD

GRENDON GDNS

THE SQUARE

YARM RD

Dinsdale Sta

THE MEADOWS

SALISBURY DINSDALE
PL

DINSDALE CL

Middleton
St George

7

Maidendale
Farm

Maidendale
Gill

Morton
Farm

Thorntree
Farm

Thorntree
GDNS

POUNTEYS
CL

WESTACRES

CEDARWOOD

CHAPEL ST

Felix
House

MIDDLETON LA

PINETREE CL

High Scrog
Farm

ST MARGARETS
CL

ST ANNES GDNS

COATHAM AVE

13

6

Thorny Close

Almora
Hall

HUNTERS GN

CHURCH LA

CASTLE CL

DESMOND RD

THE PADDOCK

East Flat
Plantation

Hunger Hill
Farm

Low Maidendale
Farm

Brass
Castle

Dinsdale Spa
Golf Course

Dinsdale
Park

Bath
Cottage

Dinsdale
Spa

CHURCH CL

Tower
Hill

THE
FRONT

5

12

Neasham Stell

Hen
Slacks

CH

Teesdale Way

River Tees

Over Dinsdale
Grange

4

Birch Carr
Plantation

Dinsdale
Wood

Bridge
Cottage

NEASHAM RD

Neasham
Springs

Sunny
Bank

NEASHAM COVERT

The Old
Rectory

Manor
House

Low
Dinsdale

3

Cold Comfort
Farm

Dibdale
House

Manor House
Farm

11

Stoneybank
Plantation

Dibdale
Plantation

DIBDALE RD

THE CLOSE

Neasham Hill
Farm

NEASHAM HILL

2

Neasham

Low Neasham
Springs

Nursery

NEASHAM RD

NEW LA

TEESWAY

Teesdale
Way

Rose
Hill

SCARBURN LA

Teesdale Way

1

Abbey Farm
Cottage

HURWORTH RD

Kent
Bridge

PH

River Tees

Spa Well
(Sulphur)

10

32 A 33 B C 34 D E F

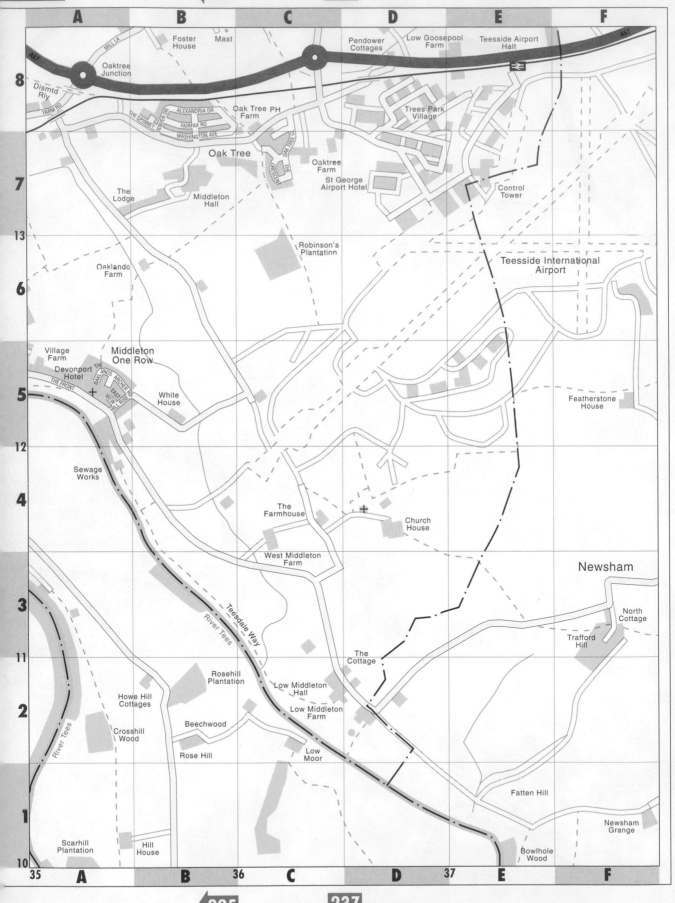

A B C D E F

8

Teesside Airport Halt

A67

Oaktree Junction

Dismtd Rly

YARN RD

MILL LA

Foster House

Mast

THE SPINNEY

DENVER DR

ALEXANDRIA DR

FAIRFAX RD

WASHINGTON AVE

Oak Tree PH Farm

THE CRESCENT

OAK TREE CL

Pendower Cottages

Low Goosepool Farm

Trees Park Village

7

Oak Tree

The Lodge

Middleton Hall

Oaktree Farm

St George Airport Hotel

Control Tower

13

Robinson's Plantation

Teesside International Airport

6

Oaklands Farm

5

Village Farm

Devonport Hotel

Middleton One Row

THE OAKLANDS

ARCHER RD

EAST VIEW

HILL RISE

THE FRONT

White House

Featherstone House

12

Sewage Works

4

The Farmhouse

Church House

West Middleton Farm

Newsham

3

River Tees

Teesdale Way

North Cottage

11

The Cottage

Trafford Hill

Rosehill Plantation

Low Middleton Hall

2

River Tees

Howe Hill Cottages

Crosshill Wood

Beechwood

Rose Hill

Low Middleton Farm

Low Moor

Fatten Hill

1

Scarhill Plantation

Hill House

Newsham Grange

Bowlhole Wood

10

35 A 36 B C 37 D E F

212
228

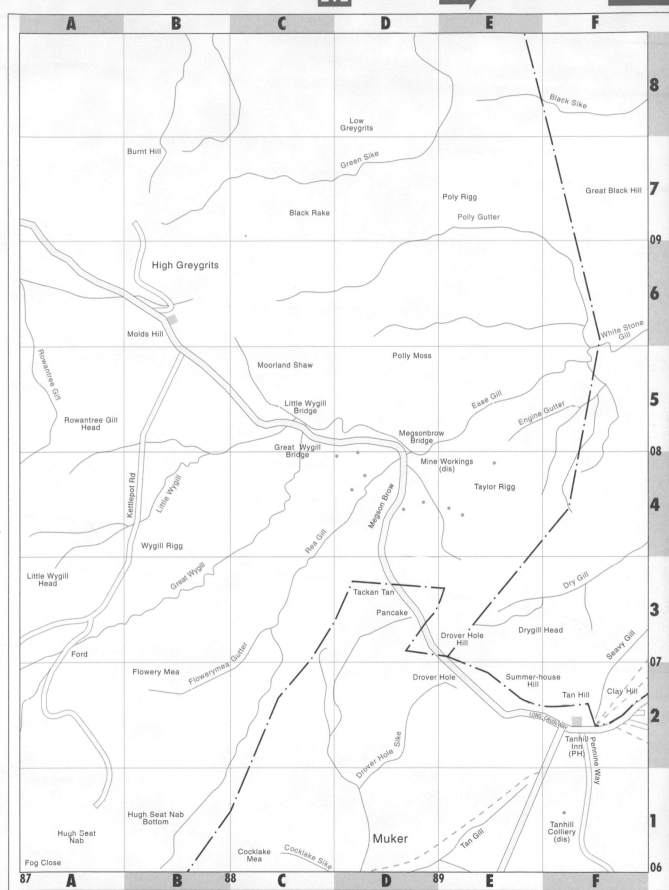

228

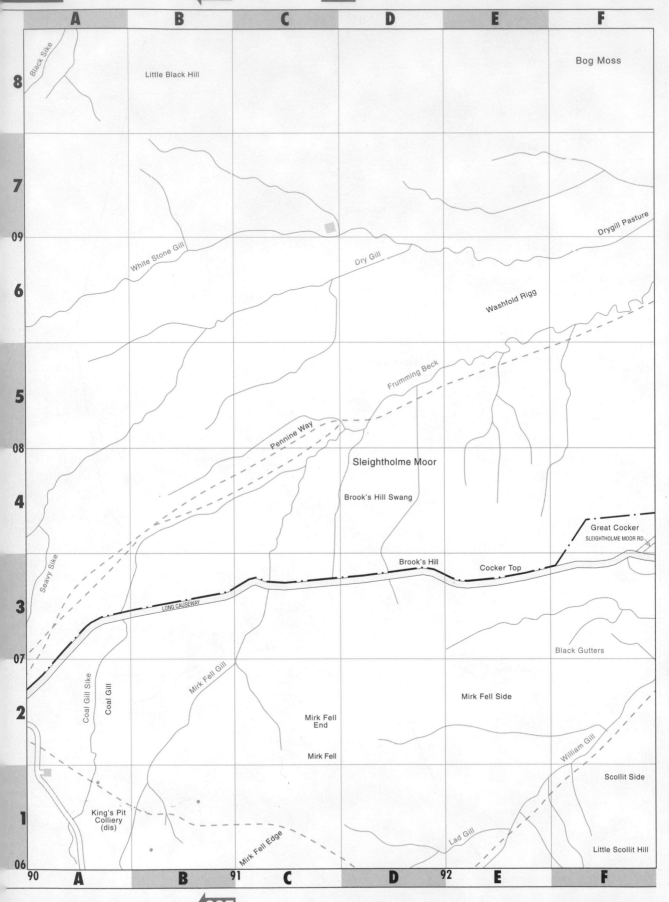

Black Sike

Bog Moss

Little Black Hill

8

White Stone Gill

Drygill Pasture

09

7

Dry Gill

6

Washfold Rigg

Frumming Beck

Pennine Way

5

Sleightholme Moor

08

Brook's Hill Swang

4

Great Cocker

SLEIGHTHOLME MOOR RD

Seavy Sike

Brook's Hill

Cocker Top

LONG CAUSEWAY

3

Black Gutters

07

Coal Gill Sike

Coal Gill

Mirk Fell Gill

Mirk Fell Side

2

Mirk Fell End

William Gill

Mirk Fell

Scollit Side

King's Pit Colliery (dis)

1

Mirk Fell Edge

Lad Gill

Little Scollit Hill

06

90
91
92

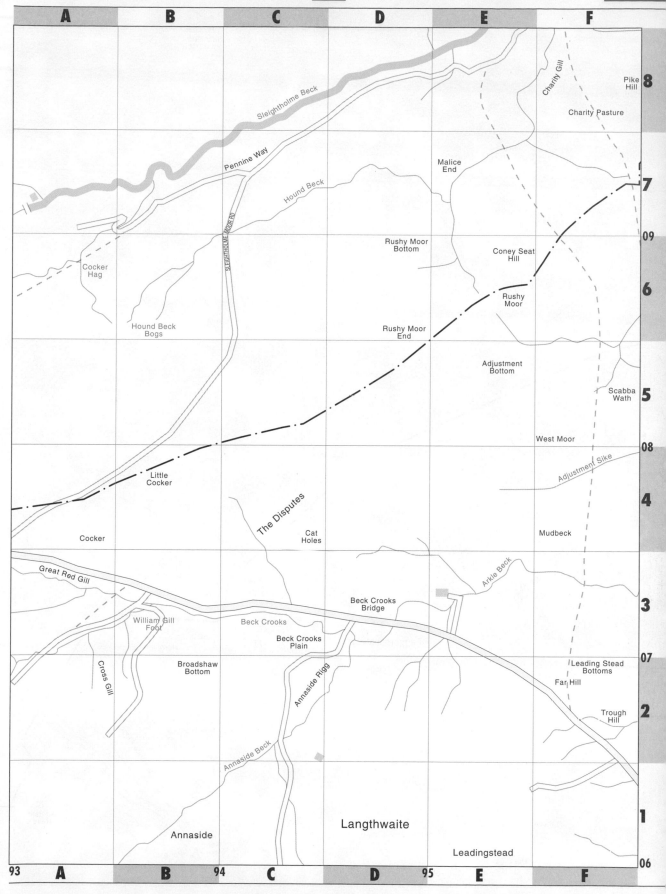

A   B   C   D   E   F

Sleightholme Beck

Pennine Way

Hound Beck

Pike Hill

Charity Gill

Charity Pasture

Malice End

Rushy Moor Bottom

Coney Seat Hill

09

7

Cocker Hag

SLEIGHTHOLME MOOR RD

Rushy Moor

6

Hound Beck Bogs

Rushy Moor End

Adjustment Bottom

Scabba Wath

5

West Moor

08

Little Cocker

Adjustment Sike

The Disputes

Cat Holes

Mudbeck

4

Cocker

Great Red Gill

Arkle Beck

Beck Crooks Bridge

3

William Gill Foot

Beck Crooks

Cross Gill

Broadshaw Bottom

Beck Crooks Plain

Annaside Rigg

Leading Stead Bottoms

07

Far Hill

Trough Hill

2

Annaside Beck

Langthwaite

1

Annaside

Leadingstead

06

93   A   B   94   C   D   95   E   F

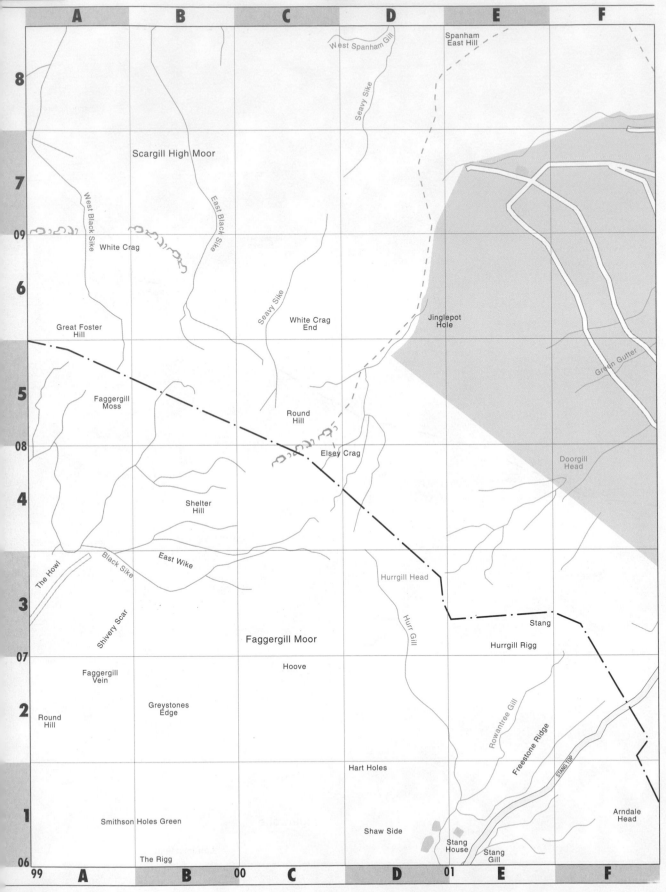

A **B** **C** **D** **E** **F**

8

Scargill High Moor

West Spanham Gill

Spanham
East Hill

7

West Black Sike

East Black Sike

Seavy Sike

09

White Crag

6

Seavy Sike

White Crag
End

Jinglepot
Hole

Green Gutter

Great Foster
Hill

5

Faggergill
Moss

Round
Hill

08

Elsey Crag

Doorgill
Head

4

Shelter
Hill

Black Sike

East Wike

The Howl

Hurrgill Head

Hurr Gill

3

Shivery Scar

Faggergill Moor

Stang

07

Hurrgill Rigg

Faggergill
Vein

Hoove

2

Greystones
Edge

Round
Hill

Rowantree Gill

Freestone Ridge

STANG TOP

Hart Holes

1

Smithson Holes Green

Shaw Side

Stang
House

Stang
Gill

Arndale
Head

06

The Rigg

A **B** 00 **C** **D** 01 **E** **F**

A B C D E F

Gregory Beck

Tad Hill

Scargill Beck

Garnathwaite

Summer Hill

Gutters Bridge

Gutters Plantation

Hurst Hill

8

Stang Foot

Peak Hole

West Hope

Hope Plantation

Hill Beck

7

Middle Rigg

East Hope

In Pasture Hill

09

Murker Hill

Stoneuckley Hill

Far East Hope

East Hope

Woodclose Gill

6

Marl Hill

STANG LA

Doorgill Bridge

Stang Gill

Long Gill

The Stang

Black Hill Gate

5

Door Gill

P

08

Cross Gill

4

Cold Seal Gill

Hope Scar

Hope Edge

High Band

STANG TOP

P

Hush Head

3

Peat Moor

Rowantree Hole

07

Hope Moor

Cocker Hill

2

Arndale Hill

Cocker Stake Nook

Black Sike

Black Hag

Arndale Beck

Arndale Bog

1

02 A B 03 C D 04 E F 06

231 218

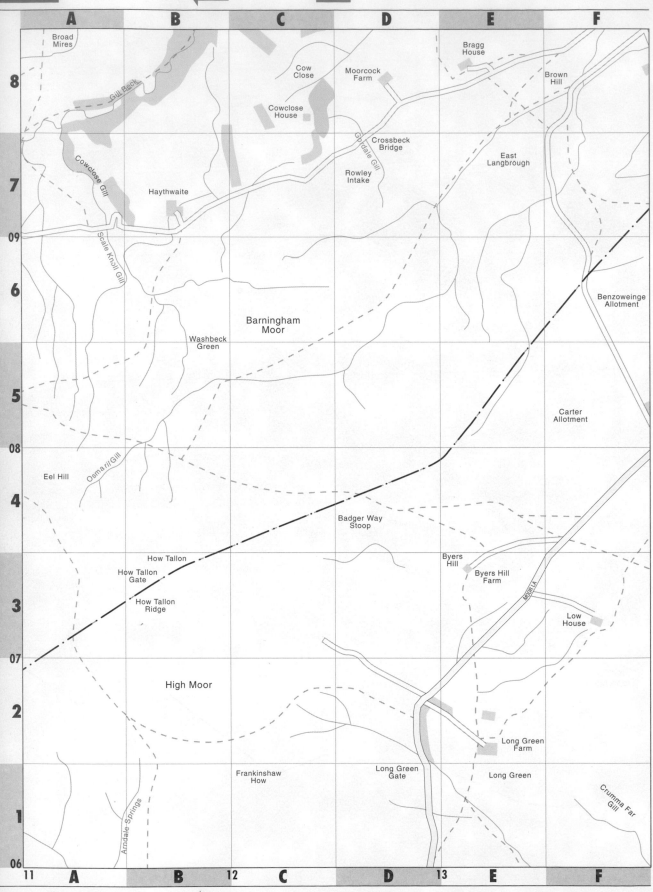

Broad Mires

Cow Close

Moorcock Farm

Bragg House

Brown Hill

Cowclose House

Gill Beck

Crossbeck Bridge

East Langbrough

Cowclose Gill

Haythwaite

Rowley Intake

Scale Knoll Gill

Gpidale Gill

Benzoweinge Allotment

Barningham Moor

Washbeck Green

Carter Allotment

Osmaril Gill

Eel Hill

Badger Way Stoop

How Tallon

Byers Hill

How Tallon Gate

Byers Hill Farm

MOOR LA

How Tallon Ridge

Low House

High Moor

Long Green Farm

Frankinshaw How

Long Green Gate

Long Green

Arndale Springs

Crumma Far Gill

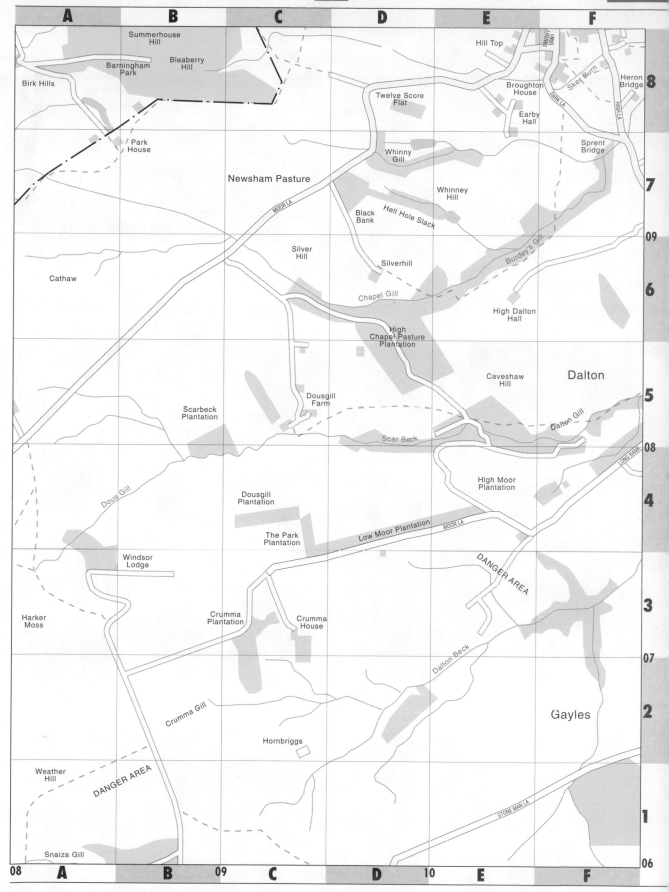

A   **B**   **C**   **D**   **E**   **F**

Summerhouse Hill

Bleaberry Hill

Barningham Park

Birk Hills

Park House

Newsham Pasture

MOOR LA

Cathaw

Silver Hill

Twelve Score Flat

Whinny Gill

Whinney Hill

Black Bank

Hell Hole Slack

Silverhill

Chapel Gill

Burdey's Gill

High Dalton Hall

High Chapel Pasture Plantation

Caveshaw Hill

Dalton

Dalton Gill

Scarbeck Plantation

Dousgill Farm

Scar Beck

08

Dous Gill

Dousgill Plantation

The Park Plantation

Low Moor Plantation

MOOR LA

High Moor Plantation

LONG BANK

DANGER AREA

Windsor Lodge

Harker Moss

Crumma Plantation

Crumma House

Dalton Beck

07

Gayles

Crumma Gill

Hornbriggs

Weather Hill

DANGER AREA

STONE MAN LA

Snaiza Gill

Hill Top

SMITHY LONID

Broughton House

SKEF BURN

DARK LA

Earby Hall

Heron Bridge

HIGH LA

Sprent Bridge

09

06

08   **A**   **B**   09   **C**   **D**   10   **E**   **F**

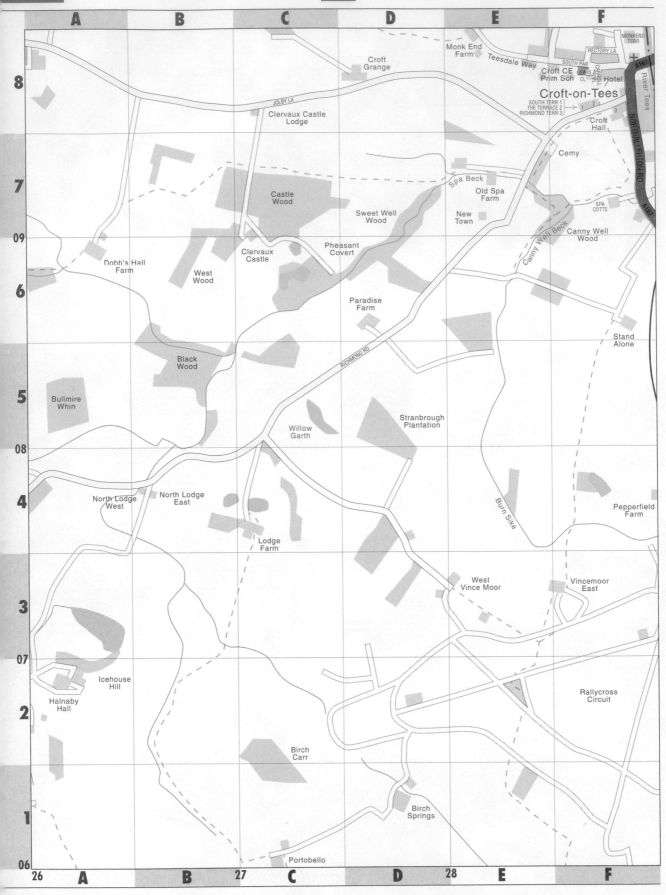

Croft-on-Tees

Monk End Farm
Teesdale Way
Croft CE Prim Sch
Hotel
MONKEND TERR
RECTORY LA
SOUTH PAR
LEWIS CL
CARROLL CL
A167
Croft Grange
Croft Hall
Cemy
SOUTH TERR 1
THE TERRACE 2
RICHMOND TERR 3
Clervaux Castle Lodge
JOLBY LA
Spa Beck
Old Spa Farm
New Town
SPA COTTS
Castle Wood
Sweet Well Wood
Canny Well Wood
Canny Well Beck
Pheasant Covert
Clervaux Castle
Dobb's Hall Farm
West Wood
Paradise Farm
Stand Alone
Black Wood
Bullmire Whin
Willow Garth
Stranbrough Plantation
RICHMOND RD
North Lodge West
North Lodge East
Burn Sike
Pepperfield Farm
Lodge Farm
West Vince Moor
Vincemoor East
Halnaby Hall
Icehouse Hill
Rallycross Circuit
Birch Carr
Birch Springs
Portobello

River Tees
NORTHALLERTON RD

26   27   28

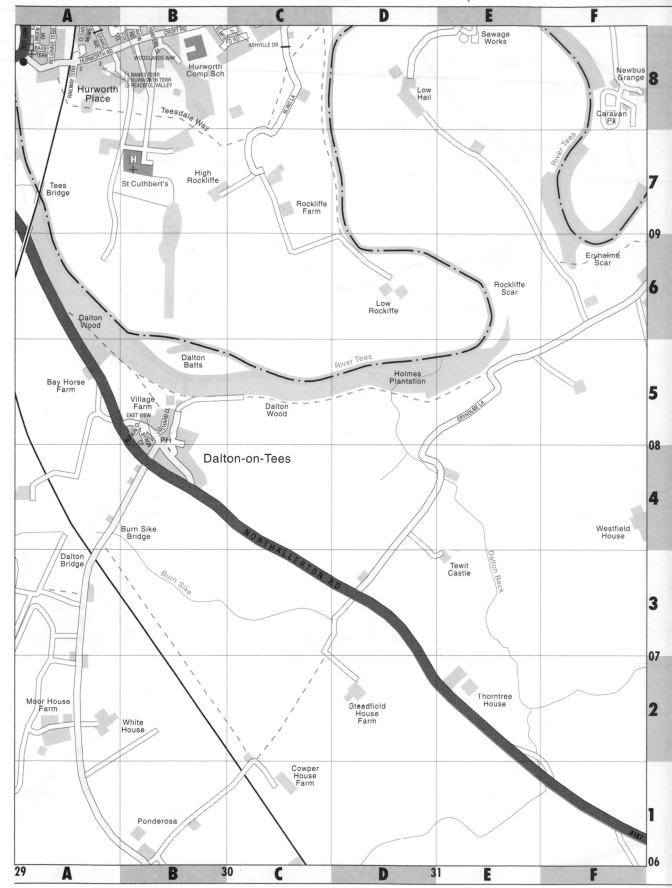

A   B   C   D   E   F

8

PEERY ENN   CEDAR MEWS   CROFT RD   ASHVILLE DR   Sewage Works   Newbus Grange
LINDEN   GRANGE   RD   ELMFIELD RD
BAXBY   AVON   WOODLANDS WAY   Low Hail   Caravan Pk
BELGRAVE TERR   HUNTER CL   Hurworth Comp Sch
RAILWAY TERR   HURWORTH RD   1 BANKS TERR   BUNGLA
Hurworth Place   2 HURWORTH TERR   3 PEACEFUL VALLEY

Teesdale Way   High Rockliffe   River Tees

7

Tees Bridge   St Cuthbert's   Rockliffe Farm   09

Dalton Wood   Low Rockliffe   Rockliffe Scar   Eryholme Scar

6

Dalton Batts   River Tees   Holmes Plantation

Bay Horse Farm   Village Farm   Dalton Wood   ERYHOLME LA   5

EAST VIEW   ORCHARD CL   08
RUSKIN CL   BYRON CT   PH

Dalton-on-Tees

Burn Sike Bridge   Westfield House   4

Dalton Bridge   NORTHALLERTON RD   Tewit Castle   Dalton Beck

Burn Sike   07

3

Thorntree House

Moor House Farm   Steadfield House Farm   2

White House

Cowper House Farm   1

Ponderosa   A167

06

A. J. Cook Terr. Shot Co DH6 ...... 84 C5
A. J. Cook's Cotts. R Gill NE39 ...... 1 B2
Abbey Cl. St on T TS21 .... 195 F4
Abbey Cty Jun Sch. Darl DL3 ...... 208 C1
Abbey Inf Sch. Darl DL3 .... 208 D1
Abbey La. Gr Br DL12 .... 201 A3
Abbey La. Start DL12 .... 201 B3
Abbey Rd. Bish Au DL14 .... 148 B5
Abbey Rd. Darl DL2 .... 210 F6
Abbey Rd. Darl DL3 .... 208 D1
Abbey Rd. Murton SR7 .... 58 B8
Abbey Road Ind Est.
  Durham DH1 .... 58 C8
Abbey Terr. Start DL12 .... 201 A4
Abbeywoods. Durham DH1 .... 58 B8
Abbots' Row. Belm DH1 .... 58 F3
Abbots Way. St on T TS21 .... 195 F4
Abbots Wlk. Beam DH9 .... 18 F8
Abbotsfield Way. Darl DL3 .... 208 B7
Abbotside Cl. Urpeth DH2 .... 8 D2
Abercorn Ct. Darl DL3 .... 208 B7
Aberdeen. Ouston DH2 .... 8 F1
Aberdeen Rd. Darl DL1 .... 209 F2
Aberfoyle. Stanl DH9 .... 18 B6
Aberfoyle. Ouston DH2 .... 8 F1
Abernethy. Ouston DH2 .... 8 F2
Abingdon. Ouston DH2 .... 8 F1
Acacia Ave. Peter SR8 .... 86 B6
Acacia Gdns. Crook DL15 .... 100 D4
Acacia Rd. Bish Au DL14 .... 148 B7
Acacia St. Darl DL3 .... 208 E4
Academy Gdns. Gain DL2 .... 205 A7
Accrington Terr. Even DL14 .... 167 D6
Acer Dr. Hasw DH6 .... 61 F3
Acle Burn. New Ay DL17 .... 150 C3
Acle Meadows. New Ay DL17 .... 150 C3
Aclet Cl. Bish Au DL14 .... 148 B4
Acorn Cl. Sacr DH7 .... 35 B4
Acorn Dr. Will DL15 .... 102 A6
Acorn Pl. Brand DH7 .... 79 B4
Acorn St. Beam DH9 .... 19 B7
Acornclose La. Sacr DH7 .... 34 F4
Acornclose La. Wit Gil DH7 .... 34 F4
Acre Rigg Rd. Peter SR8 .... 85 B8
Acton Dene. Stanl DH9 .... 18 C7
Acton Rd. Esh W DH7 .... 77 E8
Ada St E. Murton SR7 .... 40 D2
Ada St W. Murton SR7 .... 40 D2
Adam St. 3 Peter SR8 .... 86 B6
Adams Terr. Medom DH8 .... 4 A2
Adamson St. Shild DL4 .... 170 A7
Addison Rd. Cound DL14 .... 127 C1
Addison Rd. Hunw DL14 .... 125 D3
Addison St. Bish Au DL14 .... 148 F5
Addison St. Crook DL15 .... 100 E4
Adelaide Bank.
  Shild DL14 & DL4 .... 148 E3
Adelaide Row. 4 Seaham SR7 .... 41 D7
Adelaide St. 5 Bish Au DL14 .... 148 C5
Adelaide St. C le S DH3 .... 20 C2
Adelaide St. 11 Darl DL1 .... 209 B1
Adelaide Terr. Shild DL4 .... 148 E3
Adelphi St. 18 Darl DL1 .... 209 B1
Adfrid Pl. Peter SR8 .... 85 D7
Adolphus St W. Seaham SR7 ...... 41 D7
Adrian Pl. Peter SR8 .... 85 E5
Adventure La. W Rain DH4 .... 37 F2
Aged Miner's Home.
  Shild DL14 .... 149 A3
Aged Miner's Homes.
  Bear DH7 .... 57 A3
Aged Miner's Homes.
  Burnop NE16 .... 6 A6
Aged Miner's Homes.
  C le St DH2 .... 36 B7
Aged Miner's Homes.
  E Rain DH5 .... 38 C4
Aged Miner's Homes.
  H le H DH5 .... 38 F6
Aged Miner's Homes.
  H le H DH5 .... 39 A2
Aged Miner's Homes. 5
  H le Sp DH4 .... 38 C8
Aged Miner's Homes. 3
  H le Sp DH5 .... 38 F8
Aged Miner's Homes.
  Quebec DH7 .... 55 B4
Aged Miner's Homes.
  Ryhope SR2 .... 22 E7
Aged Miner's Homes. Sacr DH7 35 D3
Aged Miner's Homes. 2
  Seaham SR7 .... 22 F1
Aged Miner's Homes.
  Seaham SR7 .... 41 D6
Aged Miner's Homes.
  Bourn DH4 .... 21 E2
Aged Miner's Homes.
  Brand DH7 .... 79 B5
Aged Miner's Homes.
  Brand DH7 .... 79 C3
Aged Miner's Homes.
  Even DL14 .... 167 C7
Aged Miner's Homes.
  Fishb TS21 .... 131 D5
Aged Miner's Homes.
  Gr Lum DH3 .... 21 B1
Aged Miner's Homes.
  H Spen NE39 .... 1 A4
Aged Miner's Homes.
  Kibble NE11 .... 8 C6
Aged Miner's Homes.
  Kimble DH2 .... 35 F4
Aged Miner's Homes. 8
  Lang Pk DH7 .... 56 C6
Aged Miner's Homes.
  Leadg DH8 .... 15 C5
Aged Miner's Homes.
  Murton SR7 .... 40 B3

Aged Miner's Homes.
  Pelton DH2 .... 19 C6
Aged Miners' Homes. Peter SR8 85 F7
Aged Miner's Homes.
  Qua Hi DH6 .... 106 C1
Aged Miners' Homes. R Gill NE39 1 F1
Aged Miner's Homes.
  S Hill DH6 .... 60 C1
Aged Miners' Homes.
  Spenny DH16 .... 127 C6
Aged Miners' Homes.
  The Mid DH9 .... 18 B4
Aged Workers' Homes.
  Crook DL15 .... 100 D4
Agnes St. Stanl DH9 .... 17 F7
Agnew Way. New Ay DL5 .... 150 D1
Agricola Ct. Darl DL1 .... 208 C7
Aidan Cl. Stanl DH9 .... 18 B7
Aidans Wlk. Ferry DL17 .... 129 A7
Aiden Way. H le H DH5 .... 39 A5
Ainsley Gr. Darl DL3 .... 208 C7
Ainsley St. Durham DH1 .... 58 B2
Ainsty Hunt. New Ay DL5 .... 170 F8
Ainthorpe Cl. N Silk SR3 .... 22 B7
Aintree Ct. Darl DL1 .... 209 F3
Aintree Dr. Cons DH8 .... 14 D7
Airedale Gdns. H le H DH5 .... 38 F2
Aireys Cl. H le Sp DH4 .... 38 C8
Airton Pl. New Ay DL5 .... 171 B7
Airville Mount. N Silk SR3 .... 22 A4
Ajax St. Darl DL1 .... 209 C6
Alamein Ave. H le Sp DH5 .... 38 F8
Albatross Way. Darl DL1 .... 209 D1
Albert Cl. Bar Cas DL12 .... 201 A6
Albert Hill. Bish Au DL14 .... 148 C7
Albert Hill Ind Est. Darl DL1 .... 209 B4
Albert Rd. Cong DH8 .... 14 F2
Albert Rd. Darl DL1 .... 209 A4
Albert St. C le S DH3 .... 20 C3
Albert St. Crook DL15 .... 100 E4
Albert St. 12 Darl DL1 .... 209 B1
Albert St. Durham DH1 .... 58 B2
Albert St. Esh W DH7 .... 77 E8
Albert St. R Gill NE39 .... 1 A1
Albert St. Seaham SR7 .... 41 E6
Albert St. Shild DL4 .... 149 A2
Albert St. Thorn DH6 .... 83 D4
Albert St. W Pel DH2 .... 19 A5
Albert Terr. Billy R DL15 .... 100 E7
Albert Terr. Stanh DL13 .... 71 B2
Albery Pl. 16 Darl DL1 .... 209 B1
Albion Ave. Shild DL4 .... 148 F2
Albion Gdns. Burnop NE16 .... 5 F5
Albion Pl. Will DL15 .... 101 F3
Albion St. Spenny DH16 .... 127 C6
Albion Terr. Bish Au DL14 .... 148 C7
Albion Terr. Wit Pk DL14 .... 125 A1
Alcote Gr. Shot Co DH6 .... 84 D6
Aldam St. Darl DL1 .... 209 A4
Aldbrough Cl. 11 Ryhope SR2 .. 22 F6
Aldbrough Wlk. 4 Darl DL2 .... 224 C8
Alder Cl. H le H DH5 .... 38 F3
Alder Cres. Tant DH9 .... 5 F2
Alder Gr. Leadg DH8 .... 15 D3
Alder Lea Cl. Belm DH1 .... 59 A3
Alder Pk. Brand DH7 .... 79 A3
Alder Rd. Peter SR8 .... 86 B6
Alderdene Cl. Ush M DH7 .... 57 B1
Alderdene La. Lanch DH8 .... 32 E3
Alderman Leach Cty Jun Sch.
  Darl DL3 .... 208 C5
Alderman Wood Rd. Tanf L DH9 17 E8
Alderside Cres. Lanch DH7 .... 32 E4
Alderson St. 4 Bish Au DL14 .. 148 B6
Alderwood. Wash NE38 .... 21 B8
Alderwood Cl. Darl DL1 .... 209 E6
Alderwood Cl. Hartle TS27 .... 111 C4
Aldhome Ct. Durham DH1 .... 58 A6
Aldhun Cl. Bish Au DL14 .... 148 B4
Aldin Grange Terr. Bear DH7 .... 57 C3
Aldridge Ct. Ush M DH7 .... 57 A2
Aldwin Cl. Chilt DL17 .... 151 A8
Aldwyn Wlk. 3 New Ay DL5 .... 171 F8
Alexander Dr. H le H DH5 .... 38 F3
Alexander St. Darl DL1 .... 209 C3
Alexander Terr. Even DL14 .... 167 D6
Alexandra Cl. Durham DH1 .... 58 A6
Alexandra Gdns. 5 Shild DL4 .. 149 A2
Alexandra St. Cons DH8 .... 14 C2
Alexandra St. Pelton DH2 .... 19 C6
Alexandra St. R Gill NE39 .... 1 A1
Alexandra St. Shild DL4 .... 149 A2
Alexandra Terr. Crook DL15 ...... 100 F4
Alexandra Terr. Hasw DH6 .... 61 F3
Alexandra Terr. Wh Hi DH6 .... 83 F3
Alexandria Cres. Durham DH1 .... 58 B1
Alexandria Dr. M St G DL2 .... 226 A5
Alexandrina St. 1 Seaham SR7 . 41 D6
Alford. Ouston DH2 .... 8 F2
Alfred St. Darl DL1 .... 209 A4
Alfred St. Eas SR8 .... 63 E4
Alfred St. Seaham SR7 .... 41 E6
Alfred St E. Seaham SR7 .... 41 E6
Alfreton Cl. Brand DH7 .... 79 A2
Alfrid Pl. New Ay DL5 .... 171 D8
Alhambra Terr. Fishb TS21 .... 131 C5
Alice St. Pelton DH2 .... 19 F8
Aline St. N Silk SR3 .... 22 B7
Aline St. Seaham SR7 .... 41 E7
Alington Cl. Chilt DL17 .... 151 A8
Alington Dr. Durham DH1 .... 59 A2
Alington Rd. New Ay DL5 .... 171 C7
All Saints Cty Jun Sch.
  Shild DL4 .... 148 F5
All Saints Dr. H le H DH5 .... 39 A5
All Saints Ind Est. Shild DL4 .... 170 B7
All Saints' Rd. Shild DL4 .... 170 A7
Allan St. Darl DL1 .... 209 B3
Allen St. C le S DH3 .... 20 C2
Allen St. Eas SR8 .... 63 F5
Allendale Rd. Brand DH7 .... 79 C4

Allendale St. H le H DH5 .... 39 A2
Allendale Terr. Ann Pl DH9 .... 16 F4
Allendale Terr. Hasw DH6 .... 61 F3
Allensford Bank. Cons DH8 .... 29 F8
Allergate. Durham DH1 .... 58 B1
Allerton Pl. Whick NE16 .... 2 F5
Alliance Ind Est. Darl DL3 .... 208 A4
Alliance St. Darl DL3 .... 208 A4
Allison Gdns. Cons DH8 .... 14 F4
Allison St. Cons DH8 .... 14 F4
Alloy Terr. R Gill NE39 .... 1 C1
Alma Pl. Belm DH1 .... 59 B3
Alma Rd. Shild DL4 .... 170 A8
Alma Terr. Eas SR8 .... 63 F5
Alma Terr. Belm DH1 .... 80 A8
Alma Terr. Stan Cr DL15 .... 100 E8
Almond Cl. Hasw DH6 .... 61 F3
Almond Rd. Shild DL4 .... 170 B8
Almond Terr. 5 Peter SR8 .... 86 B6
Almoner's Barn. Durham DH1 .... 80 A7
Almshouses. Even DL14 .... 167 C7
Almshouses. Staind DL2 .... 186 D6
Alnwick Ave. Trim TS29 .... 107 E4
Alnwick Cl. Bish Au DL14 .... 148 A6
Alnwick Cl. C le S DH2 .... 20 A1
Alnwick Cl. Ferry DL17 .... 129 B5
Alnwick Cl. Hartle TS27 .... 111 D3
Alnwick Gr. New Ay DL17 .... 150 E1
Alnwick Pl. Darl DL1 .... 209 C5
Alnwick Rd. Durham DH1 .... 58 C7
Alnwick Rd. Eas SR8 .... 63 E4
Alnwick St. R Gill NE39 .... 85 F8
Alpine Terr. Cockf DL13 .... 166 C5
Alpine Terr. Cons DH8 .... 14 C6
Alpine Way. Tow Law DL13 .... 75 C2
Alston Cres. New Ay DL5 .... 171 A7
Alston Moor Cl. Darl DL1 .... 224 D8
Alston Rd. Cons DH8 .... 14 C4
Alston Rd. Mid in T DL12 .... 160 C8
Alston Terr. Cons DH8 .... 14 C4
Alston Way. Brand DH7 .... 79 C4
Alston Wlk. New Ay DL5 .... 171 A7
Alston Wlk. Peter SR8 .... 85 E7
Alston Wlk. Sherb DH6 .... 60 A1
Alum Waters. N Bran DH7 .... 79 A8
Alverton Cl. New Ay DL5 .... 150 B1
Alverton Dr. Darl DL3 .... 208 C7
Alwent Cl. Darl DL3 .... 207 F2
Alwent Mill La. Winst DL2 .... 187 B1
Alwin. Bourn DH4 .... 21 E3
Alwin. Wash NE38 .... 9 F1
Alwinton Dr. C le S DH2 .... 20 A1
Alwyn Gdns. Cons DH8 .... 14 F1
Alwyn Rd. Darl DL1 .... 209 A7
Amberwood Cl. 2 Hartle TS27 111 C4
Ambleside Ave. Seaham SR7 ...... 40 F8
Ambleside Cl. Peter SR8 .... 85 E7
Ambleside Mews. Leadg DH8 ...... 15 D4
Amersham Cres. Peter SR8 .... 85 D7
Amiens Cl. Darl DL3 .... 208 C5
Ampleforth Way. Darl DL3 .... 208 A5
Ancaster Rd. Whick NE16 .... 2 F4
Anchorage Terr. Durham DH1 .... 80 D8
Anchorage The. C le S DH3 .... 20 D3
Ancroft Garth. H Shin DH1 .... 81 B4
Ancrum Way. Whick NE16 .... 2 F5
Andrew St. Eas SR8 .... 63 E4
Andrew Terr. Wh Hi DH6 .... 83 E1
Andrew's La. Eas SR8 .... 63 B2
Anesty Ct. Bish TS21 .... 194 C7
Anfield Ct. Darl DL1 .... 209 F3
Angate Sq. Wols DL13 .... 97 F7
Angate St. Wols DL13 .... 97 F7
Anglesey Av. Hartle TS26 .... 111 E1
Angus. Ouston DH2 .... 8 F2
Angus Sq. Darl DL3 .... 79 D5
Angus St. Eas SR8 .... 63 F4
Angus Terr. Peter SR8 .... 63 F3
Ann Ave. Kelloe DH6 .... 106 D6
Ann St. 2 Cons DH8 .... 14 F2
Ann's Terr. Darl DL3 .... 208 F4
Annand Rd. Durham DH1 .... 58 F3
Annandale. Darl DL1 .... 209 E7
Annandale Cres. Hartle TS24 .... 111 F2
Annaside Mews. Leadg DH8 .... 15 D4
Anne Swyft Rd. New Ay DL5 .... 171 E5
Annfield Pl. Ann Pl DH9 .... 16 E4
Annfield Plain Cty Inf Sch.
  Ann Pl DH9 .... 16 F3
Annfield Plain Cty Jun Sch.
  Ann Pl DH9 .... 17 A3
Annfield Terr. Ann Pl DH9 .... 16 E5
Annums The. Bowes DL12 .... 216 B7
Anson Wlk. Cound DL4 .... 149 B8
Anthony St. Eas SR8 .... 63 F5
Anthony St. Stanl DH9 .... 17 E7
Antliff Terr. Ann Pl DH9 .... 16 F4
Antrim Gdns. Seaham SR7 .... 41 C8
Apperley Ave. H Shin DH1 .... 81 C4
Appleby St. Bish Au DL14 .... 148 D5
Appleby Way. Peter SR8 .... 85 A3
Appledore Gdns. C le S DH3 .... 20 D5
Appledore Gdns. Edmon DH7 ...... 35 B7
Applegarth. Coxhoe DH6 .... 106 A3
Appleton Cl. Darl DL3 .... 208 F5
Appleton Cres. Will DL15 .... 101 F3
Appletree Cl. Hur on T DL2 .... 224 D1
Applewood Cl. Hartle TS27 .... 111 B4
Aquinas Ct. Darl DL3 .... 209 A6
Arbourcourt Ave. Esh W DH7 .... 77 D8
Arcadia Cres. Darl DL3 .... 208 B4
Arcadia Ave. C le S DH3 .... 20 C5
Arcadia. Ouston DH2 .... 8 F1
Archdeacon Cres. Darl DL3 ...... 208 B4
Archer Ave. Bish Au DL14 .... 148 A4
Archer Rd. M St G DL2 .... 226 A5
Archer St. Darl DL3 .... 208 F2
Archery Rise. Durham DH1 .... 80 A8
Arden St. Shot Co DH6 .... 84 C7
Ardmore Dr. Darl DL1 .... 209 D1

Ardrossan. Ouston DH2 .... 8 F1
Arena Bsns Pk. H le Sp DH4 .... 38 C7
Argent St. Eas SR8 .... 63 F5
Argyle Ct. Tanf DH9 .... 7 A1
Argyle Pl. S Hett DH6 .... 61 F7
Argyll. Ouston DH2 .... 8 F1
Arisaig. Ouston DH2 .... 8 F1
Arkendale St. Darl DL1 .... 209 A5
Arkle Cres. Darl DL1 .... 223 F6
Arlington Cl. Bourn DH4 .... 21 E3
Armadale Ct. St on T TS21 .... 195 F4
Armondside Rd. B Mill NE17 .... 4 C6
Armoury St. 5 Spenny DL16 ...... 103 F1
Armstrong Ave. Wing TS28 .... 108 E8
Armstrong Cl. New Ay DL5 .... 171 F8
Armstrong Ct. Darl DL3 .... 208 D4
Armstrong Ind Est. Wash NE37 .. 9 F7
Armstrong Rd. Peter SR8 .... 85 D8
Arncliffe Gr. Darl DL2 .... 207 F2
Arncliffe Pl. New Ay DL5 .... 171 B7
Arndale House. 11 Birt DH3 .... 9 C4
Arnison Ctr The. Durham DH1 .... 58 C8
Arnold Cl. Stanl DH9 .... 18 A6
Arnold Rd. Darl DL1 .... 209 C3
Arnold St. Bish Au DL14 .... 147 C2
Arran Cl. Silk SR3 .... 22 A6
Arran Wlk. Darl DL1 .... 209 D7
Arrowsmith Sq. New Ay DL5 .... 171 E7
Arthur Ave. Ryhope SR2 .... 23 A6
Arthur St. Beam DH9 .... 19 A7
Arthur St. Bish Au DL14 .... 148 A4
Arthur St. Chilt DL17 .... 151 A7
Arthur St. Crook DL15 .... 100 F4
Arthur St. Darl DL3 .... 208 F4
Arthur St. Eas SR8 .... 63 F5
Arthur St. 11 Ryhope SR2 .... 23 A6
Arthur St. Ush M DH7 .... 56 F2
Arthur Terr. Bish Au DL14 .... 148 B5
Arthur Terr. Ferry DL17 .... 129 C4
Arthur Terr. Stan Cr DL17 .... 76 E1
Arun Cl. Peter SR8 .... 85 C5
Arundel Cl. Bish Au DL14 .... 148 A6
Arundel Dr. Darl DL3 .... 208 B5
Arundel Way. Brand DH7 .... 79 C4
Arundel Wlk. Pelton DH2 .... 19 F7
Ascot Cl. Pelton DH2 .... 19 F7
Ascot Rd. Cons DH8 .... 14 E7
Ascot St. Eas SR8 .... 63 F4
Ascot View. Darl DL1 .... 209 E4
Ash Ave. Lang Pk DH7 .... 56 C6
Ash Ave. Ush M DH7 .... 57 A2
Ash Cres. Seaham SR7 .... 41 C5
Ash Dr. Will DL15 .... 102 C3
Ash Gr. Chilt DL17 .... 150 E8
Ash Gr. Shild DL4 .... 149 A1
Ash Gr. Spenny DL16 .... 127 E7
Ash Gr. Wing TS29 .... 108 A5
Ash Meadows. C le S DH3 .... 20 E7
Ash St. Cons DH8 .... 14 F2
Ash St. 12 Lang Pk DH7 .... 56 C6
Ash Terr. Ann Pl DH9 .... 16 E5
Ash Terr. Bowb DH6 .... 105 D8
Ash Terr. Cornf DL17 .... 129 E8
Ash Terr. Leadg DH8 .... 15 D4
Ash Terr. Murton SR7 .... 40 D3
Ash Terr. Tant DH9 .... 6 B2
Ash Terr. The Mid DH9 .... 18 B3
Ash Tree Cl. Darl DL3 .... 208 B2
Ash Tree Terr. Holm DH7 .... 34 D7
Ashbrook Cl. Brand DH7 .... 78 F3
Ashbrooke Ct. Hut Hen TS27 .... 109 C4
Ashbrooke Est. Shot Co DH6 ...... 84 C6
Ashby Cres. Cons DH8 .... 14 D5
Ashby La. Cons DH8 .... 14 D4
Ashcroft Gdns. Bish Au DL14 .... 148 C6
Ashcroft Rd. Darl DL3 .... 223 D8
Ashcroft. Stanh DL13 .... 71 A4
Ashdale Rd. Cons DH8 .... 15 A3
Ashdown Ave. Belm DH1 .... 59 B3
Ashfield. Cons DH8 .... 14 D6
Ashfield. New Ay DL5 .... 171 C6
Ashfield Ct. H Spen NE39 .... 1 A4
Ashfield Terr. C le S DH3 .... 20 D2
Ashford Dr. Sacr DH7 .... 35 B4
Ashford Gr. Thorn DH6 .... 83 E4
Ashgrove Terr. Birt DH3 .... 9 B5
Ashkirk Cl. C le S DH2 .... 20 A1
Ashleigh Ave. Durham DH1 .... 58 B5
Ashleigh. C le S DH2 .... 20 A5
Ashleigh Gr. Lanch DH7 .... 32 E4
Ashley Ct. Tanf L DH9 .... 17 C8
Ashley Terr. C le S DH3 .... 20 C4
Ashmore Terr. Wh Hi DH6 .... 83 F3
Ashton Rise. Peter SR8 .... 85 E7
Ashton St. Eas SR8 .... 63 F4
Ashtree Cl. R Gill NE39 .... 1 F3
Ashtree La. H Spen NE21 & NE39 .. 1 B5
Ashvale Ave. Kibble NE11 .... 8 C6
Ashville Dr. Hur on T DL2 .... 235 C8
Ashwood Cl. Hartle TS27 .... 111 C4
Askerton Dr. Peter SR8 .... 85 A3
Askrigg Cl. New Ay DL5 .... 171 C8
Askrigg Cl. Urpeth DH2 .... 8 E2
Askrigg St. Darl DL1 .... 209 A5
Aspen Ave. 7 Peter SR8 .... 86 B6
Aspen Cl. Belm DH1 .... 59 A3
Aspen Ct. Cons DH8 .... 14 E4
Aspen Ct. Gr Lum DH3 .... 37 A7
Aspen Ct. Shild DL4 .... 170 B8
Aspley Cl. Silk SR3 .... 22 A6
Asquith St. Thorn DH6 .... 83 E4
Asquith Terr. Ann Pl DH9 .... 16 E5
Association St. Shild DL4 .... 148 F2
Aston Terr. Darl DL3 .... 208 C3
Aston Way. Whick NE16 .... 2 F5
Athelstan Rigg. Ryhope SR2 ...... 23 A7
Atherstone Way. Darl DL3 .... 208 A5
Atherton Cl. Spenny DH16 .... 127 F7
Atherton Dr. Fence DH4 .... 38 A7

Atherton St. Durham DH1 .... 58 B2
Atherton Terr. Bish Au DL14 ...... 148 E5
Athlone Pl. Birt DH3 .... 9 D1
Athol Gdns. Ryhope SR2 .... 23 A6
Athol Gr. N Silk SR3 .... 22 A7
Atholl Cl. Darl DL1 .... 209 D6
Atholl. Ouston DH2 .... 8 F2
Atkinson Gdns. New Ay DL5 ...... 171 E7
Atkinson Gr. Shot Co DH6 .... 84 B7
Atkinson Rd. C le S DH3 .... 20 D5
Atlee Sq. Sherb DH6 .... 59 F2
Attlee Ave. B Rocks SR7 .... 86 F1
Attlee Cres. Hasw DH6 .... 61 E1
Attlee Ct. Tow Law DL13 .... 75 C1
Attlee Est. Tow Law DL13 .... 75 C1
Attlee Gr. Sland SR2 .... 22 E8
Attwood Pl. Tow Law DL13 .... 75 B3
Attwood Rd. Tow Law DL13 .... 75 B3
Attwood Terr. Spenny DL16 ...... 104 B4
Attwood Terr. Wols DL13 .... 98 A7
Auckland Ave. Darl DL3 .... 208 D4
Auckland. C le S DH2 .... 20 A3
Auckland Mews. New Ay DL5 .... 171 E7
Auckland Oval. Darl DL3 .... 208 D5
Auckland Pl. New Ay DL5 .... 171 E7
Auckland Rd. Bish Au DL14 .... 148 D5
Auckland Rd. Durham DH1 .... 58 D7
Auckland Rd. Ferry DL17 .... 129 B6
Auckland Terr. Shild DL4 .... 148 E2
Auckland View. Hi Eth DL14 ...... 146 F5
Auckland Wynd. Shild DL4 .... 148 E2
Audrey Gr. Darl DL1 .... 209 D1
Augusta Cl. Darl DL1 .... 209 E6
Austen Pl. Stanl DH9 .... 18 B4
Austen Way. Crook DL15 .... 100 C3
Austin St. Eas SR8 .... 63 F5
Auton Cl. Bear DH7 .... 57 B3
Auton Field. Bear DH7 .... 57 C3
Auton Stile. Bear DH7 .... 57 B3
Avenue 1. Chilt DL17 .... 128 E1
Avenue 2. Chilt DL17 .... 128 E1
Avenue 3. Chilt DL17 .... 128 E1
Avenue 4. Chilt DL17 .... 128 D1
Avenue St. H Shin DH1 .... 81 B4
Avenue The. Ann Pl DH9 .... 16 E3
Avenue The. Birt DH3 .... 9 C4
Avenue The. Bourn DH3 & DH4 .. 21 E6
Avenue The. Burnh DH7 .... 33 E5
Avenue The. C le S DH3 .... 20 B3
Avenue The. Cons DH8 .... 15 A2
Avenue The. Coxhoe DH6 .... 106 A4
Avenue The. Durham DH1 .... 58 A7
Avenue The. Durham DH1 .... 58 B1
Avenue The. H le H DH5 .... 39 B4
Avenue The. Murton SR7 .... 40 D3
Avenue The. Pelton DH2 .... 19 F7
Avenue The. R Gill NE39 .... 1 F1
Avenue The. Seaham SR7 .... 41 A7
Avenue The. Staint DL12 .... 201 D8
Avenue The. Wh Hi DH6 .... 83 E3
Avenue Vivian. Gr Lum DH4 .... 21 F1
Aviemore Ct. Darl DL1 .... 209 F3
Avon Cl. R Gill NE39 .... 1 F3
Avon Cres. Fence DH4 .... 38 A8
Avon Rd. Hur on T DL2 .... 235 B8
Avon Rd. Peter SR8 .... 85 C5
Avon Rd. Stanl DH9 .... 17 F5
Avon St. Eas SR8 .... 63 E4
Avon Way. Darl DL1 .... 224 A6
Avoncroft St. Seaton DH4 .... 40 D8
Avondale Rd. 2 Cons DH8 .... 14 F3
Avondale Terr. C le S DH2 & DH3 20 C3
Axford Terr. Hams NE17 .... 4 B6
Aycliffe Ctr for Children.
  New Ay DL5 .... 172 A7
Aycliffe Hospl. New Ay DL5 ...... 171 A3
Aycliffe Ind Est. New Ay DL5 .... 171 C3
Aycliffe La. Braf DL1 .... 192 A7
Aycliffe La. Mordon TS21 .... 152 B1
Aycliffe Village Cty Jun Inf Sch.
  New Ay DL5 .... 171 E2
Aykley Ct. Durham DH1 .... 58 A4
Aykley Gn. Durham DH1 .... 58 A4
Aykley Heads Sports Gd.
  Durham DH1 .... 58 C4
Aykley Rd. Durham DH1 .... 58 B6
Aykley Vale. Durham DH1 .... 58 B5
Aylesbury Dr. Silk SR3 .... 22 A5
Aylmer Gr. New Ay DL5 .... 171 C7
Aylsham Ct. Silk SR3 .... 22 A4
Aylward Pl. Stanl DH9 .... 18 B5
Aynsley Terr. Cons DH8 .... 14 F3
Ayresome Way. Darl DL1 .... 209 D3
Aysgarth Ct. New Ay DL5 .... 171 B7
Aysgarth Rd. Darl DL1 .... 224 B8
Ayton Dr. Darl DL3 .... 223 D7
Ayton Prim Sch. Wash NE38 .... 9 F3
Ayton Rd. Wash NE38 .... 9 F4
Azalea Ave. 6 Peter SR8 .... 86 B6

Babbacombe Dr. Ferry DL17 ...... 129 C5
Back Church St. Cound DL14 .... 149 B8
Back Coronation Terr.
  Coxhoe DH6 .... 105 F5
Back Coronation Terr.
  H le H DH5 .... 39 A2
Back East Par. Cons DH8 .... 15 A2
Back Eldon Terr. Ferry DL17 ...... 129 C4
Back La. G Stain TS21 .... 173 D1
Back La. Gr Lum DH3 .... 37 A8
Back La. Head DL2 .... 188 B3
Back La. L Con DL2 .... 222 D8
Back La. Lang DL2 .... 188 B3
Back La. Leadg DH8 .... 15 F2
Back La. Longn TS21 .... 211 F7
Back La. Satley DH7 & DL13 .... 53 C3
Back La. Walw DL2 .... 190 C3
Back Mount Joy. Durham DH1 .... 80 D8
Back North Railway St.
  Seaham SR7 .... 41 D8
Back North Terr. Seaham SR7 .... 41 D8

Back Palmerston St. Cons DH8 . 14 F2
Back Ryhope St. Ryhope SR2 .... 22 E7
Back Silver St. Durham DH1 ...... 58 C2
Back South Railway St.
  Seaham SR7 .... 41 D7
Back Sussex St. Cound DL14 .... 149 B6
Back Victoria Terr. Ann Pl DH9 . 16 E5
Back Western Hill. Durham DH1 58 D2
Backhouse St. Darl DL1 .... 209 A1
Backstone Burn. Cons DH8 .... 14 C5
Backstone Rd. Cons DH8 .... 14 C4
Baden St. C le S DH3 .... 20 C2
Badger Cl. Silk SR3 .... 22 A5
Badminton Cl. Darl DL1 .... 209 F4
Badminton Gr. New Ay DL17 .... 150 E1
Baff St. Spenny DL16 .... 127 F8
Bail Hill Rd. Mick DL12 .... 161 C2
Bail Hill Rd. Romald DL12 .... 161 C2
Bailey Rise. Peter SR8 .... 85 D8
Bailey St. Tant DH9 .... 6 B2
Bailey Way. H le H DH5 .... 39 B2
Bainbridge Ave. Will DL15 ...... 102 A3
Bainbridge Ct. Bish Au DL14 .... 147 D2
Bainbridge St. Belm DH1 .... 59 D4
Bakehouse Hill. Bish Au DL14 .. 126 C1
Bakehouse Hill. 6 Darl DL1 .... 208 F1
Bakehouse La. Durham DH1 ...... 58 D2
Baker Cl. Hartle TS27 .... 111 D3
Baker St. Leadg DH8 .... 15 C4
Bakewell Pl. New Ay DL5 .... 171 C8
Baldwin St. Eas SR8 .... 63 F4
Bale Hill. Hunst DH8 .... 25 F6
Balfour Gdns. 4 Cons DH8 ...... 14 F4
Balfour St. Cons DH8 .... 14 F4
Balfour Terr. Chopw NE17 .... 4 B8
Baliol Ave. New Ay DL5 .... 171 E5
Baliol Rd. New Ay DL5 .... 171 E5
Baliol Sq. Durham DH1 .... 80 A7
Baliol St. Bar Cas DL12 .... 201 A6
Ballarat The. New Ay DL5 .... 150 D1
Ballater Cl. Stanl DH9 .... 18 B6
Balliol Cl. Peter SR8 .... 85 B5
Balliol Ct. 2 Darl DL1 .... 209 B6
Balmer Hill. Gain DL2 .... 205 A7
Balmoral. Gr Lum DH3 .... 37 A8
Balmoral Ave. H le Sp DH5 .... 38 F7
Balmoral Ct. Bish Au DL14 ...... 148 A6
Balmoral Rd. Darl DL1 .... 209 D6
Balmoral Rd. Ferry DL17 .... 129 B7
Balmoral Terr. Trim TS29 .... 107 D3
Baltic The. Wit Pk DL14 .... 147 A8
Baltimore Way. Darl DL1 .... 209 B6
Bamburgh Ave. Bish Au DL14 .. 148 A6
Bamburgh Ave. Peter SR8 .... 85 F8
Bamburgh Cres. New Ay DL17 .. 150 E1
Bamburgh Ct. Hartle TS27 ...... 111 D3
Bamburgh Par. Spenny DL16 .... 128 A8
Bamburgh Pl. Darl DL1 .... 209 C5
Bamburgh Rd. Durham DH1 ...... 58 C7
Bamburgh Rd. Ferry DL17 .... 129 B7
Bamburgh Rd. Hartle TS27 ...... 111 D3
Banesley La. Kibble NE11 .... 8 A8
Bangor Gr. Darl DL1 .... 209 E5
Bank Foot Cl. Crook DL15 .... 100 D5
Bank Side. Mick DL12 .... 161 B4
Bank Terr. Thor Th TS21 .... 175 E3
Bank The. Bar Cas DL12 .... 201 A5
Bank Top. Bish Mi DL17 .... 130 B3
Bank Top Mews. Darl DL1 .... 224 B8
Bank Top Terr. Trim TS29 .... 107 C1
Bank Well. Hi Eth DL14 .... 146 F6
Bankhead Terr. Fence DH4 .... 38 A8
Banklands Cl. Darl DL3 .... 208 D4
Banklands Rd. Darl DL3 .... 208 D4
Banks Rd. Darl DL1 .... 209 D2
Banks Terr. Hur on T DL2 .... 235 A8
Bankwell Dr. Hi Eth DL14 .... 146 F6
Bannerman Terr. S Hill DH6 ...... 60 C1
Bannerman Terr. 3 Ush M DH7 56 F2
Barbary Cl. Pelton DH2 .... 19 E7
Barcusclose La.
  Burnop DH9 & NE16 .... 6 D5
Barden Moor Rd. Darl DL1 ...... 224 C7
Barford Dr. C le S DH2 .... 20 A1
Bargate Bank. Lanch DH7 .... 54 F8
Baring Ct. Tow Law DL13 .... 75 B2
Barker's Bldgs. Coxhoe DH6 .... 105 F3
Barkwood Rd. R Gill NE39 .... 1 D2
Barley Mill Cres. Cons DH8 ...... 14 B4
Barley Mill Rd. Cons DH8 .... 14 B4
Barley Mow. C le S DH3 .... 20 D8
Barlow Cres. Barlow NE21 .... 1 C5
Barlow Fell Rd. Barlow NE21 ...... 1 C5
Barlow La. Barlow NE21 .... 1 C4
Barlow St. Darl DL3 .... 208 D3
Barlowfield Cl. Blay NE21 .... 2 A8
Barmpton La. Darl DL1 .... 209 F7
Barn Hill. Stanl DH9 .... 17 E7
Barn Hollows. Haw SR7 .... 63 C7
Barnard Ave. Bish Au DL14 ...... 148 B6
Barnard Ave. Ludw DH6 .... 83 C7
Barnard Castle Jun & Inf C of E
  Cont Schs. Bar Cas DL12 ...... 201 B6
Barnard Castle Sch.
  Bar Cas DL12 .... 201 B5
Barnard Cl. Durham DH1 .... 58 D7
Barnard Cl. New Ay DL5 .... 150 E1
Barnard Cl. Spenny DL16 .... 104 A2
Barnard Ct. Hartle TS24 .... 111 D4
Barnard Grove Inf & Jun Schs.
  Hartle TS24 .... 111 D4
Barnard Pk. H le H DH5 .... 39 A4
Barnard Rd. Ferry DL17 .... 129 C7
Barnard St. Darl DL3 .... 208 F2
Barnard St. Staind DL2 .... 186 D6
Barnard Wynd. Peter SR8 .... 85 B3
Barnes Cl. Darl DL3 .... 208 B3
Barnes Ct. Hartle TS24 .... 111 E3
Barnes Rd. Darl DL3 .... 208 B3
Barnes Rd. Murton SR7 .... 40 C3
Barnes St. H le H DH5 .... 39 A4

Barnes Wlk. 4 New Ay DL5 ...... 171 D8
Barnfield Rd. Spenny DL16 ...... 104 A1
Barningham Rd. Newsh DL11 ... 219 E1
Barningham St. Darl DL3 .... 208 F3
Barns The. Stanl DH9 .... 17 F7
Barpett Sq. Hasw DH6 .... 61 F3
Barr Hills. 6 Cons DH8 .... 14 F3
Barr House Ave. Cons DH8 .... 14 F2
Barrack Terr. Kibble NE11 .... 8 D6
Barrasford Rd. Durham DH1 ...... 58 C7
Barratt Way. Cornf DL17 .... 105 E2
Barrett Rd. Darl DL3 .... 208 B1
Barrhead Cl. St on T TS21 ...... 195 F4
Barrington Ct. H le H DH5 .... 39 A4
Barrington Rd. New Ay DL5 .... 171 C6
Barrington Terr. H le H DH5 ...... 39 A4
Barrington Terr. Ferry DL17 .... 128 E6
Barron St. Darl DL3 .... 208 F4
Barsloan Gr. Peter SR8 .... 85 B8
Bartlemere. Bar Cas DL12 .... 201 B6
Bartlett St. Darl DL1 .... 208 F3
Barton St. Darl DL1 .... 209 B4
Barwick St. Cold He SR7 .... 40 E1
Barwick St. Eas SR8 .... 63 F4
Basic Cotts. Coxhoe DH6 .... 105 F5
Basingstoke Rd. Peter SR8 .... 85 C7
Bassenthwaite Ave. C le S DH2 . 20 B1
Bassenthwaite Gr.
  Bish Au DL14 .... 147 B1
Bates Ave. Darl DL3 .... 208 C5
Bates Cl. New Ay DL5 .... 171 C8
Batey St. Ann Pl DH9 .... 16 E5
Bath La. Cons DH8 .... 14 F3
Batt La. Heigh DL5 .... 170 C1
Batts Terr. Bish Au DL14 .... 126 C1
Batts The. Frost DL13 .... 96 C6
Baxby Terr. Hur on T DL2 .... 235 A8
Bay Ave. Peter SR8 .... 86 B6
Bay Ct. Ush M DH7 .... 57 B1
Bay Tree Dr. Darl DL1 .... 209 A8
Baydale Rd. Darl DL3 .... 223 B8
Baysdale Cl. Bish Au DL14 ...... 147 E6
Baysdale Gdns. Shild DL4 .... 149 C1
Baysdale. Pens DH4 .... 21 E8
Baytree Terr. Beam DH9 .... 19 B7
Beach Gr. Peter SR8 .... 86 B6
Beachdale Cl. Hut Hen TS28 .... 108 F5
Beacon Ave. Sedge TS21 .... 153 C6
Beacon Grange Pk. Sadb DL2 .. 210 E6
Beacon Hill. Sadb DL2 .... 210 D6
Beacon La. Sedge TS21 .... 153 C6
Beaconsfield Ct. Bar Cas DL12 . 201 A6
Beaconsfield St. 2 Cons DH8 ... 14 F4
Beaconsfield St. Darl DL3 .... 208 E3
Beaconsfield St. Stanl DH9 .... 17 F7
Beadnell Cl. Blay NE21 .... 2 A8
Beadnell Cl. C le S DH2 .... 20 A1
Beagle Sq. 6 N Silk SR3 .... 22 A7
Beal Wlk. H Shin DH1 .... 81 B5
Beamish Cl. Lang Pk DH7 .... 56 B6
Beamish Ct. Pelton DH2 .... 19 C6
Beamish Cty Sch. Stanl DH9 .... 18 D7
Beamish Hills. Stanl DH9 .... 18 D7
Beamish Open Air Mus.
  Beam DH9 .... 7 D2
Beamish St. Stanl DH9 .... 17 E7
Beamish View. C le S DH2 .... 19 C3
Beamish View. Stanl DH9 .... 18 C7
Beamishburn Rd.
  Beam DH9 & NE16 .... 7 B3
Beaney La. Kimble DH7 .... 36 A6
Beaney La. Wald DH2 .... 35 F6
Bearpark Colliery Rd. Bear DH7 57 C3
Bearpark Cty Jun & Inf Sch.
  Bear DH7 .... 57 B4
Beatrice Terr. Pens DH4 .... 21 E8
Beatty St. Eas SR8 .... 63 F4
Beaumont Cl. Durham DH1 .... 58 A7
Beaumont Cl. New Ay DL17 ...... 150 D1
Beaumont Cres. Peter SR8 .... 63 E1
Beaumont Ct. Sedge TS21 .... 153 C6
Beaumont Hill. Darl DL1 & DL3 . 192 A2
Beaumont Pl. Peter SR8 .... 85 E5
Beaumont St. 9 Bish Au DL14 .. 148 B6
Beaumont St. Darl DL1 .... 208 F1
Beaumont St. Ferry DL17 .... 128 E6
Beaumont St. Seaham SR7 .... 41 D6
Beaumont St W. Darl DL1 .... 208 F1
Beaumont Way. New Ay DL5 .... 171 D3
Beaurepaire. Bear DH7 .... 57 A3
Beaver Cl. Durham DH1 .... 58 C0
Beck Pl. Peter SR8 .... 85 D7
Beck Rd. Darl DL1 .... 209 A3
Beckett Cl. Bish Au DL14 .... 147 E7
Beckwith's La. Kir Me DL16 .... 128 A3
Beda Cotts. Tant DH9 .... 6 A2
Beda Cotts. Belm DH1 .... 59 D4
Bedale Hunt. New Ay DL5 .... 170 F8
Bedale St. H le H DH5 .... 39 A2
Bedburn Cl. Crook DL15 .... 101 A3
Bedburn Dr. Bish Au DL14 ...... 147 E5
Bedburn Rd. Darl DL3 .... 207 F2
Bedburn. Wash NE38 .... 9 F1
Bede Ave. Durham DH1 .... 59 B1
Bede Cl. Escomb DL14 .... 125 D1
Bede Cl. Stanl DH9 .... 18 B7
Bede Coll. Durham DH1 .... 58 E2
Bede Cres. New Ay DL5 .... 171 D5
Bede Gr. Cornf DL17 .... 105 D1
Bede Hospl. Bar Cas DL12 ...... 201 B6
Bede Kirk. Bar Cas DL12 .... 201 B7
Bede Pl. Kir Me DL16 .... 128 A3
Bede Rd. Bar Cas DL12 .... 201 B7
Bede Rd. Eas SR8 .... 63 F4
Bede Terr. Bowb DH6 .... 81 D1
Bede Terr. C le S DH2 .... 20 B3
Bede Terr. 1 Ferry DL17 .... 129 A5

Bede Way. Durham DH1 .... 58 C6
Bede Way. Peter SR8 .... 85 D6
Bede Way. Peter SR8 .... 85 E5
Bedford Ave. Birt DH3 .... 9 D1
Bedford Pl. N Silk SR3 .... 148 B5
Bedford Pl. N Silk SR3 .... 22 A8
Bedford Pl. Peter SR8 .... 85 C8
Bedford Pl. Will DL15 .... 102 A3
Bedford St. H le H DH5 .... 38 F4
Bedford St. N Silk SR3 .... 224 A8
Bedfordshire Dr. Belm DH1 ...... 59 D3
Beech Ave. Birt DH3 .... 9 D1
Beech Ave. Chilt DL17 .... 150 E8
Beech Ave. Cons DL15 .... 100 E4
Beech Ave. 4 H le Sp DH4 .... 38 D8
Beech Ave. Spenny DL16 .... 127 E7
Beech Cl. Durham DH1 .... 58 E8
Beech Cres. Ferry DL17 .... 129 A5
Beech Cres. Heigh DL5 .... 170 E2
Beech Cres. Seaham SR7 .... 41 C6
Beech Crest. S Durham DH1 ...... 58 B1
Beech Ct. Lang Pk DH7 .... 56 C6
Beech Gr. B Mill NE17 .... 4 B6
Beech Gr. Burnh DH7 .... 33 D4
Beech Gr. Dipton DH9 .... 16 C7
Beech Gr. Ferry DL17 .... 129 A5
Beech Gr. Trim TS29 .... 107 E3
Beech Gr. Ush M DH7 .... 57 B1
Beech Gr. Wing TS29 .... 108 A5
Beech Gr. Wit le W DL14 .... 124 B3
Beech Oval. Sedge TS21 .... 153 B7
Beech Par. Cornf DL17 .... 105 E1
Beech Pk. Brand DH7 .... 79 A3
Beech Rd. Bish Au DL14 .... 148 C7
Beech Rd. Darl DL1 .... 209 E6
Beech Rd. Durham DH1 .... 58 B5
Beech Rd. Leadg DH8 .... 15 D3
Beech Terr. Ann Pl DH9 .... 16 E5
Beech Terr. Bish Au DL14 .... 148 F4
Beech Terr. Burnop NE16 .... 6 C6
Beech Terr. 4 Peter SR8 .... 86 A6
Beech Terr. Stanl DH9 .... 17 E4
Beech Terr. The Mid DH9 .... 18 B3
Beechburn Pk. Crook DL15 ...... 100 F2
Beechcroft Ave. Brand DH7 ...... 79 A3
Beechcroft St. Darl DL3 .... 59 A3
Beechdale Rd. Belm DH1 .... 59 D4
Beechdale Rd. Cons DH8 .... 15 A3
Beechers Gr. New Ay DL5 .... 150 E2
Beechfield. New Ay DL5 .... 171 B6
Beechfield Rise. Coxhoe DH6 .. 106 A5
Beechgrove La.
  Edmon DH7 & DH9 .... 18 F2
Beechgrove Terr.
  Edmon DH9 .... 18 E1
Beechside. Staind DL2 .... 186 F5
Beechwood Ave. Darl DL3 .... 208 E1
Beechwood Dr. Bish Au DL14 .. 148 C5
Beechwood Rd. Fishb TS21 ...... 131 C4
Beechwoods. C le S DH2 .... 20 B5
Bek Rd. Durham DH1 .... 58 C6
Bek Rd. New Ay DL5 .... 171 E7
Belford Gdns. Darl DL14 .... 209 C6
Belford St. Peter SR8 .... 63 F1
Belford Way. New Ay DL5 .... 170 F7
Belgrave Ave. Coxhoe DH6 ...... 106 A4
Belgrave Ct. Coxhoe DH6 .... 106 A3
Belgrave St. Darl DL1 .... 224 B8
Belgrave Terr. Hur on T DL2 .... 235 A8
Bell Meadow. Brand DH7 .... 79 A3
Bell Sq. Still TS21 .... 174 E3
Bell St. Bish Au DL14 .... 148 B6
Bell St. Cornf DL17 .... 105 D1
Bell St. Crook DL15 .... 100 F3
Bell Wlk. New Ay DL5 .... 171 F6
Bell's Folly. Durham DH1 .... 80 A7
Bell's Pl. Darl DL3 .... 208 F2
Bellasis Cl. New Ay DL5 .... 171 E7
Bellburn La. Darl DL3 .... 208 C5
Belle View Dr. Cons DH8 .... 30 A6
Belle Vue. Crook DL15 .... 100 F3
Belle Vue. Qua Hi DH6 .... 106 D8
Belle Vue Gdns. 7 Cons DH8 ... 14 F3
Belle Vue St. Spenny DL16 ...... 127 E7
Belle Vue Terr. Belm DH1 .... 59 B3
Belle Vue Terr. Hunw DL15 ...... 125 E6
Belle Vue Terr. M St G DL2 ...... 225 F8
Belle Vue Terr. Will DL15 .... 101 F3
Bellerby Dr. Urpeth DH2 .... 8 E2
Bellister Pl. Peter SR8 .... 85 E4
Bellows Burn La.
  Hut Hen TS27 .... 110 B5
Bells' Ville. Durham DH1 .... 59 A2
Bellwood Terr. Leadg DH8 .... 15 C3
Belmont Ave. Haw SR7 .... 40 F1
Belmont CE (Controlled) Jun Sch.
  Belm DH1 .... 59 C3
Belmont Comp Sch. Belm DH1 .. 59 C3
Belmont Ind Est. Belm DH1 ...... 59 B4
Belmont Inf Sch. Belm DH1 ...... 59 C3
Belmont Rise. H le H DH5 .... 39 A1
Belsay. Wash NE38 .... 9 F4
Belsay Ave. Peter SR8 .... 85 F5
Belsay Cl. Ferry DL17 .... 129 B6
Belsay Ct. Sedge TS21 .... 153 A7
Belsay Wlk. Darl DL1 .... 209 C6
Belvedere Rd. Darl DL1 .... 224 A8
Belvedere Gdns. Shot Co DH6 .. 84 B7
Belvoir Gr. Bish Au DL14 .... 148 A6
Benbow Wlk. Cound DL4 .... 149 B8
Bendle Terr. Mick DL12 .... 161 C4
Benevente St. 2 Seaham SR7 .... 41 D6
Benfield Cl. Cons DH8 .... 14 D6
Benfieldside Cty Inf Sch.
  Cons DH8 .... 14 C5
Benfieldside Cty Jun Mix Sch.
  Cons DH8 .... 14 D5

Benfieldside Rd. Cons DH8 .... 14 C6
Benfieldside Sec Sch.
  Cons DH8 .... 14 C5
Benridge Bank. W Rain DH4 ...... 38 A2
Bensham Rd. Darl DL1 .... 209 B7
Benson St. C le S DH3 .... 20 C2
Benson St. Stanl DH9 .... 17 E7
Bent House La. Durham DH1 ...... 81 A8
Benville Terr. N Bran DH7 .... 78 E8
Beresford St. Shild DL4 .... 170 A7
Berkeley Cl. Bish Au DL14 ...... 148 A6
Berkeley Rd. Darl DL14 .... 224 A7
Berkshire Cl. Belm DH1 .... 59 C3
Berkshire Rd. Peter SR8 .... 85 C8
Berksyde. Cons DH8 .... 15 A1
Bernard Shaw St. 8
  H le Sp DH4 .... 38 D8
Bernard St. H le Sp DH4 .... 38 D8
Bernard Terr. Pelton DH2 .... 19 E5
Berriedale Dr. Darl DL1 .... 209 B7
Berry Ave. Trim TS29 .... 107 E4
Berry Bank. Oving DL11 .... 204 B4
Berry Edge Factories.
  Cons DH8 .... 14 E2
Berry Edge Rd. Cons DH8 .... 14 F2
Berrybank Crest. Darl DL3 ...... 208 B4
Berryfield Cl. Silk SR3 .... 22 A5
Bertha St. Cons DH8 .... 14 F3
Bertha St. Ferry DL17 .... 129 A5
Bertie Rd. New Ay DL5 .... 171 C7
Bertram St. Birt DH3 .... 9 C4
Berwick Chase. Peter SR8 .... 85 B3
Berwick Ct. Trim TS29 .... 107 E4
Berwick Rd. Bish Au DL14 ...... 208 B5
Berwick. Wash NE38 .... 9 F4
Bessemer Park Cty Inf Sch.
  Spenny DL16 .... 104 A1
Bessemer Rd. S Hett DH6 .... 61 F7
Bessemer St. Cons DH8 .... 14 E3
Bessemer St. Ferry DL17 .... 128 C5
Bethany Gdns. Ann Pl DH9 .... 16 F5
Bethany Terr. Ann Pl DH9 .... 16 F5
Bethune Ave. Seaham SR7 .... 41 A7
Betjeman Cl. Darl DL1 .... 18 A6
Beumaris. Bourn DH4 .... 21 D3
Bevan Ave. Ryhope SR2 .... 22 E6
Bevan Cres. Wh Hi DH6 .... 83 E1
Bevan Gr. Belm DH1 .... 59 B3
Bevan Grove. Shot Co DH6 .... 84 C6
Bevan Sq. Murton SR7 .... 40 C4
Beveridge Cl. Fishb TS21 .... 131 C5
Beveridge Way. New Ay DL5 .... 171 D7
Beverley Gdns. C le S DH3 .... 20 C2
Beverley Gdns. Chilt DL17 ...... 150 E8
Beverley Gdns. Cons DH8 .... 14 D5
Beverley Gdns. 4 Cons DH8 .... 14 F3
Beverley Terr. Ann Pl DH9 .... 16 E5
Beverley Terr. 5 Cons DH8 ...... 14 F3
Beverley Way. Peter SR8 .... 85 C7
Bevin Gr. B Rocks TS27 .... 86 F2
Bevin Sq. S Hett DH6 .... 62 B7
Bewick Cl. C le S DH2 .... 36 A8
Bewick Cres. New Ay DL5 .... 171 D6
Bewley Gr. Peter SR8 .... 85 A3
Bewley Terr. N Bran DH7 .... 78 E8
Bickford Terr. New Ay DL5 ...... 171 E2
Biddick La. Wash NE38 .... 21 D8
Bigland Terr. Bish Au DL14 .... 148 D5
Billy Hill. Billy R DL15 .... 100 E8
Billy La. Kinn DL12 .... 164 A1
Billy La. Wood DL12 & DL13 .... 163 F3
Binchester Croft. New Ay DL5 .. 170 F4
Birch Ave. Bish Au DL14 .... 148 B5
Birch Ave. Shild DL4 .... 149 A1
Birch Cres. Burnop NE16 .... 6 A6
Birch Dr. Will DL15 .... 102 C2
Birch Gr. Cons DH8 .... 31 C7
Birch Pl. Esh W DH7 .... 77 D8
Birch Rd. Bar Cas DL12 .... 201 A5
Birch Rd. Cornf DL17 .... 105 E1
Birch Rd. Darl DL1 .... 209 B8
Birch St. Cons DH8 .... 14 F2
Bircham St. Stanl DH9 .... 17 D5
Birches The. E Lane DH5 .... 39 C1
Birches The. Hur on T DL2 ...... 224 E1
Birches The. Stanl DH9 .... 17 E8
Birchgrove Ave. Belm DH1 .... 59 B3
Birchmere. Spenny DL16 .... 103 E2
Birchwood Cl. Beam DH9 .... 18 E8
Birkdale Cl. 6 Hartle TS27 ...... 111 C4
Birkdale Gdns. Belm DH1 .... 59 D3
Birkdale Rd. Darl DL3 .... 208 B3
Birkhead Cotts. Kibble NE11 ...... 7 E6
Birkheads La. Kibble NE11 .... 7 E6
Birkland La.
  Kibble DH9 & NE11 & NE16 .... 7 E7
Birtley Barley Mow Cty Jun & Inf
  Schs. Birt DH3 .... 9 D1
Birtley East Cty Jun & Inf Sch.
  Birt DH3 .... 9 C6
Birtley Golf Course. Birt DH3 .... 9 D2
Birtley La. Birt DH3 .... 9 D3
Birtley Lord Lawson Comp Sch.
  Birt DH3 .... 9 D3
Birtley Portobello Cty Jun & Inf
  Sch. Birt DH3 .... 9 C4
Birtley Prim Sch. Birt DH3 .... 9 B4
Birtley Ravensworth Terrace Cty
  Jun & Inf Sch. Birt DH3 .... 9 C4
Birtley St Joseph's RC Inf Sch.
  Birt DH3 .... 9 C5
Birtley St Joseph's RC Jun Sch.
  Birt DH3 .... 9 C5
Birtley Villas. 1 Birt DH3 .... 9 C5
Biscop Cres. New Ay DL5 .... 171 E7
Bishop Auckland Tech Coll.
  Bish Au DL14 .... 147 F5
Bishop Barrington Comp Sch.
  Bish Au DL14 .... 147 F6

Bishop Cl. Darl DL1 .... 209 D5
Bishop Ian Ramsey C of E Sch.
  Medom DH8 .... 4 C1
Bishop Middleham CE Jun & Inf
  Sch. Bish Mi DL17 .... 130 C3
Bishop St. 8 Bish Au DL14 ...... 148 B8
Bishop's Cl. Spenny DL16 .... 127 F8
Bishopdale. Pens DH4 .... 21 E8
Bishopgarth. Darl DL1 .... 130 B3
Bishops Ct. H Shin DH1 .... 80 F6
Bishops Way. Durham DH1 .... 58 B7
Bishopton La. L Stain TS21 ...... 193 D2
Bishopton Rd W. St on T TS21 . 195 F4
Bishopton & Redmarshall C of E
  Sch. Bishopt TS21 .... 194 D7
Bisley Ct. Darl DL1 .... 209 F4
Black Boy Rd. Gr Lum DH4 .... 37 E7
Black Dr. Bourn DH3 .... 21 B5
Black Hall. Fir T DL15 .... 99 E2
Black Horse Terr. Wood DL3 . 143 D1
Black House La. Edmon DH7 .... 34 F8
Black Rd. Billy R DL15 .... 100 F7
Black Rd. Brand DH7 .... 79 E6
Black Rd. Ryhope SR2 .... 22 F7
Black Squares Dr. Grind TS22 . 154 F3
Black Thorn Cl. Brand DH7 ...... 79 A3
Blackcap Cl. Wash NE38 .... 9 F3
Blackdown Cl. Peter SR8 .... 85 B5
Blackett Rd. Darl DL1 .... 209 C4
Blackett St. Ann Pl DH9 .... 16 E4
Blackett St. Bish Au DL14 .... 148 C7
Blackfell Rd. Wash NE37 .... 9 F6
Blackhall Cty Inf Sch. Cons DH8 14 D4
Blackhill RC (Aided) Inf Sch.
  Cons DH8 .... 14 D4
Blackhill RC Jun Sch. Cons DH8 14 D4
Blackhills Rd. Peter SR8 .... 86 A7
Blackhills Terr. Peter SR8 .... 86 A7
Blackthorne Ave. 9 Peter SR8 . 86 B6
Blackton Cl. New Ay DL5 .... 171 A4
Blackwell. Darl DL3 .... 223 C6
Blackwell Cl. Darl DL3 .... 223 D7
Blackwell Gr. Darl DL3 .... 223 C7
Blackwell Grange Golf Course.
  Darl DL3 .... 223 D6
Blackwell La. Darl DL3 .... 223 D7
Blackwell Scar. Darl DL3 .... 223 C7
Blackwellgate. 9 Darl DL1 ...... 208 F1
Blackwood Cl. Hartle TS27 ...... 111 C4
Bladeside. Crook DL15 .... 100 F3
Blagdon Gr. Bish Au DL14 ...... 147 E5
Blaidwood Dr. Durham DH1 ...... 80 A5
Blair Gr. Bish Au DL14 .... 148 B6
Blake St. Eas SR8 .... 63 F4
Blake St. 8 Shild DL4 .... 170 A8
Blakes Cl. Stanl DH9 .... 18 A6
Blakeston La. Grind TS21 .... 175 F4
Blakiston Cl. New Ay DL17 ...... 150 C2
Blanche Gr. Peter SR8 .... 85 D5
Blanche Terr. Tant DH9 .... 6 B2
Blanchland Ave. Durham DH1 .... 58 E6
Blanchland Gn. Darl DL3 .... 208 A5
Bland Wlk. New Ay DL5 .... 171 F7
Blandford Pl. Seaham SR7 .... 41 D7
Blandford St. Ferry DL17 .... 128 E5
Blaxton Pl. Whick NE16 .... 2 F5
Blaykeston Cl. Seaham SR7 ...... 22 E1
Bleach House Bank.
  Mordon TS21 .... 174 A3
Bleak Terr. 4 Cockf DL13 .... 166 C5
Blencathra Cres. Crook DL15 ... 100 F2
Blenkinsopp Ct. Peter SR8 ...... 85 B5
Blessed John Ducket RC Prim Sch.
  Tow Law DL13 .... 75 C3
Blind La. C le S DH3 .... 20 D6
Blind La. Hur on T DL2 .... 235 C8
Blind La. N Silk SR3 .... 22 B7
Blind La. Summ DL2 .... 189 B6
Blindy La. E Lane DH5 .... 39 C1
Bloemfontein Cty Jun & Inf Sch.
  The Mid DH9 .... 18 A3
Bloemfontein Pl. The Mid DH9 .. 18 B3
Bloom Ave. Stanl DH9 .... 17 E6
Bloomfield Dr. E Rain DH5 .... 38 D3
Bloomfield Rd. Darl DL3 .... 208 D3
Blossomfield Way. Hasw DH6 .... 61 F3
Blue Coat C of E Sch.
  Durham DH1 .... 58 C6
Blue House Bldgs. Belm DH1 .... 59 C4
Blue House Est. Kir Me DL16 .. 128 A3
Bluebell Cl. B Coll TS27 .... 86 D3
Bluebell Cl. New Ay DL5 .... 171 B8
Bluebell Meadow. New Ay DL5 171 B8
Bluebell Way. New Ay DL5 ...... 171 B8
Bluehouse Bank.
  W Pel DH2 & DH9 .... 19 A3
Blumer St. Fence DH4 .... 38 A8
Blythe Ave. Bish Au DL14 .... 147 D3
Blyton Ave. Ryhope SR2 .... 22 E5
Boat La. Oving DL11 & DL2 ...... 205 A4
Boathouse La. Cleas DL2 .... 222 D7
Bob Hardisty Dr. Bish Au DL14 . 148 B7
Boddy St. Bish Au DL14 .... 148 A3
Bogma Ave. Coxhoe DH6 .... 105 C3
Bolam St. Eas SR8 .... 63 F4
Bolam. Wash NE38 .... 9 F4
Boldron La. Start DL12 .... 200 E5
Bollihope Gr. Bish Au DL14 .... 147 D5
Bolton Cl. Darl DL3 .... 208 B4
Bolton Cl. Durham DH1 .... 58 C8
Bolton Gr. Bish Au DL14 .... 148 A6
Bolton's Bglw. Chopw NE17 ...... 4 B8
Boltsburn Cres. Rook DL13 ...... 47 B2
Boltsburn Terr. Hunst DH8 ...... 25 E4
Bondgate. Darl DL3 .... 208 F2

Bondisle Terr. Stanh DL13 71 B2
Bondisle Way. Stanh DL13 71 A2
Bone Mill Bank. Bish Au DL14 148 E6
Bonemill La. Bourn NE38 & DH3 20 F8
Bonemill La. C le S NE38 & DH3 20 F8
Bonemill La. Wash NE38 & DH3 21 C8
Bonemill La. Wash NE38 & DH3 20 F8
Booth Wlk. New Ay DL5 171 C8
Borough Rd. Darl DL1 209 A2
Borough Road Ind Est. Darl DL1 209 A2
Borrowdale. Leadg DH8 15 D4
Borrowdale Cl. Belm DH1 59 E4
Borrowdale Cres. Blay NE21 2 B8
Borrowdale Dr. Belm DH1 59 C4
Borrowdale Gr. Crook DL15 100 F2
Borrowdale St. H le H DH5 39 A2
Boston Cl. Darl DL1 209 C6
Boston St. Eas SR8 63 F4
Botany Rd. Romald DL12 181 B8
Botham Gr. 3 Darl DL3 209 A7
Bottle Works Rd. Seaham SR7 41 E6
Bouch St. Shild DL4 170 A7
Boulby Cl. N Silk SR3 22 C7
Boulmer Ct. C le S DH2 20 C2
Boundary La. Newl DH8 3 A3
Bourne Ct. Stanl DH9 18 B7
Bourne St. Eas SR8 63 F4
Bourne Terr. Ann Pl DH9 16 F4
Bourne Way. Will DL15 102 A3
Bournemouth Dr. Hartle TS24 111 D4
Bournemouth Dr. Seaham SR7 40 F6
Bournmoor Cty Jun & Inf Sch. Bourn DH4 21 E3
Bousfield Cres. New Ay DL5 171 D8
Bow La. Durham DH1 58 C1
Bow Sch. Durham DH1 80 C8
Bow St. Bowb DH6 81 D1
Bow St. Thorn DH6 83 D4
Bowburn Cty Inf Sch. Bowb DH6 105 D8
Bowburn Cty Jun Sch. Bowb DH6 81 D1
Bowburn South Ind Est. Bowb DH6 105 C8
Bowen Rd. Darl DL3 208 C5
Bowes Ave. H le H DH5 39 B1
Bowes Ave. Seaham SR7 40 F6
Bowes Cl. Ferry DL17 129 B6
Bowes Cres. Byer NE16 6 D8
Bowes Ct. Durham DH1 58 D7
Bowes Gr. Bish Au DL14 148 A6
Bowes Gr. Hartle TS24 111 D4
Bowes Gr. Spenny DL16 103 F2
Bowes Hill. Even DL14 146 B3
Bowes Hutchinsons CE Aided Prim Sch. Bowes DL12 216 A8
Bowes Lea. S Row DH4 21 F4
Bowes Moor Cl. Darl DL1 224 E7
Bowes' Mus. Bar Cas DL12 201 B5
Bowes Rd. New Ay DL5 171 D6
Bowes Rd. Start DL12 200 E5
Bowes Rly. Spring NE9 9 E8
Bowesville. Burnop NE16 6 B5
Bowles Terr. Dipton DH9 16 D8
Bowman St. Darl DL3 209 A7
Bowmont Dr. Tanf L DH9 17 C8
Bowmont Wlk. C le S DH2 20 A1
Bowness Cl. Peter SR8 85 E7
Bowness Gr. Ferry DL17 128 F6
Boyd St. Cons DH8 15 A1
Boyd St. Durham DH1 80 D8
Boyd St. Eas SR8 63 F4
Boyd Terr. Stanl DH9 17 D5
Boyden Cl. Bish Au DL14 147 C2
Boyes Hill Gr. Darl DL3 208 D2
Boyne Ct. Brand DH7 79 D5
Boyne Ct. Sedge TS21 153 A7
Boyne St. Will DL15 102 A4
Boyne View. Trim TS29 107 E1
Boyne View. Trim TS29 131 E8
Boynston Gr. Sedge TS21 153 B7
Boyntons. Kimble DH2 35 F4
Brack's Rd. Bish Au DL14 148 F7
Bracken Cl. Stanl DH9 17 E6
Bracken Ct. Ush M DH7 57 A2
Bracken Field Rd. Durham DH1 58 B5
Bracken Hill Rd. Hunw DL15 125 C7
Bracken Hill. Shot Co SR8 84 F5
Bracken Rd. Darl DL3 208 D3
Brackenbeds Cl. Pelton DH2 19 F6
Brackendale Ct. Hut Hen TS28 108 F5
Brackendale Rd. Belm DH1 59 D4
Brackenhill Ave. Shot Co DH6 84 E6
Brackenridge. Burnop NE16 5 E6
Bracknell Cl. N Silk SR3 22 C8
Bradbury Cl. Tanf L DH9 17 C8
Bradbury Rd. New Ay DL5 171 D4
Bradford Cl. New Ay DL5 171 D5
Bradford Cres. Durham DH1 58 F3
Bradley Ave. H le Sp DH5 38 E6
Bradley Bglws. Leadg DH8 15 C6
Bradley Cl. Urpeth DH2 8 E2
Bradley Cotts. Leadg DH8 15 C6
Bradley Ct. 5 Bish Au DL14 148 B8
Bradley Lodge Dr. Dipton DH9 16 E8
Bradley St. Eas SR8 63 F4
Bradley St. Leadg DH8 15 C4
Bradley Terr. Dipton DH9 16 E7
Bradley Terr. E Lane DH5 39 C1
Bradley Workshops Ind Est. Leadg DH8 15 C4
Bradman Dr. C le S DH3 20 E1
Bradshaw Ct. Hartle TS24 111 F2
Braemar Ct. Darl DL1 209 E7
Braemar Terr. 1 Peter SR8 86 B6
Braes The. Cons DH8 14 C1
Braeside. Burnh DH7 33 D4
Braeside. Edmon DH7 35 B7
Brafferton Cl. New Ay DL5 150 E1
Brafferton La. Coat Mu DL1 192 A6
Braithwaite Rd. Peter SR8 85 F6
Braithwaite St. 10 Bish Au DL14 148 B8
Braithwaite St. Shild DL4 148 E1
Brakespeare Pl. Peter SR8 85 E5
Bramall La. Darl DL1 209 F3
Bramham Chase. New Ay DL5 170 F8
Brampton Ct. Eas SR8 63 B3
Bramwell Terr. Cons DH8 15 A4
Brancepath Wlk. Hartle TS24 111 F3
Brancepeth Castle Golf Course. Brance DH7 102 F7
Brancepeth Chare. Peter SR8 85 B3
Brancepeth Cl. Durham DH1 58 E6
Brancepeth Cl. New Ay DL17 150 E1
Brancepeth Gr. Bish Au DL14 148 A6
Brancepeth Rd. Ferry DL17 129 A6
Brancepeth Terr. Will DL15 102 A4
Brancepeth View. Brand DH7 78 F3
Brancpeth Cl. Ush M DH7 57 C1
Brandlings Way. Peter SR8 85 D6
Brandon Cl. Blay NE21 2 A8
Brandon Cl. C le St DH2 19 F1
Brandon Cl. H le Sp DH4 38 D7
Brandon Cty Jun & Inf Sch. Brand DH7 79 C4
Brandon La. Brand DH7 79 C5
Brandon La. N Bran DH7 & DL15 78 B5
Brandon Rd. Esh W DH7 77 E8
Brandon View. Ush M DH7 79 C8
Brankin Dr. Darl DL1 224 C7
Brankin Rd. Darl DL1 224 C7
Branksome Gn. Darl DL3 207 F5
Branksome Hall Dr. Darl DL3 208 A5
Branksome Lodge. Darl DL3 208 B5
Branksome Sch. Darl DL3 208 A4
Branksome Terr. Darl DL3 208 F3
Bransdale. Pens DH4 21 E8
Bransdale. Spenny DL16 103 E1
Brantwood. C le St DH2 19 F2
Brantwood Cres. Bish Au DL14 148 A3
Brass Thill. Durham DH1 58 B1
Braunespath Est. N Bran DH7 78 F8
Brawton Gr. Darl DL3 208 E4
Breakhouse Bank. Ery DL2 236 C6
Breamish Dr. Wash NE38 20 F8
Breck Rd. Darl DL3 208 D2
Brecken Way. Brand DH7 79 C4
Breckon Hill. Butter DL13 165 E8
Breckon Terr. Fishb TS21 131 C5
Brecon Cl. Peter SR8 85 B5
Brecon Pl. Pelton DH2 19 F8
Brecon Rd. Durham DH1 58 E7
Brecon Side. Darl DL1 209 E5
Brendon Pl. Peter SR8 85 B7
Brentwood Ct. Stanl DH9 18 C6
Brewer St. Bish Au DL14 148 B6
Brewer Terr. Ryhope SR2 23 A6
Brewery Sq. Stanl DH9 17 F7
Brian Rd. Darl DL1 209 A6
Briar Ave. Brand DH7 79 A3
Briar Ave. 2 H le Sp DH4 38 D8
Briar Cl. Darl DL3 223 C6
Briar Cl. Gr Lum DH4 21 E1
Briar Cl. Kimble DH2 35 F3
Briar Cl. S Row DH4 21 F4
Briar Cl. Spenny DL16 127 D6
Briar Dale. Cons DH8 31 C8
Briar Gdns. Crook DL15 100 D3
Briar Gr. Trim TS29 131 D8
Briar Hill. St J Ch DL13 66 F2
Briar Lea. Wit Gil DH7 35 B1
Briar Mews. Cons DH8 14 D5
Briar Rd. Belm DH1 59 D4
Briar Rd. R Gill NE39 1 D2
Briar Terr. Burnop NE16 6 C6
Briar Wlk. Darl DL3 223 D6
Briardene. Burnop NE16 5 E6
Briardene. Durham DH1 58 B1
Briardene. Esh W DH7 55 C1
Briardene. Lanch DH7 32 E3
Briarhill. C le S DH2 20 A5
Briarside. Cons DH8 14 D5
Briarsyde Cl. Whick NE16 2 E5
Briarwood Ave. C le St DH2 19 E3
Briarwood St. Gr Lum DH4 21 E1
Briary Gdns. Cons DH8 14 C6
Briary The. Cons DH8 14 D6
Brick Garth. E Lane DH5 39 C1
Brick Row. Ryhope SR2 22 E7
Bridge Ct. Shadf DH6 82 E7
Bridge End. Coxhoe DH6 105 F5
Bridge End. Pier DL2 206 B4
Bridge House Est. Ferry DL17 128 F5
Bridge Inn Yd. Bar Cas DL12 201 A5
Bridge Rd. Bish Au DL14 148 A8
Bridge Rd. Cornf DL17 105 E2
Bridge Rd. Shot Co DH6 84 D6
Bridge Rd. Stapl DL2 223 C6
Bridge Rd Bglws. Shot Co DH6 84 D5
Bridge St. Bish Au DL14 126 B1
Bridge St. Cons DH8 14 D3
Bridge St. Durham DH1 58 B2
Bridge St. Ferry DH6 & DL17 105 B2
Bridge St. How le W DL15 124 E7
Bridge St. Lang Pk DH7 56 C7
Bridge St. Mid in T DL12 160 D7
Bridge St. Stanl DH9 17 E4
Bridge St. Tow Law DL13 75 C2
Bridge St. Will DL15 101 E1
Bridge Terr. Darl DL1 209 B1
Bridge Terr. Hut Hen TS28 108 F5
Bridge View. Fishb TS21 131 D4
Bridge Way. Lang Pk DH7 56 D6
Bridgegate. Bar Cas DL12 200 F5
Bridgemere Dr. Durham DH1 58 A6
Bridle The. New Ay DL17 150 D2
Brier Ave. Peter SR8 85 F8
Brierley Dr. Sedge TS21 & TS22 154 D3
Brierville. 4 Durham DH1 58 B1
Brighouse Ct. New Ay DL5 171 D3
Bright St. Cons DH8 14 F4
Bright St. Darl DL1 209 C1
Brighton Rd. Darl DL1 224 B8
Brighton Terr. S Hill DH6 60 D1
Brignall Cl. Gr Lum DH3 37 B7
Brignall La. Brig DL12 218 C5
Brignall Moor Cres. Darl DL1 224 D8
Brindley Rd. Shot Co SR8 84 F6
Brinkburn. C le S DH2 20 A3
Brinkburn Ave. Darl DL3 208 D4
Brinkburn Cl. Bish Au DL14 147 E5
Brinkburn Cl. Blay NE21 2 A8
Brinkburn Dr. Darl DL3 208 D5
Brinkburn Rd. Darl DL3 208 E4
Briscoe La. Coth DL12 181 C3
Britannia Rd. N Silk SR3 22 A7
Britannia Terr. Fence DH4 38 A8
Britten Cl. Stanl DH9 18 A5
Brixham Cl. Seaham SR7 41 A6
Broadgate Rd. Lang Pk DH7 56 C3
Broadmeadows. Bowb DH6 81 E1
Broadmeadows. Darl DL3 208 B2
Broadmires La. Scar DL12 218 A1
Broadmires Terr. Kimble DH2 35 E4
Broadoak Dr. Lanch DH7 32 E3
Broadoaks. Bish Mi DL17 130 B3
Broadview Villas. Sherb DH6 60 A1
Broadviews. Gr Lum DH3 37 A7
Broadway. C le S DH3 20 D5
Broadway. Cons DH8 31 B7
Broadway Ave. Trim TS29 107 C1
Broadway S The. Darl DL1 209 E2
Broadway The. Darl DL1 209 D2
Broadway The. H le Sp DH4 38 E8
Broadwood La. Satley DH7 & DL13 53 D8
Broadwood View. C le S DH3 20 D2
Broadwood View. Cons DH8 14 C5
Brockett Cl. New Ay DL5 171 C8
Brockwell Cl. New Ay DL5 150 C1
Brockwell Ct. Bish Au DL14 149 A5
Brockwell Rd. Wash NE38 9 F5
Broken Banks. Bish Au DL14 148 B8
Broken Way. St J Ch DL13 67 C1
Bromley Cl. H Shin DH1 81 B4
Brompton Cl. Urpeth DH2 8 E2
Brompton Wlk. Darl DL3 208 C1
Bronte Ct. Crook DL15 100 C2
Bronte Pl. Stanl DH9 18 B4
Brook Cl. New Ay DL17 150 E1
Brook St. Bish Au DL14 148 F5
Brook St. 2 Spenny DL16 103 F1
Brook Terr. Bish Au DL14 148 F4
Brook Terr. Darl DL3 208 F4
Brook View. Lanch DH7 32 E3
Brookdale. Belm DH1 59 E4
Brookes Rise. Brand DH7 79 D5
Brooklands. Bish Au DL14 148 B4
Brooklyn Rd. Chilt DL17 150 F7
Brooklyn St. Murton SR7 40 D2
Brooklyn Terr. Murton SR7 40 D2
Brooks Cl. Stanl DH9 18 A6
Brookside. Even DL14 167 D7
Brookside. H le Sp DH5 38 D6
Brookside. Sacr DH7 35 C4
Brookside. Wit Gil DH7 57 B8
Brookside Ave. Crook DL15 100 E2
Broom Cl. Blay NE21 2 B8
Broom Cl. Stanl DH9 18 B7
Broom Cottages Cty Jun & Inf Sch. Ferry DL17 129 A6
Broom Cotts. 5 Ferry DL17 129 A5
Broom Cres. Ush M DH7 57 B1
Broom Ct. Spring NE9 9 F8
Broom Farm West. Ush M DH7 79 C8
Broom Hall Dr. Ush M DH7 57 C1
Broom La. Ush M DH1 & DH7 79 D8
Broom Rd. Ferry DL17 129 A6
Broom St. Spenny DL16 104 C1
Broom Terr. Burnop NE16 6 C6
Broom Terr. Crook DL15 100 E4
Broome Ct. Ush M DH7 79 C8
Broome Rd. Belm DH1 59 D4
Broomfield Cres. Chopw NE17 4 B8
Broomhill. Tanf L DH9 17 E7
Broomhill Est. H le H DH5 38 F6
Broomhill Terr. H le H DH5 38 F5
Broomhill Terr. Medom DH8 15 A8
Broomlee Cl. 4 New Ay DL5 171 A7
Brooms La. Leadg DH8 15 F4
Brooms RC Jun & Inf Sch. Leadg DH8 15 D4
Brooms RC Jun Mix Sch. Leadg DH8 15 F5
Brooms The. Ouston DH2 8 F2
Broomside. Ferry DL17 129 A5
Broomside Ct. Belm DH1 59 D4
Broomside La. Belm DH1 59 D4
Brough Cl. New Ay DL5 172 A7
Brough Ct. Hartle TS27 111 D3
Brough Gr. Bish Au DL14 148 A6
Brougham Ct. Peter SR8 85 B3
Brougham St. Darl DL3 209 A5
Broumley Ct. Staind DL2 186 E5
Browbank. Sacr DH7 35 D2
Brown Ave. Will DL15 101 F2
Brown St. R Gill NE39 1 C2
Brown St. Shild DL4 148 F2
Brown's Bldgs. Birt DH3 9 C1
Brown's Terr. 3 Lang Pk DH7 56 C6
Browney Bank. Satley DH7 53 F7
Browney Cty Jun & Inf Sch. Brand DH7 79 D3
Browney La. Brand DH7,DH1 & DH6 79 E2
Browning Cl. Stanl DH9 18 A6
Browning Hill. Coxhoe DH6 106 A4
Browning Pl. Crook DL15 100 C3
Browning St. Eas SR8 63 F4
Brownney Ct. Lang Pk DH7 56 C7
Browns Bldgs. M St G DL2 225 F8
Browns Cl. Coxhoe DH6 106 A5
Brownside La. Bolam DL2 169 A2
Bruce Cres. Wing TS28 108 D8
Bruce Glasier Terr. Shot Co DH6 84 C5
Bruce Kirkup Rd. Peter SR8 85 F8
Bruce Pl. Peter SR8 85 C8
Bruce Rd. New Ay DL5 171 C6
Bruce St. Edmon DH7 35 B6
Brunel Rd. Darl DL1 209 B2
Brunel St. Ferry DL17 128 E6
Brunel Way. Darl DL1 209 B2
Brunswick St. Darl DL1 209 A2
Brunswick St N. Darl DL1 209 A2
Bruntoft Ave. Hartle TS24 111 F3
Brunton St. Darl DL1 209 B1
Brunton Wlk. New Ay DL5 171 C5
Brusselton La. Shild DL4 169 C7
Bryan Cl. Hur on T DL2 224 D1
Bryan St. Spenny DL16 104 A1
Bryan's Leap. Burnop NE16 6 A7
Brydon Cres. S Hett DH6 62 B6
Buck Sq. Heigh DL5 170 D1
Buckham St. Cons DH8 14 E4
Buckingham Ave. Hart TS27 110 F2
Buckingham Ct. Darl DL1 223 E8
Buckingham Rd. Peter SR8 85 B8
Buckingham Terr. Cound DL14 149 D8
Buckinghamshire Rd. Belm DH1 59 C3
Buckton's Yd. 3 Darl DL3 208 F1
Buddle Cl. Peter SR8 85 D8
Buddle St. Cons DH8 15 A2
Buddle Wlk. New Ay DL5 171 C5
Bude Sq. Murton SR7 40 D4
Buess La. Darl DL1 210 A5
Bull Wynd. Darl DL1 208 F1
Bullion La. C le S DH2 20 B3
Bulmer Cl. New Ay DL5 171 F7
Bulmer Pl. Hartle TS24 111 F2
Bulmers Sq. Darl DL3 208 F5
Bungalows The. Birt DH3 9 B6
Bungalows The. Cons DH8 30 B7
Bungalows The. Crook DL15 100 E4
Bungalows The. Ebch DH8 3 F4
Bungalows The. H le H DH5 38 F6
Bungalows The. Kibble NE11 8 E8
Bungalows The. Medom NE17 4 B4
Bungalows The. N Bran DH7 78 F8
Bungalows The. Peter SR8 85 F8
Bungalows The. S Hett DH6 62 B6
Bungalows The. Tanf L DH9 17 C8
Burdon Ave. H le Sp DH5 39 A8
Burdon Cl. New Ay DL5 171 C7
Burdon Cres. Ryhope SR2 22 E6
Burdon Cres. Seaham SR7 22 F1
Burdon Cres. Wing TS28 84 E1
Burdon Dr. Eas SR8 84 E7
Burdon Gr. N Silk SR3 22 B7
Burdon La. Burdon SR2 & SR3 22 C5
Burdon La. Ryhope SR2 & SR3 22 C5
Burdon Pl. Peter SR8 85 E6
Burdon Plain. Sunn NE16 7 B7
Burdon Rd. Burdon SR3 22 B5
Burdon Rd. N Silk SR3 22 B6
Burghley Mews. New Ay DL17 150 E1
Burke St. Shild DL4 148 F1
Burlawn Cl. 3 Sland SR2 22 F8
Burleigh Pl. Darl DL3 208 E1
Burma Rd. Hur on T DL2 224 E4
Burn Crook. H le Sp DH5 38 D6
Burn Foot. St J Ch DL13 67 D1
Burn Gdns. Eas SR8 63 C4
Burn La. H le H DH5 39 A3
Burn La. New Ay DL5 171 D8
Burn Oval. Trim TS29 107 C1
Burn Park Rd. H le Sp DH4 38 D8
Burn Pl. Will DL15 101 F3
Burn Prom. 5 H le Sp DH4 38 E8
Burn St. Bowb DH6 81 D1
Burn Terr. 1 Spenny DL16 103 F1
Burn Valley Gdns. Hut Hen TS28 108 F5
Burn's Cl. Hart TS27 110 F3
Burn's Terr. Shot Co DH6 84 D6
Burnbeck Pl. Heigh DL5 170 C1
Burnell Rd. Esh W DH7 77 E8
Burnett Cres. Kelloe DH6 106 E5
Burnhall Dr. Seaham SR7 23 A1
Burnhill Way. New Ay DL5 & DL17 171 B7
Burnhills La. Green NE40 1 B8
Burnhope. New Ay DL5 171 A7
Burnhope Cl. Crook DL15 100 D2
Burnhope Cty Jun & Inf Sch. Burnh DH7 33 D4
Burnhope Way. Peter SR8 85 C6
Burnhopeside Ave. Lanch DH7 33 A3
Burnie Gdns. Shild DL4 149 A1
Burnigill. Brand DH7 79 C3
Burnington Dr. Will DL15 101 E3
Burnip Rd. Murton SR7 40 C4
Burnlea. 4 H le Sp DH4 38 C8
Burnmere. Spenny DL16 103 E2
Burnmill Bank. Shot DH8 13 D6
Burnop Terr. H Spen NE39 1 A2
Burnopfield Cty Jun Mix & Inf Sch. Burnop NE16 6 A6
Burnopfield RC Mix & Inf Sch. Byer NE16 6 D7
Burnopfield Rd. R Gill NE39 1 F1
Burns Ave N. H le Sp DH5 38 E7
Burns Ave S. H le Sp DH5 38 E7
Burns Cl. Stanl DH9 18 A6
Burns Cl. W Rain DH4 38 A2
Burns Rd. Chilt DL17 150 E8
Burns St. Wh Hi DH6 83 E2
Burnshouse La. Shild DL14 168 E8
Burnside. Esh W DH7 55 D1
Burnside. Lanch DH7 32 E4
Burnside. Peter SR8 85 D6
Burnside. Wit Gil DH7 57 B8
Burnside Ave. Peter SR8 86 A6
Burnside Cotts. Rook DL13 47 A2
Burnside Rd. Darl DL1 224 D7
Burnside Rd. R Gill NE39 1 D2
Burnt Ho. Cockf DL13 166 C3
Burnt Houses La. Cockf DL13 & DL2 166 E3
Burnthouse Bank. C le St DH2 19 F4
Burnthouse Cl. Blay NE21 2 A8
Burnway. Seaham SR7 23 A1
Burnynghill Cl. New Ay DL5 170 F5
Burt Cl. Hasw DH6 61 E3
Burt Cl. Peter SR8 85 D8
Burtree Ford. Cows DL13 66 C6
Burtree La. Coat Mu DL2 191 D2
Burtree La. Darl DL3 191 D2
Burtree Rd. New Ay DL5 171 D3
Bury Rd. New Ay DL5 171 E6
Bushblades La. Ann Pl DH9 16 F7
Bushel Hill Ct. Darl DL3 208 B3
Bushel Hill Dr. Darl DL3 208 B2
Busty Bank. Burnop NE16 6 B7
Busty Bank. Burnop NE16 & NE39 6 A8
Busty Terr. Shild DL4 148 E3
Butchers Race. Spenny DL16 104 C2
Bute Ct. 3 Silk SR3 22 A6
Bute St. Tant DH9 6 A2
Butler Rd. New Ay DL5 171 D6
Butler St. Eas SR8 63 F4
Butsfield La. Cons DH8 31 C6
Butsfield La. Satley DL13 52 F7
Butterknowle Cty Sch. Butter DL13 165 F8
Buttermere. Peter SR8 85 A3
Buttermere. Spenny DL16 103 E2
Buttermere Ave. E Lane DH5 61 C8
Buttermere Cl. C le S DH2 20 C2
Buttermere Cres. Blay NE21 2 B8
Buttermere Cres. S Hett DH6 61 E8
Buttermere Gr. Bish Au DL14 147 B1
Buttermere Gr. Crook DL15 100 F2
Butterwick Ct. New Ay DL5 171 D8
Butterwick Rd. Fishb TS21 131 D5
Butterwick Rd. Hartle TS24 111 E3
Butterwick Rd. Sedge TS21 131 F2
Butterwick Rd. Sedge TS21 153 D8
Button's Bank. Esh W DH7 & DL15 77 B5
Butts Cr. Stanh DL13 71 B3
Butts La. Hart TS27 110 F3
Butts The. Stanh DL13 71 B3
Buxton Moor Cres. Darl DL1 224 D7
Bye The. Cons DH8 30 C8
Byer Sq. H le H DH5 39 A6
Byer St. H le H DH5 39 A6
Byerley Park Cty Jun Sch. New Ay DL5 171 A8
Byerley Rd. Shild DL4 169 F8
Byerleyhouse La. Satley DL13 52 E5
Byers Ct. N Silk SR3 22 B8
Byers Green Cty Jun & Inf Sch. By Gr DL14 102 D1
Byland Cl. Bish Au DL14 147 D2
Byland Ct. Bear DH7 57 B3
Byland Towers. Spenny DL16 128 A8
Bylands Way. Darl DL3 208 A4
Byony Toft. Ryhope SR2 23 A7
Byrne Terr. 4 N Silk SR3 22 B7
Byrne Terr W. 2 N Silk SR3 22 B7
Byron Ave. Bish Au DL14 148 B6
Byron Ave. C le St DH2 19 E3
Byron Cl. Stanl DH9 18 A6
Byron Ct. Crook DL15 100 C2
Byron Ct. Da on T DL2 235 B5
Byron Lodge Est. 6 Seaham SR7 22 E1
Byron Rd. Chilt DL17 150 E8
Byron Rd. Darl DL1 209 C3
Byron St. Eas SR8 63 F4
Byron St. Ouston DH2 8 F1
Byron St. Wh Hi DH6 83 F2
Byron Terr. H le Sp DH5 38 E7
Byron Terr. Seaham SR7 22 F1
Byron Terr. Shot Co DH6 84 D6
Byway The. Darl DL1 209 D1
Bywell Dr. Peter SR8 85 C3

Cadger Bank. Lanch DH7 32 E3
Cadogan Sq. 1 New Ay DL5 171 C7
Cadwell La. Eas SR8 63 B4
Caedmon Cres. Darl DL3 208 B1
Cain Terr. Wh Hi DH6 83 E2
Cairngorm Dr. Darl DL1 209 C6
Cairns Rd. Murton SR7 40 A3
Caithness Way. Darl DL1 209 E7
Cakesmire La. Head DL2 188 C3
Calder Cl. Bish Au DL14 147 E6
Caldermere. Spenny DL16 103 E2
Caldew Ct. H le H DH5 39 B2
Caldwell Gn. 2 Darl DL2 224 C8
Caledonia. Gr Lum DH3 37 A8
Caledonian Way. Darl DL1 209 E7
California. Escomb DL14 147 C8
California Row. Mid in T DL12 160 E7
Callaley Ave. Whick NE16 2 F6
Callander. Ouston DH2 9 A2
Callerton Pl. Crag DH9 18 D2
Callerton Rise. New Ay DL5 150 C1
Calley Cl. Peter SR8 85 C3
Callington Cl. Bourn DH4 21 E2
Callington Dr. Sland SR2 22 F7
Calow Way. Whick NE16 2 F5
Calvert St. Crook DL15 100 E4
Calvert Terr. Murton SR7 40 C3
Cam Mead. Silk SR3 22 A4
Camberley Cl. N Silk SR3 22 C8
Camberley Dr. Brand DH7 78 F3
Cambridge Ave. Cons DH8 30 A6
Cambridge Ave. Will DL15 101 F3

Cambridge Dr. Gr Lum DH3 ...... 37 A6
Cambridge Pl. Birt DH3 ...... 9 C1
Cambridge Rd. N Silk SR3 ...... 22 A7
Cambridge Rd. Peter SR8 ...... 85 C8
Cambridge St. Cound DL14 ...... 127 D1
Cambridge St. Spenny DL16 ...... 127 F8
Cambridge Terr. Bowb DH6 ...... 105 D8
Cambridgeshire Dr. Belm DH1 ...... 59 C2
Camden Sq. Seaham SR7 ...... 41 C6
Camelot Cl. Seaham SR7 ...... 41 C8
Camp St. Eas SR8 ...... 63 F4
Campbell St. Eas SR8 ...... 63 F4
Campbell St. Tow Law DL13 ...... 75 C2
Campbell Terr. H le H DH5 ...... 39 B1
Camperdown Ave. C le S DH3 ...... 20 D5
Campion Ct. New Ay DL17 ...... 150 E2
Campion Dr. Tanf L DH9 ...... 17 D8
Campion Rd. Darl DL1 ...... 209 B5
Candlish Terr. Seaham SR7 ...... 41 E6
Cann Rd. Peter SR8 ...... 85 D7
Cann St. Eas SR8 ...... 63 C4
Canney Hill. Bish Au DL14 ...... 148 F8
Cannobie Cl. Darl DL3 ...... 208 C1
Canterbury Cl. Gr Lum DH3 ...... 37 A6
Canterbury Cl. Spenny DL16 ...... 103 E3
Canterbury Cres. Will DL15 ...... 101 F2
Canterbury Gr. Darl DL1 ...... 209 E5
Canterbury Rd. Durham DH1 ...... 58 E7
Caradoc Rd. Wing TS28 ...... 108 E8
Caragh Rd. C le S DH2 ...... 20 C1
Cardigan Gr. Hartle TS27 ...... 111 E1
Cardinal Gdns. Darl DL3 ...... 208 C2
Cardinal Gr. St on T TS21 ...... 195 F4
Carey Cl. Bowb DH6 ...... 105 D8
Caribbees. Cons DH8 ...... 31 C7
Carileph Cl. New Ay DL5 ...... 171 C6
Carisbrooke Cres.
  Bish Au DL14 ...... 147 E6
Carisbrooke Wlk. Darl DL3 ...... 208 A2
Carlbury Cres. Darl DL3 ...... 208 B2
Carlbury Rd. New Ay DL5 ...... 171 E3
Carleton Dr. Darl DL3 ...... 208 B2
Carleton Gr. Darl DL3 ...... 208 B2
Carlingford Rd. C le S DH2 ...... 20 B1
Carlisle Gr. Bish Au DL14 ...... 148 A6
Carlisle Rd. Durham DH1 ...... 58 E7
Carlton Cl. Urpeth DH2 ...... 8 E2
Carlton Cl. 5 Darl DL1 ...... 209 B1
Carlton Moor Cres. Darl DL1 ...... 224 D7
Carlton St. Ferry DL17 ...... 129 C3
Carlton Terr. Eas SR8 ...... 63 B3
Carlyle Cres. Shot Co DH6 ...... 84 D6
Carmel Gdns. Darl DL3 ...... 208 C2
Carmel Gdns. Darl DL3 ...... 223 C8
Carmel Gr. Darl DL3 ...... 223 D7
Carmel RC Comp Sch.
  Darl DL3 ...... 208 B1
Carmel Rd. Stanl DH9 ...... 17 D6
Carmel Rd N. Darl DL3 ...... 208 C2
Carmel Rd S. Darl DL3 ...... 223 D7
Carnaby Rd. Darl DL1 ...... 209 D1
Carnation Ave. Bourn DH4 ...... 21 E3
Carnforth Gdns. R Gill NE39 ...... 1 E3
Carnoustie. Ouston DH2 ...... 9 A1
Carnoustie Gr. Darl DL1 ...... 209 C7
Carole Dunes. Qua Hi DH6 ...... 106 D7
Caroline St. Bish Au DL14 ...... 148 B6
Caroline St. H le H DH5 ...... 39 A4
Caroline St. Seaham SR7 ...... 41 D7
Carr Ave. Brand DH7 ...... 79 B4
Carr House Dr. Durham DH1 ...... 58 D7
Carr La. Mordon DL1 & DL5 ...... 172 E6
Carr La. Spenny DL16 ...... 103 E2
Carr Pl. New Ay DL5 ...... 171 F6
Carr Row. W Rain DH4 ...... 37 E3
Carr Side. Darl DL3 ...... 208 F6
Carr St. Spenny DL16 ...... 103 E1
Carr's Terr. Wit le W DL14 ...... 124 B3
Carrhouse La. H le H DH5 & SR7 ...... 39 F4
Carrick St. Hartle TS24 ...... 111 F2
Carrmere Rd. 1 Sland SR2 ...... 22 E8
Carrmyers. Ann Pl DH9 ...... 16 E6
Carrock Cl. Peter SR8 ...... 85 D4
Carroll Pl. Cr on T DL2 ...... 234 F8
Carroll Rd. Darl DL3 ...... 208 B1
Carrowmore Rd. C le S DH2 ...... 20 C1
Carrs The. Durham DH1 ...... 58 C7
Carrside Rd. Trim TS29 ...... 131 D7
Carrsides La. New Ay DL17 ...... 150 F4
Carrsway. Belm DH1 ...... 59 D5
Carrsyde Cl. Whick NE16 ...... 2 F5
Cartington Cl. Peter SR8 ...... 85 D3
Cartington Rd. Durham DH1 ...... 58 D5
Cartmel Cl. C le S DH2 ...... 20 A2
Cartmel Ct. Spenny DL16 ...... 103 E3
Cartmel Terr. Beam DH9 ...... 19 B7
Cartmel Terr. Darl DL3 ...... 208 E4
Carville St. Will DL15 ...... 101 E4
Carville Terr. Will DL15 ...... 101 E4
Carvis Cl. Brand DH7 ...... 79 A3
Carwardine Cl. New Ay DL17 ...... 150 C2
Carway Bank. St J Ch DL15 ...... 66 F3
Cassel Bank. Mid in T DL12 ...... 139 A1
Cassop Cty Jun & Inf Sch.
  Qua Hi DH6 ...... 106 D8
Castle Ave. Bowb DH6 ...... 81 C1
Castle Bank. Tow Law DL13 ...... 75 C3
Castle Chare. 3 Bish Au DL14 ...... 148 C8
Castle Chare. 2 Durham DH1 ...... 58 C2
Castle Cl. C le S DH3 ...... 20 D2
Castle Cl. H le H DH5 ...... 39 B2
Castle Cl. M St G DL2 ...... 225 F6
Castle Close Flats. Stanh DL13 ...... 71 B3
Castle Dene Gr. H le Sp DH4 ...... 38 D8
Castle Eden Dene (Nature
  Reserve). Cast Eden TS27 ...... 85 E3
Castle Eden Walkway.
  Grind TS21 ...... 175 D8

Castle Howard Cl. Hartle TS27 ...... 111 D3
Castle Riggs. C le S DH2 ...... 20 B3
Castle St. Eas SR8 ...... 63 F4
Castle Terr. Bowes DL12 ...... 216 A8
Castle View. Esh W DH7 ...... 55 D1
Castle View. C le S DH3 ...... 20 C5
Castle View. How le W DL15 ...... 125 A6
Castle View. Ush M DH7 ...... 57 C1
Castle View. Wit le W DL14 ...... 124 B3
Castlebay Ct. Darl DL1 ...... 209 E7
Castledene Rd. Cons DH8 ...... 15 B1
Castlegarth. Spenny DL16 ...... 127 C5
Castlereagh. Grind TS22 ...... 155 C2
Castlereagh Cl. New Ay DL5 ...... 171 C6
Castlereagh Homes The.
  Seaham SR7 ...... 23 D1
Castlereagh Rd. Seaham SR7 ...... 41 D7
Castlereagh St. N Silk SR3 ...... 22 A7
Castlereigh Cl. Bourn DH4 ...... 21 D3
Castleside Cty Jun & Inf Sch.
  Cons DH8 ...... 29 F6
Castleside Ind Est. Cons DH8 ...... 30 B7
Cat Castle Cotts. Lartt DL12 ...... 199 F6
Catchgate Cty Jun & Inf Schs.
  Ann Pl DH9 ...... 16 E4
Catchwell Rd. Dipton DH9 ...... 16 D8
Caterhouse Rd. Durham DH1 ...... 58 C6
Cathedral View. Sacr DH7 ...... 35 D2
Catherine Cl. Spenny DL16 ...... 128 A8
Catherine Terr. Ann Pl DH9 ...... 17 B4
Catherine Terr. Stanl DH9 ...... 17 F8
Causeway Rd. St J Ch DL13 ...... 66 D2
Causeway The. Darl DL1 ...... 209 D2
Causeway The. Wols DL13 ...... 97 E7
Causey Arch. Tanf DH9 ...... 7 A4
Causey Rd. Stanl DH9 ...... 18 A8
Causey Rd. Tanf DH9 & NE16 ...... 7 A2
Causey View. Stanl DH9 ...... 18 B7
Cavell Cl. Stanl DH9 ...... 18 A5
Cavell Sq. Eas SR8 ...... 63 D5
Cavendish Ct. Brand DH7 ...... 79 A3
Cavendish Ct. 4 Darl DL1 ...... 209 B6
Cavendish Ct. Ferry DL17 ...... 128 E5
Cavendish Dr. 3 Darl DL1 ...... 209 B6
Cavendish Pl. 2 N Silk SR3 ...... 22 A7
Cawthorne Terr. Burnop NE16 ...... 6 A4
Caxton Way. C le S DH3 ...... 20 D8
Cecil Cres. Lanch DH7 ...... 32 F3
Cecil Rd. Bar Cas DL12 ...... 200 F6
Cedar Ave. Kimble DH2 ...... 35 F3
Cedar Cres. Burnop NE16 ...... 5 F6
Cedar Cres. E Lane DH5 ...... 39 D1
Cedar Cres. Seaham SR7 ...... 41 C6
Cedar Ct. Will DL15 ...... 102 C3
Cedar Ct. Lang Pk DH7 ...... 56 A6
Cedar Dr. Durham DH1 ...... 80 B5
Cedar Gdns. Cons DH8 ...... 14 C1
Cedar Gdns. Crook DL15 ...... 100 D4
Cedar Gr. Shild DL4 ...... 149 A1
Cedar Mews. Hur on T DL2 ...... 235 A8
Cedar Rd. Bish Au DL14 ...... 148 C7
Cedar Rd. Darl DL3 ...... 208 D4
Cedar St. Peter SR8 ...... 86 B6
Cedar St. Wald DH2 ...... 19 E1
Cedar Terr. 7 Fence DH4 ...... 38 A8
Cedars. C le S DH2 ...... 20 B5
Cedars Cres. Murton SR7 ...... 40 D3
Cedars The. Coxhoe DH6 ...... 106 A3
Cedars The. Darl DL3 ...... 208 D3
Cedarwood. Gr Lum DH4 ...... 21 E1
Cedarwood. M St G DL2 ...... 225 E7
Cemetery La. Darl DL3 ...... 208 C1
Cemetery Rd. Stanl DH9 ...... 17 F7
Cemetery Rd. Wh Hi DH6 ...... 83 F2
Cemetery Rd. Wit le W DL14 ...... 124 B3
Central Ave. Bish Au DL14 ...... 147 D3
Central Ave. Brand DH7 ...... 79 C3
Central Ave. New Ay DL5 ...... 171 E7
Central Dr. Spenny DL16 ...... 127 D6
Central Par. Shild DL4 ...... 149 A1
Centre The. Even DL14 ...... 167 D6
Century Terr. Ann Pl DH9 ...... 16 E5
Cestria Way. New Ay DL5 ...... 171 A8
Chains The. 3 Durham DH1 ...... 58 D2
Chair La. Spenny DH6 & DL16 ...... 104 A5
Chalfont Way. Brand DH7 ...... 79 C4
Challener Way. Bish Au DL14 ...... 147 D2
Chancery La. 1 Darl DL1 ...... 208 F1
Chandler Cl. New Ay DL5 ...... 171 E8
Chandlers Ford. Pens DH4 ...... 21 F8
Chandos. Silk SR3 ...... 22 A4
Chandos St. Darl DL3 ...... 208 F4
Chantilly Ave. Darl DL1 ...... 209 E6
Chantry Cl. W Rain DH4 ...... 38 A2
Chapel Ave. Burnop NE16 ...... 6 B6
Chapel Cl. Hamst DL13 ...... 123 B3
Chapel Cl. Kibble NE11 ...... 8 D6
Chapel Ct. Sherb DH6 ...... 60 A1
Chapel Gdns. Carl TS21 ...... 195 D8
Chapel Hill Rd. Peter SR8 ...... 85 F6
Chapel La. Cleas DL2 ...... 222 E7
Chapel La. Hasw DH6 ...... 61 F3
Chapel La. Scar DL12 ...... 218 B2
Chapel Row. Birt DH3 ...... 9 E3
Chapel Row. Hur in T DL12 ...... 160 D7
Chapel Row. Sadb DL2 ...... 210 D7
Chapel Row. Stanh DL13 ...... 99 B7
Chapel St. Bish Au DL14 ...... 147 C1
Chapel St. Even DL14 ...... 167 C7
Chapel St. H le H DH5 ...... 39 B4
Chapel St. Hunw DL15 ...... 125 D7
Chapel St. Kir Me DL16 ...... 128 A3
Chapel St. M St G DL2 ...... 225 F7
Chapel St. Shild DL4 ...... 169 F8
Chapel St. Stan Cr DL15 ...... 100 F8
Chapel St. Stanh DL13 ...... 71 B3
Chapel St. Tant DH9 ...... 6 B2
Chapel St. Toro DL14 ...... 125 F2

Chapel St. Will DL15 ...... 101 F3
Chapel St. Wols DL13 ...... 108 E6
Chapel Terr. Copley DL13 ...... 165 A7
Chapel Terr. Gain DL2 ...... 205 A6
Chapel Terr. Rook DL13 ...... 47 C2
Chapel View. R Gill NE39 ...... 1 E3
Chapel View. W Rain DH4 ...... 37 F1
Chapel Wlk. Will DL15 ...... 101 F1
Chaplin St. Seaham SR7 ...... 41 D5
Chapman Cl. New Ay DL5 ...... 171 E7
Chare La. Shadf DH6 ...... 82 E7
Chare The. Peter SR8 ...... 85 D6
Charlaw Cl. Sacr DH7 ...... 35 B4
Charlaw La. Wit Gil DH7 ...... 34 E4
Charlaw Terr. Sacr DH7 ...... 35 B3
Charles Perkins Memorial Cottage
  Homes. Birt DH3 ...... 9 C3
Charles Row. Midd DL4 ...... 149 E1
Charles St. Darl DL1 ...... 209 A4
Charles St. Eas SR8 ...... 63 F4
Charles St. 12 Ryhope SR2 ...... 23 A6
Charles St. Seaham SR7 ...... 41 D7
Charles St. Shild DL4 ...... 170 A8
Charles St. Spenny DL16 ...... 127 F8
Charles St. Stanl DH9 ...... 17 E5
Charles Terr. Pelton DH2 ...... 19 E6
Charlotte St. Stanl DH9 ...... 17 E4
Charlotte Terr. Darl DL17 ...... 150 F8
Charnwood. Stanl DH9 ...... 17 E8
Charters Cres. S Hett DH6 ...... 61 F7
Charters Cres. S Hett DH6 ...... 62 A7
Chartwell Pl. Cons DH8 ...... 14 F4
Chase Cl. Darl DL3 ...... 208 A4
Chase End. Hur on T DL2 ...... 224 C1
Chase The. Hur on T DL2 ...... 224 C1
Chase The. Wash NE38 ...... 9 F1
Chatsworth Ave. 7
  Bish Au DL14 ...... 148 B6
Chatsworth Terr. Darl DL1 ...... 224 A8
Chatton Cl. C le S DH2 ...... 20 A1
Chaucer Cl. Stanl DH9 ...... 18 A6
Chaucer Rd. Darl DL1 ...... 224 A7
Chaucer St. 9 H le Sp DH4 ...... 38 D8
Chaytor Cl. Darl DL3 ...... 208 F7
Chaytor Rd. Cons DH8 ...... 14 C4
Chaytor Terr. Fishb TS21 ...... 131 C4
Chaytor Terr N. The Mid DH9 ...... 18 C3
Chaytor Terr S. The Mid DH9 ...... 18 C3
Cheapside. Shild DL4 ...... 149 A2
Cheapside. Spenny DL16 ...... 127 F8
Cheddar Cl. Ann Pl DH9 ...... 16 F3
Chelmsford St. 4 Darl DL3 ...... 208 F3
Chelmsford St. 5 N Silk SR3 ...... 22 A8
Chepstow Cl. Cons DH8 ...... 14 D7
Chepstow Rd. Darl DL1 ...... 209 F4
Chepstow Wlk. Hartle TS26 ...... 111 E1
Cherribank. Ryhope SR2 ...... 22 E6
Cherry Banks. C le S DH3 ...... 20 D5
Cherry Cotts. Tant DH9 ...... 6 B2
Cherry Knowle Hospl.
  Ryhope SR2 ...... 22 E4
Cherry Pk. Brand DH7 ...... 79 A3
Cherry Tree Dr. Sedge TS21 ...... 153 B7
Cherry Tree Dr. Will DL15 ...... 101 E2
Cherry Tree Sq. Seaham SR7 ...... 22 E8
Cherrytree Rd. C le S DH2 ...... 20 A5
Cherwell Rd. Peter SR8 ...... 85 B5
Cheshire Ave. Birt DH3 ...... 9 C1
Cheshire Dr. Belm DH1 ...... 59 C2
Cheshire Pl. Bish Au DL14 ...... 148 B5
Chesnut St. Darl DL1 ...... 209 A3
Chester Cres. Cornf DL17 ...... 129 F8
Chester Dr. Wit Gil DH7 ...... 35 B1
Chester Gdns. Wit Gil DH7 ...... 35 B1
Chester Gr. Darl DL3 ...... 208 B3
Chester Pl. Peter SR8 ...... 85 B7
Chester Rd. Bourn DH3 & DH4 ...... 21 D3
Chester Rd. C le S DH3 ...... 20 F5
Chester Rd. Cons DH8 ...... 30 A7
Chester Rd.
  S Row DH3 & DH4 ...... 21 D3
Chester Rd. Durham DH1 ...... 58 A7
Chester Road Est. Stanl DH9 ...... 18 A7
Chester St. Bish Au DL14 ...... 148 C7
Chester St. Wald DH2 ...... 19 E1
Chester Terr. Eas SR8 ...... 63 D4
Chesterton. Hur on T DL2 ...... 224 C1
Chester-le-Street Sta.
  C le S DH3 ...... 20 C3
Chester-le-Street Bullion La Sch.
  C le S DH2 ...... 20 B3
Chester-le-Street C of E Jun Sch.
  C le S DH3 ...... 20 B5
Chester-le-Street Cestria City
  Jun & Inf Sch. C le S DH3 ...... 20 D3
Chester-le-Street General Hospl.
  C le S DH3 ...... 20 C2
Chester-le-Street Hermitage
  Comp Sch. C le S DH2 ...... 20 A2
Chester-le-Street Newker Cty
  Jun Sch. C le S DH2 ...... 20 B2
Chester-le-Street Park View
  Comp Sch. C le S DH3 ...... 20 D3
Chester-le-Street Pelaw Cty
  Inf Sch. C le S DH2 ...... 20 B5
Chester-le-Street Red Rose Cty
  Jun & Inf Sch. C le S DH2 ...... 20 D1
Chester-le-Street West La Sch.
  C le S DH2 ...... 20 B2
Chesters Dene. Ebch DH8 ...... 3 E3
Chesters The. Ebch DH8 ...... 3 E3
Chestnut Ave. Ferry DL17 ...... 129 A6
Chestnut Ave. Spenny DL16 ...... 127 E7
Chestnut Cl. Shild DL4 ...... 149 A1
Chestnut Dr. Hasw DH6 ...... 62 A3
Chestnut Gr. Billy R DL15 ...... 100 D7
Chestnut Gr. Ush M DH7 ...... 57 A1
Chestnut Rd. Sedge TS21 ...... 153 B7
Cheveley Park Jun & Inf Schs.
  Belm DH1 ...... 59 E4

Cheveley Park Sh Ctr.
  Belm DH1 ...... 59 E4
Cheveley Wlk. Belm DH1 ...... 59 D3
Cheviot Ct. Ann Pl DH9 ...... 16 F3
Cheviot Cl. 3 Darl DL1 ...... 209 C6
Cheviot Ct. Seaham SR7 ...... 41 A8
Cheviot Gdns. Seaham SR7 ...... 41 B8
Cheviot La. Ryhope SR2 ...... 22 E7
Cheviot Pl. New Ay DL5 ...... 171 B7
Cheviot Pl. Peter SR8 ...... 85 B6
Cheviot Rd. C le S DH2 ...... 20 B1
Cheviot Terr. Ann Pl DH9 ...... 18 A5
Cheviot View. C le S DH2 ...... 36 A8
Cheyne The. Silk SR3 ...... 22 A5
Chichester Rd. Durham DH1 ...... 58 D8
Chichester Wlk. Darl DL1 ...... 209 F5
Chillingham Dr. C le S DH2 ...... 20 A1
Chillingham Gr. New Ay DL17 ...... 150 E1
Chillingham Rd. Durham DH1 ...... 58 D6
Chiltern Ave. C le S DH2 ...... 20 B2
Chiltern Rd. Cound DL14 ...... 149 C8
Chilton Cl. Darl DL3 ...... 208 B1
Chilton Cl. New Ay DL5 ...... 150 E1
Chilton Cty Inf Sch. Chilt DL17 ...... 150 F8
Chilton Cty Jun Sch.
  Chilt DL17 ...... 150 F7
Chilton Garth. Peter SR8 ...... 85 F5
Chilton Gdns. 10 Fence DH4 ...... 38 A8
Chilton Ind Est. Chilt DL 17 ...... 128 E2
Chilton La. Ferry DL17 ...... 129 C4
Chilton Way. Chilt DL17 ...... 128 E1
China St. Darl DL3 ...... 209 A6
Chipchase. Wash NE38 ...... 9 F4
Chirnside Terr. Ann Pl DH9 ...... 16 E3
Chopwell Rd. B Mill NE17 ...... 4 C6
Christchurch Cl. 5 Darl DL1 ...... 209 B6
Christchurch Pl. Peter SR8 ...... 85 C5
Christopher Wlk. 2
  New Ay DL5 ...... 171 C7
Church Bank. Cons DH8 ...... 14 C6
Church Bank. Egg DL12 ...... 162 B4
Church Bank. Stanl DH9 ...... 17 F7
Church Bank. Start DL12 ...... 200 F4
Church Chare. C le S DH3 ...... 20 D3
Church Cl. Ebch DH8 ...... 3 E3
Church Cl. Kir Me DL16 ...... 128 A3
Church Cl. M St G DL2 ...... 225 F5
Church Cl. New Ay DL5 ...... 171 D6
Church Cl. Peter SR8 ...... 85 E5
Church Cl. Seaham SR7 ...... 41 C8
Church Cl. Seaham SR7 ...... 41 A8
Church Dr. Bish Au DL14 ...... 148 D6
Church Farm Flats.
  Redmar TS21 ...... 195 B7
Church Gn. Seaham SR7 ...... 41 C8
Church Gr. Cound DL14 ...... 149 B8
Church Hill. Crook DL15 ...... 100 F4
Church La. Durham DH1 ...... 58 E2
Church La. Ferry DL17 ...... 128 F6
Church La. Hunw DL15 ...... 125 E6
Church La. M St G DL2 ...... 225 F5
Church La. Murton SR7 ...... 40 C2
Church La. Nent CA9 ...... 42 A4
Church La. New Ay DL5 ...... 171 E1
Church La. Redmar TS21 ...... 195 B7
Church La. Sadb DL2 ...... 210 E6
Church La. Shadf DH6 ...... 82 E7
Church La. Stanh DL13 ...... 71 B3
Church La. Tow Law DL13 ...... 75 C2
Church La N. Murton SR7 ...... 40 B3
Church Mews. Winst DL2 ...... 204 A6
Church Par. Sacr DH7 ...... 35 B4
Church Rd. Cons DH8 ...... 14 D4
Church Rd. Ferry DL17 ...... 128 F6
Church Rd. H le H DH5 ...... 39 A4
Church Rd. Pelton DH2 ...... 19 D6
Church Row. 5 Darl DL1 ...... 208 F1
Church Row. Hur on T DL2 ...... 224 E1
Church Row. Ingle DL2 ...... 188 A6
Church Row. Stanh DL13 ...... 71 A5
Church Sch. Hur on T DL2 ...... 224 C1
Church Sq. Cockf DL13 ...... 166 D5
Church Sq. Hi Eth DL14 ...... 146 F5
Church St. Ann Pl DH9 ...... 16 F4
Church St. Birt DH3 ...... 9 C4
Church St. Bish Mi DL17 ...... 130 B3
Church St. By Gr DL 16 ...... 126 F8
Church St. Cons DH8 ...... 14 F2
Church St. Cound DL14 ...... 149 B8
Church St. Crook DL15 ...... 100 F4
Church St. Durham DH1 ...... 80 D8
Church St. Ferry DL17 ...... 129 C3
Church St. 7 H le Sp DH4 & DH5 ...... 38 E8
Church St. Hasw DH6 ...... 61 E3
Church St. Hesl TS27 ...... 86 A1
Church St. Hi Eth DL14 ...... 146 F5
Church St. How le W DL15 ...... 124 E7
Church St. Lang Pk DH7 ...... 56 C6
Church St. Leadg DH8 ...... 15 C4
Church St. Murton SR7 ...... 40 C2
Church St. 1 Qua Hi DH6 ...... 106 D8
Church St. Sacr DH7 ...... 35 B3
Church St. Seaham SR7 ...... 41 D7
Church St. Shild DL4 ...... 148 F2
Church St. Spenny DL16 ...... 127 F8
Church St. Staind DL2 ...... 186 E6
Church St. Trim TS29 ...... 107 D1
Church St. W Rain DH4 ...... 38 A2
Church St. W Hi DH6 ...... 84 A3
Church St. Will DL15 ...... 101 C3
Church St E. Coxhoe DH6 ...... 106 A4
Church Street Head.
  Durham DH1 ...... 80 D8

Church Street Villas.
  Durham DH1 ...... 80 D8
Church Vale. H Pitt DH6 ...... 60 C4
Church View. Belm DH1 ...... 59 D4
Church View. Bish TS21 ...... 194 D7
Church View. Cons DH8 ...... 14 E2
Church View. Hasw DH6 ...... 61 F3
Church View. Heigh DL5 ...... 170 D1
Church View. 2 Hi Eth DL14 ...... 146 F5
Church View. Hur on T DL2 ...... 224 D1
Church View. Ingle DL2 ...... 188 A6
Church View. Kimble DH2 ...... 36 A3
Church View. Lanch DH7 ...... 32 F3
Church View. N Silk SR3 ...... 22 A7
Church View. Quebec DH7 ...... 55 B4
Church View. Sadb DL2 ...... 210 E6
Church View. Sedge TS21 ...... 153 A6
Church View. Shot Co DH6 ...... 84 C7
Church View. Thor DL13 ...... 99 B7
Church View. Thorn DH6 ...... 83 D4
Church View. Will DL15 ...... 102 B3
Church Wlk. Eas SR8 ...... 63 A3
Church Wynd. Sherb DH6 ...... 59 F1
Churchgarth La. Rook DL13 ...... 47 C1
Churchill Ave. Durham DH1 ...... 58 F2
Churchill Cl. Cons DH8 ...... 14 C6
Churchill Rd. Bar Cas DL12 ...... 201 B6
Churchill Sq. Durham DH1 ...... 58 F3
Churchill Sq. Fence DH4 ...... 38 B8
Churchill Terr. S Hill DH6 ...... 82 E8
Cinnamon Dr. Wing TS29 ...... 108 A5
Clanny Rd. New Ay DL5 ...... 171 E5
Clap Shaw. Blanch DH8 ...... 10 A1
Clappersgate. Eas SR8 ...... 63 A3
Clara St. Seaham SR7 ...... 41 B8
Clare Ave. Darl DL3 ...... 208 B2
Clare Rd. Peter SR8 ...... 85 B5
Claremont Gr. Sedge TS21 ...... 153 A5
Claremont Rd. Darl DL1 ...... 224 C7
Clarence Cl. New Ay DL5 ...... 171 E5
Clarence Cl. New Ay DL5 ...... 171 E5
Clarence Cnr. New Ay DL5 ...... 171 E5
Clarence Gdns. Bish Au DL14 ...... 148 B8
Clarence Gdns. Cons DH8 ...... 14 F4
Clarence Gn. New Ay DL5 ...... 171 E5
Clarence House. Spenny DL16 ...... 127 F8
Clarence St. Bish Au DL14 ...... 148 B8
Clarence St. Bowb DH6 ...... 105 F6
Clarence St. 3 Seaham SR7 ...... 41 D7
Clarence St. Spenny DL16 ...... 127 F8
Clarence St. Tant DH9 ...... 6 B2
Clarence Terr. C le S DH3 ...... 20 C3
Clarence The. 11
  Bish Au DL14 ...... 148 B8
Clarence Villas. Bowb DH6 ...... 105 F6
Clarendon Rd. Darl DL1 ...... 209 E6
Clarendon St. 13 Cons DH8 ...... 14 F3
Clareville Rd. Darl DL3 ...... 208 C2
Clark Terr. Leadg DH8 ...... 15 B6
Clark Terr. Stanl DH9 ...... 17 F8
Clark's Terr. 2 Seaham SR7 ...... 22 E1
Clarke Terr. Murton SR7 ...... 40 C3
Claude St. H le H DH5 ...... 39 A3
Claude Terr. Murton SR7 ...... 40 D3
Clavering Pl. Ann Pl DH9 ...... 16 F3
Clavering Prim Sch.
  Hartle TS24 ...... 111 C3
Clavering Rd. Hartle TS24 ...... 111 D3
Claxton Ave. Darl DL3 ...... 208 B3
Claxton Ct. New Ay DL5 ...... 150 A1
Claxton St. 5 Peter SR8 ...... 86 A7
Clay La. Durham DH1 ...... 80 A8
Clay La. Durham DH1 ...... 80 B8
Claypath. Durham DH1 ...... 58 D2
Claypath Rd. H le H DH5 ...... 39 B2
Claypool Farm Cl.
  Hut Hen TS27 ...... 109 D5
Clayton Ave. Bish Au DL14 ...... 126 E1
Clayton St. 1 Bish Au DL14 ...... 148 B8
Cleadon St. 8 Cons DH8 ...... 14 F3
Cleasby La. Stapl DL2 ...... 222 E3
Cleasby La. Stapl DL2 ...... 223 A5
Cleasby View. Darl DL3 ...... 208 B4
Cleatlam Back La. Cleat DL2 ...... 185 F2
Clemmy Bank. Wit le W DL14 ...... 124 B3
Clervaux Terr. Fishb TS21 ...... 131 D5
Cleve Cotts. 1 Ferry DL17 ...... 129 B5
Clevecoat Wlk. Hart TS27 ...... 110 F2
Cleveland Ave. Bish Au DL14 ...... 148 B6
Cleveland Ave. C le S DH2 ...... 20 B2
Cleveland Ave. Darl DL3 ...... 208 E1
Cleveland Ave. Shild DL4 ...... 149 B1
Cleveland Ave. Trim TS29 ...... 107 D1
Cleveland Ct. Ferry DL17 ...... 129 C5
Cleveland Pl. Peter SR8 ...... 85 B6
Cleveland Rd. Bar Cas DL12 ...... 201 B7
Cleveland St. Darl DL3 ...... 209 A4
Cleveland St. Darl DL3 ...... 208 D1
Cleveland Terr. Stanl DH9 ...... 18 A5
Cleveland Trad Est. Darl DL1 ...... 209 A4
Cleveland View. Cound DL14 ...... 149 C8
Cleveland View. Ferry DL17 ...... 129 B5
Cleveland View. Fishb TS21 ...... 131 C4
Cleves Ave. Ferry DL17 ...... 129 C5
Cleves Cl. Ferry DL17 ...... 129 B7
Cleves Cross Cty Jun & Inf Sch.
  Ferry DL17 ...... 129 B6
Cleves Cross Grange.
  Ferry DL17 ...... 129 B6
Cleves Ct. Ferry DL17 ...... 129 B7
Cliff Rd. Ryhope SR2 ...... 23 A6
Cliff Terr. Eas SR8 ...... 63 B4
Cliff Terr. Ryhope SR2 ...... 23 A6
Cliff View. Ryhope SR2 ...... 23 A7
Cliffe Way. Darl DL1 ...... 224 C8
Clifford Ave. Bish Au DL14 ...... 148 B5

Clifford Cl. Hartle TS24 ...... 111 F2
Clifford Rd. Stanl DH9 .... 17 F6
Clifford St. C le S DH3 .... 20 C2
Clifford St. Lang Pk DH7 .... 56 B6
Clifford Terr. C le S DH3 .... 20 C2
Clifford's Bank. Quebec DH7 ..... 55 C3
Clifford's View. Oving DL11 .... 203 D2
Cliffords Gate. Esh W DH7 .... 55 C1
Clifton Ave. Darl DL1 .... 224 A7
Clifton Gn. Will DL15 .... 101 E2
Clifton Rd. Darl DL1 .... 224 A8
Clifton Sq. Peter SR8 .... 85 D6
Clint La. Bowes DL12 .... 198 F1
Clive St. Ferry DL17 .... 129 C4
Clockburn Lonnen. Whick NE16 .... 2 E4
Clockburnside Cl. Whick NE16 .... 2 E5
Close E The. C le S DH2 .... 20 C5
Close House Jun & Inf Sch.
Bish Au DL14 .... 149 A5
Close House. Shild DL14 .... 149 A4
Close St. Darl DL1 .... 209 A5
Close The. Belm DH1 .... 59 D3
Close The. Brance DH7 .... 78 E1
Close The. Burnop NE16 .... 6 C7
Close The. C le S DH2 .... 20 C5
Close The. Cons DH8 .... 14 D6
Close The. Coth DL12 .... 182 E3
Close The. H le Sp DH5 .... 38 F8
Close The. Hi Eth DL14 .... 146 F6
Close The. Lanch DH7 .... 32 E4
Close The. Longn TS21 .... 211 F5
Close The. Neas DL2 .... 225 B2
Close The. Spenny DL16 .... 104 A2
Closeburn Sq. Silk SR3 .... 22 B6
Clough Dene. Tant NE16 .... 6 A3
Clover Ave. Win M NE21 .... 2 C6
Clover Ct. New Ay DL5 .... 150 D2
Clover Laid. Brand DH7 .... 79 A3
Cloverdale. Darl DL1 .... 209 E6
Cloverhill. C le S DH2 .... 19 F2
Cloverhill Jun & Inf Sch.
Whick NE16 .... 2 F4
Clowes Terr. Ann Pl DH9 .... 16 F4
Clowes Wlk. Stanl DH9 .... 18 B7
Club La. Durham DH1 .... 58 A3
Clyde Terr. Cound DL14 .... 149 C8
Clyde Terr. Spenny DL16 .... 127 E2
Clydesdale Garth. Durham DH1 ... 58 D8
Clydesdale St. H le H DH5 .... 39 A2
Co-operative Bldgs. Dipton DH9 16 C8
Co-operative St. C le S DH3 ...... 20 C4
Co-operative St. Shild DL4 ...... 148 E2
Co-operative Terr. Beam DH9 .... 19 A7
Co-operative Terr. Burnh DH7 .... 33 E5
Co-operative Terr. Burnop NE16 .. 6 B6
Co-operative Terr. Cons DH8 ..... 14 C7
Co-operative Terr. 4
Coxhoe DH6 .... 106 A4
Co-operative Terr. Crook DL15 .. 100 F3
Co-operative Terr. Dipton DH9 .. 16 C8
Co-operative Terr. Gr Lum DH4 .. 21 F1
Co-operative Terr. Hunw DL15 125 D7
Co-operative Terr. Medom DH8 .. 4 B1
Co-operative Terr. N Bran DH7 .. 78 F8
Co-operative Terr. Shot Co DH6 84 D6
Co-operative Terr.
Stan Cr DL15 .... 100 F8
Co-operative Terr. Trim TS29 .... 107 D5
Co-operative Terr. W Pel DH2 .... 19 B4
Co-operative Terr. Wols DL13 .. 97 F7
Co-operative Terr E.
Dipton DH9 .... 16 D8
Co-operative Terr W.
Dipton DH9 .... 16 C8
Co-operative Villas. Brand DH7 79 E5
Co-operative Villas. S Hill DH6 . 60 D1
Coach La. Hur on T DL2 .... 224 D1
Coal La. Elwick TS27 & TS22 .... 133 E6
Coal La. Longn TS22 .... 155 F2
Coal La. Hut Hen TS27 & TS22 ... 133 E6
Coal Rd. Thor DL13 .... 99 D4
Coalbank Rd. H le H DH5 .... 38 F2
Coalbank Sq. H le H DH5 .... 38 F2
Coalford La. H Pitt DH6 .... 60 C4
Coalford La. Satley DL13 .... 53 A3
Coalford Rd. Sherb DH6 .... 59 F2
Coast Rd. B Coll TS27 .... 86 B5
Coast Rd. B Rocks TS27 .... 86 E2
Coast Rd. Peter SR8 & TS27 ...... 86 B5
Coates Cl. Stanl DH9 .... 18 A5
Coatham Ave. M St G DL2 .... 225 F6
Coatham Ave. New Ay DL5 .... 171 D4
Coatham Cres. Darl DL1 .... 209 B6
Coatham La.
Coat Mu DL1 & DL3 .... 191 D5
Coatsay Moor La. Heigh DL2 .... 190 E6
Cobbler Gate La. Mick DL12 .... 161 A5
Cobby Castle La. Bish TS21 ..... 194 D8
Cobden Ct. Darl DL1 .... 224 C8
Cobden St. Cons DH8 .... 15 A3
Cobden St. Darl DL1 .... 209 C1
Cobey's Carr La.
Newf DL14 & DL15 .... 102 B1
Coburg St. Darl DL1 .... 209 A2
Cochrane Ct. Ferry DL17 .... 129 C2
Cochrane Terr. Ush M DH7 .... 57 A1
Cochrane Terr. Will DL15 .... 101 E3
Cock La. Head DL2 .... 205 B4
Cock La. Pier DL2 .... 206 A6
Cock's Cotts. 2 Ush M DH7 ...... 56 F2
Cocken La. Gr Lum DH1 & DH3 .. 37 B5
Cocken Rd. Durham DH1 .... 37 C3
Cocken Rd. W Rain DH4 .... 37 C3
Cockerton C of E Prim Sch.
Darl DL3 .... 208 C4
Cockerton Gn. Darl DL3 .... 208 C4
Cockfield Cty Sch.
Cockf DL13 .... 166 C5

Cockhouse La. Ush M DH7 .... 56 F3
Cockshaw Nook. Bish Au DL14 . 126 B1
Cockton Hill Cty Inf Sch.
Bish Au DL14 .... 148 C6
Cockton Hill Cty Jun Sch.
Bish Au DL14 .... 148 C6
Cockton Hill Rd. Bish Au DL14 . 148 B6
Cohort Cl. Ebch DH8 .... 3 E3
Colburn Ave. New Ay DL5 .... 171 A8
Colby House. 13 Darl DL2 .... 224 C8
Cold Hesledon Ind Est.
Cold He SR7 .... 40 F3
Coldstream. Ouston DH2 .... 9 A2
Coldstream Dr. Blay NE21 .... 2 A8
Coldwell Cl. S Hett DH6 .... 61 F7
Colebrooke. Birt DH3 .... 9 D2
Colepike Rd. Lanch DH7 .... 32 E3
Coleridge Cl. Will DL15 .... 101 F1
Coleridge Gdns. Darl DL1 .... 224 A7
Coleridge Gdns. Dipton DH9 ..... 16 D8
Coleridge Pl. C le St DH2 .... 19 E3
Coleridge Rd. Chilt DL17 .... 150 E8
Colin Terr. 7 Ryhope SR2 .... 22 F6
College Cl. Elwick TS27 .... 134 E3
College Ct. Darl DL3 .... 208 E2
College Rd. Lang Pk DH7 .... 56 D4
College St. Shild DL4 .... 148 E2
College View. Bear DH7 .... 57 A4
College View. Cons DH8 .... 31 C8
College View. Esh W DH7 .... 77 D7
Collier Cl. Crook DL15 .... 100 D3
Collier La. E Lay DL11 .... 221 A2
Collierley Cty Jun & Inf Sch.
Dipton DH9 .... 16 C8
Collierley La. Dipton DH9 .... 5 D1
Colliery La. H le H DH5 .... 39 B2
Colling Ave. Seaham SR7 .... 41 A7
Colling Wlk. New Ay DL5 .... 171 D6
Collingdon Gn. H Spen NE39 ...... 1 A4
Collingdon La. H Spen NE39 ...... 1 A4
Collingwood Bank.
Romald DL12 .... 162 A3
Collingwood Coll. Durham DH1 . 80 C6
Collingwood St. Cound DL14 .... 149 B8
Collingwood St. H le H DH5 ...... 39 A6
Collison St. Cons DH8 .... 14 F3
Collyers Cl. Hur on T DL2 ...... 224 D1
Colorado Gr. Darl DL1 .... 209 B6
Colston Rise. Peter SR8 .... 85 C7
Colt Pk. Hams NE17 .... 4 B5
Coltspool. Kibble NE11 .... 8 D6
Columbia St. Darl DL3 .... 208 E4
Colville Ct. Stanl DH9 .... 18 B6
Colwell Cl. New Ay DL5 .... 170 F7
Comer Terr. Cockf DL13 .... 166 D5
Comet Dr. Eas SR8 .... 63 C4
Comet Sq. N Silk SR3 .... 22 A7
Commercial Rd E. Coxhoe DH6 105 F5
Commercial Rd W.
Coxhoe DH6 .... 105 F5
Commercial Sq. Brand DH7 ...... 79 C4
Commercial Sq. Brand DH7 ...... 79 C5
Commercial St. Corn Co DH7 .... 55 A3
Commercial St. Crook DL15 ..... 100 E4
Commercial St. Darl DL3 .... 208 F2
Commercial St. Ferry DL17 ..... 129 C3
Commercial St. Trim TS29 ...... 108 A5
Commercial St. Will DL15 ...... 102 A3
Commercial St. Wing TS29 ...... 108 A5
Compton Gr. Bish Au DL14 ...... 148 A6
Compton St. Darl DL3 .... 208 C3
Concorde Sq. 5 N Silk SR3 ...... 22 A7
Cone Terr. C le S DH3 .... 20 D4
Coney Ave. Bish Au DL14 .... 148 A5
Congburn Bank. Edmon DH7 ..... 35 B7
Congreve Terr. New Ay DL5 .... 171 E2
Conifer Ave. Sedge TS21 .... 153 B7
Conifer Cl. Belm DH1 .... 59 A3
Conifer Cl. Blay NE21 .... 2 B8
Conifer Rise. Peter SR8 .... 85 B8
Coniscliffe Rd. Darl DL3 .... 208 F1
Coniscliffe Rd. Darl DL3 .... 223 C8
Coniscliffe St. Stanl DH9 .... 17 D6
Conishead Terr. S Hett DH6 ...... 61 F8
Coniston. Birt DH3 .... 9 D2
Coniston Ave. Bish Au DL14 .... 147 B1
Coniston Ave. E Lane DH5 .... 61 C8
Coniston Cl. Belm DH1 .... 59 E4
Coniston Cl. C le S DH2 .... 20 C2
Coniston Cl. Peter SR8 .... 85 E6
Coniston Cres. Blay NE21 .... 2 B8
Coniston Cres. Crook DL15 ..... 100 F3
Coniston Cres. Redmar TS21 ... 195 B7
Coniston Dr. Sacr DH7 .... 35 B3
Coniston Rd. Ferry DL17 .... 128 F5
Coniston St. Darl DL3 .... 208 D4
Coniston Way. Leadg DH8 .... 15 D4
Connolly Terr. B Mill NE17 .... 4 C6
Consett Blackfyne Comp Sch.
Cons DH8 .... 14 F4
Consett Bsns Pk. Cons DH8 ..... 15 B4
Consett Cty Inf Sch. Cons DH8 .. 14 F3
Consett Cty Jun Mix Sch.
Cons DH8 .... 15 A3
Consett Cty Jun Sch. Cons DH8 15 A3
Consett & District Golf Course.
Cons DH8 .... 14 F6
Consett Grove Cty Jun & Inf Sch.
Cons DH8 .... 14 C1
Consett Grove RC (Aided) Jun
& Inf Sch. Cons DH8 .... 14 C1
Consett La. Cons DH8 .... 14 B2
Consett Moorside Jun & Inf Sch.
Cons DH8 .... 30 A7
Consett Moorside Sec Sch.
Cons DH8 .... 30 B8
Consett Park Terr. Cons DH8 .... 30 B7
Consett RC Inf Sch. Cons DH8 .. 14 F3
Consett RC Jun Mix Sch.
Cons DH8 .... 14 F2
Consett Rd. Cons DH8 .... 29 F6
Consett Terr. Esh DH7 .... 56 A5

Consett Villa Real Sch.
Cons DH8 .... 15 B4
Constable Cl. Stanl DH9 .... 17 F6
Constables Garth. 6 Birt DH3 .... 9 C4
Constance St. Cons DH8 .... 14 F2
Constance St. Pelton DH2 .... 19 E7
Constantine Rd.
How le W DL15 .... 125 A6
Convers Terr. 4 Ferry DL17 .... 129 A5
Conway Gr. Bish Au DL14 .... 148 B6
Conway Pl. Pelton DH2 .... 19 F8
Conway Wlk. Hartle TS26 .... 111 E1
Conyers Ave. C le S DH2 .... 20 B5
Conyers Ave. Darl DL3 .... 208 B3
Conyers Cl. Darl DL3 .... 208 B3
Conyers Cres. Peter SR8 .... 63 E1
Conyers Gdns. C le S DH2 .... 20 B5
Conyers Gr. Darl DL3 .... 208 B3
Conyers Pl. C le S DH2 .... 20 B5
Conyers Rd. C le S DH2 .... 20 C5
Cook Ave. Bear DH7 .... 57 B3
Cook Cres. Murton SR7 .... 40 B3
Cook Gr. Peter SR8 .... 63 E1
Cook Way. Eas SR8 .... 84 F7
Cooke's Wood. Ush M DH7 .... 79 D8
Cookshold La. S Hill DH6 .... 60 B2
Cookshold La. Sherb DH6 .... 60 B2
Cookson Terr. C le S DH3 .... 20 C3
Coombe Dr. Darl DL1 .... 209 E3
Cooper Sq. Durham DH1 .... 58 F3
Cooper's Terr. Thorn DH6 .... 83 D4
Coopers Cl. Thorn DH6 .... 83 D4
Copeland Ct. Durham DH1 .... 80 C7
Copeland La. Even DL14 .... 167 E7
Copeland Rd. Bish Au DL14 .... 147 B1
Copeland Rd. Even DL14 .... 167 D7
Copley Bent. Copley DL13 ...... 165 F7
Copley La. Copley DL13 .... 165 C7
Copperfield. Durham DH1 .... 80 A7
Copperwood Cl. 1
Hartle TS27 .... 111 C4
Coppice Hill. Esh W DH7 .... 77 F8
Coppice The. Grind TS22 .... 155 D2
Coppice Wlk. Darl DL3 .... 208 A4
Coppy La. Beam DH9 .... 7 C4
Copse Side. Darl DL3 .... 208 A1
Copse The. Bish Au DL14 .... 148 A7
Copse The. Burnop NE16 .... 5 F6
Copse The. H le W DL14 .... 124 B3
Copthill. Cons DH8 .... 66 C6
Coptleigh. H le Sp DH5 .... 39 A7
Coquet Dr. Pelton DH2 .... 19 E8
Coquet Gdns. Stanl DH9 .... 17 E4
Coquet. Wash NE38 .... 9 F1
Corbett St. Seaham SR7 .... 41 B8
Corbridge Cres. Darl DL1 ...... 209 C5
Corbridge Rd. Medom DH8 .... 15 A7
Corby Gr. Peter SR8 .... 85 A3
Corcyta St. 3 Seaham SR7 .... 41 D6
Cormorant Cl. 4 Wash NE38 ...... 9 F1
Corn Cl. Start DL12 .... 200 E5
Corn Mill Dr. H le Sp DH5 .... 38 D6
Cornbank Cl. Silk SR3 .... 22 A5
Cornelia Cl. 7 N Silk SR3 .... 22 A7
Cornelia Terr. Seaham SR7 ...... 41 D6
Corner Bank La. Heigh DL2 .... 169 E4
Cornfieldgarth. Peter SR8 .... 85 F5
Cornforth By-Pass. Cornf DL17 129 C8
Cornforth La. Cornf DH6 .... 105 F2
Cornforth La. Coxhoe DH6 ...... 105 F3
Cornforth Lane Cty Sch.
Coxhoe DH6 .... 105 F3
Cornmill Ctr. 10 Darl DL1 ...... 208 F2
Cornmoor. C le St DH2 .... 19 F2
Cornriggs. Laneh DL13 .... 66 B7
Cornsay La. Corn DH7 .... 54 B5
Cornwall Ave. Darl DL1 .... 209 C4
Cornwall Cl. Murton SR7 .... 40 D3
Cornwall Pl. Bish Au DL14 ...... 148 B5
Cornwall St. Eas SR8 .... 63 F4
Cornwall Wlk. Belm DH1 .... 59 D3
Coronation Ave. Belm DH1 ...... 59 D4
Coronation Ave. Fishb TS21 .... 131 C4
Coronation Ave. 2 Peter SR8 .... 86 A6
Coronation Ave. 6 Ryhope SR2 22 F6
Coronation Ave. Shild DL4 ..... 149 B1
Coronation Ave. Stanh DL13 .... 71 C2
Coronation Ave. Tow Law DL13 .. 75 B3
Coronation Cotts. Shot Co DH6 .. 84 C6
Coronation Gdns. Staind DL2 .. 186 C5
Coronation Gn. E Lane DH5 ...... 61 D8
Coronation Homes. She'wf DH7 77 F8
Coronation Rd. Chilt DL17 ..... 151 A8
Coronation Rd. Wing TS28 ..... 108 D8
Coronation Sq. S Hett DH6 ...... 62 B7
Coronation St. Bar Cas DL12 .. 201 A7
Coronation St. C le S DH3 .... 20 D1
Coronation St. Crook DL15 ..... 100 E4
Coronation St. Darl DL3 .... 208 E4
Coronation Terr. Ann Pl DH9 .... 17 B4
Coronation Terr. Belm DH1 ...... 59 C1
Coronation Terr. C le S DH3 .... 20 C2
Coronation Terr. Cockf DL13 ... 166 C5
Coronation Terr. Cornf DL17 ... 105 D1
Coronation Terr. Coxhoe DH6 .. 105 F5
Coronation Terr. Fir T DL15 .... 100 A1
Coronation Terr. H le H DH5 .... 39 A2
Coronation Terr. Hunw DL15 ... 125 D7
Coronation Terr. Kibble NE11 .... 8 C6
Coronation Terr. Kir Me DL16 .. 128 A3
Coronation Terr. Trim TS29 .... 107 E1
Coronation Terr. W Pel DH2 ..... 19 B4
Coronation Terr. Will DL15 .... 101 C3
Coronation Terr. Wing TS29 .... 107 F6
Corporation Rd. Darl DL3 ...... 208 F3
Corporation Road Prim Sch.
Darl DL3 .... 208 F3
Corriedale Cl. Durham DH1 ..... 58 C8
Corrighan Terr. E Rain DH5 ..... 38 C4

Corry Cl. B Coll TS27 .... 86 E3
Corsair. Whick NE16 .... 2 F6
Corscombe Cl. Ferry DL17 ...... 129 C5
Cort St. Cons DH8 .... 14 E3
Cortett St. Eas SR8 .... 63 F4
Cortland Rd. Cons DH8 .... 14 C4
Corvan Terr. Tant DH9 .... 6 A2
Cosgrove Ave. Bish Au DL14 ... 148 A4
Cosin Cl. New Ay DL5 .... 171 E5
Cote House Rd. Mick DL12 ..... 160 F4
Cotherstone Cty Jun & Inf Sch.
Coth DL12 .... 182 E4
Cotherstone Moor Dr.
Darl DL1 .... 224 D7
Cotherstone Rd. Durham DH1 ... 58 D5
Cotsford Cres. 3 Peter SR8 ..... 86 A6
Cotsford La. Peter SR8 .... 86 B6
Cotswold Ave. C le S DH2 .... 20 B1
Cotswold Cl. Cound DL14 ...... 149 C8
Cotswold Pl. Peter SR8 .... 85 B6
Cotswold Terr. Stanl DH9 .... 18 A5
Cotswolds The. Chilt DL17 ..... 150 F7
Cottage Rd. 8 Shild DL4 .... 148 F1
Cottages Rd. Seaham SR7 .... 41 D6
Cottages The. Heigh DL5 .... 170 D1
Cottingham Cl. Peter SR8 .... 85 B7
Cottingham St. Darl DL3 .... 208 B4
Coulson St. Spenny DL16 ...... 128 B8
Coulton Terr. Kir Me DL16 ..... 128 A3
Coundon Cty Jun & Inf Sch.
Cound DL14 .... 149 C8
Coundon St Joseph's RC Inf
& Jun Sch. Cound DL14 .... 149 C8
County Hospl. Durham DH1 ..... 58 B2
Court La. Durham DH1 .... 58 D1
Court St. Eas SR8 .... 63 F4
Courtine The. Heigh DL5 .... 170 D1
Courtlands Rd. Darl DL3 .... 208 D4
Courtney Dr. 1 N Silk SR3 ...... 22 A7
Courtney Dr. Pelton DH2 .... 19 F7
Courtyard The. Tanf L DH9 ...... 17 C8
Coventry Rd. Durham DH1 ...... 58 E7
Coverdale Ct. New Ay DL5 ..... 171 B8
Coverley. Gr Lum DH3 .... 37 A8
Covert The. New Ay DL5 .... 170 F8
Cowclose La. Barn DL11 & DL12 218 D1
Cowell St. Peter SR8 .... 85 F7
Cowen St. Blay NE21 .... 2 B8
Cowen Terr. R Gill NE39 .... 1 F3
Cowfold La. Walw DL2 .... 190 B5
Cowgarth Hill. 1 Stanh DL13 .... 71 A3
Cowley Cres. E Rain DH5 .... 38 C4
Cowley La. Wood DL13 .... 164 C7
Cowley St. Shot Co DH6 .... 84 D6
Cowsley La. Corn DH7 .... 54 A1
Coxwold Dr. Darl DL1 .... 224 C7
Coxwold La. Bish Au DL14 ...... 148 C6
Coxwold House. 9 Darl DL2 ... 224 C8
Craddock St. Spenny DL16 ..... 127 E8
Cradock St. Bish Au DL14 ...... 148 C6
Crag La. Bolam DL2 .... 168 F3
Crag Works. Leadg DH8 .... 15 C6
Cragg View. Mick DL12 .... 161 B4
Craggyknowe. Wash NE37 .... 9 F6
Craghead La. Crag DH9 .... 18 E3
Craghead La. H le H DH9 .... 18 E3
Cragleas. Burnop NE16 .... 6 A4
Cragside. C le S DH2 .... 20 A4
Cragside. Chilt DL17 .... 151 A8
Cragside. Sedge TS21 .... 153 A5
Cragside. Wit Gil DH7 .... 57 B8
Cragside Cl. Ann Pl DH9 .... 16 F3
Cragside Cl. Cons DH8 .... 14 C4
Cragside Ct. 4 H le Sp DH5 ...... 38 F8
Cragwell Dr. Sacr DH7 .... 35 B2
Craig Lea Rd. Billy R DL15 ..... 100 A6
Craig St. 1 Birt DH3 .... 9 C4
Craig St. Darl DL3 .... 208 E3
Craig Terr. Eas SR8 .... 63 B3
Craig Terr. Wols DL13 .... 98 A7
Craigland Villas. Sacr DH7 ...... 35 C2
Craigwell Dr. Silk SR3 .... 22 A4
Crake Way. Wash NE38 .... 9 F2
Cramond Cl. Darl DL1 .... 208 A1
Crane Row La. Hamst DL13 .... 144 E4
Cranford Terr. Eas SR8 .... 63 B4
Cranleigh. Gr Lum DH3 .... 37 A7
Cranston Pl. 9 Ryhope SR2 ...... 23 A6
Craster Cl. C le St DH2 .... 19 F1
Crathie. Birt DH3 .... 9 C7
Craven's Bldgs. Hut Hen TS28 .. 108 F5
Crawford Ave. Peter SR8 .... 85 D8
Crawford Cl. Bish Au DL14 ..... 148 A4
Crawford St. Sherb DH6 .... 59 F1
Crawford Rd. New Ay DL5 ...... 171 E6
Crawlaw Bglws. Eas SR8 .... 63 E5
Crawlaw Rd. Eas SR8 .... 63 E5
Creighton Rd. New Ay DL5 ..... 171 E6
Crescent The. B Coll TS27 .... 86 D3
Crescent The. C le S DH2 .... 20 B3
Crescent The. Carl TS21 .... 195 C8
Crescent The. Chilt DL17 ...... 150 F8
Crescent The. Cons DH8 .... 14 C4
Crescent The. Cons DH8 .... 14 C6
Crescent The. Cons DH8 .... 14 F4
Crescent The. Cound DL14 ..... 149 C8
Crescent The. Durham DH1 ..... 58 B3
Crescent The. Eas SR8 .... 63 E5
Crescent The. H le H DH5 .... 39 A3
Crescent The. Hi Eth DL14 ..... 146 F5
Crescent The. Kibble NE11 .... 8 C6
Crescent The. Kimble DL5 .... 34 F4
Crescent The. Lang Pk DH7 ..... 56 A6
Crescent The. M Law DH7 .... 33 A8
Crescent The. R Gill NE39 .... 1 F2
Crescent The. Sherb DH6 .... 59 F1
Crescent The. Staint DL12 ..... 201 D8
Crescent The. Tanf L DH9 .... 17 D8
Crescent The. W Rain DH4 ...... 37 F2

Crescent The. Wald DH2 .... 36 A7
Crescent The. Wit Gil DH7 .... 35 B1
Cresswell Ave. Peter SR8 .... 86 A6
Cresswell Cl. Blay NE21 .... 2 A8
Crewe Ave. Durham DH1 .... 59 B1
Crewe Rd. New Ay DL5 .... 171 E6
Crichton Ave. C le S DH3 .... 20 D1
Cricket Field Row. Darl DL3 ... 208 F5
Cricket Terr. Burnop NE16 .... 6 A6
Crimdon Gr. H le Sp DH4 .... 38 C7
Crimdon Terr. B Rocks TS27 ..... 87 A1
Crime Rigg Bank. Shadf DH6 .... 82 D8
Cringlemoor Cres. Darl DL1 .... 224 D7
Crispin Ct. Sedge TS21 .... 153 B6
Croft Ave. Crook DL15 .... 100 E3
Croft CE Prim Sch. Cr on T DL2 234 F8
Croft Gdns. Ferry DL17 .... 129 C4
Croft Rd. Hur on T DL2 .... 223 D3
Croft Rd. Hur on T DL2 .... 224 B1
Croft Rigg. Brand DH7 .... 79 A3
Croft Side. Bish Au DL14 ...... 147 D6
Croft St. Crook DL15 .... 100 E3
Croft Terr. Ann Pl DH9 .... 17 A4
Croft Terr. Cound DL4 .... 149 B8
Croft Terr. Frost DL13 .... 96 B6
Croft The. Kir Me DL16 .... 127 F3
Croft The. New Ay DL17 .... 150 E2
Croft The. S Hill DH6 .... 60 D1
Croft View. Coth DL12 .... 182 E4
Croft View. Lanch DH7 .... 32 E4
Croft Yoke La. Mick DL12 ..... 161 F3
Croft Yoke La. Romald DL12 ... 162 A3
Crofts The. Still TS21 .... 174 F3
Crofts The. Wols DL13 .... 97 E7
Croftside. Birt DH3 .... 9 C5
Cromarty Cl. Darl DL1 .... 209 E7
Cromer Lea. Frost DL13 .... 96 B6
Crompton Cl. Ferry DL17 ...... 128 C5
Cronniewell. Hams NE17 .... 4 B5
Crook (Beechburn) Ind Est.
Crook DL15 .... 100 E2
Crook Cty Jun Mix Sch.
Crook DL15 .... 100 E3
Crook Inf Sch. Crook DL15 ..... 100 E3
Crook La. Bar Cas DL12 .... 201 B5
Crookhall La. Leadg DH8 .... 15 C3
Crookhall Rd. Cons DH8 .... 15 A3
Crosby Rd. New Ay DL5 .... 171 C5
Crosby St. Darl DL3 .... 209 A6
Cross Hill Flats. 4 Stanh DL13 . 71 A4
Cross Hill. 3 Stanh DL13 .... 71 A3
Cross La. Cows DL13 .... 66 C7
Cross La. Sacr DH7 .... 35 C4
Cross Lanes. Heigh DL2 .... 190 B7
Cross Row. Durham DH1 .... 58 C7
Cross Row. Hunw DL15 .... 125 D5
Cross St. Bish Au DL14 .... 147 D2
Cross St. Cons DH8 .... 14 D4
Cross St. Crook DL15 .... 101 B3
Cross St. Eas SR8 .... 63 F4
Cross St. 8 Fence DH4 .... 38 A8
Cross St. H Pitt DH6 .... 60 D3
Cross St. Sedge TS21 .... 153 B6
Cross St. Shild DL4 .... 170 A8
Cross St. Sland B DH6 .... 104 B7
Cross St. Stanh DL13 .... 71 A3
Cross Terr. R Gill NE39 .... 1 D1
Cross View Terr. Durham DH1 ... 80 A8
Crossfield Cl. Hur on T DL2 .... 224 D1
Crossfield Cres. Shot Co DH6 ... 84 C7
Crossfield Rd. Darl DL3 .... 208 C5
Crossfield. Sacr DH7 .... 35 C2
Crossgate. Durham DH1 .... 58 C1
Crossgate Moor Gdns.
Durham DH1 .... 57 F3
Crossgate Peth. Durham DH1 ... 58 B1
Crossgate Rd. H le H DH5 .... 39 A2
Crosslea. Sacr DH7 .... 35 C3
Crosslet La. Westg DL13 .... 92 B8
Crossway The. Darl DL1 .... 209 D2
Crossways. Lang Pk DH7 .... 56 C6
Crossways. Sacr DH7 .... 35 C2
Crow Trees La. Bowb DH6 ..... 105 D8
Crowley Pl. New Ay DL5 .... 171 D7
Crown St. Bish Au DL14 .... 148 D5
Crown St. Darl DL1 .... 209 A2
Crowther Ind Est. Wash NE38 .... 9 F5
Crowther Rd. Wash NE38 .... 9 F5
Croxdale Gr. Bish Au DL14 ..... 147 C5
Croxton Cl. St on T TS21 ...... 195 F3
Crystal Cl. Chilt DL17 .... 150 F8
Cullen Cl. Darl DL1 .... 209 D6
Culloden Terr. Peter SR8 .... 63 F3
Culross Gr. St on T TS21 ...... 195 F3
Culzean Ct. Cons DH8 .... 14 D4
Cumberland Pl. Birt DH3 .... 9 D1
Cumberland Rd. Cons DH8 .... 30 A7
Cumberland Rd. N Silk SR3 .... 22 A8
Cumberland St. Bish Au DL14 .. 148 F5
Cumberland St. Darl DL3 ...... 209 A5
Cumberland Terr. Will DL15 ... 101 F3
Cumbie Way. New Ay DL5 ...... 171 D2
Cumbria Pl. Stanl DH9 .... 18 A7
Cumbrian Way. Peter SR8 .... 85 E6
Cumby Rd. New Ay DL5 .... 171 C5
Cummings Ave. Sherb DH6 ...... 59 F2
Cummings Sq. Wing TS28 ...... 108 D8
Cunningham Pl. Durham DH1 ... 58 F3
Curtain La. Epp DL11 .... 205 B2
Cut Throat La. Medom NE17 ..... 4 C4
Cuthbert Ave. Durham DH1 ...... 59 B1
Cuthbert Rd. Cornf DL17 ...... 105 E1
Cuthbert St. Spenny DL16 ..... 104 A2
Cutler's Ave. Cons DH8 .... 14 C5
Cutlers' Hall Rd. Cons DH8 ..... 14 C5
Cutting St. 3 Seaham SR7 .... 22 F1
Cyclamen Gr. Darl DL1 .... 209 C6
Cypress Cl. Darl DL1 .... 223 C2
Cypress Gr. Brand DH7 .... 79 B3
Cypress Gr. Belm DH1 .... 59 A3

Cypress Pk. Esh W DH7 ..... 77 D8
Cypress Sq. N Silk SR3 ..... 22 A8
Cyril St. Cons DH8 ..... 14 F4

D'Arcy Sq. Murton SR7 ..... 40 E4
D'Arcy St. Lang Pk DH7 ..... 56 C7
Dabble Duck Ind Est.
Shild DL4 ..... 170 A8
Dacre Gdns. Cons DH8 ..... 15 A2
Daffodil Ave. Peter SR8 ..... 85 F7
Daffodil Cl. B Coll TS27 ..... 86 D3
Dairy La. H le Sp DH4 ..... 38 C8
Daisy Cotts. 9 Birt DH3 ..... 9 C4
Daisy Hill. Medom DH8 ..... 14 F8
Dalden Gr. Seaham SR7 ..... 41 D8
Dale Cl. Hur on T DL2 ..... 224 D1
Dale Rd. Bar Cas DL12 ..... 201 B6
Dale Rd. Darl DL3 ..... 208 D2
Dale Rd. Sadb DL2 ..... 210 F7
Dale Rd. Shild DL4 ..... 170 B7
Dale Road Ind Est. Shild DL4 ..... 170 B8
Dale St. Bish Au DL14 ..... 147 E3
Dale St. Chilt DL17 ..... 150 F8
Dale St. Cons DH8 ..... 14 D3
Dale St. Lang Pk DH7 ..... 56 C7
Dale St. Ush M DH7 ..... 56 F2
Dale Terr. Billy R DL15 ..... 100 D6
Dale Terr. Dal le D SR7 ..... 41 A5
Dale Terr. Wood DL13 ..... 164 A6
Dale View. Crook DL15 ..... 101 A3
Dale View. Hi Eth DL14 ..... 146 E6
Dale View. Mick DL12 ..... 161 B4
Dale View. Mid in T DL12 ..... 160 E7
Dales St. Stanh DL13 ..... 71 B3
Dales Terr. Stanh DL13 ..... 71 B2
Daleside. Sacr DH7 ..... 35 C5
Dalkeith Cl. Darl DL3 ..... 208 A1
Dallymore Dr. Bowb DH6 ..... 81 C2
Dalton Ave. Bish Au DL14 ..... 147 E3
Dalton Ave. Seaham SR7 ..... 41 A7
Dalton Back La. Dalt P TS27 ..... 134 E1
Dalton Cl. Bish Au DL14 ..... 147 E3
Dalton Cotts. Shild DL4 ..... 170 A7
Dalton Cres. Shild DL4 ..... 170 A8
Dalton Hts. Dalt P TS27 ..... 134 E3
Dalton Hts. Seaham SR7 ..... 40 E6
Dalton St. Darl DL1 ..... 209 A2
Dalton Terr. Chopw NE17 ..... 4 B8
Dalton Terr. Murton SR7 ..... 40 D2
Dalton Terr. Wh Hi DH6 ..... 83 E1
Dalton Way. New Ay DL5 ..... 171 D7
Dan's Castle. Tow Law DL13 ..... 75 B3
Danby Cl. N Silk SR3 ..... 22 B6
Danby Cl. Wash DH3 & NE38 ..... 20 F8
Danelaw. Gr Lum DH3 ..... 37 A8
Danesmoor Cres. Darl DL3 ..... 208 C2
Daniel La. Even DL13 & DL14 ..... 145 D7
Daniel La. Hamst DL13 ..... 145 D7
Daphne Cres. Seaham SR7 ..... 41 C5
Dark La. Newsh DL11 ..... 233 F8
Dark La. Start DL12 ..... 200 E5
Darley Ct. Kimble DH2 ..... 36 A5
Darling Pl. Stanl DH9 ..... 18 B5
Darlington Arts Ctr. Darl DL3 .. 208 E2
Darlington Ave. Peter SR8 ..... 85 F7
Darlington Back La.
Longn DL2 & TS21 ..... 194 E1
Darlington Back La.
Redmar TS21 ..... 195 C4
Darlington Back La.
St on T TS19 & TS21 ..... 195 C4
Darlington (Bank Top) Sta.
Darl DL1 ..... 209 A1
Darlington Coll of Tech.
Darl DL3 ..... 208 E2
Darlington Golf Course.
Darl DL1 ..... 209 D8
Darlington Memorial Hospl.
Darl DL3 ..... 208 E3
Darlington Queen Elizabeth Sixth Form Coll. Darl DL3 ..... 208 E2
Darlington Railway Athletic Gd.
Darl DL3 ..... 208 D4
Darlington Railway Mus.
Darl DL3 ..... 208 F4
Darlington Rd.
Bar Cas DL12 & DL2 ..... 202 C6
Darlington Rd. Bish Au DL14 ..... 147 C1
Darlington Rd. Durham DH1 ..... 80 A8
Darlington Rd. Ferry DL17 ..... 128 F5
Darlington Rd. Heigh DL5 ..... 170 D1
Darlington Rd. Longn TS21 ..... 211 F5
Darlington Rd. Sadb DL2 ..... 210 E6
Darlington Rd. Whorl DL2 ..... 202 C6
Darlington Ret Pk The.
Darl DL1 ..... 209 E1
Darlington Skerne Park Cty Inf Sch.
Darl DL2 ..... 224 A7
Darlington Skerne Park Cty Jun Sch. Darl DL1 ..... 223 F7
Darrowby Dr. Darl DL3 ..... 208 E4
Dart Rd. Peter SR8 ..... 85 C5
Dartmouth Cl. Seaham SR7 ..... 41 A6
Darwin Gr. Darl DL1 ..... 224 C7
Daryngton Cl. Darl DL1 ..... 209 D6
David Terr. Bish Au DL14 ..... 148 E4
David Terr. Bowb DH6 ..... 81 D2
David Terr. Qua Hi DH6 ..... 106 D7
Davis Ave. Bish Au DL14 ..... 147 E3
Davis Cres. Lang Pk DH7 ..... 56 A7
Davis Terr. Eas SR8 ..... 63 D4
Davis Wlk. Peter SR8 ..... 85 E8
Davison Ave. N Silk SR3 ..... 22 B7
Davison Cres. Murton SR7 ..... 40 B4
Davison Dr. Hartle TS24 ..... 111 F2
Davison Rd. Darl DL1 ..... 209 B7
Davison Terr. Sacr DH7 ..... 35 B4
Davy Dr. Eas SR8 ..... 84 F8
Davy Dr. Peter SR8 ..... 84 F8
Davy St. Ferry DL17 ..... 128 E6
Dawdon Cres. Seaham SR7 ..... 41 D6
Dawson Rd. Bar Cas DL12 ..... 201 A6
Dawson Rd. Wing TS28 ..... 108 E8
Dawson St. Crook DL15 ..... 100 F4
Daylesford Gr. Darl DL3 ..... 208 C7
Deaf Hill Prim Sch. Wing TS29 ..... 107 F6
Deaf Hill Terr. Wing TS29 ..... 107 F6
Dean Bank Cty Jun & Inf Sch.
Ferry DL 17 ..... 128 E6
Dean & Chapter Ind Est.
Ferry DL 17 ..... 128 E6
Dean Cl. Peter SR8 ..... 85 F5
Dean Cl. Shild DL4 ..... 148 F2
Dean Court Grange.
Ferry DL17 ..... 128 E5
Dean Gdns. Shild DL4 ..... 148 F2
Dean Rd. Ferry DL17 ..... 129 A5
Dean St. Lang Pk DH7 ..... 56 D8
Dean St. Shild DL4 ..... 148 F2
Deanery Ct. Bish Au DL14 ..... 148 F4
Deans' Wlk. Belm DH1 ..... 58 F3
Deepdale Cl. Whick NE16 ..... 2 F4
Deepdale St. H le H DH5 ..... 39 A2
Deepdale Way. Darl DL1 ..... 209 F3
Deerbolt Bank. Start DL12 ..... 200 F5
Deerness Ct. Brand DH7 ..... 79 C4
Deerness Est. Tow Law DL13 ..... 75 C3
Deerness Estate Bglws.
Tow Law DL13 ..... 75 C3
Deerness Gr. Esh W DH7 ..... 55 D2
Deerness Hts. Brand DH7 ..... 79 B5
Deerness Rd. Bish Au DL14 ..... 148 A6
Deerness Valley Comp Sch.
Bear DH7 ..... 57 A3
Deerness View. E Hed DL13 ..... 76 D5
Deerness View. Ush M DH7 ..... 56 D2
Defoe Cres. New Ay DL5 ..... 171 E8
Dehlia Cres. Eas SR8 ..... 63 D3
Delamere Ct. 7 Silk SR3 ..... 22 A6
Delamere Gdns. Eas SR8 ..... 63 D4
Delaval. C le S DH2 ..... 20 A3
Delavale Cl. Peter SR8 ..... 85 F5
Delaware Ave. Even DL14 ..... 167 C7
Deleval Cl. New Ay DL5 ..... 150 C1
Delight Bank. Dipton DH9 ..... 16 D7
Delight Ct. Dipton DH9 ..... 16 D7
Delight Row. Dipton DH9 ..... 16 D8
Dell Side. Will DL15 ..... 102 B2
Dell The. Bish Au DL14 ..... 148 C8
Delvedere. Cons DH8 ..... 15 B1
Delves La. Cons DH8 ..... 15 A2
Delves La. Cons DH8 ..... 31 B7
Delves Lane Cty Inf Sch.
Cons DH8 ..... 31 B8
Delves Lane Cty Jun Mix Sch.
Cons DH8 ..... 31 B8
Delves Lane Ind Est. Cons DH8 .. 31 B7
Demesne Ct. Wols DL13 ..... 97 F7
Demesne La. Coth DL12 ..... 182 E4
Dene Ave. Eas SR8 ..... 63 E6
Dene Ave. H le Sp DH5 ..... 39 A7
Dene Ave. R Gill NE39 ..... 1 D1
Dene Ave. Shot Co DH6 ..... 84 D6
Dene Bank Ave. Peter SR8 ..... 86 A6
Dene Bank. Wit Gil DH7 ..... 57 B8
Dene Bridge. How le W DL15 ..... 124 E8
Dene Bridge Row. Chilt DL17 .. 128 D1
Dene Cotts. Edmon DH2 ..... 19 D1
Dene Cres. R Gill NE39 ..... 1 D1
Dene Cres. Sacr DH7 ..... 35 D3
Dene Cres. Shot Co DH6 ..... 84 D6
Dene Ct. Birt DH3 ..... 9 C7
Dene Ct. Hams NE17 ..... 4 B6
Dene Dr. Belm DH1 ..... 59 D5
Dene Garth. Dalt P TS27 ..... 134 E3
Dene Gdns. H le Sp DH5 ..... 38 F7
Dene Gr. Bish Au DL14 ..... 148 C7
Dene Gr. Darl DL3 ..... 208 D3
Dene Hall Dr. Bish Au DL14 ..... 147 F7
Dene House Rd. Seaham SR7 ..... 41 C8
Dene Park Ct. 1 Darl DL3 ..... 208 F3
Dene Pk. Esh W DH7 ..... 77 D8
Dene Rd. B Rocks TS27 ..... 86 E3
Dene Rd. Bar Cas DL12 ..... 200 F6
Dene Rd. R Gill NE39 ..... 1 D1
Dene Rd. Seaham SR7 ..... 41 B5
Dene St. H le H DH5 ..... 39 B6
Dene St. Peter SR8 ..... 86 A7
Dene Terr. Chilt DL17 ..... 150 E8
Dene Terr. Nent CA9 ..... 42 A4
Dene Terr. Shot Co DH6 ..... 84 D6
Dene The. C le St DH2 ..... 36 B8
Dene The. Medom DH8 ..... 4 A2
Dene The. W Rain DH4 ..... 38 A2
Dene View. Burnop NE16 ..... 6 A6
Dene View. Ca Eden TS27 ..... 109 D7
Dene View. Cassop DH6 ..... 82 F2
Dene View. H Spen NE39 ..... 1 A3
Dene View. R Gill NE39 ..... 1 C2
Dene View. Stanl DH9 ..... 18 C7
Dene View. Will DL15 ..... 101 E3
Dene Villas. C le S DH3 ..... 20 D1
Dene Villas. Kir Me DL16 ..... 128 C1
Dene Villas. Peter SR8 ..... 86 B6
Dene Way. Seaham SR7 ..... 41 C8
Deneburn Terr. Cons DH8 ..... 30 C8
Denecrest. Medom DH8 ..... 4 A2
Deneholme Terr. Holm DH7 ..... 34 D7
Deneside. Bish Au DL14 ..... 148 C6
Deneside. How le W DL15 ..... 124 E8
Deneside. Lanch DH7 ..... 33 A3
Deneside. Sacr DH7 ..... 35 C4
Deneside. Spenny DL16 ..... 103 F1
Deneside. Wit Gil DH7 ..... 57 B8
Deneside Jun Mix & Inf Sch.
Seaham SR7 ..... 41 A6
Deneside Rd. Darl DL3 ..... 208 D3
Denesyde. Medom DH8 ..... 4 A2
Deneway. R Gill NE39 ..... 2 A4
Denewood Cl. Will DL15 ..... 101 F3
Denham Gr. Blay NE21 ..... 1 F8
Denham Pl. New Ay DL5 ..... 171 E7
Denmark St. Darl DL3 ..... 209 A5
Dennis St. Wh Hi DH6 ..... 83 F3
Dennison Cres. Birt DH3 ..... 9 C6
Dennison Terr. Ferry DL17 ..... 129 C4
Dent Bank. Mid in T DL12 ..... 139 A1
Dent Cl. Hasw DH6 ..... 61 E3
Dent Gate La.
Copley DL12 & DL13 ..... 165 A5
Dent Gate La. Staint DL12 ..... 184 D6
Dent St. Bish Au DL14 ..... 148 A3
Dent St. Shild DL4 ..... 149 A2
Dent Wlk. New Ay DL5 ..... 171 D7
Dent's Villas. Wit Pk DL14 ..... 147 B8
Dentdale. Pens DH4 ..... 21 E8
Denton Ave. New Ay DL5 ..... 171 D2
Denton Cl. Darl DL3 ..... 208 B4
Denton Cotts. Beam DH9 ..... 19 B7
Denton Cross Roads.
Summ DL2 ..... 189 B2
Denton Hall Cotts. Denton DL2 189 D2
Denver Dr. M St G DL2 ..... 226 B8
Denwick Cl. C le St DH2 ..... 36 A8
Deorna Ct. Darl DL1 ..... 209 B5
Derby Cres. Cons DH8 ..... 30 A7
Derby Dr. Cons DH8 ..... 30 A7
Derby Rd. Stanl DH9 ..... 17 E5
Derby St. Darl DL3 ..... 208 F5
Derbyshire Dr. Belm DH1 ..... 59 D2
Dere Ave. Bish Au DL14 ..... 148 A3
Dere Pk. Leadg DH8 ..... 15 C4
Dere Rd. Cons DH8 ..... 15 B1
Derwent Ave. Bish Au DL14 ..... 147 B1
Derwent Ave. Crook DL15 ..... 100 F3
Derwent Ave. R Gill NE39 ..... 1 E1
Derwent Cl. Redmar TS21 ..... 195 B7
Derwent Cl. Sacr DH7 ..... 35 B3
Derwent Cl. Seaham SR7 ..... 41 C8
Derwent Cote. Hams NE17 ..... 4 B5
Derwent Cres. Gr Lum DH3 ..... 37 B7
Derwent Cres. Hams NE17 ..... 4 B5
Derwent Cres. Leadg DH8 ..... 15 D5
Derwent Dale. Cons DH8 ..... 14 C6
Derwent Haven. Hams NE17 ..... 4 B5
Derwent Mews. Cons DH8 ..... 14 D4
Derwent Pl. Cons DH8 ..... 14 C6
Derwent Pl. New Ay DL5 ..... 171 A7
Derwent Rd. Ferry DL17 ..... 128 F6
Derwent Rd. Peter SR8 ..... 85 E7
Derwent Resr Sailing Club.
Bale H DH8 ..... 11 C7
Derwent St. B Mill NE17 ..... 4 C6
Derwent St. Cons DH8 ..... 14 D4
Derwent St. 6 Darl DL3 ..... 208 F3
Derwent St. H le H DH5 ..... 39 B2
Derwent St. Tant L DH9 ..... 17 E8
Derwent Terr. Ann Pl DH9 ..... 16 E4
Derwent Terr. Burnop NE16 ..... 6 B7
Derwent Terr. S Hett DH6 ..... 61 E8
Derwent Terr. Spenny DL16 ..... 104 A1
Derwent Valley Villas.
Hams NE17 ..... 4 A6
Derwent View. Burnop NE16 ..... 6 B6
Derwent View Terr. Dipton DH9 ..... 5 D1
Derwentdale Ct. Cons DH8 ..... 14 D3
Derwentdale Ind Est. Cons DH8 14 D3
Derwentwater Ave. C le S DH2 .. 20 B1
Desmond Rd. M St G DL2 ..... 225 F6
Devon Cres. Birt DH3 ..... 9 B6
Devon Cres. Cons DH8 ..... 30 B7
Devon Dr. N Silk SR3 ..... 22 A8
Devon Dr. Will DL15 ..... 102 A3
Devon Pl. Bish Au DL14 ..... 148 C5
Devon St. H le H DH5 ..... 38 F4
Devonshire Rd. Belm DH1 ..... 59 C2
Devonshire Rd. Darl DL1 ..... 209 C4
Deyncourt. Durham DH1 ..... 80 A6
Dial Stob Hill. Bish Au DL14 ..... 126 C1
Diamond Cl. Chilt DL17 ..... 150 F8
Diamond Hill. Butter DL13 ..... 165 F8
Diamond St. Shild DL4 ..... 148 F1
Diamond Terr. Butter DL13 ..... 165 F8
Diamond Terr. Durham DH1 ..... 58 C2
Dibdale Rd. Neas DL2 ..... 225 B2
Dickens Rd. Bar Cas DL12 ..... 201 B7
Dickens St. H le Sp DH4 ..... 38 D8
Dickens St. Hartle TS24 ..... 111 F3
Dickens St. Spenny DL16 ..... 127 F8
Dickens Wynd. Durham DH1 ..... 80 A7
Dickenson Rd. Bish Au DL14 ..... 168 A8
Dickins Wlk. Peter SR8 ..... 85 E5
Dickinson St. Darl DL1 ..... 209 B1
Diddridge La.
Hamst DL13 & DL14 ..... 123 E1
Dilks St. Bish Au DL14 ..... 148 A3
Dillon St. Seaham SR7 ..... 41 D7
Dilston Cl. Peter SR8 ..... 85 C3
Dilston Rd. Durham DH1 ..... 58 D6
Dinsdale Cl. M St G DL2 ..... 225 F7
Dinsdale Cotts. 3 Ryhope SR2 .. 22 F6
Dinsdale Cres. Darl DL1 ..... 209 C1
Dinsdale Ct. M St G DL2 ..... 225 F8
Dinsdale Dr. Belm DH1 ..... 59 E4
Dinsdale Spa Golf Course.
M St G DL2 ..... 225 D5
Dinsdale St. Ryhope SR2 ..... 22 F6
Dinsdale St S. 9 Ryhope SR2 ..... 22 F6
Dinsdale Sta. M St G DL2 ..... 225 F7
Dinting Cl. Peter SR8 ..... 85 B5
Dipton RC Jun & Inf Sch.
Dipton DH9 ..... 16 E8
Dipwood Rd. R Gill NE39 ..... 1 E1
Dipwood Way. R Gill NE39 ..... 5 D8
Disraeli St. Fence DH4 ..... 38 B8
Dixon Ave. Ebch DH8 ..... 3 F4
Dixon Est. Shot Co DH6 ..... 84 C5
Dixon Estate Bglws.
Shot Co DH6 ..... 84 C5
Dixon Rd. H le Sp DH5 ..... 38 D6
Dixon Rd. New Ay DL5 ..... 171 D5
Dixon Rise. Peter SR8 ..... 86 B6
Dixon St. Bish Au DL14 ..... 148 C7
Dixon St. Cons DH8 ..... 14 E4
Dixon Terr. 6 Cockf DL13 ..... 166 C5
Dobinson's La. Even DL14 ..... 145 D3
Dobson Pl. Hartle TS24 ..... 111 E3
Dobson Terr. Murton SR7 ..... 40 C3
Dobson Terr. Wing TS28 ..... 84 D1
Dodd Hill La. Wals DL13 ..... 73 F2
Dodd Terr. Ann Pl DH9 ..... 16 F3
Dodds Cl. Wh Hi DH6 ..... 84 A3
Dodds St. Darl DL3 ..... 208 F3
Dodds Terr. Birt DH3 ..... 9 C6
Dodds Terr. Wing TS28 ..... 84 D1
Dodmire Cty Inf Sch. Darl DL2 224 C8
Dodmire Cty Jun Sch.
Darl DL2 ..... 224 C8
Dodsworth St. Darl DL1 ..... 209 B4
Dodsworth Wlk. Hartle TS27 ..... 111 D3
Dolphin Ctr The. 12 Darl DL1 ..... 208 F1
Dominies Cl. R Gill NE39 ..... 1 F3
Dominion Rd. Brand DH7 ..... 79 B3
Don Cres. Gr Lum DH3 ..... 37 B7
Donald Ave. S Hett DH6 ..... 61 F8
Donkin Rd. Wash NE37 ..... 9 F7
Donnini Pl. Durham DH1 ..... 58 F3
Dorchester Dr. Hartle TS24 ..... 111 D4
Dorchester Pk. Gr Lum DH3 ..... 37 A7
Doreen Ave. Seaham SR7 ..... 40 F6
Doric Rd. N Bran DH7 ..... 78 F7
Dorlonco Villas. Brand DH7 ..... 79 C3
Dormand Ct. Hut Hen TS28 ..... 108 F5
Dormand Dr. Peter SR8 ..... 85 D3
Dorothy Terr. Sacr DH7 ..... 35 C2
Dorset Ave. Birt DH3 ..... 9 D1
Dorset Cres. Cons DH8 ..... 30 B8
Dorset Dr. Darl DL1 ..... 209 C4
Dorset Dr. Will DL15 ..... 102 A3
Dorset La. N Silk SR3 ..... 22 B7
Dorset Pl. Bish Au DL14 ..... 148 C5
Dorset St. E Lane DH5 ..... 61 C8
Douai Dr. Cons DH8 ..... 31 C8
Douglas Ave. Peter SR8 ..... 85 F7
Douglas Cres. Bish Au DL14 ..... 148 E6
Douglas Ct. Ann Pl DH9 ..... 16 E3
Douglas Gdns. Durham DH1 ..... 80 A7
Douglas La.
How le W DL14 & DL15 ..... 124 B6
Douglas Terr. Crook DL15 ..... 100 E5
Douglas Terr. Dipton DH9 ..... 16 A6
Douglas Villas. 3 Durham DH1 . 58 E2
Douthwaite Rd. Bish Au DL14 ..... 148 A4
Dove Cl. Brand DH7 ..... 79 A4
Dove Ct. 8 Birt DH3 ..... 9 C5
Dovecot Hill. Bish Au DL14 ..... 148 D4
Dovecote Farm. C le St DH2 ..... 19 F2
Dovecote St. Staind DL2 ..... 186 D6
Dovedale Ave. Will DL15 ..... 101 F2
Dovedale Rd. Seaham SR7 ..... 41 B6
Down Terr. Trim TS29 ..... 107 E3
Downing Ct. Darl DL1 ..... 209 B5
Downs La. H le H DH5 ..... 39 B5
Downs Pit La. H le H DH5 ..... 39 C5
Dowsey Rd. Sherb DH6 ..... 59 F2
Dowson Rd. Hartle TS24 ..... 111 F3
Dowson Sq. Murton SR7 ..... 40 A3
Doxford Ave. H le H DH5 ..... 38 F6
Doxford Cl. New Ay DL5 ..... 171 C5
Doxford Dr. Shot Co SR8 ..... 84 F6
Doxford Park Way. Silk SR3 ..... 22 A5
Doxford Terr. H le H DH5 ..... 38 F6
Doxford Terr N. Murton SR7 ..... 40 A3
Doxford Terr S. Murton SR7 ..... 40 A3
Dragon La. Belm DH1 ..... 59 B2
Dragonville Ind Est. Belm DH1 .. 59 B2
Dragonville Pk. Belm DH1 ..... 59 B2
Drake Ave. Cound DL14 ..... 149 B8
Drake St. Spenny DL16 ..... 127 F8
Draycote Cres. Durham DH3 ..... 223 D7
Drinkfield Cres. Darl DL3 ..... 208 F7
Drive The. Birt DH3 ..... 9 D1
Drive The. Cons DH8 ..... 14 D6
Dronfield Cl. C le S DH2 ..... 20 A1
Drover Rd. Cons DH8 ..... 30 A6
Drover Terr. Cons DH8 ..... 30 A6
Droverhouse La. Satley DL13 ..... 52 E2
Drum Ind Est. C le S DH2 ..... 20 B7
Drum Rd. C le S DH2 ..... 20 B7
Drum Rd. C le S DH2 & DH3 ..... 20 B8
Drummond Cl. Darl DL1 ..... 209 E7
Drury St. Darl DL3 ..... 208 F3
Drybeck Sq. Silk SR3 ..... 22 B6
Drybourne Ave. Shild DL4 ..... 148 F1
Drybourne Pk. 2 Shild DL4 ..... 148 F1
Dryburgh View. Darl DL3 ..... 208 B4
Dryburn Hill. Durham DH1 ..... 58 A5
Dryburn Hospl. Durham DH1 ..... 58 A4
Dryburn Pk. Durham DH1 ..... 58 A5
Dryburn Rd. Durham DH1 ..... 58 A5
Dryden Cl. Stanl DH9 ..... 18 A6
Dublin St. Darl DL3 ..... 209 A6
Dubmire Cotts. Fence DH4 ..... 38 A8
Dubmire Ct. Fence DH4 ..... 38 A8
Dubmire Jun & Inf Schs.
Fence DH4 ..... 38 A8
Duddon Cl. Peter SR8 ..... 85 E6
Dudley Dr. New Ay DL17 ..... 150 D2
Dudley Gr. Bish Au DL14 ..... 148 A6
Dudley Pl. Allen NE47 ..... 44 E7
Dudley Rd. Darl DL1 ..... 210 A2
Duffy Terr. Ann Pl DH9 ..... 17 A3
Duke St. Ann Pl DH9 ..... 16 F5
Duke St. Bish Au DL14 ..... 148 B6
Duke St. Darl DL3 ..... 208 F2
Duke St. Seaham SR7 ..... 41 B8
Duke St. Staind DL2 ..... 186 D6
Dumfries St. Darl DL1 ..... 209 A3
Duncan Rd. Ferry DL17 ..... 128 F6
Duncombe Bank. Ferry DL17 ..... 129 C5
Duncombe Cl. Spenny DL16 ..... 127 D7
Duncombe Cres. Stanl DH9 ..... 17 F8
Duncombe Terr. 2 Ferry DL17 129 B5
Duncow La. Durham DH1 ..... 58 C1
Dundas St. Spenny DL16 ..... 127 F8
Dundee St. Darl DL1 ..... 209 B3
Dunelm. Sacr DH7 ..... 35 C2
Dunelm Ave. Will DL15 ..... 102 A3
Dunelm Chare. Escomb DL14 ..... 125 E1
Dunelm Cl. 5 Birt DH3 ..... 9 C4
Dunelm Cl. Leadg DH8 ..... 15 D3
Dunelm Ct. Bar Cas DL12 ..... 201 A5
Dunelm Ct. Brand DH7 ..... 79 A3
Dunelm Ct. Durham DH1 ..... 58 C1
Dunelm Ct. Sedge TS21 ..... 153 A6
Dunelm Ct. Spenny DL16 ..... 103 E3
Dunelm Dr. H le Sp DH4 ..... 38 D7
Dunelm Gr. Shild DL4 ..... 148 E2
Dunelm Pl. Shot Co DH6 ..... 84 D7
Dunelm Rd. Cons DH8 ..... 30 B8
Dunelm Rd. H le H DH5 ..... 38 F4
Dunelm Rd. Thorn DH6 ..... 83 B3
Dunelm Rd. Trim TS29 ..... 107 D1
Dunelm Terr. 4 Ferry DL17 ..... 129 A6
Dunelm Way. Leadg DH8 ..... 15 D3
Dunelm Wlk. Darl DL1 ..... 209 D5
Dunelm Wlk. Leadg DH8 ..... 15 D3
Dunelm Wlk. Peter SR8 ..... 85 D7
Dunholme Sch. Durham DH1 ..... 58 B4
Dunkirk Ave. H le Sp DH5 ..... 38 F7
Dunlin Dr. Wash NE38 ..... 9 F3
Dunn Rd. Peter SR8 ..... 85 D7
Dunn St. Ann Pl DH9 ..... 16 F4
Dunnock Dr. Wash NE38 ..... 9 F2
Dunrobin Cl. Darl DL1 ..... 209 E7
Dunsany Terr. C le St DH2 ..... 19 E4
Dunsfield Farm Est. Stanh DL13 71 B3
Dunstan Cl. C le S DH2 ..... 20 A1
Dunster Cl. Darl DL3 ..... 208 A5
Dunvegan Ave. C le S DH2 ..... 20 B1
Dunvegan. Birt DH3 ..... 9 E2
Dunwell La. Bolam DL2 ..... 168 F1
Durham Agricultural Coll.
Durham DH1 ..... 80 E7
Durham Ave. Peter SR8 ..... 85 F8
Durham Castle. Durham DH1 ..... 58 C1
Durham Cath Chorister Sch.
Durham DH1 ..... 80 C8
Durham Cath. Durham DH1 ..... 58 C1
Durham Chare. 2
Bish Au DL14 ..... 148 C8
Durham Ct. Sacr DH7 ..... 35 D2
Durham Cty Constabulary HQ.
Durham DH1 ..... 58 B5
Durham Cty Cricket Gd.
C le S DH3 ..... 20 E2
Durham Gdns. Wit Gil DH7 ..... 35 B1
Durham High Sch. Durham DH1 80 B5
Durham Johnston Comp Sch.
Durham DH1 ..... 58 A2
Durham Johnston Comp Sch.
Durham DH1 ..... 80 E8
Durham La. Eas SR8 ..... 62 F3
Durham La. Eas SR8 ..... 63 A3
Durham La. Hasw DH6 ..... 61 C1
Durham La. Hasw DH6 & SR8 ..... 62 D1
Durham La. S Hill DH6 ..... 82 F8
Durham La. Shadf DH6 ..... 82 F8
Durham Light Infantry Mus & Arts Ctr. Durham DH1 ..... 58 C3
Durham Moor Cres.
Durham DH1 ..... 58 A5
Durham Newton Hall Cty Inf Sch.
Durham DH1 ..... 58 C6
Durham Pl. Birt DH3 ..... 9 D1
Durham Rd. Ann Pl DH9 ..... 17 A3
Durham Rd. Birt DH3 ..... 9 C3
Durham Rd. Bish Au DL14 ..... 148 E8
Durham Rd. Bowb DH6 ..... 105 D8
Durham Rd. Brance DH7 ..... 78 E1
Durham Rd. C le S DH3 ..... 20 C1
Durham Rd. C le S DH3 ..... 20 C8
Durham Rd. Chilt DL17 ..... 150 F7
Durham Rd. Coat Mu DL1 & DL3 192 A4
Durham Rd. Cons DH8 ..... 14 E4
Durham Rd. Crook DL15 ..... 101 A3
Durham Rd. Durham DH1 ..... 58 A5
Durham Rd. E Rain DH5 ..... 38 C4
Durham Rd. Esh W DH7 ..... 77 E8
Durham Rd. Ferry DL17 ..... 128 F6
Durham Rd. Gates NE9 ..... 9 B8
Durham Rd. H le Sp DH5 ..... 38 E7
Durham Rd. Lanch DH7 ..... 32 F3
Durham Rd. Leadg DH8 ..... 15 D3
Durham Rd. New Ay DL5 ..... 171 E3
Durham Rd. Sacr DH7 ..... 35 C2
Durham Rd. Sedge TS21 ..... 153 A7
Durham Rd. Spenny DL16 ..... 104 A2
Durham Rd. Spenny DL16 ..... 127 C5
Durham Rd. Stanl DH9 ..... 18 A4
Durham Rd. Thor Th TS21 ..... 175 C6
Durham Rd. Thor Th TS21 ..... 175 E3
Durham Rd. Wing TS28 ..... 84 D1
Durham Rd. Wols DL13 ..... 98 A7
Durham Rd W. Bowb DH6 ..... 105 D8
Durham Sch (Annexe).
Durham DH1 ..... 58 B1
Durham Sch. Durham DH1 ..... 80 B8
Durham Sixth Form Ctr.
Durham DH1 ..... 58 D2
Durham St. Bish Au DL14 ..... 148 B8
Durham St. Fence DH4 ..... 38 A8
Durham St. Lang Pk DH7 ..... 56 C7
Durham St. Seaham SR7 ..... 41 B8
Durham St. Spenny DL16 ..... 127 C6
Durham Sta. Durham DH1 ..... 58 B2
Durham Terr. Durham DH1 ..... 58 A6
Durham Terr. 2 N Silk SR3 ..... 22 A8
Durham Univ (Dept of Psychology).
Durham DH1 ..... 80 D7
Durham Univ. Durham DH1 ..... 58 C1
Durham Univ (Science Labs).
Durham DH1 ..... 80 D8

Durham Way. New Ay DL5 ...... 171 D3
Durham Way. Peter SR8 ...... 85 C3
Durham Way N. New Ay DL5 ...... 171 E3
Durham Way S. New Ay DL5 ...... 171 D2
Dwyer Cres. Ryhope SR2 ...... 22 F6
Dykes Wlk. New Ay DL5 ...... 171 E6
Dyson La. Newsh DL11 & DL12 ...... 219 F2

E. D. Morel Terr. Chopw NE17 ...... 4 C8
Eaglesdene. H le H DH5 ...... 39 A4
Eamont Rd. Ferry DL17 ...... 128 F6
Eardulph Ave. C le S DH3 ...... 20 D3
Earl Cl. Darl DL1 ...... 209 B7
Earl St. Ann Pl DH9 ...... 16 F5
Earl St. Seaham SR7 ...... 41 A8
Earl's House Hospl. Wit Gil DH1 ...... 57 E7
Earls Gn. E Rain DH5 ...... 38 D3
Earnwell. St J Ch DL13 ...... 67 A2
Earsdon Rd. H le Sp DH5 ...... 38 F8
Earsdon Terr. 2 Ryhope SR2 ...... 22 F6
Easby Cl. Bish Au DL14 ...... 147 E6
Easby Ct. Spenny DL16 ...... 103 E3
Easby Pl. Darl DL3 ...... 208 B4
Easington CE Jun & Inf Sch.
  Eas SR8 ...... 63 A3
Easington Colliery Cty Jun Sch.
  Eas SR8 ...... 63 E4
Easington Colliery Welfare Gd.
  Eas SR8 ...... 63 E4
Easington Comp Sch. Eas SR8 .. 63 B3
Easington Lane Prim Sch.
  E Lane DH5 ...... 61 D8
Easington Rd.
  Hartle TS24 & TS27 ...... 111 C3
Easington Sec Sch. Eas SR8 ...... 63 C4
Easington St. Eas SR8 ...... 63 D4
Easson Rd. Darl DL1 ...... 208 F3
East Ave. Cound DL14 ...... 149 B8
East Ave. Wald DH2 ...... 36 A7
East Blackdene. St J Ch DL13 ...... 67 C1
East Block. Wit Gil DH7 ...... 57 A8
East Bridge St. Crook DL15 ...... 100 F4
East Butsfield La. Satley DL13 ...... 53 B6
East Cl. Sadb DL2 ...... 210 E6
East Clere. Lang Pk DH7 ...... 56 C6
East Coronation St. Murton SR7 40 D3
East Ellen St. Murton SR7 ...... 40 D2
East End. Sedge TS21 ...... 153 B6
East End. Wols DL13 ...... 97 F7
East Gn. Heigh DL5 ...... 170 E1
East Gn. Shot Co DH6 ...... 84 D6
East Grange Ct. Eas SR8 ...... 63 B3
East Green. Bish Au DL14 ...... 147 C1
East Haswicks. Westg DL13 ...... 92 C8
East Hetton Aged Workmen's
  Homes. Kelloe DH6 ...... 106 E5
East La. Stanh DL13 ...... 71 C3
East Law. Ebch DH8 ...... 3 D1
East Lea. Blay NE21 ...... 2 C8
East Lea. Thorn DH6 ...... 83 C5
East Mount Rd. Darl DL1 ...... 209 A4
East Par. Bish Au DL14 ...... 148 B8
East Par. Cons DH8 ...... 15 A2
East Par. Kimble DH2 ...... 35 F3
East Par. Sedge TS21 ...... 153 B6
East Par. Stanl DH9 ...... 18 A7
East Raby St. 1 Darl DL3 ...... 208 F1
East Rainton Prim Sch.
  E Rain DH5 ...... 38 C4
East Row. 4 Darl DL1 ...... 208 F1
East Side Ave. Bear DH7 ...... 57 A3
East St. B Coll TS27 ...... 86 D4
East St. Cons DH8 ...... 15 A2
East St. Cons DH8 ...... 15 B2
East St. Darl DL1 ...... 209 A4
East St. Hett DH6 ...... 104 E6
East St. Sacr DH7 ...... 35 B4
East St. Shot Co DH6 ...... 84 D6
East St. Stanl DH9 ...... 18 B7
East St. Thorn DH6 ...... 83 E4
East St. W Pel DH2 ...... 19 A5
East Stanley Cty Sch. Stanl DH9 18 A7
East Terr. Billy R DL15 ...... 100 D6
East Terr. Chopw NE17 ...... 4 C7
East Terr. Cound DL14 ...... 126 F1
East Terr. Hesl TS27 ...... 86 A1
East View. Brand DH7 ...... 79 C3
East View. Burnop NE16 ...... 6 A6
East View. Cons DH8 ...... 14 F4
East View. Da on T DL2 ...... 235 B6
East View. Dipton DH9 ...... 16 D8
East View. E Lane DH5 ...... 39 D1
East View. Eas SR8 ...... 63 E5
East View. 8 Ferry DL17 ...... 129 A6
East View. Fishb TS21 ...... 131 D5
East View. Gain DL2 ...... 205 A4
East View. M St G DL2 ...... 226 A5
East View. Murton SR7 ...... 40 D2
East View. 1 Peter SR8 ...... 86 A7
East View. R Gill NE39 ...... 1 C2
East View. Ryhope SR2 ...... 22 E6
East View. S Hill DH6 ...... 60 D1
East View. Sadb DL2 ...... 210 E6
East View. 1 Seaham SR7 ...... 22 F1
East View Terr. Shild DL4 ...... 148 F2
East View. Trim TS29 ...... 107 D3
East View. Will DL15 ...... 101 C3
East Villas. Hasw DH6 ...... 61 F4
Eastbourne Comp Sch.
  Darl DL1 ...... 209 C2
Eastbourne Rd. Darl DL1 ...... 209 C1
Eastcroft. Stanl DL13 ...... 71 A3
Eastdene Rd. Seaham SR7 ...... 40 F7
Eastdene Way. Peter SR8 ...... 85 F5
Eastern Ave. Lang Pk DH7 ...... 56 C6
Eastfield. Peter SR8 ...... 85 F5
Eastfields. Stanl DH9 ...... 17 E5
Eastfields Rd. New Ay DL5 ...... 170 F4

Eastlands. C le S DH3 ...... 20 E7
Eastlea Ave. Bish Au DL14 ...... 148 C6
Eastlea Cres. Seaham SR7 ...... 41 A7
Eastlea Rd. Seaham SR7 ...... 40 F7
Eastwell Cl. Sedge TS21 ...... 153 B6
Eastwood. Sacr DH7 ...... 35 C2
Ebba Cl. New Ay DL5 ...... 171 C6
Ebberston Ct. Spenny DL16 ...... 103 E3
Ebchester C of E Jun & Inf Sch.
  Ebch DH8 ...... 3 E3
Ebchester Hill. Ebch DH8 ...... 3 F2
Eden Ave. Burnop NE16 ...... 6 C8
Eden Ave. Leadg DH8 ...... 15 D5
Eden Cl. Cound DL14 ...... 149 C8
Eden Cl. Heigh DL5 ...... 170 C1
Eden Cl. Hur on T DL2 ...... 224 A1
Eden Cres. Darl DL1 ...... 223 F7
Eden Crest. Gain DL2 ...... 205 A6
Eden Croft. W Pel DH2 ...... 19 A6
Eden Ct. 6 Bish Au DL14 ...... 148 B8
Eden Dr. Sedge TS21 ...... 153 B5
Eden Gr. Bish Au DL14 ...... 147 B1
Eden Gr. Midd DL5 ...... 149 E1
Eden La. Gain DL2 ...... 205 B7
Eden La. Peter SR8 ...... 85 E8
Eden Pk. Gain DL2 ...... 205 B6
Eden Rd. Durham DH1 ...... 58 C6
Eden Rd. New Ay DL5 ...... 171 E2
Eden Rd. Spenny DL16 ...... 127 F7
Eden St. Peter SR8 ...... 86 A7
Eden St. Spenny DL16 ...... 127 E7
Eden Terr. Belm DH1 ...... 59 B3
Eden Terr. Chilt DL17 ...... 150 F8
Eden Terr. Kir Me DL14 ...... 127 F3
Eden Terr. Kir Me DL14 ...... 149 F8
Eden Terr. Stanl DH9 ...... 17 D5
Eden Terr. Will DL15 ...... 102 A2
Eden Vale. Peter SR8 ...... 85 F6
Eden View. Cound DL14 ...... 127 E3
Eden View. Shot Co DH6 ...... 84 D6
Edendale Cres. How le W DL15 124 D7
Edendale Terr. Peter SR8 ...... 85 F6
Edenfield. Beam DH9 ...... 19 A7
Edenhill Rd. Peter SR8 ...... 85 E7
Edgar Gr. Bish Au DL14 ...... 148 B8
Edge Ct. Durham DH1 ...... 58 F2
Edge Hill. Bish Au DL14 ...... 148 B8
Edge La. Lanch DH7 ...... 33 B6
Edgecombe Dr. Darl DL3 ...... 208 A3
Edgecombe Gr. Darl DL3 ...... 208 A3
Edgemoor Rd. Darl DL1 ...... 224 D6
Edgmond Ct. Sland SR2 ...... 22 E8
Edinburgh Dr. Darl DL3 ...... 208 A1
Ediscum Garth. Bish Au DL14 ... 147 F6
Edison St. Murton SR7 ...... 40 D3
Edith St. Cons DH8 ...... 14 F2
Edith St. Seaham SR7 ...... 41 E5
Edith Terr. Bish Au DL14 ...... 147 B1
Edlingham Cl. 6 H le Sp DH5 .. 38 F8
Edlingham Cty Jun & Inf Sch.
  Edmon DH7 ...... 35 B7
Edmondsley La. Edmon DH7 ...... 35 B5
Edmondsley La. Sacr DH7 ...... 35 B5
Edmund St. Darl DL1 ...... 209 A4
Edna St. Bowb DH6 ...... 105 D8
Edward Ave. Bish Au DL14 ...... 148 B8
Edward Ave. Peter SR8 ...... 85 F6
Edward Cain Ct. 9 Peter SR8 .. 86 A7
Edward Rd. Birt DH3 ...... 9 B5
Edward St. Bish Au DL14 ...... 148 B8
Edward St. Bish Au DL14 ...... 148 F4
Edward St. Burnop NE16 ...... 6 A4
Edward St. C le S DH3 ...... 20 C3
Edward St. Crag DH9 ...... 18 C2
Edward St. Darl DL1 ...... 209 B4
Edward St. Durham DH1 ...... 58 F2
Edward St. Esh W DH7 ...... 77 E8
Edward St. H le H DH5 ...... 39 A4
Edward St. N Silk SR3 ...... 22 A7
Edward St. 6 Seaham SR7 ...... 41 B6
Edward St. Spenny DL16 ...... 127 E8
Edward Terr. Ann Pl DH9 ...... 17 B4
Edward Terr. N Bran DH7 ...... 78 F8
Edward Terr. Pelton DH2 ...... 19 C6
Edwardson Rd. Brand DH7 ...... 79 D4
Egerton Gr. New Ay DL17 ...... 150 D1
Eggleston Cl. Durham DH1 ...... 58 D6
Eggleston Cl. Gr Lum DH4 ...... 3 B7
Eggleston La. Romald DL12 ...... 162 B2
Eggleston View. Darl DL3 ...... 208 A4
Egglestone Wlk. Bish Au DL14 147 D2
Egremont Gr. Peter SR8 ...... 85 A3
Egton Terr. Birt DH3 ...... 9 C5
Egton Way. Darl DL1 ...... 209 E6
Eight Houses. Hut Hen TS27 ... 109 C5
Eighth Ave. C le S DH2 ...... 20 B3
Eighth St. B Coll TS27 ...... 86 D4
Eighth St. Peter SR8 ...... 86 A7
Elcoat Terr. Crook DL15 ...... 101 A2
Elder Cl. Ush M DH7 ...... 57 C1
Elderberry Mews. Fishb TS21 .. 131 C5
Eldon Bank. Shild DL14 & DL4 ... 149 A3
Eldon Bank Top. Shild DL4 ...... 149 A3
Eldon Cl. Lang Pk DH7 ...... 56 A6
Eldon Cl. New Ay DL5 ...... 171 E7
Eldon Lane Cty Jun & Inf Sch.
  Bish Au DL14 ...... 148 A4
Eldon Pl. Darl DL3 ...... 208 B1
Eldon Rd. New Ay DL5 ...... 171 D4
Eldon St. Darl DL3 ...... 208 B1
Eldon Terr. Ferry DL17 ...... 129 C4
Eldon Terr. Fishb TS21 ...... 131 C4
Elemore Cl. Lang Pk DH7 ...... 56 B6
Elemore Hall Sch. H Pitt DH6 ... 61 A5
Elemore La. E Lane DH5 ...... 61 A7
Elemore La. H Pitt DH6 ...... 60 E6
Elemore Pl. New Ay DL5 ...... 150 C1
Elemore View. S Hett DH6 ...... 61 F7
Eleventh Ave. C le S DH2 ...... 20 B3

Eleventh St. B Coll TS27 ...... 86 C4
Eleventh St. B Coll TS27 ...... 86 D4
Eleventh St. 8 Peter SR8 ...... 86 A7
Elgar Cl. Stanl DH9 ...... 18 A5
Elgin Ave. Seaham SR7 ...... 40 F7
Elgin Cl. Darl DL1 ...... 209 E7
Elgin Gr. Stanl DH9 ...... 18 B6
Elisabeth Ave. Birt DH3 ...... 9 B6
Elisabeth Barrett Wlk.
  New Ay DL5 ...... 171 D5
Elizabeth Pl. Darl DL1 ...... 209 A4
Elizabeth St. Ann Pl DH9 ...... 17 A4
Elizabeth St. Seaham SR7 ...... 41 C7
Ellam Ave. Durham DH1 ...... 80 A8
Elland Ct. Darl DL1 ...... 209 F3
Ellerbourne Terr.
  Hut Hen TS28 ...... 108 F5
Ellerton Cl. Darl DL3 ...... 208 A5
Ellesmere. Bourn DH4 ...... 21 D3
Ellesmere. Spenny DL16 ...... 103 E2
Ellesmere Dr. Seaham SR7 ...... 40 F7
Ellett Ct. Hartle TS24 ...... 111 F2
Ellington Cl. Urpeth DH2 ...... 8 E2
Elliot St. Thorn DH6 ...... 83 D4
Elliott Rd. Peter SR8 ...... 85 D7
Elliott St. Crook DL15 ...... 100 E4
Elliott St. Sacr DH7 ...... 35 C3
Elliott Terr. Bish Au DL14 ...... 148 F4
Ellis Leazes. 6 Durham DH1 ...... 58 E2
Ellison Rd. Peter SR8 ...... 85 E7
Elm Ave. B Rocks TS27 ...... 86 E2
Elm Ave. Brand DH7 ...... 79 B3
Elm Ave. Pelton DH2 ...... 19 C6
Elm Ave. Sedgc TS21 ...... 153 B7
Elm Cl. Spenny DL16 ...... 104 A3
Elm Cl. Will DL15 ...... 101 E2
Elm Cres. Kimble DH2 ...... 35 F3
Elm Cres. Seaham SR7 ...... 41 C5
Elm Cres. Sacr DH7 ...... 35 C3
Elm Dr. Shild DL4 ...... 148 E2
Elm Gdns. Billy R DL15 ...... 100 D7
Elm Gr. Burnop NE16 ...... 5 F6
Elm Gr. Ush M DH7 ...... 57 B1
Elm Park Rd. Cons DH8 ...... 14 F7
Elm Park Terr. Cons DH8 ...... 14 F7
Elm Park Terr. Tow Law DL13 ... 75 D1
Elm Rd. Cornf DL17 ...... 105 E1
Elm Rd. Ferry DL17 ...... 129 A5
Elm Rd. Shild DL4 ...... 148 E2
Elm St. C le S DH3 ...... 20 C3
Elm St. Cons DH8 ...... 14 F4
Elm St. Lang Pk DH7 ...... 56 C7
Elm St. Stanl DH9 ...... 17 D4
Elm Terr. Ann Pl DH9 ...... 16 E5
Elm Terr. Birt DH3 ...... 9 B6
Elm Terr. Bish Au DL14 ...... 148 C6
Elm Terr. Bish Au DL14 ...... 148 F4
Elm Terr. Leadg DH8 ...... 15 D4
Elm Terr. Tant DH9 ...... 6 B2
Elm Terr. The Mid DH9 ...... 18 B3
Elmdale Rd. Cons DH8 ...... 15 A3
Elmfield. Lanch DH7 ...... 32 E4
Elmfield Ave. Belm DH1 ...... 59 B3
Elmfield Pl. New Ay DL5 ...... 171 B5
Elmfield Rd. Cons DH8 ...... 14 F4
Elmfield Rd. Hur on T DL2 ...... 235 B8
Elmfield St. Darl DL3 ...... 208 F3
Elmfield Terr. Darl DL3 ...... 208 F3
Elmfield Terr. Shild DL4 ...... 148 E2
Elms Rd. Darl DL3 ...... 208 E2
Elms The. E Lane DH5 ...... 61 D8
Elmtree St. Darl DL3 ...... 208 F6
Elmway. C le S DH2 ...... 20 A5
Elmwood. C le St DH2 ...... 19 F2
Elmwood St. Gr Lum DH4 ...... 21 E1
Elsdon Cl. C le S DH2 ...... 19 F1
Elsdon Cl. Peter SR8 ...... 85 C3
Elsdon Gdns. Cons DH8 ...... 14 F5
Elsdon Rd. Durham DH1 ...... 58 D6
Elstob Cl. New Ay DL5 ...... 171 B8
Elstob La. G Stain TS21 ...... 173 C4
Elstob La. Mordon TS21 ...... 173 C4
Elstob Rd. New Ay DL5 ...... 171 E3
Elterwater Rd. C le S DH2 ...... 20 B1
Elton Gr. Darl DL1 ...... 208 D1
Elton Par. Darl DL1 ...... 223 D8
Elton Rd. Darl DL1 ...... 208 D1
Elvet Bridge. Durham DH1 ...... 58 D1
Elvet Cl. Cornf DL17 ...... 105 D1
Elvet Cres. Durham DH1 ...... 58 D1
Elvet Gn. C le S DH2 ...... 20 C2
Elvet Gn. H le H DH5 ...... 39 A1
Elvet Hill Rd. Durham DH1 ...... 80 C7
Elvet Moor. Durham DH1 ...... 80 A7
Elvet St. Durham DH1 ...... 58 D1
Elvet Waterside. Durham DH1 ... 58 D1
Elwick Ave. New Ay DL5 ...... 150 A1
Elwick Hall CE Sch.
  Elwick TS27 ...... 134 C5
Elwick View. Trim TS29 ...... 131 E8
Elwin Pl. Pelton DH2 ...... 19 E7
Elwin St. Pelton DH2 ...... 19 E7
Ely Cl. Darl DL1 ...... 209 F5
Ely Rd. Durham DH1 ...... 58 D8
Ely Terr. Ann Pl DH9 ...... 17 C5
Embankment Rd. Seaham SR7 ... 41 B8
Embankment Rd. Seaham SR7 .. 41 E6
Embles La. New Ay DL5 ...... 171 F2
Embleton Cl. Durham DH1 ...... 58 D6
Embleton Dr. C le St DH2 ...... 19 F1
Embleton St. Seaham SR7 ...... 41 D5
Emerald Wlk. Chilt DL17 ...... 150 F8
Emerson Ct. Hartle TS24 ...... 111 F2
Emerson St. 4 Peter SR8 ...... 86 A7
Emerson Terr. Hur on T DL2 ...... 224 D1

Emerson Way. New Ay DL5 ...... 171 D5
Emery Cl. Hur on T DL2 ...... 224 D2
Emily St E. 2 Seaham SR7 ...... 41 D7
Emley Moor Rd. Darl DL1 ...... 224 D7
Emma St. Cons DH8 ...... 14 F4
Emmanuel Cl. Darl DL1 ...... 209 B5
Emmbrook Cl. E Rain DH5 ...... 38 D4
Emmerson Sq. Thorn DH6 ...... 83 C5
Emmerson St. Crook DL15 ...... 100 F4
Emmerson Terr. 3 N Silk SR3 .. 22 B7
Emmerson Terr W. N Silk SR3 .. 22 B7
Emms Hill La. Hamst DL13 ...... 144 D6
Empire Bldgs. Durham DH1 ...... 59 A2
Encombe Terr. Ferry DL17 ...... 129 C4
Enfield Rd. Seaham SR7 ...... 40 F7
Engel St. R Gill NE39 ...... 1 B2
Engels Terr. Stanl DH9 ...... 18 A5
Engineman's Terr.
  Wit le W DL15 ...... 124 F4
Enid Gdns. B Rocks TS27 ...... 86 E3
Ennerdale. Birt DH3 ...... 9 D2
Ennerdale Cl. Belm DH1 ...... 59 E4
Ennerdale Cl. Peter SR8 ...... 85 D7
Ennerdale Cl. Seaham SR7 ...... 40 F7
Ennerdale Cres. Blay NE21 ...... 2 B8
Ennerdale Dr. Crook DL15 ...... 100 F3
Ennerdale Gr. Bish Au DL14 ...... 147 B1
Ennerdale Pl. C le S DH2 ...... 20 C1
Ennerdale Rd. Darl DL1 ...... 224 B8
Ennerdale St. H le H DH5 ...... 38 F2
Ennerdale Terr. Hams NE17 ...... 4 A5
Ennerdale Wlk. Whick NE16 ...... 2 F5
Enterprise City. Spenny DL16 ... 104 D3
Enterprise Way. Spenny DL16 ... 104 C2
Epping Cl. Seaham SR7 ...... 40 F6
Eppleby Way. 3 Darl DL2 ...... 224 C8
Eppleton Cl. Lang Pk DH7 ...... 56 B6
Eppleton Hall Cl. Seaham SR7 .. 40 E8
Eppleton Prim Sch. H le H DH5 39 A6
Eppleton Row. H le H DH5 ...... 39 B4
Eppleton Terr. Beam DH9 ...... 19 B7
Eppleton Terr E. H le H DH5 ...... 39 B4
Eppleton Terr W. H le H DH5 ...... 39 B4
Epsom Cl. Cons DH8 ...... 14 E7
Epsom Ct. Darl DL1 ...... 209 F3
Epworth. Tanf L DH9 ...... 17 C8
Ernest St. Pelton DH2 ...... 19 C7
Ernest Terr. C le S DH3 ...... 20 C2
Ernest Terr. 5 Ryhope SR2 ...... 23 A6
Ernest Terr. Stanl DH9 ...... 17 F8
Errington Bglws. Sacr DH7 ...... 35 B3
Errington Dr. Tanf L DH9 ...... 17 C8
Errol Pl. Birt DH3 ...... 9 D2
Eryholme La. Da on T DL2 ...... 235 E5
Eryholme La. Ery DL2 & DL6 ...... 236 C5
Escallond Dr. Seaham SR7 ...... 40 F6
Escomb Cl. New Ay DL5 ...... 171 B8
Escomb Cty Jun Mix & Inf Sch.
  Escomb DL14 ...... 147 D7
Escomb Rd. Bish Au DL14 ...... 148 B7
Esdale. Ryhope SR2 ...... 22 E6
Esh Bank. Esh DH7 ...... 55 E5
Esh CE Sch. Esh DH7 ...... 55 F5
Esh Hillside. Lang Pk DH7 ...... 56 B6
Esh Laude RC Sch. Esh DH7 ...... 55 F4
Esh Terr. 10 Lang Pk DH7 ...... 56 C6
Esh Winning Cty Jun & Inf Sch.
  Esh W DH7 ...... 77 D7
Esk Ave. Gr Lum DH3 ...... 37 B7
Esk Gdns. Crook DL15 ...... 100 F2
Esk Rd. Darl DL1 ...... 224 A6
Eskdale. Birt DH3 ...... 9 E1
Eskdale Cl. Seaham SR7 ...... 40 F7
Eskdale Gdns. Shild DL4 ...... 149 C1
Eskdale Pl. New Ay DL5 ...... 171 A6
Eskdale St. Darl DL3 ...... 208 E2
Eskdale St. H le H DH5 ...... 38 F2
Eskdale Wlk. Peter SR8 ...... 85 E6
Esperley. Cockf DL13 ...... 166 F5
Esperley La.
  Cockf DL13 & DL14 & DL2 ... 167 B4
Espin Wlk. 2 New Ay DL5 ...... 171 E8
Essex Ave. Cons DH8 ...... 30 B7
Essex Cres. Seaham SR7 ...... 40 F7
Essex Gr. N Silk SR3 ...... 22 A8
Essex Pl. Peter SR8 ...... 85 C8
Essex Pl. Will DL15 ...... 102 A3
Essex St. H le H DH5 ...... 38 F4
Essex Way. Darl DL1 ...... 209 C4
Essington Way. Peter SR8 ...... 85 C7
Esthwaite Ave. C le S DH2 ...... 20 B1
Esthwaite Gr. Cound DL14 ...... 147 A1
Eston Moor Cres. Darl DL1 ...... 224 E7
Estoril Rd. Darl DL1 ...... 209 E1
Estoril Rd S. Darl DL1 ...... 224 E8
Ethel Ave. Ryhope SR2 ...... 23 A6
Etherley Bank. Bish Au DL14 ... 146 F3
Etherley Cl. Durham DH1 ...... 58 D6
Etherley Grange. Hi Eth DL14 ... 147 C6
Etherley La. Bish Au DL14 ...... 147 E6
Etherley Lane Jun & Inf Sch.
  Bish Au DL14 ...... 148 B7
Etherley Rd. H le H DH5 ...... 147 B6
Ettersgill Dr. Darl DL3 ...... 208 A1
Ettrick Terr N. The Mid DH9 ...... 18 B3
Ettrick Terr S. The Mid DH9 ...... 18 B3
Evans St. R Gill NE39 ...... 1 C2
Evansleigh Rd. Cons DH8 ...... 30 C8
Eve St. 4 Peter SR8 ...... 86 B6
Evelyn Terr. Stanl DH9 ...... 17 E6
Evenwood CE Jun & Inf Sch.
  Even DL14 ...... 167 C7
Evenwood Gate. Even DL14 ...... 167 E5
Evenwood Ind Est. Even DL14 . 167 D7
Evenwood La. Even DL14 ...... 167 D6
Everton Dr. Seaham SR7 ...... 40 F7
Evesham Gr. Hur on T DL2 ...... 224 C2
Evesham Rd. Seaham SR7 ...... 40 F7
Ewbank Cl. New Ay DL5 ...... 171 E8
Ewe Hill Cotts. Fence DH4 ...... 21 F1

Ewe Hill Terr. Fence DH4 ...... 21 F1
Ewe Hill Terrace W. Fence DH4 21 F1
Ewehurst Cres. Dipton DH9 ...... 5 E1
Ewehurst Gdns. Dipton DH9 ...... 5 E1
Ewehurst Par. Dipton DH9 ...... 5 E2
Ewehurst Rd. Dipton DH9 ...... 5 E2
Ewesley. Wash NE38 ...... 21 A8
Exeter Ave. Seaham SR7 ...... 41 B7
Exeter Cl. Gr Lum DH3 ...... 37 A6
Exeter Dr. Darl DL1 ...... 209 F5
Exmouth Cl. Seaham SR7 ...... 41 A6
Eyre St. Stanl DH9 ...... 17 D5

Faber Cl. New Ay DL5 ...... 171 D8
Factory. Ca Eden TS27 ...... 85 B1
Fair View. Burnh DH7 ...... 33 D3
Fair View. Burnop NE16 ...... 5 E6
Fair View. Esh W DH7 ...... 55 E1
Fair View. W Rain DH4 ...... 37 F2
Fair View. Wit Gil DH7 ...... 35 B1
Fairbairn Rd. Peter SR8 ...... 85 D8
Fairburn Ave. H le Sp DH5 ...... 38 C6
Fairclough Ct. Peter SR8 ...... 85 B5
Fairfalls Terr. N Bran DH7 ...... 78 E8
Fairfax Rd. M St G DL2 ...... 226 B8
Fairfield. Ann Pl DH9 ...... 16 F5
Fairfield. Cons DH8 ...... 15 B1
Fairfield. Even DL14 ...... 167 D6
Fairfield. Pelton DH2 ...... 19 D7
Fairfield Rd. Bar Cas DL12 ...... 201 A7
Fairfield St. Darl DL3 ...... 208 E4
Fairfield Wlk. Will DL15 ...... 101 E1
Fairhills Ave. Dipton DH9 ...... 16 C7
Fairisle. Ouston DH2 ...... 9 A1
Fairlawn Ave. Cound DL14 ...... 127 C1
Fairmile Dr. Silk SR3 ...... 22 A4
Fairport Terr. Peter SR8 ...... 63 F3
Fairview Dr. Medom DH8 ...... 15 A8
Fairview Dr. Spenny DL16 ...... 128 A8
Fairview Terr. Ann Pl DH9 ...... 16 E3
Fairway The. Darl DL1 ...... 209 C1
Fairways. Cons DH8 ...... 14 F5
Fairways. 1 N Silk SR3 ...... 22 B7
Fairways The. Beam DH9 ...... 19 A7
Fairways The. Qua Ho DH9 ...... 17 E2
Fairwell View. Brand DH7 ...... 79 E6
Fairy St. H le H DH5 ...... 39 A4
Falcon Cl. Darl DL1 ...... 209 E2
Falcon Way. Esh W DH7 ...... 55 C1
Falkous Terr. Wit Gil DH7 ...... 57 A8
Fallow Rd. New Ay DL17 ...... 150 E2
Fallowfield Terr. S Hett DH6 ...... 62 A7
Fallows The. Cockf DL15 ...... 166 D5
Fallsway. Belm DH1 ...... 59 D5
Falmer Rd. Darl DL1 ...... 224 B8
Falmouth Cl. Seaham SR7 ...... 41 A6
Falsgrave Pl. Whick NE16 ...... 2 F5
Falstaff Ct. Darl DL1 ...... 209 A2
Falstone Dr. C le St DH2 ...... 19 F1
Falstone Terr. Darl DL1 ...... 209 C6
Faraday Rd. Peter SR8 ...... 85 E8
Faraday St. Murton SR7 ...... 40 D3
Faraday St. Ferry DL17 ...... 128 E6
Faraday Terr. Hasw DH6 ...... 61 E3
Farbridge Cres. Ebch DH8 ...... 3 F3
Farfield Terr. Trim TS29 ...... 107 F5
Farfields Cl. Longn TS21 ...... 211 F5
Farm Cl. Bish Au DL14 ...... 148 A4
Farm Cotts. Shot Co DH6 ...... 84 D7
Farm Rd. Durham DH1 ...... 80 D5
Farmer St. Murton SR7 ...... 40 B3
Farnborough Dr. N Silk SR3 ...... 22 B8
Farncombe Terr. Even DL14 ...... 167 D6
Farndale. Spenny DL16 ...... 103 E2
Farndale Cl. Blay NE21 ...... 1 B8
Farndale Cres. Darl DL3 ...... 208 C3
Farndale Gdns. Shild DL4 ...... 149 B1
Farndale Sq. Bish Au DL14 ...... 147 E4
Farnham Cl. Durham DH1 ...... 58 C5
Farnham Cl. New Ay DL17 ...... 150 E1
Farnham Rd. Durham DH1 ...... 58 C5
Farnley Hey Rd. Durham DH1 ... 58 A1
Farnley Mount. Durham DH1 ...... 58 A1
Farnley Ridge. Durham DH1 ...... 58 A1
Farr Holme. Darl DL3 ...... 223 C6
Farrer St. Darl DL3 ...... 208 F4
Fatfield Prim Sch. Wash NE38 ... 21 D8
Fatherly Terr. Fence DH4 ...... 38 B8
Faulkner Rd. New Ay DL5 ...... 171 D7
Faverdale. Darl DL3 ...... 208 D6
Faverdale Ind Est. Darl DL3 ...... 208 D6
Faverdale N. Darl DL3 ...... 208 D6
Faverdale Rd. Darl DL3 ...... 208 C6
Faverdale W. Darl DL3 ...... 208 D6
Fawcett Cl. Bish Au DL14 ...... 147 F4
Fawcett Hill Terr. Crag DH9 ...... 18 C2
Fawcett Terr. 7 Ryhope SR2 ...... 23 A6
Fawn Cl. New Ay DL17 ...... 150 E2
Feather Bed La. Ryhope SR2 ...... 23 A6
Featherstone. Gr Lum DH3 ...... 37 B8
Featherstone. Wash NE38 ...... 9 F5
Featherstone Rd. Durham DH1 ... 58 D5
Featherstones. Coxhoe DH6 ...... 106 A3
Federation Sq. Murton SR7 ...... 40 D2
Federation Terr. Tant DH9 ...... 6 B2
Fee Terr. Ryhope SR2 ...... 22 E6
Feetham Ave. Darl DL1 ...... 209 E5
Feethams. 17 Darl DL1 ...... 208 F1
Feethams S. 18 Darl DL1 ...... 208 F1
Feethams Sports Gd. Darl DL1 223 F8
Fell Bank. Birt DH3 ...... 9 D4
Fell Cl. Birt DH3 ...... 9 E3
Fell La. Romald DL12 ...... 181 E8
Fell Rd. C le St DH2 ...... 19 E4
Fell Side. Cons DH8 ...... 31 B7
Fell Terr. Burnop NE16 ...... 6 B6
Fell View. Cons DH8 ...... 14 C1
Fell View. H Spen NE39 ...... 1 A3
Fellcross. Birt DH3 ...... 9 C5
Fellrose Ct. C le St DH2 ...... 19 E4
Fellside. Birt DH3 ...... 9 D3

Fellside Cl. Stanl DH9 .... 18 B7
Fellside Cl. Tow Law DL13 ...... 75 B4
Fellside Gdns. Belm DH1 .... 59 C4
Fellside Rd. Byer NE16 .... 6 C8
Fellside Rd. Sunn NE16 .... 2 F3
Fellside Terr. Qua Ho DH9 ...... 17 D2
Fellside View. Sacr DH7 .... 35 C2
Felltop. Cons DH8 .... 14 D3
Felton Cl. New Ay DL5 .... 171 E8
Fenby Ave. Darl DL1 .... 224 C8
Fence Houses Woodlea Cty Jun
   & Inf Sch. Gr Lum DH4 .... 21 E1
Fence Rd. Bourn DH3 .... 21 E5
Fenhall Gn. New Ay DL5 .... 150 C1
Fenhall Pk. Lanch DH7 .... 32 E4
Fens The. Hart LS27 .... 111 B3
Fenside Rd. Sland SR2 .... 22 F8
Fenton Cl. C le S DH2 .... 20 A2
Fenton Well La. Gr Lum DH3 .... 36 F7
Fenwick Cl. C le St DH2 .... 19 F1
Fenwick St. Spenny DL16 .... 128 B8
Fenwick Terr. Durham DH1 ...... 80 A8
Ferens Cl. Durham DH1 .... 58 D3
Ferens Pk. Durham DH1 .... 58 E3
Ferens Terr. Shild DL4 .... 170 A7
Fern Ave. Stanl DH9 .... 17 D5
Fern Cres. Seaham SR7 .... 41 C4
Fern Gr. Spenny DL16 .... 127 D6
Fern Rd. Sacr DH7 .... 35 D3
Fern St. Cons DH8 .... 14 F3
Fern Terr. Tant DH9 .... 5 F1
Fern Valley. Crook DL15 .... 100 D2
Ferndale. Belm DH1 .... 59 D4
Ferndale. Wols DL13 .... 98 A4
Ferndale Cl. Hut Hen TS28 .... 108 F5
Fernlea Ct. Darl DL1 .... 224 B7
Fernleigh. Gr Lum DH3 .... 37 A7
Fernwood. Sacr DH7 .... 35 B2
Fernwood Cl. Silk SR3 .... 22 A5
Ferrand Dr. H le Sp DH4 .... 38 D8
Ferryhill Comp Sch.
   Ferry DL 17 .... 128 C5
Ferryhill Rosebank Sch.
   Ferry DL17 .... 129 A5
Feversham Terr. Ferry DL17 .... 129 C3
Festival Wlk. Spenny DL16 .... 127 F8
Fewston Cl. New Ay DL5 .... 170 F7
Field Fare Cl. Burnop NE16 ...... 6 C5
Field House Terr. Hasw DH6 .... 61 F3
Field St. Darl DL1 .... 209 A4
Field View Terr. Bear DH7 ...... 57 B3
Fieldfare Cl. Wash NE38 .... 9 F3
Fieldhouse La. Durham DH1 .... 58 B3
Fieldhouse Terr. Durham DH1 .. 58 B3
Fielding Ct. Crook DL15 .... 100 C3
Fieldon Dr. Bish Au DL14 ...... 147 C2
Fieldside. E Rain DH5 .... 38 C3
Fieldside. Pelton DH2 .... 19 E7
Fife Ave. C le S DH2 .... 20 C3
Fife Rd. Bar Cas DL12 .... 201 A7
Fife Rd. Darl DL3 .... 208 E1
Fife St. Murton SR7 .... 40 D2
Fife Terr. B Mill NE17 .... 4 B6
Fifth Ave. C le S DH2 .... 20 B3
Fifth St. B Coll TS27 .... 86 D4
Fifth St. Cons DH8 .... 15 B2
Fifth St. Peter SR8 .... 86 A7
Filby Dr. Belm DH1 .... 59 D5
Fillpoke La. B Rocks TS27 ...... 111 A8
Finchale Ave. Durham DH1 ...... 58 F8
Finchale Cl. H le Sp DH4 .... 38 D8
Finchale Cres. Darl DL3 .... 208 A4
Finchale Ct. W Rain DH4 .... 37 F2
Finchale Cty Jun & Inf Sch.
   Durham DH1 .... 58 E7
Finchale Rd. Durham DH1 .... 58 B5
Finchale Rd. Durham DH1 .... 58 D8
Finchale Rd. New Ay DL5 .... 171 D5
Finchale Sq. Bish Au DL14 .... 147 D3
Finchale Terr. Gr Lum DH4 ...... 21 E1
Finchale Training Ctr.
   Durham DH1 .... 36 D1
Finchale View. Durham DH1 .... 58 B7
Finchale View. W Rain DH4 ...... 37 F2
Finchdale Terr. C le S DH3 ...... 20 C2
Findon Ave. Sacr DH7 .... 35 C3
Findon Ave. Wit Gil DH7 .... 35 B1
Findon Hill. Sacr DH7 .... 35 C2
Fine La. Newl DH8 .... 3 B3
Fines Pk. Ann Pl DH9 .... 16 F5
Fines Rd. Medom DH8 .... 4 B1
Finings Ave. Lang Pk DH7 ...... 56 A6
Finings St. Lang Pk DH7 .... 56 B6
Finkle St. Bish Au DL14 .... 126 B1
Finneys Terr. Durham DH1 ...... 58 D2
Fir Ave. Brand DH7 .... 79 B3
Fir Ave. Durham DH1 .... 59 A1
Fir Pk. Ush M DH7 .... 57 B2
Fir Terr. Burnop NE16 .... 6 B6
Fir Terraces. Esh W DH7 .... 55 D1
Fir Tree Cl. Belm DH1 .... 59 A3
Fir Tree Cty Sch. Fir T DL15 .... 99 F2
Fire and Rescue Station Cotts.
   Billy R DL15 .... 100 E6
Firs Terr. Lang Pk DH7 .... 56 D7
Firs The. Darl DL1 .... 209 D6
First Ave. C le S DH2 .... 20 B8
First St. B Coll TS27 .... 86 D3
First St. Cons DH8 .... 15 B2
First St. Leadg DH8 .... 15 C5
First St. Leadg DH8 .... 15 C6
First St. Peter SR8 .... 86 A7
First St. Wh Hi DH6 .... 83 F3
Firth Moor Cty Inf Sch.
   Darl DL2 .... 224 E7
Firth Moor Cty Jun Sch.
   Darl DL2 .... 224 E7
Firthmoor Cres. Darl DL1 ...... 224 E8
Firtree Dr. How le W DL15 ...... 124 D7
Firtree. Shild DL4 .... 149 A1

Firwood Cres. H Spen NE39 ...... 1 A3
Firwood Gr. Hunw DL15 .... 125 E6
Firwood Terr. Ferry DL17 .... 129 C2
Fishburn Cty Prim Sch.
   Fishb TS21 .... 131 D5
Fishburn Ind Est. Fishb TS21 .. 131 C5
Fishburn Terr. Fishb TS21 ...... 131 B5
Fitzhugh Ct. Coth DL12 .... 182 E3
Fitzwilliam Dr. Darl DL1 .... 209 B6
Flag Terr. Sunni DL13 .... 75 F1
Flambard Rd. Durham DH1 ...... 58 B5
Flamingo Cl. Darl DL1 .... 209 E1
Flanders Way. Crook DL15 ...... 100 E4
Flass Ave. 7 Ush M DH7 .... 56 F2
Flass St. Durham DH1 .... 58 B2
Flass Terr. Esh W DH7 .... 56 A1
Flass Terr. 6 Ush M DH7 .... 56 F2
Flassburn Rd. Durham DH1 ...... 58 A3
Flasshall La. Esh W DH7 .... 56 B2
Flatts Farm. Toro DL14 .... 126 B2
Flatts Rd. Bar Cas DL12 .... 200 F6
Flaxfield. Start DL12 .... 200 F6
Flaxmill Ct. Newsh DL11 .... 219 E1
Fleece Cotts. Edmon DH7 .... 35 B6
Fleece Terr. Edmon DH7 .... 35 B7
Fleet St. Bish Au DL14 .... 148 B6
Fleetham Cl. C le St DH2 .... 19 F1
Fleming Cl. Shot Co DH6 .... 84 B7
Fleming Pl. Peter SR8 .... 85 D6
Flint Hill Bank. Dipton DH9 ...... 5 E1
Flintoff St. 8 Bish Au DL14 .... 148 C8
Flodden Cl. C le St DH2 .... 19 F1
Flora Ave. Darl DL3 .... 223 D8
Flora St. Spenny DL16 .... 127 E8
Floralia Ave. 1 Ryhope SR2 .... 23 A6
Fold. Quebec DH7 .... 55 C4
Fold The. Burnop NE16 .... 6 A7
Folds The. E Rain DH5 .... 38 D4
Folds The. Fence DH4 .... 38 B8
Folly Bank. Bish TS21 .... 194 C6
Folly Bank. Egg DL12 .... 162 D3
Folly Terr. Durham DH1 .... 58 A7
Folly View. Butter DL13 .... 165 E8
Fondlyset La. Dipton DH9 .... 16 C7
Fonteyn Pl. Sland DH9 .... 18 B5
Forbes Terr. Ryhope SR2 .... 22 E6
Forcett St. Darl DL3 .... 208 C4
Ford Cres. Lanch DH7 .... 32 F2
Ford Dike La. Gain A2 .... 188 A1
Ford Dike La. Lang A2 .... 188 A2
Ford Rd. Durham DH1 .... 58 D7
Ford Rd. Lanch DH7 .... 32 F2
Ford St. Cons DH8 .... 31 B8
Ford St. Lanch DH7 .... 32 F3
Ford St. Chilt DL17 .... 150 E8
Ford Way. Bish Au DL14 .... 148 A4
Fordham Rd. Durham DH1 .... 58 A5
Fore Bondgate. Bish Au DL14 .. 126 B1
Forest Dr. Wash DH3 & NE38 .. 20 F8
Forest Gate. Wing TS28 .... 108 D8
Forest Moor Rd. Darl DL1 ...... 224 D7
Forest of Teesdale Cty Jun Mix
   & Inf Sch. For in T DL12 .... 136 F8
Forest View. Brand DH7 .... 78 F3
Forfar Cl. Darl DL1 .... 209 D7
Forge Cl. B Mill NE17 .... 4 B6
Forge La. Bourn DH3 .... 21 B2
Forge La. H Mill NE17 .... 4 E5
Forge Terr. The. Hunw DL15 .... 125 E8
Forge Way. Darl DL1 .... 209 B4
Formby Cl. 7 Hartle TS24 ...... 111 C4
Formby Gr. Hartle TS24 .... 111 D4
Forres Ct. Stanl DH9 .... 18 B6
Forresters Path. New Ay DL5 .. 170 F4
Forster Ave. Cold He SR7 .... 40 E1
Forster Ave. Sherb DH6 .... 60 A2
Forster Cres. S Hett DH6 .... 62 B6
Forster Sq. Wing TS28 .... 108 D8
Forster St. Cons DH8 .... 15 A2
Forster St. Darl DL3 .... 208 F3
Forth Cl. Peter SR8 .... 85 D5
Foss Way. Ebch DH8 .... 3 E3
Foster Terr. Sland B DH6 .... 104 B6
Fother Ingay Dr. Darl DL1 ...... 209 E7
Foumarts La. Bish Mi DL17 .... 130 B3
Foundry Fields. Crook DL15 .... 100 E4
Foundry Rd. Seaham SR7 .... 41 E7
Foundry St. Shild DL4 .... 149 A2
Fountains Meadow.
   Spenny DL16 .... 128 A8
Fountains Sq. Bish Au DL14 .... 147 D2
Fountains View. Darl DL3 ...... 208 B4
Four Lane Ends. Cons DH8 ...... 30 A6
Four Lane Ends. H le H DH5 .... 39 B2
Four Lane Ends. H le Sp DH5 .. 38 E6
Four Lanes End. Hi Eth DL14 .. 147 D6
Four Riggs. Darl DL1 .... 208 F2
Fourth Ave. C le S DH2 .... 20 B3
Fourth St. B Coll TS27 .... 86 D4
Fourth St. Cons DH8 .... 15 B2
Fourth St. Leadg DH8 .... 15 C5
Fourth St. Leadg DH8 .... 15 C6
Fourth St. Peter SR8 .... 86 A7
Fourth St. Qua Ho DH9 .... 17 D2
Fourway St. Wing TS28 .... 84 E1
Fowler Rd. New Ay DL5 .... 171 E7
Fox Cl. Hur on T DL2 .... 235 B8
Fox Hills Cres. Lanch DH7 ...... 32 D3
Fox Pl. New Ay DL5 .... 171 C8
Fox St. Seaham SR7 .... 41 D6
Foxes Row. Brance DH7 .... 102 E8
Foxhills Covert. Whick NE16 .... 2 E5
Foxhills The. Whick NE16 .... 2 E6
Foxlair Cl. Silk SR3 .... 22 A4
Foxton Cl. New Ay DL5 .... 171 D8
Foxton La. Fishb TS21 .... 174 B7
Foxton Way. H Shin DL1 .... 81 B5
Framwelgate Bridge. 1
   Durham DH1 .... 58 C1
Framwelgate. Durham DH1 ...... 58 C2

Framwelgate Peth. Durham DH1 58 B3
Framwelgate Waterside.
   Durham DH1 .... 58 C2
Framwellgate Moor Comp Sch.
   Durham DH1 .... 58 B6
Framwellgate Moor Cty Inf Sch.
   Durham DH1 .... 58 B6
Framwellgate Moor Cty Jun Sch.
   Durham DH1 .... 58 B6
Frances Terr. Bish Au DL14 .... 148 B6
Francis St. Stan Cr DL15 .... 100 F8
Frank Ave. Seaham SR7 .... 41 A7
Frank St. Belm DH1 .... 59 A2
Frankland La. Durham DH1 ...... 58 D3
Frankland Rd. Durham DH1 ...... 58 B5
Franklyn Rd. Peter SR8 .... 85 C7
Fred Peart Sq. Wh Hi DH6 ...... 83 F2
Frederick St. Chopw NE17 .... 4 B8
Frederick St. Cound DL14 ...... 149 B8
Frederick St. Seaham SR7 .... 41 D7
Frederick St N. Brand DH7 ...... 79 C4
Frederick St S. Brand DH7 ...... 79 C4
Frederick Terr. H le H DH5 ...... 39 B1
Frederick Terr. S Hett DH6 ...... 61 F6
Freeman's Pl. Darl DL1 .... 209 A2
Freeman's Pl. Durham DH1 ...... 58 C2
Frensham Way. Brand DH7 ...... 79 C4
Freville Gr. Shild DL4 .... 148 E1
Friar St. Shot Co DH6 .... 84 D6
Friar's Row. Belm DH1 .... 58 F3
Friar's Row. Burnop NE16 .... 5 F5
Friars Pardon. Hur on T DL2 .... 224 C1
Friarside. Wit Gil DH7 .... 57 B8
Friarside Gdns. Burnop NE16 .... 5 F6
Friarside. R Gill NE39 .... 5 D8
Front Row. Shild DL14 .... 149 A4
Front St. Ann Pl DH9 .... 16 F4
Front St. Bish Au DL14 .... 147 C1
Front St. Bish Mi DL17 .... 130 B3
Front St. Brand DH7 .... 79 E6
Front St. Burnop NE16 .... 5 E6
Front St. Burnop NE16 .... 6 A4
Front St. Burnop NE16 .... 6 B6
Front St. C le S DH3 .... 20 C3
Front St. Cockf DL13 .... 166 D5
Front St. Cons DH8 .... 14 C6
Front St. Coxhoe DH6 .... 106 A3
Front St. Crag DH9 .... 18 B7
Front St. Crag DH9 .... 18 C3
Front St. Dipton DH9 .... 16 C8
Front St. Durham DH1 .... 58 A7
Front St. Edmon DH7 .... 35 B7
Front St. Fence DH4 .... 38 A8
Front St. Fishb TS21 .... 131 C5
Front St. Frost DL13 .... 96 B6
Front St. Gr Lum DH3 .... 37 A7
Front St. H le H DH5 .... 38 E1
Front St. H le H DH5 .... 39 A3
Front St. H Pitt DH6 .... 60 B6
Front St. Hart TS27 .... 111 A2
Front St. Hasw DH6 .... 61 F3
Front St. Hesl DH6 .... 86 A1
Front St. Hut Hen TS27 .... 109 C5
Front St. Hut Hen TS28 .... 108 E6
Front St. Hut Hen TS28 .... 108 F5
Front St. Ingle DL2 .... 188 A6
Front St. Kelloe DH6 .... 106 D5
Front St. Kir Me DL16 .... 128 A3
Front St. Lang Pk DH7 .... 56 B5
Front St. Lang Pk DH7 .... 56 C7
Front St. Leadg DH8 .... 15 C4
Front St. Pelton DH2 .... 19 D5
Front St. Pelton DH2 .... 19 D7
Front St. Pelton DH2 .... 19 F8
Front St. Qua Hi DH6 .... 106 D8
Front St. Quebec DH7 .... 55 B4
Front St. Rook DL13 .... 87 B2
Front St. S Hett DH6 .... 61 F7
Front St. S Hett DH6 .... 60 D1
Front St. Sacr DH7 .... 35 B3
Front St. Sedge TS21 .... 153 B6
Front St. Sherb DH6 .... 60 A1
Front St. Shot Co DH6 & SR8 .. 84 D7
Front St. Sland B DH6 .... 104 B6
Front St. Spenny DL16 .... 104 B4
Front St. Spenny DL16 .... 128 A8
Front St. St J Ch DL13 .... 66 F2
Front St. St J Ch DL13 .... 91 E8
Front St. Staind DL2 .... 186 D6
Front St. Stanh DL13 .... 71 B3
Front St. Stanl DH9 .... 17 E6
Front St. Sunni DL13 .... 76 A1
Front St. Tanf DH9 .... 6 D3
Front St. Trim TS29 .... 107 F5
Front St. Ush M DH7 .... 79 C8
Front St. Wear DL13 .... 66 D4
Front St. Wh Hi DH6 .... 83 F3
Front St. Will DL15 .... 101 C3
Front St. Will DL15 .... 101 F1
Front St. Wit Gil DH7 .... 57 A8
Front St. Wols DL13 .... 97 E7
Front St E. Coxhoe DH6 .... 106 A4
Front St E. Sland B DH6 .... 104 B6
Front St N. Trim TS29 .... 107 D1
Front St N. Trim TS29 .... 107 E1
Front St S. Qua Hi DH6 .... 106 D7
Front St S. Trim TS29 .... 107 D1
Front St S. Trim TS29 .... 107 E1
Front The. M St G DL2 .... 226 A5
Frosterley Cl. Durham DH1 ...... 58 D6
Frosterley Cl. E Lane DH5 ...... 61 D8
Frosterley Cl. Gr Lum DH3 ...... 37 B7

Frosterley Gdns. Ann Pl DH9 .... 16 F4
Frosterley South Cty Sch.
   Frost DL13 .... 96 A6
Fryer Cl. Darl DL1 .... 209 E5
Fujitsu Way. New Ay DL3 ...... 191 D8
Fulbeck Rd. New Ay DL5 .... 171 D3
Fulford Pl. Darl DL1 .... 209 A6
Fulforth Way. Sacr DH7 .... 35 B4
Fulmar Dr. Wash NE38 .... 9 F3
Fulthorpe Ave. Hartle TS24 .... 111 E3
Fulthorpe Ave. Darl DL3 .... 208 B2
Fulthorpe Cl. Darl DL3 .... 208 B2
Fulthorpe Gr. Darl DL3 .... 208 A2
Fulton Ct. Shild DL4 .... 148 F2
Fulwell Rd. Peter SR8 .... 85 F5
Furness Cl. Bish Au DL14 ...... 147 E5
Furness Cl. Peter SR8 .... 85 B6
Furness Pit Ind Est. Shild DL4 . 169 F8
Furness St. 2 Darl DL1 .... 209 C6
Fylingdale Dr. N Silk SR3 .... 22 C7
Fyndoune Community Coll.
   Sacr DH7 .... 35 C2
Fyndoune. Sacr DH7 .... 35 C2
Fyndoune Way. Wit Gil DH7 .... 35 B1
Fynes Cl. Peter SR8 .... 85 D8
Fynway. Sacr DH7 .... 35 C2

Gable Terr. Wh Hi DH6 .... 83 F2
Gables The. Burnh DH7 .... 33 C4
Gables The. Hur on T DL2 .... 224 D1
Gables The. Sedge TS21 .... 153 A8
Gainford. C le S DH2 .... 20 A3
Gainford Controlled Prim Sch.
   Gain DL2 .... 204 F6
Gainford Rd. Ingle DL2 .... 188 B5
Gainsborough Ct. Darl DL14 .. 126 B1
Gainsborough Ct. Darl DL2 .... 224 A8
Gainsborough Rd. Stanl DH9 .... 17 F5
Gair Ct. Kimble DH2 .... 35 A4
Gairloch Dr. Pelton DH2 .... 19 F7
Gairsay Cl. 5 Sland SR2 .... 22 E8
Galbraith Terr. Trim TS29 ...... 107 E4
Gale St. Stanl DH9 .... 17 D5
Galfrid Cl. Seaham SR7 .... 40 F6
Galgate. Bar Cas DL12 .... 201 A6
Gallagher Cres. Peter SR8 .... 85 F6
Gallow Hill. Bowes DL12 .... 217 D8
Galloway. Darl DL1 .... 209 E7
Galloway Rd. Peter SR8 .... 85 D7
Galt St. Thorn DH6 .... 83 D4
Garburn Pl. New Ay DL5 .... 171 B7
Garbutt Cl. Shild DL4 .... 148 E2
Garbutt Sq. Darl DL1 .... 209 B1
Garbutt St. Shild DL4 .... 148 E2
Garden Ave. Durham DH1 .... 58 A6
Garden Ave. Lang Pk DH7 .... 56 B6
Garden Cl. 11 Cons DH8 .... 14 F3
Garden Cres. Ebch DH8 .... 3 F4
Garden Est. H le H DH5 .... 39 B4
Garden House La. Cockf DL13 .. 166 C5
Garden Pl. 12 Cons DH8 .... 14 F3
Garden Pl. Crook DL15 .... 100 F4
Garden Pl. 7 Darl DL1 .... 209 A7
Garden Pl. Leadg DH8 .... 15 C4
Garden St. Darl DL1 .... 209 A2
Garden St. Newf DL14 .... 126 B7
Garden Terr. Coxhoe DH6 .... 105 F3
Garden Terr. Leadg DH8 .... 15 C4
Garden Terr. Mid in T DL12 .... 160 E7
Garden Terr. Stanl DH9 .... 17 E5
Garden Terr. Sunni DL13 .... 76 A1
Garden Terr. Thorn DH6 .... 83 D4
Garden View. Butter DL13 ...... 165 E8
Garden Villas. Will DL15 .... 101 F3
Gardens The. C le S DH2 .... 20 B3
Gardens The. Hunw DL15 ...... 125 D5
Gardiner Cres. C le St DH2 ...... 19 E4
Gardiner Sq. Kibble NE11 .... 8 C6
Gardner Ave. Will DL15 .... 101 F2
Gardners Pl. Brand DH7 .... 79 D5
Garesfield Gdns. R Gill NE39 .... 1 E3
Garesfield La. Barlow NE21 & NE39 1 E6
Garland Terr. 6 Fence DH4 ...... 38 A8
Garmondsway Rd. Cornf DL17 . 129 E8
Garrick Ct. 17 Darl DL1 .... 209 B1
Garron St. Seaham SR7 .... 41 D6
Garsdale. Birt DH3 .... 9 E1
Garside Ave. Birt DH3 .... 9 C6
Garside Gr. Peter SR8 .... 85 B8
Garth Cl. Carl TS21 .... 195 C8
Garth Meadows. 1 Hi Eth DL14 146 F5
Garth The. Ferry DL17 .... 128 F5
Garth The. Ingle DL2 .... 188 A6
Garth The. Medom DH8 .... 4 C2
Garth The. New Ay DL5 .... 170 F4
Garth The. Pelton DH2 .... 19 E7
Garth The. Sedge TS21 .... 153 B7
Garth The. Spenny DL16 .... 104 B1
Garth The. Wols DL13 .... 97 F3
Garthlands. Heigh DL5 .... 170 D1
Garthlands Rd. Darl DL3 .... 208 C4
Garthorne Ave. Darl DL3 .... 208 A2
Garths The. Lanch DH7 .... 32 F3
Gas La. Mid in T DL12 .... 160 E7
Gas Works Rd. Seaham SR7 .... 41 E6
Gaskell Way. Crook DL15 ...... 100 C3
Gate La. 2 Cons DH8 .... 222 D8
Gatehouse Cl. Darl DL1 .... 209 E6
Gatehouse Factories.
   Cons DH8 .... 14 F2
Gateway The. Darl DL1 .... 209 B6
Gateways. Wols DL13 .... 97 F3
Gaunless Terr. 1 Bish Au DL14 148 C8
Gaunless Terr. Bish Au DL14 .. 148 C5
Gaunless Terr. Copley DL13 .... 165 B7
Gayfield Terr. Peter SR8 .... 63 F3
Gayhurst Cres. Silk SR3 .... 22 B6
Gelt Cres. H le H DH5 .... 39 B2

General Bucher Ct.
   Bish Au DL14 .... 148 C7
General Hospl The.
   Bish Au DL14 .... 148 B6
General's Wood The.
   Wash NE38 .... 21 B8
Geneva Cres. Darl DL1 .... 224 B7
Geneva Dr. Darl DL1 .... 224 B7
Geneva Gdns. Darl DL1 .... 224 B7
Geneva La. Darl DL1 .... 224 B7
Geneva Rd. Darl DL1 .... 224 C7
Geneva Terr. Darl DL1 .... 224 A8
Gent Rd. Bish Au DL14 .... 148 C6
Geoffrey Ave. Durham DH1 ...... 80 A8
Geoffrey Terr. Stanl DH9 .... 17 D5
George Parkinson Memorial
   Homes. Sherb DH6 .... 59 F1
George Pit La.
   Gr Lum DH3 & DH4 .... 37 C6
George Reynolds Ind Est.
   Shild DL4 .... 170 B6
George Short Cl. Darl DL1 ...... 209 A4
George Sq. Shadf DH6 .... 82 E6
George Sq. Shot Co DH6 .... 84 D6
George St. Bar Cas DL12 .... 201 A5
George St. Birt DH3 .... 9 B4
George St. Bish Au DL14 .... 147 B1
George St. 2 Bish Au DL14 .... 148 B8
George St. Bowb DH6 .... 81 D2
George St. C le S DH3 .... 20 C2
George St. Cons DH8 .... 14 D4
George St. Cons DH8 .... 14 F3
George St. Crag DH9 .... 18 C2
George St. 8 Darl DL1 .... 209 A1
George St. Dipton DH9 .... 16 D8
George St. Durham DH1 .... 58 A1
George St. Esh W DH7 .... 77 E8
George St. Ferry DL17 .... 129 C2
George St. H le H DH5 .... 39 A5
George St. Hasw DH6 .... 61 F3
George St. Lang Pk DH7 .... 56 C7
George St. Murton SR7 .... 40 D2
George St. N Silk SR3 .... 22 A8
George St. Ryhope SR2 .... 23 A6
George St. S Hill DH6 .... 82 E8
George St. Seaham SR7 .... 41 D7
George St. Sherb DH6 .... 60 A1
George St. Shild DL4 .... 148 E1
George St. Trim TS29 .... 107 F5
George St W. 10 N Silk SR3 .... 22 A8
George Street Ind Est.
   Seaham SR7 .... 41 C7
George Terr. Bear DH7 .... 57 C3
George Terr. Crook DL15 .... 100 F4
George Terr. Will DL15 .... 101 E3
Gerard St. Spenny DL16 .... 104 A1
Gervaulx Ct. Spenny DL16 ...... 103 E3
Ghent St. By Gr DL16 .... 126 E8
Ghyll Field Rd. Durham DH1 .... 58 B5
Gib Chare. Bish Au DL14 .... 148 C8
Gibbon St. Bish Au DL14 .... 148 B8
Gibbon St. Spenny DL16 .... 127 C5
Gibbs Ct. 2 C le S DH2 .... 20 C2
Gibside Cl. Stanl DH9 .... 18 B7
Gibside Cres. Byer NE16 .... 6 D8
Gibside Terr. Burnop NE16 .... 6 B6
Gibside View. Blay NE21 .... 2 B8
Gibson Gr. Hartle TS24 .... 111 D4
Gibson St. Cons DH8 .... 14 F3
Gibson St. Shild DL14 .... 149 A4
Gilbert Rd. Peter SR8 .... 85 C7
Gilberti Pl. Hartle TS24 .... 111 F3
Gilderdale. Pens DH4 .... 21 E8
Gilesgate Comp Sch.
   Belm DH1 .... 59 A3
Gilesgate Ct. 5 Durham DH1 .... 58 D2
Gilesgate Cty Inf Sch.
   Belm DH1 .... 59 A3
Gilesgate Cty Jun Sch.
   Belm DH1 .... 59 A3
Gilesgate. Durham DH1 .... 58 D2
Gilesgate. Durham DH1 .... 58 E2
Gilesgate Rd. H le H DH5 .... 39 B1
Gill Crescent N. Gr Lum DH4 .... 21 E1
Gill Crescent S. Gr Lum DH4 .... 21 E1
Gill Croft. C le St DH2 .... 19 F2
Gill La. Start DL12 .... 200 F5
Gill Side View. Cons DH8 .... 14 C5
Gill St. Cons DH8 .... 15 A2
Gill-lands La. Coth DL12 .... 181 B3
Gillas La. H le H DH5 .... 39 A7
Gillas La E. H le Sp DH5 .... 38 E6
Gillas La W. H le Sp DH5 .... 38 E6
Gillas Lane Inf Sch. H le Sp DH5 38 E7
Gilliland Cres. Birt DH3 .... 9 C6
Gilling Cres. Darl DL1 .... 224 C8
Gilling Cres. Spenny DL16 ...... 128 A8
Gilpin Ct. New Ay DL5 .... 171 E5
Gilpin Rd. New Ay DL5 .... 171 E5
Gilpin St. H le Sp DH4 .... 38 D8
Gilsland Cres. Darl DL1 .... 209 C6
Gipsy La. Ferry DL17 .... 151 E7
Girlington Bank. Hut Ma DL11 . 220 E8
Girlington Bank. Oving DL11 .. 203 E1
Girton Cl. Peter SR8 .... 85 B5
Girton Wlk. Darl DL1 .... 209 B5
Girvan Cl. Stanl DH9 .... 18 B6
Girvan Terr. E Lane DH5 .... 39 B1
Girvan Terr W. E Lane DH5 ...... 39 B1
Gladstone Gdns. Cons DH8 ...... 15 A3
Gladstone St. Cons DH8 .... 15 A3
Gladstone St. Crook DL15 ...... 100 E4
Gladstone St. Darl DL1 .... 208 F2
Gladstone St. Fence DH4 .... 38 B8
Gladstone St. Stanl DH9 .... 17 D5
Gladstone St. Stanl DH9 .... 18 D7

Gladstone Terr. Binch DL14 ...... 127 A4
Gladstone Terr. Birt DH3 .... 9 B4
Gladstone Terr. Coxhoe DH6 .... 105 F3
Gladstone Terr. 9 Ferry DL17 . 129 B5
Gladstone Villas. Ferry DL17 .... 129 B5
Glaisdale. Spenny DL16 .... 103 E1
Glaisdale Gdns. Shild DL4 .... 149 B1
Glamis Cl. R Gill NE39 .... 2 B4
Glamis Rd. Darl DL1 .... 209 D6
Glamis Terr. Even DL14 .... 167 C7
Glamis Villas. Birt DH3 .... 9 C6
Glanton Cl. C le S DH2 .... 20 A2
Glanton Terr. 2 Peter SR8 ...... 86 B6
Glastonbury Cl. Spenny DL16 .... 103 E3
Gleaston Ct. Peter SR8 .... 85 B3
Glebe Ave. Eas SR8 .... 63 D4
Glebe Dr. Seaham SR7 .... 22 F2
Glebe Est. Seaham SR7 .... 22 F2
Glebe Houses. Ferry DL17 .... 128 F6
Glebe Rd. G Stain TS21 .... 173 D1
Glebe Sch. Darl DL1 .... 209 B8
Glebe Terr. Eas SR8 .... 63 D4
Glebe View. Frost DL13 .... 96 B6
Glebe View. Murton SR7 .... 40 E4
Glebe Villas. Cornf DL17 .... 105 E1
Glebeside. Satley DL13 .... 53 B3
Glebeside. Wit Gil DH7 .... 57 B8
Glen Barr. C le S DH2 .... 20 B4
Glen Cl. R Gill NE39 .... 1 E3
Glen Hill Sch. Eas SR8 .... 63 A4
Glen Hill Sch. Eas SR8 .... 63 D5
Glen Terr. C le S DH2 .... 20 A4
Glen's Flats. H Pitt DH6 .... 60 B5
Glenavon Ave. C le S DH2 .... 20 B4
Glenburn Cl. Wash NE38 .... 9 F3
Glencoe Ave. C le S DH2 .... 20 B4
Glencoe Terr. R Gill NE39 .... 1 C1
Glencot Gr. Haw SR7 .... 63 A7
Glendale Cl. Blay NE21 .... 1 F8
Glendale Dr. Darl DL3 .... 223 D7
Gleneagles Rd. Darl DL1 .... 209 E7
Gleneagles Rd. 8 Hartle TS27 . 111 C4
Glenfield Rd. Darl DL3 .... 223 D7
Glenholme Cl. Wash NE38 .... 9 F3
Glenholme Dr. Crook DL15 .... 100 F3
Glenhurst Cotts. Eas SR8 .... 63 D4
Glenhurst Dr. Whick NE16 .... 2 F4
Glenhurst Rd. Eas SR8 .... 63 D4
Glenhurst Terr. Murton SR7 ...... 40 D3
Glenlude Ct. Cons DH8 .... 14 C3
Glenmeads. Kimble DH2 .... 35 F4
Glenmere. Spenny DL16 .... 103 E2
Glenmore. Cons DH8 .... 31 C8
Glenmore Ave. C le S DH2 .... 20 C4
Glenroy Gdns. C le S DH2 .... 20 B4
Glenside. Cons DH8 .... 14 D6
Glenside Terr. C le St DH2 .... 19 F4
Glenuce. Birt DH3 .... 9 E3
Globe Cl. 10 Darl DL1 .... 209 B1
Gloucester Cl. Gr Lum DH3 .... 37 A6
Gloucester Pl. Darl DL1 .... 209 C4
Gloucester Pl. Peter SR8 .... 85 B7
Gloucester Rd. Cons DH8 .... 15 B1
Gloucester Terr. Hasw DH6 ...... 61 E1
Gloucestershire Dr. Belm DH1 .. 59 C3
Goatbeck Terr. Brand DH7 .... 79 D5
Goathland Cl. N Silk SR3 .... 22 C7
Goathland Dr. N Silk SR3 .... 22 B6
Goldcrest Rd. Wash NE38 .... 9 F3
Golden Acre. Cons DH8 .... 14 D5
Golden Ave. C le S DH2 .... 20 B4
Golden Gr. Chilt DL17 .... 150 F8
Goldhill La. Mugg DH8 .... 29 A4
Goldsmith Ave. Hartle TS24 ..... 111 E4
Golf Course Rd. S Row DH4 ...... 21 F5
Gomer Terr. Bish Au DL14 .... 126 B1
Gonville Ct. Darl DL1 .... 209 B6
Good Ave. Trim TS29 .... 107 E4
Good St. Tanf L DH9 .... 17 E8
Goodburn Rd. Mid in T DL12 ..... 160 D7
Goodison Way. Darl DL1 .... 209 E3
Goodwell Lea. Brance DH7 .... 78 E1
Goodwood Cl. Cons DH8 .... 14 E6
Goodyear Cres. Durham DH1 ..... 59 B1
Gordon Ave. Peter SR8 .... 85 F7
Gordon Bank. Egg DL12 .... 162 B5
Gordon Cl. Darl DL1 .... 209 E7
Gordon La. Even DL14 .... 167 B8
Gordon Terr. 3 Bish Au DL14 . 148 B8
Gordon Terr. Ferry DL17 .... 128 F6
Gordon Terr. 3 Ryhope SR2 ... 23 A6
Gordon Terr. Stanl DH9 .... 17 F8
Gordon Terr. Wols DL13 .... 97 F7
Gore Hill Est. Thorn DH6 .... 83 C4
Gorecock La. M Law DH7 & DH9 . 32 B8
Gorleston Way. Silk SR3 .... 22 A4
Gorsedale Gr. Belm DH1 .... 59 D3
Gort Pl. Durham DH1 .... 58 F3
Gort Rd. New Ay DL5 .... 171 D7
Gouldsmith Gdns. Darl DL1 ...... 209 E5
Goundry Ave. Ryhope SR2 .... 23 A6
Gower Wlk. Hartle TS26 .... 111 E1
Gowland Sq. Murton SR7 .... 40 B3
Graham Ct. 1 Darl DL1 .... 209 B1
Graham Ct. Sacr DH7 .... 35 C3
Graham Sports Ctr The.
   Durham DH1 .... 80 E7
Graham St. Stanh DL13 .... 71 B3
Graham Terr. H Pitt DH6 .... 60 B5
Graham Way The. Seaham SR7 . 41 B6
Graham's Cotts. Sunni DL13 ..... 76 A1
Grainger St. Bish Au DL14 .... 126 B1
Grainger St. Darl DL1 .... 224 A8
Grainger St. Spenny DL16 .... 104 B1
Grampian Ave. C le S DH2 .... 20 B2
Grampian Ct. Ann Pl DH9 .... 16 E3
Grampian Dr. Peter SR8 .... 85 B5

Grampian Way. Chilt DL17 .... 151 A8
Granaries The. Fence DH4 .... 38 B8
Granary The. Grind TS22 .... 155 C2
Granby Terr. Wing TS28 .... 84 E1
Grand View. Sherb DH6 .... 81 F8
Grange Ave. Bish Au DL14 .... 148 E6
Grange Ave. Eas SR8 .... 63 B3
Grange Ave. Hur on T DL2 .... 235 A8
Grange Bank. Hunw DL15 .... 125 A4
Grange Cl. Peter SR8 .... 85 D8
Grange Cotts. Whorl DL12 .... 202 F3
Grange Cres. Coxhoe DH6 .... 106 A4
Grange Ct. New Ay DL5 .... 171 E8
Grange Ct. W Pel DH2 .... 19 B5
Grange Est. Kibble NE11 .... 8 C6
Grange Park Cres. Bowb DH6 ... 105 E8
Grange Rd. Belm DH1 .... 59 C4
Grange Rd. Darl DL1 & DL2 ...... 223 E7
Grange Rd. Stanl DH9 .... 17 D6
Grange St. Cons DH8 .... 31 B7
Grange St. Pelton DH2 .... 19 E7
Grange St. Wilt Pk DL14 .... 125 A1
Grange Terr. C le St DH2 .... 19 D4
Grange Terr. Kibble NE11 .... 8 C6
Grange Terr. Medom DL8 .... 4 B1
Grange Terr. Shot Co DH6 .... 84 C7
Grange Terr. Trim TS29 .... 107 D3
Grange Terr. Whorl DL12 .... 202 F3
Grange The. New Ay DL5 .... 150 D2
Grange The. Tanf L DH9 .... 17 C8
Grange View. Bish Au DL14 ...... 148 F8
Grange View. E Rain DH5 .... 38 D5
Grangeside. Darl DL3 .... 223 D7
Grangeside. Heigh DL5 .... 170 C4
Grant St. 3 Peter SR8 .... 86 A7
Grantham Ave. Seaham SR7 ..... 41 A7
Granton Cl. Darl DL3 .... 208 B1
Grants Cres. Seaham SR7 .... 41 D7
Granville Ave. Ann Pl DH9 .... 16 F4
Granville Ave. 3 Shild DL4 .... 148 F1
Granville Cl. Chilt DL17 .... 151 A8
Granville Cl. Shild DL4 .... 148 F1
Granville Rd. Bish Au DL14 ...... 148 A6
Granville Rd. Peter SR8 .... 85 F5
Granville Terr. Binch DL14 .... 126 F5
Granville Terr. Wh Hi DH6 .... 83 F3
Grape La. Durham DH1 .... 58 C1
Grasmere. Birt DH3 .... 9 E2
Grasmere. Spenny DL16 .... 103 E2
Grasmere Ave. Bish Au DL14 .... 147 B1
Grasmere Ave. E Lane DH5 ...... 61 C8
Grasmere Cres. Blay NE21 .... 2 B8
Grasmere Gr. Crook DL15 .... 100 F3
Grasmere Mews. Leadg DH8 .... 15 D4
Grasmere Rd. C le S DH2 .... 20 B1
Grasmere Rd. Darl DL1 .... 224 B8
Grasmere Rd. Ferry DL17 .... 128 F5
Grasmere Rd. Peter SR8 .... 85 E7
Grasmere Terr. Murton SR7 ..... 40 D2
Grasmere Terr. S Hett DH6 ...... 62 B7
Grasmere Terr. Stanl DH9 .... 17 D4
Grass St. Darl DL1 .... 209 A4
Grassdale. Belm DH1 .... 59 D3
Grasshill Cswy. St J Ch DL13 ... 90 A8
Grassholme. 12 Darl DL2 .... 224 C8
Grassholme La. Holw DL12 .... 179 E8
Grassholme. 3 New Ay DL5 ... 171 A7
Grasslees. Wash NE38 .... 20 F8
Gravel Wlks. H le Sp DH5 .... 38 F8
Gray Ave. C le S DH2 .... 20 B2
Gray Ave. Durham DH1 .... 58 B5
Gray Ave. Murton SR7 .... 40 C3
Gray Ave. Sherb DH6 .... 59 F2
Gray Ct. Eas SR8 .... 63 D4
Gray La. Bar Cas DL12 .... 201 A5
Gray Sq. Wing TS28 .... 108 E8
Gray St. Bish Au DL14 .... 148 F4
Gray St. Cons DH8 .... 14 E3
Gray Terr. Ann Pl DH9 .... 17 C5
Gray's Terr. Durham DH1 .... 58 A1
Graylands. Wash NE38 .... 20 E8
Grayson Rd. Spenny DL16 .... 127 D6
Graythwaite. C le St DH2 .... 19 F3
Great Gates. Bish Au DL14 ...... 148 C8
Great North Rd. Darl DL1 .... 209 A8
Greathead Cres. New Ay DL5 ... 171 E6
Green Cres. Coxhoe DH6 .... 106 A4
Green Ct. Esh DH7 .... 55 F4
Green La. Bar Cas DL12 .... 201 C6
Green La. Bish Au DL14 .... 148 B3
Green La. Bish Au DL14 .... 148 B8
Green La. Darl DL1 .... 209 B8
Green La. Darl DL1 .... 209 C7
Green La. Durham DH1 .... 58 E1
Green La. Durham DH1 .... 58 F2
Green La. Hasw DH6 .... 61 B3
Green La. Holm DH7 & DH9 ...... 33 E7
Green La. Hunw DL15 .... 125 B5
Green La. New Ay DL5 .... 172 A2
Green La. Satley DL13 .... 52 E5
Green La. Satley DL13 .... 52 E8
Green La. Seaton DH5 & SR7 ... 39 F6
Green La. Shild DL4 .... 148 F4
Green La. Shild DL4 .... 149 A2
Green La. Spcnny DL16 .... 104 C1
Green La. Wing TS29 .... 107 E8
Green La. Wycl DL12 .... 220 B7
Green Lane Ind Est.
   Spenny DL16 .... 104 C2
Green Lea. Wit Gil DH7 .... 35 B1
Green Leas. Carl TS21 .... 195 C8
Green Rise. By Gr DL16 .... 102 E1
Green Rising. Hunw DL15 .... 125 D5
Green St. Cons DH8 .... 14 C7
Green St. Cons DH8 .... 14 F3
Green St. Darl DL1 .... 209 B1
Green St. Leadg DH8 .... 15 C4
Green St. Seaham SR7 .... 41 D7
Green The. Bish TS21 .... 194 C7
Green The. Bish Mi DL17 .... 130 C4
Green The. Braf DL13 .... 192 B7
Green The. C le S DH2 .... 20 B3

Green The. Chopw NE17 .... 4 B8
Green The. Cleas DL2 .... 222 E7
Green The. Cockf DL13 .... 166 D5
Green The. Cornf DL17 .... 105 E2
Green The. Elwick TS27 .... 134 D5
Green The. Even DL14 .... 167 D6
Green The. H Con DL2 .... 206 F3
Green The. 2 H le Sp DH5 ..... 38 F8
Green The. H Shin DH1 .... 81 B4
Green The. Haw SR7 .... 63 B7
Green The. Head DL2 .... 188 B2
Green The. Hett DH6 .... 104 E6
Green The. Hur on T DL2 .... 224 D1
Green The. Kimble DH2 .... 35 F4
Green The. New Ay DL5 .... 171 E1
Green The. Peter SR8 .... 85 A4
Green The. R Gill NE39 .... 1 C2
Green The. Spenny DL16 .... 104 A3
Green The. Staint DL12 .... 201 E8
Green The. Stapl DL2 .... 223 A5
Green The. Wit Pk DL14 .... 125 A1
Green's Bank. Beam DH9 .... 19 A7
Greenacres. Pelton DH2 .... 19 D7
Greenacres Rd. Cons DH8 .... 14 D5
Greenbank Cl. Trim TS29 .... 131 D8
Greenbank Hospl. Darl DL3 ...... 208 E3
Greenbank Rd. Darl DL3 .... 208 E3
Greenbank St. C le S DH3 .... 20 D4
Greencroft. S Hett DH6 .... 62 B7
Greencroft. Darl DL3 .... 208 D1
Greencroft Comp Lower Sch.
   Ann Pl DH9 .... 17 B4
Greencroft Comp Sch.
   Ann Pl DH9 .... 16 E4
Greencroft Ind Est. Ann Pl DH9 . 16 E2
Greencroft Ind Pk. Ann Pl DH9 . 16 E2
Greencroft Rd. Cons DH8 .... 31 C8
Greencroft Terr. Ann Pl DH9 .... 16 E3
Greendale Gdns. H le H DH5 .... 38 F2
Greenfield Cl. Hur on T DL2 ..... 224 C2
Greenfield Comp Sch.
   New Ay DL5 .... 170 F7
Greenfield Cotts. Crook DL15 ... 100 F4
Greenfield St. By Gr DL16 .... 102 E1
Greenfield Terr. Ann Pl DH9 .... 16 F4
Greenfield Way. New Ay DL5 ... 170 F7
Greenfields. Bish Au DL14 .... 147 A4
Greenfields. Coth DL12 .... 182 E3
Greenfields. 7 Ferry DL17 .... 129 A6
Greenfields. Ouston DH2 .... 9 A2
Greenfields Ind Est.
   Bish Au DL14 .... 147 F4
Greenfields Rd. Bish Au DL14 .. 147 D5
Greenfinch St. Wash NE38 ...... 9 F3
Greenford. Kibble NE11 .... 8 D6
Greenford La. Kibble DH2 & NE11 . 8 F6
Greengates La. Mick DL12 .... 161 C5
Greenhead. Cons DH8 .... 14 D5
Greenhead. Wash NE38 .... 9 F4
Greenhill Rd. Heigh DL5 .... 170 C1
Greenhills Est. Wing TS28 .... 84 E1
Greenhills Terr. Wh Hi DH6 ...... 83 F3
Greenland Rd. Esh DH7 .... 55 D4
Greenlands. Stanl DH9 .... 17 D4
Greenlea. Elwick TS27 .... 134 C5
Greenlea Cl. H Spen NE39 .... 1 A3
Greenlee Garth. New Ay DL5 ... 171 A8
Greenless La. E Lay DL11 .... 221 C5
Greenless La. Force DL11 .... 221 C5
Greenmount Rd. Darl DL3 .... 223 E8
Greenrigg La. Mick DL12 .... 161 A2
Greenside Ave. Peter SR8 .... 85 F7
Greenside Cl. Hur on T DL2 ..... 224 C1
Greenside Pl. Crook DL15 .... 101 A2
Greentree La. Ann Pl DH9 .... 16 E5
Greenway Ct. Cons DH8 .... 31 C8
Greenway The. M St G DL2 ...... 225 E7
Greenways. Cons DH8 .... 31 C8
Greenways. Will DL15 .... 101 E2
Greenways. Wols DL13 .... 97 F8
Greenwell Rd. New Ay DL5 ...... 171 D7
Greenwell St. Darl DL1 .... 224 A8
Greenwells Garth. Cound DL14 . 149 C8
Greenwood Ave. Brand DH7 .... 33 D4
Greenwood Cl. Wh Hi DH6 .... 84 A3
Gregory Terr. 4 Fence DH4 ... 38 A8
Gregory Terr. 10 Ferry DL17 . 129 A6
Gregson St. Sacr DH7 .... 35 C3
Gregson Terr. S Hett DH6 .... 62 B6
Gregson Terr. Seaham SR7 ..... 22 F1
Grendon Gdns. M St G DL2 ..... 225 E8
Grenwood Ave. H le Sp DH5 .... 38 C8
Gresham Cl. Darl DL1 .... 209 B5
Gresley Rd. Shot Co SR8 .... 85 A6
Greta Bridge Bank. Gr Br DL12 . 219 A7
Greta Pl. Bar Cas DL12 .... 201 B6
Greta Rd. Bar Cas DL12 .... 201 B6
Greta St N. Pelton DH2 .... 19 C6
Greta St S. Pelton DH2 .... 19 C6
Greville Way. New Ay DL5 .... 171 E6
Grewburn La. Copley DL13 ...... 165 C8
Grey Coll. Durham DH1 .... 80 C7
Grey Gables. Brand DH7 .... 79 C5
Grey Gdns. Cound DL14 .... 149 B8
Grey Ridges. Brand DH7 .... 79 C4
Grey St. Bish Au DL14 .... 148 B8
Grey St. Crook DL15 .... 100 F4
Grey St. Darl DL1 .... 209 B3
Grey St. Newf DL14 .... 126 B7
Grey Terr. 3 Ferry DL17 .... 129 B5
Grey Terr. 10 Ryhope SR2 .... 22 F6
Grey Terr. 2 Ryhope SR2 ...... 23 A6
Greyfriars Cl. Darl DL3 .... 208 A1
Greylingstadt Terr. The Mid DH9 18 A3
Greystones. Ludw DH6 .... 83 C7
Greywood Cl. Hartle TS27 .... 111 C5
Grindon Cl. New Ay DL5 .... 150 E1
Grindon Way. New Ay DL5 .... 171 D1
Grinstead Way. Darl DL1 .... 209 D5
Grinton Park Way. 4 Darl DL1 224 C7
Grisedale Rd. Peter SR8 .... 85 E6

Groat Ave. New Ay DL5 .... 171 E4
Groat Dr. New Ay DL5 .... 171 E5
Groat Rd. New Ay DL5 .... 171 E4
Groat Way. New Ay DL5 .... 171 E4
Grosmont. Gr Lum DH3 .... 37 A7
Grosvenor Terr. Cons DH8 ...... 15 A3
Grosvenor Cl. Stanh DL13 .... 71 A3
Grosvenor Terr. 4 Darl DL14 . 224 A8
Grosvenor Terr. Trim TS29 ...... 107 F5
Grove Cotts. 8 Birt DH3 .... 9 C4
Grove Ct. Hett DH6 .... 104 E5
Grove Ct. Shot Co DH6 .... 84 C5
Grove Pk. Bar Cas DL12 .... 201 A6
Grove Rd. Bish Au DL14 .... 148 A7
Grove Rd. Brand DH7 .... 79 B3
Grove Rd Flats. Brand DH7 ..... 79 A3
Grove Rd. Tow Law DL13 .... 75 B3
Grove St. Spenny DL16 .... 104 A3
Grove Terr. Brand DH1 & DH7 .. 79 E6
Grove Terr. Burnop NE16 .... 6 B6
Grove The. Burnh DH7 .... 33 D4
Grove The. Chilt DL17 .... 150 F7
Grove The. Cornf DL17 .... 105 E1
Grove The. Coxhoe DH6 .... 106 A3
Grove The. Durham DH1 .... 58 A3
Grove The. Eas SR8 .... 63 A4
Grove The. H le Sp DH5 .... 38 D6
Grove The. R Gill NE39 .... 1 F1
Grove The. Ryhope SR2 .... 22 F6
Gudmunsen Ave. Bish Au DL14 . 148 A4
Guildford Cl. Darl DL1 .... 209 E5
Gullane Cl. Stanl DH9 .... 18 B6
Gully Rd. Wing TS28 .... 108 E8
Gunn La. New Ay DL5 .... 171 F6
Gurlish Terr. Cound DL14 .... 127 B1
Gurney Pease Cty Prim Sch.
   Darl DL1 .... 209 B4
Gurney St. Darl DL1 .... 209 A4
Gurney Terr. Bish Au DL14 ...... 149 A5
Gurney Valley. Bish Au DL14 ... 149 A5
Gurney Way. New Ay DL5 .... 171 D4
Guthrum Pl. New Ay DL5 .... 150 C1
H. W. Cocks Memorial Homes The.
   M St G DL2 .... 225 E8
Hackworth Cl. Ferry DL17 .... 128 E5
Hackworth Cl. New Ay DL5 ...... 171 E5
Hackworth Cl. Shild DL4 .... 170 A8
Hackworth Ind Est. Shild DL4 .. 169 F8
Hackworth Rd. B Coll TS27 ..... 86 C3
Hackworth Rd. Eas SR8 .... 62 F1
Hackworth St. Ferry DL17 .... 128 E5
Hackworth St. Shild DL4 .... 149 A1
Hadleigh Cl. Sedge TS21 .... 153 A5
Hadrian Ave. C le S DH3 .... 20 D5
Hadrian Ct. Darl DL3 .... 223 E8
Hadrians Way. Ebch DH8 .... 3 E3
Hagg La. By Gr DL16 .... 103 A1
Hagg Rd. By Gr DL16 .... 126 F8
Haggs La. Shild DL14 & DL4 .... 169 B8
Haig Cres. Durham DH1 .... 59 A1
Haig Rd. Ferry DL17 .... 129 C4
Haig St. Ferry DL17 .... 128 E6
Haig Terr. Ferry DL17 .... 128 E6
Haldon Pl. Peter SR8 .... 85 B5
Hale Rise. Peter SR8 .... 85 E6
Hales Cl. B Coll TS27 .... 86 D3
Half Moon La. Spenny DL16 ..... 104 C1
Hall Ave. Ush M DH7 .... 57 A2
Hall Cl. Seaton SR7 .... 22 D1
Hall Cl. W Rain DH4 .... 38 A2
Hall Cres. Peter SR8 .... 63 F1
Hall Farm Ct. Trim TS29 .... 107 D1
Hall Farm. H Shin DH1 .... 80 F6
Hall Farm Rd. Silk SR3 .... 22 A5
Hall Gdns. Sherb DH6 .... 60 A1
Hall La. Cald DL11 .... 221 E8
Hall La. H le Sp DH5 .... 38 F7
Hall La. H Shin DH1 .... 80 F5
Hall La. Hasw DH6 .... 61 F3
Hall La. Heigh DL5 .... 170 D2
Hall La. W Rain DH4 .... 38 A2
Hall Lane Est. Will DL15 .... 101 F2
Hall Lea. Sedge TS21 .... 153 A7
Hall Rd. Cons DH8 .... 14 C2
Hall Rd. Esh DH7 .... 55 F4
Hall St. Bar Cas DL12 .... 201 A5
Hall Terr. Will DL15 .... 102 A2
Hall View Gdns. How le W DL15 124 D8
Hall View Gr. Darl DL3 .... 208 A3
Hall View. Hunw DL15 .... 125 D7
Hall Wlks. Eas SR8 .... 63 A3
Hallam Rd. Peter SR8 .... 85 D7
Hallfield Cl. Silk SR3 .... 22 A5
Hallfield Dr. Eas SR8 .... 63 A3
Hallgarth. Kir Me DL16 .... 128 A3
Hallgarth La. H Pitt DH6 .... 60 B5
Hallgarth Rd. Trim TS29 .... 131 D8
Hallgarth St. Durham DH1 ...... 80 D8
Hallgarth St. Sherb DH6 .... 59 F1
Hallgarth Terr. Ferry DL17 ...... 129 A6
Hallgarth The. Durham DH1 .... 80 D8
Hallgarth View. H Pitt DH6 ..... 60 C5
Hallgarth View. H Pitt DH6 ..... 60 C5
Hallgarth Villas. Sherb DH6 .... 60 A1
Halliday Gr. Brand DH7 .... 79 D5
Hallimond Rd. Escomb DL14 ... 147 D7
Hallington Head. New Ay DL5 .. 170 F7
Hallnaby Ave. Darl DL3 .... 207 F2
Halton Rd. Durham DH1 .... 58 D5
Hambledon Ave. C le S DH2 .... 20 B2
Hambledon Pl. Peter SR8 .... 85 A5
Hambleton Ct. New Ay DL5 ..... 171 A8
Hambleton Dr. Seaham SR7 .... 41 D8
Hambleton Gr. 4 Darl DL1 .... 209 C6
Hambleton Rd. Cound DL14 .... 149 C8
Hambleton Way. Chilt DL17 .... 151 A8
Hamilton Ct. Shot Co DH6 ...... 84 C6
Hamilton Dr. Thor Th TS21 ..... 175 E3
Hamilton Dr. Darl DL1 .... 209 C7

Hamilton St. Peter SR8 .... 85 F7
Hamilton Terr. Edmon DH7 ...... 35 B6
Hammer Square Bank.
   Beam DH9 .... 7 F1
Hammermill La. Shot DH8 .... 13 D7
Hammond Dr. Darl DL1 .... 223 F6
Hampshire Pl. Bish Au DL14 .... 148 C5
Hampshire Pl. Peter SR8 .... 85 B7
Hampshire Rd. Peter SR8 .... 59 C3
Hampton Ct. C le S DH3 .... 20 D7
Hamsteels Bank. Lanch DH7 ... 55 A6
Hamsteels Cty Jun & Inf Sch.
   Esh W DH7 .... 55 C1
Hamsteels La. Lanch DH7 .... 55 C1
Hamsteels Cl. Lanch DH7 .... 37 B7
Hamsteels Cres. Durham DH1 .. 58 D6
Hamsteels Cl. 6 Silk SR3 ...... 22 A6
Hamsteels Cty Jun Mix & Inf Sch.
   Hamst DH7 .... 123 A3
Hamsterley Dr. Crook DL15 ..... 100 D3
Hamsterley Gdns. Ann Pl DH9 . 16 F4
Hamsterley Gdns. Ann Pl DH9 . 16 F4
Hamsterley Rd. New Ay DL5 .... 171 B8
Hamsterley St. 4 Darl DL4 .... 208 E4
Handel Terr. Wh Hi DH6 .... 83 E2
Handley Cres. E Rain DH5 .... 38 C4
Handley St. Peter SR8 .... 85 F7
Hangingstone La.
   Ann Pl DH8 & DH9 .... 16 C3
Hanover Cl. Darl DL3 .... 208 A1
Hanover Ct. Bish Au DL14 ...... 148 C6
Hanover Ct. 1 Durham DH1 ... 58 B1
Hanover Gdns. Bish Au DL14 ... 148 C6
Hansard Cl. New Ay DL5 .... 170 F4
Hansons Bldgs. M St G DL2 .... 225 F8
Harap Rd. Fishb DL17 & TS21 .. 131 B7
Harap Rd. Kelloe DL17 .... 130 E8
Harbour Wlk. Seaham SR7 ...... 41 C7
Harcourt St. Darl DL3 .... 208 F4
Harding Terr. Darl DL3 .... 208 A1
Hardinge Rd. New Ay DL5 .... 171 D8
Hardings. Hund DL12 .... 182 B6
Hardisty Cres. Bish Au DL14 ... 148 A5
Hardwick Cl. Darl DL1 .... 209 D6
Hardwick Ct. New Ay DL5 .... 171 D8
Hardwick Hall Ctry Pk.
   Sedge TS21 .... 152 F7
Hardwick Rd. Sedge TS21 .... 153 A7
Hardwick St. B Coll TS27 .... 86 C3
Hardwick St. Peter SR8 .... 86 A6
Hardy St. Seaham SR7 .... 41 D7
Hardy Terr. Crook DL15 .... 100 E4
Hardy Terr. Stanl DH9 .... 17 C4
Hare Law Sch. Ann Pl DH9 ...... 16 E6
Harebell Meadows.
   New Ay DL17 .... 150 D2
Harelaw. Pelton DH2 .... 19 D6
Harelaw Gdns. Ann Pl DH9 ...... 16 E6
Harelaw Ind Est. Dipton DH9 ... 16 E7
Harewood Gr. Darl DL3 .... 223 E8
Harewood Hill. Darl DL3 .... 223 E8
Harewood Terr. Darl DL1 & DL3 223 E8
Hargill Dr. Wash NE38 .... 21 A8
Hargill Gr. How le W DL15 ...... 124 D7
Hargill Haven. How le W DL15 .. 124 D7
Hargill Rd. How le W DL15 ...... 124 D7
Hargreave Terr. Darl DL1 .... 209 A1
Harker St. 5 Shild DL4 .... 148 F1
Harlech Wlk. Hartle TS26 .... 111 E1
Harley Gr. Darl DL1 .... 209 E6
Harley St. Brand DH7 .... 79 D3
Harley Terr. Sherb DH6 .... 59 F2
Harmire Cl. Bar Cas DL12 .... 201 A7
Harmire Enterprise Pk.
   Bar Cas DL12 .... 201 A8
Harmire Rd. Bar Cas DL12 ...... 201 A7
Harold Wilson Dr. Hesl TS27 ... 85 F1
Harper Bglws. Wh Hi DH6 .... 83 E1
Harperley Gdns. Ann Pl DH9 ... 16 E5
Harperley La. Tant DH9 .... 17 B7
Harperley Rd. Ann Pl DH9 ...... 16 F5
Harperley Terr. Fir T DL15 ...... 100 A1
Harpers Terr. M St G DL2 .... 210 E1
Harpington View.
   Mordon TS21 .... 152 C1
Harras Bank. Birt DH3 .... 9 C3
Harraton Terr. 12 Birt DH3 ... 9 C4
Harraton Terr. Bourn DH3 .... 21 C7
Harringay Cres. Darl DL1 .... 209 E3
Harris St. Darl DL1 .... 224 D8
Harrison Cl. Peter SR8 .... 85 E5
Harrison Cl. Shild DL4 .... 170 A7
Harrison Cres. Bish Au DL14 ... 147 F4
Harrison Ct. Birt DH3 .... 9 C3
Harrison Garth. Sherb DH6 ..... 59 F2
Harrison Pl. Hartle TS24 .... 111 F4
Harrison St. Tow Law DL13 ..... 75 B2
Harrison Terr. Darl DL3 .... 208 A4
Harrison Terr. Eas SR8 .... 63 D4
Harrogate Terr. Murton SR7 .... 40 C3
Harrowgate Hill Cty Inf Sch.
   Darl DL3 .... 209 A6
Harrowgate Hill Cty Jun Sch.
   Darl DL3 .... 208 F6
Harrowgate Hill Cty Jun Sch.
   Darl DL3 .... 209 A6
Harrowgate Village. Darl DL3 . 209 A8
Harry St. Darl DL3 .... 208 F5
Hart Cres. B Rocks TS27 .... 86 F1
Hart Pastures. Hart TS27 .... 111 A2
Hart Rd. Hartle TS24 & TS27 ... 111 D3
Hart View. Trim TS29 .... 131 E8
Hart Village Prim Sch.
   Hart TS27 .... 110 F3
Hartburn Cl. Trim TS29 .... 131 E8
Hartburn La. Hi Eth DL14 .... 146 E3
Hartford Rd. Darl DL3 .... 223 D8
Harthope Cl. Wash NE38 .... 20 F8
Harthope Carr. Bish Au DL14 .. 147 F5
Harthope Rd. St J Ch DL13 ..... 91 C8
Hartington St. Cons DH8 .... 15 A3
Hartland Dr. Birt DH3 .... 9 D3
Hartlea Ave. Darl DL1 .... 192 A2

Hartlepool Ave. Peter SR8 .... 85 F8
Hartlepool Rd.
  Elwick TS22 & TS21 .... 155 C5
Hartlepool Rd. Sedge TS21 .... 154 C7
Hartlepool St. Thorn DH6 .... 83 D4
Hartley Ave. Cound DL14 .... 127 C1
Hartley Cl. Staind DL2 .... 186 E6
Hartley Rd. New Ay DL5 .... 171 D7
Hartley Terr. Spenny DL16 .... 104 A1
Harts Bldgs. M St G DL2 .... 225 F8
Hartside. Birt DH3 .... 9 D1
Hartside. Crook DL15 .... 100 D4
Hartside Cl. Crook DL15 .... 100 E4
Hartside Cotts. Ann Pl DH9 .... 16 F4
Hartside Cres. Blay NE21 .... 2 A8
Hartside Cty Jun & Inf Sch.
  Crook DL15 .... 100 D4
Hartside Gdns. E Lane DH5 .... 39 C1
Hartside View. Durham DH1 .... 58 A7
Hartville Rd.
  Hartle TS24 & TS27 .... 111 C5
Harvey Cl. Peter SR8 .... 85 D7
Harvey Cl. Wash NE38 .... 9 F5
Harwick Cl. Stanl DH9 .... 18 C6
Harwood Ct. Trim TS29 .... 107 E4
Haselrigg Cl. New Ay DL5 .... 170 F4
Hasledon Gr. Sedge TS21 .... 153 A5
Hasledon Wlk. Murton SR7 .... 40 E4
Haslewood Rd. New Ay DL17 ...... 150 C2
Hastings Ave. Durham DH1 .... 80 A7
Hastings Pl. Hartle TS24 .... 111 F2
Haswell Cty Jun Mix Sch.
  Hasw DH6 .... 61 E3
Hatfield Cl. Durham DH1 .... 58 A6
Hatfield Coll. Durham DH1 .... 58 D1
Hatfield Pl. Peter SR8 .... 85 E5
Hatfield Rd. New Ay DL5 .... 171 E7
Hatfield Way. Bish Au DL14 .... 148 D4
Haughton Comp Sch.
  Darl DL1 .... 209 D5
Haughton Gn. Darl DL1 .... 209 E4
Haughton Rd. Darl DL1 .... 209 C3
Hauxley Dr. Wald DH2 .... 35 F8
Havelock Cl. New Ay DL5 .... 171 E6
Havelock St. Darl DL1 .... 209 A4
Havelock Terr. Tant DH9 .... 6 B2
Haven Ct. Durham DH1 .... 58 C8
Haven House. Leadg DH8 .... 15 C4
Haven The. Burnh DH7 .... 33 D4
Haven The. Lang Pk DH7 .... 56 A7
Haven The. Leadg DH8 .... 15 C4
Haverley Dr. Seaham SR7 .... 40 E8
Haveson Rd. New Ay DL5 .... 171 A8
Hawes Ave. C le S DH2 .... 20 C1
Hawes Cres. Crook DL15 .... 100 F2
Hawes Pl. New Ay DL5 .... 171 B7
Hawes Rd. Peter SR8 .... 85 D7
Hawesdale Cres. Blay NE21 .... 2 B8
Haweswater Gr. Bish Au DL14 .... 147 B1
Hawick Ct. Stanl DH9 .... 18 B6
Hawk Terr. Birt DH3 .... 9 E2
Hawkesbury Mews. Darl DL3 ...... 208 E3
Hawkhill Cl. C le S DH2 .... 36 A8
Hawkins Rd. Cold He SR7 .... 40 E1
Hawkshead Ct. New Ay DL5 .... 171 B7
Hawkshead Pl. New Ay DL5 .... 171 B7
Hawkswood. Hur on T DL2 .... 224 A1
Hawsker Cl. N Silk SR3 .... 22 C7
Hawthorn Ave. N Silk SR3 .... 22 B8
Hawthorn Cl. Kimble DH2 .... 35 F3
Hawthorn Cotts. 4 Cons DH8 ..... 14 D4
Hawthorn Cotts. S Hett DH6 ...... 62 B7
Hawthorn Cres. Belm DH1 .... 59 A3
Hawthorn Cres. Qua Hi DH6 .... 106 D7
Hawthorn Dr. Bar Cas DL12 .... 201 A4
Hawthorn Pk. Brand DH7 .... 79 B4
Hawthorn Rd. Belm DH1 .... 59 D4
Hawthorn Rd. Bish Au DL14 .... 148 C7
Hawthorn Rd. Sedge TS21 .... 153 B7
Hawthorn Rd. Spenny DL16 .... 127 D7
Hawthorn St. 2 Cons DH8 .... 14 D4
Hawthorn St. Darl DL1 .... 224 A8
Hawthorn St. Eas SR8 .... 63 D5
Hawthorn Terr. Ann Pl DH9 .... 17 B4
Hawthorn Terr. Bish Mi DL17 ..... 130 C4
Hawthorn Terr. C le S DH3 .... 20 D2
Hawthorn Terr. Cons DH8 .... 14 D4
Hawthorn Terr. Durham DH1 .... 58 B1
Hawthorne Cl. Lang Pk DH7 .... 56 B6
Hawthorne Cl. Murton SR7 .... 40 D2
Hawthorne Rd. Ferry DL17 .... 129 A6
Hawthorne Sq. Seaham SR7 ...... 41 B8
Hawthorne Terr. Cornf DL17 ...... 129 E8
Hawthorne Terr. Lang Pk DH7 .... 56 D8
Hawthorne Terr. N Bran DH7 ...... 78 E8
Hawthorne Terr. Pelton DH2 ...... 19 E5
Hawthorne Terr. Shot Co DH6 .... 84 C6
Hawthorne Terr. Tanf DH9 .... 6 D3
Hawthorns The. Darl DL3 .... 208 D5
Haxby Rd. M St G DL2 .... 210 E1
Hayling Way. St on T TS21 .... 195 F2
Hayricks The. Tanf DH9 .... 6 D4
Hazard La. H le H DH5 .... 38 E3
Hazard La. W Rain DH5 .... 38 E3
Hazel Ave. Brand DH7 .... 79 A3
Hazel Ave. Darl DL3 .... 208 E4
Hazel Ave. 3 H le Sp DH4 .... 38 C8
Hazel Ave. N Silk SR3 .... 22 B8
Hazel Ave. Qua Hi DH6 .... 106 D7
Hazel Cres. Eas SR8 .... 63 D3
Hazel Dr. Hesl TS27 .... 86 A1
Hazel Gr. Bish Au DL14 .... 148 B7
Hazel Gr. Burnop NE16 .... 6 C6
Hazel Gr. C le S DH2 .... 20 A5
Hazel Grove Terr. Fir T DL15 ...... 99 F2
Hazel Terr. Crook DL15 .... 100 D4
Hazel Terr. Shot Co DH6 .... 84 C6
Hazel Terr. The Mid DH9 .... 18 B3
Hazeldale Ave. Shild DL4 .... 149 B1
Hazelgrove Cres. Cockf DL13 ..... 166 C5
Hazelmere. Spenny DL16 .... 103 E2

Headingley Cres. Darl DL1 .... 209 E3
Headlam Rd. Darl DL1 .... 224 C8
Headlands The. Darl DL3 .... 208 C1
Healeyfield La. Heal DH8 .... 29 D4
Heath Cl. Bowb DH6 .... 105 D8
Heath Cl. Peter SR8 .... 85 F5
Heath Rd. Spenny DL16 .... 127 E6
Heath View. Hut Hen TS28 .... 109 A6
Heather Dr. H le H DH5 .... 39 A5
Heather Gr. Hartle TS26 .... 111 F1
Heather Gr. Spenny DL16 .... 127 D6
Heather La. Crook DL15 .... 100 C3
Heather Lea. Dipton DH9 .... 5 E2
Heather Terr. Burnop NE16 .... 6 B6
Heather Way. Stanl DH9 .... 17 C6
Heatherburn Ct. New Ay DL5 ..... 171 D8
Heatherdale Cres. Belm DH1 ...... 59 D4
Heatherdene Rd. Fishb TS21 ..... 131 D4
Heatherlaw. Wash NE37 .... 9 F6
Heatherwood Gr. Darl DL3 .... 208 D3
Heathfield Inf Sch. Darl DL1 ...... 209 D2
Heathfield Jun Sch. Darl DL1 ..... 209 D2
Heathfield Pk. M St G DL2 .... 210 E1
Heathmeads. Pelton DH2 .... 19 D6
Heathway. Seaham SR7 .... 41 C5
Heathways. H le H DH5 .... 81 B5
Heaton Terr. Hut Hen TS28 .... 108 F5
Heaviside Pl. Durham DH1 .... 58 F2
Hebburn St. Eas SR8 .... 63 C4
Hedgelea Rd. E Rain DH5 .... 38 C3
Hedleigh Ct. Coxhoe DH6 .... 106 A3
Hedley Cl. 2 New Ay DL5 .... 171 C8
Hedley La. Kibble NE11 & NE16 .. 7 C6
Hedley Terr. Dipton DH9 .... 16 A6
Hedley Terr. Ryhope SR2 .... 23 A6
Hedleyhill Colliery. E Hed DH7 .. 76 E6
Hedleyhill La. Corn Co DH7 .... 55 A2
Hedleyhill La. E Hed DH7 .... 54 E1
Hedleyhill Terr. Esh W DH7 .... 77 A5
Hedworth St. C le S DH3 .... 20 C3
Heighington CE Prim Sch.
  Heigh DL5 .... 170 D2
Heighington La. Heigh DL5 .... 170 E1
Heighington La. New Ay DL5 ...... 171 C2
Heighington St. New Ay DL5 ...... 171 E1
Heighington Sta (Halt).
  New Ay DL5 .... 171 C2
Heild Cl. New Ay DL5 .... 171 E7
Helena Terr. Bish Au DL14 .... 148 B6
Helford Rd. Peter SR8 .... 85 C4
Hellvellyn Ct. Ann Pl DH9 .... 16 F3
Helmington Gr. Will DL15 .... 101 E1
Helmington Sq. Hunw DL15 .... 125 D7
Helmington Terr. Hunw DL15 ..... 125 D7
Helmsley Cl. Ferry DL17 .... 129 B5
Helmsley Dr. New Ay DL17 .... 150 E1
Helmsley Moor Way. Darl DL1 ... 224 D8
Helmsley Rd. Durham DH1 .... 58 D7
Hemel St. C le S DH3 .... 20 C2
Hemlington Cl. 12 Ryhope SR2 ... 22 F6
Hemmel Courts. Brand DH7 .... 79 C5
Henderson Ave. Wh Hi DH6 .... 83 E2
Henderson Rd. New Ay DL5 .... 171 E6
Henderson St. Darl DL1 .... 224 A8
Hendren Cl. 5 Darl DL3 .... 209 A7
Henknowle Jun & Inf Sch.
  Bish Au DL14 .... 148 C5
Henley Ave. C le S DH2 .... 19 E3
Henley Gdns. Cons DH8 .... 15 A2
Henry Ave. Bowb DH6 .... 81 D2
Henry Smith Sch. Hartle TS24 ... 111 E3
Henry St. Cons DH8 .... 14 E3
Henry St. Darl DL1 .... 209 A5
Henry St. H le H DH5 .... 39 A5
Henry St. Seaham SR7 .... 41 D8
Henry St. Shild DL4 .... 148 F1
Henry St N. Murton SR7 .... 40 D3
Henry Terr. Gr Lum DH4 .... 21 F2
Henson Gr. New Ay DL5 .... 171 D8
Henson Rd. Darl DL1 .... 209 E7
Herbert St. 21 Cons DH8 .... 14 F3
Herbert St. 7 Darl DL1 .... 209 A1
Herbert Terr. Seaham SR7 .... 41 D7
Hercules St. Darl DL1 .... 209 C6
Herdinghill. Wash NE37 .... 9 F6
Hereford St. Cound DL14 .... 127 D1
Herefordshire Dr. Belm DH1 ...... 59 C3
Hermitage Pk. C le S DH3 .... 20 C1
Heron Dr. Darl DL1 .... 209 D1
Herrington Cl. Lang Pk DH7 .... 56 B6
Herrington Cl. 2 New Ay DL5 ..... 171 D8
Herriot Ct. Darl DL1 .... 209 E7
Hertford Cres. H le H DH5 .... 38 F4
Hertford Pl. Peter SR8 .... 85 C8
Herton Cl. Peter SR8 .... 85 C7
Heseldene Ave. Hunw DL15 .... 125 D6
Hesleden Rd. B Coll TS27 .... 86 D3
Hesleden Rd. Hesl TS27 .... 86 B2
Hesley Rise. Staint DL12 .... 184 D2
Heslop Dr. Darl DL1 .... 223 F7
Heslop St. Bish Au DL14 .... 149 A5
Hessewelle Cres. Hasw DH6 ...... 61 E1
Hett La. Sland DH6 .... 104 C7
Hetton Lyons Ind Est.
  H le H DH5 .... 39 B3
Hetton Lyons Inf Sch.
  H le H DH5 .... 39 A2
Hetton Lyons Jun Sch.
  H le H DH5 .... 39 A2
Hetton Prim Sch. H le H DH5 ..... 38 F3
Hetton Rd. H le Sp DH5 .... 38 E2
Hetton Sch. H le H DH5 .... 38 F3
Heugh Edge. Sacr DH7 .... 35 B5
Heugh Hall Row. Qua Hi DH6 ..... 105 F8
Hever Cl. Bish Au DL14 .... 147 E6
Hewitson Rd. Darl DL1 .... 209 D1
Hewitson Rd S. 4 Darl DL1 .... 224 D8
Hewitt Ave. Sland SR2 .... 22 E8

Heworth La. New Ay DL5 .... 172 A3
Hexham. Wash NE38 .... 9 F4
Hexham Ave. Seaham SR7 .... 41 B6
Hexham Dr. Ann Pl DH9 .... 16 F5
Hexham St. Bish Au DL14 .... 148 B8
Hexham Way. Darl DL3 .... 208 A5
Hickstead Ct. Darl DL1 .... 209 F4
Hickstead Rise. New Ay DL17 .... 150 E2
Higgins Terr. N Silk SR3 .... 22 B7
High Barn Rd. New Ay DL5 .... 170 F4
High Barnes. Gr Lum DH3 .... 37 A7
High Bondgate. Bish Au DL14 ..... 126 B1
High Carr Cl. Durham DH1 .... 58 B5
High Carr Rd. Durham DH1 .... 58 A5
High Chare. C le S DH3 .... 20 D3
High Cross St. Escomb DL14 ...... 82 F1
High Downs Sq. H le H DH5 .... 39 A5
High Escomb. Escomb DL14 .... 147 D8
High Farm Cl. Carl TS21 .... 195 C8
High Garth. Winst DL2 .... 203 F6
High Gn. Darl DL3 .... 208 B3
High Gn. Gain DL2 .... 205 A6
High Graham St. Sacr DH7 .... 35 C3
High Grange. Hunw DL15 .... 125 A4
High Grange Rd. Spenny DL16 .... 103 F1
High Hamsterley Rd. H Mill NE39 . 5 A5
High Hope St. Crook DL15 .... 100 E5
High Horse Cl. R Gill NE39 .... 2 A4
High Horse Close Wood.
  R Gill NE39 .... 2 A4
High House La. Braf DL13 .... 192 C7
High House La. Heal DH8 .... 30 E3
High Job's Hill. Crook DL15 .... 101 B3
High La. Newsh DL11 .... 233 F8
High Lands. Even DL13 .... 166 D8
High Meadows. Brand DH7 .... 79 A5
High Melbourne St. 12
  Bish Au DL14 .... 148 B6
High Mill Rd. H Mill NE39 .... 5 A5
High Northgate. Darl DL1 .... 209 A3
High Primrose Hill. Bourn DH4 ... 21 D3
High Queen St. Wit Pk DL14 .... 125 A1
High Rd. Cound DL14 .... 127 E3
High Rd. Heigh DL5 .... 170 B3
High Rd. Stan Cr DL15 .... 100 F8
High Riggs. Bar Cas DL12 .... 201 C2
High Row. Cald DL11 .... 221 E7
High Row. Darl DL1 .... 208 F2
High Row. Gain DL2 .... 204 F6
High Row. Gr Lum DH4 .... 21 E1
High Row. Grwf DL14 .... 126 B8
High Shaws. Brand DH7 .... 79 C5
High Spen Ct. H Spen NE39 .... 1 A4
High St. Belm DH1 .... 59 C4
High St. Bish TS21 .... 194 D7
High St. Bish Au DL14 .... 148 F4
High St. Bish Mi DL17 .... 130 C4
High St. Brand DH7 .... 79 E5
High St. By gl Gr DL 16 .... 126 E8
High St. Cornf DL17 .... 105 E1
High St. E Lane DH5 .... 39 C1
High St. Ferry DL17 .... 129 C4
High St. H Pitt DH6 .... 60 B6
High St. H Shin DH1 .... 81 A6
High St. H Shin DH1 .... 81 B5
High St. How le W DL15 .... 124 E7
High St. New Ay DL5 .... 171 E1
High St. Sedge TS21 .... 153 B6
High St. Spenny DL16 .... 127 F8
High St. Stanh DL13 .... 71 B3
High St. Stanl DH9 .... 17 F7
High St. Thorn DH6 .... 83 C4
High St. Tow Law DL13 .... 75 C2
High St. Will DL15 .... 101 F3
High St. Wit le W DL14 .... 124 B3
High St. Wols DL13 .... 97 E7
High St N. Brand DH7 .... 79 D5
High St N. Murton SR7 .... 40 D3
High St S. Brand DH7 .... 79 E6
High St S. Murton SR7 .... 40 D3
High Street S Bk.
  Brand DH7 .... 79 E5
High Terr. Billy R DL15 .... 100 D6
High Town. Westg DL13 .... 68 B1
High View. 8 Ush M DH7 .... 56 F2
High West La. Haw SR7 .... 63 A7
High West Rd. Crook DL15 .... 100 C3
High Winning Cotts. Wing TS28 .. 84 F1
High Wood Terr. Durham DH1 .... 80 D8
High Wood View. Durham DH1 ... 80 D8
Highbury Rd. Darl DL3 .... 208 C3
Highcliffe Edge. Winst DL2 .... 203 F6
Highcliffe Terr. 6 Ferry DL17 ..... 129 A6
Highcroft. Spenny DL16 .... 127 D6
Highfield. Birt DH3 .... 9 C6
Highfield. Sacr DH7 .... 35 C3
Highfield Cres. C le S DH3 .... 20 C5
Highfield Day Hospl.
  C le S DH3 .... 20 C5
Highfield Dr. Fence DH4 .... 38 B7
Highfield Gdns. C le S DH3 .... 20 C5
Highfield Gr. How le W DL15 ...... 124 D7
Highfield Grange. Fence DH4 ...... 38 B7
Highfield Jun & Inf Schs.
  R Gill NE39 .... 1 C2
Highfield Rd. Darl DL3 .... 208 B5
Highfield Rd. R Gill NE39 .... 1 C1
Highfield Rise. C le S DH3 .... 20 C5
Highfield Terr. Ush M DH7 .... 56 F1
Highland Gdns. Shild DL4 .... 148 F2
Highland Terr. 5 Ferry DL17 ...... 129 A6
Highmoor Rd. Darl DL1 .... 224 E7
Highridge. Birt DH3 .... 9 C5
Highridge. Cons DH8 .... 14 C3
Highroad Ave. Bish Mi DL17 .... 130 C4
Highside Rd. Heigh DL2 & DL5 ... 170 B2
Hilda Ave. Durham DH1 .... 59 A1
Hilda Pk. C le S DH2 .... 20 B5
Hilda St. Ann Pl DH9 .... 16 E5
Hilda St. Darl DL1 .... 209 A2
Hilda Terr. C le S DH2 .... 20 B4

Hildon Dr. Darl DL1 .... 224 C7
Hill Brow. N Silk SR3 .... 22 B6
Hill Cres. Murton SR7 .... 40 C3
Hill Cres. Seaham SR7 .... 41 E5
Hill Crest. Burnh DH7 .... 33 D4
Hill Crest. Burnop NE16 .... 6 B6
Hill Crest. Sacr DH7 .... 35 D2
Hill Crest Mews. 1
  Durham DH1 .... 58 D2
Hill End. Frost DL13 .... 95 F5
Hill Fields. New Ay DL5 .... 170 F4
Hill Meadows. H Shin DH1 .... 81 A5
Hill Rise. M St G DL2 .... 226 A5
Hill Side. Stapl DL2 .... 223 A5
Hill St. N Silk SR3 .... 22 A7
Hill Terr. Billy R DL15 .... 100 E8
Hill Terr. Mid in T DL12 .... 160 D7
Hill Top. Birt DH3 .... 9 D4
Hill Top. Stanl DH9 .... 18 B7
Hill View. Copley DL13 .... 165 B7
Hill View. Esh W DH7 .... 77 E8
Hill View. Stanl DH9 .... 18 D7
Hillbeck St. Bish Au DL14 .... 148 D5
Hillcrest. Cons DH8 .... 29 F6
Hillcrest. Durham DH1 .... 58 D2
Hillcrest. H Shin DH1 .... 81 B5
Hillcrest. Tow Law DL13 .... 75 C2
Hillcrest Gr. Elwick TS27 .... 134 C6
Hillcrest Pl. Hesl TS27 .... 86 A1
Hillcroft. 4 Birt DH3 .... 9 C5
Hillcroft. R Gill NE39 .... 1 C2
Hillersdon Terr. Nent CA9 .... 42 A4
Hillfield. Cons DH8 .... 14 D3
Hillgarth. Cons DH8 .... 30 B6
Hillhead La. Byer NE16 .... 2 D2
Hillhouse. Sadb DL2 .... 210 E6
Hillhouse La. Sadb DL2 .... 210 E7
Hillmeads. Kimble DH2 .... 35 F4
Hillrise Cres. Seaton SR7 .... 40 D8
Hillside. C le S DH3 .... 20 C4
Hillside. Ingle DL2 .... 188 A6
Hillside. Wit Gil DH7 .... 35 B1
Hillside Cl. R Gill NE39 .... 1 E3
Hillside Cres. Thorn DH6 .... 83 C4
Hillside Gdns. Stanl DH9 .... 18 A8
Hillside Grove. H Pitt DH6 .... 60 B5
Hillside Rd. Cound DL14 .... 149 B7
Hillside Rd. Darl DL3 .... 223 D8
Hillside Terr. Sadb DL2 .... 210 E6
Hillside View. Sherb DH6 .... 59 F2
Hillside Villas. Peter SR8 .... 85 F7
Hillside Way. 1 H le Sp DH4 ...... 38 E8
Hilltop. Nent CA9 .... 42 A3
Hilltop Bglws. Thorn DH6 .... 83 B3
Hilltop Gdns. N Silk SR3 .... 22 C7
Hilltop Rd. Bear DH7 .... 57 A3
Hilsdon Dr. Shild DL4 .... 170 B8
Hilton Dr. Peter SR8 .... 85 D5
Hilton Moor La. Hilton DL14 .... 167 F3
Hilton Rd. Bar Cas DL12 .... 201 B6
Hilton Rd. Bish Au DL14 .... 148 C6
Hilton Rd. New Ay DL5 .... 171 B8
Hind Ct. New Ay DL17 .... 150 E2
Hinkley Cl. N Silk SR3 .... 22 B6
Hird St. Darl DL1 .... 209 A1
Hirdman Gr. Hartle TS24 .... 111 E4
Hirst Ct. Spenny DL16 .... 127 D6
Hirst Gr. 3 Darl DL1 .... 224 D8
HM Prison Durham.
  Durham DH1 .... 58 D1
HM Remand Ctr Low Newton.
  Durham DH1 .... 58 F8
Hodge La. Holw DL12 .... 138 A2
Hogarth Terr. Cound DL14 .... 149 C8
Holberry Terr. Cound DL14 .... 149 C8
Holborn. Spenny DL16 .... 103 F1
Holburn Cl. Esh W DH7 .... 77 E8
Holburn Ct. Ush M DH7 .... 57 B1
Holderness. New Ay DL5 .... 170 F8
Holdforth Cl. Hartle TS24 .... 111 F1
Holdforth Crest. Bish Au DL14 ... 148 C7
Holdforth Dr. Bish Au DL14 .... 148 C7
Holdforth Rd. Hartle TS24 .... 111 F1
Hole La. Whick NE16 .... 2 F4
Holehouse La. Lanch DH7 .... 54 A7
Holgate Moor Gn. Darl DL1 .... 224 D7
Holindale. Spenny DL16 .... 127 F7
Hollin Cres. Romald DL12 .... 182 B8
Hollin Way. New Ay DL5 .... 171 D2
Hollingside La. Durham DH1 ...... 80 C6
Hullinhhill. R Gill NE39 .... 2 A5
Hollinhill La. R Gill NE39 .... 1 F4
Hollinside Terr. Lanch DH7 .... 32 C1
Hollinside Terr. R Gill NE39 .... 1 D2
Hollow The. Crook DL15 .... 100 E1
Hollowdene. Crook DL15 .... 100 E2
Hollowdene. H le H DH5 .... 39 A3
Hollowdene Garth. Crook DL15 .. 100 E2
Holly Ave. H le Sp DH5 .... 38 F8
Holly Ave. N Silk SR3 .... 22 B8
Holly Ave. Win M NE21 .... 2 C6
Holly Cres. Sacr DH7 .... 35 D2
Holly Gdns. Cons DH8 .... 30 C8
Holly Haven. E Rain DH5 .... 38 D4
Holly Hill. Shild DL4 .... 149 B1
Holly Hill Gdns E. Stanl DH9 ...... 18 A5
Holly Hill Gdns W. Stanl DH9 ..... 17 F4
Holly Pk. Brand DH7 .... 79 B4
Holly Pk. Ush M DH7 .... 57 A2
Holly St. Darl DL3 .... 208 F2
Holly Terr. Ann Pl DH9 .... 16 E5
Holly Terr. Burnop NE16 .... 6 C5
Holly Terr. Crook DL15 .... 100 C4
Holly Terr. How le W DL15 .... 124 E8
Holly Terr. Stanl DH9 .... 17 D5
Hollycarrside Rd. Sland SR2 ...... 22 E8

Hollycrest. C le S DH2 .... 20 B5
Hollydene. Kibble NE11 .... 8 D6
Hollydene. R Gill NE39 .... 1 F2
Hollyhock Terr. Bowb DH6 .... 105 E6
Hollyhurst Rd. Cornf DL17 .... 105 D1
Hollyhurst Rd. Darl DL3 .... 208 E3
Hollys The. Birt DH3 .... 9 B7
Hollywell Cl. Ush M DH7 .... 57 B1
Hollywell Gr. Bish Au DL14 .... 147 E5
Holme Dene. Hunw DL15 .... 125 D5
Holme Lea Terr. Wing TS29 .... 108 A5
Holmefield. Frost DL13 .... 96 B6
Holmewood Dr. R Gill NE39 .... 5 D8
Holmfield Villas. Bowb DH6 .... 105 E6
Holmhill La. C le S DH2 & DH3 ... 36 C7
Holmhill La. Eas SR8 .... 63 D5
Holmlands Cres. Durham DH1 .... 58 A5
Holmlands Pk. C le S DH3 .... 20 C2
Holmlands Rd. Darl DL3 .... 208 D4
Holmlea. Burnh DH7 .... 33 D4
Holms La. Thor Th TS21 .... 175 C2
Holmsand Villas. Sacr DH7 .... 35 C2
Holmside Ave. Lanch DH7 .... 32 F3
Holmside Hall Rd.
  Holm DH7 & DH9 .... 34 B7
Holmside La. Holm DH7 .... 34 C6
Holmside & South Moor Hospl.
  The Mid DH9 .... 18 A4
Holmside Terr. Crag DH9 .... 18 C2
Holmwood Gr. Darl DL1 .... 209 A8
Holwick Rd. Darl DL1 .... 209 A6
Holy Family RC Prim Sch.
  Darl DL3 .... 208 C4
Holy Well La. Crook DL15 .... 101 B2
Holyoake Gdns. Birt DH3 .... 9 C4
Holyoake St. Ferry DL17 .... 128 E6
Holyoake St. Pelton DH2 .... 19 C6
Holyoake Terr. Stanl DH9 .... 17 E4
Holyrood. Gr Lum DH3 .... 37 A8
Holyrood Ave. Darl DL3 .... 208 A1
Holyrood Cres. Hart TS27 .... 110 F2
Homelands Hospl.
  Crook DL15 .... 101 B2
Homer Terr. Durham DH1 .... 80 A8
Homerton Ct. Darl DL1 .... 209 B5
Homeside Ave. Trim TS29 .... 107 E3
Honeypot La. Darl DL3 .... 208 E5
Honeysuckle Cl. Silk SR3 .... 22 A5
Honeywood Gdns. Darl DL3 .... 208 E4
Honister Pl. New Ay DL5 .... 171 B7
Honister Sq. Crook DL15 .... 100 F2
Hood Cl. Hartle TS24 .... 111 E4
Hood St. St J Ch DL13 .... 67 C1
Hoode Cl. New Ay DL5 .... 171 B8
Hookergate Comp Sch.
  H Spen NE39 .... 1 B3
Hookergate La. H Spen NE39 ..... 1 A2
Hooper Terr. Shot Co DH6 .... 84 C6
Hope Cl. Trim TS29 .... 131 D8
Hope Shield. Wash NE38 .... 9 F1
Hope St. Cons DH8 .... 14 E4
Hope St. Crook DL15 .... 100 E4
Hope St. Sherb DH6 .... 59 F1
Hope View. Sland SR2 .... 22 F7
Hopelands Ct. Heigh DL5 .... 170 D1
Hopelands. Heigh DL5 .... 170 D1
Hopemoor Pl. Darl DL1 .... 224 D7
Hopetown La. Darl DL3 .... 208 F4
Hopgarth Ct. C le S DH3 .... 20 D4
Hopgarth Gdns. C le S DH3 .... 20 D4
Hopkinson Pl. Kir Me DL16 .... 127 F3
Hopkinson Rd. Kir Me DL16 .... 128 A3
Hopper Pl. Durham DH1 .... 58 C5
Hopper Rd. New Ay DL5 .... 171 D5
Hopper St. Eas SR8 .... 63 C4
Hopper Terr. Trim TS29 .... 107 E3
Horn Hall Hospl. Stanh DL13 ...... 70 F3
Hornby Ave. Sedge TS21 .... 153 A5
Hornby Cl. Hur on T DL2 .... 224 C8
Hornby House. 8 Darl DL2 .... 224 C8
Horndale Ave. New Ay DL5 .... 171 C4
Horndale Cty Inf Sch.
  New Ay DL5 .... 171 A7
Hornsea Cres. H le H DH5 .... 39 B1
Hornsey Terr. H le H DH5 .... 39 B1
Horse Close La. Trim TS29 .... 107 F2
Horse Market. Bar Cas DL12 ..... 200 F6
Horse Market. 7 Darl DL1 .... 208 F1
Horseclose La. Carl TS19 .... 195 E7
Horsemarket. Mid in T DL12 ...... 160 D7
Horsley Gr. Bish Au DL14 .... 147 F5
Horsley Pl. Hartle TS24 .... 111 F2
Horton Cres. Bowb DH6 .... 81 D2
Hospital Rd. Lang Pk DH7 .... 56 B6
Hotts La. St J Ch DL13 .... 67 A1
Houghton Bank La. H le Si DL2 .. 169 C1
Houghton Enterprise Ctr.
  H le Sp DH5 .... 38 E8
Houghton Gate. Bourn DH3 .... 21 B3
Houghton Kepier Sch.
  H le Sp DH4 .... 38 D8
Houghton La. Denton DL2 .... 189 D5
Houghton La. H le Si DL2 .... 189 E5
Houghton La. Walw DL2 .... 189 D5
Houghton Prim Sch.
  H le Sp DH5 .... 38 E8
Houghton Rd. H le H DH5 .... 39 A4
Houghton Rd W. H le H DH5 .... 39 A4
Houghton-le-Spring Golf Course.
  H le Sp DH4 .... 39 B7
Houghton-Le-Spring Sch.
  H le Sp DH5 .... 38 D7
Houghwell Gdns. Tanf L DH9 ..... 17 D8
Houlskye Cl. N Silk SR3 .... 22 C7
Hound Hill. Wols DL13 .... 97 F7
Houndgate. Darl DL1 .... 208 F1
Houndgate Mews. 10 Darl DL1 .. 208 F1
Housing La. Medom DH8 & DH9 .. 4 D1

Hovingham Cl. Peter SR8 ...... 85 E5
Howard Cl. Bish Au DL14 ...... 148 A5
Howarth Terr. Hasw DH6 ...... 61 F3
Howden. Cons DH8 ...... 14 D3
Howden Bank. M Law DH7 ...... 32 F6
Howden Gdns. Wing TS28 ...... 108 E8
Howden Rd. Hartle TS24 ...... 111 E4
Howden Rd. New Ay DL5 ...... 171 E4
Howden Sq. How le W DL15 ...... 124 E7
Howden-le-Wear Cty Jun Mix
 & Inf Sch. H le W DL15 ...... 124 E7
Howlea La. Hamst DL13 ...... 122 F7
Howlea La. Wols DL15 ...... 98 C2
Howletch La. Peter SR8 ...... 85 C6
Howlish La. Cound DL14 ...... 149 C7
Howlish View. Cound DL14 ...... 149 C8
Hownsgill Dr. Heal DH8 ...... 31 B6
Howson Cres. New Ay DL17 ...... 150 D1
Hoy Cres. Seaham SR7 ...... 22 F1
Hoyle Fold. Silk SR3 ...... 22 A4
Hude. Mid in T DL12 ...... 160 D8
Hudson Ave. Peter SR8 ...... 85 F7
Hudspeth Cres. Durham DH1 ...... 58 A7
Hugar Rd. H Spen NE39 ...... 1 A3
Hulam La. Lang DL2 ...... 187 E5
Hullock Rd. New Ay DL5 ...... 171 D7
Hulme St. Peter SR8 ...... 85 C5
Humber Hill. Stanl DH9 ...... 18 A5
Humber Pl. Darl DL1 ...... 223 F6
Humberhill Dr. Lanch DH7 ...... 32 E3
Humberhill La. Lanch DH7 ...... 31 F4
Humble Carr La. Heigh DL2 ...... 190 C8
Humbleburn La. Edmon DH7 ...... 18 E1
Hummerbeck La. Bolam DL14 ...... 160 D7
Hummerbeck La. Hilton DL14 ...... 168 A4
Hummersknott Ave. Darl DL3 ...... 208 C1
Hummersknott Comp Sch.
 Darl DL3 ...... 208 A1
Humphrey Cl. New Ay DL5 ...... 171 C7
Hunden's La. Darl DL1 ...... 209 C2
Hundens Day Hospl. Darl DL1 ...... 209 C1
Hunstanworth Rd. Darl DL3 ...... 208 B4
Hunt Lea. Whick NE16 ...... 2 E5
Hunter Ave. Ush M DH7 ...... 57 A4
Hunter Rd. New Ay DL5 ...... 171 D6
Hunter Rd. Shot Co SR8 ...... 85 A5
Hunter Terr. Chilt DL17 ...... 150 F8
Hunters Cl. Hur on T DL2 ...... 224 B1
Hunters Gn. Bish Au DL14 ...... 225 F6
Hunters Gn. New Ay DL5 ...... 170 F8
Huntershaw Way. Darl DL3 ...... 208 F7
Huntingdon Rd. Peter SR8 ...... 85 C8
Huntingdonshire Dr. Belm DH1 ...... 59 D3
Huntley Ave. Murton SR7 ...... 40 B3
Huntley Cres. Blay NE21 ...... 2 A8
Huntley St. Darl DL1 ...... 209 A1
Huntley Terr. ◢ Ryhope SR2 ...... 22 F6
Huntsgarth. Will DL15 ...... 101 E1
Huntshield Ford. St J Ch DL13 ...... 67 D1
Hunwick La. Hunw DL15 ...... 125 E6
Hunwick La. Will DL15 ...... 101 D2
Hurbuck Cotts. Lanch DH7 ...... 31 E5
Hurworth Burn Rd.
 Hut Hen TS28 ...... 133 B7
Hurworth Burn Rd. Trim TS29 ...... 108 A1
Hurworth Burn Rd.
 Wing TS28 & TS29 & TS27 ...... 132 D7
Hurworth Cl. Trim TS29 ...... 131 D8
Hurworth Comp Sch.
 Hur on T DL2 ...... 235 B8
Hurworth Cty Inf Sch.
 Hur on T DL2 ...... 224 C1
Hurworth Cty Jun Sch.
 Hur on T DL2 ...... 224 C1
Hurworth House Sch.
 Hur on T DL2 ...... 224 C1
Hurworth Hunt. New Ay DL5 ...... 170 F8
Hurworth Rd. Hur on T DL2 ...... 235 A8
Hurworth Rd. Neas DL2 ...... 225 A1
Hurworth Rd. New Ay DL5 ...... 171 C4
Hurworth St. ◢ Bish Au DL14 .. 148 B6
Hurworth Terr. Hur on T DL2 ... 235 A8
Hustledown Gdns. Stanl DH9 ...... 17 E4
Hustledown Rd. Stanl DH9 ...... 17 E4
Hutchinson Ave. Cons DH8 ...... 14 F3
Hutchinson St. Bish Au DL14 ...... 148 B7
Hutchinson Wlk. New Ay DL5 ...... 171 F8
Hutone Pl. Hartle TS24 ...... 111 E4
Hutton Ave. Darl DL1 ...... 209 C5
Hutton Cl. Bish Au DL14 ...... 148 C4
Hutton Cl. H le Sp DH4 ...... 38 C8
Hutton Cl. Wash NE38 ...... 9 F5
Hutton Cres. Hut Hen TS27 ...... 109 C5
Hutton Henry C of E Sch (Jun &
 Inf). Hut Hen TS27 ...... 109 C5
Hutton Pl. New Ay DL5 ...... 150 D1
Hutton Terr. Will DL15 ...... 101 F3
Huxley Gr. Darl DL1 ...... 224 C7
Hydenside Gr. Cons DH8 ...... 30 C8
Hylton Cl. Lang Pk DH7 ...... 56 B6
Hylton Cl. New Ay DL5 ...... 171 F8
Hylton Rd. Durham DH1 ...... 58 D6
Hylton Rd. Ferry DL17 ...... 129 B6
Hylton Terr. Pelton DH2 ...... 19 E7
Hylton Terr. Rook DL13 ...... 47 B2
Hylton Terr. Ryhope SR2 ...... 22 E6
Hysehope Terr. Cons DH8 ...... 15 A2

I'anson St. Darl DL3 ...... 208 F6
Ianson Sq. Darl DL3 ...... 209 A2
Ida Pl. New Ay DL5 ...... 150 C1
Idaho Gdns. Darl DL1 ...... 209 B6
Ilchester St. Seaham SR7 ...... 41 C6
Imperial Bldgs. 🆗 H le Sp DH4 ... 38 E8
Inchcape Terr. Peter SR8 ...... 63 F3
Industrial St. Pelton DH2 ...... 19 C6
Ingleby Moor Cres. Darl DL1 .. 224 D7

Inglesgarth Ct. Spenny DL16 ...... 127 E7
Ingleside. Whick NE16 ...... 2 F6
Ingleton C of E Controlled Sch.
 Ingle DL2 ...... 188 A6
Inglewood Cl. Darl DL1 ...... 209 B5
Ingram Cl. C le S DH2 ...... 20 A1
Inkerman St. By Gr DL16 ...... 102 E1
Institute St. Will DL15 ...... 102 A6
Institute Terr. Bear DH7 ...... 57 C3
Institute Terr. Billy R DL15 ...... 100 E7
Institute Terr. F T DL15 ...... 100 A1
Institute Terr. Newf DL14 ...... 126 B7
Institute Terr. Toro DL14 ...... 125 F2
Institute Terr. E Pelton DH2 ...... 19 F8
Institute Terr. Pelton DH2 ...... 19 F8
Insula Cotts. Bish Mi DL17 ...... 130 C4
Intake La. Frost DL13 ...... 96 A8
Inveraray St. Darl DL1 ...... 209 E7
Irene Terr. Lang Pk DH7 ...... 56 C6
Irestone La. St J Ch DL13 ...... 66 D2
Iris Cres. Ouston DH2 ...... 8 F2
Iris Terr. Bourn DH4 ...... 21 E3
Ironmasters Way. Still TS21 ...... 174 E4
Ironworks Rd. Tow Law DL13 ...... 75 B2
Irvin Ave. Bish Au DL14 ...... 148 A5
Isherwood Cl. New Ay DL5 ...... 171 D6
Isis Rd. Peter SR8 ...... 85 C5
Ivanhoe Terr. C le S DH3 ...... 20 C2
Ivanhoe Terr. Dipton DH9 ...... 5 E1
Ivesley Cotts. Esh W DH7 ...... 77 B6
Ivesley La. Esh W DH7 ...... 77 A7
Iveson St. Sacr DH7 ...... 35 C3
Iveston La. Ives DH8 ...... 16 A1
Iveston La. Cons DH8 ...... 15 B1
Iveston Terr. Stanl DH9 ...... 17 F7
Ivy Ave. Seaham SR7 ...... 41 B6
Ivy Cl. Spenny DL16 ...... 127 F7
Ivy Cres. Billy R DL15 ...... 100 D7
Ivy Gr. Hartle TS24 ...... 111 F1
Ivy Pl. Tant DH9 ...... 6 C3
Ivy Terr. Lang Pk DH7 ...... 56 C6
Ivy Terr. Stanl DH9 ...... 17 D4
Ivy Terr. The Mid DH9 ...... 18 B3
Ivyway. Pelton DH2 ...... 19 E7
Ivywood Ct. Darl DL3 ...... 208 E5

Jack Lawson Terr. Wh Hi DH6 ...... 83 E2
Jackson Pl. New Ay DL5 ...... 171 F7
Jackson St. Bish Au DL14 ...... 148 F5
Jackson St. Spenny DL16 ...... 127 F8
Jackson Terr. Eas SR8 ...... 63 A4
Jacques Terr. C le S DH2 ...... 20 B4
Jade Wlk. Chilt DL17 ...... 151 A8
James St. Ann Pl DH9 ...... 17 A4
James St. Bish Au DL14 ...... 148 B6
James St. Darl DL1 ...... 209 A4
James St. Dipton DH9 ...... 16 B7
James St. Eas SR8 ...... 63 D5
James St. Seaham SR7 ...... 41 D6
James St. Spenny DL16 ...... 127 F8
James St. Tanf L DH9 ...... 6 F1
James St N. Murton SR7 ...... 40 D3
James St S. Murton SR7 ...... 40 D3
James Terr. Bish Au DL14 ...... 148 E4
James Terr. E Lane DH5 ...... 61 B8
James Terr. Fence DH4 ...... 38 A8
James Terr. N Silk SR3 ...... 22 B7
Jameson St. ◨ Cons DH8 ...... 14 F3
Jamieson St. S Hett DH6 ...... 62 B6
Jane St. H le H DH5 ...... 39 A6
Jane St. Stanl DH9 ...... 17 D4
Jarvis Rd. Peter SR8 ...... 85 D8
Jasmine Ave. Shild DL4 ...... 149 A1
Jasmine Cres. Seaham SR7 ...... 41 C5
Jasmine Cres. Trim TS29 ...... 131 D8
Jasmine Terr. Birt DH3 ...... 9 D4
Jasper Ave. Seaham SR7 ...... 41 B6
Jaywood Cl. Hartle TS24 ...... 111 C4
Jedburgh Cl. Murton SR7 ...... 40 A2
Jedburgh Dr. Darl DL3 ...... 208 A5
Jenison Cl. New Ay DL5 ...... 170 F4
Jenkins Dr. Bish Au DL14 ...... 148 A4
Jesmond Cl. New Ay DL5 ...... 171 A8
Jesmond Gdns.
 Hartle TS24 & TS26 ...... 111 F1
Jesmond Rd. Darl DL1 ...... 209 E6
Job's Hill Bank. Crook DL15 ...... 101 A3
Jobson Terr. Stanl B DH6 ...... 100 F8
John Dixon La. Darl DL1 ...... 209 B2
John Dobbin Rd. Darl DL1 ...... 209 A3
John St. Bar Cas DL12 ...... 201 A6
John St. Bish Au DL14 ...... 148 F4
John St. Cons DH8 ...... 14 D4
John St. Cons DH8 ...... 14 F3
John St. Crag DH9 ...... 18 C2
John St. Darl DL1 ...... 209 A3
John St. Durham DH1 ...... 58 B1
John St. Eas SR8 ...... 63 E5
John St. Fence DH4 ...... 38 A4
John St. H le H DH5 ...... 39 A3
John St. H le Sp DH5 ...... 38 F8
John St. 🔢 Ryhope SR2 ...... 23 A6
John St. Shild DL4 ...... 148 F2
John St. Stanl DH9 ...... 17 D4
John St. Stanl DH9 ...... 18 D7
John St N. Brand DH7 ...... 79 D4
John St S. Brand DH7 ...... 79 D4
John Street Sq. ◨ Cons DH8 ...... 14 F2
John Terr. Bish Au DL14 ...... 148 E4
John Wilson Ct. Peter SR8 ...... 86 A7
Johnson Cl. Peter SR8 ...... 85 D8
Johnson Est. Thorn DH6 ...... 83 D4
Johnson St. Bish Au DL14 ...... 148 F4
Johnson Terr. Ann Pl DH9 ...... 17 A3
Johnson Terr. Leadg DH8 ...... 104 B7
Johnson's Bldgs. Cons DH8 ...... 15 E1
Johnson's St. Wing TS28 ...... 108 A6
Joicey Gdns. Stanl DH9 ...... 17 F7
Joicey Pl. New Ay DL5 ...... 171 F7

Joicey Terr. Tanf L DH9 ...... 17 D8
Jolby La. Cr on T DL2 & DL10 ...... 234 C8
Jolliffe St. C le S DH3 ...... 20 D1
Jones Rd. Hartle TS24 ...... 111 F2
Jones St. ◤ Birt DH3 ...... 9 C4
Joseph Hopper Aged Miners'
 Homes. Birt DH3 ...... 9 C7
Joseph Hopper Terr.
 Cornf DL17 ...... 105 E1
Joseph St. Stanl DH9 ...... 17 E5
Jowitt Rd. Hartle TS24 ...... 111 F2
Jowsey Pl. New Ay DL16 ...... 128 A3
Joyce Rd. Hartle TS24 ...... 111 E3
Joyce Terr. Esh W DH7 ...... 56 B2
Jubilee Ave. Seaham SR7 ...... 40 F6
Jubilee Cl. Edmon DH7 ...... 35 B7
Jubilee Cotts. Darl DL3 ...... 222 F8
Jubilee Cotts. H le Sp DH4 ...... 38 D8
Jubilee Cres. Shild DL4 ...... 149 B1
Jubilee Cres. S Hill DH6 ...... 60 D1
Jubilee House. E Lane DH5 ...... 39 C1
Jubilee Pl. H Shin DH1 ...... 80 F6
Jubilee Pl. Mid in T DL12 ...... 160 E7
Jubilee Pl. Shot Co DH6 ...... 84 C7
Jubilee Rd. Shild DL4 ...... 149 A1
Jubilee Sq. E Lane DH5 ...... 39 C1
Jubilee Sq. S Hett DH6 ...... 61 F7
Jubilee Terr. Toro DL14 ...... 125 F2
Jubilee Terr. Even DL14 ...... 167 D7
Jubilee Terr. Tant DH9 ...... 6 A2
Jubilee Terr. Will DL15 ...... 102 A2
Jude Pl. Peter SR8 ...... 85 C8
Jude St. Eas SR8 ...... 63 C4
Judith Cl. Heigh DL5 ...... 170 D1
June Ave. Win M NE21 ...... 2 C6
Jupiter Ct. Eas SR8 ...... 63 C4
Jura Dr. Darl DL1 ...... 209 D7
Jutland Terr. Tanf L DH9 ...... 17 D8

Kalafat. Bar Cas DL12 ...... 201 B6
Kate's Cl. Hunw DL15 ...... 125 E6
Kateregina. Birt DH3 ...... 9 D4
Katherine St. Darl DL1 ...... 209 A4
Katrine Cl. C le S DH2 ...... 20 B1
Katrine Ct. Silk SR3 ...... 22 A5
Katrine Wlk. Bish Au DL14 ...... 147 B1
Kay Gr. Darl DL1 ...... 209 C1
Kay St. Stanl DH9 ...... 17 F7
Keating Cl. B Coll TS27 ...... 86 D3
Keats Cl. Stanl DH9 ...... 18 A6
Keats Ct. Darl DL1 ...... 224 C8
Keats Rd. Shot Co DH6 ...... 84 D6
Keir Hardie Ave. Stanl DH9 ...... 17 F5
Keir Hardie Se. Fence DH4 ...... 38 B8
Keir Hardy Terr. Birt DH3 ...... 9 B6
Keld Rd. New Ay DL5 ...... 171 B7
Keldmere. Spenny DL16 ...... 103 E2
Kell Cres. S Hill DH6 ...... 60 C1
Kell Rd. Peter SR8 ...... 85 F6
Kell's Terr. Durham DH1 ...... 80 A8
Kell's Way. R Gill NE39 ...... 1 E1
Kellaw Rd. New Ay DL5 ...... 209 F1
Kellawe Pl. New Ay DL5 ...... 171 E7
Kellet Sq. Crook DL15 ...... 100 E4
Kelloe Cty Sch Jun Mix & Inf.
 Kelloe DH6 ...... 106 E5
Kelso Wlk. Darl DL3 ...... 208 A5
Kelton La. Mick DL12 ...... 179 F7
Kelvin Gdns. ◷ Cons DH8 ...... 14 F2
Kelvin St. Ferry DL17 ...... 128 E6
Kemble Gn. New Ay DL5 ...... 171 F7
Kemp Rd. Peter SR8 ...... 85 C7
Kempton Cl. Cons DH8 ...... 14 D7
Kempton Ct. Darl DL1 ...... 209 F4
Kenber Dr. B Coll TS27 ...... 86 D3
Kendal. Birt DH3 ...... 9 E2
Kendal Cl. Darl DL1 & DL3 ...... 223 E8
Kendal Cl. Pens DH4 ...... 85 A3
Kendrew Cl. New Ay DL5 ...... 171 D8
Kendrew St. Darl DL3 ...... 208 F2
Kenilworth. Gr Lum DH3 ...... 37 A8
Kenilworth Ave. Bish Au DL14 .. 147 F6
Kenilworth Cl. New Ay DL17 ...... 150 E1
Kenilworth Dr. Darl DL3 ...... 208 B5
Kenmir Ct. Spenny DL16 ...... 128 A8
Kenmir's Bldgs. Coxhoe DH6 ...... 105 F3
Kennel La. Darl DL1 ...... 209 D4
Kenny Pl. Durham DH1 ...... 58 F3
Kenny Wlk. New Ay DL5 ...... 171 F6
Kensington. 🔢 Bish Au DL14 .. 148 B6
Kensington Ct. Hartle TS24 ...... 111 F1
Kensington Gdns. Darl DL1 ...... 209 C1
Kensington Gdns. Ferry DL17 .. 128 F6
Kensington S. 🔟
 Bish Au DL14 ...... 148 B6
Kensington Terr. Cockf DL13 ...... 166 C5
Kensington Terr. Will DL15 ...... 101 F3
Kensington Villas. Will DL15 ...... 101 F3
Kent Gdns. H le H DH5 ...... 38 F4
Kent Rd. Cons DH8 ...... 30 B8
Kent St. Cound DL14 ...... 127 C1
Kent Terr. Hasw DH6 ...... 61 E1
Kent Wlk. Peter SR8 ...... 85 C8
Kentmere. Belm DH1 ...... 59 A3
Kentmere. Spenny DL16 ...... 103 E2
Kentmere Pl. Peter SR8 ...... 85 E6
Kepier Cres. Belm DH1 ...... 59 A3
Kepier Ct. Durham DH1 ...... 58 D2
Kepier Terr. ◢ Durham DH1 ...... 58 D2
Kerr Cres. Sedge TS21 ...... 153 A6
Kerryhill Dr. Durham DH1 ...... 58 C8
Kestrel Cl. Darl DL1 ...... 209 E1
Kestrel Ct. 🔢 Birt DH3 ...... 9 C4
Keswick Dr. Spenny DL16 ...... 104 B1
Keswick Rd. Peter SR8 ...... 85 C7
Keswick Rd. Stanl DH9 ...... 17 D4

Keswick Terr. S Hett DH6 ...... 61 E8
Ketton Ave. Darl DL3 ...... 209 A8
Ketton La. Braf DL1 & DL3 ...... 192 B3
Ketton Way. New Ay DL5 ...... 171 D2
Keverstone Bank. Staind DL2 .. 166 F1
Kew Rise. Darl DL3 ...... 208 B3
Kexwith Moor Cl. Darl DL1 ...... 223 D7
Kibblesworth Bank. Kibble NE11 .. 8 B6
Kibblesworth Cty Jun & Inf Sch.
 Kibble NE11 ...... 8 D6
Kidd Ave. Sherb DH6 ...... 59 F2
Kielder. Wash NE38 ...... 9 F4
Kielder Dr. Darl DL1 ...... 209 D6
Kielder Dr. Trim TS29 ...... 107 E3
Kielder Dr. Trim TS29 ...... 107 E4
Kier Hardie St. R Gill NE39 ...... 1 B2
Kilburn Cl. ◢ Ryhope SR2 ...... 23 A6
Kilburn Dr. Peter SR8 ...... 64 A1
Kilburn House. 🔟 Darl DL2 ...... 224 C8
Kilburn St. Shild DL4 ...... 170 A7
Kilchurn. Cons DH8 ...... 14 D3
Kildale Moor Pl. Darl DL1 ...... 224 D8
Kildale. Pens DH4 ...... 21 E8
Killhope Gr. Bish Au DL14 ...... 147 E5
Killhope Wheel (Mus).
 Killh DL13 ...... 43 D2
Killin Rd. Darl DL1 ...... 209 D6
Killinghall Row. M St G DL2 ...... 225 F8
Killinghall St. Darl DL1 ...... 209 B3
Kilmarnock Rd. Darl DL1 ...... 209 D7
Kiln Cres. Bish Mi DL17 ...... 130 B4
Kiln La. Ingle DL2 ...... 188 D5
Kiln La. Kill D5 ...... 188 C5
Kiln La. Lang DL2 ...... 187 F3
Kilnhill Wlk. Peter SR8 ...... 85 E6
Kimberley Gdns. The Mid DH9 .. 18 C3
Kimberley St. Bish Au DL14 ...... 148 F5
King Albert Pl. Cons DH8 ...... 100 F4
King Edward Rd. Seaham SR7 .. 41 D6
King Edward St. Shild DL4 ...... 149 A2
King Edward Terr. Tanf L DH9 .. 6 C1
King Edward VIII Terr.
 Stanl DH9 ...... 18 A8
King James I Sch.
 Bish Au DL14 ...... 148 C8
King James St. ◢ Spenny DL16 103 F1
King Oswy Dr.
 Hartle TS24 & TS27 ...... 111 E4
King St. Ann Pl DH9 ...... 16 F5
King St. Bar Cas DL12 ...... 201 A6
King St. Birt DH3 ...... 9 A4
King St. Darl DL2 ...... 208 F2
King St. Sherb DH6 ...... 59 F1
King St. Shot Co DH6 ...... 84 D6
King St. Cons DH8 ...... 14 D5
King's La. Pelton DH2 ...... 19 D7
King's Rd. Wing TS28 ...... 108 D8
King's Rd. Mid in T DL12 ...... 139 D1
King's Wlk. Mid in T DL12 ...... 139 D1
Kings Dr. New Ay DL5 ...... 171 C8
Kings Gr. Durham DH1 ...... 80 A6
Kings Lodge. Bish Au DL14 ...... 126 C1
Kingsley Cl. Stanl DH9 ...... 18 B7
Kingsley Dr. Crook DL15 ...... 100 C3
Kingsmead. Will DL15 ...... 102 B2
Kingsmere. C le S DH3 ...... 20 C7
Kingston Ave. Bear DH7 ...... 57 B3
Kingston St. Darl DL3 ...... 208 F3
Kingston Terr. Hasw DH6 ...... 61 E3
Kingsway. Bish Au DL14 ...... 148 C8
Kingsway. Darl DL1 ...... 209 B6
Kingsway. H le Sp DH5 ...... 38 F8
Kingsway. Lang Pk DH7 ...... 56 C6
Kingsway Villas. Pelton DH2 ...... 19 D7
Kinley Rd. Belm DH1 ...... 59 D5
Kinloch Ct. C le S DH2 ...... 20 B1
Kinnock Cl. Sherb DH6 ...... 60 A1
Kinross Cl. Birt DH3 ...... 9 D2
Kinross Dr. Stanl DH9 ...... 18 B6
Kintyre Cl. Darl DL1 ...... 209 E7
Kiphill Ct. Stanl DH9 ...... 18 A8
Kipling Cl. Stanl DH9 ...... 18 A6
Kipling's Terr. Durham DH1 ...... 79 F7
Kira Dr. Durham DH1 ...... 58 C8
Kirby Ave. Durham DH1 ...... 58 C8
Kirk Merrington Cty Jun Mix
 & Inf Sch. Kir Me DL16 ...... 128 A3
Kirk Rise. Frost DL13 ...... 96 B7
Kirk St. Cons DH8 ...... 14 E3
Kirk St. Still TS21 ...... 174 E3
Kirk View. Bar Cas DL12 ...... 201 B6
Kirkby Cl. Darl DL1 ...... 209 B3
Kirkby House. ◢ Darl DL2 ...... 224 C8
Kirkdale. Spenny DL16 ...... 103 E1
Kirkdale St. H le H DH5 ...... 38 F2
Kirkfield Gdns. Ann Pl DH9 ...... 16 E5
Kirkfield Rd. Darl DL3 ...... 209 A7
Kirkham Cl. New Ay DL17 ...... 150 D1
Kirkham Rd. Durham DH1 ...... 58 D6
Kirkham Way. Bish Au DL14 ...... 148 E6
Kirkland Hill. Peter SR8 ...... 85 E7
Kirklea Rd. H le Sp DH4 ...... 38 F8
Kirkstall Ct. Darl DL3 ...... 208 B4
Kirkstall Wlk. Bish Au DL14 ...... 147 D2
Kirkstone. Birt DH3 ...... 9 E2
Kirkstone Ave. Peter SR8 ...... 85 E6
Kirkstone Cl. Kir Me DL16 ...... 128 A3
Kirkstone Dr. Belm DH1 ...... 59 D5
Kirkstone Pl. New Ay DL5 ...... 171 B6

Kirkwall Cl. St on T TS21 ...... 195 F4
Kirkwood. Sacr DH7 ...... 35 B3
Kirtley Terr. Bish Mi DL17 ...... 130 C4
Kitchen Ave. Bish Au DL14 ...... 148 A5
Kitchener St. Darl DL3 ...... 208 F3
Kitchener Terr. Ferry DL17 ...... 129 A5
Kitching Gr. Eas SR8 ...... 62 F1
Kitson Cl. Lanch DH7 ...... 32 C5
Kittiwake Dr. Wash NE38 ...... 9 F3
Knaresborough Cl.
 Hartle TS17 ...... 111 D3
Knaresborough Rd. Murton SR7 40 C3
Knaresdale. Birt DH3 ...... 9 D1
Kneller Cl. Stanl DH9 ...... 17 F6
Knightsbridge Ave. Darl DL1 ...... 209 E6
Knitsley Gdns. Cons DH8 ...... 14 F1
Knitsley La. Cons DH8 ...... 30 F8
Knitsley La. Heal DH8 ...... 30 D4
Knitsley La. Satley DH8 ...... 31 B1
Knobbyends La. Blay NE21 ...... 1 F8
Knoll Ave. Darl DL3 ...... 223 D8
Knoulberry Rd. Wash NE37 ...... 9 F6
Kyo Heugh Rd. Ann Pl DH9 ...... 17 A6
Kyo La. Ann Pl DH9 ...... 17 B5
Kyo Rd. Ann Pl DH9 ...... 16 F5

L'Arbre Cres. Whick NE16 ...... 2 F7
Laburnum Pk. Brand DH7 ...... 78 F3
Laburnham Ct. Ush M DH7 ...... 57 B1
Laburnum Ave. Cons DH8 ...... 14 E4
Laburnum Ave. Crook DL15 ...... 100 D4
Laburnum Ave. Durham DH1 ...... 58 B1
Laburnum Cres. Eas SR8 ...... 63 C4
Laburnum Cres. Kibble NE11 ...... 8 C6
Laburnum Cres. Seaham SR7 ...... 41 C4
Laburnum Cres. Wing TS29 ...... 108 B5
Laburnum Cres. Sacr DH7 ...... 35 B3
Loburnum Gdns. Will DL15 ...... 102 C3
Laburnum Rd. Bish Au DL14 ...... 148 C7
Laburnum Rd. Chilt DL17 ...... 129 C2
Laburnum Rd. Cornf DL17 ...... 129 E8
Laburnum Rd. Darl DL1 ...... 209 B8
Laburnum Sq. Wing TS29 ...... 108 B5
Laburnum Terr. Ann Pl DH9 ...... 16 E5
Laburnum Terr. Shot Co DH6 ...... 84 C6
Ladock Cl. Sland SR2 ...... 23 A8
Lady Anne Rd. Sherb DH6 ...... 59 F2
Lady Kathryn Gr. Darl DL3 ...... 208 E4
Lady St. H le H DH5 ...... 39 A5
Lady's Piece La. H Pitt DH6 ...... 60 A5
Ladybower. ◤ New Ay DL5 ...... 171 A7
Ladyclose Croft. Staind DL2 ...... 186 C6
Ladyclose. Staind DL2 ...... 186 C6
Ladysmith Ct. Stanl DH9 ...... 18 A5
Ladysmith St. Bish Au DL14 ...... 148 B8
Ladywell. Hamst DL13 ...... 123 C2
Ladywell Rd. Cons DH8 ...... 31 C8
Ladywood Pk. Pens DH4 ...... 21 F8
Laing Sq. C le S DH3 ...... 20 D1
Laing St. Cons DH8 ...... 14 F4
Laing St. Darl DL3 ...... 208 D4
Lake Bank Terr. Hut Hen TS28 .. 108 E6
Lake Ct. Silk SR3 ...... 22 A6
Lake Rd. H le Sp DH5 ...... 38 E8
Lake View. Hut Hen TS28 ...... 108 E6
Lakeside. Darl DL1 ...... 223 F7
Lamb Cl. New Ay DL5 ...... 171 E8
Lamb's Pl. Bowb DH6 ...... 105 D8
Lamberd Rd. Hartle TS24 ...... 111 F3
Lambert Cl. Darl DL3 ...... 209 A7
Lambert Rd. Wash NE37 ...... 9 F7
Lambourne Cl. Bourn DH4 ...... 21 E3
Lambton Ave. Cons DH8 ...... 31 B8
Lambton Cl. New Ay DL5 ...... 171 D5
Lambton Cres. Sedge TS21 ...... 153 A6
Lambton Ct. Peter SR8 ...... 85 C3
Lambton Ct. Wash DH3 & NE38 .. 20 E8
Lambton Dr. Bish Au DL14 ...... 148 A6
Lambton Dr. H le H DH5 ...... 39 A1
Lambton Gdns. Burnop NE16 ...... 5 E5
Lambton Rd. Ferry DL17 ...... 129 B5
Lambton St. C le S DH3 ...... 20 D2
Lambton St. Darl DL1 ...... 209 A3
Lambton St. ◢ Durham DH1 ...... 58 B2
Lambton St. Shild DL4 ...... 148 E1
Lambton Terr. Crag DH9 ...... 18 D2
Lambton Terr. Pens DH4 ...... 21 F8
Lammermuir St. ◷ Darl DL1 ...... 209 C6
Lanark Terr. Ferry DL17 ...... 129 A4
Lancashire Dr. Belm DH1 ...... 59 D3
Lancaster Cl. Bish Au DL14 ...... 147 E6
Lancaster Hill. Peter SR8 ...... 85 B8
Lancaster Rd. Cons DH8 ...... 30 A7
Lancaster Terr. C le S DH3 ...... 20 D2
Lanchester Rd.
 M Law DH7 & DH9 ...... 33 A8
Landreth Gr. Trim TS29 ...... 107 E1
Lands Rd. Butter DL13 ...... 166 B8
Landsdowne Comp Sch.
 Coxhoe DH8 ...... 105 F3
Landsdowne Cres. Bowb DH6 .. 105 E8
Landsdowne Rd. Coxhoe DH6 .. 105 F4
Landseer Cl. Stanl DH9 ...... 17 F6
Landswood Terr. Win M NE21 ...... 2 F7
Lane Head. Copley DL13 ...... 165 A8
Lane The. Sedge TS21 ...... 153 B7
Lanehead La. Hut Ma DL11 ...... 220 B3
Lanehill. St J Ch DL13 ...... 66 E2
Lanethorpe Cres. Darl DL1 ...... 224 D8
Lanethorpe Rd. Darl DL1 ...... 224 D8
Langdale. Birt DH3 ...... 9 E1
Langdale Ave. Crook DL15 ...... 100 F3
Langdale Cl. Leadg DH8 ...... 15 D4
Langdale Cres. Belm DH1 ...... 59 C5
Langdale Cres. Blay NE21 ...... 2 B8
Langdale Oval. Trim TS29 ...... 108 A4
Langdale Pl. New Ay DL5 ...... 171 A6
Langdale Pl. Peter SR8 ...... 85 E6
Langdale Rd. Darl DL1 ...... 224 B8
Langdale St. H le H DH5 ...... 39 A2

Langdale Terr. Hams NE17 .... 4 A5
Langdale Way. Lang Pk DH7 ...... 56 D6
Langdale Wlk. Bish Au DL14 .... 147 F4
Langdon Gdns. Ann Pl DH9 .... 16 E5
Langholm Cres. Darl DL3 .... 208 E1
Langhurst. Sland SR2 .... 22 E8
Langley Ave. Burnh DH7 .... 33 D4
Langley Cres. Brand DH7 .... 79 D5
Langley Dr. Spenny DL16 .... 128 A8
Langley Garth. Staind DL2 .... 186 F5
Langley Gr. Bish Au DL14 .... 148 A6
Langley La. Lang Pk DH7 .... 34 B2
Langley Moor Ind Est.
   Brand DH7 .... 79 E5
Langley Moor Jun & Inf Sch.
   Brand DH7 .... 79 E6
Langley Park Cty Inf Sch.
   Lang Pk DH7 .... 56 C7
Langley Park Sch. Lang Pk DH7 . 56 C6
Langley Rd. Durham DH1 .... 58 C6
Langley Rd. New Ay DL5 .... 171 E7
Langley St. Lang Pk DH7 .... 56 C7
Langley Terr. Ann Pl DH9 .... 17 A4
Langley Terr. Burnh DH7 .... 33 D5
Langley View. Stanl DH9 .... 17 C3
Langleydale CE Controlled Sch.
   Kinn DL12 .... 164 C1
Langmere. Spenny DL16 .... 103 E2
Langton. Lang DL2 .... 188 A3
Langton Lea. H Shin DH1 .... 81 C5
Langton Terr. Bourn DH4 .... 21 E2
Langton Wlk. [11] Darl DL2 ...... 224 C8
Lanivet Cl. [4] Sland SR2 .... 22 F8
Lansbury Cl. 9 B6
Lansbury Dr. Birt DH3 .... 9 B5
Lansbury Dr. Murton SR7 .... 40 C3
Lansdown Way. Will DL15 ...... 101 E1
Lansdowne. Sland SR2 .... 22 E7
Lansdowne Cl. Darl DL3 .... 209 A5
Lapwing Cl. Wash NE38 .... 9 F3
Lapwing Ct. Burnop NE16 .... 6 C5
Larch Ave. [2] H le Sp DH4 .... 38 C8
Larch Ave. Shild DL4 .... 149 B1
Larch St. Cons DH8 .... 14 F3
Larch Terr. Tant DH9 .... 6 A1
Larch Terr. The Mid DH9 .... 18 B3
Larches Rd. Durham DH1 .... 58 A3
Larches The. Burnop NE16 .... 6 A7
Larches The. Esh W DH7 .... 77 D8
Larchfield Gdns. Crook DL15 ... 100 D4
Larchfield House. [13]
   Darl DL3 .... 208 F1
Larchfield St. Darl DL3 .... 208 F1
Larkspur Cl. Tanf L DH9 .... 17 D8
Larkspur Dr. Darl DL1 .... 209 C2
Lartington Cl. Gr Lum DH3 .... 37 B6
Lartington Green La.
   Lart DL12 .... 199 D8
Lartington La. Lart DL12 .... 200 C7
Larwood Ct. Ann Pl DH9 .... 16 E3
Lascelles Ave. New Ay DL5 ..... 171 A8
Latimer Rd. Darl DL1 .... 209 D5
Laude Bank. Esh DH7 .... 55 D4
Launceston. Gr Lum DH3 .... 37 A7
Laura St. Seaham SR7 .... 41 D6
Laurel Ave. Durham DH1 .... 59 A1
Laurel Ave. Seaham SR7 .... 41 B7
Laurel Avenue Cty Inf Sch.
   Durham DH1 .... 59 A1
Laurel Avenue Cty Jun Sch.
   Durham DH1 .... 58 F1
Laurel Cres. Beam DH9 .... 19 B7
Laurel Cres. Thorn DH6 .... 83 C3
Laurel Cres. Trim TS29 .... 107 F5
Laurel Ct. C le S DH2 .... 20 B5
Laurel Ct. Shild DL4 .... 170 B8
Laurel Dr. Leadg DH8 .... 15 D3
Laurel Gdns. Crook DL15 .... 100 D4
Laurel Rd. Chilt DL17 .... 129 C2
Laurel St. Darl DL3 .... 208 E3
Laurel Terr. Burnop NE16 .... 5 F6
Laurel Terr. Sadb DL2 .... 210 E6
Lauren Ct. Eas SR8 .... 63 C4
Lauriston Cl. Darl DL3 .... 208 A1
Lavender Gdns. Sacr DH7 .... 35 D3
Laverick Terr. Ann Pl DH9 .... 17 A3
Lavers Rd. Birt DH3 .... 9 C5
Lawnhead Sq. Silk SR3 .... 22 B6
Lawns The. E Lane DH5 .... 39 C1
Lawns The. Seaham SR7 .... 41 A6
Lawnswood. H le Sp DH5 .... 38 F7
Lawrence St. Darl DL1 .... 209 B1
Lawson Ct. [4] C le S DH2 .... 20 C2
Lawson Rd. Bowb DH6 .... 81 D1
Lawson Terr. Durham DH1 .... 58 B1
Lawson Terr. H le H DH5 .... 39 B1
Lawson's St. Trim TS29 .... 108 A4
Lax Terr. Crook DL15 .... 100 D3
Laxford. Birt DH3 .... 9 D2
Laxford St. Silk SR3 .... 22 A5
Layburn Pl. Peter SR8 .... 85 C7
Layton Ct. New Ay DL5 .... 150 D1
Lazenby Cl. Darl DL3 .... 208 B3
Lazenby Cres. Darl DL3 .... 208 B3
Lazenby Gr. Darl DL3 .... 208 B3
Lazenby Rd. Hartle TS24 .... 111 E4
Lea Gn. Birt DH3 .... 9 E1
Lea Gn. Wols DL13 .... 97 E7
Lea La. Eas SR8 .... 63 B6
Lea Riggs. W Rain DH4 .... 38 A2
Lea Side. Cons DH8 .... 31 B8
Leach Gr. Darl DL3 .... 208 C5
Lead La. Newl DH8 & NE43 .... 9 F3
Leadenhall St. Darl DL1 .... 209 A3
Leadgate Cty Inf Sch.
   Leadg DH8 .... 15 C3
Leadgate Cty Jun Sch.
   Leadg DH8 .... 15 D3
Leadgate Ind Est. Leadg DH8 ... 15 E2
Leadgate Rd. Cons DH8 .... 15 B4

Leadgate Rd. Leadg DH8 .... 15 B4
Leadgate Terr. Wols DL13 .... 98 A7
Leadpipe La. Coth DL12 .... 182 D4
Leafield Rd. Darl DL1 .... 224 A8
Leamside Cty Jun Sch.
   W Rain DH4 .... 37 F1
Leander Ave. C le S DH3 .... 20 D7
Leas The. Darl DL1 .... 209 A6
Leas The. Sedge TS21 .... 153 B5
Leases The. Bowb DH6 .... 105 D8
Leaside. New Ay DL5 .... 171 D4
Leaside N. New Ay DL5 .... 171 D4
Leatham. Sland SR2 .... 22 E8
Leazes Cl. Durham DH1 .... 58 D2
Leazes Hospl. Wols DL13 .... 97 D8
Leazes La. Bish Au DL14 .... 147 C3
Leazes La. Durham DH1 .... 58 E2
Leazes La. Wols DL13 .... 97 D7
Leazes Pl. Durham DH1 .... 58 D2
Leazes Rd. Durham DH1 .... 58 D2
Leazes Rise. Peter SR8 .... 85 F5
Leazes The. Burnop NE16 .... 5 F6
Leazes View. R Gill NE39 .... 1 D2
Leazes View. Wols DL13 .... 97 E7
Leazes Villas. Burnop NE16 .... 6 A6
Lee Gn. New Ay DL5 .... 171 D5
Lee Hill Ct. Lanch DH7 .... 32 E3
Lee Terr. Eas SR8 .... 63 C4
Lee Terr. H le H DH5 .... 39 B2
Lee Terr. Shot Co DH6 .... 84 C6
Leechmere Cres. Seaham SR7 ... 22 F1
Leechmere Ind Est. Sland SR2 ... 22 F8
Leechmere View. [5] Sland SR2 . 22 F8
Leechmere Way. Sland SR2 ...... 22 F8
Leeds La. Mordon DL1 & DL5 ... 172 E4
Leeholme. H le Sp DH5 .... 38 F7
Leeholme Ct. Ann Pl DH9 .... 17 A3
Leeholme Rd. Cound DL14 .... 149 D8
Leekworth Gdns. Mid in T DL12 160 E7
Leekworth La. Mid in T DL12 .... 160 F7
Leeman's La. Hett DH6 .... 104 F5
Lees St. Stanl DH9 .... 17 F7
Lees Wlk. Cound DL14 .... 149 C8
Leesfield Dr. Brand DH7 .... 79 C3
Leesfield Gdns. Brand DH7 .... 79 C3
Leesfield Rd. Brand DH7 .... 79 D3
Leicester Gr. Darl DL1 .... 209 E5
Leicester Wlk. Peter SR8 .... 85 C8
Leicestershire Dr. Belm DH1 ..... 59 D1
Leighton Terr. Birt DH3 .... 9 B5
Leith Gdns. Tanf L DH9 .... 6 D1
Leith Rd. Darl DL1 .... 208 B1
Lendings The. Start DL12 .... 201 A4
Lenin Terr. Chopw NE17 .... 4 C8
Lenin Terr. Stanl DH9 .... 17 F5
Leonard Ropner Dr.
   St on T TS21 .... 195 F3
Leonard St. Darl DL1 .... 224 B8
Leopold Pl. Bish Au DL14 .... 148 C7
Lerwick Cl. St on T TS21 .... 195 F3
Lesbury Cl. C le S DH2 .... 19 F1
Lesbury Terr. Chopw NE17 .... 4 B8
Leslie St. Bish Au DL14 .... 147 D2
Letch Ave. Haw SR7 .... 63 B8
Letch La. Carl TS19 & TS21 ..... 195 E8
Leuchars Ct. Birt DH3 .... 9 C3
Leven Ave. C le S DH2 .... 20 B1
Leven Rd. Bish Au DL14 .... 147 B1
Leven Wlk. Peter SR8 .... 85 C4
Levisham Cl. N Silk SR3 .... 22 C7
Lewes Rd. Darl DL1 .... 224 B8
Lewis Cl. Cr on T DL2 .... 234 F8
Lexington Ct. Brand DH7 .... 79 A2
Leybourne Hold. Birt DH3 .... 9 C6
Leyburn Cl. Urpeth DH2 .... 8 D1
Leyburn Pl. Birt DH3 .... 9 B6
Leyburn Rd. Darl DL1 .... 209 A6
Leyfield Cl. Burdon SR3 .... 22 B5
Leyland Cl. Bowb DH6 .... 81 E2
Liberty Terr. Tant DH9 .... 6 B2
Library Terr. Ann Pl DH9 .... 16 F4
Library Wlk. Ann Pl DH9 .... 16 F4
Lichfield Cl. Gr Lum DH3 .... 37 A6
Lichfield Rd. Cornf DL17 .... 129 F8
Lidcombe Cl. N Silk SR3 .... 22 C7
Liddell Cl. New Ay DL5 .... 171 F6
Liddle Ave. Sherb DH6 .... 59 F1
Liddle Cl. Peter SR8 .... 85 B8
Lidell Terr. Wh Hi DH6 .... 83 E1
Lightfoot Cres.
   Hartle TS24 & TS26 .... 111 F2
Lightfoot Rd. New Ay DL5 .... 171 C7
Lightfoot Terr. Ferry DL17 .... 128 E5
Lilac Ave. B Rocks TS27 .... 86 F2
Lilac Ave. Durham DH1 .... 58 B5
Lilac Ave. [10] H le Sp DH5 .... 38 E8
Lilac Ave. N Silk SR3 .... 22 B8
Lilac Ave. Sacr DH7 .... 35 C3
Lilac Ave. Sedge TS21 .... 153 B7
Lilac Cl. Carl TS21 .... 175 D1
Lilac Cres. Burnop NE16 .... 6 A6
Lilac Cres. Wing TS29 .... 108 B5
Lilac Ct. Shild DL4 .... 170 B8
Lilac Gdns. Beam DH9 .... 19 B7
Lilac Gdns. Crook DL15 .... 100 D3
Lilac Gr. C le S DH2 .... 20 A5
Lilac Gr. C le S DH2 .... 107 D1
Lilac Pk. Ush M DH7 .... 57 A1
Lilac Pl. Leadg DH8 .... 15 D3
Lilac Rd. Chilt DL17 .... 129 C2
Lilac Sq. Bourn DH4 .... 21 E3
Lilac Terr. Ann Pl DH9 .... 16 E5
Lilac Terr. Shot Co DH6 .... 84 C6
Lilac Way. Hi Eth DL14 .... 146 E5
Lilburn Cl. [9] Shild DL4 .... 148 F1
Lilburne Cres. New Ay DL5 ...... 171 D7
Lile Gdns. Sedge TS21 .... 153 B6

Lilian Ave. Sland SR2 .... 22 E8
Lilian Terr. [4] Lang Pk DH7 ...... 56 C6
Lilley Terr. R Gill NE39 .... 1 F3
Lilleycroft. R Gill NE39 .... 1 F2
Lillie Terr. Trim TS29 .... 107 F3
Lilwhite Terr. H le H DH5 .... 39 B1
Lime Ave. B Rocks TS27 .... 86 E3
Lime Ave. Darl DL1 .... 209 A8
Lime Ave. H le Sp DH4 .... 38 C8
Lime Gr. Bish Au DL14 .... 148 B4
Lime Gr. Darl DL4 .... 149 B1
Lime La. Mordon DL1 .... 172 C1
Lime La. New Ay DL5 .... 191 F8
Lime Pk. Brand DH7 .... 79 B4
Lime Rd. Ferry DL 17 .... 128 F6
Lime St. Stanl DH9 .... 17 C4
Lime Terr. Bish Au DL14 .... 148 F4
Limecragg Ave. Belm DH1 .... 59 B3
Limehurst Rd. Darl DL3 .... 208 E3
Limekiln La. E Lay DL11 .... 221 D1
Limes The. E Lane DH5 .... 39 D1
Linacre Cl. Peter SR8 .... 85 B5
Linacre Way. Darl DL1 .... 209 B6
Linburn. Wash NE38 .... 9 E8
Linburn Dr. Bish Au DL14 .... 147 F5
Lincoln Cl. N Silk SR3 .... 22 A8
Lincoln Cl. New Ay DL5 .... 171 C7
Lincoln Cres. H le H DH5 .... 38 F4
Lincoln Ct. Darl DL1 .... 209 E4
Lincoln Dr. Will DL15 .... 101 F2
Lincoln Pl. Cons DH8 .... 30 A7
Lincoln Rd. Cons DH8 .... 30 A7
Lincoln Rd. Durham DH1 .... 58 D7
Lincoln St. Cound DL14 .... 149 D8
Lincoln Wlk. Gr Lum DH3 .... 37 A7
Lincoln Wlk. Peter SR8 .... 85 C8
Lincolnshire Cl. Belm DH1 .... 59 C3
Linden Ave. Darl DL3 .... 223 D8
Linden Cl. Shild DL4 .... 170 B8
Linden Ct. Spenny DL16 .... 128 A8
Linden Dr. Darl DL3 .... 223 D8
Linden Gr. Coxhoe DH6 .... 105 F4
Linden Gr. H le Sp DH4 .... 38 C8
Linden Pk. Brand DH7 .... 79 B4
Linden Pl. New Ay DL5 .... 171 A6
Linden Rd. Bear DH7 .... 57 B3
Linden Rd. Bish Au DL14 .... 148 C6
Linden Rd. Cornf DL17 .... 129 E8
Linden Rd. Ferry DL17 .... 129 B5
Linden Terr. Coxhoe DH6 .... 105 F4
Linden Way. Cons DH8 .... 14 E4
Lindesfarne. H Shin DH1 .... 81 B5
Lindisfarne. Peter SR8 .... 85 D4
Lindisfarne Ave. C le S DH3 ...... 20 D3
Lindisfarne Cl. Bish Au DL14 ... 147 E6
Lindisfarne Cl. C le S DH2 .... 20 A1
Lindisfarne Cl. Hartle TS27 ..... 111 D3
Lindisfarne Rd. Durham DH1 ..... 58 D5
Lindom Ave. C le S DH3 .... 20 D3
Lindon Rd. Stanl DH9 .... 17 E5
Lindrick Dr. Hartle TS27 .... 111 C4
Lindsay St. Bish Au DL14 .... 148 B7
Lindsay St. H le H DH5 .... 39 B5
Lingard Wlk. New Ay DL5 .... 171 E5
Lingdale. Belm DH1 .... 59 D3
Lingey Cl. Sacr DH7 .... 35 B4
Lingfield Cl. Darl DL1 .... 209 F2
Lingfield Rd. Cons DH8 .... 14 E3
Lingfield Way. Darl DL1 .... 209 F1
Lingholme. C le S DH2 .... 20 A4
Lingmell Dene. Cound DL14 ..... 127 B1
Links The. Belm DH1 .... 59 D3
Linkway. Sacr DH7 .... 35 C3
Linley Hill. Whick NE16 .... 2 E4
Linskell. Sland SR2 .... 22 E8
Lintfort. C le S DH3 .... 20 E7
Linton Terr. Crook DL15 .... 100 F4
Lintz Green La.
   Burnop NE16 & NE39 .... 5 C6
Lintz La. Burnop NE16 .... 5 E4
Lintz Terr. Burnop NE16 .... 5 F6
Lintz Terr. Stanl DH9 .... 17 C5
Lintzford Gdns. R Gill NE39 .... 5 B8
Lintzford La. R Gill NE39 .... 1 B1
Lintzford Rd. H Mill NE39 .... 5 C7
Lintzford Rd. R Gill NE39 .... 5 C7
Linwood Gr. Darl DL1 .... 223 D7
Lishman Ave. Crook DL15 .... 100 C4
Lisle Rd. New Ay DL5 .... 171 A8
Lismore Dr. Darl DL1 .... 209 D7
Lister Cl. H le Sp DH5 .... 38 D6
Lister Rd. Peter SR8 .... 85 A8
Lister Terr. Crook DL15 .... 100 E5
Lister Terr E. Wols DL13 .... 97 F7
Litchfield Rd. Durham DH1 .... 58 D8
Little Eden. Peter SR8 .... 85 D7
Little Hutton La. Hut Ma DL11 .. 220 E2
Littlebeck Dr. Darl DL1 .... 209 C5
Littleburn Ind Est. Brand DH7 ... 79 F4
Littleburn La. Brand DH7 .... 79 E5
Littleburn Rd. Brand DH7 .... 79 E4
Littletown. H Pitt DH6 .... 60 D3
Livingstone St. [17] Cons DH8 ... 14 F3
Lloyd Ave. E Lane DH5 .... 38 C4
Lloyds Terr. [5] Lang Pk DH7 ..... 56 C6
Lobley Hill Rd. Brand DH7 .... 79 D4
Lobleyhill Rd. Byer NE16 .... 6 D8
Lobleyhill Rd. Sunn NE16 .... 6 D8
Local Ave. S Hill DH6 .... 60 C1
Lochfield Gdns. Kibble NE11 ...... 8 C5
Lock St. Darl DL3 .... 208 F6
Lockhaugh Rd. R Gill NE39 .... 2 A1
Lockyer Cl. New Ay DL5 .... 171 B8
Locomotive St. Darl DL1 .... 209 C6
Lodge Cl. H Mill NE39 .... 5 A5

Lodge La. Mordon DL1 & TS21 .. 172 E1
Lodge St. By Gr DL16 .... 102 E1
Lodge St. Darl DL1 .... 209 A2
Loefield. Gr Lum DH3 .... 37 A8
Logan St. H le H DH5 .... 39 A3
Logan St. Lang Pk DH7 .... 56 C7
Logan Terr. S Hett DH6 .... 61 E8
Lombard Dr. C le S DH3 .... 20 D7
Lomond Cl. [8] Silk SR3 .... 22 A6
Lomond Pl. C le S DH2 .... 20 B1
Lomond Wlk. Bish Au DL14 ...... 147 C1
Londonderry Ave. Durham DH1 .. 59 A1
Londonderry St. N Silk SR3 .... 22 A7
Londonderry St. Seaham SR7 .... 41 E6
Londonderry Terr. Eas SR8 .... 63 D5
Londonderry Terr. N Silk SR3 .... 22 B7
Long Acres. Durham DH1 .... 58 F3
Long Bank. Birt DH3 .... 9 C7
Long Bank. Dalton DL11 .... 233 F4
Long Burn Dr. C le S DH2 .... 19 F2
Long Close La. Gilm DL12 .... 216 A6
Long Close Rd. H Mill NE39 .... 4 F5
Long Cswy. Langth DL11 .... 228 B3
Long Edge. Burnh DH7 .... 34 C4
Long Edge. Sacr DH7 .... 34 C4
Long Gair. Blay NE21 .... 2 A8
Long Garth. Durham DH1 .... 57 F4
Long La. Cockf DL13 & DL2 ..... 166 E4
Long La. Newf DL14 .... 126 D7
Long Row. How le W DL15 .... 125 A6
Long Tens Way.
   New Ay DL3 & DL5 .... 171 C1
Longacre. H le Sp DH4 .... 38 C8
Longclose Bank.
   Medom DH8,DH9,NE17 & NE39 .. 4 E3
Longdale Dr. St J Ch DL13 .... 67 C1
Longdean Pk. C le S DH3 .... 20 D6
Longedge La. Heal DH7 & DH8 .. 31 C2
Longedge La. Lanch DH7 & DH8 31 C2
Longfellow Ct. Crook DL15 ...... 100 C2
Longfellow St. H le Sp DH5 .... 38 E7
Longfield Comp Sch. Darl DL3 . 208 F7
Longfield Rd. Bish Au DL14 ..... 148 D5
Longfield Rd. Darl DL3 .... 208 F6
Longfield Stad. Darl DL3 .... 208 F7
Longhorn Ends. Cows DL13 .... 66 D6
Longlands Dr. H le Sp DH5 .... 38 E7
Longnewton St. Seaham SR7 .... 41 D5
Longshank Cl. Kibble DH3 .... 9 A6
Longslade Ave. Trim TS29 .... 107 E4
Lonsdale. Birt DH3 .... 9 E1
Loop La. Butter DL13 .... 144 F2
Loraine Cres. Darl DL1 .... 223 F7
Loralne Wlk. [1] New Ay DL5 ... 171 C8
Lord Byrons Wlk. Seaham SR7 ... 23 B1
Lord Hyndley Terr.
   Copley DL13 .... 165 A8
Lord Neville Dr. New Ay DL5 .... 170 F4
Lord St. N Silk SR3 .... 22 B7
Lord St. Seaham SR7 .... 41 D7
Lorimers Cl. Peter SR8 .... 85 B4
Lorn Wlk. Darl DL1 .... 209 D7
Lorne St. E Lane DH5 .... 61 B8
Lorne Terr. Cound DL14 .... 149 C8
Lothian Cl. Birt DH3 .... 9 D1
Lothian Cl. Spenny DL16 .... 127 E7
Loud Terr. Ann Pl DH9 .... 16 D4
Loud View Terr. Ann Pl DH9 .... 16 E3
Louisa Ctr The. Stanl DH9 .... 17 E6
Louisa St. Darl DL1 .... 209 B1
Louisa Terr. Bish Au DL14 .... 147 E3
Louisa Terr. Stanl DH9 .... 17 E6
Louisa Terr. Wit Gil DH7 .... 57 B8
Louise Terr. C le S DH3 .... 20 C3
Louvain Terr. Crook DL15 .... 100 D3
Louvain Terr. H le H DH5 .... 39 A5
Louvain Terr W. H le H DH5 .... 39 A5
Lovaine St. Pelton DH2 .... 19 C6
Lovaine Terr. [8] Ferry DL17 .... 129 B5
Low Albert Terr. Billy R DL15 .. 100 D7
Low Bowes Cl. Even DL14 .... 146 B1
Low Chare. C le S DH3 .... 20 D3
Low Church St. Ann Pl DH9 .... 16 F5
Low Dowfold. Crook DL15 .... 101 A5
Low Downs Rd. H le H DH5 .... 39 A6
Low Dyke St. Trim TS29 .... 108 A4
Low Etherley. Hi Eth DL14 ...... 146 F6
Low Flatts Rd. C le S DH2 & DH30 20 C6
Low Gn. Gain DL2 .... 205 A6
Low Gn. H Shin DH1 .... 80 F6
Low Gn. New Ay DL1/ 150 E2
Low Graham St. Sacr DH7 .... 35 C3
Low Grange Rd. Spenny DL16 .. 104 A1
Low Greenfields. Bish Au DL14 147 B4
Low Hogg St. Trim TS29 .... 108 A4
Low La. Barn DL11 .... 218 E2
Low La. Newsh DL11 .... 220 A1
Low La. Wit le W DL14 & DL15 .. 124 D7
Low Melbourne St.
   Bish Au DL14 .... 148 B5
Low Mill. Bar Cas DL12 .... 201 A5
Low Moor Cotts. Durham DH1 ... 36 D1
Low Moor Rd. Lanch DH7 .... 55 E6
Low Moor Rd. Lang Pk DH7 .... 56 B6
Low Queen St. With Pk DL14 ... 125 A1
Low Rd. Bowes DL12 .... 216 B2
Low Rd. Cound DL14 .... 127 C3
Low Rd. Eas SR8 .... 63 B3
Low Rd. Gain DL2 .... 204 F6
Low Rd. H Shin DH1 .... 80 F6
Low Redgate Bank. Wols DL13 .. 97 B5
Low Side. Mick DL12 .... 161 C4
Low Startforth Rd. Start DL12 .. 200 F5
Low Station Rd. W Rain DH4 ..... 37 E2
Low West Ave. R Gill NE39 .... 1 D1
Low Willington. Will DL15 .... 102 B2
Lowdale La. Hartle TS24 .... 111 D4
Lowe St. Darl DL3 .... 208 F2

Lowe's Barn Bank. Durham DH1 . 80 A7
Lower Bridge St. Bish Au DL14 . 126 B1
Lowery La. Crag DH7 & DH9 ...... 18 D1
Lowery Rd. New Ay DL5 .... 171 C5
Lowes Ct. Durham DH1 .... 80 A8
Lowes Fall. Durham DH1 .... 80 A8
Lowes Rise. Durham DH1 .... 80 A8
Loweswater Ave. C le S DH3 ...... 20 B1
Loweswater Ave. E Lane DH5 ..... 61 C8
Lowfields. New Ay DL5 .... 170 F4
Lowhills Rd. Peter SR8 .... 85 B8
Lowick Cl. Birt DH3 .... 9 D1
Lowland Rd. Silk SR3 .... 22 A5
Lowland Rd. Brand DH7 .... 79 B4
Lowmoor Rd. Darl DL1 .... 224 D7
Lowson St. Darl DL3 .... 209 A7
Lowson St. Still TS21 .... 174 F4
Lowther Ave. C le S DH2 .... 20 B2
Lowther Cl. Peter SR8 .... 85 D7
Lowther Ct. Peter SR8 .... 85 B2
Lowther Dr. New Ay DL17 .... 150 E1
Lowther Rd. Bish Au DL14 .... 148 A4
Lucknow St. Darl DL1 .... 209 B4
Lucy St. C le S DH3 .... 20 C4
Ludworth Cty Sch. Ludw DH6 .... 83 B7
Luke Ave. Cassop DH6 .... 82 E1
Luke Cres. Murton SR7 .... 40 B3
Luke St. Wing TS29 .... 107 F5
Luke Terr. Wh Hi DH6 .... 83 E2
Lulworth Gr. Hartle TS24 .... 111 D4
Lumley Cl. C le S DH2 .... 20 B3
Lumley Cl. New Ay DL5 .... 171 D6
Lumley Cres. Ferry DL17 .... 129 B5
Lumley Cty Jun Sch.
   Gr Lum DH3 .... 37 B7
Lumley Dr. Cons DH8 .... 31 C8
Lumley Dr. Peter SR8 .... 85 D3
Lumley Gdns. Burnop NE16 .... 5 E5
Lumley Gr. Bish Au DL14 .... 148 A6
Lumley Medway Cty Inf Sch.
   Gr Lum DH3 .... 37 A8
Lumley New Rd.
   Gr Lum DH3 & DH4 .... 21 C1
Lumley Rd. Durham DH1 .... 58 C7
Lumley Terr. C le S DH3 .... 20 C2
Lumley Terr. Coxhoe DH6 .... 105 F3
Lumley Terr. [1] Ryhope SR2 ..... 22 F6
Lumsden Sq. Murton SR7 .... 40 C3
Lumsden Terr. Ann Pl DH9 .... 16 E5
Lund Ave. Durham DH1 .... 58 B6
Lund's La. Ives DH8 .... 16 A1
Lunedale Dr. Gr Lum DH3 .... 37 B6
Lunedale Rd. Darl DL1 .... 208 B3
Lunesdale St. H le H DH5 .... 39 A2
Lusby Cres. Bish Au DL14 .... 147 F4
Lutterington La. Bolam DL14 ... 168 D6
Luttryngton Ct. New Ay DL5 .... 171 A8
Luxmoore Ave. Will DL15 .... 101 F3
Lych Gate. Hur on T DL2 .... 224 D1
Lydford Way. Birt DH3 .... 9 D3
Lydgate Ave. Wols DL13 .... 97 F8
Lydgate La. Wols DL13 .... 97 F8
Lydgate La. Wols DL13 .... 98 A7
Lydia St. Will DL15 .... 101 F3
Lydia Terr. Newf DL14 .... 126 B8
Lynden Rd. [6] Sland SR2 .... 22 F8
Lyndhurst Ave. C le S DH3 .... 20 C6
Lyndhurst Cl. Blay NE21 .... 2 A8
Lyndhurst Dr. Darl DL1 .... 58 A1
Lyndhurst Rd. Chilt DL17 .... 150 F7
Lyndhurst Rd. Stanl DH9 .... 17 D6
Lyne Cl. Pelton DH2 .... 19 C8
Lyne Rd. Spenny DL16 .... 127 D6
Lyne's Dr. Brand DH7 .... 79 D5
Lyngrove. Sland SR2 .... 22 F8
Lynn Cres. Cassop DH6 .... 82 E1
Lynn Park Cres. Coxhoe DH6 .... 105 F3
Lynn St. C le S DH3 .... 20 C2
Lynn Terr. Wh Hi DH6 .... 84 A4
Lynndale. Wols DL13 .... 98 A7
Lynne Cl. Darl DL3 .... 209 A7
Lynthorpe. Sland SR2 .... 22 F8
Lynton Gdns. Darl DL1 .... 209 D1
Lyon Wlk. New Ay DL5 .... 171 D6
Lyonette Rd. Darl DL1 .... 209 D6
Lyons Ave. H le H DH5 .... 39 B2
Lyons La. H le H DH5 .... 39 C1
Lyster Cl. Seaham SR7 .... 22 E1
Lytham Rd. Darl DL1 .... 209 D7

Maben Ave. Bish Au DL14 .... 147 D3
Mackenzie Pl. New Ay DL5 ...... 171 C8
Macmillan Ave. New Ay DL5 .... 171 C7
Maddison St. Shild DL4 .... 169 F8
Mafeking Pl. Shild DL4 .... 149 A1
Mafeking Terr. Shild DL4 .... 35 B2
Magdalene Ave. Belm DH1 .... 59 D4
Magdalene Ct. [2] Durham DH1 .. 58 E2
Magdalene Dr. Hart TS27 .... 110 F3
Magdalene Hts. [1] Durham DH1 58 E2
Magdalene St. Durham DH1 .... 58 E2
Magdalene Terr. [7] Ferry DL17 129 B5
Maglona St. Seaham SR7 .... 41 D6
Magnet St. [5] Shild DL4 .... 170 A8
Magnolia Way. Shild DL4 .... 149 B1
Mahogany Row. Beam DH9 .... 7 D1
Maiden Castle. Durham DH1 ...... 80 E8
Maiden Law. Fence DH7 .... 38 A7
Maiden Law Hospl. M Law DH7 . 32 F6
Main Rd. Gain DL2 .... 205 A6
Main Rd. Heigh DL5 .... 170 C3
Main St. Bish Au DL14 .... 148 D5
Main St. Cons DH8 .... 15 B2
Main St. Ferry DL17 .... 128 F6
Main St. Shild DL4 .... 148 F1
Main St. Wit Pk DL14 .... 147 B8

Mains Ct. Durham DH1 .... 58 A5
Mains Park Rd. C le S DH3 .... 20 D3
Mainsforth Front Row.
　Ferry DL17 .... 129 C3
Mainsforth Rd. Ferry DL17 ...... 129 D4
Mainside. Redmar TS21 .... 195 B7
Major St. Darl DL3 .... 208 E4
Malcolm Ave. Qua Hi DH6 .... 106 D7
Malcolm St. 5 Seaham SR7 ..... 41 D6
Malham Cres. New Ay DL5 .... 171 C7
Malim Rd. Darl DL1 .... 209 E1
Mallard Cl. Wash NE38 .... 9 F4
Mallard Rd. Darl DL1 .... 209 E1
Mallory Ct. Darl DL1 .... 209 E4
Malone Gdns. Birt DH3 .... 9 D6
Malt Cres. Peter SR8 .... 85 F7
Maltby Cl. Bish Au DL14 .... 148 E6
Maltings The. N Silk SR3 .... 22 C7
Maltkiln La. New Ay DL5 .... 171 E2
Malton Terr. Sedge TS21 .... 153 B6
Malvern. Chilt DL17 .... 151 A8
Malvern Ave. C le S DH2 .... 20 B2
Malvern Cl. Peter SR8 .... 85 B5
Malvern Cres. Darl DL3 .... 207 F5
Malvern Cres. Seaham SR7 ...... 41 A7
Malvern Cres. Wing TS29 .... 108 A5
Malvern Terr. Stanl DH9 .... 18 A5
Malvern Villas. Durham DH1 .... 58 F2
Malvern Way. New Ay DL5 .... 170 F7
Malvern Wlk. Cound DL14 .... 149 C8
Mandela Cl. Stanl DH9 .... 17 D5
Manfield House. 6 Darl DL2 .... 224 C8
Manisty Terr. Eas SR8 .... 63 D4
Mann Cres. Murton SR7 .... 40 D4
Manor Cl. Elwick TS27 .... 134 D5
Manor Cl. Trim TS29 .... 131 D8
Manor Cl The. H Shin DH1 .... 81 A6
Manor Cotts. Ingle DL2 .... 188 A6
Manor Cotts. Thor Th TS21 ...... 175 E3
Manor Ct. Even DL14 .... 167 D6
Manor Ct. Ferry DL17 .... 129 A6
Manor Ct. Heigh DL5 .... 170 E1
Manor Ct. Lanch DH7 .... 33 A2
Manor Dr. Ann Pl DH9 .... 16 F5
Manor Dr. Still TS21 .... 174 F3
Manor Field. Dalt P TS27 .... 134 E3
Manor Gr. Cockf DL13 .... 166 D5
Manor Grange. Lanch DH7 ...... 33 A3
Manor Hall Cl. Seaham SR7 ..... 40 E8
Manor House Est.
　Hut Hen TS27 .... 109 C5
Manor House Est.
　Hut Hen TS27 .... 109 D6
Manor Rd. Bish Au DL14 .... 147 D2
Manor Rd. Darl DL3 .... 223 E8
Manor Rd. Hur on T DL2 .... 224 A1
Manor Rd. Ingle DL2 .... 188 A6
Manor Rd. Medom DH8 .... 4 C1
Manor Rd. Stanl DH9 .... 17 F7
Manor Rd. Will DL15 .... 102 B3
Manor St. Even DL14 .... 167 D6
Manor Terr. Win M NE21 .... 2 C7
Manor View. 3 Ferry DL17 ...... 129 A6
Manor View. H Pitt DH6 .... 60 B4
Manor Way. Peter SR8 .... 85 E5
Manor Wlk. Still TS21 .... 174 F3
Manorfields. Hur on T DL2 ...... 224 D1
Manse St. Cons DH8 .... 14 E4
Mansell Cres. Peter SR8 .... 85 E7
Maple Ave. Durham DH1 .... 59 A2
Maple Ave. N Silk SR3 .... 22 B8
Maple Ave. Shild DL4 .... 149 B1
Maple Cl. Will DL15 .... 101 E2
Maple Cres. Crook DL15 .... 100 D4
Maple Cres. Seaham SR7 .... 41 C4
Maple Ct. Brand DH7 .... 78 F3
Maple Ct. Hi Eth DL14 .... 146 E5
Maple Gdns. Cons DH8 .... 14 C4
Maple Gr. Cornf DL17 .... 105 E1
Maple Gr. Stanl DH9 .... 17 D4
Maple Grove. Sedge TS21 .... 153 B7
Maple Pk. Ush M DH7 .... 57 B1
Maple Rd. Darl DL1 .... 209 B8
Maple St. 18 Cons DH8 .... 14 F3
Maple St. Stanl DH9 .... 17 D4
Maple Terr. Ann Pl DH9 .... 16 E5
Maple Terr. Burnop NE16 .... 5 F6
Maplewood. C le S DH2 .... 20 B4
Maplewood St. Gr Lum DH4 .... 21 E1
Marcia Ave. Shot Co DH6 .... 84 C7
Mardale St. H le H DH5 .... 39 A2
Margaret Ct. Bowb DH6 .... 81 D1
Margaret St. Ludw DH6 .... 83 C7
Margaret St. 7 Seaham SR7 .... 41 D6
Margaret Terr. Bish Au DL14 ... 148 E4
Margaret Terr. R Gill NE39 ...... 1 C1
Margaret Terr. Tanf L DH9 ...... 6 C1
Margaret Terr. Wing TS29 .... 108 A5
Margate St. N Silk SR3 .... 22 A8
Margery La. Durham DH1 .... 58 B1
Maria St. N Silk SR3 .... 22 A7
Maria St. 8 Seaham SR7 .... 41 D7
Marigold Cres. Bourn DH4 ...... 21 E3
Marigold Ct. Darl DL1 .... 209 C2
Marina Rd. Darl DL1 .... 209 A8
Marina Terr. 8 Ryhope SR2 .... 22 F4
Marine Cres. B Rocks TS27 ..... 86 F2
Marine Dr. Sland SR2 .... 23 A8
Maritime Cres. Peter SR8 .... 63 D4
Mariville E. Ryhope SR2 .... 23 A5
Mariville W. Ryhope SR2 .... 23 A5
Mark Rise. H le H DH5 .... 39 A5
Mark's La. W Rain DH4 .... 37 F4
Market Cres. Hut Hen TS28 ..... 108 E6
Market Pl. Bar Cas DL12 .... 201 A5
Market Pl. Bish Au DL14 .... 126 C1
Market Pl. 8 Darl DL1 .... 208 F1
Market Pl. 4 Durham DH1 ...... 58 C2
Market Pl. Esh W DH7 .... 77 E8
Market Pl. H le Sp DH5 .... 38 F8
Market Pl. Mid in T DL12 .... 160 D8
Market Pl. Shild DL4 .... 149 A2
Market St. Cons DH8 .... 14 D4
Market St. Ferry DL17 .... 128 F6
Market St. H le H DH5 .... 39 B4
Markham Pl. New Ay DL5 .... 171 F7
Markington Dr. Ryhope SR2 .... 22 F6
Markle Gr. E Rain DH5 .... 38 D5
Marlborough. 1 Seaham SR7 .. 41 D7
Marlborough Ct. Darl DL1 .... 223 E8
Marlborough Ct. H le Sp DH5 .. 38 E6
Marlbrough Cres. 8
　Peter SR8 .... 86 B6
Marlene Ave. Bowb DH6 .... 81 D2
Marley Hill Cty Jun & Inf Sch.
　Sunn NE16 .... 7 A8
Marley Rd. New Ay DL5 .... 171 D6
Marley Way. Hartle TS27 .... 111 D3
Marley Wlk. Hartle TS27 .... 111 D3
Marley's Cotts. Quebec DH7 ... 55 B4
Marlow Way. Whick NE16 .... 2 F5
Marlowe Pl. H le Sp DH5 .... 38 F7
Marmaduke St. Spenny DL16 .. 104 A1
Marrick Ave. Darl DL3 .... 207 F5
Marrick Cl. 2 New Ay DL5 ...... 171 B7
Marsden Cl. H le Sp DH4 .... 38 C8
Marsden Wlk. Darl DL3 .... 208 F7
Marshall St. Hartle TS24 .... 111 E3
Marshall Rd. New Ay DL5 .... 171 C7
Marshall St. Bar Cas DL12 .... 201 A6
Marshall St. Darl DL3 .... 208 F3
Marshall Terr. Belm DH1 .... 59 A2
Marske Gr. Darl DL3 .... 208 F5
Marson Ave. Crook DL15 .... 100 E2
Marston Moor Rd. Darl DL1 .... 224 E8
Marston Wlk. Whick NE16 ...... 2 F5
Martin Ave. Tant DH9 .... 6 B2
Martin Ct. Wash NE38 .... 9 F2
Martindale Cl. Elwick TS27 ..... 134 D6
Martindale Pk. H le Sp DH5 ..... 38 E8
Martindale Rd. Darl DL5 .... 209 C5
Marwood Cres. Darl DL3 .... 208 D5
Marwood Dr. Bar Cas DL12 ..... 201 A7
Marwood Gr. Peter SR8 .... 85 C3
Marwood Terr. Coth DL12 .... 182 E3
Marwood Wlk. Coth DL12 .... 182 E3
Marx Cres. Stanl DH9 .... 17 F5
Marx Terr. Chopw NE17 .... 4 C8
Mary Ave. Birt DH3 .... 9 B6
Mary Cres. Kelloe DH6 .... 106 E6
Mary Ct. Darl DL3 .... 208 B4
Mary St. Ann Pl DH9 .... 17 A4
Mary St. N Silk SR3 .... 22 A8
Mary St. Seaham SR7 .... 41 E7
Mary St. Stanl DH9 .... 17 E6
Mary Terr. Bish Au DL14 .... 148 E4
Mary Terr. Bowb DH6 .... 81 C1
Masefield Cl. Stanl DH9 .... 18 B7
Masefield Cres. Will DL15 .... 101 F1
Masefields. C le St DH7 .... 19 E4
Masham Moor Way. Darl DL1 .. 224 D7
Mason Cres. Peter SR8 .... 85 F6
Mason St. Cons DH8 .... 14 F2
Masterman Pl. Mid in T DL12 .. 160 D7
Matfen Cl. C le S DH3 .... 20 A3
Matfen Ct. Sedge TS21 .... 153 A7
Matterdale Rd. Peter SR8 .... 85 F6
Matthew Cl. New Ay DL5 .... 171 F8
Matthews Cres. S Hett DH6 .... 62 B6
Matthews Rd. Cold He SR7 ..... 40 E1
Maud Terr. Even DL14 .... 167 C8
Maud Terr. Tanf DH9 .... 6 D3
Maude St. Darl DL3 .... 208 F2
Maude Terr. Bish Au DL14 .... 147 E3
Maudville. Cons DH8 .... 30 A6
Maugham St. 7 Shild DL4 ...... 148 F1
Maughan Cl. Cornf DL17 .... 105 D1
Maughan Terr. Fishb TS21 ...... 131 C4
Maureen Terr. Belm DH1 .... 59 C6
Maureen Terr. Seaham SR7 ..... 41 C7
Mavin St. Durham DH1 .... 80 D8
Maxwell Cl. Darl DL1 .... 224 D8
May Ave. Win M NE21 .... 2 C7
May Cres. Wing TS29 .... 108 B5
May Lea. Wit Gil DH7 .... 35 B1
May St. Birt DH3 .... 9 C4
May St. Bish Au DL14 .... 148 B8
May St. Durham DH1 .... 58 B1
May Terr. Lang Pk DH7 .... 56 C6
Mayfair Rd. Darl DL1 .... 209 A8
Mayfair Sch. Darl DL1 .... 209 B8
Mayfield. Bar Cas DL12 .... 201 A6
Mayfield. Darl DL3 .... 208 E1
Mayfield Terr. Cockf DL13 .... 166 C5
Maylands. Thor DL13 .... 99 A7
Maynard's Row. Durham DH1 .. 58 D2
Maynes Way. Stanl DH9 .... 18 B7
Mayorswell Cl. 7 Durham DH1 . 58 D2
Mayorswell Field. 4
　Durham DH1 .... 58 E2
Mayorswell St. 6 Durham DH1 . 58 D2
Mazine Terr. Hasw DH6 .... 61 E2
McAteer Ct. Hasw DH6 .... 61 E1
McCullagh Gdns. Bish Au DL14 148 C6
McCutcheon St. 7 Seaham SR7 22 E1
McGuinness Ave. Peter SR8 .... 85 E8
McIntyre Terr. Bish Au DL14 .... 148 E6
McMullen Rd. Darl DL1 .... 209 E2
McNally Pl. Durham DH1 .... 58 F2
McNay St. Darl DL3 .... 208 F4
Mead The. Darl DL1 .... 209 C1
Meadhope St. Wols DL13 .... 97 F7
Meadow Cl. Coxhoe DH6 .... 105 F4
Meadow Cl. H le Sp DH5 .... 38 F7
Meadow Cl. Mid in T DL12 ...... 160 E7
Meadow Dr. C le St DH2 .... 19 F2
Meadow Grange. Bourn DH4 .. 21 E2
Meadow Rd. Trim TS29 .... 131 D7
Meadow Rise. Darl DL3 .... 208 B2
Meadow St. E Rain DH5 .... 38 C3
Meadow View. Bish Au DL14 ... 147 C2
Meadow View. Cons DH8 .... 31 C7
Meadow View. Coxhoe DH6 .... 105 F3
Meadow View. Dipton DH9 ..... 5 E1
Meadow View. Egg DL12 .... 162 C4
Meadow View. Sacr DH7 .... 35 C3
Meadow Way. Lanch DH7 .... 32 E3
Meadowbank. Lang Pk DH7 .... 56 B6
Meadowdale. Chilt DL17 .... 150 F7
Meadowfield Ave.
　Spenny DL16 .... 104 D2
Meadowfield Ind Est.
　Brand DH7 .... 79 D3
Meadowfield Rd. Darl DL3 ...... 208 B5
Meadowfield Way.
　New Ay DL5 .... 171 A8
Meadowlands Way.
　Tanf L DH9 .... 17 C8
Meadows La. W Rain DH4 & DH5 38 B3
Meadows The. Bourn DH4 .... 21 D3
Meadows The. M St G DL2 ...... 225 F7
Meadows The. Midd DL5 .... 149 E1
Meadows The. Sedge TS21 ..... 153 B6
Meatleasburn Cl. New Ay DL5 . 170 F4
Medomsley Cross Rds.
　Medom DH8 .... 15 A8
Medomsley Rd. Cons DH8 ...... 14 F4
Medway. Gr Lum DH3 .... 37 A7
Medway Cl. Peter SR8 .... 85 C4
Medway Gdns. Stanl DH9 .... 17 E4
Medwyn Cl. Bourn DH4 .... 21 E3
Meet The. New Ay DL5 .... 170 F6
Melbeck Dr. Urpeth DH2 .... 8 E2
Melbourne Pl. Wols DL13 .... 97 F7
Melbourne Terr. Sacr DH7 .... 35 B5
Melbury St. Seaham SR7 .... 41 E5
Meldon Ave. Sherb DH6 .... 60 A1
Meldon Cl. Darl DL1 .... 209 D6
Meldon Way. Ann Pl DH9 .... 17 B4
Meldon Way. Blay NE21 .... 1 F8
Meldon Way. H Shin DH1 .... 81 B5
Melgrove Way. Sedge TS21 .... 153 A5
Mellanby Cres. New Ay DL5 .... 171 F7
Melland St. Darl DL1 .... 209 A1
Mellbutts Bank. Frost DL13 .... 96 A1
Mellor Cl. Darl DL5 .... 209 A5
Melrose Ave. Darl DL3 .... 209 A7
Melrose Ave. Murton SR7 .... 40 A3
Melrose Cres. Seaham SR7 ..... 40 F8
Melrose Ct. Cons DH8 .... 14 C4
Melrose Dr. Bish Au DL14 .... 147 D3
Melsonby Cres. Darl DL1 .... 224 C8
Melville St. C le S DH3 .... 20 C2
Melville St. 2 Darl DL1 .... 208 F3
Memorial Ave. Eas SR8 .... 63 E4
Memorial Cotts. Butter DL13 .. 165 F8
Memorial Homes. Tanf L DH9 . 17 D8
Mendip Ave. C le S DH2 .... 20 C2
Mendip Cl. Peter SR8 .... 85 B6
Mendip Gn. Chilt DL17 .... 150 F8
Mendip Gr. Darl DL1 .... 209 C5
Mendip Terr. Stanl DH9 .... 18 A5
Mendip Wlk. Cound DL14 .... 149 C8
Menom Rd. New Ay DL5 .... 171 D2
Menville Cl. New Ay DL5 .... 170 F4
Mercantile Rd. H le Sp DH4 .... 38 C7
Mercia Ct. Darl DL3 .... 208 F2
Mercia Ret Pk. Durham DH1 ... 58 C8
Mere Dr. Durham DH1 .... 58 B7
Merlin Cl. Seaham SR7 .... 41 C8
Merlin Ct. Esh W DH7 .... 77 D8
Merlin Dr. C le S DH3 .... 20 D7
Merriman Gr. Hartle TS24 .... 111 D3
Merrington Cl. Kir Me DL16 .... 128 A3
Merrington Hts. Spenny DL16 . 127 F3
Merrington Lane Ind Est.
　Spenny DL16 .... 128 B7
Merrington Rd.
　Ferry DL16 & DL17 .... 128 C5
Merrington Rd. Kir Me DL17 ... 128 C5
Merrington View. Spenny DL16 128 A8
Merrybent. L Con DL2 .... 207 C2
Merrybent Dr. L Con DL2 .... 207 D1
Mersey St. Leadg DH8 .... 15 D5
Merton Cl. Darl DL1 .... 209 B6
Merz Rd. New Ay DL5 .... 171 D6
Messenger Bank. Cons DH8 ... 14 C6
Messines La. Still TS21 .... 174 E3
Metcalfe Cres. Murton SR7 ..... 40 B3
Metcalfe Rd. Cons DH8 .... 15 B1
Methold Houses. Beam DH9 ... 18 E8
Mewburn Ct. Darl DL3 .... 208 F7
Mewburn Rd. Darl DL3 .... 208 F7
Mews The. Hartle DH4 .... 38 A7
Mews The. H Shin DH1 .... 80 F6
Meynell Rd. Darl DL3 .... 208 F5
Mickle Gr. Cound DL14 .... 149 C8
Mickle Hill Rd. D Rocks TS27 .. 86 F1
Mickle Hill Rd. Hesl TS27 .... 86 D1
Mickleton Cl. Gr Lum DH3 ...... 37 B7
Middle Bank. Thor Th TS21 ..... 175 E3
Middle Chare. C le S DH3 .... 20 D3
Middle Farm. Staint DL12 .... 184 E2
Middle St. B Coll TS27 .... 86 D4
Middle St. Cons DH8 .... 14 F2
Middlefield. Pelton DH2 .... 19 E7
Middlefield Terr. Ush M DH7 ... 56 F1
Middleham Cl. Darl DL1 .... 209 B6
Middleham Rd. Cornf DL17 ..... 105 C1
Middleham Rd. Darl DL1 .... 209 B7
Middleham Rd. Durham DH1 ... 58 D7
Middleham Way. New Ay DL5 .. 171 F8
Middleham Wlk. Spenny DL16 . 104 A2
Middlehope Gr. Bish Au DL14 . 147 E5
Middles Rd. The Mid DH9 .... 18 B3
Middlestone Moor Cty Jun Mix
　Sch. Spenny DL16 .... 127 C5
Middleton Ave. R Gill NE39 ..... 1 F1
Middleton Cl. Seaham SR7 ...... 22 E1
Middleton Ct. Darl DL1 .... 209 A2
Middleton La. M St G DL2 .... 225 F6
Middleton Rd. Sadb DL2 .... 210 E6
Middleton Rd. Shild DL4 .... 169 F8
Middleton Rd. Wood DL13 ...... 143 C1
Middleton St. Darl DL1 .... 209 A2
Middleton St George Cty Prim
　Sch. M St G DL2 .... 225 F7
Middleton-in-Teesdale Jun
　& Inf Sch. Mid in T DL12 ..... 160 E7
Middlewood Ave. Bish Au DL14 147 D2
Middlewood Cl. 3 Hartle TS27 111 C4
Middlewood Rd. Lanch DH7 ... 32 E3
Middridge Rd.
　New Ay DL17 & DL5 .... 150 C4
Middridge Rd. New Ay DL5 ..... 150 A1
Midfields. New Ay DL5 .... 170 F4
Midhill Cl. Brand DH7 .... 79 B5
Midhill Cl. 7 Lang Pk DH7 ...... 56 C6
Miers Ave. Hartle TS24 .... 111 F2
Milbank Cres. Darl DL3 .... 208 D2
Milbank Rd. Darl DL3 .... 208 C2
Milbank Rd. Darl DL3 .... 208 D2
Milbank Terr. Hut Hen TS28 .... 108 F5
Milbank Terr. Shot Co DH6 ..... 84 D6
Milbanke Cl. Ouston DH2 .... 8 F1
Milbanke St. Ouston DH2 .... 8 F1
Milburn Cl. C le S DH3 .... 20 C2
Milburn St. Crook DL15 .... 100 E4
Mildred St. Darl DL3 .... 208 F3
Milford Dr. Sherb DH6 .... 60 A2
Milford La. Bish Au DL14 .... 148 D4
Milford Terr. 9 Ferry DL17 ..... 129 A6
Milkwood Ct. Darl DL3 .... 208 E4
Mill Cl. Bourn DH4 .... 21 E2
Mill Farm Rd. H Mill NE39 ...... 5 A5
Mill Hill. Eas SR8 .... 63 A1
Mill Hill. H le Sp DH5 .... 38 D6
Mill Hill. Sherb DH6 .... 60 A1
Mill Hill Prim Sch. Silk SR3 .... 22 A5
Mill Hill Rd. Silk SR3 .... 22 A6
Mill House Ct. Belm DH1 .... 59 A2
Mill La. Bish TS21 .... 194 E8
Mill La. Bish Au DL14 .... 148 D5
Mill La. Darl DL1 .... 209 E4
Mill La. Durham DH1 .... 59 A2
Mill La. Ebch DH8 .... 3 E4
Mill La. Frost DL13 .... 96 B6
Mill La. H Con DL2 .... 206 F3
Mill La. H Shin DH1 .... 81 A7
Mill La. Heigh DL4 & DL5 .... 170 C4
Mill La. Kimble DH2 & DH3 ..... 36 B4
Mill La. Longn DL2 & TS21 ..... 211 D3
Mill La. M St G DL2 .... 211 D3
Mill La. Mick DL12 .... 161 C5
Mill La. N Bran DH7 .... 79 A8
Mill La. Sherb DH6 .... 60 A1
Mill La. Spenny DL16 .... 103 E4
Mill La. Urpeth DH2 & DH9 ..... 8 D1
Mill La. Win M NE21 .... 2 B7
Mill Race Cl. 3 B Mill NE17 .... 4 B6
Mill Rd. B Mill NE17 .... 4 B8
Mill Rd. Brand DH7 .... 79 E5
Mill Rd. Chopw NE17 .... 4 B8
Mill Rd. Seaham SR7 .... 40 F8
Mill St. Cons DH8 .... 31 B8
Mill St. Crook DL15 .... 100 F4
Mill St. Shild DL4 .... 170 A8
Mill St. Will DL15 .... 101 F3
Mill Terr. H le Sp DH5 .... 38 D6
Mill Terr. Thor Th TS21 .... 175 D3
Mill The. Hunst DH8 .... 25 E3
Mill Wynd. Staind DL2 .... 186 D6
Millbank. Heigh DL5 .... 170 D1
Millbank Cl. Bish Au DL14 ...... 147 C1
Millbank Cl. Hart TS27 .... 111 A3
Millbank Ct. Durham DH1 .... 58 B3
Millbank Terr. Bish Au DL14 ... 148 F4
Millbank Terr. Still TS21 .... 175 A2
Millbeck Gr. H le Sp DH5 .... 38 D6
Millburngate. Durham DH1 .... 58 C2
Millburngate Sh Ctr.
　Durham DH1 .... 58 C2
Milldale. Seaham SR7 .... 40 F8
Miller Cres. Hartle TS24 .... 111 D4
Miller Gdns. C le S DH3 .... 19 D4
Miller Terr. N Silk SR3 .... 22 A8
Millershill La. Heal DH8 .... 30 E2
Millfield. Lanch DH7 .... 32 E4
Millfield Cl. C le S DH2 .... 20 A1
Millfield Ct. Cons DH8 .... 14 C3
Millfield Gr. Crook DL15 .... 100 E4
Millfield Rd. Fishb TS21 .... 131 D4
Millfields. New Ay DL5 .... 171 F2
Millford Way. Bowb DH6 .... 81 E1
Millhill La. Durham DH1 .... 80 B7
Millom Ct. Peter SR8 .... 85 A3
Millrace Ct. Darl DL1 .... 209 F6
Mills Bldgs. Ferry DL17 .... 129 C4
Mills Cl. New Ay DL5 .... 171 C1
Milner Rd. Darl DL1 .... 224 A8
Milton Ave. Bish Au DL14 .... 148 B6
Milton Ave. H le Sp DH5 .... 38 F7
Milton Cl. Seaham SR7 .... 41 B7
Milton Cl. Stanl DH9 .... 18 B6
Milton Gr. Shot Co DH6 .... 84 D6
Milton La. Eas SR8 .... 63 C4
Milton St. Crook DL15 .... 100 E5
Milton St. Darl DL1 .... 224 C8
Minehead Gr. N Silk SR3 .... 22 A8
Miners' Bglws. Cockf DL13 ..... 166 C5
Miners' Homes. Bish Au DL14 . 147 E3
Miners' Homes. Will DL15 ...... 102 A2
Mingarry. Birt DH3 .... 9 E2
Mingary Cl. E Rain DH5 .... 38 C4
Minors Cres. Darl DL3 .... 208 B5
Minstarley. Gr Lum DH3 .... 37 A7
Minster Ct. Belm DH1 .... 59 C3
Minster Wlk. Hur on T DL2 ..... 224 D1
Mire La. Coth DL12 .... 182 F3
Miry La. Newb DL12 .... 138 D4
Mission Pl. Kir Me DL16 .... 128 A3
Mistletoe St. Durham DH1 ...... 58 B1
Mistral Dr. Darl DL1 .... 209 B7
Mitchell Cl. Peter SR8 .... 85 B8
Mitchell St. Ann Pl DH9 .... 17 A4
Mitchell St. Birt DH3 .... 9 C4
Mitchell St. 4 Durham DH1 .... 58 B2
Mitchell St. Stanl DH9 .... 17 D4
Mitchell Terr. Tant DH9 .... 6 B2
Mitford Cl. C le S DH3 .... 20 D8
Mitford Cl. H Shin DH1 .... 81 B5
Mitford Ct. Peter SR8 .... 85 C4
Mitford Dr. Sedge TS21 .... 153 A8
Mitford Dr. Sherb DH6 .... 60 A2
Model Pl. 4 Darl DL1 .... 209 A1
Model Terr. 2 Cockf DL13 ...... 166 C5
Moffat Cl. Darl DL1 .... 209 D7
Mona St. Stanl DH9 .... 17 F7
Monarch Gn. Darl DL1 .... 209 B7
Moncreiff Terr. Eas SR8 .... 63 D4
Money Slack. Durham DH1 .... 80 B5
Monk Ct. Peter SR8 .... 85 B3
Monkend Terr. Cr on T DL2 .... 234 F8
Monks' Cres. Belm DH1 .... 58 F3
Monks End. New Ay DL5 .... 171 F2
Monkswood Sq. Silk SR3 .... 22 B6
Monmouth Gr. Hartle TS26 .... 111 E1
Montalbo Rd. Bar Cas DL12 ... 201 A7
Monteith Cl. Bish Au DL14 ..... 147 C1
Montfalcon Cl. Bish Au DL14 . 147 C1
Montgomery Rd. Bar Cas DL12 200 F7
Montgomery Rd. Durham DH1 . 58 F3
Montrose St. Darl DL1 .... 209 B3
Monument Terr. 10 Birt DH3 .. 9 C4
Moor Cotts. H Pitt DH6 .... 60 D4
Moor Cres. Belm DH1 .... 59 B3
Moor Cres. Ludw DH6 .... 83 C7
Moor Edge. Brand DH7 .... 79 B3
Moor Edge. Durham DH1 .... 57 F2
Moor Farm Est. Spenny DL16 . 127 E6
Moor Houses. Stan Co DH6 ... 76 E1
Moor La. Cleas DL2 .... 222 E5
Moor La. Dalton DL11 .... 233 E4
Moor La. Hilton DL4 & DL2 .... 167 F2
Moor La. Midd DL5 .... 150 A2
Moor La. Newsh DL11 .... 233 C7
Moor La. Scar DL12 .... 217 F2
Moor La. Shild DL4 & DL5 ...... 149 E3
Moor La. Staind DL2 .... 185 C7
Moor La. Staint DL2 .... 185 C7
Moor La. Stapl DL2 .... 222 E5
Moor La. Wing TS28 .... 108 E7
Moor Rd. Staind DL2 .... 186 C5
Moor View. Cockf DL13 .... 166 C5
Moor View. Thorn DH6 .... 83 E4
Moor View. Wh Hi DH6 .... 83 F3
Moor View Terr. Ann Pl DH9 ... 16 E3
Moore Cres. Birt DH3 .... 9 C6
Moore Cres N. H le Sp DH5 .... 38 E7
Moore Cres S. H le Sp DH5 .... 38 E7
Moore La. New Ay DL5 .... 171 F6
Moore Sq. Wing TS28 .... 84 D1
Moore St. Bish Au DL14 .... 148 F4
Moore St. Stanl DH9 .... 17 E4
Moore St. Wh Hi DH6 .... 83 E4
Moore Terr. Shot Co DH6 .... 84 D5
Moorfield. Butter DL13 .... 144 E1
Moorfoot Ave. C le S DH2 ...... 20 C2
Moorhead Way. New Ay DL5 .. 171 E4
Moorhouse Gdns. H le H DH5 . 39 B2
Moorhouse La. Brig DL12 ...... 218 A5
Moorland Cl. Will DL15 .... 101 E1
Moorland Cres. Cons DH8 ...... 30 A6
Moorland View. Chopw NE17 . 4 B8
Moorland View. Cons DH8 ...... 29 F6
Moorlands. Cons DH8 .... 14 D5
Moorlands Cres. Cons DH8 .... 14 D4
Moorlands Rd. Darl DL3 .... 208 C4
Moorlands The. Dipton DH9 ... 5 E1
Moorlands The. Durham DH1 .. 59 A2
Moormill. Kibble NE11 .... 8 D6
Moormill La. Kibble NE11 ...... 8 E6
Moors Cl. Fence DH4 .... 38 B8
Moorsfield. Fence DH4 .... 38 B8
Moorside. Spenny DL16 .... 127 D6
Moorside Cres. Fishb TS21 .... 131 D4
Moorsley Rd. H le H DH5 .... 38 F2
Moorview. Cons DH8 .... 14 E4
Moraine Cres. B Mill NE17 ..... 4 B6
Moravian St. Crook DL15 .... 100 E4
Moray Cl. Birt DH3 .... 9 D1
Moray Cl. Darl DL1 .... 209 C7
Moray Cl. Peter SR8 .... 85 C5
Mordue Terr. Ann Pl DH9 .... 17 A3
Morland St. Bish Au DL14 ...... 148 A5
Morley Cres. Kelloe DH6 .... 106 E6
Morley Gdns. 3 Cons DH8 ..... 14 F4
Morley La. Brance DH7 .... 78 D2
Morley Terr. 3 Fence DH4 ..... 38 A8
Morningside. C le S DH3 .... 20 C4
Morningside. Sacr DH7 .... 35 C4
Morningside. Wash NE38 .... 20 E8
Mornington La. Darl DL3 .... 208 D4
Morpeth Ave. Darl DL1 .... 209 C6
Morpeth Cl. Ferry DL17 .... 129 B6
Morpeth Cl. Wash DH3 .... 9 F4
Morpeth Gr. Bish Au DL14 ...... 148 A6
Morpeth St. Peter SR8 .... 85 F8
Morris Cres. Thorn DH6 .... 83 C4
Morris Sq. Eas SR8 .... 63 C3
Morris St. Birt DH3 .... 9 C4

Morrison Cl. New Ay DL5 .... 150 D1
Morrison Road North Ind Est.
  Ann Pl DH9 .... 17 A3
Morrison St. Still TS21 ...... 174 F4
Morrison Terr. Ferry DL17 ..... 129 D4
Morriss Terr. H le Sp DH5 ..... 38 F7
Mortham La. Gr Br DL12 ...... 202 A1
Mortimer St. Cons DH8 .... 14 D3
Morton Cres. Gr Lum DH4 ...... 21 F1
Morton Grange Terr.
  Gr Lum DH4 .... 21 E1
Morton Rd. Darl DL1 .... 210 A1
Morton Sq. Peter SR8 .... 85 C7
Morton Wlk. New Ay DL5 ...... 171 E7
Mossbank Gr. Darl DL1 .... 209 C5
Mossdale. Belm DH1 .... 59 E4
Mossmere. Spenny DL16 .... 103 E3
Mossway. Pelton DH2 .... 19 D7
Mosswood Cotts. Shot DH8 .... 13 D2
Mostyn Terr. Cockf DL13 ...... 166 D5
Moule Cl. New Ay DL5 .... 171 C5
Moulton Way. **1** Darl DL2 .... 224 C8
Mount Eff La. Bar Cas DL12 .... 201 D5
Mount Eff Rd. Bar Cas DL12 ... 201 E5
Mount Joy Cres. Durham DH1 ... 80 D8
Mount La. Spring NE9 .... 9 E8
Mount Lonnen. Spring NE9 ..... 9 E8
Mount Oswald Golf Course.
  Durham DH1 .... 80 B6
Mount Park Dr. Lanch DH7 ..... 32 E4
Mount Pleasant. Birt DH3 ...... 9 C5
Mount Pleasant. Burnh DH7 .... 33 D4
Mount Pleasant. Cockf DL13 ... 166 B5
Mount Pleasant. Dipton DH9 .... 5 E1
Mount Pleasant. H le Sp DH5 ... 38 F8
Mount Pleasant. Lanch DH7 .... 32 E4
Mount Pleasant. Sacr DH7 ..... 35 B4
Mount Pleasant. Stan Cr DL15 .. 100 F8
Mount Pleasant. Still TS21 .... 174 E3
Mount Pleasant Bglws. 5
  Birt DH3 .... 9 C5
Mount Pleasant Cl. M St G DL2 225 E8
Mount Pleasant Cl.
  Spenny DL16 .... 104 B1
Mount Pleasant Cl. Still TS21 . 174 E3
Mount Pleasant Ct.
  Spenny DL16 .... 104 B1
Mount Pleasant Cty Prim Sch.
  Darl DL3 .... 208 A5
Mount Pleasant Gr. Still TS21 . 174 F3
Mount Pleasant Rd. Still TS21 . 174 F3
Mount Pleasant View.
  Spenny DL16 .... 104 B1
Mount Pleasant Wlk. Still TS21 174 E3
Mount Rd. Birt DH3 .... 9 D5
Mount Rd. Gates NE9 .... 9 E8
Mount Stewart St. Seaham SR7 . 41 D5
Mount The. Cons DH8 .... 14 D6
Mount View. Lanch DH7 .... 32 E4
Mountside. Cons DH8 .... 14 D6
Moutter Cl. Peter SR8 .... 85 E8
Mowbray Dr. Hur on T DL2 .... 224 C2
Mowbray St. Durham DH1 ...... 58 B2
Mowden Hall Dr. Darl DL3 ..... 208 B3
Mowden Inf Sch. Darl DL3 ..... 208 B2
Mowden Jun Sch. Darl DL3 .... 208 B3
Mowden St. Darl DL3 .... 208 F3
Mowden Terr. Darl DL3 .... 208 F3
Mowden Wlk. Darl DL3 .... 208 A3
Mown Meadows Rd. Crook DL15 99 F4
Mown Meadows Rd.
  Crook DL15 .... 100 A3
Moyle Terr. Burnop NE16 ...... 6 A4
Muirfield Cl. Hartle TS27 ..... 111 C4
Muirfield Wlk. Hartle TS27 .... 111 C4
Muirkirk Gr. Darl DL1 .... 209 C6
Muirlands. Even DL14 .... 167 C8
Mulberry. Coxhoe DH6 .... 106 A4
Mulberry Terr. Ann Pl DH9 ..... 17 B4
Mulgrave Ct. New Ay DL17 .... 150 E1
Mulheim Cl. Darl DL3 .... 208 C5
Mullin Cl. Will DL15 .... 102 A6
Muncaster Mews. Peter SR8 .... 85 A3
Mundell St. Stanl DH9 .... 17 E4
Mundle Ave. Win M NE21 ...... 2 C6
Muriel St. Qua Ho DH9 .... 17 E3
Murphy Cres. Bish Au DL14 .... 148 A5
Murphy Crescent Sch.
  Bish Au DL14 .... 148 A5
Murphy Gr. Ryhope SR2 .... 22 E7
Murray Ave. Bish Au DL14 ..... 148 A5
Murray Ct. Cons DH8 .... 14 D5
Murray Pl. C le S DH2 .... 20 B3
Murray Rd. C le S DH2 & DH3 .. 20 C3
Murray St. Peter SR8 .... 86 A6
Murray Terr. Dipton DH9 ...... 16 D8
Murray Wlk. Darl DL3 .... 208 B2
Murrayfield Dr. Brand DH7 .... 79 A3
Murrayfield Way. Darl DL1 .... 209 E3
Murton Cl. New Ay DL5 .... 171 E2
Murton Cty Sch. Murton SR7 .. 40 C3
Murton Jubilee Cty Jun Sch.
  Murton SR7 .... 40 C3
Murton La. E Lane DH5 .... 39 D1
Murton Sea View Cty Inf Sch.
  Murton SR7 .... 40 E4
Musgrave Gdns. Durham DH1 .. 59 A2
Musgrave St. Bish Au DL14 .... 147 E3
Myre Hall. **8** H le Sp DH5 .... 38 E8
Myrtle Gdns. Darl DL1 .... 209 B8
Myrtle Gr. Billy R DL15 .... 100 D7
Myrtle Gr. Burnop NE16 .... 5 F6
Myrtle Gr. N Silk SR3 .... 22 B7
Myrtle Gr. Trim TS29 .... 107 D3
Myrtles. C le S DH2 .... 20 B5

Naby La. Coth DL12 .... 182 E1
Nairn Cl. Birt DH3 .... 9 D2
Nairn Cl. Darl DL1 .... 209 E2
Naisbitt Ave. Peter SR8 .... 85 E8
Naismith Gr. Tow Law DL13 ... 75 B2

Nanny Pop Lonnen.
  Spenny SR7 .... 127 E5
Nansen St. Cons DH8 .... 15 A3
Napier Cl. C le S DH3 .... 20 D8
Napier Cl. Ferry DL17 .... 128 E5
Napier Rd. Seaham SR7 .... 41 A8
Napier St. Darl DL3 .... 208 E2
Nattress Terr. Wing TS28 ..... 108 E8
Nattress Terr. Wing TS29 ..... 108 B5
Navenby Cl. Seaham SR7 ...... 23 A1
Naworth Ct. Peter SR8 .... 85 B3
Naylor Ave. Win M NE21 ...... 2 C6
Naylor Bldgs. Win M NE21 .... 2 C6
Naylor Rd. Spenny TS21 ...... 153 B6
Neale St. Ann Pl DH9 .... 17 A4
Neale St. Ferry DL17 .... 128 E5
Neale St. Tant DH9 .... 6 B2
Neasham Covert. Neas DL2 ... 225 C3
Neasham Dr. Darl DL1 .... 224 C7
Neasham Hill. Neas DL2 ...... 225 D2
Neasham Rd. Darl DL1 & DL2 . 224 B7
Neasham Rd.
  Hur on T DL1 & DL2 .... 224 E3
Neasham Rd. M St G DL2 ..... 225 D5
Neasham Rd. Neas DL2 .... 225 A1
Neasham Rd. Neas DL2 .... 225 D5
Neasham Rd. Seaham SR7 .... 23 A1
Nebraska Cl. Darl DL1 .... 209 B6
Neil Cres. Qua Hi DH6 .... 106 D7
Neil St. E Lane DH5 .... 39 C1
Neile St. New Ay DL5 .... 171 E8
Nell Terr. R Gill NE39 .... 1 C1
Nelson St. Peter SR8 .... 86 A7
Nelson St. **9** Bish Au DL14 . 148 B8
Nelson St. C le S DH3 .... 20 C2
Nelson St. Cons DH8 .... 14 F2
Nelson St. Crook DL15 .... 100 E4
Nelson St. Ferry DL17 .... 129 C4
Nelson St. H le H DH5 .... 39 A3
Nelson St. Leadg DH8 .... 15 C4
Nelson St. Ryhope SR2 .... 22 F7
Nelson St. Seaham SR7 .... 41 B8
Nelson Terr. Darl DL1 .... 224 A8
Nelson Terr. Sherb DH6 ...... 60 A1
Nenthead Cl. Gr Lum DH3 ..... 37 B7
Neptune Way. Eas SR8 .... 63 C4
Nesbit Rd. Peter SR8 .... 85 E5
Nesbyt Rd. Hartle TS24 ...... 111 F3
Nesham Pl. H le H DH5 .... 38 F8
Nestfield Ind Est. Darl DL1 ... 209 B4
Nestfield St. Darl DL1 .... 209 B4
Nestfield St. Darl DL1 .... 209 C4
Netherby Rise. Darl DL3 ...... 208 C1
Netherton Cl. C le St DH2 ..... 19 F2
Netherton Cl. Lang Pk DH7 .... 56 B6
Nettlebed La.
  Even DL13 & DL14 ...... 145 D5
Nettles La. Burdon SR3 .... 22 B6
Nettles La. N Silk SR3 .... 22 B6
Nettlesworth Jun & Inf Sch.
  Kimble DH2 .... 35 F4
Nevada Gdns. Darl DL1 .... 209 B6
Neville Cl. Even DL14 .... 167 D6
Neville Cl. Spenny DL16 ...... 104 B1
Neville Cres. Birt DH3 .... 9 C6
Neville Dene. Durham DH1 .... 57 F1
Neville Dr. Sedge TS21 .... 153 A8
Neville Par. New Ay DL5 ...... 171 E6
Neville Rd. Darl DL3 .... 208 D1
Neville Rd. Peter SR8 .... 85 C6
Neville Sq. Durham DH1 ...... 80 A7
Neville St. Durham DH1 ...... 58 C1
Neville Terr. Bowb DH6 .... 105 E8
Neville Terr. Durham DH1 .... 58 A2
Neville's Cross Bank.
  Durham DH1 .... 80 A8
Neville's Cross Villas.
  Durham DH1 .... 80 A8
Nevilledale Terr. Durham DH1 . 58 B1
Nevilles Cross Cty Jun & Inf Sch.
  Durham DH1 .... 80 A8
New Acres. Ush M DH7 .... 57 A2
New Blackett St. Ann Pl DH9 .. 16 E5
New Brancepeth Cty Jun & Inf Sch.
  N Bran DH7 .... 78 F7
New Burn Ave. Bowb DH6 .... 81 D1
New Cl. New Ay DL5 .... 171 F7
New Coll. Durham DH1 .... 80 A8
New Coll Durham. Durham DH1 58 A5
New Cross Row. Wing TS28 .. 108 E8
New Durham Rd. Ann Pl DH9 .. 17 A3
New Elvet. Durham DH1 ...... 58 D1
New Front St. Tant DH9 .... 6 C1
New Grange Terr.
  C le S DH2 .... 19 D4
New La. Denton DL2 .... 189 D2
New La. Heigh DL5 .... 170 F2
New La. Neas DL2 .... 225 B1
New Rd. Beam DH9 .... 19 A7
New Rd. Burnop NE16 .... 6 B7
New Rd. Crook DL15 .... 100 E2
New Rd. Hut Ma DL11 .... 220 C3
New Rd. Wash NE38 .... 21 C8
New Rd. Wit Pk DL14 .... 125 A1
New Row. M St G DL2 .... 225 F8
New Row. Shild DL14 .... 149 A4
New Row. Will DL15 .... 102 A4
New Row. Will DL16 .... 103 A4
New Seaham Byron Terrace Cty
  Sch. Seaham SR7 .... 22 F1
New Seaham St Cuthbert's RC Sch.
  Seaham SR7 .... 40 F8
New Silksworth Inf Sch.
  N Silk SR3 .... 22 B7
New Silksworth Jun Sch.
  N Silk SR3 .... 22 B7
New South Terr. Birt DH3 ..... 9 D4
New South View. Chilt DL17 .. 150 F7
New St. Durham DH1 .... 58 B1
New St. Sherb DH6 .... 60 A1

New Strangford Rd.
  Seaham SR7 .... 41 C7
New Watling St. Leadg DH8 ... 15 D4
Newacres Rd. Qua Ho DH9 ... 17 E1
Newark Ave. Bish Au DL14 ... 147 E6
Newark Cl. Peter SR8 .... 85 C7
Newark Cres. Seaham SR7 .... 23 A1
Newbiggin La. Heigh DL2 .... 169 D4
Newbiggin La. Lanch DH7 .... 32 C4
Newbottle La. Gr Lum DH4 ... 37 F7
Newbottle St. **4** H le Sp DH4 . 38 E8
Newbridge Bank. Bourn DH3 .. 20 F5
Newbridge Banks. W Pel DH2 . 19 A4
Newburgh Ct. Spenny DL16 .. 103 E3
Newburn Ct. New Ay DL5 .... 171 C7
Newburn Rd. Stanl DH9 ...... 18 A8
Newbury Dr. Cons DH8 ...... 14 E7
Newby La. H Pitt DH6 .... 60 C5
Newcastle Ave. Peter SR8 .... 85 F8
Newcastle Bank. Birt NE9 .... 9 B7
Newcastle Rd. Birt DH3 ...... 9 C6
Newcastle Rd. C le S DH3 .... 20 C5
Newcastle Rd. Durham DH1 .. 58 A1
Newcastle Terr. Durham DH1 . 58 A6
Newcomen St. Ferry DL17 ... 128 E6
Newfield Terr. Pelton DH2 .... 19 C5
Newfoundland St. Darl DL3 .. 208 E4
Newgate. Bar Cas DL12 ...... 201 A5
Newgate St. Bish Au DL14 ... 148 C8
Newholme Cres. Even DL14 .. 167 C7
Newholme Terr. Hut Hen TS28 108 F5
Newhouse Ave. Esh W DH7 ... 55 D1
Newhouse RC (Aided) Jun & Inf
  Sch. Esh W DH7 .... 77 E8
Newhouse Rd. Esh W DH7 .... 77 E8
Newker Cty Inf Sch. C le S DH2 20 B2
Newlands. Cons DH8 .... 14 D4
Newlands Ave. Bish Au DL14 . 148 B6
Newlands Rd. Belm DH1 ...... 59 C4
Newlands Rd. Darl DL3 .... 208 D4
Newlands Rd. Trim TS29 ..... 131 D8
Newlands Rd E. Seaham SR7 .. 41 A8
Newlands Rd W. Seaham SR7 . 41 A8
Newlands View. Crook DL15 .. 100 F2
Newmarket St. Cons DH8 .... 14 F3
Newmin Way. Whick NE16 .... 2 F5
Newport Ct. Darl DL1 .... 209 E4
Newport Gr. **6** N Silk SR3 ... 22 A8
Newsham Hill. Hut Ma DL11 . 220 C4
Newstead Rise. Durham DH8 .. 14 C5
Newstead Sq. Silk SR3 .... 22 A6
Newton Aycliffe Sta (Halt).
  New Ay DL5 .... 171 B5
Newton Cap Bank.
  Bish Au DL14 .... 126 B1
Newton Dr. Durham DH11 .... 58 B6
Newton Hanzard Long Dr.
  Elwick TS22 .... 155 B4
Newton La. Darl DL2 & DL3 .. 208 A5
Newton La. Walw DL2 .... 207 F7
Newton St. Ferry DL17 .... 128 E6
Newton St. Wit Gil DH7 ...... 57 A8
Newton Villas. Bowb DH6 .... 105 E6
Newtown. Mid in T DL12 .... 160 D7
Newtown Villas. Sacr DH7 .... 35 C3
Nicholas St. H le H DH5 ...... 39 B5
Nicholson Terr. Coth DL12 ... 182 E4
Nicholson Way. Hartle TS24 . 111 E3
Nicholson's Terr. Beam DH9 .. 18 F8
Nickleby Chare. Durham DH1 . 80 B7
Nickstream La. Darl DL3 ..... 208 B5
Nidderdale Ave. H le H DH5 .. 38 F2
Nightingale Ave. Darl DL1 ... 209 D6
Nightingale Pl. Stanl DH9 .... 18 B5
Nile St. Cons DH8 .... 14 F2
Nimbus Ct. **10** Silk SR3 ..... 22 A6
Nine Acres. Hart TS27 .... 110 E2
Nine Lands. H le Sp DH4 ..... 38 C8
Ninefields. Bish Au DL14 ..... 148 B8
Ninian Terr. Dipton DH9 ...... 16 C7
Ninth Ave. C le S DH2 .... 20 B3
Ninth St. C le St DH2 .... 86 D4
Ninth St. **6** Peter SR8 ...... 86 A7
Noble St. Eas SR8 .... 63 E5
Noel Ave. Win M NE21 .... 2 C6
Noel St. Stanl DH9 .... 18 B7
Noel Terr. Win M NE21 .... 2 D7
Nook La. Holw DL12 .... 160 A2
Norbeck Bank. Barn DL11 .... 219 A2
Norburn La. Wit Gil DH7 ..... 34 F2
Norburn Pk. Wit Gil DH7 ..... 35 A1
Norfolk Ave. Birt DH3 .... 9 D1
Norfolk Ave. **8** N Silk SR3 .. 22 A8
Norfolk Cl. Seaham SR7 ...... 23 A1
Norfolk Pl. Birt DH3 .... 9 D1
Norfolk Pl. Bish Au DL14 .... 148 C5
Norfolk Rd. Cons DH8 .... 30 B7
Norfolk St. H le H DH5 .... 38 F4
Norfolk Wlk. Peter SR8 ...... 85 C8
Norham Dr. Peter SR8 .... 85 C3
Norham Rd. Durham DH1 .... 58 D7
Norhurst. Whick NE16 .... 2 E5
Norman Ave. N Silk SR3 ..... 22 B7
Norman Rd. R Gill NE39 ...... 1 F1
Norman Terr. Chilt DL17 ..... 150 F8
Norman Terr. Cons DH8 ...... 14 E3
Norman Terr. H Pitt DH6 ..... 60 C5
Normanby Cl. Seaham SR7 ... 23 A1
Normandy Cres. H le Sp DH5 . 38 F8
North App. C le S DH2 .... 20 B4
North Ave. Peter SR8 .... 85 F7
North Bailey. Durham DH1 ... 58 C1
North Bitchburn Bank.
  How le W DL15 .... 124 F7
North Bitchburn Terr.
  How le W DL15 .... 125 A6
North Bondgate. Bish Au DL14 126 C1
North Brancepeth Cl.
  Brand DH7 .... 79 E6
North Burns. C le S DH3 ...... 20 C4
North Cl. Elwick TS27 .... 134 C5

North Cl. Thor Th TS21 ...... 175 E4
North Close Rd. Spenny DL16 . 127 F5
North Coronation St. 9
  Murton SR7 .... 40 D3
North Cotts. New Ay DL5 .... 171 A4
North Cres. Durham DH1 ..... 58 B3
North Cres. Eas SR8 .... 63 C3
North Cross St. Leadg DH8 ... 15 C4
North Dr. C le S DH3 .... 20 C7
North East Ind Est. Peter SR8 . 63 D1
North Eastern Terr. 3
  Darl DL1 .... 209 A1
North End. Brand DH7 .... 79 A5
North End. Durham DH1 ..... 58 A3
North End. Sedge TS21 ...... 153 B7
North End Gdns. Bish Au DL14 148 D6
North End Ind Est. Peter SR8 . 85 C8
North Field. Bar Cas DL12 ... 201 B7
North Gn. Staind DL2 .... 186 D6
North La. Elwick TS27 .... 134 C6
North La. Gain DL2 .... 205 A8
North La. H le H DH5 .... 39 E5
North La. Kill DL2 .... 188 F5
North La. Sunni DL13 & DL15 . 76 C1
North La. Will DL15 .... 101 C6
North Leigh. Tanf L DH9 ...... 6 D1
North Lodge. C le S DH3 ..... 20 D7
North Lodge Terr. Darl DL3 .. 208 F3
North Magdalene. Medom DH8 . 4 B1
North Moor Ave. Trim TS29 .. 107 F4
North Park Rd. Sedge TS21 .. 153 C7
North Railway St. Seaham SR7 . 41 D7
North Rd. Ann Pl DH9 .... 16 E6
North Rd. C le S DH3 .... 20 C7
North Rd. Darl DL1 .... 209 A6
North Rd. Durham DH1 ...... 58 B2
North Rd. H le H DH5 .... 38 C4
North Rd. H le Sp DH5 ...... 38 E4
North Rd. Seaham SR7 ...... 41 D8
North Rd. Spenny DL16 ..... 104 B1
North Rd. Tow Law DL13 .... 75 A4
North Rd. Wing TS28 .... 108 E8
North Rd E. Wing TS28 ..... 108 E8
North Rd W. Wing TS28 ..... 108 E7
North Rise. Darl DL3 .... 209 A5
North Road Cty Prim Sch.
  Darl DL1 .... 209 A5
North Road Sta. Darl DL3 .... 208 F4
North Side. Midd DL4 .... 149 E1
North St. B Coll TS27 .... 86 D3
North St. Birt DH3 .... 9 E3
North St. By Gr DL16 .... 102 E1
North St. Cons DH8 .... 15 B2
North St. E Rain DH5 .... 38 D4
North St. Ferry DL17 .... 128 F6
North St. Hett DH6 .... 104 E6
North St. N Silk SR3 .... 22 A8
North St. Spenny DL16 ..... 127 F8
North St. W Rain DH4 ...... 38 A2
North Stead Dr. Cons DH8 ... 14 C5
North Terr. Ann Pl DH9 ..... 17 C5
North Terr. Crook DL15 ..... 100 F4
North Terr. Durham DH1 .... 58 A6
North Terr. Eas SR8 .... 63 B4
North Terr. **11** N Silk SR3 .. 22 A8
North Terr. New Ay DL5 .... 171 E2
North Terr. Seaham SR7 .... 41 D8
North View. Will DL15 ...... 102 A2
North View. Wit Gil DH7 .... 57 A8
North View. Bear DH7 ...... 57 A3
North View. Bish Mi DL17 .. 130 C4
North View. Bourn DH4 ..... 21 E2
North View. Brand DH7 ..... 79 C3
North View. Ca Eden TS27 .. 85 B1
North View. Cons DH8 ...... 14 D4
North View. Dalt P TS27 .... 134 E3
North View. E Lane DH5 .... 39 C1
North View. Eas SR8 .... 63 E5
North View. Hasw DH6 ..... 61 E1
North View. Hunw DL15 .... 125 D5
North View. Lang Pk DH7 ... 56 B6
North View. Medom DH8 .... 4 B1
North View. Murton SR7 .... 40 D2
North View. Ouston DH2 .... 8 F1
North View. Pelton DH2 .... 19 C5
North View. R Gill NE39 ..... 1 C2
North View. S Hill DH6 ..... 60 D1
North View. The Mid DH9 ... 18 B3
North View Terr. Fence DH4 . 38 B8
North View W. R Gill NE39 ... 1 C2
North West Ind Est. Eas SR8 . 63 A1
North West Ind Est. Peter SR8 . 85 A8
Northallerton Rd. Da on T DL2 . 235 C3
Northampton Rd. Peter SR8 .. 85 C8
Northamptonshire Dr.
  Belm DH1 .... 59 D3
Northburn Gr. How le W DL15 . 124 D3
Northcote Terr. Darl DL3 .... 208 E4
Northdene Ave. Seaham SR7 . 41 D8
Northdene. Birt DH3 .... 9 C7
Northfield Cl. Whick NE16 ... 2 F5
Northfield View. Cons DH8 ... 15 A3
Northfield Way. New Ay DL5 . 171 C5
Northgate. Ann Pl DH9 ...... 16 F3
Northgate. Darl DL1 .... 209 A3
Northgrain. Wear DL13 ...... 66 D4
Northlands. C le S DH3 ...... 20 C5
Northlea Rd. Seaham SR7 .... 41 A8
Northlea. Seaham SR7 ...... 41 D8
Northside Cl. Midd DL5 ..... 149 E1
Northside Cl. Midd DL5 ..... 149 E1
Northside Terr. Trim TS29 ... 107 E3
Northumberland Ave.
  Bish Au DL14 .... 148 B6
Northumberland Pl. Birt DH3 . 9 D1

Northumberland Pl. Peter SR8 . 85 B8
Northumberland St. 14
  Darl DL1 .... 208 F1
Northumberland St. Peter SR8 . 85 F8
Northumbria Pl. Stanl DH9 ... 18 B7
Northwood Rd. Seaham SR7 .. 41 B8
Norton Ave. Bowb DH6 ...... 81 D1
Norton Ave. Seaham SR7 .... 23 A1
Norton Back La. Sadb DL2 ... 211 A8
Norton Cl. C le St DH2 .... 19 F1
Norton Cres. Sadb DL2 ...... 210 E7
Norton Rd. Sadb DL2 .... 210 E7
Norwich Cl. Gr Lum DH3 .... 37 B7
Norwich Gdns. Will DL15 ... 101 F2
Norwich Gr. Darl DL1 ...... 209 E5
Norwich Rd. Durham DH1 ... 58 D7
Norwood Cres. R Gill NE39 ... 1 F2
Nottingham Pl. Peter SR8 .... 85 B8
Nottingham St. Cound DL14 . 127 C1
Nottinghamshire Rd. Belm DH1 59 C3
Nuffield Cl. Darl DL1 .... 209 B6
Number One Ind Est. Cons DH8 15 A4
Nunnery Cl. Darl DL1 .... 208 B2
Nunnery La. Darl DL3 ...... 208 C2
Nuns Cl. Bish Au DL14 ...... 148 D5
Nuns' Row. Belm DH1 ...... 58 F3
Nursery Cl. B Mill NE17 ..... 4 B6
Nursery Dr. Grind SR22 ..... 154 F3
Nursery The. Bish Au DL14 .. 147 C1

O Hanlan St. **4** Spenny DL16 . 103 F1
O'Neil Dr. Peter SR8 .... 85 E5
Oak Ave. B Rocks TS27 ...... 86 E3
Oak Ave. Seaham SR7 .... 59 A1
Oak Ave. **5** H le Sp DH4 .... 38 D8
Oak Ave. Will DL15 .... 102 B2
Oak Cres. Kimble DH2 ...... 36 A3
Oak Ct. Sacr DH7 .... 35 C3
Oak Gdns. Billy R DL15 ..... 100 D6
Oak La. Cons DH8 .... 14 C7
Oak Lea. Shild DL4 .... 149 B1
Oak Lea. Wit Gil DH7 ...... 35 B1
Oak Rd. Eas SR8 .... 63 D3
Oak St. Bish Au DL14 ...... 148 F4
Oak St. Cons DH8 .... 14 F2
Oak St. Gr Lum DH4 .... 21 E1
Oak St. Lang Pk DH7 .... 56 C7
Oak St. Wald DH7 .... 19 E1
Oak Terr. Ann Pl DH9 ...... 16 E5
Oak Terr. Bish Au DL14 .... 148 C5
Oak Terr. Burnop NE16 ..... 6 C6
Oak Terr. Cornf DL17 ...... 129 E8
Oak Terr. Holm DH7 .... 34 D7
Oak Terr. Leadg DH8 ...... 15 D4
Oak Terr. Murton SR7 ...... 40 D2
Oak Terr. Pelton DH2 ...... 19 C6
Oak Terr. Spenny DL16 .... 127 E8
Oak Terr. Tant DH9 .... 6 B2
Oak Terr. The Mid DH9 .... 18 B3
Oak Tree Cl. M St G DL2 ... 226 C7
Oak Tree Cres. Sedge TS21 . 153 B7
Oakdale Rd. Cons DH8 ..... 15 A3
Oakdale Terr. C le S DH3 ... 20 C2
Oakdene Ave. Darl DL3 .... 223 E8
Oakdene Rd. Fishb TS21 ... 131 D4
Oakdene Terr. Spenny DL16 . 127 C5
Oakerside Dr. Peter SR8 .... 85 C4
Oakeys Rd. Stanl DH9 ...... 17 F8
Oakfield. C le S DH7 .... 19 F2
Oakfield Wlk. New Ay DL5 .. 171 B6
Oakfield Cres. Bowb DH6 ... 81 E1
Oakfield La. Cons DH8 ..... 14 C1
Oakfields. Burnop NE16 .... 6 B7
Oakgreen Flats. Brand DH7 . 79 B4
Oakham Ave. Whick NE16 ... 2 F6
Oakham Dr. Belm DH1 ..... 59 D5
Oakhurst Rd. Darl DL3 ..... 208 B3
Oakland Gdns. Darl DL1 .... 209 B7
Oaklands Terr. **5** Darl DL3 . 208 F3
Oaklands The. M St G DL2 .. 226 A5
Oaklea. C le S DH7 .... 20 A5
Oaklea Ct. **19** Darl DL1 ... 208 F1
Oaklea Terr. **2** Bish Au DL14 . 148 B6
Oakley Cross Sch.
  Bish Au DL14 .... 147 C1
Oakley Gn. Bish Au DL14 ... 147 D1
Oakridge. Whick NE16 ...... 2 F6
Oakridge Rd. Ush M DH7 .... 57 A1
Oaks Bank. Even DL14 ..... 167 C8
Oaks House. Even DL14 .... 167 C8
Oaks The. Darl DL3 .... 208 D3
Oaks The. E Lane DH5 ..... 39 D1
Oaks The. Esh W DH7 ...... 77 D7
Oaks The. H Spen NE39 .... 1 A3
Oaks The. Hut Hen TS27 ... 109 C5
Oaks The. New Ay DL17 ... 150 E2
Oakwood. Ann Pl DH9 ..... 16 E4
Oakwood. Coxhoe DH6 ..... 106 A3
Oakwood. S Hett DH6 ...... 62 B6
Oakwood Cl. Sacr DH7 ..... 35 C3
Oakwood Cl. Ann Pl DH9 ... 16 E4
Oakwood Dr. Darl DL1 ..... 209 B7
Oatlands Way. Durham DH1 . 58 C8
Oban Ct. Darl DL1 .... 209 D6
Obelisk La. Durham DH1 ... 58 B2
Ocean Rd. Hartle TS24 ..... 111 C5
Ocean View. B Rocks TS27 .. 86 F2
Ocean View. Sland SR2 .... 22 F8
Office Pl. H le H DH5 ...... 39 A3
Office Row. Shild DL14 .... 149 B4
Office Sq. Staind DL2 ..... 186 D6
Office St. Eas SR8 .... 63 E4
Office St. Wh Hi DH6 ..... 84 B3
Official Terr. Lanch DH7 ... 33 B1
Old Blackett St. Ann Pl DH9 . 16 E5
Old Elvet. Durham DH1 .... 58 D1
Old Engine Houses. Shild DL4 169 D8
Old Forge The. Brance DH7 . 78 E1

Old Fulling Mill Mus.
Durham DH1 .... 58 C1
Old Hall Rd. Cons DH8 .... 15 B1
Old Mill La. Gr Lum DH3 .... 36 F6
Old Park Terr. Spenny DL16 ... 127 A7
Old Pit Terr. Durham DH1 .... 58 C7
Old Shire Hall. Durham DH1 .... 58 D1
Oley Meadows. Cons DH8 .... 14 C2
Olga Terr. R Gill NE39 .... 1 C1
Olive Terr. Wald DL4 .... 19 E1
Oliver Cres. Birt DH3 .... 9 C6
Oliver Cres. Shadf DH6 .... 82 E6
Oliver Pl. Durham DH1 .... 80 A7
Oliver St. Cold He SR7 .... 40 E1
Oliver St. Seaham SR7 .... 41 B8
Oliver St. Stanl DH9 .... 17 E4
Olympic Dr. Darl DL3 .... 208 D4
Onslow Terr. Brand DH7 .... 79 E5
Opal Ave. Chilt DL17 .... 150 F8
Orchard Ave. R Gill NE39 .... 1 D1
Orchard Cl. Carl TS21 .... 195 D8
Orchard Cl. Crook DL15 .... 100 E3
Orchard Cl. Da on T DL2 .... 235 B5
Orchard Cl. R Gill NE39 .... 5 D8
Orchard Cl. Sedge TS21 .... 153 B6
Orchard Cl. W Pel DH9 .... 19 A6
Orchard Ct. Darl DL3 .... 208 E3
Orchard Dene. R Gill NE39 .... 1 D1
Orchard Dr. Durham DH1 .... 58 E3
Orchard Gdns. C le S DH3 .... 20 C1
Orchard Gr. Gain DL2 .... 205 A7
Orchard House. Durham DH1 ... 58 D1
Orchard Pk. 7 Birt DH3 .... 9 C4
Orchard Rd. Darl DL3 .... 208 D3
Orchard Rd. R Gill NE39 .... 1 D1
Orchard St. Birt DH3 .... 9 C4
Orchard St. Pelton DH2 .... 19 E7
Orchard Terr. C le S DH3 .... 20 C1
Orchard Terr. R Gill NE39 .... 5 D8
Orchard The. C le S DH3 .... 20 D4
Orchard The. Durham DH1 .... 58 B7
Orchard The. Heigh DL5 .... 170 D2
Orchard The. Sadb DL2 .... 210 E6
Orchard The. Sedge TS21 .... 153 B6
Orchard Way. 8 Shild DL4 ...... 149 A2
Orchards The. Staind DL2 .... 186 D5
Oriel Ct. Darl DL1 .... 209 B6
Orkney Dr. Sland SR2 .... 22 D8
Orlands The. New Ay DL5 .... 171 E2
Orr Ave. N Silk SR3 .... 22 B6
Orwell Cl. Peter SR8 .... 85 B4
Orwell Gdns. Stanl DH9 .... 17 F4
Osbert Pl. New Ay DL5 .... 171 E8
Osborne Rd. C le S DH3 .... 20 C3
Osborne St. 4 Shild DL4 .... 148 F1
Osborne Terr. Cound DL14 ...... 149 D8
Osborne Terr. Eas SR8 .... 63 B3
Osborne Terr. Even DL14 .... 167 C4
Osborne Terr. 6 Ferry DL17 .. 129 B5
Osbourne Ct. Darl DL3 .... 208 C2
Osprey Cl. Esh W DH7 .... 77 C8
Osric Pl. New Ay DL5 .... 171 D8
Oswald Ave. Durham DH1 .... 59 A1
Oswald Cl. Cornf DL17 .... 105 L1
Oswald Ct. Durham DH1 .... 80 D8
Oswald Pl. Ferry DL17 .... 128 F6
Oswald Rd. H le H DH5 .... 39 A5
Oswald Rd. Bish Au DL14 .... 147 D2
Oswald St. Crag DH9 .... 18 D2
Oswald Terr. Chilt DL17 .... 150 E1
Oswald Terr. Eas SR8 .... 63 D4
Otley Terr. Darl DL3 .... 208 F4
Otterburn Cl. Darl DL1 .... 209 C6
Otterington Cl. Hart TS27 ...... 111 A3
Our Lady & St Thomas RC Jun
Mix & Inf Sch. Will DL15 .... 101 F3
Our Lady's Jun & Inf Sch.
Peter SR8 .... 63 F1
Ouse Cres. Gr Lum DH3 .... 37 B7
Ouseburn Cl. Sland SR2 .... 22 F8
Ouselaw. Kibble NE11 .... 8 D6
Ouslaw La. Kibble NE11 .... 8 B6
Ousterley Terr. Crag DH9 .... 18 C2
Ouston Jun Sch.
Ouston DH2 .... 8 F1
Ouston La. Pelton DH2 .... 19 F8
Outdoor Pursuits Ctr.
Lang Be DL13 .... 114 C2
Outputs La. Heal DH8 .... 31 A4
Outram St. Darl DL3 .... 208 E2
Oval Pk. Spenny DL16 .... 104 B3
Oval The. Bish Au DL14 .... 147 E3
Oval The. C le S DH2 .... 36 B7
Oval The. Cornf DL17 .... 129 F8
Oval The. H le Sp DH4 .... 38 D8
Oval The. Hur on T DL2 .... 224 D1
Oval The. Ouston DH2 .... 8 F2
Oval The. Shild DL4 .... 148 F2
Oval The. Staint DL12 .... 201 D8
Overdene. Dal le D SR7 .... 40 F5
Ovington Cl. Oving DL11 .... 203 F2
Owen St. Ferry DL17 .... 128 F6
Owen Terr. Chopw NE17 .... 4 C8
Owen Terr. Tant DH9 .... 6 B2
Owengate. Durham DH1 .... 58 C1
Ox Close Cres. Spenny DL16 .. 103 F1
Ox Close Cty Jun & Inf Sch.
Spenny DL16 .... 103 F1
Oxford Cl. H le H DH5 .... 38 F4
Oxford Pl. Birt DH3 .... 9 C1
Oxford St. Spenny DL16 .... 103 F1
Oxford St. Ann Pl DH9 .... 16 F5
Oxford St. Bish Au DL14 .... 148 F4
Oxford St. Darl DL1 .... 209 A3
Oxford St. Hunw DL15 .... 125 D7
Oxford St. Seaham SR7 .... 41 A7
Oxford St. Shild DL4 .... 169 F8

Oxford Terr. 7 Bish Au DL14 .. 148 B8
Oxford Terr. Bowb DH6 .... 105 D8
Oxford Terr. 3 Cockf DL13 .... 166 D5
Oxfordshire Dr. Belm DH1 ...... 59 C3
Oxhill Villas. Ann Pl DH9 .... 17 B5
Oxley St. Cons DH8 .... 14 D4
Oxley Terr. Durham DH1 .... 58 A7

Pacific Hall. Seaham SR7 .... 40 E8
Paddock Cl. S Row DH4 .... 21 F5
Paddock La. N Silk SR3 .... 22 C7
Paddock The. Coxhoe DH6 ...... 106 A3
Paddock The. Elwick TS27 ...... 134 C5
Paddock The. Lanch DH7 .... 32 E3
Paddock The. M St G DL2 .... 225 F6
Paddock The. New Ay DL17 .... 150 E2
Paddock The. Staint DL12 ...... 184 E2
Paddock The. Tanf L DH9 .... 17 C8
Paddock The. Will DL15 .... 102 B2
Padstow Cl. 2 Sland SR2 .... 22 F8
Page Gr. Spenny DL16 .... 127 D7
Palace Row. Hart TS27 .... 110 F2
Palatine View. 2 Durham DH1 .. 58 B1
Palm Lea. Brand DH7 .... 79 A4
Palm Rd. Cornf DL17 .... 105 L1
Palm St. 16 Cons DH8 .... 14 F3
Palm St. Lang Pk DH7 .... 56 D8
Palm Terr. Tant DH9 .... 6 C3
Palm Terr. The Mid DH9 .... 18 B3
Palm Tree Villas. M St G DL2 .. 225 E8
Palmer Rd. Dipton DH9 .... 5 E1
Palmer Rd. New Ay DL5 .... 171 E5
Palmer Rd. Shot Co SR8 .... 85 A5
Palmer St. S Hett DH6 .... 62 B6
Palmer St. Stanl DH9 .... 17 D5
Palmers Garth. Durham DH1 .... 58 D1
Palmers Terr. Bish Au DL17 .... 130 B3
Palmerston St. Cons DH8 .... 14 F2
Pan La. Satley DH7 & DL13 ...... 53 C2
Panfield Terr. Bourn DH4 .... 21 E2
Pankhurst Pl. Stanl DH9 .... 18 A4
Pannell Cl. 5 Hartle TS27 ...... 111 C4
Pannell Pl. 4 Hartle TS27 ...... 111 C4
Parade The. C le S DH3 .... 20 C1
Parade The. Pelton DH2 .... 19 C6
Paradise Cotts. Wood DL13 .... 143 D1
Paradise Cres. Eas SR8 .... 63 D4
Paradise La. Eas SR8 .... 63 D4
Paradise St. Peter SR8 .... 86 B6
Paragon St. Stanh DL13 .... 71 A3
Park Ave. Bish Au DL14 .... 148 F1
Park Ave. Bowb DH6 .... 105 E6
Park Ave. Cons DH8 .... 15 A3
Park Ave. Crook DL15 .... 100 E4
Park Ave. N Silk SR3 .... 22 B7
Park Ave. Stanl DH9 .... 17 F7
Park Avenue Cl. Crook DL15 .. 100 E4
Park Cl. Ann Pl DH9 .... 17 A3
Park Cl. Lang Pk DH7 .... 56 D6
Park Cotts. B Mill NE17 .... 4 B6
Park Cres. Darl DL1 .... 224 A7
Park Cres. Still TS21 .... 174 F3
Park Dr. Lang Pk DH7 .... 56 D6
Park Hill. Bowb DH6 .... 105 E6
Park House Cl. Sherb DH6 .... 59 F2
Park House Gdns. Sherb DH6 .. 59 F2
Park House La. Heigh DL2 ...... 169 F2
Park House Rd. Durham DH1 ... 80 A7
Park La. Blay NE21 .... 2 B8
Park La. Darl DL1 .... 224 A5
Park La. Murton SR7 .... 40 B3
Park La. Peter SR8 .... 86 A7
Park Par. Spenny DL16 .... 127 E8
Park Pl. C le S DH3 .... 20 D5
Park Pl. Darl DL1 .... 209 A1
Park Rd. Cons DH8 .... 14 E3
Park Rd. Peter SR8 .... 85 E8
Park Rd. R Gill NE39 .... 1 D2
Park Rd. Sherb DH6 .... 59 F2
Park Rd. Stanl DH9 .... 17 D5
Park Rd. Trim TS29 .... 108 A4
Park Rd. Wit Pk DL14 .... 147 A8
Park Rd N. C le S DH3 .... 20 D4
Park Rd S. C le S DH3 .... 20 D1
Park Road Central. C le S DH3 .. 20 D3
Park St. Bish Au DL14 .... 148 C8
Park St. Cons DH8 .... 14 E4
Park St. Darl DL1 .... 209 A1
Park St. Seaham SR7 .... 41 D6
Park St. Will DL15 .... 102 A4
Park Terr. Bar Cas DL12 .... 201 A5
Park Terr. Burnop NE16 .... 6 A6
Park Terr. Cons DH8 .... 30 A6
Park Terr. How le W DL15 ...... 124 F7
Park Terr. Leadg DH8 .... 15 D4
Park Terr. Peter SR8 .... 86 A6
Park Terr. Tow Law DL13 .... 75 D1
Park Terr. Will DL15 .... 102 A2
Park The. Bish Mi DL17 .... 130 B3
Park View. Blay NE21 .... 2 C8
Park View. Bourn DH4 .... 21 D4
Park View. Burnop NE16 .... 6 B6
Park View. C le S DH2 .... 20 B5
Park View. Fishb TS21 .... 131 D5
Park View. H le H DH5 .... 39 A3
Park View. Kimble DH2 .... 35 F4
Park View. Pelton DH2 .... 19 E5
Park View. Peter SR8 .... 86 A7
Park View. Sedge TS21 .... 153 A6
Park View. Will DL15 .... 102 A5
Park View. Wit Gil DH7 .... 56 F8
Park View Comp Sch (North Lodge
Premises). C le S DH3 .... 20 D7
Park View Terr. Brand DH7 ...... 79 E6
Park View Terr. Cound DL14 .. 126 F1
Park Villas. Dipton DH9 .... 16 C7
Park Villas. Leadg DH8 .... 15 D4
Park Wood Ave. Bear DH7 ...... 57 A3
Parkdale. Spenny DL16 .... 103 E2
Parkdale Rise. Whick NE16 .... 2 F7

Parker Terr. Ferry DL17 .... 128 F6
Parker's Bldgs. Cons DH8 .... 15 E1
Parkgate. Darl DL1 .... 209 A1
Parkgate La. Blay NE21 .... 2 B8
Parkhead Gdns. Blay NE21 .... 2 B8
Parkhead Ave. Blay NE21 .... 2 B8
Parkland Ct. Seaham SR7 .... 41 B8
Parkland Dr. Darl DL3 .... 208 A3
Parkland Gr. Darl DL3 .... 208 A3
Parkland Terr. Seaham SR7 ..... 41 B8
Parklands. H Mill NE39 .... 4 F5
Parklands Gr. S Hett DH6 .... 62 B6
Parkside. Burnh DH7 .... 33 E6
Parkside. How le W DL15 .... 124 E8
Parkside. Longn TS21 .... 211 F5
Parkside. Sacr DH7 .... 35 C3
Parkside. Spenny DL16 .... 103 E1
Parkside. Tanf L DH9 .... 6 C1
Parkside Cotts. Tanf L DH9 .... 6 C1
Parkside Cres. Seaham SR7 ..... 41 C6
Parkstone Gr. Hartle TS24 ..... 111 D4
Parkway. Whick NE16 .... 2 E6
Parliament St. Cons DH8 .... 14 F2
Parmeter St. Stanl DH9 .... 17 E4
Parnaby St. Cons DH8 .... 14 F2
Parnell St. Fence DH4 .... 38 B8
Parsons Ct. Ferry DL17 .... 128 E5
Parsons Lonnen. Bar Cas DL12 .. 201 A5
Parsons Rd. Peter SR8 .... 63 D1
Partridge Cl. Wash NE38 .... 9 F4
Partridge Terr. Wing TS28 ..... 108 E8
Passfield Sq. Eas SR8 .... 63 C3
Passfield Sq. Thorn DH6 .... 83 D4
Passfield Way. Peter SR8 .... 85 B4
Pasteur Rd. S Hett DH6 .... 61 F7
Pasture Rows. Shild DL14 ...... 149 B4
Patches La. Coat Mu DL3 .... 191 E3
Pateley Moor Cres. Darl DL1 .. 224 C7
Patrick Cres. S Hett DH6 .... 61 E8
Patterdale Cl. Belm DH1 .... 59 E4
Patterdale Cl. Crook DL15 ..... 100 F2
Patterdale Mews. Leadg DH8 .. 15 D4
Patterdale St. H le H DH5 .... 39 A2
Pattison St. 22 Darl DL1 .... 209 B1
Patton Wlk. Wh Hi DH6 .... 84 A3
Paulinus Rd. New Ay DL5 ...... 171 C6
Pauls Gn. H le H DH5 .... 39 A4
Pavilion Terr. Burnh DH7 .... 33 D5
Pawston Rd. H Spen NE21 & NE39 .. 1 B5
Paxton Cl. New Ay DL5 .... 171 B8
Paxton St. Ferry DL17 .... 128 D5
Pea Flatts La. Gr Lum DH3 ...... 37 C2
Pea Rd. Stanl DH9 .... 17 D6
Peabody St. Darl DL3 .... 209 A6
Peaceful Valley. Hur on T DL2 .. 235 A8
Pear Lea. Brand DH7 .... 79 A4
Pear Tree Terr. Chopw NE17 ..... 4 B8
Pearl Cl. Chilt DL17 .... 150 F8
Pearl St. Shild DL4 .... 148 F1
Pears' Terr. 6 Shild DL4 .... 170 A8
Pearson St. Spenny DL16 .... 128 C8
Pearson St. Stanl DH9 .... 17 F8
Pearson Terr. Bar Cas DL12 ... 201 A6
Peartl Cl. Sherb DH6 .... 60 A1
Peartree Bglws. B Mill NE17 ..... 4 C6
Peartree Cl. B Mill NE17 .... 4 C6
Peartree Terr. Holm DH7 .... 34 B6
Pease Cotts. Darl DL1 .... 208 F1
Pease Rd. Peter SR8 .... 84 F8
Pease St. Darl DL1 .... 209 C1
Pease Way. New Ay DL5 .... 171 C6
Peaseholm Bglws. Crook DL15 .. 100 D4
Peases Row. Bish Au DL14 ..... 147 F3
Peases West. Billy R DL15 ...... 100 E7
Peases West Cty Jun Mix & Inf Sch.
Billy R DL15 .... 100 D7
Peases West Sports Ctr.
Crook DL15 .... 100 E5
Peebles Cl. Darl DL1 .... 209 C6
Peel Ave. Belm DH1 .... 59 B3
Peel Ave. Trim TS29 .... 107 E4
Peel Pl. Toro DL14 .... 125 F2
Peel St. Binch DL14 .... 127 A5
Peel St. Bish Au DL14 .... 148 C5
Peel St. 8 Darl DL1 .... 209 B1
Peggy's Wicket. Beam DH9 ...... 18 F8
Pelaw Ave. C le S DH2 .... 20 C5
Pelaw Ave. Stanl DH9 .... 18 A8
Pelaw Bank. C le S DH3 .... 20 C4
Pelaw Cres. C le S DH2 .... 20 B5
Pelaw Grange Ct. C le S DH3 ... 20 C8
Pelaw Leazes La. Durham DH1 .. 58 D2
Pelaw Pl. C le S DH2 .... 20 C5
Pelaw Rd. C le S DH2 .... 20 C5
Pelaw Sq. C le S DH2 .... 20 B5
Pelham Ct. Coxhoe DH6 .... 106 A3
Pelton Cty Inf Sch. Pelton DH2 .. 19 F7
Pelton Cty Jun Sch. Pelton DH2 19 F7
Pelton Fell Rd. C le S DH2 .... 20 B4
Pelton House Farm Estate.
Pelton DH2 .... 19 E6
Pelton La. C le S DH2 & DH3 ... 20 B5
Pelton La. Pelton DH2 .... 19 C5
Pelton Mews. Pelton DH2 .... 19 C6
Pelton Roseberry Comp Sch.
Pelton DH2 .... 19 C6
Pelton Roseberry Cty Inf Sch.
Pelton DH2 .... 19 C5
Pemberton Ave. Cons DH8 ...... 30 C8
Pemberton Bank. E Lane DH5 .. 39 C1
Pemberton Rd. Cons DH8 .... 14 B2
Pemberton Rd. New Ay DL17 .. 150 D2
Pemberton Terr. M St G DL2 ... 225 F6
Pemberton Terr S. The Mid DH9 18 B3
Pembroke Ave. Birt DH3 .... 9 C5
Pembroke Ave. N Silk SR3 .... 22 B6
Pembroke Ct. 15 Darl DL1 .... 209 B1

Pembroke Gr. Hartle TS26 ...... 111 E1
Pembroke Pl. Peter SR8 .... 85 B8
Pembroke St. Cound DL14 ...... 149 D8
Pendle Cl. Peter SR8 .... 85 B5
Pendleton Rd. Darl DL1 .... 209 A5
Pendleton Rd. Darl DL1 .... 209 A6
Pendower St. Darl DL1 .... 209 A6
Pendragon. Gr Lum DH3 .... 37 A8
Penhale Dr. Sland SR2 .... 22 F7
Penhill Cl. Urpeth DH2 .... 8 F1
Pennine Ave. C le S DH2 .... 20 B2
Pennine Cl. Darl DL3 .... 208 C3
Pennine Ct. Ann Pl DH9 .... 16 F3
Pennine Dr. Peter SR8 .... 85 A5
Pennine Gdns. Stanl DH9 .... 18 A5
Pennine View. Chopw NE17 ...... 4 B8
Pennine View. Tow Law DL13 ... 75 B4
Pennine Way. Chilt DL17 .... 151 A8
Penrith Ave. Murton SR7 .... 40 D3
Penryn Ave. Brand DH7 .... 79 C4
Penryn Way. Brand DH7 .... 79 C4
Pensbury St. Darl DL1 .... 209 A1
Penshaw Cl. Lang Pk DH7 .... 56 B6
Penshaw Gdns. Stanl DH9 .... 18 B7
Penshaw View. Birt DH3 .... 9 E3
Penshaw View. Sacr DH7 .... 35 D2
Penshaw Way. Birt DH3 .... 9 E3
Pentland Cl. Peter SR8 .... 85 A5
Pentland Ct. 3 C le S DH2 .... 20 C2
Pentland Gr. Darl DL3 .... 208 B1
Pentland Terr. Stanl DH9 .... 18 A5
Pentlands The. Chilt DL17 ...... 150 F8
Penzance Bglws. Murton SR7 ... 40 D4
Percy Ave. Ann Pl DH9 .... 16 E3
Percy Cres. Lanch DH7 .... 32 F3
Percy Gdns. Cons DH8 .... 15 B1
Percy Rd. Darl DL3 .... 208 F6
Percy Sq. Durham DH1 .... 80 A7
Percy St. Rish Au DL14 .... 148 B5
Percy St. Crook DL15 .... 100 E5
Percy St. H le H DH5 .... 39 B4
Percy St. Stanl DH9 .... 17 D5
Percy St. Thorn DH6 .... 83 D4
Percy St. Wh Hi DH6 .... 83 F3
Percy Terr. Ann Pl DH9 .... 17 B4
Percy Terr. Cons DH8 .... 15 B1
Percy Terr. Durham DH1 .... 58 A1
Perm Terr. Rish Mi DL17 .... 130 C4
Perrycrofts. Silk SR3 .... 22 A4
Pert Rd. Hartle TS24 .... 111 E4
Perth Gr. Darl DL1 .... 209 F2
Pesspool Ave. Hasw DH6 .... 61 F3
Pesspool Bglws. Hasw DH6 ..... 61 F3
Pesspool La. Eas DH6 & SR8 ... 62 C4
Pesspool La. Hasw DH6 .... 62 C4
Pesspool Terr. Hasw DH6 .... 61 F3
Peter Lee Cotts. Wh Hi DH6 .... 83 E2
Peter's Bank. Ann Pl DH9 .... 17 A7
Peterborough Rd. Durham DH1 .. 58 E7
Peterhouse Cl. Darl DL1 .... 209 B5
Peterlee Acre Rigg Cty Inf Sch.
Peter SR8 .... 85 C7
Peterlee Acre Rigg Cty Jun Mix
Sch. Peter SR8 .... 85 C7
Peterlee Acre Rigg Mix Modern
Sch. Peter SR8 .... 85 B8
Peterlee Dene House Cty Jun Sch.
Peter SR8 .... 85 C7
Peterlee Dene House Cty Mix Inf
Sch. Peter SR8 .... 85 F5
Peterlee Eden Hall Inf Sch.
Peter SR8 .... 85 D7
Peterlee Eden Hall Jun Sch.
Peter SR8 .... 85 D7
Peterlee Gram Tech Sch.
Peter SR8 .... 85 C7
Peterlee Howletch Cty Inf Sch.
Peter SR8 .... 85 B6
Peterlee Howletch Cty Jun Sch.
Peter SR8 .... 85 B6
Peterlee North Blunts Cty Inf Sch.
Peter SR8 .... 85 D6
Peterlee North Blunts Cty Jun Sch.
Peter SR8 .... 85 D6
Peterlee RC Inf Sch. Peter SR8 . 85 C6
Peterlee RC Jun Mix Sch.
Peter SR8 .... 85 C6
Peterlee Shotton Hall Cty Inf Sch.
Peter SR8 .... 85 B4
Peterlee Shotton Hall Cty Jun Sch.
Peter SR8 .... 85 B4
Peterlee Tech Coll. Peter SR8 .. 85 D6
Peth Gn. H le H DH5 .... 39 B1
Peth La. Lanch DH7 .... 33 B4
Pethside. Lanch DH7 .... 33 A4
Petterson Dale. Coxhoe DH6 .. 106 A4
Petwell Cres. Eas SR8 .... 63 C4
Petwell La. Eas SR8 .... 63 C5
Peverell St. Bish Au DL14 ...... 148 D5
Phelp St. S Hett DH6 .... 62 B6
Pheonix Ct. Cons DH8 .... 14 C3
Philip Ave. Bowb DH6 .... 81 D2
Phillips Cl. Hasw DH6 .... 61 E3
Philpotts Wlk. New Ay DL5 .... 171 E8
Phoenix Cl. Lang Pk DH7 .... 56 B6
Phoenix Ct. Darl DL1 .... 209 D1
Phoenix Pl. New Ay DL5 .... 150 C1
Phoenix Pl. 3 Shild DL4 .... 149 A2
Phoenix Rd. Wash NE38 .... 9 E6
Phoenix Row. Hi th DL14 .... 146 F7
Phoenix Way. H le Sp DH4 .... 38 C7
Pickard Cl. Peter SR8 .... 85 E7
Pickering St. Wing TS28 .... 108 D6
Picktree Cotts. C le S DH3 ...... 20 D4
Picktree Cotts E. C le S DH3 ... 20 D4
Picktree Farm Cotts. C le S DH3 20 D4
Picktree La. Wash NE38 .... 9 E1
Picktree La. C le S DH3 .... 20 E7
Picktree La. C le S DH3 & NE38 .. 20 E7
Picktree La. Wash DH3 .... 20 E5
Picktree Lodge. C le S DH3 ..... 20 D8

Picktree Terr. C le S DH3 .... 20 D4
Pickwick Cl. Durham DH1 .... 80 B7
Piele Pk. Cons DH8 .... 14 C6
Pierremont Cres. Darl DL3 ..... 208 D3
Pierremont Dr. Darl DL3 .... 208 D3
Pierremont Gdns. Darl DL3 .... 208 D2
Pierremont Rd. Darl DL3 .... 208 D3
Piggy La. Gain DL2 .... 204 F6
Pike Hill. Shot DH8 .... 13 F8
Pikesyde. Dipton DH9 .... 16 B7
Pilgrims' Way. Belm DH1 .... 58 F3
Pilmoor Gn. Darl DL1 .... 224 C7
Pimlico. Durham DH1 .... 80 C8
Pimlico Rd. H le H DH5 .... 39 B1
Pimlico Rd. H le H DH5 .... 39 B1
Pinders Way. S Hill DH6 .... 60 D1
Pine Ave. Durham DH1 .... 59 A1
Pine Ave. 3 H le Sp DH4 .... 38 D8
Pine Gr. Darl DL3 .... 223 D8
Pine Gr. Hartle TS24 .... 111 F1
Pine Lea. Brand DH7 .... 79 A4
Pine Pk. Ush M DH7 .... 57 B1
Pine Rd. Ferry DL17 .... 105 B1
Pine Ridge Ave. Sedge TS21 .. 153 B8
Pine St. Beam DH9 .... 19 B7
Pine St. Birt DH3 .... 9 C5
Pine St. C le S DH3 .... 20 C3
Pine St. Lang Pk DH7 .... 56 D7
Pine St. Stanl DH9 .... 17 D4
Pine St. W Pel DH2 .... 19 A5
Pine St. Wald DH2 .... 19 E1
Pine Terr. Ann Pl DH9 .... 16 E5
Pine Tree Cres. Shild DL4 ...... 149 B1
Pine View. Stanl DH9 .... 17 D4
Pine View Villas. Esh W DH7 ... 77 F8
Pinedale Dr. S Hett DH6 .... 61 F7
Pinetree. Esh W DH7 .... 77 D8
Pinetree Gdns. Crook DL15 .... 100 D3
Pinetree Gr. M St G DL2 .... 225 F7
Pinewood Cl. Hartle TS27 ...... 111 C4
Pinewood Cres. Heigh DL5 ..... 170 C1
Pinewood St. Gr Lum DH3 .... 21 E1
Pinfold La. Butter DL13 .... 165 E8
Pipe Ave. Burnop NE16 .... 5 F6
Pipershaw. Wash NE37 .... 9 F6
Pit La. Brand DH7 .... 78 E5
Pit La. Durham DH1 .... 58 C7
Pithouse La. Medom DH8 .... 15 B8
Pithouse La. W Rain DH4 .... 37 E3
Pitt St. Binch DL14 .... 127 A4
Pitt St. Cons DH8 .... 14 F2
Pittington Cty Jun & Inf Sch.
H Pitt DH6 .... 60 B5
Pittington La. Belm DH1 & DH6 .. 59 F5
Pittington La. H Pitt DH1 & DH6 . 59 F5
Pittington Rd.
W Rain DH5,DH6 & DH4 .... 60 A7
Pixley Dell. Cons DH8 .... 31 C7
Plane St. Cons DH8 .... 15 A2
Plantagenet Ave. C le S DH3 ... 20 D2
Plantation Ave. H Pitt DH6 ...... 60 E3
Plantation St. Leadg DH8 .... 15 D4
Plantation Terr. Fir T DL15 .... 100 A1
Plantation Terr. How le W DL15 124 E8
Plantation View.
How le W DL15 .... 124 E8
Plantation View. W Pel DH9 .... 18 F6
Plantation Wlk. S Hett DH6 ..... 61 F7
Plawsworth Cty Inf Sch.
Sacr DH7 .... 35 C3
Plawsworth Rd. Sacr DH7 .... 35 C3
Pleasant Pl. 6 Birt DH3 .... 9 C5
Pleasant View. Burnh DH7 .... 33 D4
Pleasant View. Cons DH8 .... 14 B4
Pleasant View. Darl DL3 .... 209 A6
Pleasant View. Leadg DH8 .... 15 B6
Plover Cl. 5 Wash NE38 .... 9 F3
Plover Dr. Burnop NE16 .... 6 C5
Plunkett Rd. Dipton DH9 .... 5 E1
Plunkett Terr. C le S DH2 .... 19 D4
Plymouth Cl. Seaham SR7 .... 40 F6
Polam Hall Jun Sch. Darl DL1 . 223 F8
Polam La. Darl DL1 .... 223 F8
Polam Rd. Darl DL1 .... 223 F8
Polden Cl. Peter SR8 .... 85 A5
Polemarch St. 4 Seaham SR7 ... 41 D6
Police Houses. Fir T DL15 .... 99 D2
Police Houses. Peter SR8 .... 85 C6
Pollard's Dr. Bish Au DL14 ..... 148 A7
Polpero Cl. Birt DH3 .... 9 D3
Pond Field Cl. Darl DL3 .... 223 B8
Pond St. H Shin DH1 .... 81 B4
Pont Bglws. Leadg DH8 .... 15 B6
Pont La. Leadg DH8 .... 15 C4
Pont Rd. Leadg DH8 .... 15 D5
Pont Terr. Leadg DH8 .... 15 C4
Pont View. Cons DH8 .... 15 B5
Ponteland Cl. Wash NE38 .... 9 F4
Pontop Ct. Ann Pl DH9 .... 16 F4
Pontop La. C le S DH3 .... 20 D4
Pontop St. E Rain DH5 .... 38 C4
Pontop Terr. Ann Pl DH9 .... 16 E3
Pontop View. Cons DH8 .... 15 B1
Pontop View. R Gill NE39 .... 1 D2
Pontopsyde. Dipton DH9 .... 16 C7
Poplar Ave. Burnop NE16 .... 5 F6
Poplar Ave. 1 H le Sp DH4 ...... 38 D8
Poplar Cres. Birt DH3 .... 9 B5
Poplar Dr. Belm DH1 .... 59 A3
Poplar Gr. Dipton DH9 .... 16 E8
Poplar Gr. 6 Sland SR2 .... 22 E8
Poplar Lea. Brand DH7 .... 79 A4
Poplar Rd. Belm DH1 .... 59 D4
Poplar St. Beam DH9 .... 19 B7
Poplar St. C le S DH3 .... 20 C3
Poplar St. Stanl DH9 .... 17 D4
Poplar St. Wald DH2 .... 19 E1
Poplar Terr. Billy R DL15 .... 100 D7
Poplar Terr. C le S DH3 .... 20 D4
Poplar Terr. Cornf DL17 .... 129 D8

Poplars The. Chilt DL17 150 E8
Poplars The. E Lane DH5 39 C1
Poppyfields. C le St DH2 19 F2
Popular Ct. C le S DH3 20 C2
Porrett Cl. Hartle TS24 111 E4
Porter Cl. New Ay DL5 171 E8
Porter Terr. Murton SR7 40 C3
Portland Ave. Seaham SR7 41 A7
Portland Cl. C le S DH2 20 A1
Portland Gr. Hartle TS24 111 D4
Portland Pl. Darl DL3 208 F2
Portmeads Rise. Birt DH3 9 D4
Portobello Terr. Birt DH3 9 E2
Portobello Way. Birt DH3 9 D4
Portree Cl. Birt DH3 9 D1
Portrush Cl. Darl DL1 209 E6
Portsmouth Pl. Darl DL1 209 E5
Post Horn. New Ay DL5 170 F8
Post House Wynd. 2 Darl DL3 208 F1
Post Office Row. Corn DH7 54 B3
Post Office St. Wit le W DL14 124 B3
Potter Pl. Stanl DH9 18 B5
Potterhouse La. Wit Gil DH1 57 F8
Potterhouse Terr. Durham DH1 58 A8
Potters Bank. Durham DH1 80 B7
Potters Cl. Durham DH1 80 A7
Pottery Yd. 3 H le Sp DH4 38 E8
Potto St. Shot Co DH6 84 D6
Potts Rd. Cound DL14 127 C1
Pounder Pl. Hartle TS24 111 F2
Pounteys Cl. M St G DL2 225 E7
Pow Hill Ctry Pk. Edmun DH8 11 D4
Powburn Cl. C le S DH2 20 A1
Powlett St. Darl DL3 208 F1
Prebend Row. 8 Darl DL1 208 F2
Prebend Row. Pelton DH2 19 D7
Prebends Field. Belm DH1 59 A4
Prendwick Cl. C le St DH2 36 A8
Prescott St. Darl DL1 209 B3
Preston La. Mordon DL5 172 C4
Preston Rd. New Ay DL5 171 C3
Price Ave. Bish Au DL14 148 A4
Priestfield Gdns. Burnop NE16 5 F6
Priestgate. Darl DL1 209 A2
Priestman Ave. Cons DH8 14 C1
Priestman Rd. New Ay DL5 171 C7
Primitive St. Shild DL4 148 F2
Primrose Ave. Peter SR8 85 F7
Primrose Cres. Bourn DH4 21 E3
Primrose Gdns. Ouston DH2 8 F2
Primrose Hill. Newf DL14 126 B8
Primrose St. Darl DL3 208 F1
Primrose Terr. Birt DH3 9 D4
Prince Charles Ave. Bowb DH6 81 D1
Prince's St. Ann Pl DH9 16 F5
Prince's St. Bish Au DL14 148 B8
Prince's St. 13 Darl DL1 209 B1
Princes' St. Durham DH1 58 B2
Princes' St. Shild DL4 148 E1
Princess Ave. Cons DH8 14 D5
Princess Cl. B Rocks TS27 86 E2
Princess Ct. Spenny DL16 127 E8
Princess Gdns. H le H DH5 39 A5
Princess Rd. Darl DL3 209 A8
Princess Rd. Seaham SR7 41 D6
Princess St. Spenny DL16 127 E8
Pringle Cl. N Bran DH7 78 E7
Pringle Gr. N Bran DH7 78 F7
Pringle Pl. N Bran DH7 78 F7
Prior Dene. Darl DL3 208 C4
Prior St. Darl DL3 208 C4
Priors Cl. Durham DH1 58 A2
Priors Grange. H Pitt DH6 60 B5
Priors Path. Ferry DL17 129 A7
Priory Cl. Cons DH8 14 C5
Priory Ct. Bar Cas DL12 201 A5
Priory Gdns. Will DL15 102 A3
Priory Rd. Durham DH1 58 B6
Priory Road Flats. Durham DH1 58 B5
Progress Way. Darl DL1 209 A3
Promenade. Seaham SR7 23 D1
Promenade The. Cons DH8 14 F4
Prospect Cres. E Lane DH5 61 C8
Prospect Pl. Bar Cas DL12 201 B7
Prospect Pl. 9 Cons DH8 14 F3
Prospect Pl. 7 Darl DL3 208 F2
Prospect Pl. Darl DL3 208 F5
Prospect Pl. N Bran DH7 78 E8
Prospect Pl. Wing TS29 107 F5
Prospect Rd. Crook DL15 100 E2
Prospect Sq. 1 Cockf DL13 166 C5
Prospect St. C le S DH3 20 C4
Prospect St. 10 Cons DH8 14 F3
Prospect Terr. Ann Pl DH9 17 B4
Prospect Terr. Burnop NE16 6 A4
Prospect Terr. C le S DH3 20 C4
Prospect Terr. Chilt DL17 151 A7
Prospect Terr. 3 Cockf DL13 166 C5
Prospect Terr. Durham DH1 80 A8
Prospect Terr. Egg DL12 162 B5
Prospect Terr. H Shin DH1 81 A6
Prospect Terr. Kibble NE11 8 C6
Prospect Terr. Lanch DH7 32 E3
Prospect Terr. N Bran DH7 78 F8
Prospect Terr. Will DL15 101 F3
Prospect View. W Rain DH4 37 F2
Proudfoot Dr. Bish Au DL14 148 A5
Providence Pl. Belm DH1 59 B3
Providence Row. Durham DH1 58 D2
Provident St. Pelton DH2 19 C6
Provident Terr. Crag DH9 18 D3
Provident Terr. Even DL14 167 C8
Prudhoe Ave. Fishb TS21 131 C4
Pudding Hill Rd. Oving DL11 204 E3
Pudsey Ct. Durham DH1 58 C6
Pudsey Wlk. New Ay DL5 171 E5
Purvis Terr. Wing TS29 108 B5

Quaker La. Darl DL1 223 F8
Quantock Ave. C le S DH2 20 A2
Quantock Cl. Darl DL1 209 C5
Quantock Pl. Peter SR8 85 A6
Quarrington Hill Ind Est. Qua Hi DH6 106 D7
Quarry Burn La. Hunw DL15 125 B8
Quarry Cres. Bear DH7 57 A3
Quarry Farm Cl. Hunw DL15 125 D6
Quarry House Gdns. E Rain DH5 38 C4
Quarry House La. Durham DH1 57 F1
Quarry House La. E Rain DH5 38 D4
Quarry Houses. Cound DL14 127 B3
Quarry La. Butter DL13 165 E8
Quarry Rd. N Silk SR3 22 B6
Quarry Rd. Stanl DH9 17 F7
Quarry St. N Silk SR3 22 A7
Quarry St. Shild DL4 148 F1
Quarryheads La. Durham DH1 80 C8
Quay The. H le H DH5 39 A3
Quebec St. Darl DL1 209 A2
Quebec St. 2 Lang Pk DH7 56 C6
Quebec Terr. Mick DL12 161 B4
Queen Alexandra Rd. Seaham SR7 41 D5
Queen Elizabeth Dr. E Lane DH5 61 D8
Queen St. Bar Cas DL12 201 A5
Queen St. Birt DH3 9 B4
Queen St. Cons DH8 14 F2
Queen St. Crook DL15 100 E3
Queen St. 4 Darl DL3 208 F2
Queen St. H le H DH5 39 A5
Queen St. Seaham SR7 41 C7
Queen St. Shild DL4 149 A2
Queen St. Sland SR2 22 F8
Queen St. W Pel DH2 19 A5
Queen's Ave. Seaham SR7 40 F6
Queen's Pk. C le S DH3 20 D2
Queen's Rd. Bish Au DL14 148 C7
Queen's Rd. Cons DH8 14 E5
Queen's Rd. Wing TS28 108 D8
Queens Dr. Sedge TS21 153 A5
Queens Garth. Sland B DH6 104 B7
Queens Gr. Durham DH1 80 A7
Queens Head Wynd. Staind DL2 186 D6
Queens Par. Ann Pl DH9 16 F4
Queens Way. Cons DH8 14 C5
Queensbury Rd. Seaham SR7 41 A7
Queensmere. C le S DH3 20 C7
Queensway. H le Sp DH5 38 F8
Queensway. Shild DL4 149 B1
Queensway. Will DL15 102 B2
Quetlaw Rd. Wh Hi DH6 83 E2
Quigley Terr. Birt DH3 9 B6
Quilstyle Rd. Wh Hi DH6 83 E2
Quin Cres. Wing TS28 108 D8
Quin Sq. S Hett DH6 62 A7
Quinn Cl. Peter SR8 85 D5

Raby Ave. Bar Cas DL12 200 F6
Raby Ave. Eas SR8 63 E5
Raby Cotts. Denton DL2 189 D2
Raby Dr. New Ay DL17 150 E1
Raby Gdns. Bish Au DL14 148 B6
Raby Gdns. Burnop NE16 5 E6
Raby Gdns. 7 Shild DL4 149 A2
Raby Rd. Durham DH1 58 C7
Raby Rd. Ferry DL17 129 A6
Raby St. Darl DL3 208 E1
Raby St. Even DL14 167 D6
Raby Terr. Bish Au DL14 147 B1
Raby Terr. Chilt DL17 150 E8
Raby Terr. Cockf DL13 166 C5
Raby Terr. Darl DL3 208 F2
Raby Terr. Will DL15 101 E3
Raby Way. Spenny DL16 128 A8
Racecourse The. Grind TS22 154 F2
Rachel Cl. Ryhope SR2 & SR3 22 C7
Radcliffe St. Birt DH3 9 C3
Rafton Dr. Hartle TS27 111 D3
Raglan Pl. Burnop NE16 6 B6
Raglan St. Cons DH8 14 F2
Ragpath La. Corn DH7 54 C6
Railway Cotts. Darl DL2 224 B6
Railway Cotts. Durham DH1 57 F1
Railway Cotts. Gr Lum DH4 37 F8
Railway Cotts. Wing TS28 84 F1
Railway Cotts. Wit le W DL15 124 F4
Railway Gdns. Ann Pl DH9 16 F4
Railway Houses. Bish Au DL14 148 F4
Railway Pl. Cons DH8 14 D3
Railway St. Ann Pl DH9 17 A3
Railway St. Bish Au DL14 148 C7
Railway St. Cons DH8 15 A2
Railway St. Crag DH9 18 C2
Railway St. H le H DH5 39 A4
Railway St. How le W DL15 124 E7
Railway St. Lanch DH7 32 F3
Railway St. Lang Pk DH7 56 C7
Railway St. Leadg DH8 15 D4
Railway St. Tow Law DL13 75 C2
Railway Terr. Bar Cas DL12 201 A7
Railway Terr. Cornf DL17 105 E2
Railway Terr. Hunw DL15 125 F6
Railway Terr. Hur on T DL2 235 A8
Railway Terr. Shild DL4 170 A8
Railway Terr. Stan Cr DL15 100 F7
Railway Terr. Stanh DL13 71 C1
Railway Terr. Will DL15 102 A3
Railway Terr. Wit le W DL14 124 C3
Raine St. Bish Au DL14 148 B8
Rainton Bridge Ind Est. H le Sp DH4 38 C7
Rainton Gr. H le Sp DH5 38 E6
Rainton St. Seaham SR7 41 D6
Rainton View. W Rain DH4 37 F2
Raisby Terr. Cornf DL17 105 E1
Ralph Ave. Sland SR2 22 E8
Ramilies. Ryhope SR2 22 D6
Ramona Ave. Kelloe DH6 106 C5
Ramsay Pl. New Ay DL5 171 E7
Ramsay St. Bowb DH6 105 C4
Ramsay St. H Spen NE39 1 A5
Ramsay Terr. Cons DH8 31 B8
Ramsey Cl. Durham DH1 59 A2
Ramsey Cl. Peter SR8 85 D8
Ramsey Cres. Bish Au DL14 147 F4
Ramsey Dr. Ferry DL17 128 E5
Ramsey St. C le S DH3 20 C2
Ramsey Wlk. Darl DL1 209 D5
Ramsgill. 1 Darl DL1 224 C7
Ramsgill House. 2 Darl DL2 224 C7
Ramshaw Cl. Lang Pk DH7 56 A6
Ramshaw Cty Sch. Even DL14 167 C8
Ramshaw La. Even DL14 146 C2
Ramshaw Terr. Kir Me DL16 128 A3
Ramside View. Belm DH1 59 D5
Randolph St. Bish Au DL14 148 F5
Randolph Terr. Even DL14 167 D6
Ranksborough St. Seaham SR7 41 B8
Rannoch Ave. C le S DH2 20 B1
Ranulf Ct. New Ay DL5 171 A8
Raven Ct. Esh W DH7 77 C8
Ravenscar Cl. Whick NE16 2 F5
Ravensdale Rd. Darl DL3 223 D7
Ravensdale Wlk. Darl DL3 223 D8
Ravenside Terr. Cons DH8 14 D4
Ravensworth. Birt DH3 9 D5
Ravensworth. Ryhope SR2 22 D7
Ravensworth Ave. 8 Bish Au DL14 148 B6
Ravensworth Cres. Byer NE16 6 D8
Ravensworth Cres. Hartle TS24 111 D5
Ravensworth Ct. Crook DL15 101 A3
Ravensworth Ct. S Hett DH6 61 F7
Ravensworth Rd. Birt DH3 9 B5
Ravensworth Rd. Fence DH4 21 F1
Ravensworth Rd. Ferry DL17 129 B6
Ravensworth Terr. 2 Durham DH1 58 D2
Raventhorpe Prep Sch. Darl DL3 208 C1
Ravenwood Cl. Hartle TS27 111 B4
Rayson Ct. Ingle DL2 188 A6
Reading St. Cornf DL17 105 D1
Reay Ct. 1 C le S DH2 20 C2
Rectory Gdns. Will DL15 102 B3
Rectory La. Blay NE21 2 B8
Rectory La. Cr on T DL2 234 F8
Rectory La. Wols DL13 97 F7
Rectory Rd. H le H DH5 39 A3
Rectory Row. Sedge TS21 153 B6
Rectory View. Shadf DH6 82 E7
Red Banks. C le St DH2 19 F2
Red Barnes Way. Darl DL1 209 D3
Red Cts. Brand DH7 79 C4
Red Firs. Brand DH7 79 B4
Red Hall Cty Prim Sch. Darl DL1 209 E4
Red Hall Dr. Darl DL1 209 D3
Red Hills Terr. Durham DH1 58 B1
Red House La. Heigh DL2 170 A4
Red Houses. Hi Eth DL14 146 E5
Red Ridges. Brand DH7 79 C4
Red Rose Terr. C le S DH3 20 D2
Redburn Cl. H le Sp DH4 38 C8
Redesdale Ave. Blay NE21 1 F8
Redesdale Ct. Trim TS29 107 E4
Redesdale Rd. C le S DH2 20 A1
Redford La. Hamst DL13 122 D4
Redgate Bank. Wols DL13 74 B1
Redhill Dr. Whick NE16 2 E4
Redhills La. Durham DH1 58 A2
Redhills Way. H le H DH5 39 A2
Redhouse Cl. Sacr DH7 35 D2
Redmarshall Rd. Bish TS21 194 F6
Redmarshall St. Still TS21 174 E3
Redmire Cl. Darl DL1 209 A5
Redmires Cl. Urpeth DH2 8 E1
Redshank Cl. Wash NE38 9 F2
Redwing Cl. Wash NE38 9 F3
Redwood. Brand DH7 79 B4
Redwood. Esh W DH7 77 D7
Redwood Cl. H le H DH5 38 F4
Redwood Cl. Hartle TS27 111 C5
Redwood Ct. Cons DH8 14 E4
Redworth Est. Heigh DL5 170 B3
Redworth Gr. Bish Au DL14 148 E7
Redworth Rd. Darl DL3 208 B4
Redworth Rd. Heigh DL5 170 D2
Redworth Rd. Shild DL4 170 A7
Redworth Way. New Ay DL5 171 D4
Reed Ave. Will DL15 102 A6
Reeth Moor Cl. Darl DL1 224 E8
Reeth Pl. New Ay DL5 171 B8
Regal Dr. Darl DL1 209 B7
Regency Dr. N Silk SR3 22 B8
Regency Dr. Whick NE16 2 F6
Regent Dr. Whick NE16 2 F4
Regent Rd. Ryhope SR2 23 A5
Regent St. Ann Pl DH9 16 F5
Regent St. Bish Au DL14 148 C8
Regent St. Bish Au DL14 148 F4
Regent St. H le H DH5 39 A5
Regent St. Shild DL4 148 F1
Regent Terr. Fishb TS21 131 C4
Regents Ct. Darl DL1 209 C1
Reid St. Darl DL3 208 E3
Reid Street Cty Prim Sch. Darl DL3 208 E3
Relley Cl. Ush M DH7 57 B1
Relley Garth. Brand DH7 79 D5
Relly Path. Durham DH1 80 A8
Relton Cl. Fence DH4 38 A7
Relton Terr. C le S DH3 20 C2
Rembrandt Way. New Ay DL5 171 D3
Renfrew Pl. Birt DH3 9 D2
Rennie Cl. Darl DL1 209 B2
Rennie St. Ferry DL17 128 E6
Renny St. 5 Durham DH1 58 E2
Renny's La. Belm DH1 59 B2
Rescue Station Cotts. H le Sp DH5 38 F6
Reservoir Terr. Stan Cr DL15 100 F7
Reynolds Cl. Stanl DH9 17 F6
Reynolds Ct. Peter SR8 86 B6
Rhodes' Terr. Durham DH1 79 F8
Ribble Dr. Darl DL1 223 F6
Richard Ct. Darl DL1 209 A4
Richard St. H le H DH5 39 A3
Richard Terr. Bish Au DL14 148 E4
Richardson Ave. Bish Au DL14 147 F4
Richardson Cl. Winst DL2 203 F6
Richardson Fields. Bar Cas DL12 201 A6
Richardson Hospl. Bar Cas DL12 201 A6
Richardson Pl. Kir Me DL16 128 A3
Richardson Terr. 6 Ryhope SR2 23 A6
Richardson Wlk. 6 New Ay DL5 171 E8
Richmond. Ryhope SR2 22 D7
Richmond Ave. Bish Au DL14 148 A6
Richmond Cl. Darl DL3 208 B5
Richmond Cl. Ferry DL17 129 B5
Richmond Ct. Durham DH1 58 D7
Richmond Fields. Spenny DL16 128 B8
Richmond Rd. Cr on T DL10 & DL2 234 D5
Richmond Rd. Durham DH1 58 D7
Richmond St. By Gr DL16 126 F8
Richmond Terr. Cr on T DL2 234 F8
Richmond Terr. Hasw DH6 61 F3
Rickleton Ave. C le S DH3 20 D5
Rickleton Prim Sch. Wash NE38 20 F8
Rickleton Way. Wash NE38 21 A8
Ricknall Ave. New Ay DL5 171 E4
Ricknall La. Mordon DL1 & DL5 172 C3
Ricknall La. New Ay DL1 & DL5 172 C3
Riddell Ct. 5 C le S DH2 20 C2
Ridding Ct. Esh W DH7 77 D8
Ridding Rd. Esh W DH7 77 D8
Ridgeside. Spenny DL16 128 A5
Ridgeway. Birt DH3 9 C6
Ridgeway. Darl DL3 208 F7
Ridgeway. New Ay DL5 171 C4
Ridgeway. Ryhope SR2 22 C6
Riding Hill. Gr Lum DH3 37 A7
Riding Hill Rd. Ann Pl DH9 17 A5
Riding La. Kibble DH9 & NE11 8 B4
Ridley Ave. C le S DH2 20 B2
Ridley Ave. Sland SR2 22 F7
Ridley St. Stanl DH9 17 F7
Ridley Terr. Leadg DH8 15 C3
Ridley Terr. Tow Law DL13 75 B3
Ridlington Way. Hartle TS24 111 E4
Ridsdale St. Darl DL1 209 B1
Rievaulx Ct. Spenny DL16 103 E3
Rigg Head. Lang DL2 188 A2
Rigg La. Holw DL12 159 F2
Riggs The. Brand DH7 79 C5
Riggs The. H le Sp DH5 38 F8
Riggs The. Hunw DL15 125 D5
Ripon Dr. Darl DL1 224 B7
Ripon Dr. Will DL15 101 F2
Ripon Rd. Durham DH1 58 D8
Ripon St. C le S DH3 20 C1
Ripon Terr. Kimble DH2 36 A3
Ripon Terr. Murton SR7 40 C3
Rise Carr Cty Prim Sch. Darl DL3 208 F5
Rise The. Cons DH8 30 A6
Rise The. Darl DL3 223 D8
Ritson Ave. Bear DH7 57 B3
Ritson Rd. New Ay DL5 171 D6
Ritson St. Cons DH8 14 D4
Ritson St. Stanl DH9 17 F6
Ritson's Rd. Cons DH8 14 D4
River Terr. Mid in T DL12 160 D7
River View. B Mill NE17 4 B6
River View. Will DL15 102 B2
River View Ind Est. Darl DL1 209 C4
River Wlk. Bish Au DL14 147 C2
Riverbank Trad Est. Darl DL1 209 A4
Riverdale. Wols DL13 97 F6
Rivergarth. Darl DL1 209 F6
Rivermead Ave. Darl DL1 209 F6
Riversdale. B Mill NE17 4 B6
Riverside. Bish Au DL14 148 D6
Riverside. Cons DH8 14 C6
Riverside Dr. Darl DL1 209 F5
Riverside Ind Est. Lang Pk DH7 56 C7
Riverside Way. Darl DL1 209 C5
Roast Calf La. Bish Mi DL17 130 C4
Robert Sq. Seaham SR7 41 E6
Robert St. N Silk SR3 22 B7
Robert St. Seaham SR7 41 E6
Robert St. Spenny DL16 127 E7
Robert Terr. Bowb DH6 81 D2
Robert Terr. Stanl DH9 17 F8
Roberts Sq. Cornf DL17 105 D1
Roberts Wlk. 4 Darl DL1 209 B1
Robin Ct. E Rain DH5 38 C3
Robin La. E Rain DH4 & DH5 38 C2
Robin La. W Rain DH4 & DH5 38 C2
Robinson St. Cons DH8 14 E4
Robinson Terr. Burnop NE16 6 A4
Robinson Terr. By Gr DL16 102 E1
Robinson Terr. N Silk SR3 22 B7
Robson Ave. Peter SR8 85 D7
Robson Cres. Bowb DH6 81 D2
Robson Pl. 10 Ryhope SR2 23 A6
Robson Rd. Bish Au DL14 168 B8
Robson St. Cons DH8 15 A3
Robson St. Shild DL4 149 A2
Robson Terr. H Shin DH1 80 F6
Robson Terr. H Spen NE39 1 B3
Robson Terr. Tant DH9 5 F1
Rochdale St. Even DL14 167 C7
Rochdale St. H le H DH5 39 A2
Roche Wlk. Darl DL3 208 A5
Rochester Cl. Bish Au DL14 147 E6
Rochester Rd. Durham DH1 58 D7
Rochester Way. Darl DL1 209 E5
Rock Rd. Spenny DL16 127 E6
Rock Terr. Mid in T DL12 139 E1
Rock Terr. N Bran DH7 78 F8
Rockcliffe House. 3 Darl DL2 224 C7
Rockcliffe Terr. Kir Me DL16 128 A3
Rocket St. Darl DL1 209 B1
Rockhope. Wash NE38 20 F8
Rockingham Dr. Bish Au DL14 147 E6
Rockingham Rd. Will DL15 101 F1
Rockingham St. Darl DL1 224 A8
Rockwell Ave. Darl DL1 209 D6
Rockwell House. Darl DL1 209 C5
Roddymoor Ct. Billy R DL15 100 D7
Roddymoor Rd. Billy R DL13 & DL15 100 B5
Roddymoor Rd. Billy R DL15 100 D7
Rodham Terr. Stanl DH9 17 F8
Rodney Cl. Ryhope SR2 22 C6
Rodney Wlk. Cound DL4 149 B8
Rodwell St. Wing TS29 107 F5
Roger St. Cons DH8 14 E3
Rogeri Pl. Hartle TS24 111 F3
Rogerley Terr. Ann Pl DH9 16 E5
Rogers Cl. 1 Peter SR8 86 A6
Rogerson Cl. Sland B DH6 104 B7
Rogues La. H Spen NE39 1 A5
Rokeby Pk. Gr Br DL12 202 A1
Rokeby Sq. Durham DH1 80 A7
Rokeby Terr. Hunw DL15 125 E6
Roker Cl. Darl DL1 209 E3
Roman Ave. C le S DH3 20 D3
Roman Mews. W Rain DH4 38 A2
Roman View. Pier DL2 206 B4
Romanway Ind Est. Bish Au DL14 148 A3
Romney Dr. Belm DH1 59 D5
Ronaldsay Cl. 4 Sland SR2 22 E8
Rookery Gdns. Chilt DL17 150 E6
Rookery La. Whick NE16 2 E4
Rookhope Cty Jun Mix & Inf Sch. Rook DL13 47 B2
Rookhope Gr. Bish Au DL14 147 E5
Rookswood Gdns. R Gill NE39 1 E3
Rookwood Hunt. New Ay DL5 171 A8
Roosevelt Rd. Durham DH1 58 F3
Roper's Terr. Trim TS29 107 D3
Ropery La. Bourn DH3 20 F3
Ropery La. C le S DH3 20 D2
Ropery Wlk. Seaham SR7 41 E6
Rosa St. Spenny DL16 127 E8
Rosa Street Jun & Inf Sch. Spenny DL16 127 E8
Rose Ave. Fence DH4 21 F1
Rose Ave. Stanl DH9 17 D5
Rose Cotts. Burnop NE16 5 E5
Rose Cotts. S Hett DH6 62 A7
Rose Cotts. Shot Co SR8 84 E7
Rose Cres. Bourn DH4 21 D3
Rose Cres. Sacr DH7 35 D3
Rose Ct. Esh W DH7 55 C2
Rose Ct. Peter SR8 85 B3
Rose Gdns. Kibble NE11 8 C6
Rose La. Darl DL1 209 E5
Rose Lea. Wit Gil DH7 35 B1
Rose St. 7 H le Sp DH4 38 D8
Rose St. Trim TS29 107 E4
Rose Terr. 6 Lang Pk DH7 56 C6
Rose Terr. Mid in T DL12 160 D8
Rose Terr. Pelton DH2 19 E5
Rose Terr. Stanh DL13 71 A3
Rosebank Cl. Sland SR2 22 E8
Rosebay Ct. Darl DL3 208 E3
Rosebay Rd. Brand DH7 79 E4
Roseberry Cres. Crook DL15 100 D4
Roseberry Cres. Thorn DH6 83 C4
Roseberry Grange Municipal Golf Course. W Pel DH2 19 B6
Roseberry Rd. Trim TS29 131 D8
Roseberry St. Stanl DH9 18 D7
Roseberry Villas. Pelton DH2 19 C5
Rosebery St. Darl DL3 208 E3
Rosebery Terr. 4 Cons DH8 14 F2
Rosebery Terr. 4 Shild DL4 149 A2
Roseby Rd. Peter SR8 85 F6
Rosedale. Spenny DL16 103 E1
Rosedale Ave. Cons DH8 14 D5
Rosedale Cl. Sedge TS21 153 B7
Rosedale Cres. Darl DL3 208 B4
Rosedale Cres. Shild DL4 149 B1
Rosedale Rd. Belm DH1 59 D4
Rosedale St. H le H DH5 38 E1
Rosedale Terr. Peter SR8 85 F7
Rosedale Terr. Will DL15 102 A3
Roselea Ave. Ryhope SR2 22 F7
Rosemary Ct. 7 Darl DL2 224 C8
Rosemary La. Eas SR8 63 B4
Rosemead Ave. Will DL15 102 A3
Rosemount. Durham DH1 58 D8
Rosemount Ct. Bish Au DL14 148 D5
Rosemount Rd. Bish Au DL14 148 D5
Rosewood. Chilt DL17 150 E8
Rosewood Cl. Sacr DH7 35 C3
Rosewood Gdns. C le S DH2 20 B5
Rosewood Terr. Birt DH3 9 B5
Roslin Terr. Hamst DL13 123 B3
Roslyn St. Darl DL1 224 A8
Ross. Ouston DH2 9 A1
Ross St. 9 Seaham SR7 41 D7
Ross Terr. 3 Ferry DL17 129 A5
Ross Wlk. New Ay DL5 171 F6
Ross Wlk. New Ay DL5 171 F7
Rosslyn Ave. Ryhope SR2 22 F7
Rosslyn Pl. Birt DH3 9 D2
Rossmere. Spenny DL16 103 E2

Rossway. Darl DL1 .... 209 E7
Rothbury. Ryhope SR2 .... 22 D6
Rothbury Ave. Peter SR8 .... 85 F8
Rothbury Cl. C le S DH2 .... 20 A1
Rothbury Cl. Trim TS29 .... 107 E4
Rothbury Dr. Darl DL3 .... 208 B5
Rothbury Rd. Durham DH1 .... 58 D7
Rotherham Cl. H le Sp DH5 .... 38 D6
Rothesay. Ouston DH2 .... 8 F1
Rothley Ave. Peter SR8 .... 85 F8
Rothley Terr. Medom DH8 .... 4 B1
Rough Lea Colliery.
  Hunw DL15 .... 125 E8
Rough Lea La. Hunw DL15 .... 125 E7
Rough Lea Terr. Hunw DL15 ..... 125 D7
Roundhill Cl. Hur on T DL2 .... 224 C1
Roundhill Rd. Hur on T DL2 .... 224 C3
Rowan Ave. Shild DL4 .... 149 B1
Rowan Ct. Darl DL3 .... 208 C1
Rowan Ct. Esh W DH7 .... 77 C7
Rowan Dr. Durham DH1 .... 58 E8
Rowan Dr. H le H DH5 .... 38 F4
Rowan Lea. Brand DH7 .... 79 B4
Rowan Oval. Sedge TS21 .... 153 B7
Rowan Pl. New Ay DL5 .... 171 B6
Rowell Cl. Ryhope SR2 & SR3 .... 22 C6
Rowlands Gill Cty Inf Sch.
  R Gill NE39 .... 1 F3
Rowlands Gill Jun Sch.
  R Gill NE39 .... 1 F3
Rowlands Terr. Hut Hen TS28 ... 108 E6
Rowlandson Terr. [5]
  Ferry DL17 .... 129 B5
Rowley Bank. Cons DH8 .... 29 F6
Rowley Cl. N Bran DH7 .... 78 E7
Rowley Cres. Esh W DH7 .... 55 D1
Rowley Dr. Ush M DH7 .... 57 B1
Rowley Link. Esh W DH7 .... 55 D1
Roxburgh Cl. Blay NE21 .... 2 A8
Roxby Moor Ave. Darl DL1 ...... 224 D7
Royal Gr. Crook DL15 .... 100 E4
Royal Oak Cotts. Stanh DL13 ..... 71 A5
Royal Oak Yd. Darl DL3 .... 208 F2
Royal Rd. Stanl DH9 .... 17 F7
Royal Yard. Cockf DL13 .... 166 D5
Ruby Ave. Chilt DL17 .... 150 F8
Ruby St. Darl DL3 .... 209 A6
Ruby St. Shild DL4 .... 148 F1
Ruddock Ave. Bish Au DL14 ...... 148 A5
Rudds Hill. Ferry DL17 .... 129 C5
Rudland Way. H Eth DL14 .... 146 F6
Rumby Hill Bank.
  How le W DL15 .... 124 F8
Rumby Hill La. Crook DL15 ...... 101 A2
Runcie Ave. Bowb DH6 .... 105 D8
Runciman Rd. Hartle TS24 .... 111 F2
Runcorn. Ryhope SR2 .... 22 C7
Runnymede. Gr Lum DH3 .... 37 A8
Runnymede. Ryhope SR2 .... 22 D7
Runnymede Ct. [6]
  Bish Au DL14 .... 148 C8
Runnymede Gdns. Chopw NE17 ... 4 B7
Runswick Cl. N Silk SR3 .... 22 C7
Rush Pk. Bish Au DL14 .... 147 E6
Rushey Gill. Brand DH7 .... 79 A4
Rushford. Ryhope SR2 .... 22 D6
Rushsyde Cl. Whick NE16 .... 2 E5
Rushy Lea La. Wols DL13 .... 97 D4
Rushyford Ct. [1] New Ay DL5 .. 171 D8
Ruskin Ave. C le S DH2 .... 19 E3
Ruskin Ave. E Lane DH5 .... 61 D8
Ruskin Ave. [1] Shild DL4 .... 148 F1
Ruskin Cl. Da on T DL2 .... 235 B5
Ruskin Cl. Stanl DH9 .... 18 B7
Ruskin Cres. Thorn DH6 .... 83 C4
Ruskin Rd. Birt DH3 .... 9 C4
Ruskin Rd. Darl DL1 .... 224 A6
Russ St. Will DL15 .... 101 C3
Russel Ct. Cons DH8 .... 15 A3
Russell Ct. New Ay DL5 .... 171 A8
Russell Pl. Will DL15 .... 102 A4
Russell St. Bish Au DL14 .... 148 B8
Russell St. Darl DL1 .... 209 A2
Russell St. Esh W DH7 .... 77 C6
Russell Terr. Birt DH3 .... 9 B6
Russell's Yd. Will DL15 .... 101 F3
Rustland Dr. Darl DL3 .... 223 D8
Ruswarp Dr. Silk SR3 .... 22 B6
Rutherford Ave. Seaham SR7 ..... 40 F8
Rutherford House. Eas SR8 .... 63 D4
Rutherford La. Scar DL12 .... 217 C4
Rutherford Terr. [2] Ferry DL17 129 A5
Rutland Ave. Bish Au DL14 .... 148 B6
Rutland Ave. [3] N Silk SR3 ..... 22 A7
Rutland Dr. Will DL15 .... 102 A3
Rutland Pl. Cons DH8 .... 30 B7
Rutland Rd. Cons DH8 .... 30 B7
Rutland Sq. Birt DH3 .... 9 B5
Rutland St. Cound DL14 .... 149 D8
Rutland St. H le H DH5 .... 38 F4
Rutland St. Seaham SR7 .... 41 B8
Rutland Terr. Hasw DH6 .... 61 E1
Rutland Wlk. Peter SR8 .... 85 C8
Ryan Terr. Wh Hi DH6 .... 83 E1
Rydal Ave. E Lane DH5 .... 61 C8
Rydal Ave. Stanl DH9 .... 17 D4
Rydal Cl. Sacr DH7 .... 35 B3
Rydal Cres. Blay NE21 .... 2 B8
Rydal Cres. Peter SR8 .... 85 E6
Rydal Dr. Crook DL15 .... 101 A3
Rydal Gr. Even DL14 .... 147 A1
Rydal Mews. Leadg DH8 .... 15 D4
Rydal Mount. Eas SR8 .... 63 D4
Rydal Rd. C le S DH2 .... 20 C1
Rydal Rd. Darl DL1 .... 224 B8
Rydal Rd. Ferry DL17 .... 128 F5
Rydal Way. Redmar TS21 .... 195 B7

Ryde Terr. Ann Pl DH9 .... 16 F5
Ryde Terrace Bglws. Ann Pl DH9 16 F5
Ryder Ct. New Ay DL17 .... 150 C3
Rye Hill. Darl DL3 .... 208 D4
Rye View Rd. Sland SR2 .... 22 F7
Ryedale. Belm DH1 .... 59 D3
Ryehill View. E Rain DH5 .... 38 C5
Ryelands Rd. Durham DH1 .... 58 C8
Ryemount Rd. Ryhope SR2 .... 22 D7
Ryhope General Hospl.
  Ryhope SR2 .... 22 F5
Ryhope Inf Sch. Ryhope SR2 ...... 22 F7
Ryhope Jun Sch. Ryhope SR2 .... 22 F7
Ryhope Rd. Ryhope SR2 .... 23 A7
Ryhope Rd. Sland SR2 .... 23 A8
Ryhope St. H le Sp DH5 .... 38 F8
Ryhope St. Ryhope SR2 .... 22 F7
Ryhope St S. Ryhope SR2 .... 22 F7
Ryhope Village C of E Prim Sch.
  Ryhope SR2 .... 22 F6
Rylstone Cl. New Ay DL5 .... 171 B8
Rymers Cl. Eas SR8 .... 63 A3
Ryton Cres. Seaham SR7 .... 41 A7
Ryton Cres. Stanl DH9 .... 18 A8
Sabin Terr. Ann Pl DH9 .... 17 B4
Sacriston Jun & Inf Schs.
  Sacr DH7 .... 35 C2
Sacriston La. Wit Gil DH7 .... 35 B1
Sadb St. Darl DL1 .... 210 E7
Sadberge C of E Sch.
  Sadb DL1 .... 210 E7
Sadberge Rd. M St G DL2 .... 210 E1
Saddler St. Bish Au DL14 .... 148 B8
Saddler St. Durham DH1 .... 58 C1
Saddler St. Ferry DL17 .... 128 F5
Saddlery The. New Ay DL5 .... 170 F8
Sadler La. Even DL14 .... 167 D6
Sadler La. Kinn DL12 .... 164 C1
Saint Ct. Silk SR3 .... 22 A5
St Aidan Cres. Thorn DH6 .... 83 C3
St Aidan's Ave. Durham DH1 .... 58 B5
St Aidan's Coll. Durham DH1 .... 80 B7
St Aidan's Cres. Durham DH1 ...... 58 A2
St Aidan's Pl. Cons DH8 .... 14 E4
St Aidan's St. Cons DH8 .... 14 E4
St Aidan's Terr. Wing TS29 .... 107 F6
St Aidan's Wlk. Bish Au DL14 ... 148 C6
St Aidan's Wlk. [2] New Ay DL5 171 F8
St Alban's Cl. Gr Lum DH3 .... 37 B6
St Alban's Gn. Darl DL1 .... 209 F5
St Alban's St. Tow Law DL13 ...... 75 C2
St Alban's Terr. Trim TS29 .... 107 E3
St Aldwyn Rd. Seaham SR7 .... 41 B8
St Andrew's Cl. Cons DH8 .... 14 D4
St Andrew's Cl. New Ay DL5 .... 171 E1
St Andrew's Cres. Durham DH1 .. 14 D4
St Andrew's Crest.
  Bish Au DL14 .... 148 C7
St Andrew's Gdns. Cons DH8 ..... 14 D4
St Andrew's La. Spenny DL16 ... 104 A1
St Andrew's Pl. Bish Au DL14 .. 148 C7
St Andrew's Pl. Westg DL13 .... 68 B1
St Andrew's Rd. Bish Au DL14 .. 148 C5
St Andrew's Rd. Bish Au DL14 .. 148 D5
St Andrew's Rd. Cons DH8 .... 14 D4
St Andrew's Rd. Spenny DL16 .. 104 A1
St Andrew's Rd. Tanf L DH9 .... 6 F1
St Andrew's Sq. Murton SR7 ...... 40 E4
St Andrew's St. Darl DL1 .... 209 A5
St Andrew's Terr. Bish Au DL14 148 C6
St Andrews. Fence DH4 .... 38 B8
St Andrews Cl. Darl DL1 .... 209 D4
St Andrews Cl. New Ay DL17 .... 150 C3
St Andrews Ct. New Ay DL17 .... 150 C3
St Andrews Gr. Hartle TS27 ..... 111 D4
St Andrews Way.
  New Ay DL1,DL3 & DL5 .... 191 A6
St Anne's C of E Prim Sch.
  Bish Au DL14 .... 148 A6
St Anne's Convent High Sch.
  Wols DL13 .... 97 F7
St Annes Gdns. M St G DL2 ...... 225 F6
St Aubyn's Way. Stanl DH9 .... 18 B7
St Augustine's Prim Sch.
  Darl DL1 .... 208 E1
St Augustines Way.
  Darl DL1 & DL3 .... 208 F2
St Barbara's Wlk. [1]
  New Ay DL5 .... 171 F8
St Barnabas. Bourn DH4 .... 21 D3
St Bede Ave. Fishb TS21 .... 131 C5
St Bede Cres. Thorn DH6 .... 83 B3
St Bede's Cl. Durham DH1 .... 58 A1
St Bede's Cl. H le H DH5 .... 39 A4
St Bede's Ct. Leadg DH8 .... 32 E5
St Bede's Gram Tech Sch.
  M Law DH7 .... 32 F6
St Bede's RC Comp Sch.
  Peter SR8 .... 85 C8
St Bede's RC Prim Sch.
  Darl DL1 .... 209 C6
St Bede RC Jun & Inf Sch.
  Sacr DH7 .... 35 B3
St Benet's RC Jun Mix Inf Sch.
  Ouston DH2 .... 8 F1
St Brandon's Gr. Brand DH7 .... 79 A4
St Brelades Way. Stanl DH9 .... 18 B7
St Catherine Cl. Fishb TS21 ..... 131 C5
St Chad Sq. Thorn DH6 .... 83 B3
St Chad's RC Sch. Wit Pk DL14 147 A8
St Chads Cl. Bish Au DL14 .... 148 D5
St Charles Rd. Spenny DL16 ..... 104 A1
St Clare's Abbey. Darl DL3 ...... 208 C2
St Cuthbert Ave. C le S DH3 ...... 20 D3
St Cuthbert Rd. Thorn DH6 .... 83 C3
St Cuthbert's Ave.
  Hi Eth DL14 .... 146 F5
St Cuthbert's Cl. H le H DH5 ...... 39 A4
St Cuthbert's Cres. Trim TS29 .. 107 D1
St Cuthbert's Hospl.
  Hur on T DL2 .... 235 B7

St Cuthbert's Mix Jun & Inf Sch.
  Crook DL15 .... 100 F4
St Cuthbert's Rd. Peter SR8 .... 85 D5
St Cuthbert's Rd. Sunn NE16 .... 7 B7
St Michaels. Fence DH4 .... 38 B8
St Cuthbert's Society (Coll, Durham
  Univ). Durham DH1 .... 80 C8
St Cuthbert's Terr. Dal le D SR7 40 F5
St Cuthbert's Terr. Ferry DL17 128 E6
St Cuthbert's Way. Cornf DL17 105 E1
St Cuthbert's Way. Darl DL1 .... 209 A1
St Cuthbert's Way.
  New Ay DL5 .... 171 D5
St Cuthbert's Wlk.
  Bish Au DL14 .... 148 C6
St Cuthbert's Wlk. C le S DH3 ... 20 C3
St Cuthberts Ave. Durham DH1 .. 58 A5
St Cuthberts Pk. Sunn NE16 .... 7 A8
St Cuthberts Pl. Darl DL3 .... 208 E2
St David's Cl. Spenny DL16 ...... 104 B3
St David's Gn. Darl DL1 .... 209 F5
St Ebba's Way. Bish Au DL14 ...... 3 E3
St Edmund's Terr. Dipton DH9 .. 16 C7
St Edmund's Terr. Seaham SR7 153 B6
St Edmunds Gn. Sedge TS21 .... 153 B7
St Edwin's Cl. H Con DL2 .... 206 F3
St Elizabeth's Cl. New Ay DL17 150 E2
St Francis C of E Sch.
  New Ay DL5 .... 171 A7
St George's Est. Wash NE38 .... 21 C8
St George's Dr. Cons DH8 .... 14 E3
St Giles Cl. Darl DL3 .... 208 A1
St Godric's RC (Aided) Jun & Inf
  Sch. Durham DH1 .... 58 C2
St Godrics Rd. New Ay DL5 ...... 171 C6
St Gregory Cl. Staind DL2 .... 186 C5
St Helen Auckland Jun Mix & Inf
  Sch. Bish Au DL14 .... 147 D2
St Helen's Cres. Quo Hi DH6 .... 106 D7
St Heliers Way. Stanl DH9 .... 18 B7
St Hild Cl. Darl DL3 .... 208 B1
St Hild's Coll C of E Sch.
  Belm DH1 .... 59 A4
St Hild's Coll. Durham DH1 .... 58 C2
St Hild's La. Durham DH1 .... 58 E2
St Ives Pl. Murton SR7 .... 40 D4
St Ives' Rd. Leadg DH8 .... 15 D4
St James Cl. Thor Th TS21 ...... 175 D4
St James Gdns. Wit le W DL14 124 B3
St James Gr. Hart TS27 .... 110 F2
St John Vianney RC Sch.
  Hartle TS24 .... 111 F3
St John's Chapel Cty Sch.
  St J Ch DL13 .... 67 C1
St John's Coll (Theological).
  Durham DH1 .... 80 C8
St John's Cres. Bowb DH6 .... 81 C1
St John's Ct. Kir Me DL16 .... 128 A3
St John's Gdns. Will DL15 .... 101 D2
St John's Pl. Birt DH3 .... 9 C4
St John's Pl. Darl DL1 .... 209 B1
St John's RC Comp Sch.
  Bish Au DL14 .... 147 F5
St John's Rd. Brand DH7 .... 79 B4
St John's Rd. Durham DH1 .... 58 A1
St John's Terr. Dipton DH9 .... 16 C7
St John's Terr. [3]
  Seaham SR7 .... 22 E1
St John's Wlk. Escomb DL14 ..... 125 D1
St Joseph's Catholic Sch.
  Durham DH1 .... 59 A2
St Joseph's Cl. Durham DH1 .... 59 A2
St Joseph's Cl. [7] Birt DH3 .... 9 C5
St Joseph's RC Aided Sch.
  R Gill NE39 .... 1 B2
St Joseph's RC Jun & Inf Sch.
  Murton SR7 .... 40 C2
St Joseph's RC Jun & Inf Sch.
  Ush M DH7 .... 57 A2
St Joseph's RC Prim Sch.
  New Ay DL5 .... 171 B7
St Lawrence Cl. H Pitt DH6 .... 60 C7
St Lawrence Rd. H Pitt DH6 .... 60 B5
St Leonard's Cl. Peter SR8 .... 85 B5
St Leonard's RC Comp Sch.
  Durham DH1 .... 58 B3
St Leonard's RC Prim Sch.
  N Silk SR3 .... 22 B7
St Margaret's C of E Inf Sch.
  Durham DH1 .... 58 B1
St Margaret's C of E Jun Sch.
  Durham DH1 .... 80 B8
St Margaret's Cl. M St G DL2 .. 225 F6
St Margaret's Dr. Durham DH1 .. 58 B1
St Margaret's Dr. Tanf DH9 .... 6 D4
St Margaret's (Durham Sch
  Annexe). Durham DH1 .... 58 B1
St Mark's Cl. Bish Au DL14 ...... 148 F5
St Marks Rd. Fishb TS21 .... 131 C5
St Mary Magdalen's Seaham
  Harbour RC Jun & Inf Sch.
  Seaham SR7 .... 41 C8
St Mary's Catholic Prim Sch.
  Bar Cas DL12 .... 201 A5
St Mary's Cl. Bar Cas DL12 ..... 201 A5
St Mary's Cl. Bish Au DL14 ...... 148 B5
St Mary's Cl. C le S DH2 .... 20 B1
St Mary's Cl. Cons DH8 .... 14 D4
St Mary's Cl. Eas SR8 .... 63 A3
St Mary's Cl. H Shin DH1 .... 80 F6
St Mary's Coll (Durham Univ).
  Durham DH1 .... 80 C7
St Mary's Cres. Cons DH8 .... 14 D4
St Mary's Gr. Spenny DL16 ...... 104 A3
St Mary's Prim Sch. Cons DH8 .. 14 C3
St Mary's RC Jun & Inf Sch.
  New Ay DL5 .... 171 E7
St Mary's Rd. Belm DH1 .... 59 C4
St Mary's St. Cons DH8 .... 14 D4

St Mary's Terr. Bowb DH6 .... 105 E6
St Matthews View. N Silk SR3 .... 22 A7
St Michael's Cl. Heigh DL5 ...... 170 C1
St Michael's Cres. Heigh DL5 ... 170 C1
  H le Sp DH5 .... 38 E7
St Michael's RC Jun & Inf Schs.
  Durham DH1 .... 58 A1
St Monica Gr. Durham DH1 .... 58 A1
St Nicholas' Cty Sch.
  Durham DH1 .... 58 E2
St Nicholas Dr. Durham DH1 ...... 57 F4
St Nicholas Ind Est. Darl DL1 .. 209 B4
St Nicholas Terr. Eas SR8 .... 63 D4
St Ninian's Cl. Darl DL3 .... 208 A1
St Oswald Sq. Durham DH1 .... 58 A7
St Oswald's C of E Inf Sch.
  Durham DH1 .... 80 D8
St Oswalds Cl. Bish Au DL14 .... 148 D6
St Oswalds Ct. New Ay DL5 ..... 171 F8
St Oswald's Dr. Durham DH1 ..... 80 A5
St Oswald's Wlk. [4]
  New Ay DL5 .... 171 F8
St Oswin's Pl. [3] Cons DH8 ..... 14 D4
St Patrick's RC Jun Mix & Inf Sch.
  Ryhope SR2 .... 22 F6
St Patrick's RC Prim Sch.
  Brand DH7 .... 79 E5
St Paul's Cl. Spenny DL16 .... 127 E8
St Paul's Dr. Pens DH4 .... 21 E8
St Paul's Gdns. Spenny DL16 ... 127 E8
St Paul's Pl. Darl DL1 .... 209 A5
St Paul's Rd. Wing TS29 .... 108 A5
St Paul's St. Spenny DL16 .... 127 E8
St Paul's Terr. Darl DL1 .... 209 A5
St Paul's Terr. [5] Ryhope SR2 .. 22 F6
St Paul's Terr. Shild DL4 .... 149 A2
St Paul's Terr. W Pel DH9 .... 19 A6
St Paul's Way. Hunw DL15 .... 125 D7
St Peter's Catholic Sec Mod Sch.
  Hartle TS24 .... 111 F3
St Stephen's Cl. Will DL15 .... 102 A3
St Stevens Cl. Pens DH4 .... 21 E8
St Teresa's RC Prim Sch.
  Darl DL2 .... 224 D8
St Thomas Cl. Eas SR8 .... 63 A3
St Thomas' Cl. Stanh DL13 .... 71 A4
St Thomas' Cl. Will DL15 .... 101 F3
St Thomas More RC Prim Sch.
  Belm DH1 .... 59 D3
St Thomas's RC Sch.
  Wols DL13 .... 97 F7
St Vincent Terr. [2]
  Cockf DL13 .... 166 C6
St Wilfrid's RC Prim Sch.
  Bish Au DL14 .... 148 A5
St Wilfrids Wlk. Bish Au DL14 .. 148 D5
Salcombe Cl. Seaham SR7 .... 41 A6
Salem Ave. Cons DH8 .... 31 B8
Salisbury Ave. C le S DH3 .... 20 C2
Salisbury Cl. Cons DH8 .... 14 E7
Salisbury Cl. Gr Lum DH3 .... 37 A6
Salisbury Cres. Cornf DL17 ...... 129 F8
Salisbury Pl. Bish Au DL14 .... 148 C7
Salisbury Rd. M St G DL2 .... 225 E7
Salisbury Rd. Durham DH1 .... 58 E8
Salisbury St. Cons DH8 .... 15 A3
Salisbury St. Stanl DH9 .... 17 D5
Salisbury Terr. Shild DL4 .... 148 F1
Salt Yd. Darl DL3 .... 208 F2
Salter House Dr. Grind TS22 .... 155 D2
Salter Houses. Grind TS22 .... 155 C3
Salter's Dr. Fishb TS21 .... 131 C5
Salter's Gate. Satley DL13 .... 51 F2
Salter's La. H le H DH5 & SR7 ... 39 F6
Salter's La. Hasw DH6 .... 61 E6
Salter's La.
  Seaton DH5 & SR7 & DH6 .... 39 F6
Salter's La. Sedge TS21 .... 131 C4
Salter's La.
  Shot Co DH6 & SR8 & TS28 ..... 84 C5
Salter's La. Trim TS21 .... 132 A4
Salter's La. Trim TS29 .... 107 D3
Salter's La. Wing TS28 .... 108 E3
Salter's La. Wing TS29 .... 107 D3
Salterfen La. Sland SR2 .... 23 A8
Salterfen Rd. Sland SR2 .... 23 A8
Salters Ave. Darl DL1 .... 209 D4
Salters Cl. Darl DL1 .... 209 C6
Salters La. Braf DL1 .... 192 F7
Salters La. Darl DL1 .... 209 B8
Salters La N. Darl DL1 .... 209 B7
Salters La S. Darl DL1 .... 209 D5
Salters Lane Sch. Darl DL1 ...... 209 D5
Saltersgate La. Satley DL13 ...... 51 F2
Saltersgate Rd. Darl DL1 .... 209 B7
Salutation Rd. Darl DL3 .... 223 B8
Salvin St. Sland B DH6 .... 104 B6
Salvin St. Spenny DL16 .... 104 B1
Salvin Terr. Fishb TS21 .... 131 B5
Sampson Pl. [3] New Ay DL5 ... 171 C8
Sancroft Dr. H le Sp DH5 .... 38 E7
Sandbach Cl. Wash NE38 .... 9 F2
Sandbanks Dr. Hartle TS24 ...... 111 D4
Sanders Gdns. [3] Birt DH3 .... 9 C5
Sanders' Memorial Homes.
  C le S DH3 .... 20 C3
Sanderson Cl. New Ay DL5 ...... 171 C6
Sanderson Rd. Hur on T DL2 .... 224 D1
Sanderson St. [3] Coxhoe DH6 . 106 A4
Sanderson St. Darl DL1 .... 209 A4
Sandgate. Ann Pl DH9 .... 17 B4
Sandlewood Wlk. Stanl DH9 ...... 18 A7
Sandown Dr. New Ay DL17 .... 150 C2
Sandpiper Cl. Wash NE38 .... 9 F2
Sandray Cl. Birt DH3 .... 9 D1
Sandriggs. Darl DL3 .... 208 C5

Sandringham Cres. [11]
  Peter SR8 .... 86 B6
Sandringham Dr. Ann Pl DH9 ..... 16 F5
Sandringham Rd. Crook DL15 .. 100 F4
Sandringham Terr.
  Cound DL14 .... 127 D1
Sands The. Durham DH1 .... 58 D2
Sandsay Cl. Sland SR2 .... 22 D8
Sandwell Dr. Pens DH4 .... 21 F8
Sandwich Gr. Hartle TS27 .... 111 D4
Sandwick Terr. Wh Hi DH6 .... 83 E1
Sandy Bank. Sedge TS21 .... 152 D5
Sandy Gate. Durham DH1 .... 58 A3
Sandy Leas La. Elton TS21 ...... 195 B2
Sandy Lonnen. Brance DL15 .... 77 C3
Sandyford. Pelton DH2 .... 19 E7
Sandyford Pl. Pelton DH2 .... 19 E7
Sandypath La. Burnop NE16 .... 6 A7
Satley Cl. Crook DL15 .... 100 D3
Satley Jun Mix & Inf Sch.
  Satley DL13 .... 53 B3
Saturn Cl. Eas SR8 .... 63 C4
Saturn St. Seaham SR7 .... 41 A7
Saunders Ave. Hamst DL13 ...... 123 B3
Sawley Cl. Darl DL3 .... 207 F5
Sawmill Ave. B Rocks TS27 ...... 111 B8
Sawmill La. Brand DH7 .... 79 B4
Saxby Dr. Will DL15 .... 101 E1
Saxon Gn. Escomb DL14 .... 125 D1
Saxon Terr. Cons DH8 .... 14 E3
Sayer Wlk. Peter SR8 .... 85 E5
Scafell. Birt DH3 .... 9 D1
Scafell Cl. Peter SR8 .... 85 E6
Scafell Ct. Ann Pl DH9 .... 16 E3
Scafell Gdns. Crook DL15 .... 100 F2
Scardale Way. Belm DH1 .... 59 E4
Scargill. Darl DL1 .... 224 C8
Scargill Dr. Spenny DL16 .... 103 F2
Scarth St. Darl DL3 .... 208 E1
Scholar's Path. New Ay DL5 ..... 171 A7
School Ave. Coxhoe DH6 .... 105 F3
School Ave. Kelloe DH6 .... 106 E6
School Ave. W Rain DH4 .... 37 F2
School Aycliffe. Heigh DL5 . 170 E3
School Aycliffe La.
  New Ay DL5 .... 170 E3
School Cl. Thor Th TS21 .... 175 D3
School Hill. Laneh DL13 .... 66 A8
School Houses. Ingle DL2 .... 188 A6
School Houses. R Gill NE39 .... 5 B8
School La. H Spen NE39 .... 1 A3
School La. Stanl DH9 .... 17 D5
School Rd. E Rain DH5 .... 38 C4
School Row. Will DL15 .... 102 A6
School St. Birt DH3 .... 9 C4
School St. Bowb DH6 .... 105 C4
School St. Darl DL3 .... 208 C4
School St. Eas SR8 .... 63 E4
School St. How le W DL15 .... 124 E7
School St. Seaham SR7 .... 41 D5
School St. Wit le W DL14 .... 124 B3
School Terr. Gr Lum DH4 .... 21 E1
School Terr. Stanl DH9 .... 17 D5
School View. E Lane DH5 .... 61 D8
School View. W Rain DH4 .... 37 F1
Schoolhouse La. Byer NE16 .... 6 E7
Scira Ct. Darl DL1 .... 209 B5
Scorer's La. Gr Lum DH3 .... 37 B8
Scotland Head. Blay NE21 .... 2 A8
Scotland La. Staind DL13 & DL2 166 B3
Scotland St. Ryhope SR2 .... 23 A6
Scott Pl. New Ay DL5 .... 171 C8
Scott Rd. Bish Au DL14 .... 148 B4
Scott St. Shild DL4 .... 169 F8
Scott St. Stanl DH9 .... 17 E6
Scott's Terr. Darl DL1 .... 209 A6
Scott's Terr. H le H DH5 .... 39 A4
Scripton Gill. Brand DH7 .... 79 A4
Scripton Gill Rd. Brand DH7 ..... 78 F3
Scripton La. Brance DH7 .... 103 C7
Scutterhill Bank. Westg DL13 ... 68 B2
Sea View. B Rocks TS27 .... 86 F2
Sea View. Eas SR8 .... 63 B3
Sea View. Ryhope SR2 .... 23 A6
Sea View Gdns. Peter SR8 .... 86 A8
Sea View Ind Est. Peter SR8 ...... 63 F1
Sea View Wlk. Murton SR7 .... 40 E4
Seaburn Dr. [1] H le Sp DH4 ...... 38 C8
Seaham Camden Square Inf Sch.
  Seaham SR7 .... 41 C6
Seaham Golf Course.
  Seaham SR7 .... 41 C4
Seaham Grange Ind Est.
  Seaham SR7 .... 22 F2
Seaham Kingfisher Ind Est.
  Seaham SR7 .... 41 A8
Seaham Northlea Sec Sch.
  Seaham SR7 .... 23 A1
Seaham Parkside Cty Inf Sch.
  Seaham SR7 .... 41 C7
Seaham Princess Road Jun Sch.
  Seaham SR7 .... 41 C7
Seaham Rd. H le Sp DH5 .... 39 A8
Seaham Rd. Ryhope SR2 .... 23 A6
Seaham Ropery Walk Cty Jun
  & Inf Sch. Seaham SR7 .... 41 E6
Seaham St. N Silk SR3 .... 22 A7
Seaham St. Seaham SR7 .... 41 E5
Seaham Sta. Seaham SR7 .... 41 C6
Seaham Westlea Cty Jun Mix
  & Inf Sch. Seaham SR7 .... 40 F8
Seaside La. Eas SR8 .... 63 D4
Seaside La S. Eas SR8 .... 63 E4
Seaside La. Eas SR8 .... 39 A7
Seaton Cres. Seaham SR7 .... 22 E1
Seaton Gr. Seaton SR7 .... 40 D8
Seaton La. Seaham SR7 .... 22 E1
Seaton La. Seaton SR7 .... 40 F8
Secker Pl. New Ay DL5 .... 171 F7
Second Ave. C le S DH2 .... 20 B2

Second Ave. C le S DH2 ...... 20 B8
Second St. B Coll TS27 ...... 86 D3
Second St. Cons DH8 ...... 15 B2
Second St. Leadg DH8 ...... 15 C5
Second St. Leadg DH8 ...... 15 C6
Second St. Qua Ho DH9 ...... 17 D2
Sedgefield Community Coll.
  Sedge TS21 ...... 153 B7
Sedgefield Community Hospl.
  Sedge TS21 ...... 131 B3
Sedgefield Cty Jun Mix & Inf Sch.
  Sedge TS21 ...... 153 B6
Sedgefield Enterprise Ctr.
  Spenny DL16 ...... 104 D2
Sedgefield Hardwick Cty Jun Inf
  Sch. Sedge TS21 ...... 153 B7
Sedgefield Racecourse.
  Sedge TS21 ...... 152 E5
Sedgefield Terr. Fishb TS21 ...... 131 B5
Sedgeletch Rd. 5 Fence DH4 ...... 38 A8
Sedgwick St. Darl DL3 ...... 208 E4
Selaby La. Gain DL2 ...... 187 D2
Selaby La. Lang DL2 ...... 187 D2
Selborne Gdns. Cons DH8 ...... 14 E6
Selbourne Terr. Darl DL3 ...... 208 F3
Selby Cl. Bish Au DL14 ...... 147 D2
Selby Cres. Darl DL3 ...... 208 A5
Selby Gdns. Cons DH8 ...... 14 C1
Selby's Grave. Blay NE21 ...... 1 F8
Selkirk Cres. Birt DH3 ...... 9 C6
Selset Cl. Darl DL1 ...... 224 C7
Sennings La. Romald DL12 ...... 162 B1
Seton Wlk. New Ay DL5 ...... 171 E5
Setting Stones. Wash NE38 ...... 21 A8
Sevenacres. Gr Lum DH3 ...... 37 B7
Seventh Ave. C le S DH2 ...... 20 B4
Seventh St. B Coll TS27 ...... 86 D4
Seventh St. Peter SR8 ...... 86 A6
Seventh St. Peter SR8 ...... 86 A7
Severn Cl. Peter SR8 ...... 85 C4
Severn Cres. Stanl DH9 ...... 17 E5
Severn Way. Darl DL1 ...... 224 A6
Seymour St. Bish Au DL14 ...... 148 B6
Seymour St. Cons DH8 ...... 15 A2
Seymour St. Peter SR8 ...... 86 B6
Seymour Terr. H le H DH5 ...... 39 B1
Shadforth Cl. Peter SR8 ...... 85 A4
Shadon Way. Birt DH3 ...... 9 E3
Shaftesbury Ave. B Coll TS27 ...... 86 D4
Shaftesbury Ave. Ryhope SR2 ...... 22 E7
Shaftesbury Cres. B Coll TS27 ...... 86 C4
Shaftesbury Rd. B Coll TS27 ...... 86 C5
Shafto Cl. Cons DH8 ...... 31 B8
Shafto Rd. New Ay DL5 ...... 171 E6
Shafto St. By Gr DL16 ...... 102 E1
Shafto St. Spenny DL16 ...... 127 F7
Shafto Terr. Crag DH9 ...... 18 D2
Shafto Terr. Stanl DH9 ...... 17 F8
Shafto Way. New Ay DL5 ...... 171 E7
Shaftsbury Dr. Brand DH7 ...... 79 A2
Shakespeare Cl. Stanl DH9 ...... 18 B7
Shakespeare Rd. Darl DL1 ...... 224 A7
Shakespeare St. H le Sp DH5 ...... 38 F8
Shakespeare St. 7 Seaham SR7 41 D7
Shakespeare St. Thorn DH6 ...... 83 D4
Shakespeare Terr. C le St DH2 ...... 19 E3
Shakespeare Terr. Eas SR8 ...... 63 C4
Shalcombe Cl. Silk SR3 ...... 22 A6
Shannon Way. Darl DL1 ...... 223 F6
Sharon Ave. Kelloe DH6 ...... 106 D5
Sharp Cres. Belm DH1 ...... 59 A3
Sharp Rd. New Ay DL5 ...... 171 D6
Sharpley Dr. Seaham SR7 ...... 40 E8
Shaw Cres. Mid in T DL12 ...... 160 D7
Shaw La. Barn DL11 ...... 219 A1
Shaw La. Ebch DH8 & NE17 ...... 3 F4
Shaw La. Medom NE16 ...... 4 A4
Shaw St. Seaham SR7 ...... 41 D7
Shaw St. Spenny DL16 ...... 127 F8
Shaw Wood Cl. Durham DH1 ...... 58 A3
Shawbrow View. Bish Au DL14 148 B4
Shawbrow View. Darl DL1 ...... 207 F2
Shearwater Ave. Darl DL1 ...... 209 D2
Sheelin Ave. C le S DH2 ...... 20 C1
Sheen Cl. W Rain DH4 ...... 38 A2
Sheep Hill. Burnop NE16 ...... 6 B6
Shelley Ave. E Lane DH5 ...... 61 D8
Shelley Cl. Crook DL15 ...... 100 C2
Shelley Ct. C le St DH2 ...... 19 E3
Shelley Gdns. C le St DH2 ...... 19 E3
Shelley Rd. Darl DL1 ...... 209 C3
Shelley Sq. Eas SR8 ...... 63 C3
Shelley St. Seaham SR7 ...... 41 D7
Shelley Terr. Chilt DH17 ...... 150 F7
Shelly Cl. Stanl DH9 ...... 18 A6
Sheppards Croft. New Ay DL5 ...... 170 F4
Sheppey Cl. Silk SR3 ...... 22 A6
Sheraton Bank. Hut Hen TS27 ...... 109 F3
Sheraton Cl. New Ay DL5 ...... 171 E6
Sheraton Rd. New Ay DL5 ...... 171 E6
Sheraton St. Darl DL3 ...... 208 F5
Sherborne. Gr Lum DH3 ...... 37 B8
Sherborne Cl. Darl DL3 ...... 207 F4
Sherborne House. Darl DL3 ...... 207 F4
Sherburn Cty Jun & Inf Sch.
  Sherb DH6 ...... 60 A2
Sherburn Gn. R Gill NE39 ...... 1 F3
Sherburn Hill Cty Mix Inf Sch.
  S Hill DH6 ...... 60 D1
Sherburn Hospl. Sherb DH1 ...... 81 D8
Sherburn Park Dr. R Gill NE39 ...... 1 F3
Sherburn Rd. Durham DH1 ...... 59 A2
Sherburn Road Flats.
  Durham DH1 ...... 58 F2
Sherburn Terr. Cons DH8 ...... 15 A2
Sherburn Terr. Hams NE17 ...... 3 F5
Sherburn Villas. 19 Cons DH8 ...... 14 F3
Sheridan Dr. Crook DL15 ...... 100 C2
Sheriff's Moor Ave. E Lane DH5 61 E8
Sheringham Cl. Silk SR3 ...... 22 A4
Sherwood Cl. Bar Cas DL12 ...... 201 B6

Sherwood Cl. Cons DH8 ...... 14 E7
Sherwood Ct. 5 Silk SR3 ...... 22 A6
Shetland Cl. 1 Silk SR3 ...... 22 A6
Shetland Dr. Darl DL1 ...... 209 D7
Shield Row Cty Jun Mix & Inf Sch.
  Stanl DH9 ...... 18 A8
Shield Row Gdns. Stanl DH9 ...... 17 F8
Shield Wlk. New Ay DL5 ...... 171 E7
Shieldraw La. Ann Pl DH9 ...... 17 A3
Shieldrow La. Ann Pl DH9 ...... 17 B4
Shields Rd. C le S DH3 ...... 20 D5
Shildon Cl. 4 Shild DL4 ...... 170 A8
Shildon Cty Sch. Shild DL4 ...... 148 E2
Shildon Jubilee Cty Inf Sch.
  Shild DL4 ...... 149 A1
Shildon Rd. Heigh DL5 ...... 170 B4
Shildon St. Darl DL1 ...... 209 A5
Shildon St John's C of E (Cont)
  Jun & Inf Sch. Shild DL4 ...... 149 A1
Shildon Sta. Shild DL4 ...... 170 B8
Shildon Sunnydale Comp Sch.
  Shild DL4 ...... 149 A2
Shillmoor Cl. C le St DH2 ...... 19 F1
Shincliffe C of E Jun Mix & Inf Sch.
  H Shin DH1 ...... 81 B5
Shincliffe La. Cassop DH1 ...... 81 C7
Shincliffe La. H Shin DH1 ...... 81 C7
Shincliffe La. Sherb DH1 ...... 81 D7
Shinwell Cres. Thorn DH6 ...... 83 C4
Shinwell Terr. Murton SR7 ...... 40 B3
Shinwell Terr. Wh Hi DH6 ...... 83 E2
Shipley Gr. Bish Au DL14 ...... 147 F5
Shipley Terr. Coth DL12 ...... 182 E4
Shipley Terr. Crook DL15 ...... 101 A3
Shire Chase. Durham DH1 ...... 58 D8
Shirley La. Even DL14 ...... 167 D7
Shirley Terr. Even DL14 ...... 167 C7
Short Bank. Mick DL12 ...... 161 A3
Short Gr. Murton SR7 ...... 40 A3
Short St. Bish Au DL14 ...... 148 B5
Shotley Bridge Cty Inf Sch.
  Cons DH8 ...... 14 D6
Shotley Bridge Cty Jun & Inf Sch.
  Cons DH8 ...... 14 C7
Shotley Bridge General Hospl.
  Cons DH8 ...... 14 E6
Shotley Grove Rd. Cons DH8 ...... 14 B5
Shotton Bank. Shot Co SR8 ...... 84 F3
Shotton Colliery Cty Inf Sch.
  Shot Co DH6 ...... 84 C7
Shotton Colliery Cty Jun Sch.
  Shot Co DH6 ...... 84 C7
Shotton Colliery Ind Est.
  Shot Co DH6 ...... 84 D7
Shotton Hall Comp Sch.
  Peter SR8 ...... 85 B4
Shotton La. Shot Co DH6 & SR8 ... 84 E5
Shotton RC Jun Mix & Inf Sch.
  Shot Co DH6 ...... 84 B7
Shotton Rd. Peter SR8 ...... 85 F7
Shotton Rd. Shot Co SR8 ...... 84 E7
Shrewsbury Cl. Peter SR8 ...... 85 B5
Shrewsbury St. Seaham SR7 ...... 41 D5
Shropshire Dr. Belm DH1 ...... 59 C2
Shull Bank. Hamst DL13 ...... 122 C6
Sid Chaplin Dr. New Ay DL5 ...... 171 C8
Sidegate. Durham DH1 ...... 58 C2
Sidlaw Ave. C le S DH2 ...... 20 A2
Sidmouth Cl. Seaham SR7 ...... 40 F6
Sidney Cl. Stanl DH9 ...... 18 B6
Sidney Terr. Tanf L DH9 ...... 17 D8
Siemans St. Ferry DL17 ...... 128 E6
Silent Bank. Cassop DH6 ...... 82 E4
Silkin Way. New Ay DL5 ...... 171 C7
Silkstun Ct. 8 N Silk SR3 ...... 22 A7
Silksworth Rd. N Silk SR3 ...... 22 A7
Silksworth Terr. N Silk SR3 ...... 22 A7
Silkworth La. 1 N Silk SR3 ...... 22 A8
Sills The. Start DL12 ...... 200 F5
Silver Courts. Brand DH7 ...... 79 B4
Silver Pl. Darl DL1 ...... 209 B1
Silver St. Cons DH8 ...... 14 D4
Silver St. Durham DH1 ...... 58 C1
Silver St. Spenny DL16 ...... 127 F8
Silver St. Wols DL13 ...... 97 F7
Silverdale Pl. New Ay DL5 ...... 171 A7
Silverdale. Silk SR3 ...... 22 A4
Silverdale Way. Whick NE16 ...... 2 F4
Silverwood Cl. Hartle TS27 ...... 111 C4
Simonburn. Wash NE38 ...... 9 F4
Simpasture Ct. New Ay DL5 ...... 171 C5
Simpasture Gate. New Ay DL5 171 D5
Simpson Ave. Bish Au DL14 ...... 147 E3
Simpson Rd. Bish Au DL14 ...... 168 BR
Simpson St. Stanl DH9 ...... 17 F7
Sinclair Dr. C le S DH3 ...... 20 D8
Sir E. D. Walker Homes.
  Darl DL1 ...... 223 D8
Sixth Ave. C le S DH2 ...... 20 B3
Sixth St. B Coll TS27 ...... 86 D4
Sixth St. Cons DH8 ...... 15 B2
Sixth St. Peter SR8 ...... 86 A7
Skeeby Rd. Darl DL1 ...... 224 B8
Skeldale Gr. Darl DL3 ...... 208 E4
Skelton Cl. Hartle TS24 ...... 111 E4
Skerne Ave. Trim TS29 ...... 107 C1
Skerne Cl. Peter SR8 ...... 85 C4
Skerne Gr. Leadg DH8 ...... 15 D5
Skerne Rd. New Ay DL5 ...... 171 E4
Skiddaw Cl. Peter SR8 ...... 85 E6
Skiddaw Ct. Ann Pl DH9 ...... 16 F3
Skinnergate. Darl DL3 ...... 208 F1
Skippers Meadow. Ush M DH7 .. 57 B1
Skipsea View. Ryhope SR2 ...... 22 D7
Skipton Cl. Ferry DL17 ...... 129 B5
Skipton Cl. 1 New Ay DL5 ...... 171 B7
Skipton Gr. Bish Au DL14 ...... 148 A6
Skipton Moor Cl. Darl DL1 ...... 224 D7
Skirlaw Cl. Chilt DL17 ...... 151 A8
Skirlaw Rd. New Ay DL5 ...... 171 E6

Skye Ct. 2 Silk SR3 ...... 22 A6
Slack The. Butter DL13 ...... 166 A7
Slaidburn Rd. Stanl DH9 ...... 17 F7
Slaley Ct. 4 Silk SR3 ...... 22 A6
Slater Pl. Bowb DH6 ...... 105 D8
Sledmere Cl. Peter SR8 ...... 85 D8
Sledwich Cotts. Whorl DL12 ...... 202 C3
Sleightholme Moor Rd.
  Bowes DL11 & DL12 ...... 229 C6
Sleightholme Moor Rd.
  Langth DL11 & DL12 ...... 229 C6
Slingley Cl. 4 Seaham SR7 ...... 22 E1
Sloshes La. Hi Eth DL14 ...... 146 C4
Smailes La. R Gill NE39 ...... 1 C2
Smailes St. Stanl DH9 ...... 17 E5
Smallhope Dr. Lanch DH7 ...... 32 F3
Smillie Cl. Peter SR8 ...... 85 D7
Smillie Rd. Seaham SR7 ...... 41 E1
Smillie St. Peter SR8 ...... 63 E1
Smith Gr. Ryhope SR2 ...... 22 E6
Smith St. Ryhope SR2 ...... 22 F6
Smith St. Tow Law DL13 ...... 75 C3
Smith St S. Ryhope SR2 ...... 22 F6
Smith's Terr. H le H DH5 ...... 39 B1
Smithfield Rd. Darl DL1 ...... 224 B8
Smithy Gn. Newsh DL11 ...... 233 F8
Smithy La. Kibble NE11 ...... 8 E8
Smythsons Cl. New Ay DL5 ...... 170 F4
Snackgate La. Heigh DL5 ...... 170 D1
Snaith Terr. Wing TS28 ...... 108 D8
Snipe La. Darl DL2 ...... 223 E6
Snipe La. Darl DL2 ...... 224 A4
Snipe La. Hur on T DL2 ...... 224 A4
Sniperley Gr. Durham DH7 ...... 57 F5
Snipes Dene. R Gill NE39 ...... 1 E3
Snotterton La. Staindrop DL2 ... 186 A5
Snow's Green Rd. Cons DH8 ...... 14 C7
Snowden Terr. Wild DL15 ...... 102 A2
Snowdon Cl. Ann Pl DH9 ...... 16 E3
Snowdon Gr. Hartle TS24 ...... 111 D4
Snowdon Pl. Peter SR8 ...... 85 A5
Snowdrop Ave. Peter SR8 ...... 85 F7
Sockburn La. Neas DL2 ...... 236 E7
Soho St. Shild DL4 ...... 170 A8
Somerset Cotts. 4 N Silk SR3 ... 22 A8
Somerset Ct. Darl DL1 ...... 209 C4
Somerset Rd. Cons DH8 ...... 30 A7
Somerset St. N Silk SR3 ...... 22 A8
Somerville Ct. 1 Darl DL1 ...... 209 B6
Sophia. Darl DL1 ...... 41 D7
Sophia St. Seaham SR7 ...... 41 D7
Sorrel Wynd. New Ay DL17 ...... 150 D2
South App. C le S DH2 ...... 20 C2
South Arden St. 16 Darl DL1 ...... 208 F1
South Ave. Shadf DH6 ...... 82 F8
South Ave. Still SR21 ...... 174 E3
South Bailey. Durham DH1 ...... 80 C8
South Burns. C le S DH3 ...... 20 C4
South Church Enterprise Pk.
  Bish Au DL14 ...... 148 C4
South Church Rd.
  Bish Au DL14 ...... 148 C7
South Cl. E Lane DH5 ...... 61 D8
South Cleatlam. Cleat DL2 ...... 186 D1
South Cotts. New Ay DL5 ...... 171 A4
South Cres. Durham DH1 ...... 58 B3
South Cres. Peter SR8 ...... 63 E1
South Cres. Seaham SR7 ...... 41 E7
South Cres. Wash NE38 ...... 21 B8
South Cross St. Leadg DH8 ...... 15 C4
South Down. C le S DH2 ...... 20 C2
South Downs. Stanl DH9 ...... 17 F5
South End Villas. Crook DL15 ... 100 E3
South Fields. Stanl DH9 ...... 17 E4
South Gn. Hett DH6 ...... 104 E5
South Gn. Staind DL2 ...... 186 D6
South Gr. New Ay DL5 ...... 171 F1
South Grange Pk. Seaham SR7 .. 22 F2
  S Hett DH6 ...... 61 F7
South Hetton Cty Jun Mix Inf Sch.
  S Hett DH6 ...... 61 F7
South Hetton Ind Est.
  S Hett DH6 ...... 61 F7
South Hetton Rd.
  E Lane DH5 & DH6 ...... 61 D8
South Lea. Wit Gil DH7 ...... 35 B1
South Leigh. Tanf L DH9 ...... 6 D1
South Magdalene. Medom DH8 ... 4 B1
South Market St. H le H DH5 ...... 39 B4
South Meadows. Dipton DH9 ... 16 D8
South Moor Golf Course.
  Qua Ho DH9 ...... 17 F3
South Moor Greenland Cty Jun &
  Inf Schs. Stanl DH9 ...... 17 D4
South Moor RC (Aided) Jun & Inf
  Sch. Stanl DH9 ...... 17 F4
South Moor Rd. Qua Ho DH9 ...... 17 E3
South Par. Cr on T DL2 ...... 234 F5
South Par. Thorn DH6 ...... 83 D4
South Railway St. Seaham SR7 .. 41 D7
South Rd. Durham DH1 ...... 80 C6
South Rd. Hi Eth DL14 ...... 146 F4
South Row. Shild DL14 ...... 149 A4
South Sherburn. R Gill NE39 ...... 1 E1
South Side. Butter DL13 ...... 144 F2
South Side (Dean Rd).
  Ferry DL17 ...... 128 F5
South Side. Eas SR8 ...... 63 B3
South Side. Midd DL4 ...... 149 E1
South St. C le S DH2 & DH3 ...... 20 B4
South St. Cons DH8 ...... 15 B2
South St. Crook DL15 ...... 100 E3
South St. Darl DL3 ...... 208 F4
South St. Durham DH1 ...... 58 C1
South St. E Rain DH5 ...... 38 C4
South St. 9 Fence DH4 ...... 38 A8
South St. Sherb DH6 ...... 60 A1
South St. Shild DL4 ...... 169 F8
South St. Spenny DL16 ...... 127 F8
South St. Still TS21 ...... 174 E3
South St. W Rain DH4 ...... 38 A2
South St. Will DL15 ...... 101 F1

South St. Will DL15 ...... 101 F3
South Stanley Cty Inf Sch.
  Stanl DH9 ...... 17 E5
South Stanley Cty Jun Mix Sch.
  Stanl DH9 ...... 17 E5
South Terr. Bish Au DL14 ...... 148 C8
South Terr. Chopw NE17 ...... 4 B8
South Terr. Corn Co DH7 ...... 55 A2
South Terr. Cr on T DL2 ...... 234 F8
South Terr. Crook DL15 ...... 101 A4
South Terr. Darl DL1 ...... 208 F1
South Terr. Durham DH1 ...... 58 A5
South Terr. Egg DL12 ...... 162 B5
South Terr. Esh W DH7 ...... 55 F1
South Terr. Peter SR8 ...... 86 A7
South Terr. Seaham SR7 ...... 41 E7
South Terr. Shild DL4 ...... 169 D8
South Terr. Spenny DL16 ...... 104 A1
South Terr. Staind DL2 ...... 186 C5
South Thorn. Stanl DH9 ...... 17 F8
South View. Ann Pl DH9 ...... 17 A3
South View. Beam DH9 ...... 19 A4
South View. Birt DH3 ...... 9 D4
South View. Bish Au DL14 ...... 147 D2
South View. Bish Au DL14 ...... 148 C7
South View. Bish Mi DL17 ...... 130 C4
South View. Brand DH7 ...... 79 C3
South View. Burnh DH7 ...... 33 D5
South View. Ca Eden SR27 ...... 85 B1
South View. Chilt DL17 ...... 150 F7
South View. Chopw NE17 ...... 4 A8
South View. Cons DH8 ...... 14 C4
South View. Cons DH8 ...... 30 F8
South View. E Lane DH5 ...... 61 D8
South View. Even DL14 ...... 167 C6
South View. Fishb TS21 ...... 131 C5
South View. 1 Ferry DL17 ...... 129 A6
South View. Gain DL2 ...... 205 A7
South View. Hart TS27 ...... 110 F2
South View. Heigh DL5 ...... 170 D1
South View. Hett DH6 ...... 104 E6
South View. Hunw DL15 ...... 125 D5
South View. Hut Hen TS27 ...... 109 D5
South View. Kimble DH2 ...... 35 F3
South View. Kir Me DL16 ...... 128 A3
South View. Lang Pk DH7 ...... 56 C6
South View. Murton SR7 ...... 40 D2
South View. Newf DL14 ...... 126 B7
South View. Pelton DH2 ...... 19 C5
South View. Pelton DH2 ...... 19 E7
South View. R Gill NE39 ...... 1 C2
South View. S Hill DH6 ...... 60 D1
South View. Sacr DH7 ...... 35 B4
South View. Shild DL4 ...... 149 A2
South View. Spenny DL16 ...... 127 D6
South View. Tant DH9 ...... 6 B2
South View. The Mid DH9 ...... 18 B3
South View. Trim TS29 ...... 107 E3
South View. Wh Hi DH6 ...... 83 E1
South View Gdns. Ann Pl DH9 ... 17 A3
South View Scnl. Durham DH1 ... 58 B4
South View Terr. Bear DH7 ...... 57 B3
South View Terr. Fence DH4 ...... 38 B8
South View W. R Gill NE39 ...... 1 C2
South West Ind Est.
  Shot Co SR8 ...... 84 F6
Southampton St. Darl DL1 ...... 209 A4
Southburn Cl. 4 New Ay DL5 ...... 38 C8
Southburn Gr. How le W DL15 . 124 D7
Southdowns. C le S DH2 ...... 20 C2
Southend Ave. Darl DL1 ...... 223 F8
Southend Pl. Darl DL1 ...... 208 F1
Southfield Cl. Hur on T DL2 ...... 224 D1
Southfield Cl. Hi Eth DL14 ...... 146 E5
Southfield La. Medom DH9 & NE17 .. 4 A4
Southfield Way. Durham DH1 ... 58 A4
Southgate St. 7 Bish Au DL14 . 148 C8
Southlands. Bowb DH6 ...... 105 E7
Southlands Gdns. Shild DL4 ... 148 F2
Southway. Lanch DH7 ...... 32 E4
Southway. Peter SR8 ...... 85 C5
Southwell Gn. Darl DL1 ...... 209 E4
Southwood Cres. R Gill NE39 .... 1 F2
Sowerby St. Sacr DH7 ...... 35 B2
Spa Cotts. Cr on T DL2 ...... 234 F7
Spa Dr. Cons DH8 ...... 14 C7
Spa Rd. Gain DL2 ...... 204 F6
Spa Well Cl. Blay NE21 ...... 2 B8
Spa Well Turn. Whick NE21 ...... 2 E7
Sparrow Hall Dr. Darl DL1 ...... 209 D7
Spearman Wlk. Hartle TS27 ...... 111 D3
Speeding Dr. Hartle TS24 ...... 111 F4
Speedwell Cl. Darl DL1 ...... 209 C1
Spen St. Stanl DH9 ...... 17 E5
Spencely St. Shild DL4 ...... 148 F2
Spencer Gr. Darl DL1 ...... 224 C7
Spencer St. Bish Au DL14 ...... 148 F4
Spencer St. Cons DH8 ...... 14 F3
Spennymoor Comp Lower Sch.
  Spenny DL16 ...... 127 E6
Spennymoor Comp Sch.
  Spenny DL16 ...... 127 E7
Spennymoor North Road Cty Jun
  Mix Sch. Spenny DL16 ...... 104 B1
Spennymoor West Cty Inf Sch.
  Spenny DL16 ...... 127 E7
Spinney The. Darl DL3 ...... 223 D6
Spinney The. M St G DL2 ...... 226 B8
Spinney The. New Ay DL17 ...... 150 D2
Spinney The. Spenny DL16 ...... 104 C1
Spire Hollin. Peter SR8 ...... 85 C6
Spout Bank. Hund DL12 ...... 182 D5
Spout La. Shild DL4 ...... 149 C1
Spring Ct. Darl DL3 ...... 208 C5
Spring Gdns. Bish Au DL14 ...... 147 A2
Spring Hill. Darl DL3 ...... 208 F6
Spring La. Foxton TS21 ...... 153 A3

Spring Rd. New Ay DL5 ...... 171 C2
Springbank Rd. Newf DL14 ...... 126 B7
Springdale Ave. Wing TS29 ...... 108 B5
Springfell. Birt DH3 ...... 9 D3
Springfield Cty Prim Sch.
  Darl DL1 ...... 209 C5
Springfield Gdns. C le S DH3 ...... 20 C5
Springfield Pk. Durham DH1 ...... 58 A3
Springfield Rd. Darl DL1 ...... 209 C6
Springfield Rd. Fishb TS21 ...... 131 C4
Springfield Terr. Pelton DH2 ...... 19 E5
Springfield Terr. Will DL15 ...... 63 F3
Springfield Terr. Will DL15 ...... 101 E3
Springfields. New Ay DL5 ...... 170 F4
Springhouse Cl. Ebch DH8 ...... 3 E2
Springhouse La. Ebch DH8 ...... 3 E2
Springs The. Birt DH3 ...... 9 E3
Springside. Sacr DH7 ...... 35 C3
Springsyde Cl. Whick NE16 ...... 2 E5
Springwell Ave. Durham DH1 ...... 58 A3
Springwell Ave. Lang Pk DH7 ...... 56 C6
Springwell Ave. Trim TS29 ...... 107 E1
Springwell Cl. 9 Lang Pk DH7 ... 56 C6
Springwell. Ingle DL2 ...... 188 A6
Springwell Rd. Durham DH1 ...... 58 A3
Springwell Terr. Darl DL1 ...... 209 D5
Springwell Terr. H le H DH5 ...... 39 A2
Spruce Ct. Shild DL4 ...... 170 B8
Spruce Gr. Darl DL3 ...... 208 C1
Square The. Bish Au DL14 ...... 147 D2
Square The. Blanch DH8 ...... 10 B1
Square The. Gr Br DL12 ...... 219 B2
Square The. Lanch DH7 ...... 32 F3
Square The. M St G DL2 ...... 225 D8
Square The. Sedge TS21 ...... 153 B6
Stack Garth. Brand DH7 ...... 79 C5
Stacks La. Mid in T DL12 ...... 160 C8
Stafford Gr. Ryhope SR2 ...... 22 E6
Stafford Pl. Peter SR8 ...... 85 B7
Stafford St. H le H DH5 ...... 38 F4
Staffordshire Dr. Belm DH1 ...... 59 D3
Stag La. New Ay DL17 ...... 150 E1
Staindrop C of E Jun Mix & Inf Sch.
  Staind DL2 ...... 186 E6
Staindrop Comp Sch.
  Staind DL2 ...... 186 C5
Staindrop Cres. Darl DL3 ...... 208 C3
Staindrop Rd. Bish Au DL14 ...... 147 B1
Staindrop Rd. Cockf DL13 ...... 166 D5
Staindrop Rd. Darl DL3 ...... 208 B3
Staindrop Rd. Durham DH1 ...... 58 D6
Staindrop Terr. Ann Pl DH9 ...... 16 F4
Stainmore Terr. Cound DL14 .. 127 C1
Stainforth Cl. New Ay DL5 ...... 171 B7
Stainmore La. Start DL12 ...... 200 E5
Stainmore Cres. New Ay DL5 ... 171 A7
Stainmore Dr. Gr Lum DH3 ...... 37 B7
Stainmore Wlk. 2 New Ay DL5 171 A7
Stainton Bank. Staint DL12 ...... 184 E1
Stainton View. Sadb DL2 ...... 210 E6
Stainton Way. Peter SR8 ...... 85 C6
Staintondale. New Ay DL5 ...... 170 F8
Stainwood Ct. Darl DL3 ...... 208 C3
Stampley Cl. Blay NE21 ...... 2 A8
Standerton Terr. The Mid DH9 ... 18 B3
Standish St. Stanl DH9 ...... 17 D5
Stanelaw Way. Tanf L DH9 ...... 6 F1
Stanfield Rd. New Ay DL5 ...... 171 E7
Stang La. E Hope DL11 ...... 231 A3
Stang La. Scar DL11 ...... 231 A3
Stang La. Scar DL11 & DL12 ... 217 C2
Stang Top. E Hope DL11 ...... 231 A3
Stang Top. Langth DL11 ...... 230 F1
Stanhope. Wash NE38 ...... 9 F5
Stanhope Barrington CE (Cont)
  Sch. Stanh DL13 ...... 71 A4
Stanhope Cl. Brand DH7 ...... 79 C4
Stanhope Cl. Cons DH8 ...... 58 D6
Stanhope Cl. Ferry DL17 ...... 129 B6
Stanhope Cl. H le Sp DH4 ...... 38 D7
Stanhope Cl. Spenny DL16 ...... 104 A2
Stanhope Gdns. Ann Pl DH9 ...... 17 A4
Stanhope Rd. Wols DL13 ...... 97 D7
Stanhope Rd N. Darl DL3 ...... 208 E2
Stanhope Rd S. Darl DL3 ...... 208 E1
Stanhope Terr. Crook DL15 ...... 100 F4
Stank La. Wit Gil DH1 ...... 36 A1
Stanley Burnside Cty Jun & Inf Sch.
  Stanl DH9 ...... 18 B5
Stanley Cl. Sherb DH6 ...... 59 F1
Stanley Comp Sch. Stanl DH9 ... 17 E5
Stanley (Crook) Cty Sch.
  Stan Cr DL15 ...... 76 F1
Stanley Ct. Stanl DH9 ...... 18 A6
Stanley Gdns. Cons DH8 ...... 15 A3
Stanley RC (Aided) Jun Mix & Inf
  Sch. Stanl DH9 ...... 17 F7
Stanley St. 14 Cons DH8 ...... 14 F3
Stanley St. 6 Darl DL1 ...... 209 B1
Stanley St. Seaham SR7 ...... 41 B8
Stanley St. Shild DL4 ...... 149 A4
Stanley Terr. C le S DH3 ...... 20 D2
Stanley Terr. Stan Cr DL15 ...... 76 F1
Stanley Way. Billy R DL15 ...... 100 E7
Stanner's La. Will DL16 ...... 103 A4
Stanwix Cotts. 4 Cockf DL13 ... 166 C5
Stapleton Bank. Stapl DL2 ...... 223 A4
Stargate Cl. Lang Pk DH7 ...... 56 B6
Stargate Cl. New Ay DL5 ...... 150 D1
Starmer Cres. Darl DL1 ...... 224 B7
Startforth Cl. Gr Lum DH3 ...... 37 B7
Startforth Morrit Memorial CE Sch.
  Start DL12 ...... 200 E4
Startforth Park. Start DL12 ...... 200 D5
Statham Pl. 2 Darl DL3 ...... 209 A7
Station App. Bish Au DL14 ...... 148 B7
Station App. Durham DH1 ...... 58 B2

Station Ave. Brand DH7 .... 79 C4
Station Ave. Esh W DH7 .... 77 E8
Station Ave. H le H DH5 .... 39 A3
Station Ave N. 2 Fence DH4 .... 38 A8
Station Ave N. Fence DH4 .... 21 F1
Station Ave S. 1 Fence DH4 .... 38 A8
Station Ave S. Fence DH4 .... 21 F1
Station Bank. 1 Durham DH1 .. 58 C2
Station Cotts. Beam DH9 .... 18 E8
Station Cotts. Burnop NE39 ...... 5 C6
Station Cotts. Cockf DL13 ...... 166 A6
Station Cotts. New Ay DL5 ...... 171 C1
Station Cotts. Sedge TS22 ...... 154 E5
Station Cres. Seaham SR7 .... 41 B8
Station Est E. Murton SR7 .... 40 A3
Station Est N. Murton SR7 .... 40 A3
Station Est S. Murton SR7 .... 40 A3
Station Field Rd. Tanf L DH9 ...... 6 F1
Station House Visitor Ctr.
    Grind TS21 .... 175 E5
Station Houses. Pelton DH2 .... 19 E5
Station La. Birt DH3 .... 9 B4
Station La. Durham DH1 .... 58 E2
Station La. Hut Hen TS28 ...... 108 E6
Station La. Pelton DH2 .... 19 E6
Station Rd. Ann Pl DH9 .... 17 A3
Station Rd. B Rocks TS27 .... 86 F2
Station Rd. Beam DH9 .... 18 F8
Station Rd. Bish Au DL14 ...... 147 C2
Station Rd. Brand DH7 .... 79 C3
Station Rd. C le S DH3 .... 20 C3
Station Rd. Cornf DL17 .... 105 D1
Station Rd. Coxhoe DH6 .... 106 B2
Station Rd. Darl DL3 .... 208 F4
Station Rd. Eas SR8 .... 63 F4
Station Rd. Gain DL2 .... 205 A7
Station Rd. H le H DH5 .... 39 A2
Station Rd. H Pitt DH6 .... 60 A6
Station Rd. Heigh DL5 .... 170 E1
Station Rd. Hesl TS27 .... 86 A1
Station Rd. How le W DL15 .... 124 E7
Station Rd. Hunw DL14 & DL15 .. 125 F5
Station Rd. Hut Hen TS28 ...... 108 E6
Station Rd. Lanch DH7 .... 32 F3
Station Rd. M St G DL2 .... 225 E8
Station Rd. Murton SR7 .... 40 A3
Station Rd. New Ay DL5 .... 171 C2
Station Rd. Pens DH4 & NE38 .. 21 E8
Station Rd. R Gill NE39 .... 1 F1
Station Rd. Rhype SR2 .... 23 A6
Station Rd. Seaham SR7 .... 41 A8
Station Rd. Seaham SR7 .... 41 B8
Station Rd. Sedge TS21 .... 153 A6
Station Rd. Shot Co DH6 .... 84 C7
Station Rd. Stanl DH9 .... 17 F7
Station Rd. Ush M DH7 .... 56 F1
Station Rd. W Rain DH4 .... 37 F1
Station Rd. Wing TS29 .... 107 F5
Station Rd. Wit le W DL14 ...... 124 B3
Station Rd N. H le H DH5 .... 39 A3
Station Rd S. Murton SR7 .... 40 A3
Station St. Esh W DH7 .... 77 C6
Station St. Hasw DH6 .... 61 F3
Station St. Shild DL4 .... 170 A8
Station St. Tow Law DL13 .... 75 C2
Station Terr. Cons DH8 .... 15 A2
Station Terr. Coth DL12 .... 182 E3
Station Terr. Even DL14 .... 146 C1
Station Terr. Fence DH4 .... 21 F1
Station Terr. M St G DL2 .... 210 E1
Station Terr. Stanh DL13 .... 71 C2
Station View. Bish Au DL14 .... 147 C2
Station View. Esh W DH7 .... 77 E8
Station View. H le H DH5 .... 39 A3
Station View. Wit Pk DL14 ...... 125 B1
Station Villas. Stanl DH9 .... 17 F8
Staveley Rd. Peter SR8 .... 85 E6
Stavordale St. Seaham SR7 .... 41 D5
Stavordale St W. Seaham SR7 .. 41 D5
Stead Cl. New Ay DL5 .... 171 C7
Steadings The. Whorl DL12 .... 202 E2
Steadman's La. Quebec DH7 .... 55 A4
Steavenson St. Bowb DH6 ...... 105 D8
Steel St. Cons DH8 .... 14 F3
Steels Houses. Crook DL15 .... 100 C4
Steeplejack Way. Darl DL1 .... 209 A2
Steetley Terr. Qua Hi DH6 ...... 106 D7
Stella Gill Ind Est. Pelton DH2 .. 19 F5
Stephen Bank. Dalton DL11 .... 220 B2
Stephen Ct. Darl DL1 .... 209 A4
Stephen St. Cons DH8 .... 14 F3
Stephen's Terr. Wh Hi DH6 ...... 83 F3
Stephens Rd. Murton SR7 .... 40 B3
Stephenson Cl. H le H DH5 ...... 39 B4
Stephenson Cres. Will DL15 .... 101 F2
Stephenson Rd. Peter SR8 ...... 63 D1
Stephenson Sq. Eas SR8 .... 63 B3
Stephenson St. Darl DL3 ...... 208 F4
Stephenson St. Ferry DL17 .... 128 E6
Stephenson St. Murton SR7 .... 40 C3
Stephenson Way. Blay NE21 .... 2 B8
Stephenson Way. New Ay DL5 .. 171 C6
Stephenson Way Cty Inf Sch.
    New Ay DL5 .... 171 C6
Stephenson Way Jun Mix Sch.
    New Ay DL5 .... 171 B7
Stevenson St. H le Sp DH4 ...... 38 D8
Stewart Ave. Ryhope SR2 .... 22 E6
Stewart St. Darl DL3 .... 208 E4
Stewart St. Eas SR8 .... 63 D4
Stewart St. N Silk SR3 .... 22 A7
Stewart St. Seaham SR7 .... 41 E6
Stewart St E. Seaham SR7 .... 41 C6
Stewart's Bldgs. Hunw DL15 .. 125 D5
Stewartsfield. R Gill NE39 .... 1 D1
Stillington Cl. Ryhope SR2 ...... 22 F5
Stillington Ind Est. Still TS21 .. 174 E4

Stirling Ave. R Gill NE39 .... 1 E1
Stirling Cl. Bish Au DL14 ...... 147 E6
Stirling La. R Gill NE39 .... 1 F1
Stirrup The. New Ay DL5 .... 170 F8
Stobart St. Edmon DH7 .... 35 B7
Stobart Terr. Fishb TS21 ...... 131 B5
Stobarts Ct. Hi Eth DL14 ...... 146 E6
Stobb Cross La. Coxhoe DL17 .. 130 B8
Stobb Cross Rd. Cornf DL17 .. 129 E8
Stobb Cross Villas. Cornf DL17 .. 129 E8
Stobb Hill. Gain DL2 .... 205 A7
Stobb House View. Brand DH7 .. 79 A5
Stobhill La. Bolam DL2 .... 168 D1
Stockerley La. Lanch DH7 .... 31 F6
Stockerley La. Lanch DH7 & DH8 .. 32 A7
Stockerley La. Cons DH8 .... 15 B1
Stockley Cl. Darl DL3 .... 208 F7
Stockley Cres. Frost DL13 ...... 96 C7
Stockley Ct. Ush M DH7 .... 57 C1
Stockley Gr. Brance DH7 .... 102 E7
Stockley Gr. Frost DL13 .... 96 C6
Stockley La. Will DL15 & DH7 .. 101 D7
Stocks Gn. New Ay DL5 .... 171 A7
Stockton Ave. Peter SR8 .... 85 F8
Stockton Rd. Darl DL1 .... 209 E5
Stockton Rd. Eas SR8 .... 63 A2
Stockton Rd. Haw SR7 .... 63 B7
Stockton Rd. Ryhope SR2 .... 22 F2
Stockton Rd. Sadb DL2 .... 210 F6
Stockton Rd. Seaham SR2 & SR7 .. 22 F2
Stockton Rd. Sedge TS21 ...... 153 C6
Stockton Rd. Sedge TS21 ...... 154 B1
Stockton St. Seaham SR7 .... 41 B8
Stoker Cres. Wh Hi DH6 .... 83 E1
Stoker Terr. H Spen NE39 .... 1 A3
Stokoe St. Cons DH8 .... 14 E4
Stone Cross. Fishb TS21 .... 131 D4
Stone Houses. Stanh DL13 ...... 71 B3
Stone Man La. Gayles DL11 .... 233 E1
Stone Row. Butter DL13 .... 165 F8
Stone Row. W Pel DH2 .... 19 A5
Stonebank Terr. New Ay DL5 .. 126 B8
Stonebridge. 2 Darl DL1 ...... 209 A1
Stonechat Cl. 3 Wash NE38 .... 9 F3
Stonecliffe Dr. Darl DL1 .... 223 C8
Stonedale Cres. Darl DL3 ...... 208 D2
Stonehaven Way. Darl DL1 .... 209 E7
Stonehurst Dr. Darl DL1 .... 223 C8
Stoneleigh Cl. New Ay DL17 .. 150 E1
Stones End. Even DL14 .... 167 C7
Stonesdale. Pens DH4 .... 21 E8
Stoneybeck. Bish Mi DL17 .... 130 C4
Stony Bank. Heigh DL2 .... 170 A3
Stony Bank. Will DL15 .... 102 B2
Stony La. Urpeth DH9 .... 19 A8
Stony Path. St J Ch DL13 .... 66 F2
Stonybeck La. Bish Mi DL17 .. 130 D4
Stonyheap La. Ann Pl DH8 & DH9 .. 16 B4
Stonyheap La. La Maw DH8 .... 16 B2
Stooperdale Ave. Darl DL3 .... 208 C4
Store Cotts. Edmon DH7 .... 35 B6
Store St. Cons DH8 .... 14 F3
Store Terr. E Lane DH5 .... 39 B1
Stornaway Cl. St on T TS21 .... 195 F3
Stotfold Cl. Seaham SR7 .... 40 E8
Strait La. Hur on T DL2 .... 224 E2
Strand St. Shild DL4 .... 169 F8
Strangford Ave. C le S DH2 .... 20 B1
Strangford Rd. Seaham SR7 .... 41 C7
Strangways St. Seaham SR7 .... 41 D6
Stranton St. 4 Bish Au DL14 .. 148 B8
Stratford Gdns. 1 Cons DH8 .. 14 F4
Stratford Gdns. 2 Ferry DL17 .. 129 A6
Strathmore Ave. R Gill NE39 .... 1 E1
Strathmore Cl. Stanl DH9 .... 18 B7
Strathmore Cres. Byer NE16 .... 6 D8
Strathmore Ct. Bar Cas DL12 .. 201 A6
Strathmore. Gr Lum DH3 .... 37 A8
Strathmore Rd. Bar Cas DL12 .. 201 B7
Strathmore Rd. R Gill NE39 ...... 1 E1
Stratton Cl. Sland SR2 .... 23 A8
Stratton Ct. Darl DL1 .... 223 E8
Stratton St. Spenny DL16 ...... 127 F8
Stratus Ct. 9 Silk SR3 .... 22 A6
Straw Gate. Stapl DL2 .... 223 B4
Strawberry La. H Shin DH1 .... 81 A4
Strawgate Gr. Stapl DL2 .... 223 A5
Strawgate La. Stapl DL2 .... 223 A5
Stray The. Darl DL1 .... 209 D1
Streatlam Cl. Staint DL12 ...... 184 E2
Streatlam Rd. Darl DL1 .... 224 B8
Street The. Bowes DL12 .... 216 A8
Street The. Bowes DL12 .... 217 B8
Street The. Bowes DL12 .... 217 D8
Street The. Gr Br DL12 .... 218 D8
Street The. Gr Br DL12 .... 219 B7
Stressholme Golf Course.
    Hur on T DL2 .... 223 E5
Stretton Cl. Fence DH4 .... 38 A7
Stronsay Cl. 2 Sland SR2 .... 22 B8
Stuart Cl. B Coll TS27 .... 86 D3
Studland Dr. Hartle TS24 ...... 111 D4
Sudburn Ave. Staind DL2 ...... 186 C5
Suffolk Pl. Birt DH3 .... 9 D1
Suffolk Pl. Bish Au DL14 ...... 148 B5
Suffolk St. H le H DH5 .... 38 F4
Suffolk Way. Durham DH1 ...... 58 D8
Suffolk Wlk. Peter SR8 .... 85 C8
Sugar Hill Cty Prim Sch.
    New Ay DL5 .... 171 D6
Summerdale. Cons DH8 .... 14 D7
Summerfield. Hams NE17 .... 4 A5
Summerfield. W Pel DH9 .... 19 A6
Summerfields. C le S DH2 ...... 19 F2
Summerhouse Back La.
    Kill DL2 .... 189 A5
Summerhouse Farm.
    E Rain DH5 .... 38 D5
Summerhouse Gr. Darl DL3 .... 208 A2

Summerson St. H le H DH5 ...... 39 B4
Summerville. 3 Durham DH1 .. 58 B1
Sun Rd. Copley DL13 .... 143 F1
Sun St. Bish Au DL14 .... 148 C7
Sun St. Darl DL3 .... 208 F2
Sunderland Ave. Peter SR8 .... 85 F8
Sunderland Rd. Eas SR7 & SR8 .. 63 B5
Sunderland Rd. Haw SR7&SR8 .. 63 B5
Sunderland Rd. Peter SR8 ...... 63 F2
Sunderland St. 2 H le Sp DH4 .. 38 E8
Sunderland St. Leadg DH8 ...... 15 D4
Sunnidale. Whick NE16 .... 2 E5
Sunningdale. Cons DH8 .... 31 C7
Sunningdale. New Ay DL17 .... 150 E2
Sunningdale Gn. Darl DL1 ...... 209 E6
Sunningdale Gr. Hartle TS27 .. 111 D3
Sunny Blunts. Peter SR8 .... 85 C4
Sunny Terr. Dipton DH9 .... 16 C7
Sunny Terr. Stanl DH9 .... 17 E7
Sunnybanks. Lanch DH7 .... 32 E4
Sunnybrow. 7 N Silk SR3 .... 22 A8
Sunnybrow Sch. Will DL15 .... 101 D2
Sunnyside Ave. Shild DL4 ...... 149 A2
Sunnyside Terr. Trim TS29 .... 107 E3
Sunnyview Cotts. Coth DL12 .. 182 E4
Surbiton St. St on T TS21 ...... 195 F3
Surrey Ave. N Silk SR3 .... 22 A6
Surrey Cres. Cons DH8 .... 30 B7
Surrey Pl. Bish Au DL14 .... 148 B5
Surrey Pl. Will DL15 .... 102 A3
Surrey St. H le H DH5 .... 38 F4
Surrey Terr. Birt DH3 .... 9 C1
Surtees Ave. Bowb DH6 .... 81 D1
Surtees Dr. Darl DL1 .... 58 A1
Surtees Pl. Cons DH8 .... 14 C5
Surtees Rd. Heigh DL5 .... 170 C3
Surtees Rd. Peter SR8 .... 85 E6
Surtees St. Bish Au DL14 ...... 148 B8
Surtees St. Darl DL3 .... 208 F4
Surtees Terr. Crag DH9 .... 18 D2
Surtees Terr. Ferry DL17 .... 129 C2
Surtees Wlk. New Ay DL5 ...... 171 D5
Sussex Rd. Cons DH8 .... 30 B7
Sussex St. Cound DL14 .... 149 D8
Sussex St. 3 N Silk SR3 .... 22 A8
Sussex Way. Darl DL1 .... 209 C4
Sutcliffe Ct. Darl DL3 .... 209 A7
Sutherland Pl. Durham DH1 .... 59 A1
Sutherland St. Seaham SR7 .... 41 B8
Sutton Cl. Darl DL3 .... 208 A2
Sutton St. Durham DH1 .... 58 B2
Swainby Rd. Trim TS29 .... 131 E8
Swale Cres. Gr Lum DH3 .... 37 B7
Swaledale Ave. Darl DL3 ...... 208 C3
Swaledale Cl. H le H DH5 .... 38 F1
Swallow Cl. Esh W DH7 .... 55 C1
Swallow St. Seaham SR7 .... 41 B8
Swan St. Ann Pl DH9 .... 16 E5
Swan St. 5 Darl DL1 .... 209 A1
Swan St. Even DL14 .... 167 C7
Swan Wlk. New Ay DL5 .... 171 F6
Swan Wynd. Staind DL2 .... 186 E6
Swanage Gr. Hartle TS24 ...... 111 D4
Swinburne Pl. Birt DH3 .... 9 C3
Swinburne Rd. Darl DL3 .... 208 E1
Swinburne Terr. Dipton DH9 .... 16 B7
Swindle St. R Gill NE39 .... 1 C2
Swingfield Cl. Crook DL15 .... 100 D5
Swinhope. Wash NE38 .... 21 A8
Swinside Dr. Belm DH1 .... 59 C4
Swyfte Cl. Sedge TS21 .... 153 B6
Sycamore. C le S DH2 .... 20 A5
Sycamore Ave. B Rocks SR27 .. 86 E3
Sycamore Cl. Hur on T DL2 .... 224 D1
Sycamore Cres. Wing TS29 .... 108 B5
Sycamore Gdns. Crook DL15 .. 100 D3
Sycamore Gr. Will DL15 .... 102 B3
Sycamore Pk. Brand DH7 .... 79 B5
Sycamore Rd. Cornf DL17 ...... 105 E1
Sycamore Rd. Fishb TS21 ...... 131 C4
Sycamore Rd. Kimble DH2 ...... 35 F3
Sycamore Sq. Eas SR8 .... 63 C3
Sycamore Sq. Shild DL4 .... 149 A1
Sycamore Terr. Ann Pl DH9 .... 17 B4
Sycamore Terr. Hasw DH6 ...... 61 C8
Sycamores The. Burnop NE16 .. 6 C5
Sycamores The. Darl DL3 ...... 208 D3
Sydney Gdns. Cons DH8 .... 31 B8
Sydney St. Beam DH9 .... 19 A7
Sydney St. Bourn DH4 .... 21 E2
Syke Rd. Burnop NE16 .... 5 F5
Sylvan Gr. Darl DL3 .... 208 D1
Sylvia Terr. Stanl DH9 .... 17 F8
Symington Wlk. 3 Darl DL1 .. 209 B1
Symon Terr. Chopw NE17 .... 4 B8
Symons Cl. St on T TS21 ...... 195 F2
Syron. Whick NE16 .... 2 F7
Syston Cl. Fence DH4 .... 38 A7

Tail-upon-end La. Bowb DH6 .. 81 D2
Talbot Pl. Seaham SR7 .... 41 D7
Tamar Cl. Peter SR8 .... 85 C5
Tamar St. E Lane DH5 .... 61 C8
Tamerton Dr. Birt DH3 .... 9 D2
Tamworth Cl. Bish Au DL14 .... 147 E6
Tandridge Ct. Darl DL3 .... 208 D3
Tanfield Comp Sch. Tanf L DH9 .. 17 D8
Tanfield Lea Cty Jun & Inf Sch.
    Tanf L DH9 .... 6 C1
Tanfield Lea Ind Est. Tanf L DH9 . 6 D2
Tanfield Lea South Ind Est.
    Tanf L DH9 .... 6 F1
Tanfield Rly. Sunn NE16 .... 7 B7
Tangmere. Spenny DL16 .... 103 E2
Tanmeads. Kimble DH2 .... 35 F4
Tannery Yd. Darl DL1 .... 209 A2
Tansley Gdns. Darl DL1 .... 224 D8
Tantallon. Birt DH3 .... 9 D2

Tarn Cl. Peter SR8 .... 85 E6
Tarn Dr. Sland SR2 .... 22 F8
Tarn La. Winst DL2 .... 203 C7
Tate Ave. Kelloe DH6 .... 106 D5
Tattersall Cl. New Ay DL17 .... 150 E2
Tavistock Sq. N Silk SR3 .... 22 A8
Tay St. E Lane DH5 .... 61 D8
Taylor Ave. Bear DH7 .... 57 B3
Taylor Ave. R Gill NE39 .... 1 F1
Taylor Ave. Trim TS29 .... 107 D3
Taylor Ct. Will DL15 .... 101 F3
Taylor Gr. Wing TS29 .... 84 D1
Taylor Rd. Bish Au DL14 ...... 148 C6
Taylor Sq. Bish Au DL14 ...... 148 A5
Taylor St. Ann Pl DH9 .... 16 E5
Taylor St. Cons DH8 .... 14 F2
Taylor Wlk. New Ay DL5 .... 171 E7
Taylor's Terr. Cons DH8 .... 14 C1
Tayside. Darl DL1 .... 209 E7
Teal Cl. Peter SR8 .... 85 C4
Teal Rd. Darl DL1 .... 209 E1
Teasdale St. Cons DH8 .... 15 A3
Teasdale Terr. Belm DH1 .... 59 B2
Ted Fletcher Ct. Darl DL1 ...... 209 D4
Tees Cl. Peter SR8 .... 85 C4
Tees Cres. Stanl DH9 .... 17 F5
Tees Dr. Darl DL1 .... 224 A6
Tees Grange Ave. Darl DL3 .... 208 A1
Tees St. E Lane DH5 .... 61 D8
Tees St. Peter SR8 .... 86 A7
Tees St. Seaham SR7 .... 41 D7
Tees View. Gain DL2 .... 205 A6
Tees View. Trim TS29 .... 107 C1
Teesdale Airport Halt.
    M St G DL2 .... 226 E8
Teesdale Ave. Darl DL3 .... 223 B8
Teesdale Comp Sch.
    Bar Cas DL12 .... 201 B7
Teesdale Rd. Start DL12 ...... 200 F5
Teesdale Rd. Thorn DH6 .... 17 A4
Teesdale Wlk. Bish Au DL14 .. 147 F5
Teesdale Wlk. Shild DL4 ...... 149 B1
Teesway. Neas DL2 .... 225 B1
Teign Cl. Peter SR8 .... 85 C5
Teikyo Univ of Japan.
    Durham DH1 .... 80 C7
Telford Cl. H Shin DH1 .... 81 B4
Telford Dr. Darl DL1 .... 209 B1
Temperance Ave. Shild DL4 .... 149 A2
Temperance Pl. 2 Darl DL3 .. 208 F2
Temperance Terr. Billy R DL15 .. 100 E6
Temperance Terr. Ush M DH7 .. 57 B7
Tempest Cl. Darl DL1 .... 209 B7
Tempest Rd. Hartle TS24 ...... 111 E3
Tempest Rd. Seaham SR7 .... 41 D8
Tempest St. 8 N Silk SR3 ...... 22 A7
Templar St. 1 Cons DH8 .... 14 D4
Temple Bldgs. M St G DL2 .... 225 E8
Temple Ct. M St G DL2 .... 225 E8
Temple Gdns. Cons DH8 .... 14 F1
Tenby Wlk. Hartle TS26 .... 111 E1
Tennyson Gdns. Darl DL1 ...... 224 A7
Tennyson Gdns. Dipton DH9 .. 16 C7
Tennyson Rd. C le S DH2 .... 19 E3
Tennyson Rd. Chilt DL17 ...... 150 F8
Tennyson Rd. Eas SR8 .... 63 D4
Tennyson Terr. Crook DL15 .... 100 D5
Tenter Terr. Durham DH1 .... 58 C2
Tenters St. Bish Au DL14 ...... 148 B8
Tenth Ave. C le S DH2 .... 20 B3
Tenth St. B Coll TS27 .... 86 D4
Tenth St. 7 Peter SR8 .... 86 A7
Terrace The. Cons DH8 .... 14 C6
Terrace The. Cr on T DL2 ...... 234 F8
Terrace The. Dalt P TS27 ...... 134 F3
Terrace The. Elwick TS27 ...... 134 C5
Terrace The. Shot Co DH6 ...... 84 D7
Territorial La. Durham DH1 .... 58 C1
Teviot St. E Lane DH5 .... 61 C8
Thackeray St. H le Sp DH4 .... 38 D6
Thames Cres. Fence DH4 .... 38 A8
Thames Cres. Stanl DH9 .... 17 F4
Thames Ctr. New Ay DL5 ...... 171 D6
Thames St. E Lane DH5 .... 61 C8
Thames Way. Darl DL1 .... 223 F6
Theresa St. Seaham SR7 .... 41 E5
Thickley Terr. Shild DL4 .... 149 A2
Thinford La. Ferry DH6 & DL17 .. 104 F2
Thinford Rd. Cornf DH6 .... 105 C3
Thinford Rd. Cornf DH6 .... 105 E3
Thinford Rd. Ferry DH6 & DL17 .. 105 B2
Third Ave. C le S DH2 .... 20 B3
Third St. B Coll TS27 .... 86 D3
Third St. Cons DH8 .... 15 B2
Third St. Leadg DH8 .... 15 C5
Third St. Leadg DH8 .... 15 C6
Third St. Peter SR8 .... 86 A7
Third St. Qua Ho DH9 .... 17 D2
Thireenth St. Peter SR8 .... 85 F7
Thirlmere. Birt DH3 .... 9 E2
Thirlmere. Spenny DL16 .... 103 E2
Thirlmere Ave. C le S DH2 ...... 20 B1
Thirlmere Ave. E Lane DH5 .... 61 C8
Thirlmere Cres. Blay NE21 ...... 2 B8
Thirlmere Cres. Even DL14 .... 147 A1
Thirlmere Gr. Darl DL1 .... 224 B8
Thirlmere Rd. Ferry DL17 ...... 128 F5
Thirlmere Rd. Peter SR8 .... 85 C5
Thirteenth St. Peter SR8 .... 85 F7
Thistle Rd. Brand DH7 .... 79 F4
Thistlecroft. H le Sp DH5 .... 38 E7
Thistledon Ave. Whick NE16 .... 2 E6
Thistleflat Rd. Crook DL15 .... 100 C3
Thistlewood La. Wals DL13 .... 73 F2
Thomas Cl. Darl DL1 .... 209 B1
Thomas St. Ann Pl DH9 .... 17 A4
Thomas St. C le S DH3 .... 20 C2
Thomas St. Cons DH8 .... 14 D4

Thomas St. Crag DH9 .... 18 D3
Thomas St. 21 Darl DL1 ...... 209 B1
Thomas St. Eas SR8 .... 63 C5
Thomas St. H le H DH5 .... 39 B5
Thomas St. 11 Lang Pk DH7 .. 56 C6
Thomas St. Ryhope SR2 .... 22 F6
Thomas St. Sacr DH7 .... 35 B2
Thomas St. Shild DL4 .... 170 A7
Thomas St. Spenny DL16 ...... 127 E6
Thomas St S. Ryhope SR2 .... 22 F6
Thompson Rd. Bish Au DL14 .. 148 C6
Thompson St. Peter SR8 .... 86 A7
Thompson St. 3 Spenny DL16 . 103 F1
Thompson St E. Darl DL3 ...... 209 A6
Thompson St W. Darl DL3 ...... 209 A6
Thompson Terr. 8 Ryhope SR2 .. 23 A6
Thorn Cl. Spenny DL16 .... 127 D6
Thornbank Cl. Silk SR3 .... 22 A4
Thornberry La. Bold DL12 .... 199 E3
Thornbury Rise. Darl DL3 ...... 208 D3
Thorndale Rd. Belm DH1 .... 59 D3
Thornes Cl. Peter SR8 .... 85 F5
Thorneyholme Terr. Stanl DH9 . 17 F6
Thornfield Pl. R Gill NE39 .... 1 E1
Thornfield Rd. Cons DH8 .... 30 C8
Thornfield Rd. Darl DL3 .... 208 C2
Thorngate. Bar Cas DL12 ...... 200 F5
Thorngate Wynd. Bar Cas DL12 . 200 F5
Thornhaugh Ave. Whick NE16 .. 2 F6
Thornhill Gdns. Burnop NE16 .. 5 F5
Thornhill Gdns. Shild DL4 .... 148 E2
Thornhill Rd. Shot Co DH6 .... 84 C6
Thornhill St. H le Sp DH4 .... 38 D8
Thornlaw North. Thorn DH6 .... 83 B4
Thornlaw South. Thorn DH6 .... 83 C3
Thornlea Gr. Lanch DH7 .... 32 E4
Thornley Cl. Ush M DH7 .... 57 B1
Thornley Cty Prim Sch.
    Thorn DH6 .... 83 C4
Thornley La. R Gill NE21 & NE39 .. 2 A6
Thornley Rd. Thor DL13 .... 99 A8
Thornley Rd. Thorn DL13 .... 75 B1
Thornley Rd. Tow Law DL13 .... 75 B1
Thornley Rd. Wh Hi DH6 .... 83 F3
Thornley St Godric's RC Jun
    & Inf Sch. Wh Hi DH6 .... 83 E3
Thornley Station Ind Est.
    Shot Co DH6 .... 84 D4
Thornley Terr. Tow Law DL13 .. 75 B3
Thornley View. R Gill NE39 ...... 1 F2
Thornton Cl. New Ay DL5 ...... 171 C8
Thornton Cl. Ludw DH6 .... 83 C7
Thornton Hall Cotts.
    H Con DL2 .... 207 B6
Thornton St. Darl DL3 .... 208 F3
Thorntree Gdns. M St G DL2 .. 225 E7
Thorntree Terr. Stanl DH9 ...... 18 B7
Thorpe Cres. Haw SR8 .... 63 C2
Thorpe Hall. Wycl DL12 .... 202 E1
Thorpe Hospl. Eas SR8 .... 63 B2
Thorpe Rd. Carl TS21 .... 195 D8
Thorpe Rd. Eas SR8 .... 63 C2
Thorpe Rd. Peter SR8 .... 63 F1
Thorpe St. Eas SR8 .... 63 E5
Thorpe St. Peter SR8 .... 86 A7
Three Lane Ends.
    Escomb DL14 .... 147 D7
Thrislington Cl. Cornf DL17 .... 105 D1
Thropton Cl. C le S DH2 .... 20 A1
Thropton Cl. H Shin DH1 .... 81 B5
Throstlenest Ave. Darl DL1 .... 209 C4
Throston Cl. Hartle TS26 ...... 111 F1
Throston Grange La.
    Hartle TS24 & TS26 .... 111 E1
Thrunton Cl. 5 H le Sp DH5 .. 38 F8
Thrushcross Pl. Belm DH1 ...... 59 B3
Thunderbuck Dr. Elwick TS22 .. 155 B5
Thurlow Gr. New Ay DL5 .... 171 D8
Thurlow Grange. Sedge TS21 .. 153 B6
Thurlow Rd. Sedge TS21 ...... 153 B6
Thurlow Way. H le Sp DH5 .... 38 D6
Thursby. Birt DH3 .... 9 E2
Thursby Cl. New Ay DL5 ...... 170 F8
Thurso Cl. St on T TS21 .... 195 F3
Tilbeck Sq. Silk SR3 .... 22 A5
Tilley Rd. Wash NE38 .... 9 F5
Tilleys Row. Butter DL13 ...... 165 E8
Timmys La. Hur on T DL2 ...... 224 E1
Timothy Hackworth Cty Inf Sch.
    Shild DL4 .... 169 F8
Timothy Hackworth Cty Jun Sch.
    Shild DL4 .... 169 F8
Timothy Terr. Spenny DL16 .... 127 F7
Tindale Ave. Durham DH1 ...... 58 A5
Tindale Cres. Bish Au DL14 .... 148 A3
Tindale Crescent Hospl.
    Bish Au DL14 .... 147 F4
Tindale Gn. New Ay DL5 ...... 171 A7
Tindale St. Leadg DH8 .... 15 C4
Tindle St. Cons DH8 .... 14 E4
Tinkler Terr. Gr Lum DH3 .... 21 B1
Tinmill Pl. Cons DH8 .... 14 D3
Tintagel. Gr Lum DH3 .... 37 B8
Tintagel Cl. Hartle TS27 ...... 111 C3
Tintagel Dr. Seaham SR7 .... 41 C8
Tintern Ave. Darl DL3 .... 207 F5
Tintern Rd. Bish Au DL14 ...... 147 D2
Tiree Cl. Brand DH7 .... 79 C5
Tiree St. Silk SR3 .... 22 A6
Tivoli Pl. 5 Darl DL1 .... 148 B6
Toadpool. Bish Au DL14 .... 147 B1
Tobin St. Wing TS29 .... 107 F6
Todd St. Spenny DL16 .... 127 E8
Toft Cres. Murton SR7 .... 40 C3
Toft Hill Cty Jun & Inf Sch.
    Hi Eth DL14 .... 146 E5
Toft Hill. Hi Eth DL14 .... 146 D5
Toft Hill La. Hi Eth DL14 ...... 146 B4
Tofts Rd. Mick DL12 .... 161 A4

Toll Bar Rd. Sland SR2 ..... 22 E8
Toll House Rd. Durham DH1 ..... 57 F2
Tollgate Bglws. Ann Pl DH9 ..... 16 E5
Tollgate Fields. W Rain DH4 ..... 37 F1
Tollgate Garth. Darl DL1 ..... 209 F6
Tollgate Rd. H Mill NE39 ..... 4 F5
Tollgate Terr. Ann Pl DH9 ..... 16 E5
Tom Raine Ct. Darl DL1 ..... 209 A2
Tomlin St. Shild DL4 ..... 169 F8
Topaz St. Seaham SR7 ..... 41 A7
Torrance Dr. Darl DL1 ..... 209 E7
Torver Cl. Peter SR8 ..... 85 E6
Tow Law Cty Jun Mix & Inf Sch.
Tow Law DL13 ..... 75 C2
Tow Law Ind Est. Tow Law DL13 75 B3
Tower Bank. M Law DH7 ..... 32 E8
Tower Ct. E Lane DH5 ..... 39 C1
Tower Hill. M St G DL2 ..... 225 F5
Tower Rd. Darl DL3 ..... 208 D3
Tower Rd. M Law DH7 & DH9 ..... 16 E1
Tower St. Eas SR8 ..... 63 F5
Town End. Mid in T DL12 ..... 160 E7
Town Farm Cl. Bish TS21 ..... 194 C7
Town Head. Egg DL12 ..... 162 C4
Town Head. Mid in T DL12 ..... 160 D8
Town Pasture La.
Bar Cas DL12 ..... 201 D7
Towneley Ct. Stanl DH9 ..... 17 E5
Townend Ct. Hut Hen TS28 ..... 108 F5
Townley Fields. R Gill NE39 ..... 1 F2
Townley Rd. R Gill NE39 ..... 1 D2
Trafalgar St. Cons DH8 ..... 14 F2
Trafalgar St. Ferry DL17 ..... 129 C4
Trafalgar Terr. Darl DL3 ..... 208 E4
Trafford Cl. Darl DL1 ..... 209 E4
Travellers' Gn. New Ay DL5 ..... 171 E5
Treecone Cl. Silk SR3 ..... 22 A5
Treelands. Darl DL3 ..... 208 C1
Treen Cres. Murton SR7 ..... 40 D3
Trefoil Rd. Tanf L DH9 ..... 17 D8
Tregoney Ave. Murton SR7 ..... 40 D4
Trent Cres. Gr Lum DH3 ..... 37 B7
Trent Dale. Leadg DH8 ..... 15 D5
Trent Pl. Darl DL1 ..... 223 F6
Trent St. E Lane DH5 ..... 61 C8
Trevarren Dr. Sland SR2 ..... 22 F8
Trevelyan Coll. Durham DH1 ..... 80 C7
Trevelyan Pl. Crook DL15 ..... 100 C3
Trevelyan Pl. Peter SR8 ..... 85 B5
Trevithick Cl. 2 Darl DL1 ..... 209 B1
Trevone Sq. Murton SR7 ..... 40 D3
Trevor Green N. 5
New Ay DL5 ..... 171 E8
Trevor Wlk. 3 New Ay DL5 ..... 171 E8
Trident Rd. N Silk SR3 ..... 22 A7
Trimdon Grange Cty Inf Sch.
Trim TS29 ..... 107 D3
Trimdon Jun Sch & Community
Coll. Trim TS29 ..... 131 E8
Trimdon St Williams RC (Aided)
Prim Sch. Trim TS29 ..... 131 E7
Trimdon Village Cty Inf Sch.
Trim TS29 ..... 131 D8
Trinity Rd. Darl DL3 ..... 208 E2
Trool Ct. Silk SR3 ..... 22 A5
Troon Ave. Darl DL1 ..... 209 E6
Trotter Terr. Ryhope SR2 ..... 22 F6
Trotter Terr. Shot Co DH6 ..... 84 C6
Trout's La. Wit Gil DH1 ..... 57 D7
Trout's Lane Sch. Wit Gil DH1 ..... 57 E7
Troutbeck Cl. Spenny DL16 ..... 103 E2
Troutbeck Way. Peter SR8 ..... 85 E7
Trowsdale St. Ann Pl DH9 ..... 16 E5
Trueman Gr. 4 Darl DL3 ..... 209 A7
Truro Ave. Murton SR7 ..... 40 D4
Truro Cl. Darl DL1 ..... 209 E5
Tuart St. C le S DH3 ..... 20 C3
Tubwell Row. Darl DL1 ..... 208 F1
Tudhoe Colliery Jun & Inf Sch.
Spenny DL16 ..... 104 B4
Tudhoe Grange Comp Sch.
Spenny DL16 ..... 104 A1
Tudhoe Grange Comp Sch.
Spenny DL16 ..... 104 A2
Tudhoe Ind Est. Spenny DL16 ..... 104 B4
Tudhoe La. Spenny DL16 ..... 104 A3
Tudhoe Moor Cty Inf Sch.
Spenny DL16 ..... 104 B1
Tudhoe Moor. Spenny DL16 ..... 104 C1
Tudhoe St Charles's RC Sch.
Spenny DL16 ..... 104 A2
Tudor Ct. Heigh DL5 ..... 170 E1
Tudor Ct. Shot Co DH6 ..... 84 D7
Tudor Dr. Tanf DH9 ..... 6 D3
Tudor Grange. Eas SR8 ..... 63 A3
Tudor Rd. C le S DH3 ..... 20 D5
Tudor Terr. Cons DH8 ..... 14 E3
Tummel Ct. Silk SR3 ..... 22 A6
Tunstall Ave. Bowb DH6 ..... 81 D1
Tunstall Bank. Ryhope SR2 & SR3 22 D7
Tunstall Gr. Bish Au DL14 ..... 147 F5
Tunstall Gr. Leadg DH8 ..... 15 D4
Tunstall Hope Rd. N Silk SR3 ..... 22 C8
Tunstall Rd. New Ay DL5 ..... 171 C6
Tunstall Terr. Darl DL2 ..... 224 B8
Tunstall Terr. N Silk SR2 ..... 22 B7
Tunstall Terr. Ryhope SR2 ..... 22 D7
Tunstall View. N Silk SR3 ..... 22 B8
Tunstall Village Gn. N Silk SR3 .. 22 C7
Tunstall Village Rd. N Silk SR3 .. 22 B7
Tunstall Villas. N Silk SR3 ..... 22 B7
Turnberry. Ouston DH2 ..... 8 F2
Turnberry Gr. Hartle TS27 ..... 111 C4
Turnbull Cres. Murton SR7 ..... 40 C3
Turner St. Cons DH8 ..... 14 D4
Turnpike Cl. Darl DL1 ..... 209 F6
Turnstone Dr. Wash NE38 ..... 9 F3
Tursdale Aged Mine Workers
War Meml Homes. Cornf DH6 105 C3
Tuscan Cl. N Bran DH7 ..... 78 E8
Tutta Bridge Cotts. Gr Br DL12 219 A7
Tweddle Cres. B Rocks TS27 ..... 86 F2
Tweddle Terr. Bowb DH6 ..... 81 C1
Tweed Ave. Leadg DH8 ..... 15 D5
Tweed Cl. Pelton DH2 ..... 19 F8
Tweed Cl. Peter SR8 ..... 85 D5
Tweed Cl. Sland SR2 ..... 22 F8
Tweed Pl. Darl DL1 ..... 224 A6
Tweed Rd. Spenny DL16 ..... 104 B3
Tweed St. E Lane DH5 ..... 61 C8
Tweed Terr. Stanl DH9 ..... 17 F5
Twelfth Ave. C le S DH2 ..... 20 B4
Twelfth St. Peter SR8 ..... 85 F7
Twickenham Rise. Darl DL1 ..... 209 F4
Twinsburn Cl. Heigh DL5 ..... 170 D1
Twinsburn Rd. Heigh DL5 ..... 170 D1
Twizell La. W Pel DH9 ..... 18 F5
Tyne Ave. Leadg DH8 ..... 15 D5
Tyne Cres. Darl DL1 ..... 224 A6
Tyne Cres. Spenny DL16 ..... 103 F1
Tyne Rd E. Stanl DH9 ..... 17 F5
Tyne Rd. Stanl DH9 ..... 17 E5
Tyne St. Cons DH8 ..... 15 A2
Tyne St. E Lane DH5 ..... 61 C8
Tyne St. 5 Seaham SR7 ..... 41 D7
Tyne Terr. Eas SR8 ..... 63 D4
Tyne Wlk. Cound DL14 ..... 149 C8
Tynedale St. H le H DH5 ..... 38 E1
Tynedale Terr. Ann Pl DH9 ..... 17 A4
Tynedale Wlk. Shild DL4 ..... 170 B8
Tyzack St. Edmon DH7 ..... 35 B7
Ugly La. Kimble DH2 ..... 35 F4
Ullapool Cl. St on T TS21 ..... 195 F3
Ullathorne Rise. Start DL12 ..... 200 F5
Ullerdale Cl. Belm DH1 ..... 59 E4
Ullswater Ave. E Lane DH5 ..... 61 C8
Ullswater Ave. Even DL14 ..... 147 A1
Ullswater Cl. Spenny DL16 ..... 104 B1
Ullswater Cres. Blay NE21 ..... 2 B8
Ullswater Cres. Crook DL15 ..... 100 F2
Ullswater Rd. C le S DH2 ..... 20 B1
Ullswater Rd. Ferry DL17 ..... 128 F5
Ullswater Terr. S Hett DH6 ..... 61 E8
Ulnaby La. H Con DL2 ..... 206 F6
Union La. C le St DH2 & DH3 ..... 36 B7
Union La. Stanh DL13 ..... 71 B3
Union Pl. Darl DL1 ..... 209 B1
Union St. Bish Au DL14 ..... 148 C7
Union St. 3 Darl DL3 ..... 208 F2
Union St. H le H DH5 ..... 39 A4
Union St. Seaham SR7 ..... 41 D6
Union St. 2 Stanh DL13 ..... 71 A3
Unity Terr. Ann Pl DH9 ..... 17 B4
Unity Terr. Dipton DH9 ..... 16 E7
Unity Terr. Tant DH9 ..... 6 B2
Unshaw Moor Cty Jun & Inf Sch.
Ush M DH7 ..... 56 F2
Unsworth Gdns. 7 Cons DH8 ..... 14 F2
Unsworth St. 6 Cons DH8 ..... 14 F2
Uphill Dr. Sacr DH7 ..... 35 D3
Uplands Rd. Darl DL3 ..... 208 E1
Uplands The. Birt DH3 ..... 9 D5
Upper Archer St. 1 Darl DL3 .. 208 F2
Upper Chare. Peter SR8 ..... 85 D6
Upper Church St. Spenny DL16 104 B1
Upper Russell St. Darl DL1 ..... 209 A2
Upper Town. Wols DL13 ..... 97 F8
Upper Yoden Way. Peter SR8 ..... 85 E6
Upsall Dr. Darl DL1 & DL3 ..... 223 E8
Urpeth Terr. Beam DH9 ..... 19 B7
Urwin St. H le H DH5 ..... 39 A3
Ushaw Coll. Lang Pk DH7 ..... 56 D4
Ushaw Moor Jun Sch.
Ush M DH7 ..... 57 A2
Ushaw Terr. Ush M DH7 ..... 56 F2
Ushaw Villas. Ush M DH7 ..... 56 F1
Usher Ave. Sherb DH6 ..... 59 F2
Vale St. E Lane DH5 ..... 61 B8
Vale View. Burnh DH7 ..... 33 E5
Valeside. Durham DH1 ..... 58 B2
Valley Cl. Tow Law DL13 ..... 75 B3
Valley Dene. Chopw NE17 ..... 4 B7
Valley Dr. Esh W DH7 ..... 55 C1
Valley Garth. Esh W DH7 ..... 55 C2
Valley Gdns. Cons DH8 ..... 14 C4
Valley Gr. Bish Au DL14 ..... 148 F5
Valley Gr. Lanch DH7 ..... 32 F3
Valley Rd. C le St DH2 ..... 19 E3
Valley St N. Darl DL1 ..... 209 A3
Valley Terr. How le W DL15 ..... 124 F7
Valley View. Ann Pl DH9 ..... 16 F5
Valley View. Birt DH3 ..... 9 B6
Valley View. Burnop NE16 ..... 5 F7
Valley View. Cons DH8 ..... 14 B5
Valley View. Cons DH8 ..... 31 C6
Valley View. H le H DH5 ..... 38 D1
Valley View. Leadg DH8 ..... 15 C3
Valley View. R Gill NE39 ..... 1 D2
Valley View. Sacr DH7 ..... 35 B2
Valley View. Sland B DH6 ..... 104 B6
Valley View. Thor DL13 ..... 99 B7
Valley View. Ush M DH7 ..... 57 B1
Van Mildert Cl. Peter SR8 ..... 85 B4
Van Mildert Coll. Durham DH1 ..... 80 B6
Van Mildert Rd. New Ay DL5 ..... 171 E6
Vancouver St. Darl DL3 ..... 208 E3
Vane Ct. Longn TS21 ..... 211 F5
Vane Rd. Bar Cas DL12 ..... 200 F6
Vane Rd. New Ay DL5 ..... 171 E7
Vane Road Jun & Inf Sch.
New Ay DL5 ..... 171 F7
Vane St. Eas SR8 ..... 63 E4
Vane St. N Silk SR3 ..... 22 A7
Vane Terr. 7 Cockf DL13 ..... 166 C5
Vane Terr. Darl DL3 ..... 208 E2
Vane Terr. Seaham SR7 ..... 41 D8
Vart Rd. Bish Au DL14 ..... 148 B5
Vaughan St. Darl DL3 ..... 209 A7
Vaughan St. Shild DL4 ..... 148 E1
Vedra Cl. Wear DL13 ..... 66 D3
Verdun Terr. Cornf DL17 ..... 105 D1
Vere Rd. Bar Cas DL12 ..... 200 F6
Verity Rise. 1 Darl DL3 ..... 209 A7
Verner Cl. Hartle TS24 ..... 111 C5
Verner Rd. Hartle TS24 ..... 111 C5
Vernon Gdns. Darl DL1 ..... 209 B8
Viador. C le S DH3 ..... 20 C4
Vicarage Cl. How le W DL15 ..... 124 D7
Vicarage Cl. Pelton DH2 ..... 19 E7
Vicarage Cl. S Hett DH6 ..... 62 B6
Vicarage Ct. Heigh DL5 ..... 170 D1
Vicarage Dr. Trim TS29 ..... 107 E1
Vicarage Est. Wing TS28 ..... 108 E8
Vicarage Farm Cl.
Escomb DL14 ..... 147 D8
Vicarage Flats. Brand DH7 ..... 79 B4
Vicarage Gdns. Will DL15 ..... 102 A3
Vicarage Rd. Cornf DL17 ..... 105 E1
Vicarage Rd. Darl DL1 ..... 209 B3
Vicarage Rd. N Silk SR3 ..... 22 A7
Vicarage Terr. Coxhoe DH6 ..... 106 A3
Vicarage Terr. Murton SR7 ..... 40 C2
Vicarage Terr. Nent CA9 ..... 42 A4
Vicars Cl. Thor Th TS21 ..... 175 D3
Viceroy St. Seaham SR7 ..... 41 D7
Vickers St. Bish Au DL14 ..... 148 B8
Victor St. C le S DH3 ..... 20 C3
Victor Terr. Bear DH7 ..... 57 B3
Victoria Ave. Bish Au DL14 ..... 148 C8
Victoria Ave. Brand DH7 ..... 79 C4
Victoria Ave. Crook DL15 ..... 100 F3
Victoria Cotts. Butter DL13 ..... 165 E8
Victoria Emb. Darl DL1 ..... 223 F8
Victoria Gdns. Spenny DL16 ..... 127 E7
Victoria La. Cound DL14 ..... 149 C8
Victoria Rd. Bar Cas DL12 ..... 201 A6
Victoria Rd. Darl DL1 ..... 208 F1
Victoria St. Cons DH8 ..... 14 E3
Victoria St. Crook DL15 ..... 100 E4
Victoria St. 14 Darl DL1 ..... 209 B1
Victoria St. Even DL14 ..... 167 D6
Victoria St. H le H DH5 ..... 39 A4
Victoria St. Lanch DH7 ..... 32 E4
Victoria St. Sacr DH7 ..... 35 C3
Victoria St. Seaham SR7 ..... 41 C7
Victoria St. Shild DL4 ..... 170 A8
Victoria St. Shot Co DH6 ..... 84 D6
Victoria St. Spenny DL16 ..... 127 E7
Victoria St. Will DL15 ..... 102 A4
Victoria Terr. Ann Pl DH9 ..... 16 F4
Victoria Terr. Beam DH9 ..... 19 A7
Victoria Terr. Chilt DL17 ..... 150 F8
Victoria Terr. Cockf DL13 ..... 166 D5
Victoria Terr. Coxhoe DH6 ..... 105 F3
Victoria Terr. 1 Durham DH1 ..... 58 B2
Victoria Terr. Hams NE17 ..... 4 B6
Victoria Terr. Mid in T DL12 ..... 160 D7
Victoria Terr. Murton SR7 ..... 40 D2
Victoria Terr. Pelton DH2 ..... 19 C6
Victoria Terr. R Gill NE39 ..... 1 C1
Victoria Terr. Stanh DL13 ..... 71 B2
Victoria Terr. Trim TS29 ..... 107 F5
Victory St E. H le H DH5 ..... 39 B4
Victory St W. H le H DH5 ..... 39 B4
View La. Stanl DH9 ..... 17 F7
View Tops. Beam DH9 ..... 18 F8
Viewforth Rd. Ryhope SR2 ..... 22 F5
Viewforth Villas. Durham DH1 ..... 58 A2
Vigo La. Birt DH3 ..... 20 D8
Vigodale. Birt DH3 ..... 9 E1
Villa Real Bglws. Cons DH8 ..... 15 B4
Villa Real Est. Cons DH8 ..... 15 A4
Villa Real Rd. Cons DH8 ..... 15 A4
Villa St. Spenny DL16 ..... 127 E7
Village Cl. New Ay DL17 ..... 150 E1
Village Ctr. Wash NE38 ..... 20 F8
Village The. Brance DH7 ..... 102 E8
Village The. Ca Eden TS27 ..... 85 D1
Village The. Ryhope SR2 ..... 23 A6
Villas The. Ann Pl DH9 ..... 16 E3
Villas The. Burnh DH7 ..... 33 D5
Villas The. Ferry DL17 ..... 128 E5
Villiers Cl. Chilt DL17 ..... 151 A8
Villiers Cl. Darl DL3 ..... 208 B2
Villiers Pl. 6 C le S DH3 ..... 20 C4
Villiers Pl. 3 New Ay DL5 ..... 171 D8
Villiers St. Spenny DL16 ..... 127 F8
Vincent St. Eas SR8 ..... 63 E4
Vincent St. Seaham SR7 ..... 41 D6
Vincent Terr. Ann Pl DH9 ..... 17 A3
Vindomora Road. Ebch DH8 ..... 3 E4
Vindomora Villas. Ebch DH8 ..... 3 E4
Vine Pl. 6 H le Sp DH4 ..... 38 E8
Vine St. By Gr DL16 ..... 102 E1
Vine St. Darl DL3 ..... 208 E3
Vine St. Spenny DL16 ..... 103 F1
Viola Cres. Ouston DH2 ..... 8 F2
Viola Cres. Sacr DH7 ..... 35 D3
Violet Gr. Darl DL1 ..... 209 C2
Violet St. H le Sp DH4 ..... 38 D8
Violet Terr. Bourn DH4 ..... 21 D3
Viscount Rd. 4 N Silk SR3 ..... 22 A7
Vivian Cres. C le S DH2 ..... 20 C2
Voltigeur Dr. Hart TS27 ..... 111 A3
Vulcan St. Darl DL1 ..... 209 B4
Vyner St. Spenny DL16 ..... 127 E8
Vyners Cl. Spenny DL16 ..... 128 A6
Wackerfield. Hilton DL2 ..... 167 C2
Waddington St. 1
Bish Au DL14 ..... 148 B6
Waddington St. 2
Durham DH1 ..... 58 B2
Wadham Cl. Peter SR8 ..... 85 B5
Wadham Gr. Darl DL1 ..... 209 B6
Wagtail La. Crag DH9 ..... 18 A1
Wagtail La. Qua Ho DH9 ..... 17 F1
Wagtail Terr. Crag DH9 ..... 18 C2
Waine Cres. Bish Au DL14 ..... 148 B5
Wakenshaw Rd. Durham DH1 ..... 58 F3
Walcher Rd. New Ay DL5 ..... 171 D7
Walden Cl. Urpeth DH2 ..... 8 D2
Walden Terr. Fishb TS21 ..... 131 C4
Waldridge La. C le S DH2 ..... 20 A2
Waldridge La. C le St DH2 ..... 19 F2
Waldridge La. Wald DH2 ..... 35 E7
Waldridge Rd. C le S DH2 & DH3 20 B2
Waldridge Rd. C le St DH2 ..... 19 F2
Waldron St. Bish Au DL14 ..... 148 B8
Wales St. Darl DL3 ..... 209 A5
Walk The. Elwick TS27 ..... 134 C5
Walker Dr. Bish Au DL14 ..... 148 A4
Walker La. New Ay DL5 ..... 171 D5
Walker St. Bowb DH6 ..... 105 D8
Walker Terr. Ferry DL17 ..... 129 C5
Walker's La. Midd DL5 ..... 170 E7
Walkergate. 3 Durham DH1 ..... 58 C2
Walkworth La. Spenny DL16 ..... 104 A2
Wallace St. H le Sp DH4 ..... 38 D8
Wallas Rd. New Ay DL5 ..... 171 D6
Waller St. H le Sp DH5 ..... 38 E7
Wallflower Ave. Peter SR8 ..... 85 E7
Wallington Dr. Sedge TS21 ..... 153 A7
Wallish Walls Rd. Shot DH8 ..... 13 C1
Wallnook La. Lang Pk DH7 ..... 56 D7
Walmer Ave. Bish Au DL14 ..... 148 B6
Walpole Cl. Seaham SR7 ..... 40 F6
Walter St. Shild DL4 ..... 170 A7
Walter Terr. H le H DH5 ..... 39 B1
Waltham Cl. Darl DL3 ..... 208 B4
Walton Ave. Seaham SR7 ..... 40 F6
Walton Cl. Stanl DH9 ..... 18 A5
Walton Heath. Darl DL1 ..... 209 E6
Walton St. Darl DL1 ..... 224 B8
Walton Terr. Cons DH8 ..... 15 A4
Walton Terr. Cons DH8 ..... 30 A6
Walton Terr. Wing TS28 ..... 84 D1
Walton's Bldgs. 1 Ush M DH7 ..... 56 F2
Waltons Terr. N Bran DH7 ..... 78 F8
Walworth Cres. Darl DL3 ..... 208 C5
Walworth Rd. Ferry DL17 ..... 129 A7
Walworth Rd. Heigh DL2 ..... 190 A5
Walworth Rd. New Ay DL5 ..... 171 D4
Walworth Sch. New Ay DL5 ..... 171 B8
Wanlass Terr. Durham DH1 ..... 58 D2
Wansbeck Ave. Stanl DH9 ..... 17 F5
Wansbeck Cl. Pelton DH2 ..... 19 F7
Wansbeck Cl. Spenny DL16 ..... 103 E2
Wansbeck Ct. Peter SR8 ..... 85 C4
Wansbeck Gr. Leadg DH8 ..... 15 D5
Wansford Way. Whick NE16 ..... 2 F5
Wantage Rd. Belm DH1 ..... 59 D5
Warburton Cl. New Ay DL5 ..... 171 F7
Ward Ave. R Gill NE39 ..... 1 C2
Ward Terr. Wols DL13 ..... 98 A7
Warden Gr. H le Sp DH5 ..... 38 F7
Wardle St. Qua Ho DH9 ..... 17 E3
Ware St. Bar Cas DL12 ..... 201 A6
Wareham Way. Will DL15 ..... 101 F1
Waring Terr. Seaham SR7 ..... 40 F6
Wark St. C le S DH3 ..... 20 C2
Warkworth Ave.
Bish Au DL14 ..... 148 A6
Warkworth Ave. Peter SR8 ..... 85 F8
Warkworth Cres. Seaham SR7 ..... 40 E7
Warkworth Dr. C le St DH2 ..... 36 A8
Warkworth Rd. Durham DH1 ..... 58 C7
Warkworth Way. 1
Darl DL1 ..... 209 C6
Warnbrook Ave. Murton SR7 ..... 40 D2
Warnbrook Cres. B Rocks TS27 . 86 F2
Warner Gr. 6 Darl DL3 ..... 209 A7
Warren Cl. Hartle TS24 ..... 111 F1
Warren Rd. Hartle TS24 ..... 111 F2
Warren Rd. New Ay DL5 ..... 171 D4
Warren St. Darl DL3 ..... 208 E3
Warren St. Peter SR8 ..... 86 A7
Warwick Ave. Cons DH8 ..... 30 A7
Warwick Cl. Spenny DL16 ..... 104 A2
Warwick Ct. Durham DH1 ..... 80 A7
Warwick Dr. H le Sp DH5 ..... 38 E7
Warwick Pl. Peter SR8 ..... 85 B7
Warwick Pl. Will DL15 ..... 102 A3
Warwick Rd. Bish Au DL14 ..... 148 A6
Warwick Road Sch.
Bish Au DL14 ..... 148 A6
Warwick Sq. Darl DL3 ..... 208 B5
Warwick Terr. N Silk SR3 ..... 22 A8
Warwick Terr W. N Silk SR3 ..... 22 A8
Warwickshire Dr. Belm DH1 ..... 59 D2
Wasdale Cl. Peter SR8 ..... 85 E6
Washbrook Dr. Darl DL3 ..... 209 A7
Washington Ave. M St G DL2 ..... 226 B7
Washington Birtley Service Area.
Birt DH3 & NE38 ..... 9 E3
Washington Cres. New Ay DL5 171 F8
Washington Highway.
Pens DH4 & NE38 ..... 21 E8
Washington Highway.
Wash DH4 & NE38 ..... 21 E8
Washington Hospl The.
Wash NE38 ..... 20 E8
Washington Sq. Eas SR8 ..... 63 B3
Waskdale Cres. Blay NE21 ..... 2 B8
Waskerley Gr. Bish Au DL14 ..... 147 F5
Waskerley Pl. Wols DL13 ..... 97 F7
Waskerley Wlk. New Ay DL5 ..... 171 A7
Water Gap. Romald DL12 ..... 162 B1
Water House Rd. Esh W DL15 ..... 77 E4
Water La. Heigh DL5 ..... 170 D1
Water St. Sacr DH7 ..... 35 C3
Water View. M St G DL2 ..... 225 E8
Waterford Cl. E Rain DH5 ..... 38 D4
Watergate La. Crook DL15 ..... 100 F1
Watergate Rd. Cons DH8 ..... 29 F6
Waterloo Cl. Crook DL15 ..... 100 E4
Waterloo Terr. Shild DL4 ..... 148 E2
Waters End. Gain DL2 ..... 205 A6
Waterside. Darl DL3 ..... 208 C3
Watkin Cres. Murton SR7 ..... 40 C3
Watling Ave. Seaham SR7 ..... 40 F6
Watling Rd. Bish Au DL14 ..... 148 B4
Watling St. Leadg DH8 ..... 15 D4
Watling Street Bglws.
Leadg DH8 ..... 15 C5
Watling Terr. Will DL15 ..... 101 E4
Watling Way. Lanch DH7 ..... 32 E3
Watson Cl. Seaham SR7 ..... 40 F6
Watson Cl. Wh Hi DH6 ..... 84 A3
Watson Cres. Wing TS29 ..... 108 B5
Watson Ct. Bar Cas DL12 ..... 201 A5
Watson Rd. New Ay DL5 ..... 171 C5
Watson St. Burnop NE16 ..... 6 B6
Watson St. Cons DH8 ..... 14 E4
Watson St. H Spen NE39 ..... 1 A5
Watson St. Spenny DL16 ..... 127 C5
Watson St. Stanl DH9 ..... 17 F8
Watson's Bldgs. Edmon DH7 ..... 35 B7
Watt St. Ferry DL17 ..... 128 E6
Watts St. Murton SR7 ..... 40 C3
Waveney Gdns. Stanl DH9 ..... 17 E4
Waveney Rd. Peter SR8 ..... 85 B4
Waverley Cl. Blay NE21 ..... 1 F8
Waverley Terr. Darl DL1 ..... 209 A1
Waverley Terr. Dipton DH9 ..... 5 E1
Waverley Terr. Shild DL4 ..... 149 A2
Wayland Terr. Darl DL3 ..... 208 D5
Wayside. Sland B DH6 ..... 104 B6
Wayside Ct. Bear DH7 ..... 57 B3
Wayside Rd. Darl DL1 ..... 209 B7
Wayside The. Hur on T DL2 ..... 224 C1
Wear Ave. Leadg DH8 ..... 15 D5
Wear Bank. Wols DL13 ..... 97 E5
Wear Chare. Bish Au DL14 ..... 126 C1
Wear Cres. Gr Lum DH3 ..... 37 B7
Wear Lodge. C le S DH3 ..... 20 C7
Wear Rd. By Gr DL16 ..... 102 E2
Wear Rd. Stanl DH9 ..... 17 F5
Wear St. C le S DH3 ..... 20 D2
Wear St. Cons DH8 ..... 15 A2
Wear St. Fence DH4 ..... 38 A7
Wear St. H le H DH5 ..... 39 A3
Wear St. 6 Seaham SR7 ..... 41 D7
Wear St. Spenny DL16 ..... 127 F8
Wear St. Tow Law DL13 ..... 75 C2
Wear Terr. Bish Au DL14 ..... 126 C1
Wear Terr. Stanh DL13 ..... 71 B2
Wear Terr. Wit le W DL14 ..... 124 D4
Wear View. By Gr DL16 ..... 102 E1
Wear View. Durham DH1 ..... 58 D2
Wear View. Frost DL13 ..... 96 B6
Wear View. Hunw DL15 ..... 125 E7
Wear View. Toro DL14 ..... 125 F2
Weardale Cres. Tow Law DL13 ... 75 B3
Weardale Ct. How le W DL15 ..... 124 D7
Weardale Dr. Bish Au DL14 ..... 147 F4
Weardale Pk. Wh Hi DH6 ..... 84 A3
Weardale St. H le H DH5 ..... 38 E1
Weardale St. Spenny DL16 ..... 104 B1
Weardale Terr. Ann Pl DH9 ..... 17 A4
Weardale Terr. C le S DH3 ..... 20 D2
Weardale Wlk. Shild DL4 ..... 149 B1
Weare Gr. Still TS21 ..... 174 F3
Wearhead Mix Jun & Inf Sch.
Wear DL13 ..... 66 D4
Wearside Dr. Durham DH1 ..... 58 D2
Weatherleyhill La.
Satley DL13 & DH8 ..... 52 B6
Weaver's Way. Darl DL1 ..... 209 A2
Webb Ave. Murton SR7 ..... 40 C3
Webb Ave. Seaham SR7 ..... 40 F7
Webb Cl. New Ay DL5 ..... 171 C7
Webb Sq. Peter SR8 ..... 63 E1
Webster House. Durham DH1 ..... 58 F2
Wedgwood Rd. Seaham SR7 ..... 40 F6
Weeds. Westg DL13 ..... 68 B1
Weir St. Darl DL1 ..... 209 A2
Welbeck Ave. Darl DL1 ..... 209 E5
Welbeck St. Darl DL1 ..... 224 A8
Welbury Gr. New Ay DL5 ..... 171 F7
Welbury Way. New Ay DL5 ..... 171 D2
Weldon Terr. C le S DH3 ..... 20 D2
Welfare Cl. Eas SR8 ..... 63 E4
Welfare Cres. B Coll TS27 ..... 86 C3
Welfare Cres. S Hett DH6 ..... 62 B6
Welfare Rd. H le H DH5 ..... 39 A4
Welfare Terr. Coxhoe DH6 ..... 105 F4
Welford Rd. Cons DH8 ..... 30 C8
Well Bank. Billy R DL15 ..... 100 E8
Well Bank. L Con DL2 ..... 222 E8
Well Bank. New Ay DL5 ..... 171 F2
Well Bank. St J Ch DL13 ..... 67 A2
Well Chare. Cound DL14 ..... 149 B8
Well House Dr. New Ay DL5 ..... 150 C1
Well House Ride. New Ay DL5 150 D1
Welland Cl. Peter SR8 ..... 85 C4
Wellfield A. J. Dawson Sec Sch.
Wing TS28 ..... 84 E1
Wellfield Comp Sch.
Wing TS28 ..... 108 E8
Wellfield Rd. Murton SR7 ..... 40 B3
Wellfield Rd. R Gill NE39 ..... 1 C2
Wellfield Rd. Wing TS28 ..... 84 E1
Wellfield Rd N. Wing TS28 ..... 84 E1
Wellfield Rd S. Wing TS28 ..... 84 E1
Wellfield Terr. Ryhope SR2 ..... 22 E5
Wellfield Terr. Wing TS28 ..... 84 F1
Wellgarth. Even DL14 ..... 167 C6
Wellhope. Wash NE38 ..... 20 F8
Wellington Court Mews. 15
Darl DL1 ..... 208 F1
Wellington Dr. Grind TS22 ..... 155 D1
Wellington Rd. Bar Cas DL12 ..... 201 A7
Wellington St. H Pitt DH6 ..... 60 B5
Wells Cl. Darl DL1 ..... 209 E5
Wells Cres. Seaham SR7 ..... 40 F7
Wells Gr. Will DL15 ..... 101 F2
Welsh Terr. Ann Pl DH9 ..... 17 A3
Wensley Cl. Urpeth DH2 ..... 8 E1
Wensley Terr. Ferry DL17 ..... 129 C3

Wensleydale Rd. Darl DL1 .... 209 A5
Wensleydale Sq. Bish Au DL14 .. 147 F5
Wentworth Gr. Hartle TS27 ..... 111 D3
Wentworth Way. Darl DL3 .... 208 A5
Werdohl Way. Cons DH8 .... 15 B4
Wesley Cl. Stanl DH9 .... 18 B7
Wesley Cres. 6 Shild DL4 .... 149 A2
Wesley Ct. 7 Darl DL1 .... 209 B1
Wesley Gdns. Cons DH8 .... 30 B6
Wesley Gr. Bish Au DL14 .... 148 B7
Wesley St. Bish Au DL14 .... 148 F5
Wesley St. Cons DH8 .... 14 D4
Wesley St. Cons DH8 .... 14 F2
Wesley St. Crook DL15 .... 100 E4
Wesley St. 9 Darl DL1 .... 209 B1
Wesley St. Will DL15 .... 102 A3
Wesley Terr. Ann Pl DH9 .... 16 F4
Wesley Terr. C le S DH3 .... 20 C3
Wesley Terr. Cons DH8 .... 30 B6
Wesley Terr. Dipton DH9 .... 5 D1
Wesley Terr. Mid in T DL12 .... 160 D7
Wesley Terr. S Hill DH6 .... 60 C1
Wesley Way. Seaham SR7 .... 40 F7
Wesleyan Rd. Spenny DL16 .... 127 F8
West Acre. Cons DH8 .... 14 C5
West Auckland Cty Sch.
Bish Au DL14 .... 168 B8
West Auckland Rd.
Darl DL3 & DL2 .... 208 C6
West Auckland Rd.
Shild DL14 & DL4 .... 148 C1
West Auckland Rd. Walw DL2 190 D5
West Ave. Eas SR8 .... 63 E5
West Ave. Murton SR7 .... 40 C3
West Ave. R Gill NE39 .... 1 D1
West Ave. Wald DH2 .... 36 A7
West Beck Gr. Darl DL3 .... 208 A2
West Blackdene. St J Ch DL13 ... 66 F3
West Block. Wit Gil DH7 .... 57 A8
West Brandon Rd. Esh W DL15 .. 77 E3
West Bridge St. Crook DL15 .... 100 F4
West Bridge St. Pens DH4 .... 21 E8
West Chilton Terr. Chilt DL17 .. 128 E1
West Cl. Chilt DL16 .... 128 F3
West Cl. H Con DL2 .... 206 E4
West Cl. Shild DL4 .... 148 E1
West Cornforth Cty Inf Sch.
Cornf DL17 .... 105 E1
West Cornforth Cty Jun Mix Sch.
Cornf DL17 .... 105 E1
West Coronation St. 8
Murton SR7 .... 40 D3
West Cres. Chopw NE17 .... 4 B7
West Cres. Darl DL3 .... 208 E3
West Cres. Eas SR8 .... 63 D4
West Dr. Lanch DH7 .... 32 E3
West Ellen St. Murton SR7 .... 40 D2
West End. Hunw DL15 .... 125 D7
West End. Hur on T DL2 .... 224 C1
West End. Sedge TS21 .... 153 A6
West End Terr. 5 Cockf DL13 .. 166 C5
West End Terr. Will DL15 .... 101 E3
West End Villas. Crook DL15 ..... 100 D4
West Fall. Wear DL13 .... 66 D4
West Farm. Burdon SR3 .... 22 B3
West Farm. Medom DH8 .... 4 C2
West Fields. New Ay DL5 .... 170 F4
West Garth. Carl TS21 .... 195 C8
West Gn. Heigh DL5 .... 170 D1
West Gr. Seaham SR7 .... 40 F7
West Gr. Trim TS29 .... 107 D1
West Haswicks. Westg DL13 ...... 92 B8
West Haven. Cons DH8 .... 14 E3
West High Horse Cl. R Gill NE39 .. 2 A4
West La. Bish Au DL14 .... 147 F4
West La. Bish Au DL14 .... 147 F5
West La. Blay NE21 .... 2 A8
West La. Bold DL12 .... 200 B1
West La. Byer NE16 .... 2 C1
West La. C le S DH3 .... 20 C2
West La. Cald DL11 .... 205 A2
West La. Cald DL11 .... 221 C7
West La. E Lay DL11 .... 221 C1
West La. Epp DL11 .... 205 A2
West La. Kelloe DL1 & TS29 .... 107 B1
West La. Medom NE17 .... 4 B4
West La. S Hett DH6 & SR7 .... 62 D6
West La. Satley DL13 .... 52 D7
West La. Trim DL17 & TS29 .... 107 B1
West Law Rd. Cons DH8 .... 14 D8
West Lea. Blay NE21 .... 2 C8
West Lea. Wit Gil DH7 .... 57 B8
West Leigh. Tanf L DH9 .... 17 D8
West Moor Rd. Darl DL1 .... 224 C7
West Ousterley Rd. Qua Ho DH9 17 F3
West Par. Cons DH8 .... 15 A2
West Par. Coxhoe DH6 .... 105 F5
West Par. Leadg DH8 .... 15 C4
West Park La. Sedge TS21 .... 153 A6
West Pasture Rd. Mick DL12 ...... 160 E2
West Pelton Cty Jun & Inf Sch.
W Pel DH9 .... 18 F6
West Pk. Cound DL14 .... 127 A1
West Powlett St. Darl DL3 .... 208 E1
West Rainton Cty Inf Sch.
W Rain DH4 .... 37 F2
West Rd. Ann Pl DH9 .... 16 F3
West Rd. Bish Au DL14 .... 148 B8
West Rd. Cons DH8 .... 14 C4
West Rd. Crook DL15 .... 100 D3
West Rd. Shild DL4 .... 148 E1
West Rd. Tant DH9 .... 6 A1
West Rd. Will DL15 .... 101 E3
West Row. Birt DH3 .... 9 E3
West Row. Darl DL1 .... 208 F1
West Row. Sadb DL2 .... 210 E6
West St. B Coll TS27 .... 86 D3
West St. 4 Birt DH3 .... 9 C4
West St. Cornf DL17 .... 105 D1
West St. Darl DL3 .... 208 F1
West St. Ferry DL17 .... 128 F6
West St. Hett DH6 .... 104 E6
West St. Leadg DH8 .... 15 C4
West St. N Silk SR3 .... 22 A8
West St. Seaham SR7 .... 41 D7
West St. Shot Co DH6 .... 84 C6
West St. Still TS21 .... 174 E3
West St. Tanf L DH9 .... 17 D8
West St. W Pel DH2 .... 19 A5
West Terr. Billy R DL15 .... 100 E7
West Terr. Burnh DH7 .... 33 D5
West Terr. Coxhoe DH6 .... 105 F5
West Terr. Even DL14 .... 167 C7
West Terr. Fishb TS21 .... 131 B5
West Terr. New Ay DL5 .... 171 E2
West Terr. Spenny DL16 .... 127 D7
West Terr. Staind DL2 .... 186 C5
West Terr. Stanh DL13 .... 71 A3
West View. Bish Au DL14 .... 147 F3
West View. Bish Au DL14 .... 148 D5
West View. Bish Mi DL17 .... 130 C4
West View. Brand DH7 .... 79 C3
West View. Burnop NE16 .... 6 A6
West View. Butter DL13 .... 165 E8
West View. C le S DH3 .... 20 C4
West View. Cons DH8 .... 14 D5
West View. Cornf DL17 .... 105 E1
West View. Crook DL15 .... 101 A3
West View. Darl DL3 .... 208 A1
West View. Durham DH1 .... 58 E2
West View. E Hed DL13 .... 76 D5
West View. Esh W DH7 .... 77 E7
West View. Esh W DH7 .... 77 E8
West View. Even DL14 .... 167 D6
West View. 11 Ferry DL17 .... 129 A6
West View. Gain DL2 .... 205 A7
West View. Hasw DH6 .... 61 D1
West View. Hunw DL15 .... 125 D7
West View. Kibble NE11 .... 8 D6
West View. Kir Me DL16 .... 127 F3
West View. Medom DH8 .... 15 A8
West View. Murton SR7 .... 40 C2
West View. Newf DL14 .... 126 B7
West View. 2 Peter SR8 .... 86 A7
West View. Ryhope SR2 .... 22 F6
West View. S Hill DH6 .... 60 C1
West View. Sacr DH7 .... 35 B3
West View. Shild DL14 .... 168 D8
West View Cty Jun Sch.
Hartle TS24 .... 111 F2
West View Gdns. Stanl DH9 .... 17 E7
West View Rd. Hartle TS24 .... 111 F3
West View Terr. Shild DL4 .... 148 E3
West Villas. W Pel DH9 .... 19 A6
Westacres. M St G DL2 .... 225 E7
Westbourne Gr. Darl DL3 .... 208 D1
Westbrook. Darl DL3 .... 208 F3
Westbrook Terr. 3 Darl DL3 ... 208 F3
Westcliff Cl. Eas SR8 .... 63 A3
Westcliffe Ct. Darl DL3 .... 208 E1
Westcott Dr. Durham DH1 .... 58 A5
Westcott Rd. Peter SR8 .... 85 D7
Westcott Terr. Ferry DL17 .... 128 E5
Westcott Wlk. New Ay DL5 .... 171 D5
Westcroft. Stanh DL13 .... 71 A3
Westerdale. Pens DH4 .... 21 E8
Westerdale. Spenny DL16 .... 103 E1
Westerdale Ct. Darl DL3 .... 208 C6
Westerdale Gdns. Shild DL4 ...... 149 B1
Westerhope Ct. Darl DL3 .... 208 C6
Western Ave. Esh W DH7 .... 55 D1
Western Hill. Cons DH8 .... 14 C5
Western Hill. Frost DL13 .... 96 B6
Western Hill. Ryhope SR2 .... 22 E7
Western Lodge Cotts.
Durham DH1 .... 58 A4
Western Terr N. Murton SR7 .... 40 D3
Western Terr S. Murton SR7 .... 40 D3
Westernmoor. Wash NE37 .... 9 F6
Westerton Rd. Cound DL14 .... 127 C1
Westerton View. Cound DL14 ..... 149 B8
Westfield. Frost DL13 .... 96 A7
Westfield Dr. Crook DL15 .... 100 C3
Westfield Dr. Darl DL3 .... 208 C2
Westfield Dr. Hur on T DL2 .... 224 D1
Westfield Rd. Bish Au DL14 .... 148 B6
Westfield Terr. Bish Mi DL17 ...... 130 B4
Westfields. Spenny DL16 .... 103 E1
Westfields. Stanl DH9 .... 17 E5
Westgarth Gr. Shot Co DH6 .... 84 C7
Westgarth Terr. Darl DL1 .... 209 C3
Westgate Ave. N Silk SR3 .... 22 A8
Westgate Cres. Darl DL3 .... 208 C6
Westgate Dr. Bish Au DL14 .... 148 E6
Westgate Gr. N Silk SR3 .... 22 A8
Westgate Rd. Bish Au DL14 .... 148 B8
Westgate Rd. Darl DL3 .... 208 C6
Westhills Cl. Sacr DH7 .... 35 B5
Westhills. Tant DH9 .... 6 A2
Westkirk Cl. Darl DL3 .... 208 C6
Westlands. Bowb DH6 .... 105 E6
Westlands Rd. Darl DL3 .... 208 D4
Westlea Ave. Bish Au DL14 .... 148 C6
Westlea Rd. Seaham SR7 .... 40 F7
Westline Ind Est. Ouston DH2 .... 9 B2
Westminster Rd. Darl DL1 .... 224 D7
Westmoor Cl. Spenny DL16 .... 127 D7
Westmoreland St. Darl DL3 .... 208 F5
Westmorland Cl. Spenny DL16 . 104 B2
Westmorland Ct. Darl DL3 .... 209 A5
Westmorland Pl. Will DL15 .... 102 A3
Westmorland Rise. Peter SR8 ..... 85 B8
Westmorland Way.
New Ay DL5 .... 171 D7
Weston Ave. Whick NE16 .... 2 F5
Weston View. Peter SR8 .... 85 C7
Westpark Dr. Darl DL3 .... 208 C5
Westray. C le S DH2 .... 20 B1
Westray Cl. 3 Sland SR2 .... 22 E8
Westview Terr. Ann Pl DH9 .... 16 E3
Westward View. Sacr DH7 .... 35 B2
Westway. Peter SR8 .... 85 C5
Westwick Rd. Bar Cas DL12 .... 201 C4
Westwood Ave. Heigh DL5 .... 170 C1
Westwood Cl. Burnop NE16 .... 6 B7
Westwood Cty Jun Mix Inf Sch.
Medom NE17 .... 4 B4
Westwood RC Jun & Inf Sch.
Hams NE17 .... 4 A5
Westwood View. C le S DH3 .... 20 C1
Westwood Way. Hartle TS27 ...... 111 C3
Wetherburn Ave. Murton SR7 .... 40 B3
Wetherby Cl. Cons DH8 .... 14 D7
Wetlands La. Newsh DL11 .... 219 E1
Wetsgate Sch. Westg DL13 .... 68 B1
Weymouth Dr. Hartle TS24 .... 111 D4
Weymouth Dr. Seaham SR7 .... 41 A6
Whalton Cl. Sherb DH6 .... 60 A1
Wharfe Way. Darl DL1 .... 224 A6
Wharnley Way. Cons DH8 .... 29 F6
Wharrien Sq. Wh Hi DH6 .... 83 E1
Wharton Cl. E Rain DH5 .... 38 D4
Wharton St. Cound DL14 .... 149 B8
Wheat Cl. Cons DH8 .... 14 E7
Wheatbottom. Crook DL15 .... 101 A3
Wheatear Cl. 1 Wash NE38 .... 9 F3
Wheatfield Gdns. Crook DL15 .. 101 A3
Wheatley Green La. Crag DH7 ... 34 D8
Wheatley Green La. Holm DH7 .. 34 D8
Wheatley Hill Jun & Inf Sch.
Wh Hi DH6 .... 83 E2
Wheatley Terr. Wh Hi DH6 .... 83 E2
Wheatleywell La.
Kimble DH2 & DH3 .... 36 B5
Wheeldale Cl. Darl DL1 .... 209 C5
Wheldon Terr. Pelton DH2 .... 19 E7
Wheler Gn. 1 New Ay DL5 .... 171 C8
Whessoe Rd. Darl DL3 .... 208 F6
Whickham Cl. H le Sp DH4 .... 38 C8
Whickham Fellside Cty Jun Sch.
Whick NE16 .... 2 F6
Whickham Golf Course.
Whick NE16 .... 2 D3
Whickham Ind Est. Whick NE16 ... 2 F8
Whickham Parochial Prim Sch.
Whick NE16 .... 2 F5
Whickham St. Eas SR8 .... 63 D4
Whinbank Rd. New Ay DL5 .... 171 C3
Whinbush Way. Darl DL1 .... 209 E7
Whinfield Ave. Shot Co DH6 .... 84 C6
Whinfield Dr. New Ay DL5 .... 171 D2
Whinfield Jun & Inf Sch.
Darl DL1 .... 209 E6
Whinfield Rd. Darl DL1 .... 209 D6
Whinfield Terr. R Gill NE39 .... 1 D2
Whinfield Way. R Gill NE39 .... 1 C1
Whinlatter Pl. New Ay DL5 .... 171 A6
Whinney Cl. Blay NE21 .... 2 A8
Whinney Hill. Durham DH1 .... 80 D8
Whinny La. Ebch DH8 .... 3 E1
Whinny Pl. Cons DH8 .... 30 A6
Whinside. Tanf L DH9 .... 17 D7
Whitburn Cl. Lang Pk DH7 .... 56 B6
Whitby Cl. Bish Au DL14 .... 147 E6
Whitby Way. Darl DL3 .... 208 A5
White Cedars. Brand DH7 .... 79 A3
White Cres. Hesl TS27 .... 86 A1
White Gates Dr. H le H DH5 .... 39 B2
White Hart Cres. Darl DL1 .... 209 E3
White Hart Ct. Hart TS27 .... 110 F2
White Hill Rd. E Lane DH5 .... 61 C8
White House Ave. 4 Ush M DH7 56 F2
White House Dr. Sedge TS21 ...... 153 B7
White House La. Heigh DL2 .... 169 F2
White Kirkley. Frost DL13 .... 96 B4
White Lea Cl. Peter SR8 .... 85 F5
White Lea Rd. Billy R DL15 .... 100 C8
White-le-Head Gdns. Tant DH9 .. 6 A1
Whitegates Rd. Sherb DH6 .... 59 F2
Whitehead Wlk. New Ay DL5 ...... 171 F8
Whitehill Cres. C le St DH2 .... 19 F2
Whitehill Hall Gdns. C le S DH2 20 A4
Whitehouse Ave. Burnh DH7 .... 33 D4
Whitehouse Cres. Shot Co SR8 .. 84 F6
Whitehouse Ct. Eas SR8 .... 63 B3
Whitehouse Ct. Peter SR8 .... 85 B8
Whitehouse Ct. Ush M DH7 .... 57 A2
Whitehouse La. Ush M DH7 .... 56 F2
Whitehouse Terr. Burnh DH7 .... 33 D5
Whitehouse Way. Shot Co SR8 .. 84 F6
Whiteley Gr. New Ay DL5 .... 171 D8
Whitemeadows. Darl DL3 .... 208 C2
Whiteoak Ave. Belm DH1 .... 59 B3
Whitesmocks Ave. Durham DH1 58 A3
Whitesmocks. Durham DH1 .... 58 A4
Whitethroat Cl. 6 Wash NE38 .... 9 F3
Whitfield St. Cons DH8 .... 15 A3
Whitfield St. Crook DL15 .... 100 E4
Whitrout Rd. Hartle TS24 .... 111 E3
Whitton Cl. New Ay DL5 .... 150 E1
Whitton Gr. Still TS21 .... 174 E3
Whitwell Acres. H Shin DH1 .... 81 C4
Whitwell Rd. Darl DL1 .... 209 D1
Whitwell Terr. Crook DL15 .... 100 D5
Whitworth Ave. New Ay DL5 .... 171 D3
Whitworth Cl. Spenny DL16 .... 127 D7
Whitworth Dr. New Ay DL5 .... 171 D3
Whitworth House Sch.
Spenny DL16 .... 127 D8
Whitworth La.
Brance DH7 & DL16 .... 102 F6
Whitworth Meadows.
Spenny DL16 .... 127 C5
Whitworth Rd. Shot Co SR8 .... 84 F6
Whitworth Rd. Spenny DL16 .... 127 D8
Whitworth Rd. Wash NE37 .... 9 F7
Whitworth Terr. Spenny DL16 .. 127 E8
Whorlton Moor Cres.
Darl DL1 .... 224 D7
Widdowfield St. Darl DL3 .... 208 F3
Widecombe Wlk. Ferry DL17 ... 129 C5
Widgeon Rd. Darl DL1 .... 209 E1
Wigdan Walls Rd. Hi Eth DL14 147 D6
Wigeon Cl. Wash NE38 .... 9 F2
Wigham Terr. Burnop NE16 .... 6 A4
Wilbore Croft. New Ay DL5 .... 170 F5
Wild Rd. Darl DL1 .... 210 A1
Wildgoose La. Mordon DL1 .... 172 E5
Wilfred St. C le S DH3 .... 20 C2
Wilfrid St. Birt DH3 .... 9 C3
Wilk's Hill. Quebec DH7 .... 55 A4
Wilkes St. Darl DL3 .... 208 F3
Wilkinson Rd. New Ay DL5 .... 171 E6
Wilkinson Rd. Peter SR8 .... 63 E1
Wilkinson St. By Gr DL16 .... 126 E8
Wilkinson Terr. Ryhope SR2 .... 22 E6
Willan's Bldgs. Durham DH1 .... 58 F2
Willard Gr E. Stanh DL13 .... 71 C2
Willard Gr. Stanh DL13 .... 71 C2
Willerby Cl. Peter SR8 .... 85 B7
William Cassidi (C of E) Prim Sch.
Still TS21 .... 174 F4
William Johnson St.
Murton SR7 .... 40 D2
William Keers Cres The.
Ferry DL17 .... 128 D5
William Morris Ave. R Gill NE39 ... 1 B2
William Morris Terr.
Shot Co DH6 .... 84 C5
William Pl. Durham DH1 .... 58 F2
William Russell Homes.
Brance DH7 .... 78 E1
William St. Ann Pl DH9 .... 17 A4
William St. Bish Au DL14 .... 148 F6
William St. Bowb DH6 .... 81 D1
William St. C le S DH3 .... 20 C3
William St. Crag DH9 .... 18 C2
William St. Darl DL3 .... 208 F5
William St. Ferry DL17 .... 129 D2
William St. Pelton DH2 .... 19 C5
William St. Stanl DH9 .... 17 D4
Williamfield Way. New Ay DL5 . 171 A6
Williams Cl. Stanl DH9 .... 18 A5
Williams Rd. Murton SR7 .... 40 C3
Williams Terr. Ryhope SR2 .... 22 E6
Williamson Sq. Wing TS28 .... 108 D8
Willington C of E Jun & Inf Sch.
Will DL15 .... 102 A2
Willington Cty Inf Sch.
Will DL15 .... 101 F3
Willington Cty Jun Mix Sch.
Will DL15 .... 101 F3
Willington Parkside Comp Lower
Sch. Will DL15 .... 100 E3
Willis St. H le H DH5 .... 39 A5
Willow Ave. Crook DL15 .... 100 D4
Willow Chase The. Longn TS21 211 F5
Willow Cl. Brand DH7 .... 79 B3
Willow Cres. E Lane DH5 .... 39 D1
Willow Cres. Leadg DH8 .... 15 D3
Willow Ct. Hi Eth DL14 .... 146 E5
Willow Pk. Lang Pk DH7 .... 56 A6
Willow Rd. Darl DL3 .... 208 D4
Willow Rd. Esh W DH7 .... 55 D1
Willow Rd. Ferry DL17 .... 129 A6
Willow Rd. H le Sp DH4 .... 38 C8
Willow Rd. Spenny DL16 .... 127 C6
Willow Rd E. Darl DL3 .... 208 E4
Willow Tree Ave. H Shin DH1 .... 81 A6
Willow View. Burnop NE16 .... 6 A6
Willow Wlk. Shild DL4 .... 149 B1
Willows The. Bish Au DL14 .... 148 C8
Willows The. Sedge TS21 .... 153 A5
Willowtree Ave. Belm DH1 .... 59 A3
Willowvale. C le S DH2 .... 20 A5
Wilson Ave. Birt DH3 .... 9 C5
Wilson Ave. Cound DL14 .... 149 B8
Wilson Cres. Belm DH1 .... 59 A3
Wilson Pl. Peter SR8 .... 85 D8
Wilson St. Bar Cas DL12 .... 201 A5
Wilson St. Bish Au DL14 .... 148 F4
Wilson St. Crook DL15 .... 100 E4
Wilson St. Darl DL3 .... 208 F4
Wilson St. Stan Cr DL15 .... 100 F8
Wilson Terr. N Silk SR3 .... 22 A8
Wilton Cl. Darl DL3 .... 208 B2
Wilton Ct. New Ay DL5 .... 170 F7
Wilton Dr. Darl DL3 .... 208 B2
Wiltshire Cl. Belm DH1 .... 59 C3
Wiltshire Way. Hartle TS26 .... 111 F1
Wimbledon Cl. Darl DL1 .... 209 E3
Wimborne Cl. Darl DL3 .... 208 A5
Wimpole Rd.
St on T TS19 & TS21 .... 195 F4
Winchester Cl. Gr Lum DH3 .... 37 A7
Winchester Ct. Spenny DL16 ...... 103 E3
Winchester Dr. Brand DH7 .... 79 A2
Winchester Rd. Durham DH1 .... 58 E7
Winchester Way. Darl DL1 .... 209 F5
Wind Mill. Even DL 14 .... 145 F5
Windermere. Birt DH3 .... 9 D2
Windermere. Spenny DL16 .... 103 E2
Windermere Ave. C le S DH2 .... 20 C1
Windermere Ave. E Lane DH5 .... 61 C8
Windermere Ave. Redmar TS21 195 B7
Windermere Cres. Blay NE21 .... 2 B8
Windermere Ct. Darl DL1 .... 224 B8
Windermere Dr. Bish Au DL14 .. 147 B1
Windermere Gdns. Crook DL15 100 F2
Windermere Rd. Ferry DL17 .... 128 F5
Windermere Rd. Peter SR8 .... 85 E7
Windermere Rd.
S Hett DH6 & SR7 .... 62 B7
Windermere Rd. Seaham SR7 .... 40 E7
Windermere Terr. Stanl DH9 .... 17 D5
Windlestone Hall Residential Sch.
New Ay DL17 .... 150 A6
Windlestone La. Kir Me DL17 ... 150 B8
Windlestone Wlk. 4
New Ay DL5 .... 171 E8
Windmill Hill. Durham DH1 .... 80 B7
Windrush Gr. Darl DL1 .... 209 B7
Winds La. Murton SR7 .... 40 B3
Winds Lonnen Est. Murton SR7 . 40 A3
Windsor Ave. Ferry DL17 .... 129 A6
Windsor Ave. Spenny DL16 .... 127 E7
Windsor Cres. H le Sp DH5 .... 38 F8
Windsor Ct. Bish Au DL14 .... 148 B8
Windsor Ct. Darl DL3 .... 208 A5
Windsor Ct. 2 Shild DL4 .... 170 A8
Windsor Dr. Ann Pl DH9 .... 16 F5
Windsor Dr. H le Sp DH5 .... 38 E6
Windsor Dr. N Silk SR3 .... 22 A7
Windsor Dr. S Hett DH6 .... 61 F8
Windsor Gdns. Cons DH8 .... 15 A2
Windsor Gdns. Shild DL4 .... 149 A1
Windsor Pl. Shot Co DH6 .... 84 D6
Windsor Rd. Birt DH3 .... 9 B6
Windsor Rd. Seaham SR7 .... 40 F7
Windsor Sq. Trim TS29 .... 131 D8
Windsor St. Darl DL1 .... 209 A4
Windsor St. Wing TS29 .... 107 F5
Windsor Terr. Ann Pl DH9 .... 17 B4
Windsor Terr. Cornf DL17 .... 105 E1
Windsor Terr. Cound DL14 .... 149 D8
Windsor Terr. Crook DL15 .... 100 F4
Windsor Terr. Hasw DH6 .... 61 F2
Windsor Terr. Leadg DH8 .... 15 D4
Windsor Terr. Murton SR7 .... 40 D2
Windsor Terr. Peter SR8 .... 86 B6
Windsor Terr. Shild DL4 .... 149 A1
Windsor Terr. Sland B DH6 .... 104 B7
Windy Bank Rd. Hamst DL13 ... 143 D7
Wingate Cl. H le Sp DH4 .... 38 D8
Wingate Cty Inf Sch.
Wing TS28 .... 108 E7
Wingate Cty Jun Sch.
Wing TS28 .... 108 E7
Wingate Grange Ind Est.
Wing TS28 .... 108 D7
Wingate La. Wh Hi DH6 & TS29 ... 83 E1
Wingate La. Wh Hi DH6 & TS29 ... 84 A1
Wingate RC Sch. Wing TS28 ...... 108 D6
Wingate Rd. Wing TS29 .... 108 A5
Wingrove. R Gill NE39 .... 1 D1
Wingrove Cl. Wing TS28 .... 84 E1
Wingrove Terr. Leadg DH8 .... 15 D4
Winlaton Care Village.
R Gill NE21 .... 1 F6
Winlaton Park Lane Cty Inf Sch.
Blay NE21 .... 2 C8
Winlaton Park Lane Cty Jun Sch.
Blay NE21 .... 2 C8
Winlaton West Lane Prim Sch.
Blay NE21 .... 2 A8
Winslade Cl. N Silk SR3 .... 22 B8
Winslow Cres. Seaham SR7 .... 40 E7
Winster. Wash NE38 .... 20 F8
Winston Ct. Staind DL2 .... 186 E6
Winston Gn. Pens DH4 .... 21 F8
Winston Rd. Staind DL2 .... 186 E5
Winston St. 6 Darl DL3 .... 208 F2
Winterburn Pl. New Ay DL5 .... 171 A8
Winterton Cotts. Sedge TS21 .... 131 B1
Winterton Cotts. Sedge TS21 ... 131 B2
Winterton Hospl. Sedge TS21 . 131 B2
Wiseman Wlk. New Ay DL5 .... 171 E8
Witbank Rd. Darl DL3 .... 208 E3
Withernsea Gr. Ryhope SR2 .... 22 D7
Witton Ave. Sacr DH7 .... 35 C3
Witton Cres. Darl DL3 .... 208 B5
Witton Dr. Spenny DL16 .... 103 F2
Witton Garth. Peter SR8 .... 85 C3
Witton Gilbert Cty Jun & Inf Sch.
Wit Gil DH7 .... 57 A8
Witton Gr. Durham DH1 .... 57 F5
Witton Gr. H le Sp DH4 .... 38 C7
Witton Park Environmental Ctr.
Wit Pk DL14 .... 147 A8
Witton Rd. Ferry DL17 .... 129 B7
Witton Rd. Sacr DH7 .... 35 B2
Witton St. Cons DH8 .... 31 B7
Witton Tower Gdns.
Wit le W DL14 .... 124 A3
Witton Way. Hi Eth DL14 .... 146 E6
Witton-le-Wear Cty Jun Mix
& Inf Sch. Wit le W DL14 .... 124 B3
WKM Ind Pk. Darl DL1 .... 209 B4
Woburn Ave. Darl DL3 .... 207 F5
Woburn Dr. Silk SR3 .... 22 A6
Wolseley Cl. Bowb DH6 .... 105 D8
Wolseley St. Ferry DL17 .... 129 C4
Wolsey Cl. New Ay DL5 .... 171 E8
Wolsey Rd. Seaham SR7 .... 40 E6
Wolsey Rd. Spenny DL16 .... 104 B3
Wolsingham Comp Sch.
Wols DL13 .... 97 E8
Wolsingham Cty Sch.
Wols DL13 .... 97 F8
Wolsingham Dr. Durham DH1 ..... 58 D6
Wolsingham Ind Est. Wols DL13 98 A7
Wolsingham Rd.
Brance DH7 & DL15 .... 78 C2
Wolsingham Rd. Esh W DH7 .... 77 B5
Wolsingham Rd. Stan Cr DL15 ... 76 E1
Wolsingham Rd. Tow Law DL13 . 75 B2
Wolsingham Terr. Ann Pl DH9 .... 16 F4
Wolsingham Terr. Darl DL1 .... 209 C3
Wolviston Cl. New Ay DL5 .... 171 B8
Wood La. Ferry DL17 .... 129 A7
Wood La. Gain DL2 .... 205 A8
Wood La. L Con DL2 .... 222 D8
Wood Lea. H le Sp DH5 .... 39 A7
Wood Sq. Bish Au DL14 .... 148 A5
Wood St. Bar Cas DL12 .... 201 A5
Wood St. Burnop NE16 .... 6 A6
Wood St. Cons DH8 .... 14 C6
Wood St. Pelton DH2 .... 19 E7
Wood St. Spenny DL16 .... 127 C5
Wood Terr. H Spen NE39 .... 1 A2
Wood View. Esh W DH7 .... 55 E1
Wood View. H Shin DH1 .... 80 F6

Wood View. Lang Pk DH7 .... 56 C7
Wood View. Sland B DH6 .... 104 B6
Wood View. Will DL15 .... 102 A7
Wood View. Wing TS29 .... 108 B5
Wood Vue. Spenny DL16 .... 103 F2
Wood's Terr E. Murton SR7 ...... 40 D3
Wood's Terr. Murton SR7 .... 40 D3
Wood's Terr N. Murton SR7 ...... 40 D3
Woodbine Ave. Peter SR8 .... 85 F8
Woodbine Rd. Durham DH1 ...... 58 A7
Woodbine Terr. Ann Pl DH9 ...... 17 B4
Woodbine Terr. Birt DH3 .... 9 D4
Woodbine Terr. N Bran DH7 ...... 78 E8
Woodburn. Tanf L DH9 .... 17 C8
Woodburn Cl. Blay NE21 .... 2 A8
Woodburn Dr. Darl DL3 .... 223 C8
Woodcrest Rd. Darl DL3 .... 223 D8
Woodcroft Gdns. Stanh DL13 ..... 71 C2
Woodfield. Peter SR8 .... 85 C6
Woodhall Cl. Urpeth DH2 .... 8 E2
Woodham Burn Inf Sch.
  New Ay DL5 .... 171 C7
Woodham Burn Jun Sch.
  New Ay DL5 .... 171 C7
Woodham Comp Sch.
  New Ay DL5 .... 171 E8
Woodham Gate.
  New Ay DL17 .... 150 D2
Woodham Rd. New Ay DL5 ...... 171 D3
Woodham View. Chilt DL17 ...... 150 F7
Woodham Way.
  New Ay DL17 & DL5 .... 150 E2
Woodhouse Close Cty Inf Sch.
  Bish Au DL14 .... 148 A4
Woodhouse Close Cty Jun Sch.
  Bish Au DL14 .... 148 A4
Woodhouse La. Bish Au DL14 .. 147 D3
Woodhouse La. Bish Au DL14 ... 148 A5
Woodhouses La. Whick NE16 .... 2 E6
Woodifield Hill. Crook DL15 .... 100 C3
Woodland Cl. Bear DH7 .... 57 A3
Woodland Cl. Trim TS29 .... 131 D8
Woodland Cres. Kelloe DH6 .... 106 D5
Woodland Ct. Cons DH8 .... 14 D6
Woodland Cty Jun & Inf Sch.
  Wood DL13 .... 143 E2
Woodland Grange.
  Gr Lum DH4 .... 21 F1
Woodland Mews. Sedge TS21 .. 153 B8
Woodland Pl. Esh W DH7 .... 77 E7
Woodland Rd. Darl DL3 .... 208 E3
Woodland Terr. Bear DH7 .... 57 A3
Woodland Terr. Darl DL3 .... 208 D2
Woodland Terr. Esh W DH7 ...... 77 E7
Woodland Terr. Kimble DH2 ...... 35 E4
Woodland View. W Rain DH4 ..... 37 F1
Woodland View. Wing TS28 .... 108 D8
Woodland Way. Longn TS21 .... 211 F5
Woodlands. C le S DH3 .... 20 C4
Woodlands. Gr Lum DH4 .... 21 F1
Woodlands. Seaham SR7 .... 23 A1
Woodlands. Wash DH3 & NE38 .... 20 E8
Woodlands Ave. Thorn DH6 ...... 83 D4
Woodlands Ave. Wh Hi DH6 ...... 83 F2
Woodlands Cl. H Spen NE39 .... 1 A3
Woodlands Cres. Cons DH8 ...... 14 D6
Woodlands Ct. Crook DL15 ...... 101 A3
Woodlands Ct. Kibble NE11 .... 8 D6
Woodlands Rd. Bar Cas DL12 ... 201 B7
Woodlands Rd. Bish Au DL14 ... 148 C7
Woodlands Rd. Cons DH8 .... 14 D6
Woodlands Rd. Esh W DH7 .... 77 D8
Woodlands Rd. R Gill NE39 .... 1 D2
Woodlands Terr. Dipton DH9 ...... 16 C7
Woodlands The. Kibble NE11 ...... 8 D6
Woodlands View. Cons DH8 ...... 31 C7
Woodlands Way. Hur on T DL2 . 224 A1
Woodlea. Lanch DH7 .... 32 E3
Woodlea Cl. H le H DH5 .... 39 A4
Woodlea Rd. R Gill NE39 .... 1 B2
Woodmans Way. Whick NE16 ...... 2 F4
Woodnansey Cl. Peter SR8 .... 85 B7
Woodpack Ave. Whick NE16 .... 2 F6
Woodside. Bar Cas DL12 .... 201 A7
Woodside. Beam DH9 .... 18 F8
Woodside. Sacr DH7 .... 35 B2
Woodside. Shadf DH6 .... 82 E8
Woodside. Wit Pk DL14 .... 147 B8
Woodside Ave. Bear DH7 .... 57 A3
Woodside Dr. Cons DH8 .... 31 B8
Woodside Dr. Darl DL3 .... 223 E8
Woodside Gdns. The Mid DH9 ... 18 C3
Woodside Gr. Tant DH9 .... 6 C3
Woodside La. W Rain DH4 .... 37 E1
Woodside Terr. Chopw NE17 ...... 4 B8
Woodside Terr. Qua Ho DH9 ...... 17 D2
Woodside View. Edmon DH7 ...... 35 B6
Woodside Wlk. R Gill NE39 .... 1 C1
Woodstock Terr. Bish Mi DL17 . 130 B4
Woodstock Way. Hartle TS27 ... 111 C4
Woodstone Terr. Gr Lum DH4 ... 21 D1
Woodvale Rd. Darl DL3 .... 223 D8
Woody Cl. Cons DH8 .... 15 C1
Wooler St. Darl DL1 .... 209 A3
Wooley Dr. Ush M DH7 .... 57 C1
Wooley Terr. Stan Cr DL15 ...... 100 F8
Worcester Cl. Gr Lum DH3 ...... 37 A6
Worcester Pl. Bish Au DL14 ...... 148 B5
Worcester Rd. Durham DH1 ...... 58 D7
Wordsworth Avc. 6
  Bish Au DL14 .... 148 B6
Wordsworth Ave. C le St DH2 .... 19 E3
Wordsworth Ave. E Lane DH5 .... 61 D8
Wordsworth Ave. Seaham SR7 .. 40 E7
Wordsworth Ave. Wh Hi DH6 .... 83 F2
Wordsworth Ave E. H le Sp DH5 38 E7
Wordsworth Ave W.
  H le Sp DH5 .... 38 E7
Wordsworth Ct. Crook DL15 .... 100 C2
Wordsworth Gdns. Dipton DH9 .. 16 D8
Wordsworth Rd. Chilt DL17 .... 150 F8

Wordsworth Rd. Darl DL1 .... 224 A7
Wordsworth Rd. Eas SR8 .... 63 C4
Works Rd. Spenny DL16 .... 104 B1
Worley Terr. Tant DH9 .... 6 A1
Worset La. Elwick TS27 .... 134 E8
Worton Dr. Darl DL1 .... 224 B7
Wraith Terr. Peter SR8 .... 85 F8
Wraith Terr. Ryhope SR2 .... 22 E6
Wren Ave. Darl DL1 .... 209 D6
Wren Cl. New Ay DL5 .... 171 F8
Wren Cl. 8 Wash NE38 .... 9 F3
Wrentnall Cotts.
  Lang Be DL 13 .... 114 C3
Wright Cl. New Ay DL5 .... 171 C6
Wycliffe Cl. New Ay DL5 .... 171 F8
Wycliffe Rd. Seaham SR7 .... 40 F7
Wycliffe Way. Darl DL3 .... 208 A1
Wycombe St. Darl DL3 .... 208 F2
Wykes Cl. Sedge TS21 .... 153 B6
Wylam Ave. Darl DL1 .... 209 C6
Wylam Cl. Shild DL4 .... 170 A8
Wylam Rd. Stanl DH9 .... 18 A8
Wylam St. Bowb DH6 .... 105 D8
Wylam St. Crag DH9 .... 18 C2
Wylam Terr. Bowb DH6 .... 105 E6
Wylam Terr. Stanl DH9 .... 17 F8
Wynd The. Bowes DL12 .... 216 B7
Wynd The. Grind TS22 .... 155 C2
Wynd The. New Ay DL5 .... 171 E1
Wynd The. Pelton DH2 .... 19 E6
Wyndley Cl. Whick NE16 .... 2 F5
Wynds The. Esh W DH7 .... 77 D8
Wyndways Dr. Dipton DH9 .... 5 E1
Wynyard. C le S DH2 .... 20 A3
Wynyard Ct. New Ay DL5 .... 171 A8
Wynyard Ct. Thor Th TS21 ...... 175 E3
Wynyard Gr. Bish Au DL14 ...... 148 E7
Wynyard Gr. Durham DH1 .... 58 F2
Wynyard Park C of E Sch.
  Grind TS22 .... 155 C3
Wynyard Rd. Grind TS21 .... 175 F4
Wynyard Rd. Thor Th TS21 ...... 175 E3
Wynyard Rd. Trim TS29 .... 131 D8
Wynyard St. Fence DH4 .... 38 A8
Wynyard St. N Silk SR3 .... 22 A7
Wynyard St. Seaham SR7 .... 41 D5

Yarker La. Mick DL12 .... 161 C4
Yarm Back La.
  St on T TS18 & TS21 .... 195 F2
Yarm Rd. Darl DL1 .... 209 D1
Yarm Rd. M St G DL2 .... 225 F8
Yarm Road Ind Est. Darl DL1 ... 209 F2
Yarmouth Cl. Seaham SR7 .... 41 A6
Yarrow Ct. New Ay DL17 .... 150 D2
Yeckhouse La. Lanch DH7 .... 32 B3
Yetholm Ave. C le S DH2 .... 20 B2
Yew Wlk The. Longn TS21 .... 211 F5
Yewbank Ave. Belm DH1 .... 59 B3
Yewtree Ave. Shild DL4 .... 149 B1
Yiewsley Dr. Darl DL3 .... 208 A2
Yoden Ave. Peter SR8 .... 85 F7
Yoden Cres. Peter SR8 .... 85 F8
Yoden Ct. New Ay DL5 .... 171 A8
Yoden Rd. Peter SR8 .... 85 D7
Yoden Way. Peter SR8 .... 85 D6
Yoden Way. Peter SR8 .... 85 F6
Yoredale Ave. Darl DL3 .... 208 C3
York Ave. Cons DH8 .... 30 A7
York Ave. Peter SR8 .... 85 F7
York Cl. Cound DL14 .... 127 C1
York Cres. Durham DH1 .... 58 E8
York Cres. H le H DH5 .... 38 F4
York Ct. C le S DH3 .... 20 D1
York Ct. Wit Pk DL14 .... 125 A1
York Hill Cres. Spenny DL16 .... 104 B3
York Hill Rd. Spenny DL16 ...... 104 C3
York Pl. Cons DH8 .... 30 A7
York Rd. Birt DH3 .... 9 C1
York Rd. Cons DH8 .... 14 C5
York Rd. Peter SR8 .... 85 C8
York Sq. 6 Shild DL4 .... 148 F1
York St. Ann Pl DH9 .... 16 F5
York St. Darl DL1 .... 209 B4
York St. H le H DH5 .... 38 E1
York St. N Silk SR3 .... 22 A8
York Terr. C le S DH3 .... 20 D2
York Terr. 1 Cockf DL13 .... 166 C6
York Villas. Spenny DL16 .... 104 B3
Yorkshire Dr. Belm DH1 .... 59 D3
Yorkshire Pl. Bish Au DL14 ...... 148 B5
Young St. Durham DH1 .... 58 F2

Zetland Hunt. New Ay DL5 ...... 170 F8
Zetland Rd. Bar Cas DL12 ...... 201 B6
Zetland St. Darl DL3 .... 209 A5

Ordnance Survey

STREET ATLASES

The Ordnance Survey Street Atlases provide unique and definitive mapping of entire counties

Street Atlases available

- Berkshire
- Bristol and Avon
- Buckinghamshire
- Cardiff, Swansea and Glamorgan
- Cheshire
- Derbyshire
- Durham

- Edinburgh
- East Essex
- West Essex
- Glasgow
- North Hampshire
- South Hampshire
- Hertfordshire
- East Kent
- West Kent
- Nottinghamshire

- Oxfordshire
- Staffordshire
- Surrey
- East Sussex
- West Sussex
- Tyne and Wear
- Warwickshire
- South Yorkshire
- West Yorkshire

The Street Atlases are revised and updated on a regular basis and new titles are added to the series. Each title is available in three formats and as from 1996 the atlases are produced in colour. All contain Ordnance Survey mapping except Surrey which is by Philip's.

The series is available from all good bookshops or by mail order direct from the publisher. However, the order form on the following pages may not reflect the complete range of titles available so it is advisable to check by telephone before placing your order. Payment can be made in the following ways:

By phone *Phone your order through on our special Credit Card Hotline on 01933 414000. Speak to our customer service team during office hours (9am to 5pm) or leave a message on the answering machine, quoting T608N99 C, your full credit card number plus expiry date and your full name and address.*

By post *Simply fill out the order form (you may photocopy it) and send it to: Cash Sales Department, Reed Book Services, PO Box 5, Rushden, Northants, NN10 6YX.*

OS Ordnance Survey STREET ATLASES ORDER FORM

NEW COLOUR EDITIONS

T608N99 C	HARDBACK Quantity @ £10.99 each	SPIRAL Quantity @ £8.99 each	POCKET Quantity @ £4.99 each	£ Total
BERKSHIRE	☐ 0 540 06170 0	☐ 0 540 06172 7	☐ 0 540 06173 5	➤ ☐

T608N99 C	Quantity @ £12.99 each	Quantity @ £9.99 each	Quantity @ £4.99 each	£ Total
DURHAM	☐ 0 540 06365 7	☐ 0 540 06366 5	☐ 0 540 06367 3	➤ ☐
HERTFORDSHIRE	☐ 0 540 06174 3	☐ 0 540 06175 1	☐ 0 540 06176 X	➤ ☐
TYNE AND WEAR	☐ 0 540 06370 3	☐ 0 540 06371 1	☐ 0 540 06372 X	➤ ☐
SOUTH YORKSHIRE	☐ 0 540 06330 4	☐ 0 540 06331 2	☐ 0 540 06332 0	➤ ☐
WEST YORKSHIRE	☐ 0 540 06329 0	☐ 0 540 06327 4	☐ 0 540 06328 2	➤ ☐

BLACK AND WHITE EDITIONS

T608N99 C	HARDBACK Quantity @ £12.99 each	SOFTBACK Quantity @ £8.99 each	POCKET Quantity @ £4.99 each	£ Total
BERKSHIRE	☐ 0 540 05992 7	☐ 0 540 05993 5	☐ 0 540 05994 3	➤ ☐
BUCKINGHAMSHIRE	☐ 0 540 05989 7	☐ 0 540 05990 0	☐ 0 540 05991 9	➤ ☐
EAST ESSEX	☐ 0 540 05848 3	☐ 0 540 05866 1	☐ 0 540 05850 5	➤ ☐
WEST ESSEX	☐ 0 540 05849 1	☐ 0 540 05867 X	☐ 0 540 05851 3	➤ ☐
NORTH HAMPSHIRE	☐ 0 540 05852 1	☐ 0 540 05853 X	☐ 0 540 05854 8	➤ ☐
SOUTH HAMPSHIRE	☐ 0 540 05855 6	☐ 0 540 05856 4	☐ 0 540 05857 2	➤ ☐
HERTFORDSHIRE	☐ 0 540 05995 1	☐ 0 540 05996 X	☐ 0 540 05997 8	➤ ☐
EAST KENT	☐ 0 540 06026 7	☐ 0 540 06027 5	☐ 0 540 06028 3	➤ ☐
WEST KENT	☐ 0 540 06029 1	☐ 0 540 06031 3	☐ 0 540 06030 5	➤ ☐
NOTTINGHAMSHIRE	☐ 0 540 05858 0	☐ 0 540 05859 9	☐ 0 540 05860 2	➤ ☐
OXFORDSHIRE	☐ 0 540 05986 2	☐ 0 540 05987 0	☐ 0 540 05988 9	➤ ☐
EAST SUSSEX	☐ 0 540 05875 0	☐ 0 540 05874 2	☐ 0 540 05873 4	➤ ☐
WEST SUSSEX	☐ 0 540 05876 9	☐ 0 540 05877 7	☐ 0 540 05878 5	➤ ☐

See more titles overleaf

STREET ATLASES ORDER FORM
Ordnance Survey

BLACK AND WHITE EDITIONS

T608N99 C	HARDBACK Quantity @ £10.99 each	SOFTBACK Quantity @ £8.99 each	POCKET Quantity @ £4.99 each	£ Total
SURREY	☐ 0 540 05983 8	☐ 0 540 05984 6	☐ 0 540 05985 4	➤ ☐
WARWICKSHIRE	☐ 0 540 05642 1			➤ ☐

BLACK AND WHITE EDITIONS

T608N99 C	HARDBACK Quantity @ £12.99 each	SOFTBACK Quantity @ £9.99 each	POCKET Quantity @ £4.99 each	£ Total
BRISTOL AND AVON	☐ 0 540 06140 9	☐ 0 540 06141 7	☐ 0 540 06142 5	➤ ☐
CARDIFF	☐ 0 540 06186 7	☐ 0 540 06187 5	☐ 0 540 06207 3	➤ ☐
CHESHIRE	☐ 0 540 06143 3	☐ 0 540 06144 1	☐ 0 540 06145 X	➤ ☐
DERBYSHIRE	☐ 0 540 06137 9	☐ 0 540 06138 7	☐ 0 540 06139 5	➤ ☐
EDINBURGH	☐ 0 540 06180 8	☐ 0 540 06181 6	☐ 0 540 06182 4	➤ ☐
GLASGOW	☐ 0 540 06183 2	☐ 0 540 06184 0	☐ 0 540 06185 9	➤ ☐
STAFFORDSHIRE	☐ 0 540 06134 4	☐ 0 540 06135 2	☐ 0 540 06136 0	➤ ☐

Name...

Address...

....

....Postcode

◆ Free postage and packing

◆ All available titles will normally be dispatched within 5 working days of receipt of order but please allow up to 28 days for delivery

☐ Please tick this box if you do not wish your name to be used by other carefully selected organisations that may wish to send you information about other products and services

Registered Office: Michelin House, 81 Fulham Road, London SW3 6RB.
Registered in England number: 1974080

I enclose a cheque / postal order, for a **total** of ☐
made payable to *Reed Book Services*, or please debit my

☐ Access   ☐ American Express   ☐ Visa

account by ☐

Account no ☐☐☐☐ ☐☐☐☐ ☐☐☐☐ ☐☐☐☐
Expiry date ☐☐ ☐☐

Signature...

Post to: Cash Sales Department, Reed Book Services, PO Box 5, Rushden, Northants, NN10 6YX

T608N99 C